DATE DUE			
GAYLORD			PRINTED IN U.S.A.

WITHDRAWN

A SURVEY OF CONTEMPORARY ECONOMICS

The participation of the American Economic Association in the preparation and publication of this volume has been effected through its Committees on Research and on Publications and through the appropriation of Association funds for this purpose. The Committees have had the responsibility for the continuation of the project for a survey of contemporary economics which was originally developed by the Association's Committee on Development of Economic Thinking and Information, established in April, 1945.

A SURVEY OF

CONTEMPORARY

ECONOMICS

VOLUME II

EDITED BY

BERNARD F. HALEY

STANFORD UNIVERSITY

PUBLISHED FOR THE
AMERICAN ECONOMIC ASSOCIATION

RICHARD D. IRWIN, INC.

1952

HOMEWOOD, ILLINOIS

COPYRIGHT 1952 BY RICHARD D. IRWIN, INC.

First Printing, September, 1952
Second Printing, August, 1956
Third Printing, November, 1958
Fourth Printing, February, 1960
Fifth Printing, December, 1961
Sixth Printing, October, 1963
Seventh Printing, January, 1965
Eighth Printing, December, 1966

PRINTED IN THE UNITED STATES OF AMERICA

PREFACE

This volume continues the experiment, sponsored by the American Economic Association, which began with the publication of the predecessor work of the same title edited by Howard S. Ellis.[1] Readers of the first volume will recall that the primary purpose of the experiment has been to test the usefulness of a periodic review of developments in the different fields of economics. It was quite impossible to include in the first volume a review of all of the fields of specialization that have developed within the broad subject of economics. Hence, encouraged by the fact that the first undertaking did result in a product generally regarded as useful to the profession, the Executive Committee of the Association decided in December, 1949 that a second volume, reviewing developments of the past ten to fifteen years in ten additional fields of economics should be prepared. (Even though in the two volumes twenty-three fields have been treated in this way, there remain some aspects of the subject, such as location theory and social security, that have not been reviewed.)

As in the case of the earlier volume, the primary purpose of this one is to provide the economist who is not a specialist in a particular field with ". . . an intelligible and reliable account of its main ideas—both analytical devices and their practical application to public policy—which have evolved during the last ten or fifteen years."[2] In addition, however—and here we have departed somewhat from the precedents of the first volume—the ten authors have been asked to include, whenever they saw fit, their own appraisals of the work reviewed, and to indicate directions which, in their opinion, future research might profitably take. Hence it is hoped that the essays in the current volume will make provocative reading for specialists in the several fields reviewed, as well as useful reading for nonspecialists.

It should be admitted at once, however, that the larger task of review and appraisal of the present state of our subject ". . . as in some sense and degree a unified and coherent discipline," the undertaking of

---

[1] *A Survey of Contemporary Economics*, Vol. I, H. S. Ellis, ed. (Philadelphia, 1948).

[2] *Ibid.*, p. v.

which was called for by Jacob Viner in his review of the first volume,[3] is not attempted here.[4] Perhaps this should be the next step in a continuing experiment by the Association.

Since this has been an experimental venture and since in due course some appraisal of it will need to be made, it is desirable to record here the procedure that has been followed.

The selection and rough definition of the ten fields to be surveyed, itself by no means an easy task, was assumed by the Committee on Research of the Association in collaboration with the editor. This Committee, together with members of the Executive Committee of 1950, also advised the editor with regard to the selection of prospective authors for the ten essays and of the twenty critics who were to aid the authors; but final selection was a responsibility which the editor alone bore.

As in the case of the first volume, each essay when in preliminary form was submitted to two critics as well as to the editor for review—the purpose of this first review being to provide the author with suggestions for revision of the essay. The critics were invited to give particular attention to the matter of conformity of the essay with the objectives of the volume. The author then revised his manuscript (in most cases quite extensively) and resubmitted it in final form.[5] At this point the critics prepared their short *Comments* for publication with the essays. (This step was an innovation in the present volume.)

Both authors and critics have been most conscientious in seeking to carry out the tasks assigned to them in conformity with the objectives of the volume. The difficulties involved in the preparation of one of these essays, however, are considerably greater than is likely to be realized by the reader of the final products. First, there has been in nearly every case a very extensive literature that has had to be examined and appraised before the matters to be reviewed could actually be selected and the preparation of the review itself undertaken. Second, this process of selection was rendered all the more difficult by the necessarily rigorous

---

[3] *Am. Econ. Rev.,* Sept. 1950, XL, 651–53.

[4] To the extent that the authors of these essays have followed the suggestion that they appraise the developments they are reviewing, some progress on this larger task may be facilitated. Also, Richard Ruggles' essay on "Methodological Developments" is directly pertinent.

[5] Readers of the volume should keep in mind that, although the authors have had a free hand as to whether they would utilize the suggestions of their respective critics, the latter have in fact made a considerable contribution to every one of the essays. Rather than conceding to the authors' desire to have a statement of this indebtedness appear in connection with each of the essays, the editor wishes, in behalf of the authors, to make this general acknowledgment.

limitation upon the length of the several essays. There has been in nearly all cases a major problem of compression. Although, as a result of the experience with the first volume, three fewer essays were undertaken in the present volume, the authors found the problems of selection of the developments that could be reviewed and the condensation of their review of these developments a formidable task indeed. In some of the essays whole topics belonging within the framework of the subject had to be omitted entirely or treated very briefly indeed; and in some cases bibliographical material of undoubted usefulness to the reader had to be omitted.

Readers should therefore remember—when they discover what they regard as important omissions, inadequate space given to particular topics, or excessively brief summary statements with regard to the present state of knowledge in the different fields—that the authors have been under constant pressure to come within the space limits that had to be set in accordance with the feasible size of the volume. It has only been by an exceptional exercise of patience as well as ingenuity on the authors' part that these problems have been met at all satisfactorily.

Third, there has been the difficulty of maintaining a balance between simple exposition of developments, appraisal of the progress that has occurred, and opinion as to desirable directions for future work. As D. H. Robertson said in his review of the first volume:

The degree to which the several authors have allowed themselves to stray from the plains of orderly reporting into the uplands of reasoned evaluation, and thence towards the heights of original construction, naturally varies both with their temperament and with the nature of their theme. And the degree of indulgence with which the reader will regard their acts of petty indiscipline will depend largely on his own tastes.[6]

In the case of this present volume, however, perhaps with one exception, the authors have succeeded in resisting the temptation to climb to the unquestionably tempting "heights of original construction," and have extraordinarily well conformed to the standards for this sort of essay so well defined by Viner:

The ideal performance would call for a large measure of self-abnegation, of objective reporting of what was prevalent, even if what prevailed was not wholly approved of by the contributor, but with aid provided to the non-specialist so that he could reach some judgment of his own as to the merits of recent developments in the various fields.[7]

---

[6] "A Revolutionist's Handbook," *Quart. Jour. Econ.*, Feb. 1950, LXIV, 2.

[7] *Op. cit.*, p. 650.

It is not surprising that there also have been problems of definition in the case of some of the fields for the purpose of this volume. In some cases, the definition of the field has had to be conditioned by the contents of the first volume. Thus Kenneth E. Boulding's essay on "Welfare Economics" and Paul A. Baran's "National Economic Planning" in different ways supplement Abram Bergson's "Socialist Economics" in the first volume. Similarly, Norman S. Buchanan's "International Investment" should be read with Lloyd A. Metzler's "The Theory of International Trade" (Vol. I, Ch. 6); and Lowell Harriss' "Public Finance" is complementary to Arthur Smithies' "Federal Budgeting and Fiscal Policy" (Vol. I, Ch. 5).

In other cases, the boundaries of the field have been difficult to define at all, or have had to be defined somewhat more narrowly than would otherwise be desirable in order to make the preparation of an essay within the allowable space limits at all feasible. This certainly was the case with Moses Abramovitz' essay, "Economics of Growth," Joseph J. Spengler's "Population Theory," Andreas G. Papandreou's "Some Basic Problems in the Theory of the Firm," and Ruth Mack's "Consumption Economics."

Richard Ruggles' assignment was particularly difficult. Under the title, "Methodological Developments," he was asked to review what has been taking place in economics in recent years with respect to techniques of research, as distinct from contributions to the more abstract subject of economic methodology itself. But it early became clear that this was a difficult distinction to maintain, and that furthermore it was far from easy to discuss techniques of research apart from the subject-matter of the fields to which the techniques are applied—with accompanying danger of repetition of matters already receiving attention in other essays of the two volumes. In view of these difficulties—some of which, it must be admitted, should have been anticipated by the editor—the essay has been a peculiarly difficult one for author, critics, and editor alike.

The editor is most grateful to all of those who have collaborated in the preparation of this volume: the authors and critics first of all, of course; the Committee on Research of the American Economic Association, composed of Simeon E. Leland, Chairman, and Harold A. Innis, Alfred C. Neal, Theodore W. Schultz, Joseph J. Spengler, George W. Stocking, and Donald H. Wallace; others who participated in the planning of the volume along with the Committee: Frank H. Knight, Richard B. Heflebower, Edwin G. Nourse, and James W. Bell. Grateful acknowledgment is also made of the generous financial support for the venture provided by the Carnegie Corporation of New York, Dr. Charles Dollard, President.

Bernard F. Haley

Stanford University
August 1952

CONTENTS

CONTRIBUTORS

MOSES ABRAMOVITZ, Professor of Economics, Stanford University, and Member of Research Staff, National Bureau of Economic Research. Author of: *Price Theory for a Changing Economy* (New York, 1939); *Inventories and Business Cycles* (New York, 1950).

PAUL A. BARAN, Professor of Economics, Stanford University. Author of: "National Income and Product of the U.S.S.R. in 1940," *Rev. Econ. Stat.*, Nov. 1947, XXIX, 226–33; "Britain's Economic Prospects," *American Perspective*, April, May, and June 1949, III, 28–43, 100–16, 154–71; "On the Political Economy of Backwardness," *Man. School Econ. Soc. Stud.*, Jan. 1952, XX, 66–84.

JOHN D. BLACK, Henry Lee Professor of Economics and Chairman of the Committee on Research in the Social Sciences, Harvard University. Author of: *Introduction to Production Economics* (New York, 1926); *Future Food and Agriculture Policy* (New York, 1948); *Rural Economy of New England* (Cambridge, Mass., 1950).

ROY BLOUGH, Member, Council of Economic Advisers to the President, and Professor of Economics and of Political Science, University of Chicago (on leave). Author of: (with Carl Shoup and Mabel Newcomer) *Facing the Tax Problem* (New York, 1937); *The Federal Taxing Process* (New York, 1952).

KENNETH E. BOULDING, Professor of Economics, University of Michigan. Author of: *Economic Analysis* (New York, 1941; rev. ed., 1948); *The Economics of Peace* (New York, 1945); *A Reconstruction of Economics* (New York, 1950).

NORMAN S. BUCHANAN, Professor of Economics, University of California, Berkeley. Author of: *The Economics of Corporate Enterprise* (New York, 1940); *International Investment and Domestic Welfare* (New York, 1945); (with Friedrich A. Lutz) *Rebuilding the World Economy* (New York, 1947).

JOSEPH S. DAVIS, Director, Food Research Institute and Professor of Economic Research, Stanford University. Author of: *On Agricultural Policy, 1926–1938* (Stanford, 1939); *International Commodity Agreements: Hope, Illusion, or Menace?* (New York, 1947); *The Population Upsurge in the United States* (Stanford, 1949).

EVSEY D. DOMAR, Associate Professor of Political Economy, The Johns Hopkins University, and Visiting Associate Professor of Economics, Columbia University. Author of: "The 'Burden of the Debt' and the National Income," *Am. Econ. Rev.,* Dec. 1944, XXXIV, 798–827; "The Problem of Capital Accumulation," *ibid.,* Dec. 1948, XXXVIII, 777–94; "The Effect of Foreign Investment on the Balance of Payments," *ibid.,* Dec. 1950, 805–26.

MILTON FRIEDMAN, Professor of Economics, University of Chicago, and Member of Research Staff, National Bureau of Economic Research. Author of: (with Carl Shoup and Ruth P. Mack) *Taxing to Prevent Inflation* (New York, 1943); (with Simon Kuznets) *Income from Independent Professional Practice* (New York, 1946).

J. K. GALBRAITH, Professor of Economics, Harvard University. Author of: *American Capitalism: The Concept of Countervailing Power* (Boston, 1952); *A Theory of Price Control* (Cambridge, Mass., 1952).

C. LOWELL HARRISS, Associate Professor of Economics, Columbia University, and Consultant, Finance Study, Mayor's Committee on Management Survey (New York City). Author of: *Gift Taxation in the United States* (Washington, 1940); (with W. J. Schultz) *American Public Finance* (New York, 1949); *History and Policies of the Home Owners Loan Corporation* (New York, 1951).

RICHARD B. HEFLEBOWER, Professor of Economics, Northwestern University. Author of: "The Effect of Dynamic Forces on the Elasticity of Revenue Curves," *Quart. Jour. Econ.,* Aug. 1941, LV, 652–66; (with E. F. Dummeier and Theodore Norman) *Economics with Applications to Agriculture* (3rd ed., New York, 1950); "An Economic Appraisal of Price Measures," *Jour. Am. Stat. Assoc.,* Dec. 1951, XLVI, 461–79.

D. GALE JOHNSON, Associate Professor of Economics, University of Chicago. Author of: *Forward Prices for Agriculture* (Chicago, 1947); *Trade and Agriculture* (New York, 1950).

SIMON KUZNETS, Professor of Economics and Statistics, University of Pennsylvania, and Member of Research Staff, National Bureau of Economic Research. Author of: *Secular Movements in Production and Prices* (Boston, 1930); *Seasonal Variations in Industry and Trade* (New York, 1933); *National Product since 1869* (New York, 1946).

SIMEON E. LELAND, Dean of the College of Liberal Arts and Professor of Economics, Northwestern University. Author of: *The Classified Property Tax in the United States* (Boston and New York, 1928); "Division of Costs and Responsibility, Sec. 1, Principles and Policies," *Public Works Planning,* National Resources Committee (Washington, 1936).

ADOLPH LOWE, Professor of Economics, Graduate Faculty, New School for Social Research. Author of: *Economics and Sociology* (London, 1935); "Nationalism and the Economic Order," in *Nationalism.* A Report by a Study Group of Members of the Royal Institute of International Affairs (London and New York, 1939); "On the Mechanistic Approach in Economics," *Social Research,* Dec. 1951, XVIII, 403–34.

RUTH P. MACK, Member of Research Staff, National Bureau of Economic Research. Author of: *Controlling Retailers* (New York, 1936); *The Flow of Business Funds and Consumer Purchasing Power* (New York, 1941); (with Carl Shoup and Milton Friedman) *Taxing to Prevent Inflation* (New York, 1943).

JACOB MARSCHAK, Professor of Economics, University of Chicago, and Research Associate, The Cowles Commission for Research in Economics. Author of: "Rational Behavior, Uncertain Prospects and Measurable Utility," *Econometrica,* Apr. 1950, XVIII, 111–41; *Lectures on the Theory of Income, Employment and the Price Level* (New York, 1951); "Economic Measurements for Policy and Predictions," in *Econometric Methods,* W. C. Hood and T. C. Koopmans, ed., Cowles Commission Monog. 14 (New York, 1952).

EDWARD S. MASON, Professor of Economics and Dean of the Graduate School of Public Administration, Harvard University. Author of: *Street Railways in Massachusetts* (Cambridge, Mass., 1930); editor and contributor, Committee on Price Determination, *Cost Behavior and Price Policy* (New York, 1940); *Controlling World Trade* (New York, 1946).

FRANK W. NOTESTEIN, Professor of Demography and Director, Office of Population Research, Princeton University. Co-editor: *Population Index.* Author of: (with Regine K. Stix) *Controlled Fertility; An Evaluation of Clinic Service* (Baltimore, 1940); (with Irene B. Taeuber *et al.*) *The Future Population of Europe and the Soviet Union: Population Projections, 1940–1970* (Geneva, 1944).

RAGNAR NURKSE, Professor of Economics, Columbia University. Author of: *Internationale Kapitalbewegungen* (Vienna, 1935); (with W. A. Brown) *International Currency Experience* (Geneva, 1944).

ANDREAS G. PAPANDREOU, Professor of Economics, University of Minnesota. Author of: "Market Structure and Monopoly Power," *Am. Econ. Rev.,* Sept. 1949, XXXIX, 883–97; "Economics and the Social Sciences," *Ec. Jour.,* Dec. 1950, LX, 715–23.

MELVIN W. REDER, Associate Professor of Economics, Stanford University, and Research Associate, Institute of Industrial Relations, University of California, Berkeley. Author of: *Studies in the Theory of Welfare Economics* (New York, 1947); "A Reconsideration of the Marginal Productivity Theory," *Jour. Pol. Econ.,* Oct. 1947, LV, 450–58; "The Theoretical Problems of a National Wage-Price Policy," *Can. Jour. Econ. Pol. Sci.,* Feb. 1948, XIV, 46–61.

RICHARD RUGGLES, Associate Professor of Economics, Yale University. Author of: *National Income and Income Analysis* (New York, 1949).

PAUL A. SAMUELSON, Professor of Economics, Massachusetts Institute of Technology. Author of: *Foundations of Economic Analysis* (Cambridge, Mass., 1947); *Economics: An Introductory Analysis* (New York, 1948; rev. ed., 1951).

THEODORE W. SCHULTZ, Professor of Economics and Chairman of the Department of Economics, University of Chicago. Author of: *Agriculture in an Unstable Economy* (New York, 1945); *Production and Welfare of Agriculture* (New York, 1949); *The Economic Organization of Agriculture* (New York, 1952).

JOSEPH J. SPENGLER, Professor of Economics and Business Administration, and Director of Graduate Studies in Economics, Duke University. Author of: "Monopolistic Competition and the Use and Price of Urban Land Service," *Jour. Pol. Econ.,* Oct. 1946, XLIV, 385–412; "The Problem of Order in Economic Affairs," *So. Econ. Jour.,* July 1948, XV, 1–29; "Evolutionism in American Economics," in *Evolutionary Thought in America,* Stow Persons, ed. (New Haven, 1950), pp. 202–66.

RUPERT B. VANCE, Kenan Professor of Sociology and Research Professor in the Institute for Research in Social Science, University of North Carolina. Author of: *Human Geography of the South* (Chapel Hill, 1932); *Research Memorandum on Redistribution of Population in the United States* (New York, 1938); *All These People* (Chapel Hill, 1945).

JOHN H. WILLIAMS, Nathaniel Ropes Professor of Political Economy, Harvard University, and Economic Adviser, Federal Reserve Bank of New York. Author of: *Argentine International Trade under Inconvertible Paper Money, 1880–1900* (Cambridge, Mass., 1920); "Annual Studies of the Balance of Payments of the United States," *Review of Economic Statistics* (Cambridge, Mass., 1920–23); *Postwar Monetary Plans* (New York, 1944; 3rd ed., 1947; 4th ed., Oxford, 1949).

HAROLD F. WILLIAMSON, Professor of Economics, Northwestern University. Author of: *Edward Atkinson: The Biography of an American Liberal* (Boston, 1935); (with A. H. Cole) *The American Carpet Manufacture* (Cambridge, Mass., 1941); editor and author, *The Growth of the American Economy* (New York, 1944).

1

WELFARE

ECONOMICS

Kenneth E. Boulding

It is almost as difficult to define the boundaries of welfare economics as it is to define economics itself. The subject must exist, for people write books and articles about it, but it is not easy to draw the line between what is and what is not included in it. At one extreme almost any discussion of economic policy which raises matters of principle or invokes standards of judgment might be included, and at the other the subject might be narrowed down to certain highly technical discussions of the conditions for a social optimum. Nor is it easy to delimit the topic historically. Some might argue that the work of A. C. Pigou, as represented by *Wealth and Welfare*[1] and in the various editions of his subsequent *Economics of Welfare*,[2] represents the emergence of the subject as a separate department of economic thought. Nevertheless, as Hla Myint[3] has pointed out so well, the English Classical economists had a great deal to say on subjects which could reasonably be brought within the compass of welfare economics, and Pigou's work itself is in large part a refinement and elaboration of some ideas of Marshall. It is also true that the development of welfare economics in the English language in the past fifteen or twenty years by Lerner, Hicks, Kaldor, Hotelling, Reder, Samuelson, and others[4] as something

---

[1] London, 1912.

[2] London, 1920; 4th ed., 1932.

[3] *Theories of Welfare Economics* (Cambridge, Mass., 1948).

[4] See especially: A. P. Lerner, "The Concept of Monopoly and the Measurement of Monopoly Power," *Rev. Econ. Stud.*, June 1934, I, 157–75; Abram Bergson (Burk), "A Reformulation of Certain Aspects of Welfare Economics," *Quart. Jour. Econ.*, Feb. 1938, LII, 310–34; Harold Hotelling, "The General Welfare in Relation to Problems of Taxation and of Railway and Utility Rates," *Econometrica*, July 1938, VI, 242–69; Nicholas Kaldor, "Welfare Propositions of Economics and Interpersonal Comparisons of Utility," *Econ. Jour.*, Sept. 1939, XLIX, 549–52; J. R. Hicks, "Foundations of Welfare Economics," *ibid.*, Dec. 1939, XLIX, 696–712; Tibor Scitovsky, "A Note on Welfare Propositions in

like a movement or a school of economic thought has not stemmed from Pigou, the perfection of whose thought makes it somewhat of a blind alley. It originated rather with Pareto, Barone, and Edgeworth, where it has not arisen spontaneously in response to the fine English tradition that it is much easier to think up something than to look it up. It is with this "new" welfare economics that the present article is mainly concerned. As it is getting a little too old to be called new, one may perhaps propose to call it the "Paretian" welfare economics after its forerunner (Vilfredo Pareto)[5] rather than its founders. The name of Pareto is particularly appropriate in this connection because he introduced the indifference curve (or preference function) analysis as a major instrument of economic analysis, and it is only a slight exaggeration to claim that modern welfare economics has developed largely as a result of the invention of this powerful analytical tool. It is a department of thought which owes its unity not so much to the natural boundaries of the subject matter which it is discussing as to the limitations of its tool chest, much as a carpenter is not so much interested in "furniture" as in things which can be manipulated with a saw and hammer. It is for this reason, perhaps, that the welfare economist is sometimes hard put to explain what his subject is *about*. There is a field of subject matter, presumably related to human welfare, and there is a field of technical and manipulative skill. Much of the apparently "precious" and over-refined character of welfare economics arises because the fields of subject matter and of skills do not altogether coincide. The more elegant any apparatus, the more specialized it is apt to be. Consequently it is not surprising to find welfare economists devoting their energies to tasks which may seem insignificant but which they can perform with their apparatus, rather than to the major problems of the subject matter which seem to defy analysis.

As it has developed, the Paretian welfare economics seems to have had three main objectives. One has been to clarify and quantify the vague concept of "riches" or, in the language of Adam Smith, "Opu-

Economics," *Rev. Econ. Stud.,* Nov. 1941, IX, 77–88; Oscar Lange, "The Foundations of Welfare Economics," *Econometrica,* July–Oct. 1942, X, 215–28; G. J. Stigler, "The New Welfare Economics," *Am. Econ. Rev.,* June 1943, XXXIII, 355–59; P. A. Samuelson, *Foundations of Economic Analysis* (Cambridge, Mass., 1947), Ch. 8. Probably the best three works of a systematic nature on the subject are: Hla Myint, *op. cit.;* Melvin Reder, *Studies in the Theory of Welfare Economics* (New York, 1947); and I. M. D. Little, *A Critique of Welfare Economics* (Oxford, 1950).

[5] *Cours d'économie politique* (Lausanne, 1897), Vol. I, pp. 20 ff.; Vol. II, pp. 90 ff.; *Manuel d'économie politique* (Paris, 1909; 2nd ed., 1927), pp. 354–64, 616 ff., 648 ff.

lence." A closely related objective has been to clarify what it is that economists have to say on matters of public policy. Economics has largely developed as a by-product of propaganda for policies of various kinds, and the economist has yet to be born who does not feel the urge to make his abstractions give birth to Proposals. Welfare economics then tries to set up standards of judgment by which events and policies can be judged as "economically" desirable, even though on other grounds (political, national, ethical) they might be judged to be undesirable. The search for such a standard of judgment leads to a further search for a definition of an economic "optimum," this being the position of all the economic variables at which riches are at a maximum, the test of economic desirability thus being an increase in riches. Of two events or policies then, the one which increases riches more would be judged economically the more desirable. Closely linked with these objectives is a third—to develop propositions which are "scientifically" free of ethical judgments, but which can nevertheless serve as a basis for conclusions with respect to policy alternatives by delimiting the area within which the final ethical judgment has to be made.

I. THE CONCEPT OF ECONOMIC WELFARE

The subject matter of welfare economics can be approached conveniently, therefore, by considering how the concept of "riches"—that is, economic welfare as distinct from other forms of welfare—arises out of the other interests of economists. Economics itself is an abstraction from the general melee of social phenomena based primarily on those magnitudes which are descriptive of the production, consumption, and exchange of commodities. Economics, then, is not primarily interested in men, but in commodities—in those things, material or immaterial, which are produced, distributed, exchanged, and consumed, rather than in the producers, distributers, exchangers, and consumers as people. Pure economic analysis discusses an abstract universe the constituents of which are (*i*) quantities of commodities (exchangeable assets) produced, consumed, and exchanged, and (*ii*) the derivative ratios of transformation of commodities or other exchangeables one into another through exchange or through production. Prices are rates of transformation through exchange; real costs or productivity ratios are rates of transformation through production. Thus economic analysis is a kind of astronomy of the economic universe, discussing the mutual determination of the position and magnitude of the various economic quantities much as the astronomer discusses the mutual determination of the position and magnitude of astronomical quantities. Indeed, the methods of the two sciences are strikingly similar; they both proceed by observation rather than by experiment, and both lean heavily on the concept of general equilibrium through the solution of simultaneous equations. The success of astronomy and the lack of success of economics in prediction arise mainly because of the greater stability and simplicity of the astronomer's universe—it is easier for him to discover stable difference (or differential) equations relating past to future values of the various variables.

Economists, however, in the language of David Ricardo[6] have always been interested not only in "value"—the positions of the economic magnitudes—but in "riches" or economic welfare. That is to say, they ask the question not only, "What determines the quantities of commodities produced, consumed, distributed and exchanged?" but also, "Am I—or are you—richer or poorer, better or worse off as a result of any given set of changes in the quantities of the economic universe?" This, oddly enough, is also the question which the astrologer asks of the stars. I am not suggesting of course that economists are to welfare economists what astronomers are to astrologers, at least in regard to the scientific respectability of performance! Nevertheless in regard to the *question asked* the relation of welfare economics to pure economics is almost exactly that of astrology to astronomy. The astrologer postulates a "welfare function" which relates the position of the heavenly bodies to human welfare, just as the welfare economist postulates a welfare function which relates the position of the economic "bodies" to human welfare. Whether we will regard either of these operations as nonsense depends on our confidence in the stability of the functions so postulated. For the astrologer some positions of the heavenly bodies are "better" than others; for the welfare economist some positions of the economic universe are "better" than others. If we are convinced that welfare economics is superior to astrology it is because we have better statistical and personal evidence that some "difference" is made to our states of being by shifts in the economic universe, whereas no apparent difference is made to these same states by shifts in the astronomical universe. Because astrology has in fact been bad science, deriving its hocus-pocus from traditional accretions rather than from careful observation, we do not have to conclude that its *problem* is ridiculous—

---

[6] *On the Principles of Political Economy and Taxation* (London, 1817), Ch. 20.

indeed, between sunspots and cosmic rays it is by no means clear that there could be no science of astrology, or that there could be no influences on human life of the astronomical universe.

However dubious may be the existence of an astrological welfare function we all have a strong feeling that there is something real about an economic welfare function. The proposition that Dives is richer than Lazarus but poorer than Croesus may not be true, and may be disputed, but we have a certain feeling that it is at least not entire nonsense. One of the persistent interests of welfare economics, then, is the quantification of this rather vague concept of "riches." What magnitude is it that is a larger number, or a higher order, in the case of Dives than in the case of Lazarus? This is the "welfare parameter"—some quantity, vector, or indicator which in some sense goes "up" as we move from poorer to richer positions of an economic universe, and which is at a maximum when the system is richest. The search for such a parameter is a legitimate quest, even though there is some danger in it. The danger is that the basic concept with which we are dealing is itself rather vague and ill defined, and that therefore attempts at exact quantification may result in a different concept from the one which really concerns us, and we may lose interest in the basic concept in our manipulations of the quantifiable substitute. Index numbers are a good example of such forced quantifications, and their use and misuse is a constant testimony to the value and the danger of such procedures.

Riches, then, are conceived first in terms of "dollars worth." A man with $10,000 is "richer" than a man with $5,000. We may note in passing an important ambiguity in the concept of riches. A sum of dollars may refer either to a capital stock or to an income flow. Generally speaking, it has been assumed in economics that the income flow was the more significant magnitude, and that when we said that A was richer than B we meant that in some sense he had a larger income. I have argued elsewhere that this has been a mistake, and that the capital stock is a better measure of welfare.[7] However, as this is a private feud between myself and the profession it does not deserve more than a brief reference here, especially as the principal problems of the measurement of riches apply equally whether we are considering a stock or a flow. We notice first of course that simple "dollars worth" figures are not satisfactory. We cannot say that $10,000 represents "more" than $5,000 in any more than a formal arithmetical sense. If for instance,

---

[7] K. E. Boulding, "Income or Welfare," *Rev. Econ. Stud.*, 1949–50, XVII, 77–86.

the index of the price level has risen four times we would be pretty confident that $10,000 represented in some sense "less" at the new price level than $5,000 did at the old. The question arises, however, less of what? We are here thinking not of a homogeneous sum of dollars but of a heterogeneous inventory of goods—so much cheese, so many eggs, so many Cadillacs, and so on, and the question arises, in what sense can we say that one such inventory is "less" than another. Whether the inventory is an inventory of stock or whether it is an inventory of flows does not affect the point in question; in both cases we have the problem of rating on a scale two lists of quantities of heterogeneous items.

The simplest way of reducing a heterogeneous aggregate to a single quantity or rating is by the process of valuation. This is no doubt why so many of the definitions of economic welfare center around measurability in terms of money.[8] The measuring rod of money, however, is more than we need to arrive at a meaningful aggregate of heterogeneous items. As long as there exists a system of valuation coefficients expressing the equivalence of a unit of any one item in terms of every other, the heterogeneous aggregate can be reduced to a single magnitude in terms of the unit of any one of the items. This is not the only way of doing it, but it is certainly the simplest. Thus suppose we have to aggregate 3 elephants, 15 feather beds, and 1,000 mousetraps. If we know, for instance, that 1 elephant is equivalent to 60 feather beds and to 8,000 mousetraps, we can express this aggregate as the equivalent of either $3 + \frac{1}{4} + \frac{1}{8}$ $(= 3\frac{3}{8})$ elephants, or as $180 + 15 + 7\frac{1}{2}$ $(= 202\frac{1}{2})$ feather beds, or as $24,000 + 2,000 + 1,000$ $(= 27,000)$ mousetraps. Any of these figures is as good as any other, and as long as the valuation coefficients remain unchanged any change in the individual items of the aggregate will be reflected in equal proportional changes in any of the measures. If one elephant is always equivalent to 60 feather beds, then we can measure aggregates indifferently in one or the other unit, just as the constant equivalence of 12 inches to one foot means that we can measure length indifferently in either feet or inches.

Our notions of a system of valuation coefficients or equivalents are mainly derived from the existence of transformation coefficients, either in exchange or in production. If in the market one elephant can be exchanged for 60 feather beds this creates a sense of equivalence of these two quantities. The market equivalence is further based on equiva-

---

lence in production (i.e. alternative) cost: if giving up one elephant enables us to produce 60 feather beds, again a sense of equivalence of these two quantities is created. It must be emphasized, however, that valuation equivalents as psychological magnitudes may differ from price or cost equivalents—indeed exchange would not take place if this were not so. Furthermore, these psychological valuation coefficients may themselves be functions of the component quantities of the aggregate measured—the valuation function does not have to be linear, especially where there are *gestalt* configurations and complementary or competitive relationships among the various items.

The concept of a value-aggregate presents few difficulties as long as the set of valuation coefficients is stable. It is by no means unreasonable to say that within a given system of relative values a man with $10,000 is twice as rich as a man with $5,000. Interpersonal comparisons of utility, which will descend to plague us shortly, present no difficulties here, for we are not measuring utility or happiness or significance or any psychological magnitude, but simply a valued physical aggregate of valuable items—valuable not in their sense of significance for human life but simply in the sense that a unit of each can be assigned an equivalent number of units of any other. No troublesome psychological quantities plague us, for we are moving not in the world of men at all but in the economists' paradise, an abstract universe of commodities. The difficulties in measurement arise, however, as soon as the structure of relative values—that is, of the valuation coefficients —changes in the course of time or space. Then the unambiguous character of the valuation measure of riches disappears, for the measure according to one set of relative values does not even have to be the same sign as the measure according to another set. Suppose we compare, for instance, an aggregate of 3 elephants and 15 feather beds with an aggregate of 10 elephants and 5 feather beds. If 1 elephant equals 60 feather beds the first aggregate is $3\frac{1}{4}$ elephants and the second is $10\frac{1}{12}$ elephants: the second is the larger. Suppose, however that 1 elephant equals 1 feather bed. Then the first is 18 and the second is 15 elephants: the first is the larger.

For the aggregate of two commodities or items the problem can be clarified by a diagram such as Figure 1 (p. 8). Physical quantities of two items A and B are measured along the axes. The coordinates of P_0 and of P_1 represent two different collections or constellations of these items. The problem is whether P_0 represents a larger or a smaller total amount of "riches" than P_1. In comparing P_0 with P_2, which represents more of both A and B than P_0, the answer seems fairly obvious, at least qualitatively, though the possibility of one or the other item being a "discommodity" makes even this conclusion doubtful: we might be "richer" with *less* of one or more items than with more. P_1, however, represents more of A but less of B than P_0, and the question as to which combination is the larger cannot be answered unless we have some means of expressing the value of B in terms of A or of A in terms of B. The simplest such means is the constant valuation coefficient, represented

FIGURE 1

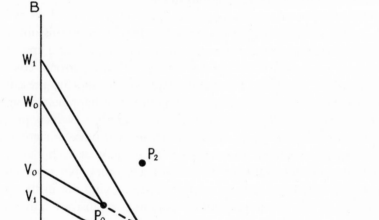

by the slope of a line in such a figure. Thus if the valuation coefficient (the amount of B that is equivalent to one unit of A) is represented by the slopes of the lines P_1V_1 and P_0V_0, OV_1 is the total value of the P_1 combination, and OV_0 is the total value of the P_0 combination, both measured in units of B. OV'_1 and OV'_0 are the corresponding values expressed in terms of A. With this valuation coefficient, P_0 is clearly "larger" than P_1. If, however, the coefficient B/A is higher, represented say by the slopes of P_0W_0 and P_1W_1, the total value of the P_0 combination (OW_0) is now smaller than the value of the P_1 combination (OW_1).

It is clear that if the fluctuations in relative values were as great as this we would lose all sense of their being a meaningful aggregate of the quantities involved. In fact we only have a sense that these aggregates—e.g. of national real capital or of national real income—are meaningful because the fluctuations in relative values are not so great as to make the limiting values meaningless. If according to one set of relative values (say "this year's" prices) the national income this year is 40% greater than last year's, while according to some other equally plausible and relevant set of values (say "last year's" prices) the difference is 50%, we would still feel that the comparison had some meaning—indeed, it would be good if the comparisons were stated in this way, saying "national income increased from 40 to 50 per cent" instead of trying to specify a more exact figure. If, however, one set of values gave an increase of 50% and another a decrease of 25%, the figures would have much less meaning. We cannot say, of course, exactly where are the boundaries of "significance" as they are not clear. It may even mean something to say: "National income increased from —25 to 50 per cent this year"!

Some readers may object that the problem I have discussed is simply one in index-number theory, which in a sense is true. I have discussed it in some detail, however, because it is the breakdown of the attempt at physical quantification of the idea of an aggregate of wealth or income which has led to the subtleties of welfare economics; did we have an unambiguous measure of physical wealth we could simply apply it in all instances where it was necessary to judge whether one situation was "economically" superior to another. The impossibility of such an unambiguous measure when relative values change is one of the drives underlying the development of utility theory: for if the objective measure fails, is there not hope in a subjective measure—that is, "utility"? Utility theory has not merely been an attempt to clarify the part played by the preference structure in the determination of relative values—there has also, from Bentham down, been the dream of a "felicific calculus" which would measure economic desirability in terms of a sum of satisfactions. It is not merely the breakdown of physical valuation which leads to a demand for utility theory. There is also a feeling that the economically superior must be judged not by any physical measure but by some measure of *significance*. Should we not say, for instance, that of two men with an identical physical inventory of assets or incomes, one is "really" richer than the other because he enjoys his riches more? And are not the valuation coefficients themselves, necessary to the calculation of any physical measure of riches, really derived from subjective valuations, and if so, in what way? The consumer's surplus analysis is an attempt to express "utility" in terms of money: its "rehabilitation" and refinement at the hands of Hicks and others[9] in the form of the various compensating payments is again an attempt to give a money value to a "utility" quantity.

It is not the business of this essay to go into the history of utility theory.[10] If, however, we are to have a psychological or subjective theory, utility or preference theory in some form is essential. As a measure of economic welfare, however, the utility concept runs into two grave difficulties. In the first place, no direct measure of utility has ever been devised, so that it can only be measured by its presumed effects on economic behavior—that is, on choices or potential choices. As choice merely implies greater or less, the thing chosen having greater utility than the thing not chosen, or two things having equal utility to which we are indifferent, a utility magnitude reflected in choices cannot be a cardinal, but can only be an ordinal magnitude.[11] That is to say, we cannot say that A has 5.867 times as much utility as B: we may say that it has more, or less, or equal utility. The fact that the measure of utility is choice leads also to a second difficulty; as nobody ever has the choice of being somebody else, the utilities of different individuals cannot be compared. This is the famous problem of "interpersonal comparisons."

---

[9] See especially, J. R. Hicks, "The Rehabilitation of Consumers' Surplus," *Rev. Econ. Stud.*, Feb. 1941, VIII, 108–16; *idem*, "The Four Consumer's Surpluses," *ibid.*, Winter 1943, XI, 31–41; *idem*, "The Generalised Theory of Consumer's Surplus," *ibid.*, 1945–46, XIII, 68–74. See also, A. M. Henderson, "Consumer's Surplus and the Compensating Variation," *ibid.*, Feb. 1941, VIII, 117–21.

[10] It may be observed that utility theory is not strictly necessary for the development of pure economics. Price theory can rest quite firmly on the assumption of demand-for-goods and supply-of-factors functions without going into the derivation of these functions from preference or utility functions. It is agreeable, of course, to find our hunches about the topography of demand and supply functions confirmed by our hunches about the topography of preference functions, but neither set of topographical hunches (e.g. the downward sloping demand curve on the one hand and the diminishing marginal rate of substitution on the other) actually demonstrates the assumed properties of the other. For an excellent history of utility theory the reader is referred to George Stigler, "The Development of Utility Theory," *Jour. Pol. Econ.*, Aug. and Oct. 1950, LVIII, 307–27, 373–96.

[11] Actually, utility is what Coombs calls an "ordered metric" magnitude: we can not only order the alternative choices in a rank of preference, but we can order the intervals between successive alternatives. Thus it makes some kind of sense to say not only, "I prefer A to B and prefer B to C" but, "My preference for A over B is greater than my preference for B over C." It seems to be curiously difficult to get a simple symbolic statement of this property. See C. L. Coombs, "Psychological Scaling without a Unit of Measurement," *Psych. Rev.*, May 1950, LVII, 145–58.

In spite of these two handicaps, however, utility theory, in its more elegant form of preference theory, has been exceedingly fruitful in the past generation. This fruitfulness is due mainly to the use of Pareto's ordinal preference function—especially in the graphic form of a system of indifference curves—as an instrument of analysis. The ordinal preference function is simply a "rubber" utility function capable of any amount of distortion in the direction of the utility axis under the limitation that the *order* of the utilities is not changed. Indifference curves (or surfaces) are contours of equal utility—i.e., they represent a set of combinations of the economic variables to which the subject is indifferent. Technically, the value of the ordinal preference function is generally supposed to be its liberation of utility theory from the assumption of cardinal utility. In fact, however, the rejection of cardinal utility has been a much less restrictive assumption than might at first appear: very few of the important properties of a cardinal utility function are not also present in its ordinal equivalent. One suspects that the fruitfulness of the indifference curve approach has been geometrical rather than analytical: it has permitted the geometric study of three-variable problems, including utility and two economic variables, and so has encouraged deeper study of the topography of the generalized functions.

II. THE SOCIAL OPTIMUM

In the case of the analysis of a single individual the restriction to an ordinal utility function is a very minor limitation, mainly because the main interest of the theory is in the position of maximum utility, and the maxima and minima of functions survive the kind of transformations which the ordinal property permits. This is even true in the case of multiple maxima: any point that is "above" another remains so through any amount of the kind of "stretching" that is permitted. The restriction imposed by the rejection of cardinal utility is somewhat more important in the case of the attempt to define a social optimum. If utility is cardinally measurable for the individual and if (what is not the same thing) the utilities of different individuals can be added, a total social utility function could be derived simply by adding the utilities of all individuals at each configuration of the economic universe. The maximum social utility in this function would then be the social optimum.

Even with the limitation of ordinal, nonaddable utilities, however, a more restricted concept of a social optimum is still possible, and it is this concept which is at the center of the Paretian welfare economics of the past fifteen years. On this view, which goes back historically to Pareto,[12] but which was introduced into English-language economics mainly by Lerner and Hicks,[13] a social optimum is defined as a situation in which nobody can move to a position which he prefers without moving somebody else to a position which is less preferred. Stated negatively, the system is said to be *not* at a social optimum if it is possible to effect a "reorganization" or rearrangement of commodities through exchange or production which will make at least one person better off, in the sense of moving him to a position which he prefers, without making others worse off in the sense of moving them to positions which they do not prefer to the original. A situation in which *A* is made better off at *B*'s expense is regarded on this criterion as nonassessable, as it would involve interpersonal comparisons.

Several points in regard to this concept of a social optimum need to be noticed. One is that it does not define a "point" but a "range" of values of the economic universe. If we suppose the economic welfare function to be an *n*-dimensional mountain in which "height" represents economic welfare, the social optimum in an absolute sense is the top of the mountain. In order to find a single peak, however, it would be necessary to assume that the economic welfare of different individuals is comparable. If this possibility is denied there is no way of finding a single peak: the best that can be done is to build a fence across the peak and say that it lies somewhere on the fence in the fog of uncertainty that covers the mountain. That is to say, the Paretian social optimum defines certain necessary conditions for the absolute social optimum, but by an act of self-abnegation it prohibits itself from finding the sufficient conditions. The main trouble with this procedure—if we admit the possibility of an absolute social optimum at all—is that points which are not on our "fence"—which do not fulfil the conditions for the Paretian optimum—may in fact be superior to points which are on the fence. Thus suppose we have two possible societies, roughly comparable in per capita income and technology, in one of which income is very highly concentrated in the hands of a small ruling class and in the other of which it is widely distributed among an independent peasantry. We might well rate the peasant society better off than the other, even though it exhibited marked maldistribution of resources, imperfect

---

[12] *Op. cit.,* note 5.

[13] See articles cited in footnote 4.

markets, and other characteristics which placed it far from its own Pare-tian optimum, while at the same time the aristocratic society exhibited a perfect Paretian optimum within its own distribution of income. The Paretian welfare economist therefore seems to have worked himself into a position where either he has to deny that interpersonal compari-sons of economic welfare have any meaning—in which case the "fence" can be supposed to run along a horizontal "ridge" and all points on it are equally good, or he has to admit that except for one unknowable point the society *might* be better off when his conditions are not satis-fied than when they are. This dilemma seems to be forcing some welfare economists (notably I. M. D. Little) to work their way back to the rejected interpersonal comparisons—without ever quite getting around to saying how it is to be done.

Another important point to notice in connection with the Paretian optimum is that it raises the question of the *payment* of compensating payments. If interpersonal comparisons are rejected, then we cannot say that one position of the economic universe is better than another unless at least one person is better off and nobody is *actually* worse off. There has been some controversy on this subject: an attempt was made by Hicks and by Kaldor to state the theory in a form in which one posi-tion is regarded as superior to another if, after compensating payments are made, nobody is worse off and somebody is better off, even if the compensating payments are not in fact made. This view represented an attempt to define a "real income" concept which should be in some sense independent of its distribution. This attempt has now generally been abandoned, and in the hands of its later exponents such as Reder, Arrow, and Samuelson there has been a general return to the earlier position of Pareto and Barone.

It should be observed that the idea of a compensating payment is a generalization of Marshall's notion of consumer's surplus as a monetary measure of utility or disutility. If a certain economic reorgani-zation necessitates Jones receiving a punch in the nose, or even more subtle disutilities, we supposedly ask Jones: "Will you let us punch you in the nose for $5?" If he says "No," we have to raise the offer: if he says "Yes," we can lower it. By a process of experiment we can presumably find that exact sum below which Jones is not willing to be punched and above which he is so willing. This is the compensating payment. Similarly, for some benefit we can find the greatest sum which Jones can be induced to pay. If the sum of these compensating pay-ments, both positive and negative is positive, i.e., if the people who benefit from the given change are willing to pay enough for the change to bribe the people who are injured by it into permitting it voluntarily, and still have something left over, then the change is judged to increase economic welfare. We can only be sure that it increases economic welfare, however, if the bribes are actually paid.

From the Paretian definition of the social optimum a number of *marginal conditions* can be derived which must be fulfilled at any position of the economic universe which conforms to the social optimum.

FIGURE 2

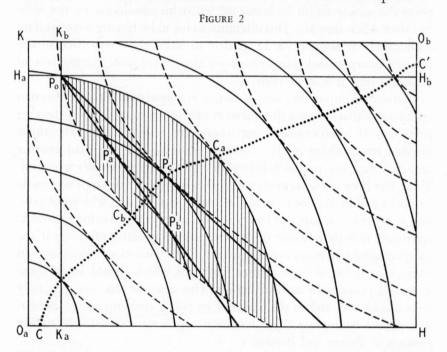

The derivation of these conditions in modern form is due mainly to A. P. Lerner and J. R. Hicks,[14] and the most complete exposition is to be found in Reder.[15] The principles can perhaps best be assessed in the simplest (and probably the best founded) case of the redistribution of existing assets among owners through exchange. This is the familiar case of Edgeworth's "contract curve." In Figure 2 the rectangle O_aHO_bK is drawn so that O_aH is the total quantity of asset H and O_aK is the total quantity of asset K in the possession of the two marketers, A and B. Any point within the rectangle then represents a given distribution of these two assets between the two marketers. Thus at the

[14] See footnote 4.
[15] *Op. cit.*, Ch. 2

point P_o A has H_aP_o of H and K_aP_o of K: B has P_oH_b of H and P_oK_b of K. Indifference curve systems can be postulated in this field for both marketers. The curved broken lines are A's indifference curves: they can be visualized as the contours of a preference surface such that A prefers any point which is "higher" on it to any point that is "lower." Points on a single indifference curve or contour are equally desirable to him. The curves are so drawn that A prefers positions which give him more of both commodities to positions which give him less: the preference surface rises as we move "out" from A's origin O_a. Similarly the curved solid lines are B's indifference curves: in Figure 2 his preference surface rises as we move away from O_b.

FIGURE 3

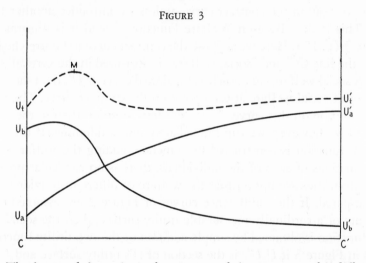

The locus of the points of tangency of the two sets of indifference curves (CC' in Figure 2) is the contract curve. From any point not on this curve, say P_o, we can move to the contract curve at C_a along a B-indifference curve P_oC_a, cutting successively higher A-indifference curves: that is, A is getting better off while B is getting no worse off. Similarly we can move along the A-indifference curve from P_o to C_b, with gain to B and no loss to A. A movement therefore from P_o to any point on the contract curve between C_a and C_b represents a gain to both parties. It is impossible to move from any point on the contract curve, however, without moving to a position in which at least one of the exchangers is worse off than before. Any point on the contract curve, then, represents a "social optimum" in the Paretian sense. The "marginal condition" in this case is the condition of tangency of the indifference curves, that is, that the marginal rates of substitution of the two exchangers should be equal. The marginal rate of substitution is the *slope* of an indifference curve: it is that amount of one commodity which can be substituted for one unit of another without feeling of loss or gain. When the indifference curves of the two exchangers are tangent, their slopes at that point are equal. The marginal condition in this case serves to *define* the contract curve. It is satisfied at any point on the contract curve and is not satisfied at any point away from it.

There still remains the significance of movement *along* the contract curve. As we move from C towards C', A is getting better off and B worse off. It is clear that we cannot say whether any point on the contract curve is "better" than any other, and so cannot define a maximum position on the contract curve, unless we introduce another function. This is the "Bergson Welfare Function,"[16] and it is illustrated in Figure 3 (p. 15). Here we suppose the contract curve to be stretched out along the line CC' and "social welfare" is measured in the vertical direction. A social welfare curve such as the dotted curve $U_tU'_t$ then shows the amount of social welfare at each point on the contract curve. The maximum position on this curve, M, is the "best" position then in the whole field. Now, however, we run immediately into a dilemma. If the social welfare function is constructed by somehow adding the welfare (utility) functions of each of the individuals, there is no particular problem apart from the assumption that the welfare of different individuals can be compared. If the indifference curves of Figure 2 are assumed to be contours of a cardinally measurable utility surface, then the social welfare function is obtained by simple addition of the two utility functions. Thus in Figure 3 if $U_aU'_a$ is the section of A's utility surface and $U_bU'_b$ is the section of B's utility surface, the social welfare function $U_tU'_t$ is obtained by adding the two curves vertically. This is clearly a highly special case of the social welfare function. In this special case we are sure that the maximum social welfare occurs somewhere on the contract curve. We can furthermore generalize the condition that limits this maximum to some point on the contract curve. It is not necessary to assume cardinal and additive utilities: as long as the social welfare is a monotonic function of individual (ordinal) utilities, the condition holds. In the most general case, however, if we visualize a generalized social welfare function as a "mountain" rising over the field of Figure 2, there is no reason to suppose that the summit of the mountain must lie somewhere over a point on the line CC'. Suppose, for instance, that

---

[16] Bergson, *op. cit.*

there is a strong social taboo against *A* having *H* and against *B* having *K*. Then the maximum social welfare, viewed in the light of the taboos and prejudices of the society, might well be at the point *K*, in spite of the fact that the individuals would prefer, as individuals, something different. The assumption that the optimum point must lie on the contract curve, therefore, itself involves an important value judgment: that people ought to get what they want.

It is evident that movement along the contract curve constitutes a redistribution of welfare in some sense, as one person is getting better off at the expense of the other. This has led to attempts to define the Paretian optimum as an "optimum of allocation" which can be defined without regard to distribution, and the fixing of a point on the contract curve as a problem in the "optimum of distribution."[17] Unfortunately the problem is not so simple, once the possibility of a generalized (Bergson) social welfare function is admitted.

These points may be clarified if the above analysis, which may seem at first sight to be very remote from real economic problems, is applied to a very practical economic question—the principles of collective bargaining. In bargaining about, say, the terms of a union contract there are a great many variables involved in the total settlement, each represented, we assume, by a clause in the contract. Let us suppose that each can be subjected to some kind of quantitative measure, and let us take a simple case in which there are only two such variables, say wages and length of vacation. Suppose the wage is measured along O_aH in Figure 2, and length of vacation along O_aK. Then, in general, the union will be better pleased as we move towards O_b, and the employer will be better pleased as we move towards O_a. Indifference curve systems can be postulated for each bargainer, and from their points of tangency a contract curve can be drawn. Then from any point not on the contract curve, agreement can be reached by *trading*, moving towards the contract curve: thus from P_o both union and employer might agree to give up some vacation in return for an addition to wages. Once the contract curve is reached, however, agreement by trading becomes impossible, and any move along the contract curve represents *conflict*—that is, a bettering of the position of one party at the expense of the other. This distinction between trading and conflict is essential in the bargaining process, and it is the main part of the skill of the

---

[17] Hicks, in his article, "Foundations of Welfare Economics," *loc. cit.*, pp. 696–712, suggests this point of view. A recent exponent is Maurice Allais, *Économie et intérêt* (Paris, 1947).

bargainer to know how to "trade"—that is, to start from a position where trading is possible and to trade in such a way, by a process akin to price discrimination, sliding down the opponent's indifference curves in a succession of small offers until he hits the contract curve at a point most favorable to himself. The theory can easily be generalized to the many-variable case: no matter how many variables there are in the bargain the contract curve with two bargainers remains a line in the n-space corresponding to the n variables, and conflict between two parties remains "one-dimensional" in the sense that it can be represented as movement along a line each point of which stands for a given collection of the bargained variables.

The introduction of more variables increases the possibility and the complexity of the "trading" process. This may well be why trade union contracts seem to get more and more complex, for the more clauses there are in the contract the more chance there is of trading clause against clause and the less likelihood there is of reaching an impasse on the contract curve. Reaching the contract curve does not necessarily involve a breakdown of bargaining: suppose for instance that the employer is willing to sign a contract on any terms more favorable than those represented by C_a, and the union will sign on any terms more favorable than those at C_b. Then a bargain can be struck anywhere within the range $C_b C_a$. If the union's sticking point were C_a and the employer's C_b, however, a bargain could not be struck, and negotiations would break down until some change had occurred in the underlying preferences. If one or both of the parties are unskilled traders, of course, there is no reason to suppose that the contract curve will be reached. In the above case where the range $C_b C_a$ represents the possible range of bargains on the contract curve, the range of possible bargains in the whole field is in the shaded area bounded by the respective indifference curves through C_b and C_a. If one of the parties is an unskilled trader the other will be able to strike a bargain at a point off the contract curve which is better for him than the position to which he could be forced, by skilled trading, on the contract curve.

The real significance of the Paretian welfare economics, then, is that it sets forth explicitly the distinction between those changes in social variables which can take place through "trading"—i.e., through a mutual benefit of all parties—and those changes which involve "conflict," or the benefit of one party at the expense of another. In a civilization which is threatened with extinction because of an inability to solve the problem of conflict this distinction may be of considerable importance. Because conflict is costly, often very costly, and there is a reasonable presumption that it is almost certain to be more costly than trading, economists in general, and welfare economists in particular, have had a strong prejudice in favor of trading; and this is why the Paretian optimum is regarded as desirable. Considered merely as analysis, however, the contribution of the Paretian type of construction is the distinction between trading and conflict, and not the judgment between them.[18]

I have illustrated the marginal conditions in the case of exchange in some detail in order to bring out the essential nature of these conditions. Reder distinguishes seven such sets of conditions, all of which must be satisfied simultaneously if they are to define the optimum position of the system. They may perhaps be illustrated most simply by means of arithmetical examples; for graphical treatment Reder can be consulted,[19] and for analytical treatment Samuelson.[20] The arithmetical exposition of all seven conditions is shown in Table 1 (p. 20). The demonstration is conducted by showing that if the marginal conditions are *not* fulfilled a reorganization can take place which will leave one party better off without injuring the other.

The first condition is the one already discussed: that the marginal rates of substitution of two commodities should be the same for any pair of owners. Thus we suppose that for owner A, 1 of H can be substituted for 2 of K without loss or gain, and for owner B, 1 of H can be substituted for 3 of K without loss or gain: this violates the first marginal equality. Then we suppose that before the reorganization A has $20H$ and $10K$, and B has $5H$ and $20K$. The reorganization consists of exchange, A giving up 1 of H to B in return for 2 of K. This leaves A with $19H$ and $12K$, and B with $6H$ and $18K$. In A's case we know from his marginal rate of substitution that the reorganization leaves him neither worse nor better off. In B's case however we could have taken $3K$ away from him and we would have left him just as well off as before: for him, therefore, $6H$ and $17K$ would be just as good as $5H$ and $20K$. The reorganization therefore leaves B better off by $1K$, and leaves A no worse off. This could not be done if the marginal rates of substitution were equal.

---

[18] The reader should perhaps be warned that I have introduced the term "trading" and "conflict" into the discussion myself, because they seem to be best descriptive of the important distinction between reorganizations which involve no loss to anyone and those which involve loss to someone.

[19] *Op. cit.*, Ch. 2.

[20] *Op. cit.*, Ch. 8.

The second marginal condition relates to the allocation of products among various producers. The producers may be conceived of as firms, or as sectors of the economy, or as "countries," though the latter aggregates are open to some objections. This condition, therefore, determines the optimum degree of specialization of production. We suppose

TABLE 1

MARGINAL CONDITIONS: OPTIMUM POSITION OF THE SYSTEM

Condition Number	Parties	Marginal Rates of Transformation	Nature of Reorganization	Situation before Reorganization	Situation after Reorganization
1	Owner A	$1H = 2K$		$20H,\ 10K$	$= 19H,\ 12K$
	Owner B	$1H = 3K$	Exchange	$5H,\ 20K$	$6H,\ 18K$
				$(5H,\ 20K$	$=\ 6H,\ 17K)$
2	Producer A	$1H$ for $2K$	Reallocation	$15H,\ 25K$	$16H,\ 23K$
	Producer B	$1H$ for $3K$	of production	$5H,\ 10K$	$4H,\ 13K$
	(Totals)			$20H,\ 35K$	$20H,\ 36K$
3	Producer A	$1f$ makes $2K$	Reallocation	$20f–40K$	$19f–38K$
	Producer B	$1f$ makes $3K$	of factors	$20f–60K$	$21f–63K$
	(Totals)			$40f–100K$	$40f–101K$
4	Producer A	$1f = 2g$	Substitution	$20f,\ 30g$	$19f,\ 32g$
	Producer B	$1f = 3g$	of factors	$10f,\ 20g$	$11f,\ 17g$
	(Totals)			$30f,\ 50g$	$30f,\ 49g$
5	Consumer A	$1H = 2K$	Substitution	$20H,\ 30K$	$= 19H,\ 32K$
	Producer B	$1H = 3K$	of products	$20H,\ 30K$	$19H,\ 33K$
6	Factors		Substitution of		
	Preference	$1t = 2H$	leisure for	$8t,\ 24H$	$= 9t,\ 26H$
	Reward Paid	$1t = 3H$	product	$8t,\ 24H$	$9t,\ 27H$
7	Lender A	$1H_1 = 2H_2$	Lending and	$20H_1,\ 10H_2$	$= 19H_1,\ 12H_2$
	Borrower B	$1H_1 = 3H_2$	borrowing	$10H_1,\ 5H_2$	$11H_1,\ 3H_2$
			without uncertainty	$(10H_1,\ 5H_2$	$= 11H_1,\ 2H_2)$

that producer A can produce $2K$ with the factors released by giving up the production of $1H$: this is his marginal rate of transformation of products under the condition that the quantity of factors used by him is constant. Similarly producer B could get $3K$ if he gave up $1H$. Before the reorganization, producer A is making $15H$ and $25K$, producer B is making $5H$ and $10K$; that is, $20H$ and $35K$ in all. We now suppose that A shifts from K to H and B from H to K, as in the table: we see that the production of K can be increased by 1 unit without lowering

WELFARE ECONOMICS · 21

the production of *H*. An example could be constructed in which the production of both goods increased as a result of the reorganization. The second marginal condition may then be stated: if the marginal rates of transformation in production of any two products are not the same for all producers, the production of some product can be increased without diminishing the production of any other, by shifting production of each commodity towards its "low cost" producer.

The third marginal condition relates to the reallocation of a single factor between two producers. Thus we suppose that for producer *A* the addition of 1*f* of a factor adds 2*K* to the product, and that for *B* the addition of 1*f* adds 3*K* to the product. Then we see by the table that if 1*f* of the factor is shifted from *A* to *B,* the amount of commodity produced by the given amount of factor is increased: thus with 40*f* of the factor before the change only 100*K* is produced, and after the change 101*K* is produced. The third marginal condition can then be stated: if the marginal physical productivity of a given factor for a given product is not the same for two producers, the total product from a given amount of the factor can be increased by shifting the factor from the low to the high productivity producer.

The fourth marginal condition deals with the substitution of factors one for another. Here we suppose two factors, *f* and *g*. Producer *A* can keep his product constant if he replaces 1*f* by 2*g;* producer *B* can do likewise if he replaces 1*f* by 3*g*. In this case therefore producer *A* can produce the same product with 20*f* and 30*g* before, or with 19*f,* and 32*g* after the change: producer B can do likewise with 10*f* and 20*g* before, and 11*f* and 17*g* after. A shift therefore of *g* towards producer *A* and of *f* towards producer *B* enables the same total product as before to be made with a smaller amount of factors. The condition may be stated: if the marginal rates of equal-product substitution of two factors are not the same for two producers, the same total product can be produced with a smaller expenditure of factors if each factor is shifted towards the producer for whom its marginal rate of substitution is least. Conditions two, three, and four can all be reduced to a single condition if factors are regarded as "negative products."

The fifth marginal condition relates to the substitution of products to conform to the structure of consumers' preferences. We suppose that consumer *A* can substitute 2*K* for 1*H* without feeling loss or gain. Producer *B* can substitute 3*K* for 1*H* without changing the amount of factors used. Then by shifting production from *H* to *K* the consumer can be made better off, without the producer being worse off; instead of the initial $20H$ and $30K$ he can have $19H$ and $33K$, whereas he would be just as well satisfied as before with $19H$ and $32K$: the change leaves him $1K$ to the good. This condition may be stated therefore: if the marginal rate of indifferent substitution of any consumer for two commodities is not equal to the marginal rate of transformation of these commodities in production, the consumer can be made better off by shifting production towards that commodity which has the greater marginal rate of equivalence in production.

The sixth condition relates to the substitution of "leisure" for product, and is concerned therefore with the *intensity of use* of factors. The concept of leisure does not only apply to labor, of course: it may refer to any factor which is withheld from use. Thus we suppose that the marginal rate of substitution of factor-use for product is $1t$ of factor use for $2H$ of product: that means that the owner of the factor would be indifferent whether the factor worked for $8t$ (say, hours) and received $24H$, or worked for $9t$ and received $26H$. The Marginal Reward is the increase in product acquired by the factor in return for a unit addition to the factor use; we suppose this is $3H$ per $1t$—i.e., working the factor another "hour" adds $3H$ to its total remuneration. In this case it will clearly pay to work another hour: $9t$ and $26H$ is just as good to the factor as $8t$ and $24H$: if it works another hour, however, it has $9t$ and $27H$—it is clearly $1H$ to the good. We can state the condition therefore: if the marginal reward of a factor exceeds the marginal rate of substitution of reward for use, the use of the factor will be increased.

The seventh condition relates to lending and borrowing in the absence of uncertainty. We suppose that H_1 and H_2 refer to qualities of asset H at times t_1 and t_2. We suppose that A is indifferent to having $1H_1$ or $2H_2$: B is indifferent to having $1H_1$ or $3H_2$. Individual A, that is to say, has a lower rate of time preference than B. Then it will pay B to borrow from A. Without borrowing we suppose A expects to have $20H_1$ and $10H_2$, B expects to have $10H_1$ and $5H_2$. Now if B borrows $1H$ from A at a rate of interest equal to A's rate of time preference A will have $19H_1$ and $12H_2$, and B will have $11H_1$ and $3H_2$, as A has transferred $1H$ to B at time t_1 and B has transferred $2H$ to A at time t_2. B however would just as soon have $11H_1$ and $2H_2$ as $10H_1$ and $5H_2$, as we know from his marginal rate of time substitution. He is therefore $1H$ to the good, and A is no worse off. The condition may be stated then: if the marginal rates of time substitution of two individuals for a given asset differ, it will pay the one with the smaller rate of time substitution to lend on the earlier date to the one with the larger.

These seven conditions correspond roughly to the list as given by

Reder. It is evident that there are others which have not been stated as yet explicitly in the literature. There may be other conditions relating to time preference, for instance: (8) that the own-rates of time preference for any one individual for two commodities must be the same; and (9) that the rate of time preference for an individual must be equal to the rate of time substitution in production (the marginal own-rate of return) for every commodity. There are also conditions relating to uncertainty and to liquidity (conditions 7, 8, and 9 assume certainty)— the marginal rates of substitution of all individuals for assets of different degrees of uncertainty and liquidity must be equal. There are also some conditions relating to equality of *rates* of uncertainty and liquidity preference, analogous to (8) and (9); the difficulties of quantifying these concepts makes these conditions rather vague. All these conditions may be summed up in two grand conditions: (*i*) wherever transformation of one variable into another is technically possible, the rate of indifferent substitution (that is, the amount of one variable which can be substituted for one unit of the other without feeling of gain or loss) must be equal to the rate of technical substitution—that is, the amount of the first variable which can be obtained technically by giving up one unit of the second; and (*ii*) all equivalent rates of technical and indifferent substitution must be equal.

The marginal equalities by themselves, of course, serve to define a minimum just as well as a maximum: that is why I have stated them in a negative rather than in a positive form, as this enables the statement of the second-order conditions to be worked into the condition itself. Stating them in this form, however, still does not guarantee that there is a real position of an optimum in which the conditions are satisfied. In the examples of Table 1, as long as the marginal inequalities persist it will always pay to make changes. If there is to be a real optimum we must invoke some "principle of diminishing returns" in each case. The generalized principle of diminishing returns may be stated thus: the movement of the system towards an optimum in the direction indicated by a divergence of marginal rates of transformation must lessen this divergence. If this law holds, the movement of the system from any position will lessen the divergence from the optimum until finally the system reaches the optimum point.

III. POLICY IMPLICATIONS OF WELFARE ECONOMICS

We may now pass on to some of the practical conclusions which have been drawn from welfare economics. The first is a strong predisposition in favor of "perfect markets"—that is, market situations in which the price of the commodity bought or sold does not vary with the *quantity* bought or sold by the individual buyer or seller. This predisposition arises from the fact that an individual operating in a perfect market maximizes his profits (or more generally his "advantage") by carrying every line of activity to the point where the price is equal to the marginal rate of transformation or substitution of money for the commodity in question. As in a perfect market the price is the same for all individuals this means that the operations of self-interest lead to an equilibrium of the universe of economic variables at a point where all the relevant marginal rates of transformation are equal to each other, because equal to the uniform price. We may illustrate from the equilibrium of exchange. Referring back to Figure 2 (p. 14), suppose that there is some price or ratio of exchange at which both parties can exchange any amounts. If we start with an initial position P_o such a price can be shown by any straight line (opportunity path) passing through P_o, such as P_oP_b or P_oP_c—the slope of the line being equal to the fixed ratio of exchange. Given this ratio of exchange, say P_oP_b, it is clear that (assuming profit or utility maximization) each party will proceed to the point at which the opportunity path touches one of his indifference curves—say P_a for A and P_b for B. We are assuming here a "market"—i.e., many other buyers and sellers—so that A and B do not have to deal only with each other. When there is a single price in the whole market at which the total amount offered for sale is equal to the total amount offered for purchase, the marginal rates of substitution for all marketers are equal and the marketers' positions lie on an n-dimensional contract function. It is not possible to illustrate this proposition graphically: however, the corresponding situation in the two-exchanger case would be the price (P_oP_c) at which both parties reach their optimum positions together on the contract curve at P_c.

We see, therefore, that welfare economics adds support to the classical case for perfect competition, as perfect competition is one form of social organization by which, theoretically, the social optimum can be achieved. This is not, of course, the main justification for a competitive economy in the minds of the classical economists, who thought much more in terms of the dynamics of social change than in terms of optimum positions of general equilibrium: the classical attack on protection is in terms of the ability of protected interests to prevent economic progress, rather than in terms of the wastes in the allocation of resources due to imperfect markets. Nevertheless, the welfare economists' case for perfect competition represents some clarification of the issues. Any argument for perfect competition immediately runs into the difficulty that perfect competition is impossible unless the size of the unit of economic decision is small relative to the market. Consequently, in cases where the efficiency of the economic unit (measured, say, by some reciprocal of average cost) increases with the size of the unit over a large range of output we run into a dilemma, that perfect competition can only be obtained at the cost of productive inefficiency. The only answer to this dilemma seems to be public operation or control of these large-scale enterprises in order to secure "marginal cost pricing"; for it is only when price is equal to marginal cost that the marginal conditions of the social optimum can be met.

This conclusion has been the subject of an extensive controversy in the journals, beginning with a famous article by Hotelling in 1938.[21] This controversy has been ably summed up by Nancy Ruggles in two articles.[22] The main issues from the point of view of welfare economics have been first, whether proportionality of price to marginal cost rather than equality would not equally well satisfy the conditions for an optimum: this was proposed by Frisch.[23] It has been shown, by Lerner, Bergson, and others, that equality is necessary if the third and fourth marginal conditions (those governing the allocation and substitution of factors) are not to be violated. A second issue of the controversy was whether complete compensation was necessary: this merely reflects the general controversy on the subject of whether the optimum conditions mean anything in the absence of full compensation. A third issue of the controversy concerned the means of raising money for the necessary subsidies: Hotelling advocated an income tax, but it can be shown that the income tax violates the sixth marginal condition, and distorts the economic equilibrium away from the optimal distribution of time between work and leisure. Perhaps the most important issue in the controversy concerns the administrative possibility of marginal cost pricing: this however lies outside the scope of welfare economics narrowly defined.

The marginal cost controversy pointed up another important con-

---

[21] *Op. cit.*

[22] Nancy Ruggles, "The Welfare Basis of the Marginal Cost Pricing Principle," *Rev. Econ. Stud.* (1949–50), XVII, 29–46; *idem*, "Recent Developments in the Theory of Marginal Cost Pricing," *ibid.*, pp. 107–26.

[23] Ragnar Frisch, "The Dupuit Taxation Theorem," *Econometrica*, Apr. 1939, VII, 145–50. See also on this point the earlier article by R. F. Kahn, "Some Notes on Ideal Output," *Econ. Jour.*, Mar. 1935, XLV, 1–35.

clusion of welfare economics: that all taxation as far as possible should be nonmarginal—that is, should be in the form of lump-sum taxes which are independent of the activity of the person or concern taxed. Thus there is a general predisposition against excise taxes on the ground that they distort the relative price and output structure away from the taxed commodities. There is a similar predisposition against income taxes on the ground that they distort the structure of activity as between "work" and "leisure." The general-welfare case against tariffs is part of the same argument, as they distort the geographic structure of economic activity. It can be shown that a tariff can benefit a single country, in the sense that it can create a situation whereby everyone within the country by a proper system of compensations, could be made better off as a result. This, however, is no more surprising than the proposition that a monopolist can benefit himself by restricting his output, even though the whole society suffers.

A rather surprising use of welfare economics has been in defense of socialism by some of the more sophisticated socialist economists. It is argued that as perfect competition is impossible in a market economy the marginal conditions for the social optimum cannot possibly be satisfied under capitalism and can only be satisfied in a socialist economy planned consciously to that end. This view—which is especially associated with the name of Oscar Lange[24]—should not be confused with the more Keynesian type of economic philosophy of Lerner,[25] in which the activity of the state is conceived as a governing mechanism, throwing a little counterweight in the directions where the system of private enterprise is failing to conform to the social optimum, rather than as the single-firm economy of the socialists. The assumption implicit in both these views, and especially in the socialist view, that there is nothing in the operations of a political and administrative system corresponding to imperfect competition in the market strikes me as naïve. Any realistic theory of the socialist or even of the governed economy must operate in terms of an equilibrium of political and administrative pressures, and I see no reason to suppose that these pressures will be any more "perfect" in a socialist than in the market economy. In any system action will affect the terms on which action is taken, whether the ac-

---

[24] "On the Economic Theory of Socialism," in *On the Economic Theory of Socialism*, B. E. Lippincott, ed. (Minneapolis, 1938). For a more detailed account of this aspect of the subject, see Abram Bergson, "Socialist Economics," *A Survey of Contemporary Economics*, Vol. I, H. S. Ellis, ed. (Philadelphia, 1948), Ch. 12.

[25] A. P. Lerner, *The Economics of Control* (New York, 1944).

tion be sales and the terms the price, or whether action be the placating of a superior and the terms the ratio of his pleasure to one's activity.

IV. AN ASSESSMENT OF WELFARE ECONOMICS

It is not perhaps the duty of the writer of one of these surveys to attempt an assessment of what he surveys. It is impossible, however, to be monarch of all one surveys without at the same time being a judge, and in a field as controversial as welfare economics the pretense of impartiality is more dangerous than the acknowledgment of bias. In the concluding pages, therefore, I propose to attempt some assessment of welfare economics, if only to warn the reader who judges differently to look for bias in my account.

In making this assessment some technical defects in the structure must first be examined. The first is of minor importance in principle, though it may be of considerable importance in practice. It is that the marginal conditions define a social optimum only marginally: i.e., the position which they define is superior to any other in the immediate vicinity, but it is not necessarily superior to any other over the whole possible range of the universe. This is the problem of the "maximum maximorum": there is nothing in the marginal conditions which can differentiate the top of a molehill from that of Mount Everest. This is a problem which has been of real concern to economists from Adam Smith on. Adam Smith's dynamics, based on the famous proposition that the division of labor depends on the extent of the market, is concerned with how one breaks out of a "low" equilibrium to a "higher" one. Marshall's case of the downward sloping supply curve intersecting the demand curve at three or more points is another example. The best treatment of this problem is that of Allyn Young:[26] since his day, until quite recently, there has been a curious lack of interest in the subject, in spite of its immense practical importance—e.g. in the development of underdeveloped areas. The preoccupation of welfare economics with the definition of a single optimum may well have done a disservice insofar as it has diverted attention from the critical problems of developmental dynamics. The problem may well be not how to get close to the top of a molehill, but how to climb *down* the molehill in order to start up the mountain. There is some recognition of this problem in Hicks' discussion of the "total conditions" in his 1939 article—a discussion

---

[26] "Increasing Returns and Economic Progress," *Econ. Jour.,* Dec. 1928, XXXVIII 527–42.

which has played some part in the marginal cost controversy. Hicks' total conditions, however, refer to the problem of whether capacity should be created; they are not adequate for dealing with the larger dynamic questions of economic development.

Somewhat related to this problem is that of the "boundary maximum." Where the actual range of variables of the economic system is sharply limited by institutional or other factors (e.g. minimum wage laws) boundary maxima are not at all improbable. That is, the boundary of the possible range of variables may represent a superior point to any other in the possible range, and yet the marginal conditions will not be satisfied at it. Thus suppose, in Figure 3 (p. 15), M represents the kind of maximum at which the marginal conditions are satisfied. It would be quite possible for U'_t to be a superior position, even though the marginal conditions would not be satisfied. One cannot assume off-hand, therefore, in the presence of a bounded universe (and the economic universe is very sharply bounded by law and by custom) that the violation of the marginal conditions is necessarily significant.

A more serious technical defect is the assumption that the structure of individual preferences (as expressed, say, in indifference curves) is independent of any variable of the system except the quantities of commodity, and in particular is independent of prices and is also invariant with respect to the paths taken towards equilibrium. These assumptions are extremely shaky. If the preference structure is itself a function, say, of the prices or other transformation ratios of the economic variables, as well as of quantities of commodity, all the marginal equalities are invalidated. I have attempted to illustrate in *A Reconstruction of Economics*[27] some of the difficulties which arise in constructing a general theory of preference in which the preference functions (e.g. the indifference curves) are assumed to vary with the absolute level of price. It is not impossible to take these modifications formally into account. When the system is so modified, however, all the simplicity and elegance of welfare economics disappears, as well as most of its present conclusions. Virtually all the constructions of welfare economics, for instance (including our Figure 2), assume that the indifference curves remain stable as change proceeds, or as prices are changed. If every change in price necessitates drawing up a new set of indifference curves, the diagrams melt into chaos. It can be argued in defense of the simpler assumption that in fact preference functions will only vary with price if

---

[27] New York, 1950, Ch. 5.

there is a "money illusion" which should be neglected in welfare considerations, or if there is purely speculative behavior which cancels out in the long run. Thus a general rise in the absolute level of money prices may make many people "feel" worse off, even if their incomes rise accordingly, because they still think of the value of money in terms of their old money incomes. This is a "money illusion," but it hardly becomes a welfare economist to neglect it. If he builds solely on revealed (or revealable) preferences, he is no more entitled (as a welfare economist) to judge this an illusion than he is to judge a taste for whiskey immoral. A shift in the preference structure with a change in the absolute price is not "illusion" if the absolute level of price is regarded as an indicator of future levels. If price is thought to be "high" relative to some norm it may be perfectly rational to revise one's preferences towards money and away from commodity, in the expectation that prices will fall. This difficulty may be merely one aspect of a general weakness of present-day welfare economics—its failure to extend its principles to include the treatment of uncertainty.

An even more fundamental technical objection to modern welfare economics is the assumption that preference structures are invariant with respect to movement among the variables. This means assuming that there is no disutility of maximizing utility, and that "trading" in any of its forms is preferentially neutral. A great deal of human behavior and attitude, however, is explicable only on the assumption that both maximizing utility or profit (i.e. "economizing") and trading are acutely disagreeable, not to say unethical proceedings. There is a general assumption in welfare economics that "trading"—i.e. moving to positions of mutual advantage—is "good" and that "conflict" is bad, or at least neutral. One can see how a Marxist might jump on this as the intellectual product of a civilization of shopkeepers, and how the principles of dialectical materialism might lead to just the opposite conclusion—that trading was bad and conflict good. Indeed, much of the conflict between capitalism and communism lies precisely in a profound difference in preference in regard to trading—it is this which makes the disagreement so intractable. The same conflict may be observed between capitalist and militarist attitudes—indeed, militarism and communism can formally be regarded as sub-forms of the same preference system. In this system trading is regarded as "appeasement": the ideal of moving to positions where everybody is better off than before is positively rejected because a great positive value is attached to some people (enemies) being *worse* off than before. On this view the wicked should not be bought off: they should be knocked down. "Millions for defense but not a penny for tribute!"—the compensating payment again! The accusation that some welfare economists assume the permanent vesting of all vested interests is also part of the above criticism.

The act of economizing, and still more, the reduction of all values to monetary terms, likewise falls under criticism. This may be called the "romantic" preference field: it registers a high value for disinterestedness, self-giving, not-counting-the-cost, daredeviltry, extravagance of life, and carelessness for consequences. It is a most important element in our civilization—witness our romantic attitude towards marriage and war. By this standard, welfare economics can be denounced as a set of variations on the shocking theme that every man has his price, and welfare economists can be stigmatized in the language of Oscar Wilde as people who know the price of everything and the value of nothing. Some things do not have a price at all, even in the form of compensating payments. It might be argued, for instance, that unmodified welfare economics would lead to the conclusion that slavery is desirable, as the establishment of any "inalienable rights" involves an interference with the ability to trade—i.e. to alienate.

The formal mathematical statement of the modifications which must be made in welfare economics to take account of these criticisms is quite beyond the scope of this paper—and of its author. It is possible, however, to see broadly some conclusions which might be expected. If the act of economizing itself is disagreeable (or agreeable!) the topography of the opportunity field itself modifies the topography of the preference field. There will be a preference for places where it does not much matter what we do, and where we do not have to hit the "right" conduct right on the head. That is to say there will be a preference for plateaus of opportunity, where we can wander around without disaster and even large errors are not fatal, to "peaks" where results are excellent *if* we make exactly the right choices but where even slightly wrong choices are disastrous. An extension of welfare economics into the fields of uncertainty and liquidity might clear up much of this problem.

The problem of the impact of the path followed on the structure of preferences is even more difficult. It may be that moving *anywhere* is painful, and produces a fall in the preference surface: this would result in a strong preference for the *status quo,* and the preference surface will bunch into peaks wherever we happen to be. Like a boy crawling about under a sheet we carry our maximum with us; in which case why bother to go anywhere! The pregnant remark of Hicks that the greatest gain of the monopolist may be a quiet life is an insight which might profitably be worked into the formal structure of welfare economics. We may run into preferences against some paths—e.g. paths of price discrimination—which do not exist for others. What is worse, even the opportunity function may not be invariant to the path chosen: means determine ends, and ends means; history is irreversible, and often there are no roads back from errors committed. Thus instead of a relatively simple problem of climbing the preference mountain along the opportunity fence until we reach the highest point—which is the essential principle of maximizing behavior and of welfare economics— we find ourselves climbing a quaking jelly of a mountain that dips and sags as we walk across it, along a nightmarish fence which shifts and wavers as we walk beside it. It is little wonder that mankind has generally retreated from the quagmire of rationality to the solid highroads of taboo and principle, even though they may not go where we want them to!

This survey may well be concluded by asking to what extent has welfare economics attained the three objectives mentioned at the outset: to define "riches," to provide a guide for social policy, and to develop a "scientific" prolegomena to ethics. For the first some success can be claimed. The concept of a social optimum and the use of a preference function have clarified somewhat the meaning of "economically better," which perhaps has certain advantages over the older concept of utility. The question must be raised however whether in the process of refining the crude idea of riches some of the metal rather than the dross has been refined out, even in the notion of a preference function for an individual. When we come to the measurement of the riches of groups, the advance seems even more dubious. Samuelson[28] has shown that we cannot even be *sure* that group A is better off than group B even if A has collectively more of everything, and once more we seem to be thrown back on the rather crude comparisons of the Colin Clark type.

Turning now to the contribution of welfare economics to the discussion of economic policy, the record is not too encouraging. On the positive side there is a certain clarification of arguments which the earlier economists left fuzzy, for example, in the theory of tariffs or of taxation. As a realistic guide to social policy, however, the concept of a social optimum and of the marginal conditions has not been particularly

---

[28] P. A. Samuelson, "The Evaluation of Real National Income," *Oxford Econ. Papers*, Jan. 1950, II, 1–29.

fruitful—as the marginal cost controversy itself witnesses. One cannot help feeling that the crude ifs and ands of plain price and monetary theory are of much more importance to the policy maker than the elegant, but fragile, pots and pans of welfare economics. The policy maker who learns that prices above some level lead to surpluses, and below lead to shortages, or that exports, on the whole, are paid for by imports, or that a large increase in the quantity of money is likely to lead to a rise in the price level, or that deflation is likely to lead to unemployment, knows something that is of use to him at least in avoiding gross and clumsy mistakes. I doubt if a knowledge of the Seven Marginal Conditions has ever proven of any value to the statesman, and an intoxication with the ideal of marginal cost pricing might mislead him severely. One wonders even if the Paretian welfare economics has come up with anything as practically useful as the famous Pigovian proposition that Smoke Is a Nuisance! And in fact all economic policy has to be based on interpersonal comparisons, as compensation is hardly ever administratively practicable. Even the conclusion of welfare economics that poll taxes are economically more desirable than income or excise taxes seems to be singularly useless as a canon of public finance— simply because of its administrative difficulty. Perhaps the best that can be said for welfare economics as a discipline is that it is virtually impossible to study it without learning a good deal of economics in the process!

Then in regard to the third objective—the curiously platonic love affair between welfare economics and ethics—one must admit that the task of making value judgments explicit is a very important one. One can dismiss fairly curtly the idea of a *wertfrei* system of evaluation: it is obviously preposterous to suppose that one can set up criteria for judgment which are somehow independent of ethical norms. Indeed, as we have seen, the ethical judgments involved in the Hicks-Kaldor variety of welfare economics—that people should get what they want and that trading is ethically neutral—are not merely ethical judgments but practically indefensible ones. In this respect the welfare economics of the Bergson-Samuelson type which postulated a general "social welfare function" is on much safer ground, even though its conclusions grow more nebulous as they become more general.

What, indeed, welfare economics seems to be turning into is not a prolegomena to ethics but a form of ethical theory itself. What we are doing in economics, or in any other abstraction, is to carve for ourselves n-k dimensional sections, along certain dimensions that interest us, of some n-dimensional "feasibility function"—the feasibility function being that which shows all those combinations of social (or other) magnitudes which are in some sense "available." "Pure" economics is essentially a discussion of the topography of a section of the whole feasibility function in the dimensions of prices and quantities of exchangeables—a very small part of the total function, of course, but one which we can explore in some degree. Welfare economics tries to add another dimension, "economic welfare" (call it W), and to discuss the problem of where in the topography of the economic feasibility function this new variable is in some sense maximized. Ethics simply adds a further dimension (call it G for "good"), and discusses where in the feasibility function this variable is also in some sense maximized; for wherever it is not maximized there are possibilities of improvement.[29] If, however, the economic welfare function is an *empirical* function, in the sense that the value of W cannot be derived by *a priori* manipulation of the economic variables (prices and quantities), it cannot be any more (or less) scientific than the G-function, for both W and G share the empirical property that they can be observed in some sense by asking people questions (Is A *better* than B? Is A *richer* than B?). They run into the same empirical difficulty—that we get different answers from different people. It should be observed that the same difficulty is actually present in *all* empirical work, as anyone who has observed students at work in a laboratory will admit. The differences among the answers to the same question are larger from person to person when we ask, "Is A richer (or better) than B?" than it is when we ask, "Is A heavier that B?" But it seems to me that no difference in principle is involved. All empirical functions are fuzzy. If somebody wants to call the less fuzzy ones "scientific" and the more fuzzy ones "unscientific" he has the right of all Humpty Dumpties to make words mean what he likes, but he will run into grave danger of making an emotional rather than an intellectual distinction.

As far as I can see we run into no difficulties in inquiring into the G-function that we do not also run into in inquiring into the W-function: indeed, I suspect that there is a better chance of constructing empirical G-functions than W-functions. In this connection the recent work of Kenneth Arrow[30] and of Duncan Black[31] in exploring the construction of general welfare functions from individual welfare func-

---

[29] I have distinguished between the W-function and the G-function to allow for the possibility that duty might not be identical with interest.

[30] *Social Choice and Individual Values* (New York, 1951).

[31] "On the Rationale of Group Decision-making," *Jour. Pol. Econ.,* Feb. 1948, LVI, 23-34.

tions is of great importance, and is just as applicable to the investigation of the general ethical judgment as to the general economic welfare judgment. Their central proposition, very briefly, is that unique and transitive general welfare functions cannot be constructed from individual welfare functions unless certain rather narrow conditions are fulfilled, such that all individuals range their choices in a single rank-order. These discussions have thrown a great deal of light on the theory of consensus and of political decision. Thus we seem to be on the verge of an expansion of welfare economics into something like a social science of ethics and politics: what was intended to be a mere porch to ethics is either the whole house or nothing at all! In so laying down its life welfare economics may be able to contribute some of its insights and analytical methods to a much broader evaluative analysis of the whole social process.

COMMENT

Melvin W. Reder

Professor Boulding's essay is an admirable summary of the recent literature on welfare economics. However, a few statements might be challenged: the assertion (p. 32) that "all economic policy has to be based on interpersonal comparisons" is of doubtful validity. Policy judgments can, and usually are, based on direct value judgments without the mediation of guesses about the properties of utility functions. The proposition that poll taxes are administratively unfeasible (p. 32) ought to be qualified; such taxes are the typical manner in which labor unions and fraternal organizations finance themselves. This is not to suggest that a government could do so (when its budget is an appreciable part of the National Income), but Boulding's statement is rather unguarded. I doubt that it is proper to contrast "the crude ifs and ands of plain price and monetary theory" with "the elegant, but fragile, pots and pans of welfare economics" (p. 32); the crude "ifs and ands," insofar as they have policy implications, are merely more vivid—and misleading—ways of expressing the ideas of welfare economics. Also, contrary to the remark on page 25, universal proportionality of price and marginal cost does imply that price and marginal cost are also everywhere equal.[32]

As the essay makes all too clear, welfare economics is currently in

---

[32] Cf. A. P. Lerner, *Economics of Control,* pp. 102–05, and Reder, *op. cit.,* p. 42.

a very unhappy state. In the past ten years or so, a succession of writers has pursued vigorously a policy of generalization through attenuation until the subject has been reduced to a shell the hollowness of which Boulding only too clearly reveals. This evisceration of welfare economics was really a by-product of the revolt against the *laissez-faire* tradition; to a considerable extent, welfare (and related) theorizing of the 1930's and '40's was an attempt to show the variety and importance of the circumstances under which *laissez-faire* was inappropriate. Put another way, the "new" welfare economics devised policy criteria that were independent of the "state of competition," the "freedom of individuals to contract," etc. Negatively, the job was well done; it made unacceptable the argument that efficient resource allocation required the institutions of capitalism;[33] that efficient management of a socially desirable enterprise always implied the covering of average cost; etc. But positively, welfare economics has been of little help; the attempt to take into account all factors that affect economic welfare has made both the Bergsonian welfare function and the Kaldor-Hicks compensation principle virtually devoid of specific policy implications. Consideration of the welfare implications of envy, for example, make it impossible even to say that welfare will be increased by everyone having more of every commodity, since we must first consider how the extra units are to be distributed; taking into account administrative costs renders suspect any scheme for increasing economic efficiency because the gains in efficiency (*ex* administrative costs) might be outweighed by the increase in administrative expense; ethical and esthetic preferences for one set of institutions may completely outweigh any "economic" gains that might be reaped from changing them; etc.

The logical critiques of Scitovsky, Little, Arrow, Samuelson *et al.* have met with relatively little resistance because there has been so little to defend. But the wreck of *formal* welfare theory has not and ought not to prevent economists from making specific policy recommendations. Such recommendations are the proper subject matter of welfare economics, and the development of a set of axioms from which these various recommendations can be deduced is merely an instrument for facilitating the rendering of still further recommendations.

The essay is quite representative of recent literature in emphasizing the difficulties and hazards of rendering welfare judgments. However, it

---

[33] I refer to the debate between Hayek, Mises and company on the one hand and Lange, Lerner *et al.*, on the other. Boulding's criticism of Lange (p. 26), although appropriate, is misleading if not considered against the background of the "proofs" then offered that a socialist society could not allocate resources rationally.

may lead the uninitiated reader to suppose that a greater part of welfare economics has been undermined than actually has. The shaky part of welfare theory is that which depends upon deciding whether one collection of (more than one kind) of goods, distributed in some manner among a given set of individuals, is greater or less (in terms of welfare, income, etc.) than some other collection, also distributed in some arbitrary manner. But the substantial part of it that refers to the optimum methods of producing a given "commodity-menu" is unscathed by this criticism and has been much utilized and developed, for example, in connection with linear programming.[34]

The recent literature on welfare economics has a controversial tone which contrasts sharply with Boulding's urbanity. This tone is the consequence of the formalization the field has been recently undergoing. From the lofty altitude of the logician, it is impossible to ascertain the practical importance of particular logical errors; one error seems as important as another and all criticism concerns fundamental matters.

While formalization is a necessary part of the development of any theory, I suspect that attempts to develop welfare criteria *ad hoc* for specific purposes will diminish the frequency of theoretical controversies which are barren of practical consequences.[35] The development of *ad hoc* welfare criteria would probably lead to a plurality of such criteria, but I would regard this as healthy.[36] *Ad hoc* criteria will arise from policy suggestions by students of concrete problems rather than by analysis of a welfare function. This is not to disparage the critical work of recent welfare theorists; they have performed a cathartic function which has been (and probably will continue to be) frequently needed. But just now the patient needs food more than purgatives.

COMMENT

Paul A. Samuelson

What is the most useful supplement that I can provide to Professor Boulding's brilliant survey of welfare economics? Upon reflection, it ap-

---

[34] Cf. *Activity Analysis of Production and Allocation,* Tjalling Koopmans, ed., Cowles Commission Monog. 13 (New York, 1951).

[35] They are barren of practical consequences in that no specific policy issue turns upon the issue under debate.

[36] This is not to deny that a single welfare criterion (in the sense of a single set of axioms sufficient for all welfare judgments) should be sought, but to assert that its achievement is no *sine qua non* for welfare theorizing.

pears to me best to provide some informal notes for the reader. For welfare economics is a rather complicated subject, with, however, the one saving grace that, once understood, it turns out to be a fairly simple theory after all.

1. The "new welfare economics" can have two entirely different meanings: (1) the now-admitted-to-be-misguided claim that welfare economics can be solidly based on objective economic criteria, independently of ethical notions about interpersonal distributions of income; (2) a systematic way of introducing from outside of economics various ethical norms (as embodied technically in what is called a social welfare function)—and so ordering the exposition of the conditions for an optimum that we first state these which require only the weakest postulates, and which therefore hold for the widest possible set of cases, and only later introduce the narrower and more restrictive hypotheses.

I know of no present-day defender of the first and narrower version of welfare economics.[37] One by one each writer, who has not remained silent, has explained the modified sense in which the doctrines are to be understood.[38]

2. Without norms, normative statements are impossible. At some point welfare economics must introduce ethical welfare functions from outside of economics. Which set of ends is relevant is decidedly *not* a scientific question of economics. This should dispel the notion that by a social welfare function is meant some one, unique, and privileged set of ends. Any prescribed set of ends is grist for the economist's unpretentious deductive mill, and often he can be expected to reveal that the prescribed ends are incomplete and inconsistent. The social welfare function is a concept as broad and empty as language itself—and as necessary.

---

[37] To understand the 1939 Kaldor and Hicks articles, we must remember that Kaldor is answering Harrod's 1938 assertion that the repeal of the Corn Laws can be justified only "if individuals are treated in some sense as equals." . . . "If the incomparability of utility to different individuals is strictly pressed, not only are the prescriptions of the welfare school ruled out, but all prescriptions whatever." All the discussants suffered from a bad case of the jitters as a result of Lionel Robbins' important 1932 *Essay on the Nature and Significance of Economic Science,* which correctly pointed out that ethical ends were ascientific by their very nature, but which lent itself to the false interpretation that welfare economics was therefore without content.

[38] The only remaining divergence of belief seems to be on pragmatic tactical questions: e.g. shall all changes which *could* make everyone better off but which might in fact hurt some people be made mandatory in the expectation or hope that the cumulative effects of following such a rule will be better (for all or some) than if some other rule is followed? Shall we set up a rule of unanimous consent for any *new* change so that compensating bribes must be in fact paid? To answer such questions we must go beyond economics.

Whether we call it W, or G, or describe it in words is, of course, immaterial.

Note that ethical notions concerning the relative deservingness of different individuals are by their nature completely ordinal. There is no necessary connection with cardinal measurable utility of the individual, or with the addibility of the independent utilities of different individuals into some grand national total. Except for a few utilitarians, drunk on poorly understood post-Newtonian mathematical moonshine, I can find in the ethical writings of recorded cultures scarcely any importance attached to the special social welfare functions of additive cardinal utility.

3. It is agreed then that the Pareto-Lerner necessary conditions for an optimum, described in Table 1 (p. 20), must be supplemented by distributional considerations if a sufficient set of conditions for an optimum and for policy prescriptions are to be given. But so long as we (1) do later supplement them, (2) assume that social welfare goes up when each and every individual becomes better off, and (3) assume that more goods and less inputs are always desirable, we can formulate these conditions independently of the interpersonal conditions. In summary:

Necessary Marginal Conditions for an Optimum. Between any two variables, the marginal rates of substitution must be (subjectively) equal for all individuals, and (technically) equal for all alternative processes, with the common technical and subjective ratios being equivalent; otherwise there exists a physically attainable position that makes everyone better off.

By calling some variables inputs and some outputs, or inputs and outputs of different time periods, etc., this rule can be expanded into many separate rules, including that of price exactly equal to marginal cost, discounted marginal productivity proportionalities, etc. In reasonably efficient societies, these necessary conditions are not very important because they are already near to being realized. But in less fortunate societies, their violation may be very important. Therefore, I dissent from much of the recent skepticism and calumny that those marginal conditions have evoked.[39]

---

[39] Part of this distrust stems from the correct feeling that it may not be feasible to price all goods at marginal costs with losses financed out of optimal lump-sum taxes; or that with many of the necessary optimum conditions violated, it is not ideal to have any particular subset of them alone satisfied. These considerations suggest that, instead of throwing out the baby with the bathwater, we solve the theoretical problem of the "feasible optimum" and deduce the relevant policy considerations.

2 ECONOMICS OF CONSUMPTION

Ruth P. Mack

The economics of consumption is really an interdisciplinary field. It involves the psychology and sociology of wants and choice, the resultant economic decisions of people as consumers, and the effect of these decisions on resource utilization in the economy. To attempt to cover recent developments over this whole gamut is, of course, impractical.

Accordingly, I propose to concentrate this review on one branch of the whole field, one in which there has been phenomenal activity during the past fifteen years: *the dynamics of consumer buying and saving*. Regrettably, it is also necessary to confine the discussion largely to the United States.

First, a matter of terminology: consumer buying has typically been called "consumption," as in "the propensity to consume," and I shall not disturb this well-established habit. In deferring to it, however, we are thinking of consumption roughly in terms of money-flows[1] and not dealing with consumption proper—using up. Nor, incidentally, are we dealing with the level at which consumers obtain satisfaction from consumption, which could be in the using up of goods in their possession, in their acquisition, or even, perhaps, in their anticipated acquisition.

In the mid-thirties three main developments in economics combined to give the particular emphasis to the work on consumption of the next fifteen years. The period inherited well-developed estimates, especially in the United States, of consumer income and buying over a considerable number of years; this work has expanded and improved throughout the period. Second, the age-old descriptive study of individual family income and disbursements (area surveys) took a new turn in

---

[1] Imputed money-flows, as in the case of home-produced food or the service of owned homes, serve to round out the concept.

39

the mid-thirties: they were designed to throw light on the factors that determine consumption and were pursued thereafter with new vigor and imagination. Third, in 1936, a book of exceptional power, *The General Theory of Employment Interest and Money,* by John Maynard Keynes, presented a theory of consumer behavior and outlined its effect on the economy as a whole in terms which promised solutions for pressing politico-economic problems of the day.

Keynes emphasized the part played by income in determining consumption. Certainly this was not a new idea. Ernst Engel had described how expenditures related to the level of family living in the middle of the nineteenth century. Henry L. Moore, in the early twentieth century, had considered the level of economic activity in empirical studies of demand, and E. E. Slutsky in 1915 had introduced apparatus in theoretical demand analysis for dealing with alterations in income. But the great depression and Lord Keynes assigned a stellar role to Income instead of to Price, which had been traditionally given top billing.

In consequence of the provocative new turn to thinking and the profusion and good quality of statistical source material, a spontaneous group investigation of the quantitative influence of income on buying or saving developed. But the Keynesian theoretical frame demanded, in the context in which it was often used, a very precise prediction of aggregate consumption, and it soon became apparent—a fact that Keynes himself recognized—that this could not be done on the basis of income alone. Accordingly, investigators studied the impact of many other factors thought capable of materially changing aggregate buying or saving at a given level of aggregate income. In these further explorations, the work of economists could benefit from that of other social scientists, and this work should perhaps be named as a fourth main stream of endeavor that has shaped recent work.

In writing this critical review, I have not followed the sequence or even the emphasis of the actual research but have tried to utilize the cumulative negative as well as positive conclusions that it yielded.

I begin the account with a discussion of the problem under investigation. The next two sections take up in sequence two levels at which study has proceeded: Section II deals with the analyses of factors influencing consumer buying or saving ("the micro-economic function"); Section III concentrates on how, as a result of these factors and their patterns of change, consumption changes from year to year ("the macro-economic function"). Section IV recounts some of the efforts to expound how changes in consumer buying or saving influence economic activity as a whole. Section V summarizes achievement and points to a few especially hopeful avenues of further work.

I. THE PROBLEM OF ANALYZING CONSUMER BUYING

The factors that influence the buying or saving of families or individuals depend fundamentally on the nature of men and women and of the society in which they live. The economist, who studies consumer buying and its association with economic variables, is primarily concerned with how *groups* of men act. But it is virtually impossible to construct a proper "macro-economic" function without at least a general understanding of individual behavior.

A. Non-Economic Man

During the past half century, and at an accelerated pace during the period here reviewed, psychoanalysts, anthropologists, psychologists, and sociologists have made impressive advances towards understanding the phenomenon, *Homo sapiens.*

Man, the psychologists tell us, is a creature of extraordinary complexity. The native equipment and basic drives with which he enters the world are from the start channelled, modified, redirected, and otherwise transformed in the course of his own developmental history. This history is characterized by a constant interaction between the individual and the world as he knows it; he is shaped by the events, values, beliefs, and minute circumstances of his daily environment at the same time that he, through a process of selective knowing, shapes it.

It is a great and illuminating discovery of twentieth-century psychology that this laborious development of the individual takes place at an unconscious as well as at a conscious level. In the unconscious part of the personality, many of the inevitably painful episodes and fantasies of childhood live on to influence the feelings and actions of adults.

Behavior, in other words, is directed in part by conscious and in part by unconscious motives. The resulting actions may differ sharply. Conduct based largely on conscious motives tends to be reasoned, predictable, flexible, experimental, adaptive. Conduct based primarily on unconscious reasons may be compulsive, inflexible, self-defeating, and therefore insatiable and repetitive. It fastens on symbolic rather than real meanings; it shapes the world to fancies. Normal adults as well as children ordinarily are motivated by both conscious and unconscious processes. Moreover, these contrapuntal themes coexist in most single acts, though the dominant motives for some may be unconscious and for others conscious.

The evolving personality depends for much of its substance on the cultural air it breathes. Concerning the character of this atmosphere, the anthropologist has assembled some highly relevant information. His researches throw light on the differences among cultures, the interrelationships of aspects or institutions within cultures, and the patterns that relate the individual to the society. Perusal of this literature seems to funnel attention toward a fact of peculiar importance to the student of consumer economics: consumption, possessions, purchasing, are matters of highly charged significance to peoples of the Western world and probably especially to North Americans. Some possessions are important in any culture. But money and goods are in ours a central core—in the sense (though not to the extent) that magic ritual to propitiate gods of fertility was central in the life of the Zuni Indians, or warlike prowess and endurance in the Sioux plains culture, or loyalty to family and friends in Confucianism.

It is characteristic of cultures that their parts are interrelated. The focal importance of goods among our life-values is bound to be imprinted on the most diverse aspects of the interaction between the unfolding individual and the world as he knows and experiences it. To mention only one example, an unsatisfied thirst for love from parents may be expressed in the greedy demand for food, clothes, or other gifts, a pattern that can persist throughout life. The goals and self-pictures that men and women try to validate for themselves and their children are as festooned as a Christmas tree by contraptions bought in shops.

The fact that some buying is so charged with meaning is accompanied almost necessarily by the fact that much of it is strongly habitual, for the organism seeks relief from the strain of making subtle decisions. But here, too, as in the distinction between conscious and unconscious motivation, most events are likely to partake of both qualities—habit and initiative.

In short, in twentieth-century America, virtually everything that influences what a person is and how he got that way—a process of constant interaction between the evolving individual and his social field—influences what and when and how much he buys or saves, and indeed in part how much he makes. Currently, his buying is a function of what he is, what he has, the recent history of his purchases, what others have or buy, what he expects, what he hopes, the habits that he has established, and very nearly anything else. The dynamics of consumption is in our society coextensive with the dynamics of personality.

The economist is interested, of course, in group behavior. He seeks knowledge of the individual in order to understand the group or to know how to study it. Before we try to summarize what this knowledge of the individual implies concerning the study of aggregate consumer buying, it will be useful to look for a moment at a set of figures that deal with simply quantitative variation in the buying of a number of individual families.

B. Dispersion and Central Tendency in the Buying of Groups

In 1934–36 the United States Bureau of Labor Statistics obtained a detailed account of income and expenditure from families of wage earners and lower salaried workers in many cities of the United States; the group was exceptionally homogeneous.[2] For six large cities, measures of dispersion of individual families around group averages were published for about a dozen classes of expenditure. Coefficients of variation for the total sample are averaged for the six cities and shown in column 1 of our table (p. 44). In column 2 the effect of family income (and anything else that is correlated with it) is roughly allowed for.[3]

The first column, line 1, of the table may be read thus: Of the families covered in the six cities, about two-thirds were within a band having total expenditures falling between plus or minus 33 per cent of the average.[4] Glancing down the column, we find that the relatively high con-

---

[2] About 80 per cent of the families had incomes between $900 and $2100 in the survey year.

[3] Measures of dispersion—coefficients of correlation for separate groups of expenditure and income—were computed by W. F. Ogburn for about 200 families in the District of Columbia in 1916: "Analysis of the Standard of Living in the District of Columbia in 1916," *Jour. Am. Stat. Assoc.,* June 1919, XVI, 374–89. James Morgan and Lawrence Klein are now correlating data for individual families from the Fed. Res. Board-Survey Research Center Survey and this will yield measures of dispersion.

Less complete but interesting studies of dispersion appear in: Faith M. Williams, "Methods of Measuring Variations in Family Expenditures," *Jour. Am. Stat. Assoc.,* Mar. 1937, XXXII, 40–46; Dorothy S. Brady, "Variations in Family Living Expenditures," *ibid.,* June 1938, XXXIII, 385–89. Information on the percentage of families in various income bands expending funds within specified ranges on stated types of expenditures are given in many survey reports. See, e.g., U.S. Bur. Labor Stat. Bull. 642, Vol. II. Tab. 50; U.S. Dept. Agric., Misc. Pub. 396, Tab. 11; 428, Tab. 1; 464, Tab. 1.

[4] This statement is a loose one. The coefficients of variation for the six cities ranged between 30 and 36; they averaged 33. Whether the distributions are normal is also not known.

centration of expenditure patterns appears for food and housing also, and then is gradually lost in diversity.

The next column shows the extent to which the scatter of individual observations is reduced if we allow roughly for the influence of income: apparently very large individual variations in expenditure remain. But here, too, income is seen to be a far more potent governor for some types of expenditure than others. In general the influence of income is

COEFFICIENTS OF VARIATION (V) OF MONEY DISBURSEMENTS, WHITE WAGE AND CLERICAL WORKERS
(Averaged for 6 large cities, 1934–36)*

ITEM	COEFFICIENT FOR		PER CENT BY WHICH V FOR TOTAL SAMPLE IS REDUCED WHEN DATA ARE GROUPED BY INCOME CLASS (COL. 2 ÷ COL. 1)
	Total Sample	Averaged for Each $300 Income Class	
All items.............................	33	17	48
Food................................	33	24	27
Housing..............................	35	30	14
Personal care........................	55	43	22
Clothing.............................	63	48	24
Recreation...........................	75	61	19
Other household......................	74	60	19
Surplus..............................	101	83	18
Deficit..............................	107	105	2
Transportation.......................	108	91	16
Medical care.........................	128	119	7
Furnishing and equipment.............	137	135	1
Other items..........................	149	124	17
Gifts and contributions..............	172	142	17

SOURCE: Based on data from Faith M. Williams and Alice C. Hanson, *Money Disbursements of Wage Earners and Clerical Workers in Eight Cities in the East North Central Region* 1934–36, U.S. Bur. Labor Stat. Bull. 636, Table 24 (A & B); data for other regions are given in Bull. 637, Vol. I, Bull. 639, 640, and 641.

* The coefficient of variation is the standard deviation divided by the group average multiplied by 100. In column 2 the coefficients of variation are computed separately for each $300 income class, multiplied by the number of families in the class, added, and divided by the number of families in the sample. The figures in columns 1 and 2 are simple averages of coefficients for six cities for which the number of families sampled ranged from 162 to 897 and totaled 2,500.

most strong for expenditures that vary least from family to family—column 3 runs generally reverse to column 1. But if we contrast the figures in column 3 with a phantom set that move smoothly from the top to the bottom, we notice some figures provocatively out of place. The reader will enjoy comparing this column with the slope of data showing the regression of spending on income for the various commodity groups.

Net saving is not given in the table—a coefficient of variation is an inappropriate measure for figures that are both negative and positive. Average saving for the group was very close to zero, and the standard deviation was ±$250. When the influence of income was allowed for, the standard deviation was ±$242. This very small amount by which income explains the total variation is not inconsistent with a strong influence of income on *average* saving by income groups, which these data, like most others, actually do display—average dissaving was $50 in the lowest income group and average saving was several hundred dollars in the top groups. It is interesting in this connection to note from the table that income was a considerably more potent determinant of average surpluses of families having net surpluses than of deficits of families who spent more than their current income.

C. An Analytic Frame

The total diversity in family buying revealed in these figures can be divided conceptually into three segments: the first involves differences in the character of individuals' sensitivity to various choice-conditioning factors; the second results from the difference among individuals in the extent to which such factors are present; the third relates to the length of time for which the factor maintained the given value. If change over time is to be included, there is a fourth segment—*change* in the character of the individual's sensitivity to each choice-conditioning factor. Finally, the nondeterminist at any rate would wish to add pure chance.

Knowledge at each of these conceptual levels can contribute to the understanding of changes in aggregate buying over time as well as of differences among groups of people at a given time. But it is not at all simple to say *how,* in view of the mixed form in which actual observations have usually to be made. It will be useful, therefore, first to view the theoretical model and then to see how the various major sources of information can be utilized in the study of changes in aggregate buying.

The foundation of changes in disbursements is the sensitivity of individuals to choice-conditioning factors. In the study of this sensitivity, the trusty tool of "the schedule" has served economists well. In this context, the schedule is a diagram or tabulation of the quantities that an individual would buy, *ceteris paribus,* were different specified amounts of some choice-conditioning factor present.

But a moment's reflection on the nature of man and his choices makes it clear that the schedule is multidimensional. Each choice-conditioning factor, operating over a specified time period, provides one dimension capable of influencing in a prescribed fashion an individual's buying of some article or group of articles, assuming nothing else changed. Actual behavior is partially determined when each factor is considered, one after the other. And there are a vast number of such factors. Yet, even this complicated notion is a gross simplification of the process underlying purchasing of one article or group of articles.[5]

But the conceptual frame must go farther and comprehend selection among articles. The maintenance of a satisfactory relationship among competing wants has traditionally been visualized as some sort of weighing of comparative utility or its rate of change at the margin of choice, on the basis of which the allocation of scarce dollars proceeds. A continuum of rationing depends on approximate homogeneity of units of utility for a given individual, and his ability to compare utility, or rates of change in utility, of marginal units of goods that might be purchased. Yet modern psychology leads us seriously to question the propriety of these notions, so that at best they ought only to be used in a very loose fashion.[6]

A third difficulty can be roughly allowed for. The schedule has ordinarily been used to apply to equilibrium conditions. But, as an aid to most empirical research, this is an awkward restriction. The length of time for which a choice-conditioning factor has maintained a given value will influence the reaction to it. This fact is securely grounded in the deeply developmental character of personality and the possibility that "change of habit is psychologically onerous."[7] Consequently first reactions are often different from later ones. We can incorporate this notion

---

[5] The structure of wants probably has very complex interrelationships so that, in effect, dimensions of the schedules would not be independent of one another. Most articles have *both* complementary and competitive aspects. Large changes—important enough to break through habitual patterns and summon fresh choice—may evoke different reactions from an equal sum of small changes the reaction to which is based largely on habit or custom.

[6] The question at issue concerns first the homogeneity of utility for a given individual. We have seen that motives in buying can be partly habitual, partly reasoned (however misinformed), and partly unconscious; utility can be a matter of fact, it can be symbolic or it can be defined in the topsy-turvy language of the unconscious; major utilities for some products may lie in the act of purchase, for others in the process of consumption, for others in possession *per se*. Do the satisfactions derived from filling these different sorts of wants differ only in extent, or is there fundamental difference in kind too?

The second question involves whether decisions at the margin are always realistic units of consumer choice. The concept seems quite inappropriate in connection with large unit purchases, and how truly it captures the essence of even small repetitive purchases has been questioned.

The matter is further complicated by the relationship between the whole and its parts. That the totality of experienced value is not merely the sum of its parts seems fairly well established in psychology and perhaps philosophy. Can "parts" be defined to avoid the difficulty in economics?

[7] Ruby T. Norris, *The Theory of Consumer's Demand* (New Haven, 1941), p. 72.

into our scheme by stipulating the time period to which a given schedule applies. To illustrate, we require at least two income dimensions, a short-term one involving reactions to new changes in income, and an inter-mediate-term one applying to reactions to levels that have been maintained for perhaps a year or more. (A true long-term dimension would tend to defy the *ceteris paribus* condition by income-linked changes in standards of living.) This dichotomy schematizes a continuum.

We end with a model which is little more than a rough conceptual counterpart of multivariate mathematical analysis for the buying of individuals. But of course, of the very essence of our requirements is a smooth transition to group behavior; concern for the individual is only a means to this end.

It has been customary to assume that individual schedules can, in effect, be *added* in order to arrive at a group schedule. But this does not seem proper for noneconomic man who is greatly influenced by what others do. James Duesenberry has elaborated this point[8] and some of its economic implications; it has been a basic concept in "field theory" as developed by Kurt Lewin. It conditions the meaning of average or representative group behavior and perhaps its statistical properties. We can sometimes include it loosely in our conceptual scheme as an additional dimension of the schedule-complex. More serious difficulties attach to fundamental changes that cannot be thus isolated and are likely to affect reactions to many other choice-conditioning factors. Changes of this sort involve, in a sense, redrawing schedules, and this might be necessitated by many sorts of changes that take place over time.

A more familiar aspect of "the problem of aggregation" involves the shape of the schedules.[9] It is easier and less hazardous to deduce the amount of aggregate buying and how it changes if individual schedules are linear rather than curved. For if they are linear (and we are willing to make certain assumptions about their distribution) we do not need to know, in order to deduce the change in aggregate buying, what sorts of people experienced how much change in some choice-conditioning fac-

---

[8] *Income, Saving and the Theory of Consumer Behavior* (Cambridge, Mass., 1949), Ch. 2, 3.

[9] I list some notable examples of this literature: Hans Staehle, "Short-Period Variations in the Distribution of Incomes," *Rev. Econ. Stat.*, Aug. 1937, XIX, 133–43; Elizabeth Gilboy, "Methods of Measuring Demand or Consumption," *ibid.*, May 1939, XXI, 69–74; Jacob Marschak, "Personal and Collective Budget Functions," *ibid.*, Nov. 1939, XXI, 161–70; Trygve Haavelmo, "Family Expenditures and the Marginal Propensity to Consume," *Econometrica*, Oct. 1947, XV, 335–41.

tor, but only the aggregate amount of the change for the group. Consequently, it is important to determine empirically whether various dimensions of the schedule-complex actually do tend to be linear.

Whether it will be possible to fasten essential characteristics of wants and choices as now understood into a theory of consumption, the future will tell. In the meantime, some sort of conceptual apparatus is necessary to steady empirical work. For without it, assumptions are encouraged to remain submerged (as in the concept "normal" or "typical" income) and errors are likely to be made (as when "micro-economic consumption functions" are read directly from the consumption-income regression in area surveys).

Turning to the source material, three major pools are available. First, psychological studies, the work of marketing research organizations and private industry, are doubtless capable of supplying a good deal of information about the schedule-complex, but they are still to be systematically canvassed. The second source, one that underwent outstanding development in the period reviewed, is area surveys. From these data we can derive (with the qualifications already made) some sort of average or representative schedule-complex. From the great quantity of dimensions, suggested in the wide scatter of the table on p. 44, we select those of interest—for the most part those capable of causing material changes in group buying from place to place or, especially, from time to time. These we endeavor to isolate and measure.

With this information we turn to the third source, time series, to learn how the choice-conditioning factor has changed with respect to its aggregate impact and, when schedules depart from linearity, its distribution. The derivation of aggregate change in disbursement is then a matter of appropriate combination of the two sorts of information with two important qualifications: First, it must be clear that the reaction to change per se does not in effect introduce additional dimensions; if so, short- as well as intermediate-term reactions must be taken into account. Second, there must be reason to believe that the individual or representative schedule-complex itself does not alter over the period; otherwise at least rough allowance for the shift in schedules must be made.

Information about how buying changes through time can also be obtained directly by the analysis of time series for buying in association with those for various choice-conditioning factors. This approach bypasses the problem of aggregation, though it may be present in reverse if these data are used, as they often are in the case of price, to learn about reactions of individuals.

We turn now first to a review of the factors that have been selected as substantially influencing what and how much people buy or save; we study the endeavor to gauge the direction and extent of their influence. In Section III we take up the efforts to describe their impact on aggregate buying over time.

II. SELECTED FACTORS THAT INFLUENCE THE DISBURSEMENTS OF INDIVIDUALS

Among the factors that influence individual buying, many are capable of causing material changes in aggregate buying through time: income, standards of living, wealth, demographic factors, habits, attitudes and expectations, goods or services offered for sale or provided outside of the market economy, availability of credit, and prices. Some of these factors have been studied intensively during the period here reviewed, some very slightly; and, of course, it is an incomplete list.

A. Income

Area surveys help to show how individuals ration their income among the wants that they would like to satisfy. Just how income ought actually to be defined is itself a moot question to which there may be no answer satisfactory in all contexts.[10] Families can be grouped by the income band in which they fall, and expenditure on any class of disbursement calculated for each income group. These data are often studied as charts—loosely termed "Engel curves"—in which average expenditure is plotted against average income for each income band. A word of warning: for lack of others, one uses, of necessity, words suggesting change over time—"vary," "increment," "elasticity"—in connection with the characteristics of functions based on area surveys. This is improper for two reasons: first, the data do not isolate the pure association of, say, income and expenditure; second, the data do not give the time duration implicit in the revealed relation—they probably show primarily what we have called the intermediate-term function (though some short-term reactions to a change in income are also present in the gross regression). But so long as the character of the data is understood, they can provide at least the first step toward useful answers to questions of value.

Three questions have often been asked, explicitly or implicitly; they are simply subdivisions of the comprehensive one, how do family

---

[10] For a very interesting discussion of this matter and a bibliography see Margaret G. Reid, "Effect of Income Concept upon Expenditure Curves of Farm Families," in Conference on Research in Income and Wealth, *Studies in Income and Wealth*, Vol. XV (New York, 1952).

disbursements of various sorts vary with family income? First, what is the relation for average quantities of family income and expenditure (the average propensity)? This relation is perhaps most descriptive of differences in the mode of life, as expressed in money disbursements, between families of different income levels. Second, what is the relation for newly added or subtracted dollars (the marginal propensity—the slope of the regression)? This relation is most useful as the foundation for calculating changes in aggregate buying likely to be associated with a given aggregate change in income. Third, what is the relation for percentage changes in disbursements and income (income elasticity)? This may serve the same purpose as the marginal propensity and is also well suited to describe the differential impact of various income levels on different sorts of needs; it is, for example, most readily translated directly into rough estimates of, say, the relative cycle-sensitivity of different sorts of goods.

The materials to which I turn for tentative answers to these questions are secondary analyses of data from surveys of individual families. I have filled in gaps by using also the basic published data where expenditures for major groups of articles had been or could readily be plotted against income, first on an arithmetic and then on a logarithmic scale; and these two charts were augmented where necessary with tables of percentages of income devoted to each disbursement.[11] Needless to say, this sort of inspection provides no more than inexact and fallible answers to the basic questions. Nevertheless I list my conclusions in the hope of stimulating more adequate ones:

(1) Expenditure on food and rent has a low income elasticity, nearer .5 than 1 around the center of the income distribution. Both the average and marginal propensities decline as income rises, though for food a constant marginal propensity sometimes appears. Average deficits of families having deficits also fall roughly in this group.

(2) At the opposite pole of behavior are disbursements on autos, education, other miscellaneous items, gifts, net saving as well as sur-

---

[11] The following materials were utilized: Elizabeth W. Gilboy, "Income-Expenditure Relations," *Rev. Econ. Stat.*, Aug. 1940, XXII, 115–21; *idem*, "Changes in Consumption Expenditures and the Defense Program," *ibid.*, Nov. 1941, XXIII, 155–64; A. D. H. Kaplan, "Expenditure Patterns of Urban Families," *Jour. Am. Stat. Assoc.*, Mar. 1938, XXXIII, 81–100; H. G. Lewis and P. H. Douglas, "Studies in Consumer Expenditures (1901, 1918–19, 1922–24)," *Jour. Bus. Univ. Chicago*, Oct. 1947, Pt. 2, Vol. XX. R. G. D. Allen and A. L. Bowley, *Family Expenditure, A Study of Its Variation* (London, 1935) give data in Tab. A, pp. 32–33. In addition, data for individual cities and groups of cities for 1935–36 could be studied from charts or tables in U.S. Bur. Labor Stat. Bull. 636–641, and data for the whole country in the two summary reports by the National Resources Planning Board on the 1935–36 study.

pluses of families having them. These groups have income elasticities of over 1 around the center of the array. Average, and typically also marginal, propensities increase with income. Clothing falls in this same class except that the income elasticity of expenditure is usually very close to 1. For net saving, the percentage of income saved often increases by uniform absolute amounts as income increases by uniform percentage amounts.

(3) For medical care, recreation, personal care, and home operation there does seem to be a tendency for marginal propensities to be constant through most of the income range. In other words, these groups conform to the "linear law." But average propensities seem to show no consistent relation to income. This last remark also holds for furniture and furnishings, though its marginal propensity sometimes decreases. Elasticities for these five commodity groups are often very close to 1 at average income.

The data do not seem to reveal a consistent tendency for elasticities to increase, decrease or remain constant with income; the same commodity class behaves differently in different samples. Two interesting exceptions are net saving, which appears very typically to show decreasing income-elasticity, and surpluses of families having positive savings, which seem often to display constant elasticity. Deficits behave erratically. Study of the differing incidence and rationale of deficits and surpluses and their components has yielded provocative results.[12]

If now we ask not simply about general principles of the relation of some disbursement to income, but about estimates of magnitudes, a puzzling variety appears among different samples.

The point can be illustrated by data on net savings. Marginal saving can be computed approximately at any specified level of income for 21 cities of different sizes for which presumably representative samples of a specified group of the population were drawn in 1935–36. Marginal propensities for, say, family incomes of \$2,500 range from a low of .17 to a high of .40 for different cities. Average propensities range from a low of .05 to a high of .17. There is some tendency for large cities to

---

[12] See George Garvy, "The Role of Dissaving in Economic Analysis," *Jour. Pol. Econ.*, Oct. 1948, LVI, 416–27; G. S. Fulcher, "Life Insurance Saving of American Families," *Rev. Econ. Stat.*, May 1944, XXVI, 93–94; George Katona, "Analysis of Dissaving," *Am. Econ. Rev.*, June 1949, XXXIX, 673–88; *idem, Psychological Analysis of Economic Behavior* (New York, 1951), Ch. 8. Various components of consumer saving are separately analyzed in a series of articles, "Survey of Consumer Finances, Distribution of Consumer Saving," *Fed. Res. Bull.*, Jan. and Nov. 1950, Sept. 1951, XXXVI, 14–34, 1441–55, XXXVII, 1061–78. See also, U.S. Bur. Labor Stat. Bull. 648, Vol. VIII, and U.S. Dept. Agric., Misc. Pub. 464.

have lower average and marginal ratios than other cities, and villages the largest of all, but the difference among individual cities within a size group tends to be wider than the difference between average ratios for different size groups.

Were we to repeat this computation for groups of disbursements other than net saving, less variation among the twenty-one cities would doubtless appear, at least for many sorts of goods. But the difference would still be material. It underscores the importance of studying variables other than income if the buying not only of individuals but of large groups is to be understood and even roughly predicted. We turn now to some of these other factors.

B. Recent Change in Income

The impact on buying of most choice-conditioning factors will typically depend in part on the recentness of the experienced change, but only in the case of income has the matter been studied.

Imagine a family whose income has been $3,000 for several years (prices constant over the period) and which now suffers a decline in income to $2,500. Suppose, alternatively, that income has been $2,000 and rises to $2,500. Would saving during the first year be the same under the two circumstances? For one thing, when income fell, one would expect that it would be difficult to reduce contractual expenses such as rent and many associated costs. Also, many routine and deeply habitual expenses would be difficult to control. This would be true not only of the class of article bought, but likewise of the quality selected; it would take a while to make the shift to the cheaper article more typically selected by people adjusted to lower incomes. Certainly, a car or vacuum cleaner would not usually be purchased. Finally, one would expect to find savings somewhat less than usual. In more severe form, this is the sort of picture that characterizes families suffering from unemployment.

The family that had experienced a rise, on the other hand, would typically be slow to increase exactly the same expenditures that were slow to decrease with a fall in income. We cannot, however, make the converse statement—that they would be quick to increase the articles that the family with fallen income had been quick to decrease. Whether the additional money would be saved or spent on some article that could not previously have been afforded would depend on where the "head" on wants had piled up most.

Empirical investigation reveals that saving is lower, *ceteris paribus*, when income has fallen. That saving is higher when income has risen is not so clearly demonstrated; logic suggests that large unit purchases ought to be considered at the same time, and so do some preliminary findings.[13] There is also some evidence that the purchase of durable goods such as autos, vacuum cleaners, electric refrigerators and washing machines, is positively associated with income change while purchases of smaller unit size as well as total purchases are negatively associated.[14]

Furthermore, it seems quite possible that differential response to income change would depend in part on other factors: a family having considerable liquid assets may be under less compulsion to reduce expenditure when income falls than one that does not. Similarly, expectations about future income must, if they are firm enough, play some part in the reaction to current changes in income. Here too, evidence is being assembled in the Federal Reserve Board-Survey Research Center data. As to how long a recent change in income will continue to deflect spending from its intermediate-term pattern, empirical study has as yet said little. On *a priori* grounds the transition must be gradual.

C. Standards of Living

"The *standard* of consumption or living is the level that is urgently desired and striven for, special gratification attending substantial success and substantial failure yielding bitter frustration."[15] Standards are conditioned both by an individual's own past and by the group in which he

---

[13] If in effect first differences in income are used as a variable in multiple correlation of time series to "explain" saving, it has a negative sign. See Jan Tinbergen, "Does Consumption Lag behind Incomes?" *Rev. Econ. Stat.,* Feb. 1942, XXIV, 1–8 (nonwage income was lagged in this study); Irwin Friend, "Relationship between Consumers' Expenditures, Savings, and Disposable Income," *ibid.,* Nov. 1946, XXVIII, 208–15.

Area surveys suggest that families having experienced a recent fall in income save less, other things the same. See D. McC. Holthausen, "Survey of Consumer Finances," *Fed. Res. Bull.,* Aug. 1947, XXXIII, 951–62; Ruth P. Mack, "The Direction of Change in Income and the Consumption Function," *Rev. Econ. Stat.,* Nov. 1948, XXX, 239–58; George Katona and Janet A. Fisher, "Postwar Changes in the Income of Identical Consumer Units," in Conference on Research in Income and Wealth, *Studies in Income and Wealth,* Vol. XIII (New York, 1951).

[14] See M. A. Girshick and Trygve Haavelmo, "Statistical Analysis of the Demand for Food: Examples of Simultaneous Estimation of Structural Equations," *Econometrica,* Apr. 1947, XV, 79–110; Mack, *op. cit.,* pp. 249–50; L. J. Atkinson, "The Demand for Consumers' Durable Goods," *Surv. Curr. Bus.,* June 1950, XXX, 5–10; Walter Jacobs and Clement Winston, "The Postwar Furniture Market and the Factors Determining Demand," *ibid.,* May 1950, XXX, 8–11; James Tobin, "A Statistical Demand Function for Food in the U.S.A.," *Jour. Royal Stat. Soc.,* 1950, CXIII (2), 113–40.

[15] J. S. Davis, "Standards and Content of Living," *Am. Econ. Rev.,* Mar. 1945, XXXV, 3. Anthropologists and psychologists have much to say on this subject. Other economists who have shown special interest in it are Elizabeth E. Hoyt, *Consumption in Our Society* (New York, 1938); *idem,* "Want Development in Underdeveloped Areas," *Jour. Pol. Econ.,* June 1951, LIX, 194–202; Duesenberry, *op. cit.*

lives. Further, standards affect not only how income is allocated to various goods and services, present and future, but the amount of income people take the trouble to earn, and the number of children they are willing to have. These matters are likely to absorb increasing attention of students as our geographic range of awareness grows. Here we can mention only a few factors that seem to bear on the picture of the self which people try to validate through their buying or saving.

One influence of particular importance to economists is income, and this has received considerable attention of late. Because buying and the plane of consumption are linked to income, when income is and has been high, the Joneses are better equipped than when it is and has been low. This causes the Joneses to develop new standards in line with the new picture of themselves that money has bought. It also causes the standards of the Smiths to rise with their exposure to the Jones's goods. Standards concerning saving are, it is assumed for one reason or another, less affected by this contagion than those supported by other goods and services. The proportion of income that is saved tends, therefore, to fall as standards rise, other things the same. This thesis in two of the three cases in which it has been forwarded, was presented substantially in the extreme form that the savings ratio is independent of the absolute level of real income and dependent only (except for the influence of factors other than the level of income) on the percentile position in the income size distribution.[16]

However one may feel about the evidence for the theory in its extreme form (and I admit I find it unconvincing), the thought that the standard of living is one of the factors that influence consumptive choices, including the choice between spending and saving, seems neces-

---

[16] Franco Modigliani, "Fluctuations in the Savings-Income Ratio; A Problem in Economic Forecasting," Conference on Research in Income and Wealth, *Studies in Income and Wealth*, Vol. XI (New York, 1949), pp. 371–441; Dorothy S. Brady and Rose D. Friedman, "Savings and the Income Distribution" in Conference on Research in Income and Wealth, *op. cit.*, Vol. X (New York, 1947), pp. 250–65; Duesenberry, *op. cit.;* an early work that presented the same notion was Horst Mendershausen's, "Differences in Family Savings between Cities of Different Size and Location, Whites and Negroes," *Rev. Econ. Stat.*, Aug. 1940, XXII, 122–35, especially p. 134.

Duesenberry develops the logic of the position with care and my statement of it is based primarily on his analysis. However, the hypothesis which he puts to the test is the extreme one (p. 45). This same position is taken (p. 248) by Brady and Friedman, who present evidence from area surveys to show that the savings ratio tends to be the same—geographically as well as over time—for families in the same decile of the income-size array. Modigliani, who works with time series for several countries, lets his data say the extent to which the savings ratio does or does not remain constant; also his rationalization seems to emphasize Smith's memory of his past glory rather than his eye on the Joneses.

sarily true. Inevitably also, standards must be affected in our culture by goods that people know friends and neighbors have bought or possess, or goods that people have had in their own homes. Exactly what effect these income-linked standards would have on buying, especially buying of status goods and saving, is a question of much interest on which all sorts of evidence can be brought to bear—experiments of psychologists and interviews with consumers, as well as area surveys and time series.

Standards may be linked to a way of life rather than to income proper. The rural-urban differences are a case in point. One of the more clearly demonstrated facts about consumer buying is that farmers seem to save a larger proportion of a given level of income than do city or village families. Further, the marginal as well as the average propensity to save as seen in area studies is greater for farm than city families. The relative allocation of income to various classes of expenditures likewise differs for farm and other families. These conclusions seem warranted in spite of the difficulty of placing income and expenditure for farm families on a truly comparable basis with that of urban or even village families.[17] In part, the differences in spending and saving patterns may be a function of the high year-to-year variability of farmers' incomes and their expectations on this score, but this can hardly be the major explanation; standards are certainly involved. Saving to a farmer means something different from what it does to a city man or his family. Farmers' saved funds buy farm machinery, fertilizer, stock, or land. What more ostentatious or enviable possessions are there, which more capable of validating a self-picture "urgently desired and striven for"?

Whether similar differences in standards or problems with respect to spending and saving exist for self-employed businessmen or other socio-economic groups is a question for the future to answer.[18]

D. Wealth: Physical Goods and Financial Assets

Physical goods: the influence of consumers' stocks of durable or semidurable goods on buying has so far eluded convincing demonstration, though it is certainly a matter of considerable interest to the study of cyclical change. Doubtless conflicting tendencies are present. For the same individual, there must be a negative association between recent and current purchases of the same item. But for other individuals there may,

---

[17] See Reid, *op. cit.*

[18] See J. N. Morgan, "The Structure of Aggregate Personal Saving," *Jour. Pol. Econ.,* Dec. 1951, LIX, 528–34.

as we have just noted, be a positive association. A positive association even for the same individual may likewise exist in some cases between one sort of purchase and others, e.g. houses and furniture, a college education and books; and a positive relation may likewise exist between purchases of refrigerators for some individuals and washing machines for others. Finally, the utility judged to remain in a stock of goods (and consequently its negative impact on current buying) is itself a function of expectations and attitudes, and therefore highly variable. This fluctuating "ownership objective"[19] would presumably be positively associated with current income (it is substantially the point about standards again); its pattern of change over time would be likely to be such as partly to neutralize the effect on current buying of the time pattern of stocks of goods. Clearly, this important subject is also a tricky one.

Financial Assets: the impact of financial assets on buying and saving creates a troublesome problem on both statistical and conceptual levels. On the one hand people who spend less of their income amass more wealth than spendthrifts. Therefore, over periods of several years, one would expect some positive correlation between annual saving and wealth of individual families, other things the same. At the same time, families having liquid assets are in a better position to meet temporary lapses in income by dissaving, and this would cause a negative short-term relation. The FRB-SRC Surveys, as analyzed by Katona, suggest that families having very small liquid assets are less likely to have large deficits; but, among families having large amounts of liquid assets, both large saving and large dissaving are common, and this seems to echo the conflicting aspects of the association of saving and assets.[20] The Survey data published in the *Federal Reserve Bulletin*[21] indicate that families with low incomes in a given year often piece out their living by reduction of such liquid assets as they possess; they likewise are more prone than are higher income families to use these funds for the purchase of food or other nondurables. Klein's work with individual schedules illu-

---

[19] C. F. Roos and Victor von Szeliski, "The Factors Governing Changes in Domestic Automobile Demand," in *Dynamics of Automobile Demand* (New York, 1939), p. 86. See also Jacobs and Winston, *op. cit.;* and N. J. Silberling, *The Dynamics of Business* (New York, 1943), Ch. 19.

[20] Katona, *Psychological Analysis*, pp. 170, 188.

[21] See articles, *op. cit.,* on the "Survey of Consumer Finances" reporting on distribution of consumer liquid assets; Aug. 1949, XXXV, 896–911 and Tab. 6, 9, pp. 904, 906; Dec. 1950, XXXVI, 1584–1611 and Tab. 13, 14, p. 1519; Dec. 1951, XXXVII, 1516–26 and Tab. 13, 15, 18, pp. 638, 639, 641.

minates the subject further. That *change* in wealth may have a different impact on disbursements from the level of wealth has been recognized by students interested in capital gains or losses, though the same problem might be posed when wealth is recorded at cost rather than market.[22]

A factor which, like wealth, provides auxiliary money funds is the ability to borrow. Unfortunately we cannot say much about how the availability of credit and the conditions under which it is offered affect disbursements. The size of down payments has been found of significance. Installment credit seems to be commonly used among lower income families as a means of deflecting income from small unit purchases to large unit purchases; or, insofar as goods are bought on installment rather than with saved funds, as a method of protecting savings by the compulsory repayment scheme.[23]

E. Demographic Factors

The needs and wants of families are influenced by the number of family members, their age, and the length of time that the family has been a going unit. But it is difficult indeed to say precisely how. One thing is clear—no satisfactory formula has as yet been devised for putting total family expenditure (expenditure on food is not quite so baffling) for families of different age and size on a comparable basis. We cannot, in other words, deflate satisfactorily for demographic factors and obtain thereby a "real per unit" measure of income or consumption, though there has been a long and continuing history of attempts to do so.[24]

We know that large families spend more on food, slightly more on

---

[22] See James Tobin, *A Theoretical and Statistical Analysis of Consumer Saving,* Doctoral Dissertation, Harvard University, 1947; G. S. Fulcher, "Annual Saving and Underspending of Individuals, 1926–1937," *Rev. Econ. Stat.,* Feb. 1941, XXIII, 28–39; J. J. Polak, "Fluctuations in United States Consumption, 1919–1932," *ibid.,* Feb. 1939, XXI, 1–12.

[23] Bureau of Applied Social Research, Columbia University, has developed some interesting findings of this sort; see also Gottfried Haberler, *Consumer Instalment Credit and Economic Fluctuations* (New York, 1942); Avram Kisselgoff, *Factors Affecting the Demand for Consumer Instalment Sales Credit,* NBER Technical Paper 7 (New York, 1952).

[24] For some of the more valiant recent attempts, see Dorothy Brady, "Budget Levels for Families of Different Sizes," *Mo. Lab. Rev.,* Feb. 1948, LXVI, 179–81; A. M. Henderson, "The Cost of a Family," *Rev. Econ. Stud.,* 1949–50, XVII, 127–48. Most of the figures for the 1934–36 B. L. S. study were published for "expenditure units." For description of the concept see Bull. 639, pp. 344–52. It is interesting to note that saving was *inversely* associated with income per expenditure unit in this study.

clothing (though less on clothing of husbands and wives), and less on most other goods; they also save less than small families at the same income level. But the picture is complicated by the fact that larger families are often older ones and that the ages of children and parents likewise affect comparisons.

For families of the same size, those headed by older husbands or wives own houses more frequently (though fewer are currently bought) and spend more for house operation, whereas most other expenditures, with the possible exception of reading, medical care, gifts, and welfare, are somewhat lower (furnishings and equipment and recreation a good deal lower). Older families save less, on the average, than those in the prime of life, and this is even true when money from annuities or pensions is counted as current income (rather than dissaving). The very young, however, perhaps in part because they often incur expenses of setting up new households and expect their incomes to rise in the future, save on the average least of all.[25]

F. Habits and Expectations

Habit is bound to be an extremely important determinant of the reaction to change of most sorts. Still, there is very little that we can say about just how buying is influenced by the fact that man is a creature of his own past. Insofar as the matter can be viewed in statistics it appears in reaction to change per se.

Expectations about the future must likewise influence buying and saving. Especially with respect to durable goods, clear expectations about prices or availability can, as has recently been sharply demonstrated, substantially influence the timing of buying. Automatically, short-term saving is affected. But saving can be directly influenced by expectations too. Insofar as saving is motivated by the wish to provide for the future, a given amount of prudence would counsel more saving if incomes are expected to fall than if they are expected to rise, *ceteris paribus*. But this influence is not easy to demonstrate, perhaps in part because the matter of how firmly expectations are held is especially hard to determine. The Michigan Surveys of consumer finances have included questions on expectations. One thing does seem fairly clearly indicated by these data:

---

[25] These two paragraphs rely heavily on two works: Day Monroe, Maryland Y. Pennell, Mary R. Pratt, and Geraldine S. DePuy, "Family Spending and Saving as Related to Age of Wife and Age and Number of Children," U.S. Dept. Agric. Misc. Pub. 489 (Washington, 1942) and Janet A. Fisher, *Economics of an Aging Population,* Doctoral Dissertation, Columbia University, April 1950, in which material from the former publication is analyzed in conjunction with data from the FRB-SRC survey.

families having recently experienced a fall in income which they expect to be temporary save less than others.[26]

G. Miscellaneous External Factors

A wide variety of factors that are not directly related either to the individual or the particular object he contemplates may nevertheless influence the decision to save or buy, other things the same. I can only illustrate.

Buying of goods is affected by the amount that is provided outside of the money economy—the services of owned homes, home-produced food, the work of housewives or children. These matters are perhaps of primary concern in the problem they create in comparing farm and urban living and that of different countries or widely different periods of time.

Buying of goods is also affected by the amount provided free (to the individual) by the State, though the relationship does not involve simple substitution. Goods provided or services provided by the State—consider education or highways—may develop more wants than they satisfy.

A related question involves how increased institutional provision of insurance, or the public provision of benefits ordinarily performed by saved private funds—insurance against illness, old age or unemployment—affect saving. These important questions we are only just starting to study.

Insofar as saving is motivated by return on investment, the interest rate may affect it. Recent literature, however, is notable for a tendency to minimize the importance of this previously emphasized factor.

Technological change is likewise important in providing new or substantially improved products that compete for the consumer dollar. Advertising is another factor that can influence the allocation of the dollar to one product or another, or perhaps from saving to buying, and how this takes place has been subjected to considerable study. Shortages are a form of external influence with which we have recently had considerable experience. As a matter of fact, external factors in the sense of the totality of goods that for one reason or another are provided by the economy exert a complicated and powerful influence on the buying of any one commodity or service. There are competitive *and* complemen-

---

[26] Katona, *Psychological Analysis,* Ch. 6 and p. 180; J. N. Morgan, "Consumer Savings," *Econometrica,* Jan. 1951, XIX, 63–64; L. R. Klein, "Estimating Patterns of Savings Behavior from Sample Survey Data," *ibid.,* Oct. 1951, XIX, 438–54.

tary aspects to the relationships of most goods to one another. In this sense, external factors are without limit in the intricate simultaneous adjustment of all expenditures to all others. But this last is a philosophic rather than practical point.

H. Price

We come finally to a factor—an external one too—that has received the oddest sort of attention. On the one hand, it has been the pampered child of a long theoretical argument—utility and later preference analysis; on the other hand, empirical investigation has been spotty and not closely integrated with the theory.

How utility analysis has endeavored to link, conceptually, consumer choice, the price system, and the supply of economic goods lies in a field covered by another chapter in this series; and how it has borne on the matter of economic welfare is dealt with in an earlier chapter in this volume.[27] This leaves for consideration here the question of the value of the construction in describing and explaining the character and implications of consumer behavior; and on this score there is virtually nothing to report. Insofar as consumer reaction to price has been studied empirically, it has been done largely by analysis of time series in which some effort has been made to hold other factors constant—the same method that has been used in the study of factors not elevated to a place in preference or demand theory. In the meantime, the minute examination of the theoretical interrelation of price and income in a stable preference field continues to pre-empt the working hours of able men. It does not seem to matter that in view of the picture of man and his interests that the scheme encompasses, most purchasing motives and behavior must lie outside of it. The preference field in actuality is as mobile as the sea.

At an empirical level, the sensitivity of consumer buying to price has proved exceptionally difficult to investigate. To see directly how the same individual would react to different prices, were all other considerations the same, is virtually impossible, since the fact of previous reactions alters later ones. Typically, therefore, experiment has been based either on how the same individual thinks he would react to various prices or how different individuals do react to them. And actually only a handful of studies of either sort have been reported.[28]

---

[27] B. F. Haley, "Value and Distribution," *A Survey of Contemporary Economics,* Vol. I, Ch. 1; and K. E. Boulding, "Welfare Economics," Ch. 1 of the present volume.

[28] Two spirited attempts to reproduce pieces of the preference field have recently been made. See S. W. Rousseas and A. G. Hart, "Experimental Verification of a Composite Indifference Map," *Jour. Pol. Econ.,* Aug. 1951, LIX, 288–318; Frederick Mosteller and Philip Nogee, "An Experimental Measurement of Utility," *ibid.,* Oct. 1951, LIX, 371–404.

In actuality, the consumer usually is required to react not to a simple change in price but to some combination of change in price and/or quality. To disentagle the two, or indeed, to appreciate either, he needs to be somewhat of a connoisseur. An interesting recent study developed some rather pessimistic conclusions as to his capacity on this score.[29] The need to make a price-quality choice is enforced by the practice of "price lining" in retail stores (carrying merchandise at well established prices or price bands, separated from one another by substantial intervals). For, when costs change, price lines are maintained for some time and quality is changed if need be.

The most common method of investigating the sensitivity of consumer buying to price has been through multiple correlation of time series.[30] To use time series for this purpose involves, in a sense, the problem of aggregation in reverse. Though there have been a few efforts to study differential choice between substitutes,[31] the majority of work has simply analyzed how the quantity purchased (or sometimes the dollar value of purchases) has varied with an index of prices, other things the same.[32] The use of variables such as consumer income and price other than that of the commodity under investigation has most usually served to enforce the *ceteris paribus* condition.

For the most part, investigators have been willing to consider the demand curve identified by the fact that it is the influences on demand, not on supply, that are isolated. The systematic aspect of the results, therefore, would apply to demand. However, others have emphasized the need to handle supply factors as well, if stable parameters are to be achieved, and have therefore worked with equation systems.

---

[29] A. R. Oxenfeldt, "Consumer Knowledge: Its Measurement and Extent," *Rev. Econ. Stat.,* Nov. 1950, XXXII, 300–14.

[30] Area surveys have been used for this purpose by comparing studies made at different times or places when prices likewise differed. But the method seems to involve a series of highly questionable assumptions—comparability of samples, linear buying-income regressions, similar supply conditions. See Abraham Wald, "The Approximate Determination of Indifference Surfaces by Means of Engel Curves," *Econometrica,* Apr. 1940, VIII, 144–75; Jacob Marschak, "Demand Elasticities Reviewed," *ibid.,* Jan. 1943, XI, 25–34. For a recent summary of methodological problems see K. A. Fox, "Relations between Prices, Consumption, and Production," *Jour. Am. Stat. Assoc.,* Sept. 1951, XLVI, 323–33.

[31] See, for example, J. N. Morgan, "Consumer Substitutions between Butter and Margarine," *Econometrica,* Jan. 1951, XIX, 18–39; Zenon Szatrowski, "Time Series Correlated with the Beef-Pork Consumption Ratio," *ibid.,* Jan. 1945, XIII, 60–78.

[32] In two studies the difference between the buying-income regression in area surveys and in time series has been related to the course of prices. Jacob Marschak, "Money Illusion and Demand Analysis," *Rev. Econ. Stat.,* Feb. 1943, XXV, 40–48; and Hans Staehle, "Relative Prices and Postwar Markets for Animal Food Products," *Quart. Jour. Econ.,* Feb. 1945, LIX, 237–79.

Calculations during the period under review have been made for about twenty different commodities or commodity groups sold to consumers. We have excluded all work dealing with demand of business intermediaries rather than consumers themselves, for the two cannot be relied upon to be identical, even in annual data, for anything other than truly perishable commodities.[33] In the findings, there are disturbing contradictions where calculations have been made for the same article by different investigators or the same investigator at different times.[34] This much, however, seems evident when the results of all of the work are viewed together:

The price elasticity of durable goods—furniture, automobiles, electrical equipment—generally appears to be over 1. At the other extreme are tobacco and tea with price elasticities of under .3. Food, as a whole, is not much higher, with individual sorts of food far less inelastic than the total. Fox's studies of different sorts of meats seem also to show considerably higher individual elasticities than for the group as a whole. Thus, in a very rough sort of way, price and income elasticity seem to parallel one another except, of course, that the one is negative and the other positive. But buyers seem to follow their price advantage more nimbly when it involves shifts between minor than major categories of goods. This is not likely to characterize income sensitivity of demand.[35]

Unfortunately, what these findings tell about motivation, and consequently about behavior in a transposed setting, is highly ambiguous. For example, we would like to know whether peoples' reactions to

[33] The elasticities calculated in (or subject to calculation from) the following studies have been included: Roos and von Szeliski, *op. cit.;* Marschak, "Money Illusion and Demand Analysis," *loc. cit.;* Richard Stone, "The Analysis of Market Demand," *Jour. Royal Stat. Soc.,* 1945, CVIII (3–4), 286–382, and, same title, Series 16, Dept. of Applied Econ., Univ. of Cambridge (Cambridge, Eng., 1948); L. R. Klein, "A Post-Mortem on Transition Predictions of National Product," *Jour. Pol. Econ.,* Aug. 1946, LIV, 289–308; Girshick and Haavelmo, *op. cit.;* A. R. Prest, "Some Experiments in Demand Analysis," *Rev. Econ. Stat.,* Feb. 1949, XXXI, 33–49; Tobin, "A Statistical Demand Function for Food," *loc. cit.;* Jacobs and Winston, *op. cit.;* K. A. Fox has had the great courtesy to make some of his findings available for this review prior to publication. They now appear in "Factors Affecting Farm Income, Farm Prices and Food Consumption," *Agric. Econ. Research,* July 1951, III, 65–82.

[34] Work of this sort runs into the fundamental problem that most prices move together with one another and with consumer income so that the influence of the price of the given commodity, other prices, and income cannot be adequately distinguished. First differences in income were used by Stone and Fox partly to lessen this difficulty and that of auto-correlated residuals.

[35] If anything, the reverse would be true insofar as when money seems more plentiful it may be spent on minor categories not previously purchased. Then the income elasticity of all subgroups might be lower than that of the group as a whole. Certainly, in any event, this last statement would apply to many subgroups.

choice-conditioning factors of all sorts are based on roughly price-deflated data or on choices conceived in current dollars. If some sort of *ad hoc* deflation is common, is it equally significant in connection with the price of the commodity whose purchase is contemplated as with the value of the income dollar? If not, theory holds, a "money illusion" is present. There is enough evidence that it is,[36] and that its character may differ for various commodities, to warrant concentrated study of the question with the tools of psychology as well as economics. The facts about the money illusion are important, not only for the analysis of demand for individual products, but likewise for total buying and saving.

All the work that, as far as I know, has been done in price sensitivity of buying deals with some sort of intermediate-term function. Yet it seems highly probable that the first reaction of buyers to a change in price will be different from later ones. Here, then, as well as in the case of income, it is likely that study of rates of change in prices as well as price proper is important to an understanding of the dynamics of change.[37]

III. CHANGE IN DISBURSEMENTS OF GROUPS THROUGH TIME

The power of each of these many considerations to produce change in aggregate buying or saving is a function, as we noted earlier, of the extent to which typical individual behavior is sensitive to each factor and the extent to which its presence undergoes variation for the aggregate as a whole.

Obviously then the relative importance of various influences will differ depending on whether attention is focused on long-term trends, cyclical change, or month-to-month variation. It would also differ depending on whether saving or the purchase of one or another class of commodity were the center of interest.

Demographic factors, standards of living, the extent to which goods and services are provided by the home or by the state, and real income may be the more important determinants of trends in buying or

---

[36] Stone found that price-elasticity of demand for articles purchased repetitively and in small units was often smaller (with a negative sign) for the commodity in question than (with a positive sign) for all others; whereas the reverse was true of large unit purchases of durable goods. The first of these findings was not duplicated in Marschak's study of meat, though it was in Fox's of meat and of livestock products. Differences of this sort, should they truly exist, seem full of information about the dynamics of buying and we would want to study reasons for the differences in terms of both the sensing of and the reaction to price change, for both the good in question and the value of the income dollar.

[37] Cf. Prest, *op. cit.,* p. 49.

saving simply because these are the factors that are subject to trend change.

Cyclical change, on the other hand, in a world in which such changes are extreme enough to include substantial fluctuations in personal income, is typically dominated by the income factor. This fact was shot anew into the stream of economic thought and work by Keynes.

A. The Consumption (or Saving) Function

Keynes held that the relationship between an increment of real income and the associated increment of consumption was one of the critical determinants of the volume of employment. After analyzing the subjective and objective factors that determine buying, he concluded that the relationship, the marginal propensity to consume, is quite stable.

As to the normal shape of the function, Keynes says: ". . . we take it as a fundamental psychological rule of any modern community that, when real income is increased, it will not increase its consumption by an equal *absolute* amount . . .";[38] the marginal propensity is less than 1. Also, several passages suggest that Keynes envisaged the possibility of a cyclical as well as a trend pattern to the marginal propensity to consume.[39]

No sooner was the concept born and its role in the determination of the level of output sketched, than efforts to clothe it in quantitative raiment got underway. Fundamentally, the work involved the study of how aggregate consumption in a country changed from year to year, on the assumption that income was the primary determinant. The question was broken into two parts: What is the typical relation between income and consumption? What factors cause systematic alterations in the relation? As the work progressed, the second question began to assume more importance than at first. As we have seen, both area surveys and time series could help in the empirical investigation of the problem.

Time series proved the most prolific source of estimate of the consumption function. The following brief résumé is based largely on a table prepared at the Department of Applied Economics, University of Cambridge, in conjunction with an excellent bibliography on the consumption function. I am deeply indebted to the authors, Guy Orcutt and A. D. Roy, for the use of this valuable unpublished document.

In general, the work proceeds in this way: An annual time series for consumer buying (or saving) is taken as the dependent variable to

---

[38] J. M. Keynes, *The General Theory of Employment Interest and Money* (New York, 1936), p. 97.

[39] *Loc. cit.*, pp. 120, 121, 319.

be "explained" by time series covering factors upon which changes in purchases are thought to depend. Multivariate analysis, usually a single equation fitted by least squares, determines the parameters of the relationship, though equation systems have sometimes been used, theoretically to take account of the generation of change in the exogenous (but not fixed) variables. Typically straight-line functions have been selected.[40] Income has for the most part been defined as consumer income (usually net of income taxes) rather than as national income. It has been worked with in current dollars or in dollars of constant purchasing power, for national aggregates or per capita. Variables other than the current level of income—time, change in income, highest past income, income of different classes of recipients, to mention some—have also been introduced.

Estimates of the coefficient of the income variable—the change in consumption associated with unit change in income—obtained in these diverse ways range for the United States from the low .90's to low .60's with the heaviest concentration around .75.[41]

As to the causes of so wide a range, generalization is difficult and

---

[40] Some especially interesting discourses on method in addition to those mentioned in other contexts are: *Statistical Inference in Dynamic Economic Models*, T. C. Koopmans, ed. (New York, 1950); Trygve Haavelmo, "The Statistical Implications of a System of Simultaneous Equations," *Econometrica*, Jan. 1943, XI, 1–12; *idem*, "Methods of Measuring the Marginal Propensity to Consume," *Jour. Am. Stat. Assoc.*, Mar. 1947, XLII, 105–22; Donald Cochrane and G. H. Orcutt, "Application of Least Squares Regression to Relationships Containing Autocorrelated Error Terms," *ibid.*, Mar. 1949, XLIV, 32–61.

[41] The summary applies to estimates using consumer income (not national income) in the United States. Estimates for other countries have not been systematically surveyed, though for the close to a dozen cases which have come to my attention, propensities are lower. But this may be due to noncomparable data. The studies to which the summary applies are the following: J. J. Polak, *op. cit.*; Tinbergen, *op. cit.*; R. B. Bangs, "The Changing Relation of Consumer Income and Expenditure," *Surv. Curr. Bus.*, Apr. 1942, XXII, 8–12; Richard Stone, "National Income in the United Kingdom and the United States of America," *Rev. Econ. Stud.*, Winter 1942–43, X, 1–27; L. J. Paradiso, "Retail Sales and Consumer Incomes," *Surv. Curr. Bus.*, Oct. 1944, XXIV, 5–14; J. Steindl, "Postwar Employment in the U.S.A.," *Bull. Oxford Univ. Inst. of Stat.*, Sept. 1944, VI, 193–202; Arthur Smithies, "Forecasting Postwar Demand: I," *Econometrica*, Jan. 1945, XIII, 1–14; S. M. Livingston, "Forecasting Postwar Demand: II," *ibid.*, 15–24; J. L. Mosak, "Forecasting Postwar Demand: III," *ibid.*, 25–53; W. S. Woytinsky, "Relationship between Consumers' Expenditures, Savings, and Disposable Income," *Rev. Econ. Stat.*, Feb. 1946, XXVIII, 1–12; V. L. Bassie, "Consumers' Expenditures in War and Transition," *ibid.*, Aug. 1946, pp. 117–30; Friend, *op. cit.*; E. G. Bennion, "The Consumption Function: Cyclically Variable?" *ibid.*, Nov. 1946, pp. 219–24; L. R. Klein, *Economic Fluctuations in the United States, 1921–1941* (New York, 1950); Modigliani, *op. cit.*; J. S. Duesenberry, "Income-Consumption Relations and Their Implications," *Essays in Honor of Alvin H. Hansen* (New York, 1948); Colin Clark, *"A System of Equations Explaining the U.S. Trade Cycle 1921 to 1941"* (Brisbane, Australia, 1948); Haavelmo, "Methods of Measuring the Marginal Prospensity to Consume," *loc. cit.*; Mack, *op. cit.*

precarious. In general, when undeflated data are used, the coefficients of income tend to be higher than when converted to constant dollars; there are few deflated estimates yielding coefficients higher than .80.

The rate of change in income, included as a rough indication of the prevalence of short-term increases or decreases in income, displays a negative sign—people buy less (save more) when income has risen to a given level than when it has fallen to it, *ceteris paribus*. The same factor is visible in the observation that when expansions and contractions are fitted separately, the coefficient of income during expansion is slightly lower than during contractions. Both of these tentative findings testify to the difference between short-term and intermediate-term adjustments to income and/or factors correlated with income in time series.[42]

The true long-term (as distinguished from intermediate-term) adjustment of buying to income may be still different. It is, of course, affected by changing income-linked standards of one sort or another, or shifts in population from the sphere of one standard to that of another. Two students have found, as has been mentioned, income-linked trends in the consumption-function, other things the same. This implies that a gradual rise in standards with rising income tends to counteract the fact that the intermediate-function (since its shape is such that consumption would be positive though income is zero) would cause the average propensity to fall as income rises.

Differential change in prices of groups of commodities for which consumer price-sensitivity differs would cause buying to be higher, other things the same, when the prices of articles having low price-elasticity, such as food, had risen relative to other prices. The theoretical case for this point has been argued, and it has also been put to a rough empirical test.[43] The net effect over time of change in liquid assets has been found by at least one investigator to be negative. And this about completes the list of those of the probable influences on buying or saving for which time series yield some support.

When a time trend has been introduced, it usually has a positive sign. This seems reasonable since both the increase in population and the

---

[42] There are some very interesting qualitative discussions of this question in the literature, of which space forbids citation. See, for example, L. H. Bean, "Relation of Disposable Income and the Business Cycle to Expenditures," *Rev. Econ. Stat.,* Nov. 1946, XXVIII, 199–207; R. V. Rosa, "Use of the Consumption Function in Short Run Forecasting," *ibid.,* May 1948, XXX, 91–105.

[43] Gardner Ackley and D. B. Suits, "Relative Price Changes and Aggregate Consumer Demand," *Am. Econ. Rev.,* Dec. 1950, XL, 785–804; Klein, "A Post-Mortem on Transition Predictions of National Product," *loc. cit.*

shift from farm to urban occupations would presumably tend to increase buying, other things the same. But since there has been an upward trend in real income over the years, the positive coefficient could also, at least in part, reflect the income-linked factor of standards of living. The evidence simply does not suffice as yet to identify the factors at work.

All in all, we cannot say with confidence what the net effect of all these factors has been on the *average* propensity over the years. Such data as we have do not seem to show a downward trend in the average buying-income ratio, but they are not as yet adequate to a firm conclusion.[44]

Theoretically, as the influence on buying of one determinant after another is taken into account, that of income should become clarified and estimates ought to gravitate toward a central figure. Actually, however, this does not seem to have taken place. The coefficients and their confidence areas based on quite reasonable manipulation of time series vary over an uncomfortably large range.

Nor can this range be narrowed by substituting calculations based on area surveys for those based on time series. Shortly after Keynes' book appeared, several investigators supplied propensities estimated from budget data.[45] Elizabeth Gilboy, for example, observed that marginal propensities calculated from the 1935–36 survey ranged from 1 for incomes below $1,000 to about .5 for incomes over $4,000; by weighting each propensity by the number of families in the income group she arrived at a collective figure of .74.

We have already pointed out that this figure does not actually isolate the income factor in buying, and so would at best constitute only a rough estimate of changes in total buying or saving associated with different levels of consumer income. But there is a further difficulty of particular significance in connection with estimates of saving (or the propensity to consume): most area surveys tell very little about the top 5 per cent of the income-size array, whereas it is these high-income families that account for most of the net saving. For example, the figures ap-

---

[44] There are interesting discussions of this problem in many of the articles previously cited. Duesenberry deals with it at length in Ch. 4 of his book; Lewis and Douglas, and Brady and Friedman in the works previously cited deal with the evidence that area surveys yield. See also, L. J. Paradiso, *op. cit.*

[45] Richard and W. M. Stone, "The Marginal Propensity to Consume and the Multiplier, a Statistical Investigation," *Rev. Econ. Stud.*, Oct. 1938, VI, 1–24; Horst Mendershausen, "The Relationship between Income and Savings of Metropolitan Families," *Am. Econ. Rev.*, Sept. 1939, XXIX, 521–37; Gilboy, "Income-Expenditure Relations," *loc. cit.*

plying to the 1935–36 urban, nonrelief sample, consisting of 18,496 families, follow: 4.1 per cent of the total population had incomes over $5,000 and 775 such families were surveyed; they had 26 per cent of the income and their saving was 85 per cent of the net total. The top 1.6 per cent of American families, those having incomes of over $10,000 (only 105 of this group were sampled) accounted for 70 per cent of the country's net saving.[46]

To judge the impact of a change in income we use the slope (marginal propensity) of the savings-income regression and weight it by the amount of the change in income received by families at each income level. The distribution of the change going to urban nonrelief families at any given time might be the same as, or more or less concentrated than, the distribution of their total income in 1935–36; and the collective marginal propensity would depend, of course, on what this proportion actually was. The matter has been submitted to intensive investigation in recent years, work that is useful in many contexts. But as an aid in predicting short-term change in the marginal propensity to save, more accurate knowledge about income distribution is probably a mere detail compared with the question of what the shape of the propensity for the top quintile of the income range actually is, a subject on which the 800-odd families surveyed in 1935–36 are still a major source of our information.

One thing about the function we do seem to know—the marginal propensity declines as income levels rise. This makes it essential to be able to describe its upper reaches in detail, and this we cannot do.[47] Indeed, the difficulties of doing so become ever clearer. Recent work with individual schedules shows more plainly than before how unstable are parameters based on area surveys. Apparently we need at least to learn a great deal more about sources of variability, and perhaps even statistical techniques, before information based on interpersonal comparisons will help us to select the proper figure for the collective propensity to consume. We return, therefore, to the quandary as to how to narrow the range of estimated marginal propensity to less than from .60 to .80.

---

[46] See National Resources Committee, *Consumer Expenditures in the United States*, p. 122, Tab. 1 B; and Natural Resources Planning Board, *Family Expenditures in the United States*, p. 130, Tab. 400.

[47] I have studied this regression for about eleven surveys or parts of them made between 1922 and 1945 in which several class averages for families in about the upper 10 per cent and often in the upper 5 per cent of the income array are available. Most of these studies do show a marked reduction of marginal prospensity in the upper income brackets, though at what point the curvature sets in, and its extent, differs considerably.

Five criteria have been put forward: (1) The height of the correlation coefficients. Though consumption functions all display extremely high coefficients, savings functions show considerable variation. Robert Ferber found this to be the case even when the same data and stretch of years were used.[48] (2) The accuracy with which consumption is predicted for years not included in the original calculation; this criterion depends, of course, on the validity of the assumption that structural relationships (for both included and excluded variables) have not changed between the period to which the equations were fitted and that to which they are to be applied. (3) Formal consistency between macro-economic functions implied by the equation and reasonable micro-economic functions; this criterion is quite useless in view of how little we know of the micro-economic function even theoretically. (4) Soundness of the logic supporting the proposed formula. The difficulty with this criterion is that it is hard to invent an implausible argument, and the chances are that most of the calculations err chiefly in their exclusions. Note that the excluded variables not only decrease the accuracy of estimation but, since there is little reason to assume a random joint-probability distribution of their influence, bias all measurements. The extent of the influence, the critical matter, is not given by argument. (5) Evidence from other sources of information in support of the selected variable. This seems to me to be the promising approach. Its application requires time and patience and concerted effort, and a good start has been made.

But let us assume for the moment that it were possible to select the best formula out of all those that have been calculated. How well could we then estimate the magnitudes? The answer, of course, depends on which magnitudes are sought.

Most of the formulas provide very respectable estimates of total consumer buying or for the average propensity to consume. The standard deviation of the coefficients in the few cases that they are published suggests that, were income known (as well as the other variables that may be included), consumption could be estimated in about two-thirds of the cases within a margin of a few billion dollars (providing the deviation is normally distributed throughout the range). This would provide a reasonably good approximation for many purposes, providing no important structural changes took place such as those that may have occurred during the war.

---

[48] *A Study in Aggregate Consumption Functions* (unpublished University of Chicago dissertation, 1951) in which several of the subjects mentioned in this paragraph are analyzed.

As an estimate of saving, these equations are obviously far less satisfactory simply because a confidence area of say two billion dollars is a larger proportion of six billion, the average interwar level of consumer saving, than of sixty billion, the approximate average interwar level of consumption in current dollars. For many purposes for which the estimates have been used, this relative error in saving is the relevant standard to apply.

As an estimate of short-term *change* in consumption or saving associated with a given change in income, a matter of considerable practical interest and one highlighted by the Keynesian investment multiplier, the equations are of hardly any use at all. Actual ratios of year-to-year change in consumption to change in income are widely variable. The Commerce figures (1922–1941) yield experienced marginal propensities for annual increments that range from 5.17 to .34; about two-thirds fall between .96 and .54 (corresponding to investment multipliers of 25.0 and 2.2); about half fall within .85 and .56 (multipliers of 6.6 and 2.3).[49]

The spectacle of failure need not jaundice the eye to the sight of success. Certainly, important knowledge has been achieved: The demonstration of the powerful influence of income on buying when income changes as much as it did in the interwar period is the first and very important achievement. It seems reasonably clear, too, that the short-term relation of consumer saving to income is such as to cause saving to represent a larger part of total consumer income in prosperity than in depression, a fact having many consequences. The less clearly demonstrated yet nevertheless strongly indicated finding that long-term influences operate which lessen the increase in saving which would, on the basis of the short-term relation, be associated with an upward trend in income is likewise of very considerable importance.

B. Buying of Various Sorts of Goods and Services

Space does not permit a summary of the investigations that have been made of the various categories of consumption, even though they

---

[49] This wide variation (and it would be only slightly reduced were an allowance made for any systematic principle in the ratios that might be detected) may seem hard to reconcile with the fact that the coefficients of the income variable, the marginal propensity as yielded by the regressions, have typically a very small standard error. The reason is that the *sequence* of pairs of observations for income and buying is largely immaterial to the calculation (unless lagged variables take it into account in part). But it is the sequence that yields the experienced ratios between increments of income and buying. Obviously, an infinite variety of these ratios would be compatible with a given coefficient for income in a regression of aggregate buying on income.

have been much rarer than studies of saving. Yet, obviously the meaning of trend and cyclical patterns of saving are conditioned by similar patterns within the consumption aggregate.

Various sorts of goods differ greatly in the extent to which buying varies from year to year. The variation is, in part, a function of how necessary the available goods are thought to be, and consequently, how willing people are to do without them when their ability to acquire goods diminishes. In part it is a function of the inflexibility in the relation between the purchase of goods and the ability to enjoy them; this relation is quite inflexible for most foods and highly flexible for many durable goods (a flexibility which is in a sense shared by saved funds). In part it is a function of the absence of impediments to change, such as contractual arrangements or strong habits. For buying measured in dollars, a fourth cause of variation is the difference among commodities in cyclical variations in prices.

Judging from a recent study,[50] these differences in the willingness and ability of consumers to shift from one sort of buying to another as aggregate income undergoes changes result in substantial cyclical shifts in the distribution of sales among products of various sorts. Comparing the averages for the two prosperity years 1929 and 1937 with the averages for the two depression years 1932 and 1933, the percentage of total sales consisting of goods of above-average income sensitivity, a group in which durable and/or luxury goods play a big part, slipped from about 27 to 21 per cent, whereas the corresponding figures for goods of below average sensitivity, a group including many small-unit habitual expenditures (e.g. tobacco, drugs, and sundries), contractual expenditures connected with dwelling places, and purchases tied to owned durable goods (e.g. gasoline and household utilities), climbed from 36 to 45 per cent of total consumption expenditures.[51]

From the study of monthly time series on sales of various sorts of stores, one arrives tentatively at a further characteristic of cyclical fluctuations in consumer buying: peaks and troughs in specific cycles of physical quantities of purchases seem to occur at about the same time as those in consumer income or business in general. A lag in retail sales measured in current prices has sometimes been observed, but this is explained by the notorious sluggishness of prices at retail.

It would be useful for heuristic reasons to attempt to reconcile in-

---

[50] Clement Winston and Mabel A. Smith, "Income Sensitivity of Consumption Expenditures," *Surv. Curr. Bus.,* Jan. 1950, XXX, 17–20.

[51] *Ibid.;* based on Tab. 2. Income sensitivity was derived from a regression of expenditure on income and time, undeflated data.

come elasticities based on area surveys with those based on time series. Obviously they could hardly be the same, and the character of differences is full of information. True, neither can be determined as exactly as one might like. Collective income elasticities read from area surveys for various sorts of goods have the same shortcomings as has the analogous figure for saving, already discussed; but they are not nearly so serious. For one thing, they are probably more stable. Further, the questions put to them are less exacting. Finally, people in the upper fifth of the income array, about which our knowledge is so meager, do a much smaller part of the buying of most commodities than they do of total net saving.

Differences in sensitivity to income as read from area surveys and time series must reflect differences in the impact of change per se. But many other factors must likewise play a part, and they will often differ depending on the type of goods or service under consideration. I wish there were space to illustrate.

Consumption functions for various commodities have been wall flowers these fifteen years because of the great popularity of the study of saving (or total consumption). This is unfortunate even for the study of saving. For, man does not save with one part of himself and spend with the rest. There is no better test for a theory of saving than the capacity to combine it gracefully with theories for inter-commodity differences in spending.

IV. CONSUMER BUYING AND CHANGES IN THE PRODUCTION OF CONSUMER GOODS

Having reviewed how the economy, among other things, influences consumer buying, we now turn to the reverse question—how consumer buying affects the economy. The problem can be attacked at both the theoretical and empirical levels.

Utility theory addressed itself partly to the question of how inter-commodity distribution of consumer buying influenced the distribution of productive resources. Indeed, it wove a poetic unity among consumption, production, and welfare, though at the expense of enlarging upon a dream. Its pallid offspring, preference analysis, seems to contribute little to the understanding of the impact on the economy of consumer choice.

Another set of ideas on this subject are those of Keynes. He focused attention on how consumer buying influences the level of employment and real output of the economy. His statement concerns not the absolute amount of buying, but its relation to income under equilibrium conditions—the propensity to consume. The marginal propensity, he believed to be, in the first place, reasonably stable and predictable. In the second place, the marginal propensity determines the total increase in income towards which a given increase in investment tends to propel the economy. The amount, under equilbrium conditions, is determined by the reciprocal of one minus the marginal propensity to consume— the investment multiplier. Only when income arrives at this point will both consumers and businessmen be under no inducement to alter their decisions about output and employment.

Our review has yielded this conclusion: empirical investigation of the consumption function has failed to disclose a degree of predictability of the marginal propensity to consume that would enable useful prediction (via the investment multiplier) of the level of employment resulting from a given short-term change in investment.

The figures on which this conclusion is based associate consumer buying with *consumer disposable income,* because it is to this relation that the psychological laws posited by Keynes would seem to apply. Multiplier theory, on the other hand, applies to the relation of consumption and *national income*—a considerably less stable or predictable function.

This review also suggests that further work may very possibly materially narrow the margin of unpredictability of the consumption function. But even were improvement to be substantial, it seems unlikely that, in effect, the theory of *production* supplied by Keynes would be adequate to explain how short-term changes in consumer buying act on the level of employment or income. Here too, and far more clearly than in the case of the consumption function, the number of parameters encompassed by the theory are not nearly adequate to depict even the major outlines of the actual process of change over short periods of time.

That the theory does, on the other hand, provide a useful analysis of long-term relationships seems far more likely. For over the years, many of the variables influencing short-term change average to zero. Certainly too, in the long run, the level of output can only be maintained or increased if resources not put to work directly by consumers are employed in the production of capital goods.

A causal link between producer and consumer that runs in a different direction from the one emphasized by Keynes has been known as the "acceleration principle," and the relation between acceleration and the multiplier has been expertly expounded in recent years. In broadest terms, the theory holds that under a given technology, the volume of output determines the size of the plant that is required. It goes on to posit a more or less fixed relationship between output and plant. This means that the demand for new plant becomes a function of the rate of change in output. Here again, the notion of long-term stability of the ratio seems realistic, if gradual technological change is allowed for.

Over short periods of time, on the other hand, all sorts of factors other than the level of output bear overpoweringly on the decisions to add to plant or inventories of consumers' goods. The acceleration principle pictures the course of the tortoise, whereas business investment moves like the hare of the fable. It alternately falls behind, spurts to catch up, rushes ahead and falls behind the current using up of plant and stocks. And many factors determine which is occurring at a particular time.

At an empirical level, since most of these factors would, like the acceleration principle, tend to cause investment to fluctuate more than consumers' takings, time series—which clearly behave this way—support uncritically this aspect of acceleration theory. But there seems little evidence in support of the more exacting implications of the cylically stable stock-output ratio—either for capital goods or stock in trade; either with respect to the ratios proper or the implied timing of investment.[52]

Lloyd Metzler has brought forward a model[53] in which production of consumers' goods for sale is assumed to lag one planning period behind consumer buying. The assumption is made that the marginal propensity to consume is constant. Initial noninduced investment causes plans to go awry. But stocks, which absorb the first impact of the difference between output and sales, are not permitted to do so for long: producers plan to restore them to their intended level, which, in the first of Metzler's models, is a fixed absolute amount unrelated to sales or output. This causes production for stock to have the pattern of the rate of change of sales. A cycle in output and buying results, though noninduced investment remains at a fixed level after an initial increase. Retail sales can either synchronize with or lead production; indeed, if the inventory objective were a given ratio of stocks to output and if

---

[52] See Moses Abramovitz, *Inventories and Business Cycles* (New York, 1950).

[53] "Factors Governing the Length of Inventory Cycles," *Rev. Econ. Stat.,* Feb. 1947, XXIX, 1–15.

stocks were large relative to sales, production could theoretically also lead sales, though Metzler is not especially concerned with the timing relationships. His interest lies primarily in the fact that cycles in output and sales are generated. Their amplitude is positively associated with the size of the marginal propensity to consume. This valuable contribution further underscores the question whether the marginal propensity has a cyclical pattern. The question is pertinent for all consumers' goods; it is also important for major classes of goods.

A study of the vertical transmission of consumer demand in the shoe-leather-hide industry[54] indicates that the question of how fluctuations in consumer buying move to earlier stages needs to be studied in segments. At the retail stage, the need to buy a substantial portion of expected sales ahead of time on the basis of a guess—often simply a projection of current volume—causes discrepancy between receipts (based on expected sales) and those required in the light of actual sales. The fact that stocks must be closely controlled, because of their large size and high degree of specificity, causes the error to be promptly corrected in current orders for immediate delivery. This correction element in orders tends to have the pattern of the rate of change of sales, and may well lead sales proper. This tendency would be present even if stocks were held at a uniform figure. The fact that they are loosely intended to move up and down with sales (though less than proportionately) underscores the tendency for orders to lead sales, as well as for them to have a wider amplitude of fluctuation.

At the manufacturing stage, some further magnification and acceleration of demand may take place, though for different reasons—ones involving primarily the problem of buying leathers at the right time and price. The effort to do so results in fluctuations in inventory investment associated with expectations about prices and availability of merchandise. In this industry these fluctuations broadly parallel those of consumer demand, though with relatively stronger minor movements and some tendency to anticipate turns. Tanners' operations as a whole damp the magnification of demand as handed back by the shoe manufacturer. This may be associated with several characteristics among which are a long manufacturing process and stock in trade which is most conveniently held in the finished or semifinished rather than the raw state.

The net result is that fluctuations in consumer buying of shoes re-

[54] Forthcoming volume, Ruth P. Mack, *Consumption and Business Cycles; A Case Study: The Shoe-Leather-Hide Industry*, Nat. Bur. Econ. Res.

sults in synchronous fluctuations in production of shoes, leather, and hides. The amplitude of fluctuations is larger at other stages than at the retail one, and largest at production of shoes or leathers. Orders, however, are harbingers of change, and precede output *and* consumer buying. Here, as in Metzler's model, though in part for different reasons, cycles in consumer buying and in output of consumer goods industries can occur and propagate independently of fluctuation in demand for durable producers' goods.

We conclude that the problem of tracing the impact of consumer buying on the economy at large is likely to be revealed by empirical study to be only somewhat simpler than that of tracing the impact of the economy (including its participants) on consumer buying.

V. SUMMARY AND PROSPECT

The picture that emerges from this excursion into the study of change in consumer buying is one of baffling complexity. Yet the subject is of so great importance that, in spite of difficulties, the effort to understand and even to predict consumer behavior must continue. And on the whole, the past augurs well for the future. In spite of the great difficulty, we have, I think, come a surprisingly long way during this short score of years.

There has been progress in four directions: First, bondage to ideas that turned out to be too restrictive has been broken; the search for "the" propensity to consume and "the" price-elasticity of demand has merged into the search for all the factors that materially influence buying or saving; including the difference between initial and later reactions to change and the interaction between the individual and the group. Second, the source material has expanded: area surveys and time series, at least in the United States, have improved prodigiously, an accomplishment the importance of which cannot be overstressed; qualitative data, too, are more plentiful; progress of high pertinence has taken place in other social sciences. Third, in the field of mathematical statistics new tools have been developed for working on problems involving many variables, with which this subject abounds. Fourth, with the expanded conception of the problem and improved materials and tools, have come more varied and resourceful methods of study.

How then may all this good work most efficiently result in more good work? I come back to the essential intricacy of the subject. How can conduct that is literally the result of everything that people are and how they got that way, and of everything in their social and physical environment, possibly be described or codified? There are I think some guides in recent work to indicate how further progress can be achieved.

The first is a negative lesson. The way to achieve understanding is not to pretend that complications do not exist and that a few rules can explain human behavior or express its central tendency in groups.

The positive lesson is a subtler one and useful in other branches of economics as well. It involves an approach and a point of view. Increasingly over the past fifteen years economists engaged in studying some problem in consumer buying have considered first the full quota of choice-conditioning factors likely to bear on the time period or aspect of buying in which interest has centered. From the total, those believed to be important are selected. Their impact is measured. The question is re-examined and submitted to further testing. A series of successive approximations produces cumulative insight.

The cumulation proceeds in several directions, even within the field to which this survey has been restricted: (1) *From one problem to another,* as when the careful study of the buying of different sorts of goods informs as to the dynamics of saving, or when the study of parts —dissaving, contractual saving, other saving—helps to illuminate the behavior of the whole, or when the conception of the developmental character of personality as understood by psychologists is applied to the study of how decisions to buy durable goods evolve. (2) *From one source material to another.* The same question (such as how do standards of living affect buying?) may be put to different materials—time series, area surveys, psychological studies of individuals, investigations by anthropologists. Between area studies and time series especially, insights have commonly flowed in a two-way stream. Even specific marginal relationships have been transplanted from an inter-family to an inter-period context; but recent work suggests that the analysis of family spending has at best not yet gone far enough to meet the precise quantitative requirements of this method. (3) *By intensive analysis of a limited body of information.* Thus, the genesis of individual decisions to make certain major purchases could profitably be described and analyzed. Histories of output and sales of important new consumer goods might help to explore the problem of market saturation. Intensive study of individual schedules from area surveys with modern tools of statistical analysis should prove highly instructive though not at all easy. For, parameters, especially for savings functions, based on interpersonal comparisons appear to be willful and jumpy even in samples of considerable size. Here is a challenge to put the inquisitive on their metal! What are the sources of the variability? Is instability due to some causes irrelevant to defined purposes for which the data are to be used? If so, can it be weeded out or subdued by especially designed statistical techniques and would parameters then grow reasonably steady? Were the answer yes, an additional step might be warranted: focused samples could be drawn in which the number of variables had been severely limited in order to flood-light relationships among those chosen for study. A final illustration, the happily increasing stock of monthly and quarterly time series on buying of various sorts and on saving possess a store of information which they could be coaxed to yield.

In sharp contrast to the many accomplishments over the period under review in the study of consumer buying is the meager exploration of the influence of consumer buying on the economy as a whole. We simply do not know and are only beginning to inquire how producers sense and react to a change in sales or orders or, perhaps, in expectations based on other things.

But here again there are many hopeful signs. The rigid preconceptions of the past are shaking loose and the attitude of the anthropologist who learns from his subjects how to phrase his questions, and, indeed, what questions to ask, is seeping into empirical investigations in our ever less dismal science.

COMMENT
Joseph S. Davis

Ruth Mack has ably illuminated one important sector of the economics of consumption. Having commented extensively on an early draft, I am loath to argue here over points in her matured treatment. I prefer to stress other important sectors of consumption economics which she deliberately ignored, in concentrating on one which has been absorbing perhaps an undue proportion of economists' energy. As will appear, however, I object to the very concept of consumption as consumption expenditures, and to the restricted perspective which this concept involves.

In my view, the central problem of postwar economics concerns the level of living of groups and peoples, and the role which consumption plays in these. How levels of consumption and living are best conceived and appraised; how they change through the life cycle of individuals, in the course of economic fluctuations, and in the various phases of war and peace; under what influences they rise and fall, and by what policies they are lowered and can be raised or otherwise enriched; how levels interact with standards of consumption and living that people have and evolve; and what are their interactions with population growth under various conditions: these are basic issues on which fresh illumination is urgently needed and on which economists can contribute much.

In this mid-century world, we need to broaden our perspective to include economies of divergent types, in which there are wide differences in the extent to which consumption goods are provided through the market, by government activities, and by self-service and by mutual service. In such a world the habit of treating consumption as if it were simply acquisition by purchase needs to be disestablished. The central aspect of consumption is utilization, though holding for use, as well as acquisition by purchase and otherwise, also deserves intensive study. Expansion in the possession and use of durable goods, and in the use of services of many kinds, amply justifies fuller analysis of utilization and possessions as distinct from acquisition.

Divergences in levels of consumption of living among groups or classes within a nation, moreover, are very imperfectly reflected in consumer expenditures per capita, per family, or per consumer spending unit, with or without allowance for household composition and ages of its members. Indeed, the whole subject of income inequalities, now in a sorry state, needs to be restudied in terms of inequalities in levels of consumption and living.

Radical changes in the age distribution of populations, notably including those in the United States in recent decades, call for much more analysis of consumption by different age groups, in order to yield results useful in forecasting demand for consumption and investment for a decade or more ahead. The upset of population forecasts and the obstinate retention of obsolete convictions make this an especially promising field.

The impacts of involvement in war, and of aggressive or defensive programs short of war, also need fuller investigation in a variety of groups and nations, with a view to replacing widely accepted notions by tested generalizations.

Several crucial questions await convincing answers:

(1) Have C. R. Noyes and others significantly dispelled our

earlier ignorance of *wants,* which Knight in 1924 termed "the most obstinately unknown of all the unknowns in the whole system of economic variables with which economic science deals"?

(2) Are "needs" for goods determinable, in scientific terms or otherwise?

(3) Are standards of consumption and living, as distinct from levels, now objectively determinable?

(4) What is the significance of "normative standards" of consumption, set by expert outsiders, as compared with the actual standards of a group?

(5) Can usable indexes of levels of consumption and living be developed for individual nations and intra-national groups over a period of time? For international comparisons at a given time?

(6) Under what conditions does production determine or limit the consumption level? Or consumption limit production?

(7) Is there, as Keynes asserted and Hansen believed, a narrow limit to the rate at which the consumption level of an advanced people, even in peace, can rise or be raised?

(8) Have postwar foreign-aid programs and the current rearmament program been essential to maintain and promote advance in the American consumption level, or have they tended to impair our consumption level or to present obstacles to its improvement?

COMMENT

Jacob Marschak

There is little to add to the inspiring "Summary and Prospect" which concludes Ruth Mack's contribution. These few remarks will deal with the nature of some predictions treated in her chapter.

Expenditure of a single family on (say) food depends admittedly on several variables such as: the family's size, composition, race, current income, past income, past food expenditure, its various assets, etc. Suppose that, on the basis of a family budget sample, an equation (Ruth Mack's "micro-economic equation") is estimated that permits predicting food expenditure when those variables are given. What is meant by "aggregating" such results? Only this: Suppose we know, for some future date, the *joint frequency distribution* of those variables, i.e. the number of families that will correspond to each possible combination of family size, current family income, past family income, etc. The "micro-economic equation" permits us to predict the food expenditure for each such combination and hence (by multiplication and addition) for the aggregate of all families as it will be on that future date. Thus the aggregate food expenditure may be predicted, in general, *not* from total national income (current and past), total cash or number of children in the nation, etc., but from these *and other* parameters (e.g., variances, correlations, etc.) of the joint frequency distribution of current family income, past family income, family cash, size, etc. The choice of such parameters will depend on one's knowledge, not only of the micro-economic equation (e.g., on whether it is linear or not), but also of the likely way in which the joint frequency distributions are going to behave in the future. Thus the use of "micro-economic equations" to derive or verify aggregative propositions presupposes a more manifold cross-classification of observed families than has been available so far.[55]

The micro-economic equation is itself not an exact one, not only because it is to be estimated from a sample but, more fundamentally, because human action depends on more variables than the investigator can list and measure. If those extra-variables are very numerous and if each is very small in its separate effect, one may regard their joint effect as a chance deviation. As is illustrated geometrically by the familiar "scatter" of points (each representing one observation on the measured variables), Ruth Mack's "micro-economic equation" merely stands for a joint probability distribution (a concept analogous to that of joint frequency distribution). The probability that the Smith family, with a given past income, current income, number of dependents, etc., would spend on food $30 to $40 a week is such-and-such. Moreover, the contagion of the Smiths by the Joneses means that the probability distributions of their respective food expenditures (given the incomes, etc.) are mutually dependent. It is because of this dependence between the chance responses of fellow-members of a community that, even when one "aggregates" for millions of people, the chance deviations do not "average out," and the "macro-economic" predictions must themselves have the form of probability distributions. The investigator can merely "bet 2:1 that aggregate savings will be between 10 and 15 billion," or some such figure.

Can such predictions be at all useful? This depends on how much

---

[55] See Trygve Haavelmo, "Family Expenditures and the Marginal Propensity to Consume," *loc. cit.* Progress is to be expected from current work such as that of the Michigan Survey Research Center.

benefit or damage can be expected, on the average, from a visualized practical decision based on such a "bet" instead of any alternative decision. (The late Sir Josiah Stamp claimed to have caught tax delinquents by assuming Paretian distribution of true incomes! Yet the standard error of a Pareto curve is well known to be large.) In this connection, a remark should be made as to Ruth Mack's treatment (Sec. III and IV) of the "multiplier" as a predictive tool; the remark would equally well apply to other empirical ratios such as the velocity of circulation of money. We want to predict, not the simultaneous change of two variables—e.g. income and investment, or income and money stock —but the effect upon one variable (income) of fixing the other variable (government expenditure, money stock) at some politically determined level. To make such a conditional prediction of one variable, the others being fixed, is clearly subject to smaller errors than to predict the ratio of two simultaneously fluctuating random variables from past observations on such ratios (Ruth Mack's "experienced marginal propensities").

The subject of consumption is common to economics, psychology, and anthropology. The author's invitation to cross boundaries must be supported. Perhaps the only useful distinction is one that would describe as economic all behavior derivable from the rule that "if A is preferred to B, and B to C, then A is preferred to C." It is not clear why the author rejects preference analysis as "pallid" (Sec. IV). The working hypothesis of consistent choices has proved (under the name of "economic theory") not at all devoid of verifiable and (if verified) useful implications.

POPULATION

3

THEORY[1]

Joseph J. Spengler

By law of nature thou art bound to breed,
That thine may live when thou thyself art dead.
SHAKESPEARE, in *Venus and Adonis*

The study of population remains relatively unstructured as to theory and relatively uncircumscribed as to scope. A variety of disciplines have contributed to its development, and their separate contributions have not yet been transformed into an integrated whole. The field of population is broader in scope, therefore, than that of economics as usually defined.

The interest of the economist in population data and their analysis

[1] Severe limitations of space have made it impossible to cite more than a very few of the contributions that are reviewed in this essay. The author has been obliged to limit his citation of the relevant literature to those items that, for one reason or another, have seemed to him to be most useful to the reader for whom this essay is primarily designed. However, readers interested in the bibliography of population may consult, besides the bibliographical reviews appearing in several of the economic journals, *Population Index,* which has provided good coverage since 1935, and a review of the literature by the Population Division of the United Nations, scheduled to appear in 1952. Post-1945 developments are reported in the journals *Population* and *Population Studies.* Population questions are treated frequently in the *Milbank Memorial Fund Quarterly,* the *Eugenics Review, Human Biology,* and the *Statistical Bulletin* of the Metropolitan Life Insurance Company; sociological aspects of these questions, in the sociological journals; and relevant statistical techniques, in the statistical and the population journals. Economists will find interesting the bibliographical appendix to Ernst Wagemann's *Menschenzahl und Völkerschicksal* (Hamburg, 1948), and the Social Science Research Council's forthcoming revised review of the literature of internal migration. Much information is provided in the findings of the Swedish and the British Royal Population Commissions on population and in the proceedings of various international demographic, historical, and sociological congresses. Many valuable papers on population measurement and change, some based upon population samples, are issued by the United States Bureau of the Census which in 1950 published *Catalog of United States Census Publications, 1790–1945,* and which now publishes an annual subject guide to its recent releases and works. Census and other governmentally sponsored population studies are reported, by sovereign state, in *Population Index.*

is conditioned both by his conception of the economic universe and by the nature of his inquiries respecting this universe. While the economist tends to be interested in the impact of economic events and processes upon all types of population movements, his interest is greatest, presumably, in processes which underlie the growth of population in time and its distribution in space. For movements of population in time and space produce changes in the conditions of supply, demand, and equilibrium at both the micro-economic and the macro-economic level; and they may, if they are periodic or irregular in character, propagate some of their periodicity or irregularity to the behavior of economic data.

Despite the significance that economists appear to attach to population movements, they have largely relinquished the study of these movements to noneconomists. In 1950–51, J. S. Siegel found, of the 430 college courses in population reported, only 9 were given in economics and cognate departments; 386 were conducted in sociology departments.

Because of the looseness with which the scope of population study has been defined and because of the variability of the economist's interest in population study, it is hard to draw a line between what is predominantly population theory and what is predominantly economic theory. For example, both the cyclical and the secular behavior of economic data may be affected by population movements. Does the analysis of this behavior, therefore, fall within the scope of population study? Or does it more properly belong to the study of cyclical and secular movements in economic data? In the present summary the latter disposition is favored. Accordingly, relatively little attention is devoted to underemployment hypotheses, or to theories which attribute economic fluctuations to population fluctuations.

In Section I we touch upon the measurement and the forecasting of population growth; in Section II recent findings respecting the socio-economic determinants of population growth are reviewed; Section III deals with the socio-economic effects of variations in population composition, density, and growth; IV, with the distribution of population in space; and V, with promising new approaches in population study.

I. POPULATION GROWTH: ITS MEASUREMENT AND PREDICTION

Since economic behavior is dominated by expectations, and prospective population movements are an important determinant of expectations, the forecasting and measurement of population growth are of considerable significance to economists. Relatively accurate population forecasts, in turn, presuppose well-premised and technically complete forecasting methods, and these presuppose the use of satisfactory measures of past and current population growth. The pertinence of these remarks is borne out by the failure of pre-1940 population forecasts to anticipate the post-1940 upsurge of births and population. It is true, of course, that the history of population forecasts has been, on the whole, a history of failure. Nonetheless, economists writing in the 1930's and the early 1940's set considerable store by contemporary population forecasts, thereby ignoring the time-bound assumptions of these forecasts and the warning implicit in the prognostic failure of earlier forecasts. Upon these untested forecasts, furthermore, economists rested both predictions respecting the probable course of economic development and recommendations concerning economic policy.

A. New Measures of Population Growth

While this is not the place to describe improvements that have been made in population-growth measures in the 1940's, the nature and the purpose of these improvements may be suggested.[2] These new measures are more elaborate than the earlier measures, and they permit more penetrating analysis of population tendencies. The new measures are not, however, always superior to the less elaborate measures, since that measure is best which is most appropriate to the purpose in hand. Thus for some purposes crude rates are the only indices that are relevant; for other purposes, the newer measures are more appropriate.

Demographers bent upon improving indices of reproduction and population growth appear to have had two main purposes in mind: (a) to rule out adventitious conditions which are temporarily affecting natality, mortality, and natural increase; (b) to distinguish long-run changes in natality, mortality, and natural increase from changes that are short-run or temporary. Experience with the sensitivity of crude birth

---

[2] On the measurement of population growth see Jean Bourgeois-Pichat, *Mesure de la fécondité des populations* (Paris, 1950); British Royal Commission on Population, *Report* (London, 1949), and *idem, Papers,* 5 vols. (London, 1949–50), hereafter cited by title only; P. R. Cox, *Demography* (Cambridge, Eng., 1951); L. I. Dublin *et al., Length of Life* (rev. ed., New York, 1949); R. R. Kuczynski, *The Measurement of Population Growth* (New York, 1936); A. J. Lotka, *Analyse démographique avec application particulière à l'espèce humaine* (Paris, 1939); U.S. Bur. Census, *Handbook of Statistical Methods for Demographers* (Washington, 1951); P. K. Whelpton, *Cohort Fertility* (Princeton, 1952); A. B. Wolfe, "The Population Problem since the World War," *Jour. Pol. Econ.,* Oct., Dec. 1928 and Feb. 1929, XXXVI, 529–59, 662–85; XXXVII, 87–120.

and death rates to changes in age composition led demographers in the 1920's to seek measures that were less subject to the influence of transient peculiarities in a population's age composition. To avoid this difficulty they devised several measures: the Gross Reproduction Rate, to represent the reproductive force characteristic of a community at a given time, and three similar rates—the Net Reproduction Rate, the Replacement Index, and the True Rate of natural increase—to represent the rate at which a population supposedly was growing.[3]

Experience and analysis subsequently disclosed these measures to be inadequate for predictive and related purposes. For various reasons age-specific fertility and mortality did not stay put as postulated. Since the new measures, being based upon age-specific fertility and mortality experienced during but one or several years, were synthetic rather than historically cumulative in character, they remained subject to the influence of adventitious conditions; and they failed to distinguish between fundamental and persisting changes in fertility and temporary changes occasioned by variations in the manner in which women passing through the childbearing period distribute their births in time. They failed in particular to take into account conditions which affect marital and childbearing patterns; e.g. the sex and the marital composition of the population; the distribution of married women by age, duration of marriage, and number of children ever borne; the fact that variations in socio-economic conditions may prompt couples to postpone or to hasten the reproduction of the number of children they desire as well as cause them to modify this number; and so on.

---

[3] Hereinafter these rates will be indicated by their initials: G.R.R.; N.R.R.; R.I.; T.R. The G.R.R., the N.R.R., and the T.R. are constructed on the premise that age-specific female fertility rates continue unchanged at current levels; the R.I. is constructed on an equivalent premise. The N.R.R., the R.I., and the T.R. are constructed on the additional premise that age-specific female mortality rates likewise continue unchanged. The G.R.R. merely indicates the maximum rate of increase per generation of which a female population is ultimately capable, given the fertility premise and provided that no female dies before she has completed the childbearing period. The N.R.R. indicates the constant rate of increase per generation that will characterize a closed (i.e. not subject to emigration or immigration) female population after its age composition has conformed to the given set of unchanging age-specific female fertility and mortality rates and become stable. An essentially similar rate of increase is indicated by the R.I. The T.R. indicates the constant annual rate of increase that is obtained when the N.R.R. is correctly translated to an annual basis. Two generations or more—i.e. 55–60 or more years—must pass before a female population's age composition can become stable (in conformity with the specified initial conditions) and the N.R.R. or the T.R. coincides with the actual rate of growth. During this interval the actual rate of growth is conditioned by the initial age distribution of the female population.

Having recognized that there exists no single all-purpose measure of reproduction or population growth, demographers in the 1940's attempted to develop measures suited either to long-period or to short-period analysis. (*i*) Under the former head fall measures intended to disclose such facts as variations in the number of live births per married woman and long-run changes in age at marriage and in the proportion of women who marry in the course of their lives: e.g. real-cohort rates, weighted birth-marriage indices, etc. Real-cohort analysis, for example, has two main objects: (*a*) to discover whether, in the course of their lives, the cohort of persons born in any given year produces births greater or less in number than those from which these persons have sprung; and of greater importance (*b*) to ascertain how this cohort of persons distributes its births over its life cycle, together with the determinants of this pattern of distribution. Real-cohort analysis thus reveals how the reproductive behavior of the representative individual responds to the cumulating total of relevant circumstances that impinge upon him in his life time. A real-cohort rate is not highly sensitive, therefore, as is the N.R.R., to the events of any single year or short period. (*ii*) A revised form of the net reproduction rate has been developed for purposes of short-period analysis. This new rate indicates within narrower limits than the N.R.R. what the population prospect appears to be; it has been standardized both for the age factor and for various conditions relating to marital state and affecting fertility. Short-period analysis may be facilitated also by comparisons of the real-cohort rates of older and younger cohorts which disclose whether births are being postponed or produced relatively early.

Improvements indicated include: (*a*) better adaptation of measures to specific purposes; (*b*) better adaptation of data to requirements of superior measures; (*c*) greater awareness of merits and limitations of specific measures.

B. Population Forecasts

The past dozen years have witnessed two changes with respect to population forecasting. First, because post-1940 demographic events in North America, Europe, Australia, and elsewhere have been radically at variance with the expectations of expert demographers, forecasts now are viewed with more scepticism than formerly and forecasting methods and assumptions are being subjected to a critical re-examination. Second, forecasters are relying in greater measure than formerly upon methods involving the projection of components of a population and in lesser measure upon growth curve (e.g. the logistic) projections. Forecasters also appear more disposed than formerly to base projections upon the supposition that a single growth rate will obtain for some time, particularly when data are not readily available for the use of elaborate methods.[4]

A population forecast is said to be based upon the projection of population components when the current enumerated population, together with its age and sex structure, is carried into the future through the addition of estimated births and immigrants and the subtraction of estimated deaths and emigrants. The correctness of a projection thus turns upon the extent to which the predicted numbers of births, deaths, and net migrants correspond to the numbers that are actually experienced as the future unrolls into the present; and these predicted numbers in turn depend upon the fertility, mortality, and migration rates and rate-trends that are postulated in the forecasting model employed. Because any particular such assumption or set of assumptions is subject to uncertainty, it is customary to combine variously a number of postulates respecting the prospective behavior of fertility, mortality, and migration, and so arrive at a range of estimates, to which varying degrees of confidence are tentatively assigned. Even so, an actual population may soon move outside the range of paths forecast. It is now recognized, therefore, that projected population movements must frequently be compared with the movements that actually take place so that the sources of discrepancy between projected and actual movements will be discovered and the projections modified accordingly.

Much uncertainty must of necessity attach to population forecasts that extend beyond the immediate future; and this uncertainty tends to be magnified when the forecaster attempts to distribute the predicted

---

[4] On population forecasts and forecasting, see F. W. Notestein et al., The Future Population of Europe and the Soviet Union (Geneva, 1944) P. K. Whelpton et al., Forecasts of the Population of the United States 1945–1975 (Washington, 1947); Margaret J. Hagood and J. S. Siegel, "Projections of the Regional Population of the United States," Agric. Econ. Research, Apr. 1951, III, 41–52; Cox, op. cit., Ch. 11–15; summary reports in Eugenics Rev., Oct. 1943—Jan. 1944, XXXV, 71–84, and Population Index, July 1948, XIV, 188–95, and ibid., Jan. 1949, XV, 2–30. See also, Papers, Vol. II, pp. 213 ff.; U.S. Bur. Census, Cur. Pop. Rep., Population Estimates, Ser. P–25, No. 43, Aug. 10, 1950, and ibid., No. 56, Jan. 27, 1952; P. K. Whelpton, Cohort Fertility, and reports on births, birth-orders, etc., in Fed. Security Agency, Nat. Office of Vital Statistics, Vital Stat.—Spec. Repts., Aug. 29, 1947, XXIII (16), Oct. 7, 1948, XXXIII (1), and Sept. 29, 1950, XXXIII (8). For evaluations of American population forecasts, see J. S. Davis, The Population Upsurge in the United States (Stanford, 1949); H. F. Dorn, "Pitfalls in Population Forecasts and Projections," Jour. Am. Stat. Assoc., Sept. 1950, XLV, 311–34.

population among regions or other parts of the country to which the forecast relates. The behavior of fertility, mortality, and migration rates is conditioned in considerable degree by the socio-economic circumstances surrounding the population in question and by the attitudes, aspirations, etc., of its members. What these circumstances, attitudes, and aspirations will be in the future is not predictable with certainty. Even if they were, the population forecaster would still be handicapped by the fact that our information is quite limited respecting the functional connections that obtain between the behavior of these elements and that of fertility, mortality, and migration.

That our power of foreseeing the prospective trend of population may be less great than Keynes and others supposed is suggested by the volatility of recent population growth and the instability and failure of population forecasts. Consider the case of the United States. At the close of the 1940's annual natural increase was about nine-tenths higher than at the beginning, while in the 1940's the average annual rate of increase was double that experienced in the 1930's. This resurgence of growth reflected both an unexpectedly large increase in life expectancy at birth and a two-fifths increase in births between the 1930's and the 1940's. This resurgence also brought about a marked upward adjustment in American population estimates, an adjustment prompted in part by the fact that population growth in the 1940's exceeded forecasts for that period by as much as 300 per cent. In 1947, the prospective American population was put at 150–162 millions as of 1960 and 151–185 millions as of 1975; by 1950 these estimates had been adjusted upward to 162–180 and 166–225 millions. It is now being suggested that by the year 2,000 the American population may number close to 300 millions;[5] yet in 1947 one authority expressed alarm lest the population decline to 100 millions by the close of the century. The recent experience of Canada, Australia, Western Europe, and other parts of the world has been somewhat similar to that of the United States. This experience suggests, therefore, that educators, military leaders, economists, businessmen and other users of population forecasts need to be aware of their contingent and uncertain character; and that flexibility rather than fixity should characterize economic plans in which the population variable plays an important part.

Both because of the prognostic failure of post-1930 population

---

[5] Given 4 million births per year and a life expectancy at birth of 75 years, the population would approach 300 millions as a limit. In 1947–51 births approximated 3.8 million per year.

forecasts and of the continuing development of demographic theory, the total role of the population projection is coming to be more clearly understood, much as the total role of the economic model came to be better appreciated. Inasmuch as every population projection, or model, rests upon certain postulates and initial conditions, a very large number of models is empirically conceivable. These models range from projections contrived to forecast what is really going to happen to projections designed to indicate what combinations of mortality, fertility, and migration will produce a stipulated change in a population. A distinction requires to be drawn, therefore, between the predictive and the analytical serviceability of a populational model, between the prognostic correctness of a projection and its usefulness as an analytical device. The function of a population forecast is to provide other disciplines with information that permits them, in the treatment of their own problems, to look upon population growth as a more or less independent variable. The function of a conditional projection of whatever degree of restriction, on the contrary, is to provide an illustrative model that discloses how a population behaves or evolves in time when it is subject to certain initial conditions and constraints. Paradoxically, the decrease in credence given to projections as forecasts and the increase in attention paid to their usefulness as analytical models should advance the art of population forecasting.

While logistic, Gompertz, and similar curves are less frequently used today than formerly to predict population growth, the logistic model, which is a corollary to the Malthusian model, is well adapted to reflect inherent stability of growth, when present, and to focus attention upon important determinants of population growth and difficulties involved in population forecasting.[6] Five assumptions underlie the theory of growth implicit in the simple logistic. (1) The physical environment (or area) utilized and/or utilizable by the population under analysis is finite. (2) The curve describing the growth of this population has a lower asymptotic limit ($= 0$) and an upper asymptotic limit K which represents the maximum population that can exist in the given finite environment under prevailing cultural conditions, which include (among other things) the aspirations of the population and the methods by which it exploits its environment. (3) In consequence of the augmenttation of the damping effect supposedly produced by the increase of the population's size N, its realized rate of increase per time period, R,

---

[6] On the logistic see Raymond Pearl, *Medical Biometry and Statistics* (3rd ed., Philadelphia, 1941), and E. C. Rhodes, "Population Mathematics," *Jour. Royal Stat. Soc.*, 1940, CIII, 369 ff., 380 ff.

steadily declines, moving from a maximum value toward zero.[7] (4) The incremental rate of growth generates a symmetrical curve, rising until a maximum is attained when $N = K/2$, and thereafter moving downward toward the asymptotic limit ($= 0$). (5) The movement of N, the size of the cumulating actual population, describes an S-shaped curve as it proceeds from a very low value to a value in the neighborhood of the asymptotic maximum K.

The logistic theory thus emphasizes the fact that, since mankind requires space into which to expand and physical environment to transform into population, both of which elements are limited, population can continue only for a limited time to grow at a compound rate which is not relatively small. It implies also that culture is a determinant of K and hence of R, since upon culture depends (a) the skill with which an environment is exploited and/or made to expand, and (b) the level and content of a population's aspirations by which both the place of children in the scale of values and wants in general are determined. The prognostic weakness of the logistic, even when it has satisfactorily described past population growth to and beyond the point of inflection (where $N = K/2$), issues primarily from the fact that the logistic cannot forecast autonomous or emergent cultural changes which may operate to increase or to decrease K.[8]

Population projections have been criticized on the ground that they

---

[7] Let b represent this biotic potential, or maximum rate of increase of which a population is capable in the absence of that environmental resistance to population growth which increases as N approaches the population maximum K and which may be represented by N/K. (Today the value of b, about .03 in Malthus' time, may be close to .045.) Let $(K - N)/K$ represent the fraction of the maximum population that remains to be brought into being before the population becomes stationary. Then the *incremental* rate of growth becomes $bN(K - N)/K$; and R becomes $b(K - N)/K$. R declines as N increases and approaches K. See G. F. Gause, *The Struggle for Existence* (Baltimore, 1934), ch. 3.

[8] Of interest in this connection is the logistic formulation of the Malthusian Franklin-Walker thesis according to which any given increment of immigration ultimately reduces by that amount natural increase on part of the population living in the country of immigration, with the result that this country's population is not finally augmented by the immigration. Let m represent the accumulated net immigrant population. Then (see n. 7) the incremental rate of increase of the domestic population becomes, in the absence of cultural change consequent upon immigration, $b(K - N - m)/K$; this rate is bm/K less than it would have been had there been no immigration. Of course, if immigration produces cultural changes which modify K, this statement must be modified accordingly. E.g., see E. N. Palmer, "Cultural Contacts and Population Growth," *Am. Jour. Soc.*, Jan. 1948, LIII, 258 ff.; and, for an evaluation of the Walker thesis in terms of an "equilibrium" theory, Corrado Gini, "Los efectos demográficos de las migraciones internacionales," *Revista internacional de sociología*, Apr.–June 1946, IV, 351–88. That immigration into a country may set in motion a compensatory emigration from a country is suggested in Mabel F. Timlin, *Does Canada Need More People?* (Toronto, 1951).

rest upon hypothesized patterns of growth which do not explicitly take into account interactions between a community's income growth and its population growth; and it has been suggested that the elasticity concept may be employed to connect these two variables. Let e represent *population elasticity*—the ratio of a small proportionate increase in population to the small proportionate increase in community income upon which the indicated population increase is consequent; and let E represent the *elasticity of productivity of population*—the ratio of a small proportionate increase in community income to the small proportionate increase in population upon which the indicated income increase is consequent. Suppose next that, for reasons unconnected with population growth, a community's income Y, initially 100 units, increases at a constant incremental rate of $k = 2$ units per year. Then, if unchanging values of 0.5 and 0, respectively, are assigned to e and E, the community's population P, initially 100 units, will grow at a constant incremental rate $ek = 1$. If, however, a value of 0.5 is assigned to E, the incremental rate of population growth will gradually rise from 1 to $1\frac{1}{3}$, in consequence of the increase in the annual increment in income occasioned by the increase in population. While we have assumed for the sake of convenience that e and E remain constant, it is more realistic to assume that they will vary. The logistic theory suggests for example, that, given unchanging cultural conditions, both e and E will fall as a country's population becomes larger. Actually, of course, they may fluctuate.[9]

Not much use has been made of the elasticity concept, presumably because of the empirical difficulties that attend its use. Population growth is affected by circumstances other than income growth, among them changes in income distribution and variation in the meaning attached by individuals to income change and in the expectations thereby generated. Only a minor fraction of income growth is attributable, in progressive countries, to the growth of the labor force, while the growth of the labor force itself reflects not recent population growth, but population growth of some 15–25 years earlier. Population growth behaves somewhat differently from income growth; the former usually is positive and much less variable than the latter which is sometimes positive and sometimes negative. While all components of population

---

[9] On the use of elasticity concepts geared to time and the generalized logistic formula in the study of the interdependence of economic and demographic evolution see Silvio Vianelli, "A Generalized Dynamic Demographic Scheme and Its Application to Italy and the United States," *Econometrica*, July 1936, IV, 269–83.

growth—natality, mortality, and migration—are sensitive to cyclical and longer-run changes in income, they differ in their capacity to change rapidly, and probably in their sensitivity to income change at various income levels. It is not easy, therefore, to relate income change and population change to one another in empirically significant ways. It is desirable, nonetheless, that considerable research be done on the responsiveness of natality, mortality, migration, and population growth to cyclical and longer-run changes in income, and on the circumstances that cause this responsiveness to vary. It probably is desirable also that further inquiry be made into the responsiveness of income growth to population growth, even though it is questionable whether empirically satisfactory results can be obtained.

While demographers have found only a limited number of populations to conform in their growth to so regular a pattern as the logistic, they still deem it useful to conceive of patterns of growth and of stages through which a population proceeds much as an economy evolves through stages.[10] Three growth patterns stand out, Cowgill suggests. the *primitive,* almost universal before 1700, with the death rate temporarily falling below and then returning to the level of natality which remains high and substantially stationary; the *modern,* essentially of post-1700 origin, with natality at first falling less rapidly and then more rapidly than mortality until a lower or a relatively low-level equilibrium is reached; and the *future,* with natality rising above and then falling back to the level of mortality which remains low and substantially stationary.

Blacker identifies five stages through which a population may pass, in the first two of which fell most if not all pre-1800 populations. These

---

[10] See C. P. Blacker, "Stages in Population Growth," *Eugenics Rev.,* Oct. 1947, XXXIX, 88–102; D. O. Cowgill, "The Theory of Population Growth Cycles," *Am. Jour. Soc.,* Sept. 1949, LV, 163–70; W. S. Thompson's classification, dating from 1929, and recently described in *Plenty of People* (New York, 1948); F. W. Notestein, "The Population of the World in the Year 2000," *Jour. Am. Stat. Assoc.,* Sept. 1950, XLV, 335 ff.; J. S. Davis' critique of this classification in *ibid.,* pp. 346–49. On the response of population before, during, and after the Industrial Revolution to increases in resources and in the skill with which they were exploited see K. W. Taylor, "Some Aspects of Population History," *Can. Jour. Econ. Pol. Sci.,* Aug. 1950, XVI, 301–13. See also J. C. Russell, *Medieval British Population* (Albuquerque, 1948); Kingsley Davis, *The Population of India and Pakistan* (Princeton, 1951); "World Population in Transition," *idem,* ed., *Annals Amer. Acad. Pol. Soc. Sci.,* Jan. 1945, CCXXXVII, 1–203; *Demographic Studies of Selected Areas of Rapid Growth,* F. W. Notestein, ed. (New York, 1944); Irene B. Tauber's papers on the countries of Asia in *Population Index,* VII–XVII, 1941–51, under "Current Items." On the power implications of the stage theories see Robert Strauz-Hupé, *The Balance of Tomorrow* (New York, 1945).

stages are: (1) high stationary, characterized by high and balancing birth and death rates; (2) early expanding, marked by birth rates which are high and death rates which are lower and (often) falling; (3) late expanding, with both death and birth rates declining, but with death rates below birth rates; (4) low stationary, characterized by low birth and death rates; and (5) declining, marked by an excess of deaths over births, with low death rates and lower birth rates. If these stages are partially consolidated, three classes of countries are identifiable: (A) those in which natality and mortality, being under control, are low and the population may be in incipient decline; (B) those in which both natality and mortality have been falling, but natality less rapidly than mortality, and the population is evolving into type A; and (C) those in which, neither mortality nor natality being under "reasonably secure control," the growth potential is high.

Since this three-category scheme is intended to describe the actual and foreshadow the potential state of world population and its growth, it has been criticized accordingly. Population elasticity, it is implied, ranges from a level that is high in the C countries wherein live close to three-fifths of the world's population, to a level that is low and unlikely to rise in the A countries wherein live about one-fifth of the world's population; it is intermediate and falling in the B countries wherein live the remaining fifth. It has been inferred, accordingly, that whereas the populations of the B and the A countries will grow, during the next fifty years, at estimated annual rates of 1 and below 0.5 per cent, respectively, the populations of the C countries may for a time grow as much as 2 per cent per year (if socio-economic conditions are sufficiently favorable) and still not evolve into the low-potential A type. Accordingly, the population of the world, which was estimated at about 2.4 billion as of 1950, may continue to grow at a yearly rate in the neighborhood of 1 per cent and increase to 3.4–3.9 billion by the year 2000.[11] Critics admit the existence of types A to C. But they maintain

---

[11] Colin Clark endorses the 1 per cent per year rate, in part, presumably, because he believes that agricultural product per man-year can be made to rise 1.5 per cent per year. A 1 per cent per year population-growth rate exceeds pre-1900 rates which rose gradually from 0.29 per cent in 1650–1750 to 0.75 in 1900–1940. As late as 1939 Pearl put the logistic asymptotic maximum for the world at 2,646 millions, to be attained about the year 2100. See Kingsley Davis, "The World Demographic Transition," *Annals Am. Acad. Pol. Soc. Sci.*, Jan. 1945, CCXXXVII, 3; Raymond Pearl, *Natural History of Population* (New York, 1939) p. 258; and, for Clark's estimate, *Proceedings* of the United Nations Scientific Conference on the Conservation and Utilization of Resources (Lake Success, 1950), Vol. I, pp. 15–28; also United Nations, *Population Bull.*, Dec. 1951, I, 1–12.

also that there exists a fourth or *D* population category made up of countries characterized by very low mortality, moderate fertility, and moderate immigration whose population will grow more rapidly than that of the world as a whole. Within this category are placed countries whose per capita income is high and prospectively rising—countries which usually are included in the *A* group: e.g. Australia, Canada, the United States, New Zealand.

It is desirable that the comparative validity of these classifications be inquired into, since it is of political, economic, and military importance to know which corresponds most closely to demographic reality. For example, given the existence of the *D* type, the politico-military security of the so-called Western World becomes more firmly anchored. Again, given existing pressure upon agricultural and raw material resources, together with the prospect that an improvement in socio-economic conditions may be accompanied by a 200 or more per cent increase in population in the *C* countries,[12] policies involving continuing assistance to *C* countries take on a significance other than they would have, given different growth prospects and raw material conditions.

II. POPULATION GROWTH: ITS SOCIO-ECONOMIC DETERMINANTS

In Section I it was indicated that knowledge of the socio-economic determinants of population growth is essential to the construction of models adequate for both the empirical analysis and the forecasting of population movements. In this section we treat of the socio-economic determinants of mortality and natality; migration is dealt with in Section IV. The past fifteen years have witnessed: (1) a steady growth in empirical knowledge of circumstances relating to the variations of fertility and mortality in time and in geographical and social space; (2) a considerable improvement in conceptualization of the elements involved in this variation; (3) a growing awareness that effective analysis of fertility behavior and (in lesser measure) of mortality behavior presupposes a theory of action that is empirically capable of assigning appro-

---

[12] "At least a threefold multiplication is implicit in the processes by which peoples hitherto *have* achieved low birth and death rates." See M. C. Balfour *et al.*, *Public Health and Demography in the Far East* (New York, 1950), p. 7; also A. J. Jaffe, "Notes on the Rate of Growth of the Chinese Population," *Human Biology*, Feb. 1947, XIX, 8. Logistic forecasts foreshadow smaller future populations for high-growth-potential countries than do forecasts based upon the assumption that transformation of a *C* into an *A* population type entails a trebling or more of the population.

priate weight to the influence exercised by man's "subjective state" (i.e. by his values, attitudes, aspirations, etc.) upon his demographic response to his physical environment.[13] The impact of price structure changes upon fertility probably has been underestimated in recent times.

Changes in a community's fertility and mortality originate in two main ways. First, community fertility and mortality change if the relative number of persons enrolled in groups characterized by comparatively low (high) fertility or mortality increases (decreases) even though the rates characteristic of each group remain unchanged. Second, the age-specific fertility and mortality rates of some or all groups may change, though not necessarily in the same proportion. Actual fertility and mortality trends reflect the operation of both types of change.

Of these two sources of change, the second is the more crucial. Why, for example, does the fertility of most if not all groups change in time? If the change in fertility is attributable immediately to changes in the culture, values, technology, and other relevant components of the psycho-physical environment of the affected population, these changes in turn must be accounted for. Have they originated with the inhabitants of the affected community, or have they arisen elsewhere and then been transmitted to this community? In the latter event, account must be taken of the fact that any specific collection of changes may affect fertility somewhat differently in the community wherein these changes originated than in the community to which they are propagated. For some changes are more easily or speedily transmitted than others; and some cultures and subcultures are more receptive than others to changes of domestic and/or foreign origin.[14] Furthermore, cultural elements may encounter more counterbalances in some communities than in others.

---

[13] A theory of action is essential to the analysis of behavior, such as that affecting fertility, which is oriented to the attainment of goals, which involves the expenditure of effort, which is conditioned by that part of the external world having meaning for the behaving individual, and which is under the regulation of values and norms present in the culture and subculture of the individual and possibly internalized in his personality. See *Toward a General Theory of Action*, Talcott Parsons and E. A. Shils, ed. (Cambridge, Mass., 1951).

[14] A subculture is significant for the study of fertility when the fertility of members of a culturally integrated subgroup (e.g. members of a deviant religious faith) differs from that of the population subscribing to the dominant culture, and this difference appears to be imputable to their membership in the subcultural group and to their consequently being more or less disposed than the population at large to adopt fertility-affecting values and practices. In time, of course, the culture of the population at large may become ascendant over the subculture even with respect to fertility. Illustrative of fertility behavior subject to the influence of a subculture is that of the Parsis, the Mormons, and the Pacific-Coast Japanese-Americans, all of which have been studied.

Since variation in fertility and mortality is subject to many seemingly separate and measurable influences some of which are in fact highly intercorrelated, it is possible at times, by means of Factor Analysis, to reduce what appears to be a larger number of influences to a smaller number of more fundamental influences. The following steps are indicated, therefore, when mortality or natality is responding to changes in a number of elements in the psychophysical environment, some of which elements are highly intercorrelated: (*a*) individual elements which are highly intercorrelated may be so grouped into sets that there is little correlation between any one and other such sets; (*b*) one or several of the elements of each set may then be converted into an index suited to reflect changes in whatever it is that the set manifests or represents; (*c*) the relative amount of influence exercised by each such set upon fertility (mortality) may then be ascertained, the influence of other relevant circumstances having been allowed for. The make-up and influence of these sets need to be examined periodically, however, since some factors which condition the influence of given sets may change.[15]

A. Mortality

Today the expectation of life at birth in low-mortality countries is 3–3.5 times what it was in the prehistoric and Graeco-Roman worlds and at least 2–2.5 times what it is in present-day high mortality countries. While mortality has declined correspondingly, the relative amount of decline has been much greater in the lower than in the upper age groups. For this reason expectation of life at birth varies much more in geographical and social space than does expectation of life at age 50.[16]

The circumstances which in the future will govern the movement of mortality in low-mortality countries are certain to differ from those operative in the past. Much of the reduction in mortality in these countries has been achieved through improvement in political order, in the quantity, quality, and regularity of the food supply, in education and the social services, in housing and working conditions, in personal hygiene,

---

[15] E.g., see E. J. Buckaztsch, "The Influence of Social Conditions on Mortality Rates," *Pop. Stud.*, Dec. 1947, I, 229–48.

[16] E.g., expectation of life at birth increased 94 per cent in Sweden in 1775–1940 while expectation at age 50 increased only 36 per cent. Corresponding percentages for England and Wales for 1841–1937 were 50 and 6; for Japan, 1899–1936, 7 and 0; and New Zealand, 1891–1938, 20 and 8. Expectation of life at birth has been at the following levels: prehistoric times, probably below 20; Graeco-Roman world, 20–30; medieval, Renaissance, and seventeenth-century times, around 33; A.D. 1800, 35–40; 1900, 45–50; in the 1950's, 70–72 or better.

and in other relevant aspects of the individual's physical environment; through the complete or partial elimination of unsanitary conditions, disease vectors (e.g. insects), and sources of infection; through the control of infectious diseases, many of which formerly often became epidemic in character; through the reduction of the incidence of deficiency diseases; and through the reduction of infections. In the past curative medicine has played a lesser role in prolonging life than has the control of infection and contagion through public health and sanitary measures, together with the correction of crucial environmental deficiencies. In low-mortality areas further declines in mortality will have to come largely from a reduction, through advances in surgery and medicine, of the impact of degenerative diseases. For example, Metropolitan Life Insurance Company analyses show, were cardio-vascular-renal diseases and cancer to cease to be causes of death the expectation of life at 40 among white American males, 30.7 years in 1948, would rise to 43; at birth, from 65.5 to 77.1. Extension of the expectation of life at birth to and beyond the upper seventies, formerly deemed improbable if not impossible, now appears to be possible. Presumably, intergroup differences in mortality, as long as they still exist, will continue to shrink, judging from past trends and from the fact that life expectancy in the American industrial population has finally become the same as that in the population as a whole. The changes in life expectancy in prospect are therefore of great economic importance, for since they involve a prolongation of human life far beyond 60–65, they will intensify retirement and related problems and make increasingly necessary a corresponding prolongation of man's active working life beyond 60–65.[17]

While the circumstances which in the future will govern the movements of mortality in countries now marked by high mortality resemble those which formerly operated in low-mortality countries, there is a difference. The introduction into the high-mortality countries of the methods of death control developed in the low-mortality countries is causing

---

[17] On mortality trends see papers on health and mortality in the *Met. Stat. Bull.,* 1949–1952, *Milbank M. F. Quart.,* 1948–1951, and Kingsley Davis, "World Population in Transition," *loc. cit.;* L. I. Dublin, *op. cit.;* F. W. Notestein, *Future Population,* pp. 183 ff.; E. C. Rhodes, "Secular Changes in Death Rates," *Jour. Royal Stat. Soc.,* 1941, CIV(1), 15 ff.; Hornell Hart and Hilda Hertz, "Expectation of Life as an Index of Social Progress," *Am. Soc. Rev.,* Dec. 1944, IX, 609–21; George Wolfe, "Tuberculosis and Civilization," *Human Biology,* Feb.–Mar. 1938, X, 106, 251 ff. On differential mortality see L. I. Dublin *et al., The Money Value of a Man* (New York, 1946); Christopher Tietze, "Life Tables for Social Classes in England," *Milbank M. F. Quart.,* Apr. 1943, XXI, 182 ff.; Jean Daric, "Mortalité, profession et situation sociale," *Population,* Oct.–Dec. 1949, IV, 671 ff.

mortality to fall more rapidly in the former than it did in the latter. Illustrative is the 35 per cent drop produced in Ceylon's mortality in 1946–48 by the use (principally) of D.D.T. in an antimalaria campaign. However, as Davis points out, "man cannot divorce the death rate from economic and demographic realities"; if he would reduce mortality, he must regulate natality and appropriately modify his environment; for, in the absence of such fundamental improvements and of increase in the supply of the needs of life therewith associated, mortality is not likely to fall to anything like the levels characteristic of advanced societies which enjoy such improvements. It is probable, of course, that world mortality will continue for some time to decline significantly. Presumably this decline will operate in turn to generate and to increase downward pressure upon fertility.[18]

B. Fertility and Natality

In low-natality countries natality is only .25–.40 of what it is in high-natality countries and what it was in prehistoric, medieval, and early modern times; today as in the past it usually lies within the 13–55 range. With the exception of French-Canada in the 1660's, when rates of 5–6 were recorded, the G.R.R. rarely moves or has moved outside the 0.8–3.5 range. The N.R.R. has rarely exceeded 2. Prior to the decline in the birth rate, which began in Western Europe in the last half of the nineteenth century and somewhat later in Eastern Europe, natality was lower in the former than in the latter, and in fact lower than it is today in much of the world.[19] The decline proceeded relatively most rapidly in those countries in which it began relatively late, but at first less rapidly, as a rule, than the decline in mortality. The decline assumed the form of a diminution in family size, specific fertility falling relatively more in the upper than in the lower age groups, with childbearing terminating

---

[18] See Kingsley Davis, *Population of India*, Pt. 2 and p. 61; T. H. Davey, "Colonial Medical Policy in Relation to Population Growth," *Eugenics Rev.*, Jan. 1951, XLII, 190–201. Mortality and natality are variously related. For example, a reduction in infant and child mortality tends to be accompanied by a diminution in the number of children borne, particularly when family size is subject to planning. Again, a decrease in the mortality of the unproductive aged might, by augmenting a family's necessary expenditures, diminish the number of children borne. The likelihood of this outcome is reduced, however, by the fact that, as family-cycle studies show, outlay upon aged dependents usually becomes significant only after the desired number of children has been borne.

[19] In eighteenth-century Western Europe, except for Finland, rates were below 40; in late nineteenth-century Eastern Europe, somewhat above 40; and at present, in Asia, Africa, and much of South America, around 40–45, probably because marriage is early and almost universal. In France and the United States the decline in natality began early in the nineteenth century.

at an earlier age than formerly. As the decline progressed men's explanations of it underwent change, a history of these explanations would reveal.

Most demographers have attributed group differences in fertility principally to group differences in the practice of family limitation, and the decline in fertility to the spread of this practice. This statement becomes more valid if it is confined to age-specific fertility, for the effect of variation in age-at-marriage, while mixed, has been significant in some groups and at some times. For example, in Ireland, where population growth has been rather effectively curbed, control appears to have been accomplished primarily through nonmarriage and deferment of marriage. In support of the view that variation in age-specific fertility is attributable primarily to variation in the practice of family limitation, it is urged that fecundity has changed very little in the past century; that age and marital composition have not become less favorable to fertility; and that miscellaneous factors (e.g. more effective personal hygiene, diminution in frequency of coitus) can account for but little of the recorded drop. While the decline has not always been closely associated in time and space with the development and spread of modern means of contraception, it is immediately attributable in large measure, as are changes in the pattern of group differences in fertility, to variation in the prevalence of contraceptive practices and in the effectiveness with which they are utilized. The ultimate origins both of the decline and of group differences in fertility must be sought, however, in the socio-economic changes that have altered man's reproductive institutions, changed the character and modified the functional role of the family, altered man's value patterns, changed the position of role of parent in the hierarchy of social roles, and increased man's disposition as well as his capacity to limit family size. The importance of these motivating factors is suggested by the fact that, although relatively effective folk methods of contraception have long been known, they were used extensively by the members of some groups which knew these methods but not by others. There is much warrant, in fact, for arguing that variation in motivation has been more significant than variation in modernity of contraceptive methods available.[20]

---

[20] The best single source of information on differential fertility is the *Milbank M. F. Quart.* The Indianapolis study, "Social and Psychological Factors Affecting Fertility," by C. V. Kiser *et al.*, has been appearing in this journal since 1943. A number of papers have appeared also in the past 15 years in *Am. Jour. Soc., Am. Soc. Rev., Soc. Rev., Human Biology, Population,* and *Pop. Stud.* Since 1943 the U.S. Bur. Census has issued a number of monographs and reports on differential fertility. See also *Report*, pp. 21–23,

Intertemporal and interclass variation in fertility-affecting motivation undoubtedly reflects in considerable measure the impact of uncompensated changes in the price structure. Since a child may be looked upon as a somewhat costly durable good whence there is likely to flow a stream of utilities variously distributed in time, the supply of children tends to be affected, other conditions given, by circumstances which modify the prospective value of the utilities flowing from offspring, or alter their cost of production. The market demand for children, therefore, is subject in varying degree to substitution and income effects. In the course of time the cost of children has risen relatively to that of many goods and services, with the result that a substitution effect has been set up against children. This effect has been accentuated, moreover, by the reduction which circumstances such as urbanization and social legislation have produced in the prospective comparative value of the utilities derivable from offspring. This effect, it is true, has been counterbalanced, but only in part, by the secular growth of per capita income, the aggregate income elasticity of demand for children being positive at any time; for the secular growth of income has usually been more than offset by secular changes in the level and content of a population's aspirations.[21] Partial corroboration of what has been said is found in group differences in fertility. For the costs as well as the prospective utilities derivable from children vary with social class, being much less favorable in some groups than in others, and these variations are not wholly offset, as a rule, by differences in income. At the same time, family size and income often tend to be positively associated within groups that are otherwise homogeneous.[22]

31–44, *Papers,* Vol. I, IV; Adolphe Landry, *Traité de démographie* (Paris, 1949); Roderich von Ungern-Sternberg and Hermann Schubnell, *Grundriss der Bevölkerungswissenschaft* (Stuttgart, 1950); Pearl, *Natural History,* pp. 285 ff., and Corrado Gini, in "Vecchie e nuove osservazioni sulle cause della natalità differenziale e sulla misura della fecondità naturale delle conjugate," *Metron,* July 1949, XV, 207 ff., and other papers, assert that fecundity has changed. See also Barbara S. Burks, "Social Promotion in Relation to Differential Fecundity," *Human Biology,* Feb. 1941, XIII, 103 ff., for support of R. A. Fisher's thesis that "the fecundity of the upper socio-economic groups is kept low by the heritable lower fecundity of persons promoted into the upper group" by a set of economic arrangements which generates "social capillarity." On family planning see, besides the Indianapolis study, Regine K. Stix and F. W. Notestein, *Controlled Fertility* (Baltimore, 1940); G. W. Beebe, *Contraception and Fertility in the Southern Appalachians* (Baltimore, 1942); *Papers,* Vol. I; and the files of *Human Fertility,* 1935–48.

[21] It has been suggested that a part of the recent upsurge of births reflects a temporary lag of aspirations behind income.

[22] See J. J. Spengler, "Some Economic Aspects of the Subsidization by the State of the Formation of 'Human Capital,'" *Kyklos,* 1950, IV (4), 316–43; also *Papers,* Vol. V, pp. 93 ff.

Major findings respecting the variation of fertility in geographical and social space are significant for the analysis of the variation of fertility in time, since the circumstances responsible for variation in space resemble closely some of those which have produced variation in time. Group differences in fertility have always characterized modern peoples; they became more pronounced in countries of European civilization in the nineteenth (or early twentieth) century, often (but not always) to diminish later in consequence of the spread of the practice of family limitation from the relatively low- to the relatively high-fertility groups and the resulting transformation of what had been a diverging fertility pattern into a converging one. While it remains to be seen whether a differential pattern will be established that (though lower in level) is similar in form to the one which obtained before the diverging movement began, this outcome is considered improbable, in part because the pattern of group differences in psycho-physical and economic environment will probably differ from that which formerly prevailed. It is of interest, in this connection, that in the United States the post-1940 increase in births has been most marked in the groups whose fertility was under effective control and relatively low. Since a decline in over-all fertility in high-fertility countries is usually preceded by an increase in rural-urban and other group differences in fertility, the appearance of a diverging pattern is looked upon as probably foretokening a decline in over-all fertility.

The historical analysis of fertility trends may be facilitated by the assembly of fertility determinants into three variable categories: (*i*) the physical environment that a population has at its disposal; (*ii*) its capacity for exploiting this environment; and (*iii*) the level and content of this population's aspirations, together with the normative restraints to which the individual's efforts to realize his aspirations are subject. While eight different combinations of these variables are possible, since each may increase or decrease, it is combinations of changes in (*ii*) and (*iii*) that are most significant, variable (*i*) being relatively constant. Variables (*ii*) and (*iii*), though capable of independent movement, may also interact, and, when they have a common origin, move together.[23]

---

[23] For example, an increase in (*ii*) resulting from an increase in the employment of fecund women might reduce their fertility; or an increase in output consequent upon an increase of (*ii*) might increase the opportunity cost of child production. Some, but not all, demographers consider small the reduction in family size attributable to the increasing entry of women into the labor force. The cost of children has been treated recently in *Papers*, Vol. V, pp. 1–34, and in *Pop. Stud.* and *Population.* Category (*iii*), here used because it fits into the theory of action (see n. 14 above), is suggested by R. K. Merton's

The analysis of group differences in fertility may contribute greatly to our understanding of the decline in over-all fertility if certain analytical requirements are met. (*a*) The fertility-affecting variable on the basis of which a population is classified should be defined with precision. (*b*) It should be represented by an index that is free of all fertility-affecting elements other than that implied in its definition. (*c*) This index should be adapted to reflect accurately the *kind* of variation whose influence upon fertility is in question, be that variation group determined or individually determined.[24] Given this information, the mechanisms through which the variable affects fertility may be uncovered.

Most important of the group differences affecting fertility directly, or indirectly are those relating to urbanization, education, occupation, socio-economic status, and, in some places, the nature of religious belief. (1) Urbanization (or deruralization), concomitant of output-increasing industrialization, has been unfavorable to fertility, presumably because there has been associated with progress in urbanization an intensification of more elements (e.g. level and content of aspirations; relative net cost of rearing children) that are or can become inimical to childbearing and childrearing, than of elements that are favorable (e.g. better medical care). As a rule fertility varies inversely with the degree of urbanization; it is higher in rural than in urban populations, and in smaller than in larger urban communities. Under some circumstances, however, rural fertility is lower than urban fertility. (2) Although education has contributed greatly to the augmentation of the world's population capacity, fertility usually varies inversely with amount of education, presumably because it rationalizes life outlook, because it often augments individual aspirations more than individual productivity, and because it frequently is associated with income and occupational conditions that appear to be unfavorable to fertility. (3) Fertility varies inversely with occupational status, though not always at relatively high income or occupational levels. (4) Although fertility tends to vary inversely with income and other

analysis in his *Social Theory and Social Structure* (Glencoe, 1949), Pt. 2. Economists may prefer J. S. Davis' "standards of consumption and living" on the ground that it is easier to define with quantitative precision. See his "Standards and Content of Living," *Am. Econ. Rev.,* Mar. 1945, XXXV, 1 ff.

[24] When an individual is a member of a social *Gestalt* or category (e.g. a religious group, the peasant class), his behavior is significantly determined by the degree of his membership in this category; but if he is merely a member of a statistical collection into which he and others have been gathered, his behavior is not affected by his membership in this collection. It probably is easier, as a rule, to devise a suitable index in the latter than in the former situation. See notes 14–15 above.

indices of socio-economic status, in part because similar conditions underlie both capacity to achieve status and disposition and ability to regulate fertility, a positive relationship frequently is found in the upper range of status and among fertility planners. (5) Variation in fertility is usually associated with variation in the nature of religious belief. This association, when not imputable to other variations connected with that in religious belief, may be attributable to the fact that religious belief can operate to diminish the extent to which individuals are under the influence of egocentric calculation, to increase the extent to which individuals give a group orientation to their socially defined roles, and to retard the upward trend of their level of aspirations. Fertility has tended to be higher among Catholics than among Protestants, and among Protestants than among Jews, though at times a part of this variation has been attributable to variation in circumstances other than religious belief.

Findings respecting group differences in fertility suggest that the decline in over-all natality has been associated primarily with the increase in the relative number of persons enrolled in occupational groups marked by relatively lower fertility and with the rise of urbanism at the expense of ruralism, and secondarily with a decline in the conduct-determining influence of religious belief and with indirect effects of advances in income. It is assumed, therefore, that fertility will fall in the predominantly agricultural high-natality countries as they become more industrialized and urbanized, better educated, and less subject to fertility-favoring religious influences. Some demographers believe, therefore, that in high-natality countries, the future course of fertility is more predictable than that of mortality. Others object that it is hazardous to infer the future demographic experience of some countries from the past experience of quite different countries.[25]

Interest in cyclical aspects of fertility and natural increase has grown stronger, in part because of their significance for population forecasting and the analysis of reproductive behavior. Because of the sensitivity of marriage rates and marital fertility to fluctuations in employment and disposable income, natality varies with economic activity, and, other conditions given, it will tend to fluctuate even more as the effectiveness of fertility control increases. This means, of course, that the

---

[25] On differential fertility see studies cited in note 20; also Kingsley Davis, *World Population* and *Population of India;* P. K. Hatt and A. J. Reiss, *Reader in Urban Sociology* (Glencoe, 1951); Dudley Kirk, *Europe's Population in the Interwar Years* (Geneva, 1946); C. V. Kiser, *Group Differences in Urban Fertility* (Baltimore, 1942); M. L. Levy, *The Family Revolution in Modern China* (Cambridge, Mass., 1949); R. B. Vance, *All These People* (Chapel Hill, 1945); W. F. Willcox, *Studies in American Demography* (Ithaca, 1940).

growth rate of the labor force will fluctuate more in the future than in the past, other conditions given, and that the behavior of the trade cycle will be affected accordingly. Other conditions may not remain given, however. Because of the disposition of the state to assume increasing responsibility for both the maintenance of employment and disposable income and the payment of expenses attendant upon the reproduction and rearing of children, natality variations of the sort described may diminish greatly. If this is the case, the rate at which the potential labor force grows in countries subject to state intervention will be less variable *ceteris paribus* in the future than in the past and the trade cycle will be damped accordingly.[26]

Much remains to be done before our understanding of reproductive behavior is complete, even in countries whose culture is European or of European origin. The available stock of empirical knowledge needs to be increased through studies of the Indianapolis type carried on in various regions and countries. The effect exercised by price structure changes upon fertility patterns needs to be isolated, in part because of their implications for government pronatality policies.[27] Information is required respecting both the connections obtaining between income-growth rates and living rates and the processes and mechanisms that underlie changes in the aspirations, living standards, or rates of living of various groups and peoples. (These processes and mechanisms resemble in part those underlying the comparative constancy of the average propensity to consume.) The implications of state intervention for reproductive behavior and its study need to be assessed, much as do the implications of state intervention for trade cycle behavior and its study. Of interest to economists is the assertion, implied already by some of Malthus' critics, that only in the presence of state intervention are the marginal private and

---

[26] See Dorothy S. Thomas, *Social and Economic Aspects of Swedish Population Movements* (New York, 1941); *idem* (with Virginia L. Galbraith), "Birth Rates and Interwar Business Cycles," *Jour. Am. Stat. Assoc.*, Dec. 1941, XXXVI, 465–76; Halvor Gille, "The Demographic History of the Northern European Countries in the Eighteenth Century," *Pop. Stud.*, June 1949, III, 3–65; Hannes Hyrenius, "The Relation between Birth-Rates and Economic Activity in Sweden, 1920–1940," *Bull. Oxford Univ. Inst. Stat.*, Jan. 1946, VIII, 15 ff.; Dudley Kirk, "The Relation of Employment to the Level of Births in Germany," *Milbank M. F. Quart.*, Apr. 1942, XX, 126–38; Wagemann, *op. cit.*; Ungern-Sternberg, *op. cit.*; August Lösch, *Bevölkerungswellen und Wechsellagen* (Jena, 1936), together with his controversy with Johan Åkerman in *Schmollers Jahrbuch*, 1936–37, LX–LXI. On pronatality legislation see files of *Population* and *Pop. Stud.*; D. V. Glass, *Population Policies and Movements* (Oxford, 1940); Alva Myrdal, *Nation and Family* (New York, 1941); J. J. Spengler, *France Faces Depopulation* (Durham, 1938).

[27] See *Papers*, Vol. V, pp. 77–120, for R. F. Harrod's proposal for taking into account intergroup differences in cost of childbearing and childrearing.

the marginal social benefit of population growth likely to be made co-incident. Of great significance is the likelihood that cheap, easily used contraceptives apparently are in the offing and that rural societies may adopt them.

III. VARIATIONS IN POPULATION COMPOSITION, DENSITY, AND GROWTH; THEIR SOCIO-ECONOMIC EFFECTS

A. Population Composition

Economically most significant of the forms of population composition which respond to variations in mortality, natality, and migration are the age, genetic, occupational, racial, ethnic, and rural-urban categories. All but the last are nonspatial in character; the last, being a spatial type, is treated in Section IV. While sexual and marital composition may be significant for labor-force analysis, this significance is conditioned by too many factors to justify analysis under the head of demography.

(a) Among the socio-economic factors which are functions of age and whose aggregate dimensions may be sensitive to changes in age composition may be included dependency, employability, absenteeism from work, and such productivity-affecting properties as strength, skill, and adaptability. The past 50–100 years have witnessed an increase in the relative number of persons aged 15–59 and a rise in the ratio of those aged 60 and over to those aged under 15. These changes, V. G. Valaoras has shown, have had their origin principally in the decline in fertility, secondarily (in some immigrant-receiving countries) in the decline in net immigration, and finally (and usually least of all) in the decline in mortality. Future changes in low-natality countries, therefore, are most likely to originate principally in the further extension of life expectancy at ages 50 and higher.

Heretofore, in advanced countries, the total effect of the changes in age composition has been favorable, improvements in age composition *ceteris paribus* having increased per capita productive capacity perhaps 10–25 per cent and having made age structures such as the American about one-sixth more productive than those of Asia and Latin America.[28]

---

[28] Change in age composition is but one of the forces governing the ratio of the labor force to the population. See A. J. Jaffe and C. D. Stewart, *Manpower Resources and Utilization* (New York, 1951), and works cited in bibliography. On the capital absorption of child mortality see Dwarkanath Ghosh, *Pressure of Population and Economic Efficiency in India* (New Delhi, 1946). On age changes see papers of V. G. Valaoras and others in *The Social and Biological Challenge of Our Aging Population*, Iago Galdston, ed. (New York, 1950).

Concern is now frequently expressed, nonetheless, lest past trends in age composition continue and (*i*) reduce the ratio of persons of productive to those of unproductive age; (*ii*) make for interoccupational imbalance; (*iii*) operate in various ways to reduce output per member of the labor force; and (*iv*) intensify difficulties associated with providing support for persons of unproductive age.

Propositions (*i*), (*ii*), and (*iv*) appear to be more nearly valid than (*iii*). (*i*) The advent of a population of stable age composition, whether stationary or declining, would be accompanied by a decline of around 5 per cent below the peak level in the relative number of persons aged 15–65, with the decline somewhat greater in the event of a declining stable population. (*ii*) Interoccupational imbalance may be fostered in two main ways. First, since the relative number of persons joining the labor force may fall by one-third or more, it may become too low to permit the preservation of an optimum interoccupational balance in the absence of a significant increase in the interoccupational transference of labor. There is not much ground for concern on this score, however, when both interoccupational and geographical mobility of labor are comparatively high, as in the United States. Furthermore, the rate of decline in the requirement for any particular kind of labor will rarely exceed the rate at which the stock of this labor is depleted, in the absence of new recruitment, by withdrawals due to death, disability, and age. Second, given a less rapid increase in the number of "preferred" jobs than in the number of older aspirants to such jobs, seniority rules may operate to restrict unduly the promotion of able younger workers. This difficulty can be overcome by improving working conditions and augmenting the relative number of jobs considered preferable. (*iii*) Since employability, productivity, and absenteeism vary with age and occupation, an increase in the average age of the labor force could appreciably affect productivity per worker. This outcome is unlikely, however, provided that entrepreneurial leadership does not pass into the hands of individuals handicapped by age; that employment and pension policies are modified to permit older workers to work as long as they are willing and able; that steps are taken to prevent worker deterioration, obsolescence of skills, etc.; and that remuneration plans are adjusted to any falling off in productivity consequent upon aging. Among means described as suited to prevent employer discrimination against older workers also fall such measures as punitive taxes, subsidies, and older-worker quotas.

(*iv*) First, the impact of dependency will be intensified. (*a*) The number of years the worker must live on a pension will increase much more than the number during which he may accumulate it. The ratio of the number of years the representative worker spent in the labor force to the number he spent in retirement between his withdrawal from the labor force and his death fell from 14.1:1 in 1900 to 7.4:1 in 1940; by 1975 it will be 6.8:1, given the 1947 employment pattern, and 4.3:1 given a continuation of 1920–40 trends. Accordingly, unless the average worker's working life is prolonged and his period of retirement is shortened, he will be hard put to make adequate provision for his years of retirement. (b) The relative number of persons of unproductive age, together with cost per dependent, will rise somewhat; for older dependents, the cost of whose support tends to exceed that of younger dependents, will increase in number more than younger dependents will decrease. Second, in highly mobile societies such as the American, in which social status and sense of well-being usually depend significantly upon an individual's pursuing his occupation, financial support, even when adequate to confer prestige, cannot compensate a worker for his premature, compulsory retirement. Third, difficulties arise out of the fact that the support of older dependents, because it commonly offers less emotional compensation than parents derive from the support of their children, tends to be shifted to impersonal agencies (e.g. retirement funds, governmental pensions, etc.) under arrangements entailing comparatively fixed money income payments. In consequence, even when consumer prices remain relatively stationary, the older dependent does not share in the fruits of technical progress, since his fixed money income lags increasingly behind rising per capita money income. Hence his consciousness of poverty, which is a result of increasing income disparity, is steadily intensified, with the result that he becomes increasingly disposed to unite with other similarly situated older dependents in groups pressing for increasing public support of the aged. Of course, were factor prices stabilized while commodity prices were allowed to fall as factor output rose, or were the older dependent given an annual public dividend roughly commensurate with his income and the rate of technical progress, he would not become a victim of increasing income disparity as at present.[29]

---

[29] In a world in which older dependents comprise 12–15 or more per cent of the population, and in which modern fiscal and financial means are available, little validity attaches to the argument that the stabilization of factor prices, or per capita money incomes, confers an undeserved boon upon *rentier* and creditor groups. On various aspects of aging see *Papers;* files of *Population;* Jaffe and Stewart, *op. cit.;* Harold Wool, *Tables of Working Life,* U.S. Dept. Labor, Bull. 1001 (Washington, 1950); Jean Daric, *Vieillissement de la population et prolongation de la vie active* (Paris, 1948); *The*

(*b*) Since populations are made up of diverse groups which differ socially, genetically, occupationally, etc., and between which mobility is imperfect, persisting and pronounced intergroup differences in the rate of natural increase may produce changes in a population's group composition which significantly affect the movement and the distribution of output. Changes in genetic structure may produce a decline (increase) in national intelligence. The uneven distribution of births by social group may generate marked changes in value-attitudes, voting behavior, etc., since these dispositions tend to be shaped by family, occupational, and related media. Differential natural increase and/or migration may tend to intensify interoccupational imbalance and to modify the wage and price structure accordingly. This would happen if two conditions occurred together: (*a*) if children tended to follow occupations similar to those pursued by their parents, because existing institutions did not appropriately distribute newcomers to the labor market among occupations; (*b*) if the rate of natural increase should be relatively high among those who pursued occupations (e.g. agriculture), the elasticity of demand for whose services was relatively low.[30]

B. Population Density

The response of output per capita, or per worker, to changes in population density has always been of major concern to students of population. For changes in population density produce, or are essential to the production of, changes in (*a*) socio-economic organization and (*b*)

Aged and Society, Milton Derber, ed. (Champaign, 1950); Galdston, *op. cit.;* Otto Pollak, *Social Adjustment in Old Age* (New York, 1948); New York State Legislative Committee on Problems of Aging, *Birthdays Don't Count* (Newburgh, 1948), and other reports; Gunnar Myrdal, *Population* (Cambridge, 1940); W. B. Reddaway, *The Economics of a Declining Population* (New York, 1939); Alfred Sauvy, "Social and Economic Consequences of the Ageing of Western European Populations," *Pop. Stud.,* June 1948, II, 115–24; Gregorz Frumkin, "Pre-war and Post-war Trends in Manpower of European Countries," *ibid.,* Sept. 1950, IV, 209–40.

[30] One-fifth of a representative cohort of females born in 1900 accounted for at least three-fifths of the children eventually produced by this cohort. The literature relating to genetic structure and intelligence is too extensive even to sample. See files of *Population, Eugenics Rev.* and *Pop. Stud.; Papers,* Vol. V, pp. 35–76; R. B. Cattell, "The Fate of National Intelligence," *Eugenics Rev.,* Oct. 1950, XLII, 136 ff.; Hans Staehle, "Ability, Wages, and Income," *Rev. Econ. Stat.,* Feb. 1943, XXV, 77 ff. On occupational balance see H. A. Simon, "Effects of Increased Productivity upon the Ratio of Urban to Rural Population," *Econometrica,* Jan. 1947, XV, 31 ff.; P. E. Davidson and H. D. Anderson, *Occupational Mobility in an American Community* (Stanford, 1937); Marcel Bresard and Alain Girard, "Mobilité sociale et dimension de la famille," *Population,* July–Sept. 1950 and Jan.–Mar. 1951, V, 533–66, VI, 103–24; *Political Arithmetic,* Lancelot Hogben, ed. (New York, 1938), Pt. 2.

the ratio of population to physical assets in use, it being given that income-affecting conditions unconnected with population growth remain unchanged.

(a) When a population group is small, an increase in its size makes specialization possible, provides protection against external attack, destroys the homogeneous and *Gemeinschaft*-like character of the society, and increases interpersonal communication and contact. As the group becomes larger, increases in population density continue to intensify specialization and division of labor, augment economies of scale, and produce better interfirm and interindustry fits until further improvement is impossible. This set of effects, which is essentially passive and mechanical in character, may be accompanied, again within limits, by another set which is essentially subjective, psychological, and sociological in character. An increase in population density, it is held, makes for an increase in personal interaction and stimulation and, therefore, for the development of morality, solidarity, new wants, knowledge, and innovations. It will cause existing political and economic forms of organization, if they cannot effectively accommodate increase in population, to be superseded by new and superior forms. This view resembles somewhat Malthus' view that the principle of population is the source of social progress. It has been criticized on a number of grounds, however: that population growth, though it may make for economic and political instability and insecurity, is not a creative force; that interpersonal interaction grows at a decreasing rate until a limit is reached even though population continues to grow; that population pressure may make for unemployment, war, and antisocial behavior. Most fundamental is the argument that the particular effects produced by an increase in population pressure are determined in very large degree by what conditions are present and what conditions are lacking in a society at the time the population increase takes place.[31]

(b) Since goods and services are the joint product of labor and complementary agents of production, and since labor is neither perfectly

---

[31] See Eugène Dupreel, *Sociologie générale* (Paris, 1948); Pierre Fromont, *Démographie économique* (Paris, 1947); E. W. Hofstee, "Population Pressure and the Future of Western Civilization in Europe," *Am. Jour. Soc.,* May 1950, LV, 523–32; R. K. Merton, "Science, Population, and Society," *Sci. Mo.,* Feb. 1937, XLIV, 165–71; M. J. Dijkmans, "Déterminisme démographique et sociologie pure," *Annales de la Société Scientifique de Bruxelles,* July–Sept. 1938, LVIII, 197–221; J. C. Russell, "The Ecclesiastical Age: A Demographic Interpretation of the Period 200–900 A.D.," *Rev. of Religion,* Jan. 1941, V, 137 ff.; Arnold Toynbee, *A Study of History* (New York, 1939), Vol. IV, pp. 207 ff.; Wagemann, *op. cit.*

substitutable for these agents nor perfectly convertible into the form of these agents, output per worker tends to fall when (*ceteris paribus*) the amount of appropriately selected and organized agents (or productive resources) in use per worker falls. This proposition is borne out by various statistical findings; it is afforded support also by studies wherein the Douglass-Cobb type of production function is used. Accordingly, other conditions (including age composition) being given, the long-run movement of per capita output depends upon the rapidity with which the amount of productive assets in use is being increased relative to the population, and upon how long an adequate rate of increase can be maintained. Furthermore, since some resources are depletable and non-replaceable, while others are augmentable only within limits, and since availability of resources conditions the amount as well as the effectiveness of technical progress, the long-run movement of per capita output depends upon how fast reproducible resources can be increased relative to population and upon the extent to which these augmentable resources can be substituted, directly or indirectly, for those which are either depletable or relatively nonaugmentable. It is because of these effects listed under (*b*) that economists, anxious to prevent either a diminution in the rate of increase in per capita income or an eventual depression of its level, have developed the concept of an income or welfare optimum population. (The probable adverse effect of population pressure upon employment is usually not taken into account in this concept.)

The term "optimum" is used to describe that population magnitude, with which is associated a maximum value for some variable that is a function of the size of a country's population. If the variable selected to be maximized is per capita "welfare," the welfare-optimum population is that population with which *ceteris paribus* maximum per capita "welfare" is associated. The magnitude of the optimum population depends, other conditions being given, upon the variable selected for maximization, being larger for some (e.g. military) than for other variables (e.g. per capita income). It varies also with other variables of which it is a function. For example, the magnitude of the income optimum depends upon (among other things) the interest rate, the response of income to investment, and the pattern of tastes. The magnitude of the "welfare" optimum depends upon these variables as well as upon the particular welfare function that is specified. Furthermore, since children are included in the pattern of tastes, and since the income elasticity of demand for children usually is positive, these facts must also be taken into account in defining income and welfare optima.

Because the magnitude of the income-optimum population (or that of any other optimum) depends upon many variables, it may change if economic or other circumstances change. It is generally agreed, for example, that the establishment of basic utilities and the mass-production industries operated, in the nineteenth century, to increase the income optimum. Many, but not all, students hold, however, that invention is no longer serving to increase the magnitude of the income optimum (as defined) in advanced countries even though it is elevating the level of living. Some students hold that the magnitude of the optimum may be undergoing change as a result of changes in the pattern of consumption that are consequent upon income increase. It is noted in particular that, in so far as the income elasticity of demand for children is positive, this fact must be taken into account when the impact of invention upon the magnitude of the optimum is estimated. Sauvy has pointed out that the subjection of a population to tribute, or to other large and continuing forms of nonproductive expenditure, increases its income optimum as viewed by that part of the population which is producing the income and which must support, through taxation, the expenditure in question. For since the *average* after-tax income of the given productive population is decreased while its *marginal* produced income is not affected, the intersection (which marks the optimum) of the marginal and the relevant average curve is shifted to the right, thereby indicating an increase in the optimum size of the producing population.

Satisfactory empirical indices of population maladjustment have not yet been devised, for the behavior of most relevant indices (e.g. per capita income, terms of trade, unemployment) is subject to the not easily isolatable influence of many nonpopulation factors. Accordingly, some writers are sceptical of the empirical usefulness of the optimum concept when it refers to situational changes more complex than mere modifications of life expectancy. The general approach has been first, to develop labor and other productivity indices suited to reflect the respective impact of an increment in population upon (i) natural resource industries subject to decreasing returns and (ii) industries still characterized by increasing returns; and second, to combine these indices into an appropriate over-all indicator. After this has been done, and some countries have been discovered to be "overpopulated" in terms of the combined index, international comparisons may be employed to disclose the relative condition of still other countries. It is also being increasingly emphasized that the population optimum must be distinguished from the politico-economic-geographical optimum, and that when a people's habitat corresponds to the latter, it will be less sensitive *ceteris paribus* to the effect of population maladjustment than when its habitat is below this optimum in size; for both economic flexibility and mobility and capacity to realize some of the noneconomic objectives associated with a large population appear to be correlated with size of political unit, population density being given.[32]

Emphasis today is placed not so much upon the achievement of an optimum population, as upon the need to avoid further maladjustment in countries in which even a moderate rate of population growth will seriously counterbalance the effect of income-increasing forces. Presumably the populations of most countries exceed the income optimum. In some of these countries, however, the income-increasing forces at work are strong enough to permit both a moderate rate of population growth and a significant increase in per capita income. But in countries wherein live more than half the world's population and where both income and resources per worker are very low, population growth operates to decelerate the rate at which per capita income can rise and sometimes even to depress it. In these countries above all, population growth serves to increase the pressure of numbers upon land and relatively fixed resource equipment, and to step up the use of depletable and nonreplaceable resources. It tends also to slow down the accumulation of substitutes, for it checks capital formation both by holding down per capita income and by transforming potential capital into population, many members of which may die before reaching productive age. Population growth also

---

[32] On the optimum and related questions discussed under (*b*) see the following studies, together with the bibliography included in many: *Papers,* Vol. III; Jan Tinbergen and J. J. Polak, *The Dynamics of Business Cycles* (Chicago, 1950), Ch. 2, 10; Alfred Sauvy, *Richesse et Population* (Paris, 1944); Wagemann, *op. cit.;* Giorgio Fua, *La conception économique de l'optimum du peuplement* (Lausanne, 1940); Manuel Gottlieb, "The Theory of an Optimum for a Closed Economy," *Jour. Pol. Econ.,* Dec. 1945, LIII, 289 ff.; *idem,* "Optimum Population, Foreign Trade, and World Economy," *Pop. Stud.,* Sept. 1949, III, 151 ff.; Radahakamal Mukerjee, *The Political Economy of Population* (Bombay, 1943); W. E. Moore, *Economic Demography of Southern and Eastern Europe* (Geneva, 1944); G. O. O'Brien, *The Phantom of Plenty* (Dublin, 1948); Georges Létinier, "Progrès technique, destructions de guerre et optimum de population," *Population,* Jan.–Mar. 1946, I, 35 ff.; Paul Vincent, "Pression démographique et ressources agricole," *ibid.,* pp. 9 ff.; J. J. Spengler, "Aspects of the Economics of Population Growth," *So. Econ. Jour.,* Oct. 1947 and Jan. 1948, XIV, 123–47, 233–65; *idem,* "The Population Obstacle to Human Betterment," *Am. Econ. Rev., Proc.,* May 1951, XLI, 343–54; *idem,* "Measures of Population Maladjustment," reprinted from *Proceedings* of the XIVth International Congress of Sociology (Rome, 1950), III. On the concept of a "minimum population," stressed by Livio Livi, see Jean Sutter and Léon Tabah, "Les notions d'isolat et de population minimum," *Population,* July–Sept. 1951, VI, 481–98; Alfred Sauvy, *Théorie générale de la population* (Paris, 1952).

reduces the rate at which a given absolute rate of capital formation can increase per capita equipment, since this capital must then be spread over more people. One may say roughly that an increase of 1 per cent in a population will absorb something like 3–5 per cent of the annual income and so prevent an increase of 0.5–1.0 per cent in per capita income.

Were more satisfactory inventories of resources available, it would be possible to describe more adequately the implications of world population growth in the light of the resources situation. Actually, estimates vary widely. Estimates of the world's cultivable land range between 2.6 and 15.6 billion acres; but O. E. Baker and R. M. Salter suggest a maximum of 4–5 billion acres, of which about two are reported under cultivation. This maximum is unevenly distributed relative to population, with most of the potential land relatively removed from the world's four main centers of population. Fertilizer supplies are adequate for a long time to come, and yields per acre can be increased 50 per cent or more. Estimates of the world's population capacity, geological change being ignored, range from under 4 to over 13 billions. This range is so wide because estimates of the world's potential food-producing capacity differ significantly and because acreage requirements vary greatly with diet (e.g. a 40 per cent meat diet calls for about twice as many acres per person as does a 10 per cent meat diet).

Whether the world's population capacity depends ultimately upon food turns on consumption patterns. In the economies of Malthus' time (as in the technologically backward economies of today) land was the population-limiting factor, since the things men used were principally of organic origin. Today, however, the limiting factor operative in high-income industrial economies appears to be composed of energy sources, iron ore, various other minerals, and leisure time. While the spread of industrialization will extend the operation of this composite factor, its extension is limited by the uneven distribution of energy and mineral sources relative to population, together with the apparent incapacity of international trade greatly to offset this inequality. Meanwhile, the stores of crucial depletable mineral resources are being used up, and their extractive costs are tending to rise. For this reason and because population and income are rising, the exchange value of raw materials is rising and will probably continue to rise unless technological progress uncovers suitable substitutes. Dissipation of the utility embodied in mineral and energy sources may operate as increasing entropy, therefore, to reduce population optima and increasingly restrict population growth, given present consumption patterns.[33]

C. Population Growth

Economists have usually been interested in the long-run rates at which population and the number of families are growing and in short-run fluctuations in these rates. In recent years long-run trends have received more attention, in part because it has been contended that, under some but not necessarily all institutional arrangements, a decline in the incremental rate of population growth tends to make for increasing underemployment. Economists have been interested in population trends and fluctuations because these may operate, mechanically or through the medium of expectations, to alter both the propensity to consume and composition of consumer demand, to change the rate of growth of the labor force, and, directly and indirectly, to modify the demand for both investment goods and labor. It has been noted, of course, that the impact of any given change in the rate of population growth will be intensified if the acceleration principle associated with derived demand comes into play. While some economists at least imply that population movements may initiate economic movements, most insist that the capacity of population movements to produce economic effects is conditioned by the manner in which various economic mechanisms are working and by whether expansive or contractive forces are ascendant. In view of the attention the supposed economic effects of population movements have received, they will merely be touched upon here.

Cyclical variations in natality and migration may damp or intensify variation in diverse kinds of economic activity. An increase (de-

---

[33] See Eugene Ayres and C. A. Scarlott, *Energy Sources—The Wealth of the World* (New York, 1952); R. M. Salter, "World Soil and Fertilizer Resources in Relation to Food Needs," *Chronica Botanica,* Summer 1948, XI, 226–35; O. E. Baker, "The Population Prospect in Relation to the World's Agricultural Resources," *Jour. Geography,* Sept. 1947, XLVI, 203–20; M. K. Bennett, "Population and Food Supply: The Current Scare," *Sci. Mo.,* Jan. 1949, LXVIII, 17–26; W. E. Boerman, "De voedselcapaciteit der aarde en de toekomstige wereldbevolking," *Tijdschrift voor economische geographie,* May 1940, XXXI, 121–32; Colin Clark, "The Future of the Terms of Trade," *Internat. Soc. Sci. Bull.,* Spring 1951, III, 37–41; W. A. Lewis, "Food and Raw Materials," *District Bank Rev.,* Sept. 1951, No. 99, pp. 1–11; and *supra,* note 32. Information about forest, mineral, and energy sources is given in various United Nations and United States government publications. Colin Clark suggests that both the capacity to form capital and the income-capital ratio rise with per capita income. See his *Conditions of Economic Progress* (2nd ed., London, 1951), Ch. 11.

crease) in natality may produce an increase (decrease) initially in the demand for products and services utilized by children and eventually (*ceteris paribus*) in both the rate at which additions need to be made to the stock of equipment used by the labor force and the rate at which families are formed and require housing, furnishings, and other durables. A population upsurge thus tends to intensify economic activity, particularly if expansive forces already are more powerful than contractive forces; and conversely. Concerning the effect of an increase (decrease) in the rate of growth of the labor force the opinions of economists differ somewhat. Economists in the Gustav Cassel tradition suppose that the intensity of trade booms will diminish as the decline in natural increase and urbanward migration reduces the rate at which labor is fed into the urban industrial reserve army. While present-day economists may accept the Cassel thesis that a relatively rapidly expanding labor force is a boom-prolonging force, they emphasize in much greater measure the associated stimulus to population-oriented investment, given that some expansive processes are already under way.[34]

The Keynes-Hansen thesis that increasing underemployment tends to be consequent upon a continuing decline in the incremental rate of population growth appears to have won considerable acceptance. Because a tapering off of population growth both diminishes the need for investment in the equipping of additions to the population and tends to affect divers other investment demands adversely, the rate of investment associated with full employment tends to fall as the rate of population growth falls. Furthermore, this fall in investment is not likely to be offset by a corresponding fall in the rate of net savings associated with full employment, even though the aging of a population does entail an increase in both dissaving and governmental expenditures upon the aged, and despite the fact that the spread of the small-family system may weaken motives to saving. In consequence of the resulting increasing imbalance between planned saving and investment at full employment, underemployment tends to increase *ceteris paribus* as the incremental rate of population growth falls. Persisting general unemployment rises and cyclical and disguised unemployment is intensified. Even structural un-

---

[34] E.g., see S. C. Tsiang, "The Effect of Population Growth on the General Level of Employment and Activity," *Economica,* Nov. 1942, IX, 325–32; A. R. Sweezy, "Population Growth and Investment Opportunity," *Quart. Jour. Econ.,* Nov. 1940, LV, 64–79; H. A. Adler, "Absolute or Relative Rate of Decline in Population Growth," *ibid.,* Aug. 1945, LIX, 626 ff.; Jorgen Pedersen, "Interest Rates, Employment and Changes in Population," *Kyklos,* 1948, II (1), 1–15; Lösch, *op. cit.;* Eric Schiff, "Family Size and Residential Construction," *Am. Econ. Rev.,* Mar. 1946, XXXVI, 97–112.

employment tends to increase, some writers believe, in industries, the per capita demand for whose products is inelastic, when technological progress becomes conjoined with comparative nongrowth of population. Such is the theory. Needless to say, information remains very inadequate respecting how investment and saving respond to quantitative and qualitative changes in populations, how this response varies with differing institutional arrangements, and what types of institutional changes are best suited to eliminate imbalance between net investment and net saving at full employment should it develop in a demographically stationary state.[35]

IV. THE DISTRIBUTION OF POPULATION IN SPACE

Empirical rules and hypotheses respecting the geographical distribution of population originally were developed somewhat independently of those relating to the constellation of economic activities in the time-space continuum. Under the impact of increasing interest in urban growth and regional development these rules and hypotheses are being transformed into a consistent body of theory.

A. Economic and Demographic Spatial Distributions Are Interrelated.[36]

(a) While all economic activities are distributed unevenly with respect to space and population, some are much more unevenly distrib-

---

[35] On the Hansen-Keynes view see B. H. Higgins, "The Theory of Increasing Under-Employment," *Econ. Jour.*, June 1950, LX, 255–74. For appraisals see M. C. Brockie, "Population Growth and the Rate of Investment," *So. Econ. Jour.*, July 1950, XVII, 1–15; George Terborgh, *The Bogey of Economic Maturity* (Chicago, 1945); William Fellner, *Monetary Policies and Full Employment* (Berkeley, 1946). On savings see Janet A. Fisher, "Postwar Changes in Income and Savings among Consumers in Different Age Groups," *Econometrica*, Jan. 1952, XX, 47–71; Leon Goldenberg, "Saving in a State with a Stationary Population," *Quart. Jour. Econ.*, Nov. 1946, LXI, 40–65, and H. W. Arndt's comments thereon, *ibid.*, Aug. 1948, LXII, 623–28. See also B. S. Keirstead, *The Theory of Economic Change* (Toronto, 1948); William Fellner's account of the Domar-Harrod and related theories in *Money, Trade, and Economic Growth; in Honor of John Henry Williams* (New York, 1951), pp. 105–34; Timlin, *op. cit.;* J. R. Hicks, *Value and Capital* (Oxford, 1939; 2nd ed., 1948), p. 302; *Papers*, Vol. III; J. J. Spengler, "Population and Per Capita Income," *Annals Am. Acad. Pol. Soc. Sci.*, Jan. 1945, CCXXXVII, 185–92.

[36] This subsection is based principally upon the works of Walter Isard, Rutledge Vining, and J. Q. Stewart: Isard, "Distance Inputs and the Space Economy," *Quart. Jour. Econ.*, May and Aug. 1951, LXV, 181–98, 373–99, together with literature cited; *idem,* "Interregional and Regional Input-Output Analysis: A Model of a Space Economy," *Rev. Econ. Stat.*, Nov. 1951, XXXIII, 318–28; Vining, "The Region as an Entity and Certain

uted than others. Three approaches have been devised to account for this general unevenness.

(*i*) When the agents of production are classified according to their ubiquitousness and their immobility, the distribution of economic activities appears to be dominated by the distribution of productive agents which are relatively nonubiquitous, place-bound, and significant for production.

(*ii*) Approach (*i*), while useful, needs to be greatly supplemented before it can account for the spatial distribution of economic activities: (1) space must be treated as an input to be economized along with jointly utilizable inputs of land, labor, capital, and enterprise; (2) there must be allowance for such agglomerative forces as economies of scale, availability of capital, external economies of conglomeration, as the logistics of transport and distribution, as the technological and economic linkages connecting economic activities, and as the cumulative effects produced in space and time by geographical, investment, and other multipliers, together with related processes; (3) governmental intervention must be allowed for; (4) account must be taken of accident and inertia, of improvements in transport and labor mobility, and of changes

---

Variations to Be Observed in the Study of Systems of Regions," *Am. Econ. Rev., Proc.,* May 1949, XXXIX, 89–104, and forthcoming papers; Stewart, "Empirical Mathematical Rules Concerning the Distribution and Equilibrium of Population," *Geog. Rev.,* July 1947, XXXVII, 461–85; *idem,* "Demographic Gravitation: Evidence and Application," *Sociometry,* Feb.–May 1948, XI, 31–58; *idem,* "Potential of Population in Its Relationship to Marketing," in Reavis Cox and Wroe Alderson, *Theory in Marketing* (Chicago, 1950). See also W. H. Dean, *The Theory of the Geographic Location of Economic Activities* (Ann Arbor, 1938); D. J. Bogue, *The Structure of the Metropolitan Community* (Ann Arbor, 1949); *idem, Metropolitan Decentralization: A Study of Differential Growth* (Oxford, Ohio, 1950); E. M. Hoover, *The Location of Economic Activity* (New York, 1948), and bibliography of governmental and other literature; G. H. Hildebrand and Arthur Mace, "The Employment Multiplier in an Expanding Industrial Market: Los Angeles County, 1940–47," *Rev. Econ. Stat.,* Aug. 1950, XXXII, 241–49, and literature cited; G. K. Zipf, *Human Behavior and the Principle of Least Effort* (Cambridge, Mass., 1949); H. W. Singer, "The 'Courbe des Populations.' A Parallel to Pareto's Law," *Econ. Jour.,* June 1936, XLVI, 254–63; August Lösch, *Die räumliche Ordnung der Wirtschaft* (Jena, 1940); Homer Hoyt, "Is City Growth Controlled by Mathematics or Physical Laws?" *Land Econ.,* Aug. 1951, XXVII, 259–62; *idem,* "Forces of Urban Centralization and Decentralization," *Am. Jour. Soc.,* Dec. 1941, XLVI, 843 ff.; A. P. Usher, "The Steam and Steel Complex," in *Technology and International Relations,* W. F. Ogburn, ed. (Chicago, 1949); S. C. Dodd, "The Interactance Hypothesis," *Am. Soc. Rev.,* Apr. 1950, XV, 245–56. J. H. Clapham and Eileen Power, *Cambridge Economic History of Europe* (Cambridge, 1941), Ch. 1, 7–8; C. F. Schmid, "The Ecology of the American City," *Am. Soc. Rev.,* Apr. 1950, XV, 264–81; papers and bibliography in Hatt and Reiss, *op. cit.* Walter Christaller's works are discussed in *ibid.,* and by Lösch, *op. cit.* See also, H. V. Meyer-Lindemann, *Typologie der Theorien des Industriestandortes* (Bremen, 1951).

in resources used, in technology and tastes, in the level and distribution of income, and in expenditure patterns; (5) sufficient weight must be given to dispersing forces: uneven distribution of resources, relatively high transport costs, consumer preference for space, costs and diseconomies consequent upon concentration in space, and diminishing returns from both natural resources and sources whence flow economies associated with agglomeration.

(*iii*) Industries, together with the workers attached to them, may be classified into the resource oriented (i.e. extractive and raw-material processing), the market or consumer oriented, and the footloose (i.e. free of heavy inflow and outflow costs and susceptible of location near power and/or labor supplies). While in accordance with this classification, in 1930, 28 per cent of the American labor force was resource oriented and 24 per cent footloose, the proportion directly or indirectly tied to resources was about two-fifths, while much of the remaining three-fifths was subject, within limits, to the forces of agglomeration.

Because regional settlement and development take time, date of occupancy and hence accessibility to early occupancy may condition the manner in which a region's spatial pattern takes shape. If it is supposed that each natural resource is distributed at random, then in only a relatively very small number of areas will enough different resources appear together to make the area a highly potential locus of diversified economic activity. Whether this locus is early chosen for settlement, however, turns in part on whether it is situated near enough, in terms of transfer costs, to already developed centers of population whence may come settlers with the necessary capital and technical training. The population-attracting power of this locus will be conditioned, furthermore, by the multiplicity of the raw materials that enter into the population's standard of living; for the greater the number of such materials, the smaller *ceteris paribus* is the pull exerted by any one, and the greater is the industry-selecting and the location-affecting influence exerted by economic forces other than the immediate availability of particular materials.

Location and settlement, being diffusion processes subject to transfer costs, tend to become relatively free of the distribution of natural resources as transfer costs fall and raw material requirements become diversified. For example, until the development of modern means of communication, location and settlement were dominated by the comparative cheapness of water transport and by the fact that, in terms of weight, the importance of food in a community's requirements significantly exceeded that of raw materials. The influence exerted by these two factors declined, however, as communications improved and transfer costs fell, as the relative importance of services and consumables other than food increased, and as additional agglomerative forces were strengthened. In general, both theory and temporal and spatial comparisons indicate that industrial development and economic progress make for the concentration of men and activity in space.

(b) Order appears to underlie the distribution of population among communities, classified as to size. In a given country, Zipf found, city-rank times city-size tends to yield a constant product that approximates the population size of the largest city in such country, particularly if city is defined in terms of metropolitan region rather than in terms of population living within corporate limits. The distribution of population among cities, classified as to size, Singer found, corresponds to a Pareto logarithmic formula, with metropolization, as measured by the proportion of large towns, tending to increase with industrial progress and size of a country's population.[37] The urban fraction of the American population, Stewart found, is an unchanging function of the number of cities, while rural population density at any point is a function of the total population potential at that point and thus dependent upon the proximity of that point to people in general. Inquiry may yet reveal a functional connection between logarithmic income distributions and logarithmic spatial population distributions.

Order also underlies the distribution of communities in space, largely because it reflects, as Christaller found, the hierarchy of market areas, a hierarchy described by Lösch as "simple market areas, nets of such areas, and systems of nets." Most of a country's population is assembled into clusters and systems of clusters of people, bound together

---

[37] The Zipf and Singer equations yield straight lines on double log paper. Let P_r represent the population of a city (or metropolitan region) of rank r in size; K, a constant approximating the population of the largest or rank 1 city (e.g. New York); and q a constant approximating 1 in value and indicating the slope of the Zipf curve. Then $\log P_r = \log K - q \log r$. When we reverse the axes we get Singer's Pareto curve: $\log r = \log A - a \log P$. Here P, measured along the abscissa, represents a certain number of inhabitants; r, measured along the ordinate, represents the number of towns with more than P inhabitants; A and a are constants, the latter of which indicates the slope of the Pareto curve. $q = 1/a$; the two are of identical value when, as in the United States, the value of q approximates one. An increase in the value of q (or a decrease in that of a) indicates an increase in the proportion of the population concentrated in the largest cities. Lorentz and other equations may also be employed to represent population distributions. In fact, the Pareto-Zipf equations may not be sensitive enough to reflect adequately the impact of urbanization upon such variables as fertility.

by transport and other media of communication. Intercluster distance is correlated positively with size of cluster. Small clusters are oriented to clusters of intermediate size; these, together with their satellites and areas of dominance, usually are oriented to still larger clusters; and so on. Out of the groupings of these clusters arise economic regions which, as they become differentiated, condition what economic activities can be carried on at various points with good prospect of success. In general, Bogue and others find, as one moves from great population concentration points, places increase in number and decrease in size in orderly fashion; but population grows much less rapidly than the area it occupies. Population density, at a local peak in the central place of any given metropolitan community, falls logarithmically, sometimes for more than a hundred miles, until the area of dominance of an adjacent metropolitan community is reached, after which density again begins to rise. Various indices of economic behavior and resource use behave similarly. Even within the units composing metropolitan areas, both the distribution and the succession of economic activities and population manifest considerable order.

(c) While order appears to underlie intranational spatial distributions of population, it does not yet follow that the present distribution is an optimum one, or one representing a relatively nonmodifiable spatial equilibrium. Our knowledge of the stochastical and other processes that have generated the present spatial distribution remains quite limited. Moreover, considerable exception is being taken to the empirical findings and the theoretical formulations of Christaller, Lösch, Zipf, and others respecting spatial distributions and their generation. While it is not believed that widespread population dispersion will develop, it is believed that, under the impact of transport and other technological developments, the number of population focal points will increase, possibly at the expense of existing metropolitan centers. It also is believed that while economic forces dominate the spatial distribution of population, this distribution may be significantly affected by institutional arrangements (e.g. system of landownership), private ventures in which many entrepreneurs cooperate, and state intervention.

Concerning the existence of cities of optimum size there is much disagreement at present, both factual information and theory remaining defective. It is admitted that because of discrepancies between marginal social benefits and costs, nonoptimum population distributions tend to arise. There is evidence that the attractiveness of a city is not associated with its size, income being held constant, while commutation time is;

and that municipal services can be supplied under optimum conditions in a city of 175–200 thousand, while no more than 200–500 thousand is required for the development of manufacture. It is presumed that an appropriately situated city of relatively small size can provide cultural advantages and satisfactory remuneration while satisfying better than the larger city demands for space, institutional and related flexibility, leisure time, recreation, and so on. On the other hand, between city size and a number of indices of welfare, there appears to be little significant correlation. Furthermore, as has been indicated, while the heaviest population growth is taking place in suburbs and outside central cities, most population growth is found in metropolitan areas and the vicinity of hinterland cities.[38]

Although it is not predicted just what form urban population distribution will assume in the future, it is predicted that within 50 years the urban fraction of the population will have risen to 80–90 per cent. The magnitude of this urban fraction will be determined by the level of employment, progress in agriculture, the extension of city boundaries to include relatively rural districts, and the disposition of people (especially elderly people) to live in rural nonfarm areas as these are made accessible to good transportation and distribution facilities. The volume of migration in prospect, together with its selectivity concerning age, education, value patterns, etc., indicate that it may produce considerable change in the value patterns and in other cultural and noncultural attributes of populations, particularly in the areas of emigration, which will be largely rural.

B. Migration

(a) While the composition of a migrant stream reflects the influence of divers factors (e.g. age, sex, race, extent to which population is urban, circumstances surrounding pursuit of livelihood), the volume of migration, in the absence of legal barriers to migration, is conditioned by interregional differences in the availability of economic opportunity and, as E. G. Ravenstein long ago noted, by distance. The volume of migration is inversely related to distance. The term distance, of course, signifies more than mere intervening space. Given correction for differences

---

[38] See Colin Clark, "The Economic Functions of a City," *Econometrica,* Apr. 1945, XIII, 97–113; E. L. Thorndike, *144 Smaller Cities* (New York, 1940); Victor Roterus, "Effects of Population Growth and Non-Growth on the Well-Being of Cities," *Am. Soc. Rev.,* Feb. 1946, XI, 90–97; R. C. Angell, "The Moral Integration of American Cities," *Am. Jour. Soc.,* July 1951, LVII, Pt. 2, 1–140; Hatt and Reiss, *op. cit.;* Meyer-Lindemann, *op. cit.*

in available transport facilities, distance constitutes a rough measure of the economic and the psychic costs of movement. The disposition of individuals to move is affected by their conceptions of distance; how far they move, together with the direction and destination point they choose, reflects the meaning distance and direction have for them in terms of opportunity. For like reason, occupational and geographical mobility are positively correlated. Perspective, too, is a function of distance: just as removal in time makes for irrational discounting so, as Vining suggests, removal in space makes for increasing underawareness of the concrete opportunities available. It follows, as Vining notes, that if actual opportunities vary proportionally with distance, while the ratio of known to actual opportunities falls with distance, the number of migrants may fall off logarithmically with distance. Several but not all studies appear to confirm S. A. Stouffer's testable formulation of the migration-distance relationship: "The number of persons going a given distance is directly proportional to the number of opportunities at that distance and inversely proportional to the number of intervening opportunities."[39] Formulation of the migration-distance relationship in terms of opportunity alone requires that opportunity be defined to take cost of movement into account. Stewart finds that the force (e.g. migrant-drawing power) which a given population cluster exercises upon another cluster, or upon a ring of clusters, diminishes with distance, just as does the marketing force emanating from a given center.

Migration, employment, and the trade cycle are interconnected. Migration varies in volume, and sometimes in direction, with the trade cycle. Migration makes for better factor allocation. Heavy migration, of the sort set in motion by transportation improvements, may, as Isard has shown, generate sustained building booms.

(*b*) While international migration may reduce international income disparity by diminishing international differences in man-resource ratios, its capacity to do this is limited by the smallness of the ratio of emigration to population in countries of emigration even when migra-

---

[39] See "Intervening Opportunities Relating Mobility and Distance," *Am. Soc. Rev.,* Dec. 1940, V, 846; D. C. Bogue and W. S. Thompson, "Migration and Distance," *ibid.,* Apr. 1949, XIV, 236–44; Zipf, *op. cit.,* Ch. 9; papers of Dodd, Isard, Stewart, and Vining cited in note 36; forthcoming Soc. Sci. Res. Coun. study cited in note 1; D. O. Price, "Some Socio-Economic Factors in Internal Migration," *Social Forces,* May 1951, XXIX, 410–15; *idem,* "Distance and Direction as Vectors of Internal Migration, 1935 to 1940," *ibid.,* Oct. 1948, XXVII, 48–53; Helen Makower *et al.,* "Studies in Mobility of Labour," *Oxford Econ. Papers,* Sept. 1940, pp. 39–62; Kirk, *Europe's Population;* Frank Lorimer, *The Population of the Soviet Union* (Geneva, 1946).

tion is not subject to rigorous, selective control as at present. Because of controls, the decline in natural increase, and the industrial development of countries (e.g. Sweden) that formerly sent out many emigrants, the volume of international migration has declined markedly. For this reason and because little new country remains, migration is no longer operating, as in the past, to shake many migrants to new countries out of inefficient traditional methods. Because skilled workers are not disposed to move in large numbers to underdeveloped countries, the latter must rely largely upon external trade, capital imports, and the gradual inculcation of relevant technical skills into the native labor force.[40]

(c) Can international trade eliminate wage and price disparities arising out of international differences in resource equipment, population-resource ratios, stage of historical development, etc., disparities which migration, were it free, might reduce? Given zero transport costs and certain other conditions, international trade in final products can equalize the prices both of these products and of productive factors, thereby removing international differences that give rise to economically motivated migration. These conditions cannot be actualized, of course, since transport cannot be made costless, and since a variety of circumstances, only some of which are completely modifiable, cause price and cost differences to persist. At the same time it is evident that, so long as transport is relatively cheap and there is ready access to raw materials in short domestic supply, an economy can enlarge its raw-material base and can very greatly diminish the impact of diminishing returns by adopting superior technological methods, exploiting economies such as those of scale, and exchanging fabricated products for the lacking raw materials. Such action entails augmentation of an economy's maximum and optimum population capacities.

In the world of reality these potentialities are not readily realizable by advanced economies which are geographically too small to permit them to exploit fully the various sources of increasing return, or by economies which, though geographically large, are heavily peopled and underindustrialized. The former type encounters economic and political obstacles; the latter, at least economic obstacles. Consider Britain, a

---

[40] See Julius Isaac, *Economics of Migration* (New York, 1947); on the shock effect, Clark, *Conditions of Economic Progress,* pp. 206–07; on the important effect of war, E. M. Kulischer, *Europe on the Move* (New York, 1948); also the files of *Population* and *Pop. Stud.;* "Reappraising Our Immigration Policy," Hugh Carter, ed., *Annals Am. Acad. Pol. Soc. Sci.,* Mar. 1949, CCLXII, 1–192.

given percentage increase in whose population entails a much greater percentage increase in her imports (and hence) exports, with a consequent increase in pressure upon her terms of trade. This pressure would be intensified if Britain should derive less benefit from the increase produced in world income by industrial progress than she experienced disadvantage from the downward pressure upon British export prices and the upward pressure on British import prices occasioned by this same progress. And yet, because specialization in the production of raw materials for export encounters opposition on the ground that such production implies inferior ("colonial") status, unfavorable terms of trade, and reduced population capacity, a country such as Britain (or Japan) tends to encounter increasingly the adverse substitution effect against its current products which spreading industrialization generates; whence resort must be had to the supply of products not so affected. While a densely populated underdeveloped area that is both relatively small and favorably situated (e.g. Puerto Rico) may greatly ease the impact of population pressure through the development of an export trade in relatively labor-embodying products, such recourse is largely denied by their size alone to underindustrialized economies which are large and heavily peopled (e.g. India). However, since such economies face shortages of capital as well as of skilled labor and various raw materials, exportation can contribute, along with external loans, to the provision of foreign exchange wherewith to meet the requirements of economic development. Domestic population growth, by intensifying the capital requirement of these economies, somewhat counterbalances the contribution that exportation can make, however, to the easing of population pressure. The rate at which capital from abroad can be utilized is conditioned by the rate at which domestic capital is formed; and this rate is checked in turn by the capital-absorbing effects of population growth.

Immigration is likely to be opposed, in a world of many sovereign states, when important groups in potential immigrant-receiving countries believe that their economic interests would be adversely affected by the coming of the immigrants in search of better situations. There is no prospect, therefore, that a world income maximizing distribution of population in space will be realized, and negligible prospect that international trade will contribute as much as it could to the diminution of international income disparity arising out of international disparity in population-resource ratios. Only in an economy that is large enough to contain most crucial raw materials and within which trade and migration are free and political status is equal can migration and exchange contribute in a maximum degree to the augmentation of aggregate income.[41]

V. PROMISING NEW APPROACHES

The most important task confronting population students is the transformation of the findings and suggestions of a great variety of descriptive and particularized inquiries into a body of explicit, systematized theory that can give economy and fruitful direction to the assembly and analysis of demographic data. Of the various approaches that seem to be indicated three may be described.

(1) A multiscience approach is required. Because the aspects of human behavior with which the demographer deals are manifold, no one social science is adequate to cope with all of them. The student of population, therefore, must draw on all the social sciences and occasionally even on cognate sciences. The study of population problems probably is more suited than any other to become an area of inquiry within which adepts in social and cognate sciences, together with engineers and practitioners, may freely mingle and merge the relevant findings of their respective sciences. There has been much discussion of the advantages to be derived from interdisciplinary approaches to subject matter and attempts at the cross-fertilization of the theory and method of the several social sciences. The study of population, if properly organized, may provide social scientists from diverse fields with opportunity to test the validity of this supposition at both the training and the research level. Development of an adequate body of population theory would be greatly aided thereby, since it cannot be done outside a multiscience framework.

(2) The study of population, like that of many economic and sociological subjects, has suffered from overemphasis upon essentially static models and underemphasis upon long-run historical and developmental processes which so far have escaped the nets of model builders. Information respecting the course of demographic change in time remains limited. Long-period historical analyses might repair present gaps in information and, by envisaging the movement of population as but

[41] See P. A. Samuelson, "International Factor-Price Equalization," *Econ. Jour.*, June 1949, LVIII, 181–97; Jan Tinbergen, "The Equalization of Factor Prices between Free-Trade Areas," *Metroeconomica*, Jan. 1949, I, 39–47; Gottlieb, *op. cit.*; *Papers*, Vol. III, pp. 8–16; S. N. Prokopovicz, *L'industrialisation des pays agricoles et la structure de l'économie mondiale après la guerre* (Paris, 1946); W. A. Lewis, *Industrial Development in the Caribbean* (Port-of-Spain, 1950).

one aspect of the phenomenon of growth, development, and change, disclose how population movements and socio-economic movements interact, how population theories affect and are affected by the course of population growth, and so on. This approach, by placing diverse phenomena in broader perspective and by emphasizing the importance of qualitative change, would avert misleading interpretations of the sort that have sometimes impaired demographic research as presently carried on. Above all it would lead the student to conceive of the objects of analysis (e.g. soil, resources, culture, technology, occupation, job, tastes, welfare, etc.) in sufficiently dynamic terms. This approach, if it utilized relevant present-day theory and information (e.g. respecting blood-group evolution, chronological measurement, action theory, personality formation, impact of hunger and disease), would greatly augment our understanding of man's demographic past.

The historical approach is well suited also to the analysis of population policies, since these policies constitute a response to the concern, of groups within nations, over lowness of natality and inequality in the capacity of families to provide adequate support for their children. Under these policies, which are founded largely upon the assumption that deficiency of family income is primarily responsible for lowness of natality and inadequacy of child support, family income is supplemented by the state out of the general revenue and, in some instances, by employers out of funds assembled under the family wage system. This system itself calls for much further analysis, because of its impact upon the price and wage structure as well as upon the allocation of productive agents, and because of the challenging political, administrative, and cost-distributing problems that it entails. Further study of the noneconomic aspects of national population policies also is indicated.

(3) With increase in the economic, cultural, and political connections obtaining among peoples, and with the spread of industrial culture, the demographic state of any one people is likely to become more dependent upon that of many other peoples, and similarly with respect to intergroup relations within countries. The analysis of the growth of any one people, therefore, must take into account the demographic behavior of other peoples, just as the analysis of the growth of any one species of life must take into account that of other species. There is opportunity here for the extension and broadening of the kinds of analysis employed within the field of international trade and for the use of various categories (e.g. substitution, complementarity, analogues of income effects) stressed in economics.

Much remains to be done, of course, besides the construction of an adequate theoretical framework. At various places in this paper gaps in theory or information have been indicated. These need to be repaired. Other types of inquiry are also indicated. For example, the theory of the optimum needs to be restated in terms that take more fully into account the recent findings of welfare economics. Again, inasmuch as state policy is placing increasing emphasis upon the subsidization of population growth, the theoretical and practical implications of various methods need to be assessed. Yet again, the practical, financial, budgetary, and other implications of population aging for public and private-industrial policy need to be examined thoroughly. And again, the implications of population movements for the theory and practice of industrial development, now politically and academically popular, need to be examined with care.[42]

COMMENT
Frank W. Notestein

Spengler has performed a constructive task of scholarship in pulling a complex and voluminous literature into organized form. His treatment will be quite as useful in giving perspective to demographers as in introducing the interested economist to an unfamiliar literature. Obviously, no two individuals undertaking the assignment would give the same account, but there are few, if any, other students of population who control the whole range of the literature with the competence shown in this summary account. On important matters, this reviewer has nothing but praise.

A main difficulty lies in the nature of the assignment. Spengler's task is to review the current position of thought in the field. Even with complete freedom to choose and reject, there is a considerable pull toward an impartial treatment of conflicting accounts simply because there is not enough space to permit a critical appraisal of pertinent evidence. The result is an impression of equally acceptable alternative positions and a lack of coherence that would be much reduced had the assignment called for a fuller and systematic presentation of his own position.

---

[42] E.g., see J. J. Spengler, "Economic Factors in the Development of Densely Populated Areas," *Proc. Am. Phil. Soc.,* Feb. 1951, XCV, 20–53; *idem,* "Generalists *versus* Specialists in Social Science," *Am. Pol. Sci. Rev.,* June 1950, XLIV, 358–79; K. E. Boulding, *A Reconstruction of Economics* (New York, 1950), Ch. 1–2, 11.

In the final section, Spengler writes: "The study of population has been made up largely of a variety of descriptive and particularized inquiries, the findings of which have not been effectively bound together by a body of pertinent theory. The construction of such a theory remains the most important task now confronting students of population." If he had said "the construction of such theories," the reviewer would agree. The subsequent discussion suggests that by "a theory" Spengler does not mean a unified overarching theoretical structure. If he does, then the reviewer disagrees sharply. Indeed, there is considerable warrant for the view that much of the progress made during the past two or three decades is due to the fact that demographers at long last managed to rid themselves of preoccupation with the overarching theories that dominated so much of nineteenth-century work in the field. It seems likely that for the foreseeable future any such intellectual construct will have more the character of an ideology than of a means of submitting reason to the test of experience. Good theoretical work is urgently needed, but at least for a considerable time the need is for a relatively low level of generality from which empirically testable propositions seem most likely to come. The reviewer suspects that Spengler would agree.

Finally, it is difficult to read Spengler's account without being impressed anew with the fact that few questions either of "economic growth" or of social change can be pursued very far in complete abstraction one from the other, or from those of population change. Because all aspects of human behavior are closely tied into the causal nexus of population change, and because such change is relatively definite and simple to measure, the field of population studies, rather broadly defined, has the distinct advantage of yielding relatively numerous points at which social and economic reasoning can be factually checked.

COMMENT

Rupert B. Vance

No pen of mine is required to assure Joseph J. Spengler's colleagues that here is a remarkable account of the present state of population study—remarkable in its brevity, in its catholic range, and its critical acumen. I heartily endorse his call for the development of integrated theory of a high order to serve as a "binder" for demography's diverse and particularized findings. This I should like to discuss in the terms set by Spengler: namely, that (1) it requires a multiscience approach; (2) it must be dynamic rather than static; and (3) it must take account of demographic interrelations as between countries and groups within nations.[43]

It is the contention of this brief discussion that such theory is now emerging. In concise statement the transition from high levels of deaths and births to the new equilibrium at a low level of vital rates furnishes the population dynamics of the last 300 years in the Western world. This Demographic Revolution unfolds and diffuses in a manner reminiscent of the Industrial Revolution. Different countries are in different stages of this transition in terms of (1) time sequence in the West and (2) culture contacts and time stages as regards Oriental countries. Population status, age, and even sex composition, can then be viewed as stages in this long sequence. Our own low crude death rates and high proportions in the working force can be seen as a transitional stage in age distribution which may later level off.

The swarming of Europe is seen as due to the demographic gap which emerged as fertility remained high for a century or more after deaths took a sharp decline. Differential fertility then emerges in the initial stage of the great decline in birth rates. Movements in succeeding countries are to be judged by the extent of economic contacts and cultural diffusion as well as the resistance to change within each culture.

It is agreed, I take it, that the function of theory is not to give dogmatic answers to all the questions which may arise; rather it is to see that in the unfolding of science the "right" questions get asked in the "right" context. Such theories of the middle range, to use Robert K. Merton's phrase, also serve to set known facts in meaningful context. Demographic fluctuations anywhere can then be viewed as short-run movements against the background of a long-run demographic transition. Beginning and ending phases of this great transition, however, will remain unclear; the first because of inadequate data, the second because it always remains in the future.

Such theory—now in process of being filled in—fulfills Spengler's requirements 2 and 3 but not number 1. Interesting to note, it has been the contribution of population specialists and does not come out of the theoretical matrix of either biology, sociology, or economics. Possibly it is the multiscience orientation of demography which has delayed the development of coherent population theory. Biological explanations of

---

[43] See pp. 126–27.

changing vital rates have sometimes proved hasty and immature; sociologists have not yet developed an adequate theory of social change; economists and others have often felt obliged to limit their work to direct economic causation. With a theoretical scheme of its own, population study has attained a certain unity of attack. It must now, however, turn to the social sciences, and seek in the dynamics of culture, the economy, and changing society itself the primary conditions of its own dynamics. And as there emerge the new demographic conditions of mature age composition, new family size, emerging and then decreasing class differentials, lowered rates of natural dependents, social scientists have the task of seeing how these factors initiate change in the culture and the economy. Truly the work of analysis and theory has just begun if we accept the task of tracing major changes through nations and classes from Occident to Orient.

Of the three major categories around which population dynamics will continue to revolve, I have neglected migration. With the passing of its "golden age," international migration, as Spengler rightly indicates, now falls more in a political than an economic context. This leaves internal migration as the one area in which a free play of forces may allow full-bodied theory. It is desperately needed. No dynamic principle comparable to that furnished by the Demographic Revolution has yet been utilized. In the transition, in Colin Clark's terminology, from primary to secondary and tertiary economy it may be we will find the dynamic principle in the growth of urbanism. As the Pacific Coast is settled and the attainment of a "mature economic stage" halts the growth of cities, presumably the "golden age" of internal migration will also pass in the United States.

ECONOMICS

OF GROWTH

4

Moses Abramovitz

Unlike most of the topics treated in this and in the first
volume of the *Survey,* the problem of economic growth lacks any organized and generally known body of doctrine whose recent development
might furnish the subject of this essay. In spite of a continuing interest
which began very early, the question has remained on the periphery of
economics. But having said so much one must add that some individuals
and schools of the nineteenth and the early twentieth centuries gave
some aspects of the problem close attention. Adam Smith, Ricardo, and
J. S. Mill analyzed the effects of different kinds of progress on the distribution of incomes and speculated about the emergence of a stationary
state. The German historians, the American institutionalists, and Marx
and his followers studied the appearance and possible decline of capitalist institutions. Weber, Tawney, Veblen, Mitchell, and more recently,
Schumpeter explained the development of the mental attitudes that fostered the growth of science and its application to industry. The theory of
capital and saving, as developed by the classical and neoclassical economists, has obvious relevance to a theory of long-term economic change,
and so has all the work on population theory and the long-run supply
curve of labor. Orthodox economics has also furnished us with theories
of diminishing and increasing returns that clearly have their place in any
general explanation of economic growth. Meanwhile, economic history
generally, and statistical work on secular trends in particular, has furnished some of the information so badly needed. Yet it is clear that these
various strands of work are not yet organized into a useful hypothesis
providing a consistent explanation of the different rates of growth characterizing given economies in different periods, different contempora-
neous economies with similar institutional framework, or economies

132

with different institutions at the same or different times. Nor have we gone far in developing detailed models of the process of growth.

Modern work on the economics of growth has been fragmentary. It deals with many varied questions. The studies have often been undertaken under the stimulus of other interests and, while their general relevance to economic growth is clear, their precise significance has not been developed. Keynesian stagnation theory is an example. It is designed to explain chronic unemployment. Presumably the forces it studies are significant for long-term growth, but their connection with secular trends in output is not immediately apparent. Other work concerns changes in the forms or patterns of economic life that accompany growth, but again the role that these changing patterns play in furthering or retarding the pace of economic advance is not clear. A good example is the hypothesis advanced by Colin Clark and others about the changing industrial composition of employment which accompanies economic development.

These characteristics of contemporary studies raise a serious problem for this essay. To attempt to deal with current literature as one finds it would imply a review of numerous studies each of which bears— often in obscure fashion—only on some special aspect of the problem. Space would prohibit any comprehensive treatment of so many heterogeneous topics and, at the same time, the general outlines of the theory of growth would not be developed. To meet this difficulty, the present writer has tried to work on a different plan, namely, to define the boundaries and describe the general content of the economics of growth and to notice current work as it bears on the development of this outline. This plan has required rather more extensive attention to older literature and rather less attention to current work than the purpose of this volume would normally make desirable. But the theory of growth is an underdeveloped area in economics. It is more important to map the chief features of the country than to concentrate on detailed descriptions of many small quadrants which together would cover but a fraction of the terrain.

Even within this general plan, however, satisfactory treatment of the entire subject proved impossible within the space available. In consequence, the essay has been divided into three parts. Part I presents an extremely condensed description of the general content of the economics of growth with occasional references to relevant literature. Part II presents a fairly full treatment of one aspect of the subject, namely, capital formation and its relation to economic growth. Part III contains some brief remarks about problems of research.

I. THE SCOPE AND CONTENT OF THE ECONOMICS OF GROWTH

A. Character of Growth Theory

The theory of economic growth has to do with the pace of sustained change in the output of economic communities measured in the aggregate, or per head of the population, or per member of the labor force, the particular variant depending on the problem in view.[1] The crucial aspects of this definition are its references to output and to sustained or long-term change. Our interest in economic growth stems from, and is relevant to, our interest in long-term changes in economic welfare. But the two subjects are not equivalent.[2]

Theories of economic growth can be constructed at various levels, all of which are useful, but which become increasingly significant the more complex and far-reaching the set of factors brought under active study. This can be illustrated if we begin with the conventional statement that the level of output at any given time is determined by the supply of resources (labor, "land," capital), the state of the arts, the organization of markets, the legal framework of economic life, and the psychological attributes of the population. Call these the *immediate determinants* of output. We can then distinguish the following levels of analysis:

Level 1. Assume that all except some one of the immediate determinants remain unchanged and examine the effects on output of some specified secular changes in the variable factor.

Level 2. Assume that two or more of the determinants are subject to secular changes of specified kinds and examine the effects on output, the other factors being assumed constant.[3] This can be varied and extended up to the point at which all determinants are assumed to change in ways specified by assumption.

Level 3. Treat the immediate determinants as variables whose movements are to be explained rather than assumed. The immediate determinants, usually treated as data by economists, now become true de-

---

[1] Compare the discussions by Simon Kuznets, J. J. Spengler, E. M. Hoover and J. L. Fisher and by J. M. Clark in *Problems in the Study of Economic Growth,* Nat. Bur. Econ. Res. (New York, July 1949; mimeographed).

[2] See the contribution by Clark cited above.

[3] This represents the level of analysis attempted by B. S. Keirstead, *The Theory of Economic Change* (Toronto, 1948).

pendent variables, and the investigation necessarily reaches into regions normally assigned to other disciplines, particularly the other social sciences.

Level 4. Theories on the first two levels are unsatisfactory to explain the observed growth of economic communities because they do not deal with the causes of the immediate determinants. The third level is unsatisfactory because it does not deal with the significance of changes in these factors. The fourth level is necessarily a combination of the first three and brings us to the point at which we obtain theories of observed changes in output at a satisfactory level of understanding.

Hypotheses at this level would presumably be able to explain observed differences in rates of growth among communities and also differences in the growth of a single community over time. These theories can also be more or less general. They may limit themselves to explaining differences between countries which differ markedly in only one particular, say those between "old" and "new" countries which may be distinguished chiefly by the ratios of land and capital per head of the population. Or the theories may go further and try to explain more complex cases, say differences between "progressive" and "backward" areas which differ partly in terms of factor supply and partly in terms of institutional and social organization.[4] Or conceivably the theories might be completely general and try to grapple with observed differences among all countries. It goes without saying that the fewer the respects in which the communities resemble each other, the more difficult the task.

B. Central Questions in the Theory of Growth

While work on the economics of growth can be usefully done on all the levels suggested above, the content of the problem can be envisaged most easily by centering attention initially on the factors identified above as the immediate determinants of the level of output. The theory of growth is then a matter of explaining long-term changes in these factors, on the one side, and the influence of such changes upon output on the other.[5]

---

[4] See P. A. Baran, "On the Political Economy of Backwardness," *Man. School Econ. Soc. Stud.,* Jan. 1952, XX, 66–84.

[5] The reader should compare the present outline with somewhat similar, though more condensed, lists of factors influencing the level of output prepared by J. J. Spengler, "Theories of Socio-Economic Growth," *Problems in the Study of Economic Growth,* p. 53; *idem,* "Economic Factors in the Development of Densely Populated Areas," *Proc. Am. Phil. Soc.,* Feb. 1951, XCV, 21–25; *idem,* "The Population Obstacle to Economic Betterment," *Am. Econ. Rev., Proc.,* May 1951, XLI, 344–46.

1. *The Supplies of the Factors.* The explanation of changes in factor supply is usually treated in connection with their long-term supply schedules. So far as concerns labor, the determinants are extremely complex. They include both the causes of population growth and the causes of change in the proportion of the population included in the labor force. The latter turns on numerous factors, including the age composition of the population, the level of income, the degree of urbanization and the character of family organization in its bearing on family responsibility for the young, the aged, and the infirm. Labor force is also influenced by social attitudes toward work by women, children, and minority groups, by educational requirements, standards, and opportunities, and by various kinds of government intervention, including the regulation of hours and working conditions, taxation, and social security arrangements. Finally, there is the large subject of union organization.[6]

Changes in the supply of land are often supposed to be nonexistent by definition; apparent changes are attributed to some form of human action—to invention and increase of knowledge generally, to enterprise, or to changes in the composition of demand—and are, therefore, classified under capital accumulation (or consumption). Even in this restricted view, however, there are real changes in the land supply of a community to be taken into account. These may result from governmental acts like conquest, seizure, or purchase or from regulations reserving land for conservation or opening a public domain to exploitation. There may also be changes in the supply of privately held land put to productive use. These may occur if there are changes in the value schemes of land owners with respect to the use of their land for commercial *versus* noncommercial use. There may be changes in the distribution of land among social classes as a result of land reform laws or otherwise, and this may affect land use significantly. Finally, land use may be affected by taxation or by government regulation.

More broadly conceived, the effective supply of land is no mere matter of area, but a value compounded of fertility, mineral content, climate, topography, and all the factors influencing accessibility. It is,

---

[6] Apart from population problems, considered elsewhere in this volume, the leading recent references of a general sort on the long-term supply of labor are: P. H. Douglas, *Theory of Wages* (New York, 1934), Pt. 3; C. D. Long, *Labor Force, Income and Employment* (New York, forthcoming). A highly interesting and important study of the influence of cultural values and social organization upon the size and capabilities of the labor force is W. E. Moore, *Industrialization and Labor* (Ithaca and New York, 1951). See also, Pei-Kang Chang, *Agriculture and Industrialization* (Cambridge, Mass., 1949), Ch. 2, 5.

therefore, highly sensitive to technological progress which affects the economic significance of all these qualities. It is a matter of choice whether the effects of technology on the supply of land are treated as an aspect of technological progress or of changing land supply. In either event, the theoretical work which grapples with the question is the recently developed dynamic location theory. Starting from the static theory of location, with its analysis of the influence of transport costs, the newer work goes on to consider the effect of technological change of specified kinds upon the spatial distribution of new activity and the spatial redistribution of old. The upshot is a body of ideas which helps to make clear the contribution of natural resources and location to the relative rates of progress of economic communities. A good example is the work of W. H. Dean, Jr.[7] who extends the older theory of location to explain a tendency observed during the last two centuries for centers of economic activity to shift from surplus food areas to places rich in sources of power and industrial raw materials.

The forces affecting the supply of capital is the subject of the bulk of the present essay, and the scope of the subject is indicated in Part II.

As to the influence of changes in factor supply on economic growth, this raises two questions. The first is the process by which changes in supply are transformed into changes in the quantities of the factors actually employed. Traditional economic theory reduced this to a matter of suitable changes in relative prices which were assumed to bring into employment as much of each factor as was satisfied by the marginal rate of real return it could produce. Keynesian theory, however, has argued that the process may be frustrated indefinitely either by price rigidities, by adverse expectations, or by inability of workers to affect their real wage rates.[8] More recent writings have revealed the theoretical adequacy of relative price changes to produce full employment, but have stressed the probable sluggishness of the process.[9] Keynesian and post-Keynesian writing has, therefore, tended to favor mild

---

[7] *The Theory of Geographic Location of Economic Activities* (Ann Arbor, 1938).

[8] J. M. Keynes, *The General Theory of Employment Interest and Money* (New York, 1936), Ch. 19; Oscar Lange, *Price Flexibility and Employment* (Bloomfield, 1944).

[9] A. C. Pigou, "The Classical Stationary State," *Econ. Jour.,* Dec. 1943, LIII, 343–51; *idem,* "Economic Progress in a Stable Environment," *Economica,* Aug. 1947, XIV, 180–90; Don Patinkin, "Price Flexibility and Full Employment," *Am. Econ. Rev.,* Sept. 1948, XXXVIII, 543–64; Franco Modigliani, "Liquidity Preference and the Theory of Interest and Money," *Econometrica,* Jan. 1944, XII, 45–88. The last three of these four articles are also in *Readings in Monetary Theory,* F. A. Lutz and L. W. Mints, ed. (Philadelphia, 1951), pp. 186–283.

price inflation as a condition facilitating the absorption of additional factor supplies. Realistic studies of the process of factor absorption are still lacking.

The second question concerns the effects of changes in the quantities of the factors actually employed. This is nothing but the hoary subject of the laws of return. Nothing need be said about it here, so far as the theory of the subject is concerned, but it is to be noted that empirical work has now begun and that more is needed.[10]

2. *Psychological and Other Qualitative Attributes of the Population.* In part, these attributes have already been raised implicitly under other headings, for example, under the determinants of labor supply. In general, they are involved in and underlie almost every economic relation. More directly than do other topics in this outline, they indicate the extent to which an understanding of economic growth rests on research outside the usual fields of economic investigation. The range of topics may be suggested by illustration.

First, the effective supply of labor is a matter not only of the numbers but also of the productivity of the labor force so far as that turns on the qualities of the workers themselves. And productivity depends on strength and health,[11] and on the social valuation assigned to income, work, and reliability. It is raised by a tradition of familiarity with mechanical operations and by habituation to cooperative activity.[12] Changes in productivity affect the growth of output directly and, by influencing its level, also help determine the volume of surplus income and, therefore, the rate of capital formation.

A second set of social-psychological traits governs the pace at which new techniques are adopted and exploited. These are the traits of mobility, adaptability, and tolerance for change. They have often been associated with environmental factors controlling exposure to new experiences like access to the sea, with recent historical experience like the influence of the frontier in new countries or of a heterogeneous popu-

---

[10] Cf. Douglas, *op. cit.,* Pt. 2; Colin Clark, *The Conditions of Economic Progress* (London, 2nd ed., 1951), Ch. 11; also a considerable amount of periodical literature developing and criticizing the work of Douglas and Clark. In addition, there is the important development of input-output analysis proceeding under the leadership of W. W. Leontief.

[11] Spengler estimates that the potential productivity of the population of underdeveloped countries would rise some 20–30 per cent if the age composition and state of health of their peoples could be "Westernized." Cf. "The Population Obstacle to Economic Betterment," *loc. cit.,* p. 344.

[12] Cf. Moore, *op. cit.,* pp. 44–47.

lation built up by immigration,[13] and with more strictly cultural factors in which religion often figures prominently.[14]

The acceptability of the new is a question of the psychic traits of the population at large. The introduction of the new, however, depends heavily on the efforts of a few who must possess a more active disposition. Enterprise, or leadership, directed to industry, seems to be the key phrase. Its sources are explored at some length in Part II.

Besides the traits that underlie a community's effectiveness as producer, and as innovator and exploiter of change, its traits as a consuming group affect growth in numerous ways. There is first the degree of its tolerance for standardized consumption in its bearing on the economics of scale and the scope for the use of capital equipment. From the same point of view, there is the relation between changes in income levels and the kind of goods demanded. Engel's Law and similar correlations between income per capita and the composition of demand connect with our problem at this point. Next, there is the fact that leisure is a form of consumption (as well as a condition for the enjoyment of goods), and the demand for leisure affects production in the most direct fashion. Again, emulation and competition in consumption influence the demand for income and, therefore, the effort devoted to production and the risks that people will accept in industry. Consumption, further, may be of a type that develops the strength, skills, and efficiency of a people, or it may be dissipative and deteriorating in its effects. Finally, there is consumption as the opponent of saving.

3. *Industrial, Commercial and Financial Organization.* Forms of organization affect growth in at least three important ways: through their influence on investment and improvement, on saving, and on finance. As to investment and improvement, there is, first, the scale and internal organization of firms which may favor or discourage the selection of enterprising leaders,[15] which may or may not provide them with scope and staff aid appropriate to their talents, and which may facilitate or hamper the efficient exercise of initiative at all levels.[16] There is, secondly, the question of market organization, the relation between monopoly power and the incentives to invest capital and to introduce new

[13] Cf. H. B. Parkes, *The American Experience* (New York, 1947).

[14] Cf. R. B. Perry, *Characteristically American* (New York, 1949).

[15] Cf. J. A. Schumpeter, "The Instability of Capitalism," *Econ. Jour.*, Sept. 1928, XXVIII, 361–86.

[16] Cf. C. A. Barnard, *The Functions of the Executive* (Cambridge, Mass., 1938); A. D. H. Kaplan, "The Influence of Size of Firms on the Functioning of the Economy," *Am. Econ. Rev., Proc.*, May 1950, XL, 74–84.

methods and products. Thirdly, there is the extent and character of labor organization in its bearing on capital formation and innovation.[17]

Organization influences saving and, therefore, capital formation through the influence of monopoly power on the distribution of income between wage earners and profit makers.[18] It also makes itself felt because of the importance of retained earnings as a source of savings when business is organized in large corporations.[19] Organization, finally, affects the types of assets available to potential savers and, therefore, the incentive to save. The essential thing, in this connection, is that the variety of modern business and financial organizations produces many kinds of assets in the form of securities the ownership of which, in different degrees, involves little or no supervision, limits risk, provides liquidity, satisfies other needs of savers besides safety and return (for example, insurance, annuities), and still furnishes a significant yield.

Between opportunities to invest and the supply of saving lie the functions of the financial sector. Upon the efficiency and variety of financial organization depends the cheapness with which business is able to raise capital and the rate of real return actually obtainable by savers. It, therefore, plays a vital role in capital formation in ways further developed in Part II.

4. *The Legal and Political Framework of Economic Life.* This is itself a huge subject and it would be impossible within a page or two to catalogue the many ways in which it probably bears on growth, let alone to discuss its bearing. The topics mentioned below can only be illustrative.

(*a*) The laws of property and contract: The essential questions here are: What may a man do with his property; what must he do by virtue of his property? What may others do to his property? In what activities may he engage? What agreements may he make? What claims can be enforced, and to what extent? With specific reference to the factors determining growth, this heading covers such matters as: (1) laws affecting the establishment and exploitation of monopolies; (2) laws

---

[17] A representative modern reference is L. G. Reynolds, *Labor Economics and Labor Relations* (New York, 1944), Ch. 10.

[18] See Michael Kalecki, *Essays in the Theory of Economic Fluctuations* (London, 1939), pp. 13–41. This is merely a matter of definition. Under perfect competition, profits would tend to disappear. It leaves open the question of what determines monopoly power and how it is exercised under different conditions and to what extent union organization can be a counterweight. See William Fellner, *Competition Among the Few* (New York, 1949).

[19] See S. S. Kuznets, *National Income and Its Composition* (New York, 1941), Ch. 4.

controlling land development: zoning, exploitation and conservation of minerals and forests, water rights; (3) debts and bankruptcy.

(b) Economic associations: the permitted areas of operation, powers, privileges and limitations of corporations, banks, labor unions, cooperatives, securities exchanges, investment trusts, etc.

(c) Indirect regulation of specific activities: the use of taxes, tariffs, subsidies, fees, etc. to discourage certain activities and to encourage others.

(d) Indirect regulation of general economic activity: the use of taxes and the laws of inheritance to control the distribution of income and wealth.

(e) Direct provision of economic facilities by public action: it is well known that private action will not exploit opportunities to increase output in certain classes of cases, or at least will not exploit such opportunities fully. The principal cases are those in which most or all of the benefits yielded by investment are difficult to appropriate and sell privately (e.g. flood control, education), those in which universal or nearly universal use is required if benefit is to be obtained (e.g. many public health facilities and controls), and those in which initial cost is heavy and returns long deferred and uncertain (e.g. railroads, harbor and power developments). These investment opportunities are among the most important open to a community; and its progress, therefore, depends on the extent to which it provides for such exploitation by direct public action.

5. *Discovery and Exploitation of Knowledge.* While it is clear enough in a general way how technical improvement leads to increases in output, and while we may be confident that, directly and indirectly, a very large share, if not the bulk, of the increase in output is to be attributed to advances in knowledge, measurement of the relation between changes in the stock of knowledge and the pace of economic growth has so far proved impossible. The chief difficulty is that no useful measures of the stock of knowledge or its changes have yet been contrived. And while interesting new attempts to measure production functions and their changes are now in progress, these have yet to come to fruition.[20] These difficulties of measurement will certainly hinder the

[20] See the series of papers submitted to the Conference on Quantitative Description of Technological Change sponsored by the Social Science Research Council, April 6–8, 1951, mimeographed. Also Anne P. Gross, "Textile Production Functions, Equipment Requirements, and Technological Change," *Econometrica,* July 1950, XVIII, 305–06; Boris Stern, "Mechanical Changes in the Cotton-Textile Industry, 1910–36," *Mo. Lab. Rev.,* Aug. 1937, XLV, 316–41.

process of increasing our understanding not only of the effects of technological advance on growth, but also of the factors making for an increase in knowledge and its economic application.

The general subject of technological change in its bearing on output growth requires study on at least two main levels: the discovery of knowledge, and its exploitation. The latter stages of the process of discovery interlace closely with the early stages of the process of commercial exploitation. This was less true some decades ago when the independent inventor still flourished and engineering was still in its infancy as a profession. But with the development of the industrial research departments of corporations, and of industry- and government-sponsored research, almost all engineering work and a considerable portion of applied scientific work is undertaken only in conjunction with the deliberate entrepreneurial decision that some new product or process can, in fact, be developed and that the various business problems involved—finance, labor, distribution—can also be satisfactorily overcome.[21]

The difficulties of commercial exploitation are at their height when a product is utterly new. This is Schumpeter's problem of innovation. After its first introduction there ensues a process of diffusion in which the new product or process is substituted for the old with increasing facility as experience is gained and knowledge of the new art becomes widespread. But there is presumably no sharp break. Innovation, however bold and pathbreaking, draws on some past experience, and there is no investment utterly devoid of novel elements. So enterprise, as well as routine calculation of differential advantages, is involved at all levels, though in different degree.

We are interested in the influences that determine the pace of all these processes, the advance of fundamental knowledge, the translation of fundamental knowledge into commercial applications, and the diffusion of such applications.[22] The factors involved include cultural char-

---

[21] W. R. Maclaurin, "The Process of Technological Innovation: The Launching of a New Scientific Industry," *Am. Econ. Rev.,* Mar. 1950, XL, 90–112; *idem, Invention and Innovation in the Radio Industry* (New York, 1949).

[22] There is, of course, much good material on the first introduction of mechanical devices and other technical advances. Cf. A. P. Usher, *History of Mechanical Inventions* (New York, 1929). But the antecedent process, as well as the factors determining the pace of diffusion remain mysterious. Cf. Yale Brozen, "Invention, Innovation, and Diffusion," paper submitted to the Conference on Quantitative Description of Technological Change, *op. cit.* Brozen, Maclaurin, *op. cit.,* and Gilfillan all emphasize the long lag, often amounting to a century or more, between an advance in fundamental knowledge and successful commercial application based on it. The meaning of these lags is not clear since

acteristics like the influence of rationality as a thought pattern, the status of science as an occupation, the place of material progress as a social and individual goal, the importance of pecuniary standards, especially in their bearing on the size, quality, and vigor of the entrepreneurial class, the mobility of the population among occupations and places, and its tolerance for novel methods and products.

Organizational and institutional arrangements form a second group of causes. These include the quantity and kind of government support for education, especially scientific education, and for research; the legal protections afforded to the interests of inventors through patent systems and otherwise; and the effects of taxes as incentives and disincentives to investment in the discovery and application of technology. They also include the organization and size of firms and the character of competition insofar as these affect the funds devoted by private firms to research and development and the incentives to introduce and exploit new methods and products. Union controls are still another institutional factor of importance.

Finally, the outcome is influenced by more narrowly economic causes. The size of the market is important since it limits the field of application of a discovery. The abundance of saving and the cheapness of finance, particularly for new firms, influence the pace of exploitation and, therefore, the pressure that is brought to bear on established firms to be technically progressive. The character and quantity of resources affects the relative economy of capital-using, land-using, and labor-using methods and, therefore, the direction if not the pace of technical advance. And the amount of such capital and its degree of obsolescence clearly influence the profitability of exploiting new goods and ways of making them.

This list of factors is only illustrative of the range of questions that are raised. It seems plausible to think that cultural factors will be most significant at the level of fundamental discovery and that the more narrowly economic causes become increasingly dominant as we approach the level of routine exploitation. But much more research will be needed before it will be possible to develop a trustworthy list of conditioning

---

our most ancient knowledge is still being applied in new inventions. But their examples emphasize both the need to clarify the factors that account for the pace with which knowledge is gained and turned to practical use, as well as the conundrums of measurement which are involved. See S. C. Gilfillan, *Sociology of Invention* (Chicago, 1935), and *idem,* "The Lag between Invention and Application, with Emphasis on Prediction of Technical Change," submitted to Conference cited above.

factors, to say nothing of assigning them proper weights at the various stages of the process of scientific discovery and application.

It is obvious that the various topics identified above as involved in the economics of growth are interrelated in a most complex fashion, which is only inadequately suggested by the discussion itself. But further illustration of the extent and importance of the interconnectedness of the several parts of the subject is furnished by Part II of the present paper, which deals with capital formation in its bearing on economic growth.

C. Mechanism and Patterns of Growth

A serious limitation of the discussion above is that it directs attention to the basic determinants of growth, but it leaves in the background or neglects entirely many portions of the subject concerned with the mechanism through which the basic factors operate and with the economic forms that growth takes. Again, there is space only to mention a very few topics.

1. *Business Fluctuations and Economic Growth.* Many scholars, notably Schumpeter,[23] have contended that business fluctuations with several distinctive periods are a necessary concomitant of growth. Their argument stresses either the effects of the uneven action of growth factors or the tendency of capitalist economies to magnify and transform slight changes in rates of growth into substantial expansions and contractions of activity. In addition to further confirmation of these ideas, there remain questions about the price in terms of growth which these fluctuations exact and about the probable influence of economic stabilization upon growth.

2. *Growth in Aggregate Production and the Changing Composition of Output.* This reveals itself in many ways. Colin Clark has emphasized the tendency for employment to shift from "primary" to "secondary" to "tertiary" industries as an economy grows.[24] Arthur F. Burns has established a marked tendency toward retardation in the growth of individual industries while progress in total output is unabated.[25] Com-

---

[23] *Business Cycles* (New York, 1939). See also D. McC. Wright, *Economics of Disturbance* (New York, 1947), the literature centering about the work of Harrod and Domar (cited p. 170), and among earlier writings, D. H. Robertson, *Banking Policy and the Price Level* (London, 1926), and J. M. Clark, *Strategic Factors in Business Cycles* (New York, 1934).

[24] *Op. cit.,* Ch. 9.

[25] *Production Trends in the United States since 1870* (New York, 1934).

position of output must be changing. Folke Hilgerdt found that the character of the goods sold in foreign trade by advanced countries tended to exhibit increasing refinement and elaboration as they and their trading partners advanced.[26] In part, these phenomena are to be attributed to the well-known tendency for the composition of consumer demand to shift as per capita income rises.[27] In part they are presumably connected with the introduction of new products and processes and their competition with the old. As for the influence of these changes in output structure on rates of growth, this connects on one side with the significance of technological improvement, for such improvement is hardly conceivable without economies in the use of some old materials, combined with more widespread consumption of other old materials and with the introduction of some new ones. From another point of view, the changing patterns bear on incentives to effort and investment. If the composition of output could not change, or if new products were not introduced, the desire for additional consumption and income and, therefore, the stimulus to economic activity would be weaker.

3. *Trends in Saving-Income Ratios in Their Relation to Growth.* The *a priori* expectation that the proportion of aggregate income saved would tend to increase as per capita incomes rose has been belied by observation. Relative constancy or decline in the ratio of saving to income seems to be the long-run rule for the few countries for which data are available. This tendency and the possible circumstances back of it will be further discussed.[28] It is clear that any such circumstances as tend to stimulate consumption affect the need for income and, therefore, the incentives to work, save and invest. The trend of consumption also influences opportunities for investment and bears on the argument that as communities become richer they tend to stagnate because of a surfeit of saving.

These and similar relations are clearly part and parcel of the mechanism of economic growth conceived of as a process of cumulative change. They are relations which would hardly be discovered in the absence of deliberate observation, and our understanding of the determinants of growth will surely be extended by further study along these

---

[26] *Industrialization and World Trade* (Geneva, 1945); also Henry Frankel, "The Industrialization of Agricultural Countries," *Econ. Jour.,* June–Sept. 1943, LIII, 188–201.

[27] Colin Clark, *op. cit.,* Ch. 8; National Resources Committee, *Consumer Expenditures in the United States* (Washington, 1939).

[28] *Infra,* pp. 149–50.

lines. Moreover, the multiplication and verification of such relations probably furnish the most fruitful opportunities for empirical work on growth in the immediate future.

II. CAPITAL FORMATION AS A CAUSE OF ECONOMIC GROWTH

This part is an attempt to suggest the scope and present state of the theory of economic growth by more intensive treatment of a single growth factor, capital formation. It is probably safe to say that only the discovery and exploitation of new knowledge rivals capital formation as a cause of economic progress. The two factors are indeed closely related. Knowledge is often characterized as the most important element in the community's stock of capital. And, insofar as new applied knowledge results from the deliberate devotion of resources to its discovery and use, the stock of knowledge is increased by a process identical with that which produces an increase in the stock of material equipment. Conversely, the actual exploitation of new knowledge virtually always involves some gross investment and, it seems probable, usually requires some net addition to the stock of capital. To some, this has justified a virtual merger of the two factors. In this essay, however, we distinguish them by making capital formation refer only to quantitative changes in the stock of instruments of production. We discuss the subject under four heads. The first three are considered from the point of view of their bearing on the level of capital formation at a given time. They are: first, saving; second, the productivity of capital; and third, the functions of finance. The fourth topic is the progress of capital formation over time.

The treatment of these subjects is limited to the conditions of countries in which governmental direction of activity is not the dominant feature of economic organization. It is especially relevant, therefore, to capitalistic economies at higher or lower levels of development, but not to Soviet Russia or to other countries in which major sectors of economic life have been subjected to control by governmental decision.

A. The Role of Saving

1. *The Influence of Saving on Capital Formation.* In the neoclassical view, an increase in the supply of saving stimulates capital accumulation by causing the rate of interest to fall. Full employment being the rule, moreover, the willingness to save leads to an effective release

of scarce resources without which the production of capital goods could not take place. It follows that capital formation at any given time varies directly with the ability and willingness to save. An increase in thrift was taken to be a universally reliable prescription for progress.

The nub of this argument is the idea that consuming and investing are exhaustive alternative uses of income. The nub of the modern view is the Keynesian idea that there is a third way to dispose of income, namely, hoarding (or adding to cash balances, or increasing liquidity). But if hoarding is a third means of disposing of income, it is no longer clear that an increase in the supply of saving will be beneficial to investment. If funds are diverted from consumption, they may be hoarded rather than invested. And conversely, since, in Keynes' view, there may be chronic unemployment, the resources exist for raising the level of capital formation without trenching further on consumption.

The logic of Keynes' view has been ably exposed by J. R. Hicks.[29] The demand for money to be hoarded (Keynes' "speculative demand") varies with the rate of interest. There is a high range of interest rates in which the speculative demand is zero. The returns from assets are too attractive to be foregone, particularly since interest rates are likely to be lower in the future. In this range, more thrift, the traditional prescription for progress, is appropriate. This is Hicks' Classical Case.

Next comes an intermediate range of interest rates in which the quantity of money people desire to hoard varies inversely with the rate of interest. If the willingness to save increases, consumption and income decline, and the released funds press for absorption in speculative balances. Hence interest rates decline and investment increases. But this rise in capital formation may be dearly bought. If speculative demand is elastic, or if the demand for new capital equipment is inelastic with respect to interest rates, the drop in income required to produce a unit rise of investment may be large. If thrift does not weaken the inducement to invest, it is still a prescription for growth, but it is costly medicine.

Finally, there is a minimum level of interest rates at which the speculative demand for money becomes indefinitely elastic. The yield of securities is too low to attract additional purchasers. More saving is wasteful or worse. It causes income to fall, but it leaves interest rates

---

[29] "Mr. Keynes and the 'Classics'; A Suggested Interpretation," *Econometrica*, Apr. 1937, V, 147–59; also in *Readings in the Theory of Income Distribution*, William Fellner and B. F. Haley, ed. (Philadelphia, 1946), pp. 461–76. Cf. Keynes, *op. cit.,* Ch. 15.

and, therefore, investment unaffected. This is Hicks' Keynesian Case.[30]

It might seem, then, that on Keynesian reasoning, thrift is beneficial to growth over the presumably wide range of situations in which rates of interest stand above the minimum. But this was not Keynes' view, for the reduction in interest rates that an increased propensity to save effects is purchased only at the expense of a reduction in income. And a reduction in income weakens the inducement to invest, a connection neglected above. If we recognize it, then lower interest rates obtained by greater thrift may not promote capital formation.[31] In Keynes' judgment they would not. So the practical conclusions from the Keynesian argument are that saving promotes capital formation in conditions of full employment or, short of full employment, when the net speculative demand for money is zero. In other conditions, saving is probably, but not necessarily, a depressant to investment.[32]

Like so much of Keynes' work, this hypothesis is plausible for the short run and in the context of business cycles. It is less clearly applicable in the construction of a theory of secular growth. In the short run, thrift reduces money and real income and may (in Keynes' judgment, probably will) reduce investment. If prices are flexible in the long run, however, as seems plausible, the eventual result should be the attainment of full employment combined with a high propensity to save—a combination that obviously yields larger real saving than full employment based on high consumption.[33]

This reasoning indicates that Keynes may be wrong, but it does not make the traditional view right. Business cycles are short-run events, but one succeeds another; they are always with us. So the question is whether a community that saves and invests a great deal at the peak of cyclical prosperity is in greater danger of being thrown into depression than an economy whose prosperities are based more largely on consumption demand. And if so, does the average investment performance of an economy with a high propensity to save tend to be worse than that of an economy with a low propensity to save? Are the same answers ap-

---

[30] This seems a somewhat misleading identification. Keynes based his argument as much on the costliness of thrift in the intermediate range as on its utter wastefulness when interest rates are at rock bottom.

[31] The connection has been well developed by Oscar Lange, "The Rate of Interest and the Optimum Propensity to Consume," *Economica*, Feb. 1938, V, 12–32; also in *Readings in Business Cycle Theory*, Gottfried Haberler, ed. (Philadelphia, 1944).

[32] Keynes, *op. cit.*, Ch. 24. Also A. P. Lerner, *The Economics of Employment* (New York, 1951), Ch. 17.

[33] Cf. Patinkin, *op. cit.;* Modigliani, *op. cit.*

propriate for the nineteenth century as in contemporary conditions? For industrial and agricultural economies? Keynesian theory has helped to clarify the role of saving, but neither Keynesian nor traditional economics has yet grappled successfully with the question of the long-term significance of thrift in an environment of business fluctuation.

2. *The Determinants of the Supply of Saving.* Whatever the precise significance of the supply of saving, it obviously has an important part to play in capital formation, and we should understand the factors that control it. But our understanding is still lamentably deficient.

Our most secure theory concerns the relation between income and saving. Marshall's dictum was that saving per capita varies directly with per capita income: not, however, with total income, but with the "excess of income over necessary expenses."[34] From this the easy inference was drawn that, as per capita income increases, savings rise more than proportionately. This proposition was long accepted for its *a priori* plausibility. But serious doubt was cast on it by the publication of S. S. Kuznets' estimates for the United States since 1869.[35] In spite of an enormous rise in *per capita* income, the ratio of saving to net national income has remained virtually constant.[36] Less reliable figures of similar import for Canada and Sweden were published by Modigliani.[37]

The reasons for this breakdown of theoretical expectations are still far from clear. Arthur Smithies has advanced the view that the savings function has been dropping secularly as a result of the trend toward urbanization and more equal distribution of income.[38] Smithies and Modigliani[39] have argued that increments to income are absorbed by expenditures on new types of products. Duesenberry[40] has contended that these factors are inadequate to account for the failure of the saving-

---

[34] *Principles of Economics* (London, 1890; 8th ed., 1920), p. 229.

[35] *National Product since 1869* (New York, 1946), Pt. 2.

[36] Kuznets, indeed, presents evidence that the savings ratio for individuals has tended to fall. See his "Proportion of Capital Formation to National Product," *Am. Econ. Rev., Proc.,* May 1952, XLII, 519–24.

[37] "Fluctuations in the Saving-Income Ratio: A Problem in Forecasting," Conference on Research in Income and Wealth, *Studies in Income and Wealth,* Vol. XI (New York, 1949), pp. 371–440.

[38] "Forecasting Postwar Demand," *Econometrica,* Jan. 1945, XIII, 1–14.

[39] "Fluctuations in the Saving-Income Ratio," *loc. cit.,* pp. 384–85.

[40] James Duesenberry, *Income, Saving and the Theory of Consumer Behavior* (Cambridge, Mass., 1949). Very similar equations consolidating the trend and cyclical relations between income and saving were independently developed by Modigliani and Duesenberry.

income ratio to rise and has argued that an individual's propensity to consume is heavily influenced by a disposition toward competitive emulation. His saving-income ratio is, therefore, related primarily to his *rank* in the income scale rather than to the absolute level of his income. If the relative inequality of income remains stable, Duesenberry's theory is consistent with the facts about the trend of the saving-income ratio. But other explanations are possible, and some independent test of the importance of emulative drives is still necessary.[41]

Another widely accepted inference from the supposed dependence of saving on excess income is the idea that the saving-income ratio tends to rise as the distribution of income becomes more unequal. This proposition is still untested by comparisons among countries or over time. It is based on the plausible assumption that "necessary expenses" do not rise as fast as individual income. And as between income classes, this seems to be true. One of the clearest results of studies of the disposition of income by members of different income groups is that the proportion devoted to saving increases as one moves from lower to higher income classes. What is doubtful for the community as a whole over time is clearly sound as among the members of a community at a given time.[42]

At least it is true for the United States and for such highly developed countries as have produced the necessary statistics. Would it be true for all South American countries? Would it have been true for Russia, Poland and the Balkans under their old regimes? It may be true for the United States because our population is relatively homogeneous as between income classes, the members of which share a common set of values and aspirations and differ mostly in their incomes. It may not be true if the highest income groups are composed of a nobility and squirearchy inheriting a noncommercial scheme of values which emphasizes the virtues of lavish hospitality, display, and extravagance, while thrift resides in a less wealthy business and professional class.

Considerations of this sort presumably gave rise to the view shared by the early nineteenth-century classicists and Marx, that the almost exclusive source of savings was profits. The workers had no excess income. The landowning gentry lacked a bent toward thrift. But the profit-making commercial classes had both. This heterogeneity in values and aspirations may also explain the alleged paucity of savings in many back-

---

[41] Cf. Kuznets' interesting suggestions in his "Proportions of Capital Formation to National Product," *loc. cit.*

[42] O. L. Altman, *Savings, Investment and National Income,* Temp. Nat. Econ. Com. Monograph 37 (Washington, 1941), p. 18.

ward areas in which the richer classes are supposed to lack a bourgeois appreciation of the satisfactions of accumulation and live instead with lordly magnificence and openhandedness.[43]

Within economically advanced communities, the importance of the distribution of income between profits and other types of income is presumably considerable, as is indicated by the figures cited in the note below.[44] Indeed, these figures probably underrate the importance of profits, for they neglect the large elements of salaries, wages, fees, and bonuses directly or indirectly attributable to profits. More of our income, particularly the income of the classes which do the bulk of our saving, has its origin in profit than is named profit. But our thinking is also colored, in this instance in a contrary sense, by an unduly restricted view of the forms of savings. Expenditure on education and on the betterment of health and skill is also a form of saving—indeed, a very important part. And in these ways, a considerable portion of the apparent consumption of the professional and working classes goes to improve the productive equipment of many communities.

The contribution of profits to saving has a twofold basis. When distributed they go largely to the rich, so they augment saving by aggravating income inequality. In addition, however, a large proportion of profits are retained by corporations and so wholly saved.[45] Indeed, the savings of corporations may well be understated if it is true, as many suspect, that depreciation allowances are normally more than adequate to maintain the productive equipment of industry.[46] How important the corporate organization of business may be in accounting for differences in savings among countries and over time is yet to be established.

Other facets of our organizational outfit, though presumably sig-

---

[43] Baran, op. cit.

[44] Making use of information about the distribution of dividends by income classes, Martin Taitel was able to estimate the amount of savings from corporate dividends in the United States for a number of years between 1920 and 1937. See Profits, Productive Activities and New Investment, TNEC Monograph 12. If we add to his data estimates of net savings by business firms, we have an approximation of total savings from profits. The order of magnitude of the results is suggested by the figures for one year. In 1925, total profits were about 10 per cent of national income; savings from profits were 41 per cent of total savings. Question arises, of course, about the stability of such a figure over the full course of a business cycle during which profits typically fluctuate far more violently than other sources of income. Cf. the article by the present writer, "Savings and Investment: Profits vs. Prosperity?" Am. Econ. Rev. Suppl., June 1942, XXXII, 53–88.

[45] S. P. Dobrovolsky, Corporate Income Retention, 1915–43 (New York, 1951), Ch. 3. Also Kuznets, National Income and Its Composition, Ch. 4.

[46] At the present time, the reverse may be true. The recent rapid price rises may have made depreciation allowances based on historical cost inadequate.

nificant, make contributions that are still unmeasured. A large volume of saving takes the form of insurance policy purchases. Another large quantity is used to purchase the securities of corporations, investment trusts, and governments. How much smaller would our savings be if these attractive kinds of assets did not exist?

Finally, even if we could allow for differences in per capita income and in the organizational structures of communities, there are still the basic problems of accounting for the level of per capita saving and for residual international and intertemporal differences. This is the aspect of the matter of which economists usually wash their hands by saying that the amount of saving that people are willing to do depends on their thriftiness, a form of words used to mark the traditional borders of economics. Of course, the border has sometimes been violated in speculative fashion, particularly by the older economists. Marshall, for example, wrote:

Thus, the causes which control the accumulation of wealth differ widely in different countries and in different ages. They are not quite the same among any two races, and perhaps not even among any two social classes in the same race. They depend much on social and religious sanctions; and it is remarkable how, when the binding force of custom has been in any degree loosened, differences in personal character will cause neighbors brought up under like conditions to differ from one another more widely and more frequently in their habits of extravagance or thrift than in any other respect.[47]

Insecurity of every kind, he added, is a most powerful hindrance to the development of habits of thrift and foresight. Family affection is the chief positive motive for accumulation. But it operates most strongly within a milieu in which an increase in wealth lifts a man and his family up the social ladder.[48]

Marshall's is a good example of the level of analysis and study to which the subject has been carried. With insignificant differences, similar remarks will be found in the writings of his contemporaries and predecessors. And among modern economists the question has been the subject of increasing neglect. The motives and conditions identified presumably are something less than established. They certainly do not exhaust the subject. And, insofar as they operate, what we really want to know is what sort of cultural and psychological forces create the required social and religious sanctions, provide the security, make wealth the hallmark of distinction, and establish family affection as the most

---

[47] *Principles of Economics* (8th ed.; London: Macmillan & Co., Ltd., 1920), p. 225.
[48] *Ibid.*, p. 228.

respectable of passions. We are, in fact, pushed beyond the limits of economics as that subject has so far developed, and it is no wonder that we find the theory in a rudimentary state.[49]

B. The Productivity of Capital and the Level of Capital Formation

If we interpret the productivity of capital to mean the net yield of additions to the capital stock, the relation between productivity and capital formation is obvious, at least qualitatively. But to do justice to the problem, we must distinguish between what may be called *potential* (or, perhaps, *ideal*) productivity and *effective* productivity. The yield under perfect competition is, perhaps, a sufficient characterization of potential productivity. It is the yield that an investor would expect if he had perfect knowledge of the present state of markets and of technical opportunities, could penetrate the future with clairvoyance, had no power to influence prices, and operated in a market in which private and social products were equivalent. Effective productivity is the yield on which potential investors will actually count, having regard to their limited knowledge of techniques and markets, present and future, their anticipations of financial rewards and dangers, and their ability, real or fancied, to control the future state of the market. Moreover, insofar as we credit potential productivity with influence over the inducement to invest, we are implicitly saying that investment will be made whenever and wherever there is an opportunity for monetary gain. When we move from potential product to effective product, however, we must depreciate the prospect of monetary gain according to the relative valuation that investors place on potential gains compared with risk, work, worry, and the strenuous life in general. Finally, we must take into account the fact that there are many opportunities to increase the productivity of society by investments which, either by their own nature, or because of institutional arrangements, or because of government action, do not have a private yield equal to their real worth. For these reasons, this section is divided into: (1) the determinants of potential productivity, and (2) the difference between potential and effective productivity.

---

[49] It can safely be said that modern economics has paid almost no serious attention to this last-mentioned portion of the subject. Among recent developments, the most hopeful are the experiments being carried out by George Katona and others at the Survey Research Center of the University of Michigan and partly reported in George Katona, *Psychological Analysis of Economic Behavior* (New York, 1951).

1. *The Determinants of Potential Productivity.* This is the area in which orthodox theory is most at home. Its starting point is the older static theory of income distribution. This theory makes the marginal productivity of the various factors depend on their relative supply. And since the canons of economy for individual firms demand that the factors be combined in such fashion that increasing use of any one brings smaller incremental products, a law of diminishing returns to changes in factor proportions is embedded in the theory. Although explicit treatment is hard to find, it is this static analysis of distribution which seems to have determined the orthodox view of the determinants of capital productivity in its bearing on the level of capital formation. We may state this view as follows: Given the structure of demand for final goods and the "state of the arts," the marginal productivity of capital will be high or low depending on the proportions of the factors. The greater the supplies of labor and natural resources, the higher the productivity of capital. The greater the volume of capital already accumulated, the lower the productivity of capital. Given the supply schedule of saving (unless it be completely inelastic), the volume of current capital formation will be greater, the higher the marginal productivity of capital. It will, therefore, vary directly with supplies of labor and other natural resources and inversely with the stock of existing capital.

An increase in the supply of a factor, however, brings an increase in aggregate output in addition to a change in factor proportions. And with an increase in scale of output there are increases in efficiency due to improvements in the organization of industry. That is to say, there are increasing returns associated with scale of output and, therefore, with the change in factor supply to which an increase in output is due. If we admit the importance of increasing returns in problems of secular growth,[50] we should have to amend the traditional conclusions to read: Capital formation will vary directly with supplies of labor and other natural resources, and *either* inversely *or* directly with the stock of existing capital depending on the relative strength of the forces making for diminishing returns—which depend on changes in factor proportions—and for increasing returns—which depend on changes in the scale of output.

Failure to take due account of the force of increasing returns—

---

[50] The classic modern statement is by A. A. Young, "Increasing Returns and Economic Progress," *Econ. Jour.*, Dec. 1928, XXXVIII, 527–42. See also, P. N. Rosenstein-Rodan, "Problems of Industrialization of Eastern and South-Eastern Europe," *ibid.*, June-Sept. 1943, LIII, 202–11.

to say nothing of factors outside the range of the discussion of potential productivity—has often led to careless thinking. One implication of the influence of scale on returns is that *a priori* there is no clear and definite reason to think that the potential productivity of capital will begin to drop when the ratio of capital to other resources increases. The demand price for capital will not necessarily be relatively high in a "new" country. Another implication is that there is no convincing reason to believe, *a priori,* that capital will flow from countries with high to countries with low ratios of capital to other resources. There is, no doubt, a tendency of that sort, but how strong is it, and how many exceptions would be found if one looked? Even at the level of potential (as distinct from effective) productivity, there is more to the problem than the capital-labor and capital-land ratios which traditional theory stressed.[51]

In recent theoretical work at the level of potential productivity, the most important development is probably Keynes' analysis of the schedule of the marginal efficiency (or productivity) of new capital.[52] From the viewpoint of economic growth, chief interest attaches to his emphasis on the cost of producing new capital equipment. In the older writings, the marginal rate of return over cost was conceived to vary with the level of investment because the marginal product of capital declined as its volume increased. Keynes emphasized a second cause for variation in the rate of return with the level of investment, namely that the cost of capital goods at any given time tends to be higher, the greater the volume of durable goods production.[53]

The practical importance of Keynes' treatment for questions of growth is simply stated. In a closed economy, the rapidity with which

---

[51] Moreover, the two factors held constant by traditional theory, the composition of demand and the state of the arts, represent important neglected areas. The productivity of capital depends on the kinds of goods to be produced, and these vary among countries and over time in a way probably related to a country's state of development. The relevance of the question may be illustrated by the fact that recent discussion has often stressed that the growing importance of services tends to reduce the inducement to invest. Cf. A. H. Hansen, *Fiscal Policy and Business Cycles* (New York, 1941), p. 357.

As to the effect of variations in the state of the arts, this too has still to be given thorough analysis. The beginnings of some necessary classification and study may be found in the various distinctions between "capital-using" and "capital-saving" inventions and in accompanying discussion. See A. C. Pigou, *Economics of Welfare* (London, 1920; 4th ed., 1932), Pt. 4, Ch. 4; J. R. Hicks, *Theory of Wages* (London, 1932), Ch. 6; R. G. Hawtrey, *Capital and Employment* (London, 1937), Ch. 3; Hansen, *op. cit.,* p. 356.

[52] *Op. cit.,* p. 135. Also, A. P. Lerner, *Economics of Control* (New York, 1946), Ch. 25.

[53] This relation was, of course, not unknown. It figures prominently in business-cycle literature. But it was not clearly recognized in general economic theory.

marginal productivity of capital declines as investment increases must depend on the ease with which capital goods production can be expanded. It must depend, therefore, on the size of a country's capital goods industry and on the number of workers who are appropriately trained and located. Keynes' view leads to the simple and obvious but important conclusion that the level of capital formation that a country can attain at any given time depends significantly on the size of the capital goods industry it has already built. It also implies that, if a backward country wishes quickly to attain a high rate of progress, what is necessary is not simply capital formation, but capital formation directed to the capital goods industries. The policy of Soviet Russia exhibits this principle in practice.

Strictly speaking, this analysis is limited to closed economies. Capital goods, however, can be bought as well as built, and in this way the capital goods industry of the world becomes available to a country. But now another limitation operates. To import more capital goods requires an expansion of exports, and this expansion will be limited at any given time by increasing costs of production which reflect the existing capacity of the export industries and by declining marginal revenues which reflect the existing demand for a country's products. In order for a country that imports capital goods to have a high rate of investment, it must have a large export industry. And to move from a low to a high rate of capital formation quickly it must concentrate on the expansion of its exports. It can escape this limitation only by restricting imports of consumer goods or by borrowing. So the need to borrow may reflect not simply a scarcity of internal sources of saving. It may also reflect a small capacity to produce capital goods at home and a small export industry.

2. *The Difference between Potential and Effective Productivity.* Resources, labor, existing capital and potentially usable knowledge define, in some sense, a set of opportunities. By themselves, however, they clearly do not determine when those opportunities will be seized or the rate at which they will be exploited. This becomes perfectly evident when we ask ourselves why the level of capital formation was greater in Britain than in France in the nineteenth century, greater in Germany than in France after 1870, and greater in Western Europe than in Russia before the Russian Revolution. The factors analyzed by traditional capital theory, therefore, provide only a partial catalogue of the incentives to invest. We may express this by saying that traditional theory provides no explanation for the gap between the potential and the effective productivity of capital.

The factors that determine how successfully that gap is leaped may be conveniently arranged under three headings. There is, first, a group of subjective attributes which together we can call *enterprise*. They control the energy with which investment opportunities are sought and exploited. Next, there are organizational, institutional, and legal arrangements which qualify the opportunities investors face. They create what are below called *institutional disparities* between potential and effective productivity. Finally, there are opportunities to raise income by investment which exist for the community but not for individuals. This subject is treated under the heading, *private versus social productivity*.

(*a*) Enterprise. As stated above, the capital theorist's data, labor supply, resources, and the rest do not define that ordered array of identified assets, each clearly labeled with its appropriate rate of return, which the conceptual device of a "schedule of the marginal productivity of capital" suggest. What it does define is a largely unexplored and unevaluated set of possibilities for useful investment of unimaginable magnitude and complexity. Hence, the effective incentives to investment do not depend on the usual data alone. They also depend on the vigor, intelligence, and open-mindedness with which the universe of unknown opportunities is searched and combed and on the willingness of potential investors to accept the work, worry, risk, and general sacrifice of ease which accompanies the establishment of a new, enlarged, changed, or relocated production unit. This constellation of qualities, combining energy in search of economic improvement, tolerance for novelty and uncertainty, and courage in the face of risk, is the group of attributes which together constitute the substance of enterprise.

The role of enterprise has been slighted by traditional theory because of the theory's generally static character which leads easily to assumptions about perfect knowledge, absence of risk, and rational calculation of profit.[54] The classic treatment of the problem is, of course, Joseph Schumpeter's.[55] Space does not permit adequate development of his

---

[54] But this is not to say that the role of enterprise was overlooked entirely. By looseness in theoretical formulation, or by adding notes on applied economics to the pure theory, neoclassical economics did develop a body of ideas. Marshall's *Principles* abounds in suggestions about the importance of a vigorous business class. But in the central structure of Marshall's work, variations in enterprise are not treated as one of the factors affecting the productivity of capital. And later writers, intent on rigorous formulation of static theory, paid it even less attention.

[55] *Theorie der wirtschaftlichen Entwicklung* (Leipzig, 1911), translation by Redvers Opie, *The Theory of Economic Development* (Cambridge, Mass., 1934); *Business Cycles;* and *Capitalism, Socialism and Democracy* (New York, 1942; 3rd ed., 1950), Pt. 2.

views, but his position may be sufficiently characterized by the statement that the marginal productivity of capital depends on enterprise to such a degree that in its absence the incremental yield of capital would fall to zero. The reason is that all important productive applications of capital involve innovation, that is, some act of search and discovery, some new departure in business life, some conquest of the active or passive resistance offered by labor, finance, or the market to new products or ways of working. Some act of enterprise is, therefore, involved; and in the absence of these special talents of leadership, it would be found that the remaining opportunities within the horizon of routine management are scant. The marginal productivity of capital would vanish.

The implication of this view is that labor supply, resources, existing capital, and the state of the arts only create a potentiality for capital productivity, while it is enterprise which performs the miracle of transforming potential into effective productivity.[56] A substantial part of the explanation of differences in the level of investment between developed and undeveloped countries, among advanced economies, and between different stages in the progress of any single country, is to be found in the size, energy, and scope of operations of the entrepreneurial or business class.

The question of the conditions controlling the vigor of enterprise is, therefore, sharply raised. On this, the leading treatments exhibit a remarkable similarity in basic theme. Whether we read Marshall's appendix on "The Growth of Free Industry and Enterprise,"[57] Karl Marx' *Capital,* Thorstein Veblen's *Theory of Business Enterprise,*[58] Schumpeter's *Capitalism, Socialism and Democracy,* or Wesley C. Mitchell's essay on "The Role of Money in Economic History,"[59] we find, with differences in emphasis and explicitness, the same central idea: that the vigor of economic enterprise or leadership under capitalism depends on the degree to which pecuniary values and pecuniary institutions have come to dominate the culture of a country.

The main expression of pecuniary culture in the limiting case is the elevation of money wealth and money income to pre-eminence among

---

[56] Schumpeter's position is, indeed, more radical. For he attributes much of the growth of basic knowledge, all of saving, and much of population growth to the activities of the entrepreneur. Cf. *Business Cycles,* Ch. 3.

[57] *Principles,* App. A. Cf. also his *Industry and Trade* (London, 1919; 3rd ed. 1920), Pt. 1.

[58] New York, 1904.

[59] *The Tasks of Economic History,* Dec. 1944 (Suppl. to the *Jour. Econ. Hist.,* Vol. IV), pp. 61–67.

the overt goals in life. The important thing is that, from the viewpoint of motivation, real assets and consumables, in bulk, if not in composition, are valued not for themselves but for their monetary equivalent. All things are thought of as exchangeable and saleable, and therefore as convertible into money, the universal solvent. The money measure of goods becomes the *real* expression of their value. Goods are money, and, from the viewpoint of capitalist motivation, it is from this equivalence that they derive their worth.[60]

Now it will readily be seen that the more completely the culture of a community is saturated with such a scheme of values, the greater will be the energy with which economic advantage is pursued and the more thoroughly and uncompromisingly will opportunities to use income to get more income be sought and exploited. The substantial needs of men for material goods are by no means insatiable, and, particularly among the richer elements in the community upon whom the function of enterprise devolves, would hardly justify and elicit the work, danger, and general woe, the sacrifice of leisure, sport, travel, and family (to name only the more obvious losses) which the effort to increase income entails. There is no specific instinct for capital accumulation, but there is in humans a powerful stream of moldable energy; and it is in the particular cultures in which prime value is attached to money that this stream becomes harnessed to the process of accumulation and that the drive for income becomes (more or less) insatiable.

In such cultures, all the avenues along which human energy may seek release—sex, distinction, power, security—are opened, or at least substantially smoothed and eased, by the possession of a relatively large income and stock of capital. The crucial phrase is, of course, "relatively large." Social distinction turns on relative income status. Political power may be wielded indirectly or obtained directly by the possession and use of money. Beauty may be purchased, and respectability and admiration achieved, by it. Indeed, to such an extent do all the facets of life reflect its influence that, at last, no specific visualization of its substantial uses is necessary. The desirability of accumulation comes to be taken for granted, an end—the end—in itself; to engage in the pursuit of money

---

[60] In this view the classical distinction between real and money economics is effectively reversed. To the classicists, the important things were pleasures and pains; commodities and services were the sources of pleasure and pain; and money was the means by which commodities are procured and services remunerated. Thus money-making is the way we get goods. All this, of course, is as it should be. But from the viewpoint of capitalist motivation, we do not make money to get goods. We make goods in order to get money.

becomes a virtue (and, therefore, beyond price) and to shrink from the costs of the chase a mark of the sloth, the fool, the eccentric, or the rebel. Thus the energy and ability which, in some societies, are directed toward religion, politics, art, or war are, in the developed capitalist milieu, channeled into business.[61]

All this is, of course, hypothesis of a particularly vague kind. The very words employed have no standard connotation in the context of the subject. It goes without saying that the force and range of application of the theory are still to be established. It poses problems of investigation most of which lie outside the normal borders of economics and will certainly resist measurement in the foreseeable future. If, blinking these difficulties, we now pass to the question of the factors controlling the origins and development of a pecuniary culture, we again enter territory which is as fascinating to visit as it is stony to cultivate. What economists know about such matters they owe to the studies and speculations of the economic historians and the students of economic institutions. From the work of Marx, Sombart, Weber, Pirenne, Veblen, Commons, Clark, their colleagues and successors, we can piece together a more or less common set of ideas. Five more or less independent but still closely related factors appear to have been of importance in the emergence of the pecuniary culture of the West. Their significance can be expressed categorically, if inadequately, in the following propositions:

First, the growth of modern science and technology, by its achievements in transport, geographical exploration, and powered machinery, broke the local subsistence economies, encouraged production for the

---

[61] Cf. Marshall, *Industry and Trade*, p. 156. Current investigations of underdeveloped areas have produced no more universal finding than that the process of investment is frustrated, not by any lack of potential opportunity for gain, and not by any lack of surplus saveable income, but rather by the lack of a vigorous business class intent on searching out and exploiting local opportunities. The energies of leading elements in such countries are instead diverted to political and social activity, sport, display, and travel. And the normal desire of a businessman is to convert himself, or his children, into members of the dominant group expending energy and income in nonproductive channels. Cf. United Nations Group of Experts, *Measures for the Economic Development of Under-Developed Countries* (New York, 1951), Ch. 3; Report to the President of the United States by the Economic Survey Mission to the Philippines (Washington, 1950); J. H. Adler, *The Under-Developed Areas: Their Industrialization*, Yale Inst. Internat. Studies, Memo. 31, Mar. 1949, pp. 20–22 and Summary.

For analysis of similar factors in a "developed" country, see D. S. Landes, "French Entrepreneurship and Growth in the Nineteenth Century," *Jour. Econ. Hist.*, May 1947, IX, 45–61; and the chapter by John Sawyer in *Modern France*, E. M. Earle, ed. (Princeton, 1951).

market and, therefore, for money, and supported the emergence of those strong national governments which were needed for the security of trade and investment.

Second, an increased supply of money, itself an offshoot of exploration and improvements in methods of extraction, placed in relatively few hands a mass of purchasing power which, in numberless ways, strained the capacity of local sources of supply, led to dramatic price rises and, therefore, greatly stimulated the movement of goods from distant areas. Profits anticipated in meeting those demands spurred emerging enterprises to organize production on commercial lines, and the profits realized furnished the saving and finance required.

Third, the institutions of private property and of economic organization based on free contract and exchange developed and spread with the material inducements which free commerce and industry could offer and with the growing influence of the business class. These institutions, in turn, widened the scope of business operations, increased the political and social power of business, and so made the pursuit of wealth and income both more rewarding and more respectable.

Fourth, more purely ideational factors encouraged the deliberate, disciplined, and rational pursuit of material progress which is the hallmark of the commercial mentality. These factors are variously taken to be of the character of religious beliefs (Weber, Tawney) or of a defensive reaction to insecurity on the part of minority groups (Sombart) or of release from the inhibitions of convention, personal relations, and vested interests which is afforded when communities are organized in new countries or when new techniques are introduced in old countries (Veblen, F. J. Turner and his followers).

Fifth, the growth of political freedom and democracy, itself a reflection of the growing power of commercial groups, made for social mobility and added the rewards of social and political distinction to economic success.

The general conclusion suggested by this survey of the factors controlling the vigor of enterprise is that a vast deal of emphasis must be placed on forces that, in the ordinary conception of the bounds of economics, would have to be classed as political, psychological, or sociological. On these matters, a fund of vague ideas has formed the background of the thinking of economists. This vagueness is regrettable, but from it we can draw one solid proposition. That is that the foundation of an adequate theory of capital formation does, in fact, involve grappling with a complex sociological tangle which can hardly be unraveled with the aid of such concepts and hypotheses as economics now furnishes.[62]

(b) Institutional disparities between potential and effective private productivity. The range of issues arising under this head and the next brings us back to topics more familiar to economists, and we merely touch on them to recall the problems involved. There is a gap between the potential and effective productivity of capital, viewed as an investment stimulus, partly because of the subjective factors already discussed, but partly also because institutional arrangements or the very nature of the assets prevent the private appropriation of part or all of the gain.

With regard to disparities of institutional origin, one large topic concerns forms and rates of taxation and subsidy in all their variants. Government regulation of business of every kind is a topic that is relevant here. Another has to do with the distribution of property and legal provisions surrounding property. In certain poorer countries, for example, the nub of the investment problem is to be found in the concentration of wealth, particularly land, in the hands of a noncommercial upper class combined with the poverty, insecurity of tenure, and ignorance of their tenants.

Still another problem concerns the kind and extent of monopoly controls over markets. The general feeling tone of orthodox economics is that competitive market structures are favorable, and monopolistic market structures inimical, to capital formation. But there has been little analysis in aggregate terms. What there is proceeds on extremely restrictive assumptions.[63] At less abstract levels, the correlation between market structure and competitive behavior breaks down.[64] Moreover, even the general contention that monopoly power and its exercise are normally unfavorable to investment has recently been challenged by

---

[62] There has, indeed, been a marked resurgence of interest in the cultural and political bases of entrepreneurial activity. The economic historians have once again been in the van, but with more conscious attention than was true a generation ago to the implications of their work for economic theory at large and, more particularly, for the theory of economic growth. See the series of papers published since 1941 in *The Tasks of Economic History,* annual supplement to the *Jour. Econ. Hist.* Also the more recent publications of the Research Center in Entrepreneurial History: *Change and the Entrepreneur* (Cambridge, Mass., 1949); and *Explorations in Entrepreneurial History,* the journal of the Center, commencing in 1949.

[63] Cf. Joan Robinson, *Economics of Imperfect Competition* (London, 1932), Bk. 10.

[64] Cf. J. M. Clark, *Economics of Overhead Costs* (Chicago, 1923), Ch. 20, 21; K. W. Rothschild, "Price Theory and Oligopoly," *Econ. Jour.,* Sept. 1947, LVII, 299–320; Fellner, *op. cit.,* and the present writer's "Monopolistic Selling in a Changing Economy," *Quart. Jour. Econ.,* Feb. 1938, LII, 191–214.

J. M. Clark[65] and Schumpeter.[66] To grapple with these questions in a realistic way evidently will require empirical work of a more penetrating sort than we have yet seen.

The facets of the problem just mentioned are, of course, only examples of the kind of questions involved. These and many more deserve further investigation for their bearing on the long-term growth of capital.

(c) Private versus social productivity. Organization, institutions, and laws affect the degree to which real productivity can be converted into private gain. But there are many types of investment, part or all of the gains from which cannot, by their nature, be appropriated and sold to furnish the reward for enterprise. If such investments are to be made, and certainly if full advantage of such opportunities is to be taken, they must be exploited by some public agency. Such agency may, of course, act directly, or indirectly by means of grants or subsidies of one kind or another.

Situations requiring social investment have been identified in Part I, Section B, 4, e. At this place, it is possible only to draw attention to one salient point. As regards an explanation of variant rates of progress, the problem is to understand why the social and political milieu in some countries and at some times lends itself to vigorous communal action, and in other places and times does not. Study of this question will lead us again to considerations of conflicts of political and economic interests and to more subtle problems connected with the intensity of group life and with the value structures of societies.[67]

---

[65] "Towards a Concept of Workable Competition," *Am. Econ. Rev.*, June 1940, XXX, 241–56.

[66] *Capitalism, Socialism and Democracy*, Ch. 7. Schumpeter did not deny the existence of those monopolistic influences which led traditional theory to an unfavorable view of monopoly. But he thought the traditional view failed to appreciate other forces which make monopoly part of the engine of progress. It is, at bottom, a quantitative matter in an area where measurement has, so far, proved impracticable. So the question for him became one of "ideology," as Mason has said. See E. S. Mason, "Schumpeter on Monopoly and the Large Firm," *Rev. Econ. Stat.*, May 1951, XXXIII, 139–44. For a rebuttal of Schumpeter's argument from the traditional side, see G. H. Hildebrand, "Monopolization and the Decline of Investment Opportunity," *Am. Econ. Rev.*, Sept. 1943, XXXIII, 591–601. For a defense, see R. V. Clemence and F. S. Doody, *The Schumpeterian System* (Cambridge, Mass., 1950), pp. 61–63.

[67] Cf. R. R. Nathan, O. O. Gass, and Daniel Creamer, *Palestine: Problem and Promise* (Washington, 1946) which provides an analysis of a dominantly capitalistic society in which intensely held and widely shared ideals and goals support a comprehensive program of public development. The capacity of Americans for group action in the face of their supposedly individualistic cast of mind has puzzled many. Ralph Barton Perry

C. The Role of Finance

Finance is the process whereby funds from whatever source are placed at the disposal of investors. It involves two chief classes of activities: financial mediation, that is, the transfer of funds from savers to investors; and credit creation, that is, the provision of credits to investors in excess of planned saving.

1. *Financial Mediation.* In the perfect market of traditional pure theory, there is no place for financial mediation. The available savings flow smoothly and costlessly to the most productive investment opportunities. The net yield of assets to savers equals the effective marginal productivity of new capital. The distinction between saver and investor essentially disappears.

In reality, however, active investment is a function confined to a special class of businessmen who command relatively good, though far from perfect, technical and market information and have the temperament to act on their knowledge. And the provision of capital traditionally takes the form of a loan contract in which the lender (saver) substitutes a risk on the general credit of the borrower (investor) for a risk on the outcome of the investment itself. Under these circumstances a spread —call it the *financial spread*—develops between the effective marginal productivity of capital, which is what borrowers can afford to pay, and the net yield of loans in the eyes of savers, which is the reward of lenders.

The size of the financial spread depends partly on the economic and social environment within which borrowing and lending proceed, and partly on the efficiency with which the capital market and its agencies are organized and operate. So far as the environment is concerned, the size of the spread turns on such matters as the level of commercial honesty, the character of the laws protecting creditors and the vigor with which they are enforced, the extent to which the habit of security buying has spread among the public, the level of development of general commercial information, the public's attitude toward risk, and the safety of the investments for which finance is actually demanded.

The size of the spread also depends heavily on the efficiency of the financial organization of a country. Indeed, in its broadest aspects, a

---

(*op. cit.*) is of the opinion that theirs is "a *collective* individualism—not the isolation of one human being, but the intercourse and cooperation of many." (P. 9.) "American self-reliance is a plural, collective, self-reliance. . . . The appropriate term is not 'organism' but 'organization.'" (P. 19.) The question for us is: Why did American conditions produce this cast of mind?

country's financial organization may be considered a device for reducing the size of the financial spread. If it works well, the cost of financing to investor-borrowers will be low while the net return to saver-lenders will be high. Investment and saving and, therefore, the volume of capital formation will tend to be large. But if it works poorly, capital formation will be discouraged.

The many ways in which financial organization helps—through the creation of liquidity, through brokerage, by providing information, by converting the securities offered by investors into forms more acceptable to savers—is too long a story for this space. But it should be noted that, besides the banks, brokers, investment houses, and other agencies of the credit and securities markets, the corporate organization of business is an important part of the organization of finance. It is not too much to say that without the invention and public acceptance of the limited liability share and the development of efficient securities exchanges, the extensive financing of large-scale firms and, therefore, the effective use of modern technology would have proved impossible. Apart from that, however, corporations, by their size and method of organization, create a divergence of interest and power between controllers and nominal owners which has encouraged the development of self-financing. Corporations desirous of financing new investment can do so by withholding net earnings which their nominal owners might be loath to permit if they had any effective choice. Perhaps of comparable importance, the fund of such automatically financed investment is swelled by conservative methods of depreciation accounting which produces large amounts of net saving that never officially appear as such.

All these agencies, institutions, and devices can be interpreted as ways and means of reducing the financial spread, that is, of increasing the net yield of securities in the eyes of savers and, therefore, increasing the supply of saving and of bringing finance to business at low cost. Now it goes without saying that the width of the spread varies from country to country and that for given countries it has changed in the course of the development of capitalist institutions. It remains for historical study to establish how wide the spread is and has been in various countries and thus to provide a measure of the contribution that financial law, institutions, and agencies have made over time and in some places to the accumulation of capital. Meanwhile, it is safe to say that the financial spread was, say 150 years ago, everywhere very wide and constituted a most serious block to saving and investment. It is also clear that it is still very wide today in many countries with undeveloped capitalist institutions and that one of the most pressing needs of backward economic communities is to promote financial integrity, establish effective and cheap protection for the rights of creditors, and create the financial institutions through which the savings of the community can be efficiently channeled into the hands of active investors.

2. *Credit Creation and the Role of Commercial Banks.* In recent years, attention has shifted from the role of financial mediation and come to be focused on the significance of the aggregate supply of money and, therefore, on credit creation through commercial banks. The older view of this matter was that in the long run the quantity of money, provided it is constant, affects only the price level, but not the level of saving or investment.[68] The reason is that the supply of productive factors, including saving, was held to be determined by the real returns they could obtain. An expansion of the money supply may push interest rates below their equilibrium levels and so temporarily stimulate investment. The benefit, however, cannot last. For in the face of lower interest rates, the real supply of saving would increase only if real output and income increased. But since real wage rates must fall as output rises, output cannot for long remain above its initial level. The real supply of saving must, therefore, tend to decline. To maintain low nominal interest rates and so to stimulate investment means that the banks have to assume an ever-larger share of the burden of financing new investment. In the end, this must lead to credit restrictions and higher interest rates. Contraction ensues. What money creation by banks causes, therefore, is an unsound cyclical spurt of investment, the real gains from which will be swallowed up in an ensuing crash and depression.[69]

The general tenor of recent, that is Keynesian, theory is that the quantity of money counts even if it is constant.[70] There are two condi-

---

[68] Cf. Marshall's testimony before the Royal Commission on the Depression of Trade and Industry (1886) and before the Gold and Silver Commission (1887–88), *Official Papers by Alfred Marshall* (London, 1926). See also the summary of the traditional view by J. R. Hicks in "Mr. Keynes and the 'Classics,'" *loc. cit.*

[69] For these reasons, neoclassical theorists thought that financial agencies, including banks, were beneficial chiefly in their role as financial intermediaries. This, of course, is still the view of that substantial body of opinion which supports the substitution of some variant of a 100 per cent reserve system for fractional reserve banking. But the chief motive of this group is economic stabilization rather than economic growth. Cf. Henry Simons, *A Positive Program for Laissez-Faire,* Public Policy Pamphlet 15 (Chicago, 1934); *idem,* "Rules *vs.* Authorities in Monetary Policy," *Jour. Pol. Econ.,* Feb. 1936, XLIV, 1–30; Irving Fisher, *100% Money* (New York, 1935); Milton Friedman, "A Monetary and Fiscal Framework for Economic Stability," *Am. Econ. Rev.,* June 1948, XXXVIII, 245–64.

[70] *General Theory,* Ch. 15.

tions required to reach this conclusion. The first is that the demand for additional hoards of cash should not be infinitely great and, therefore, that interest rates lie above their conventional minima.[71] The other is that more labor and other productive factors be available even though the real rewards of factors decline when output rises. Given these conditions, an increase in the quantity of money will reduce interest rates, stimulate investment, and so raise output. And the increased income thus generated will bring out a greater real supply of saving in spite of lower real interest rates.[72]

The supply conditions which make these results possible are concomitants of unemployment which is involuntary in the Keynesian sense. But can involuntary unemployment persist for periods long enough to be significant for economic growth? In a stable economic environment presumably not—for, in the long run, it is plausible to think that the supply of productive factors is based on real returns and, again in the long run, wages and prices are probably flexible enough to reflect the real supply prices of factors. Private enterprise economies, however, are not stable. There may be some tendency for full employment conditions to be established, but there is also an effective tendency for business cycles to recur and for technological improvements to be introduced. Unemployment due to these causes may not be an aspect of economic equilibrium, but it is a typical condition.

One question, then, is whether in an environment which typically includes some involuntary unemployment, the quantity of money makes a difference to the level of investment, even if money supply is constant. The answer would seem to turn on whether prices, in the long run, fully reflect differences in the quantity of money in spite of recurrent unemployment. If they do, the real value of the money supply would not, in the end, be altered by changes in its nominal size. Hence the rate of interest and the level of investment would be unaffected. But it is not at all clear that prices and the quantity of money are so closely tied.

Moreover, even if such a long-run tie between prices and money be admitted, it does not follow that a secularly *increasing* supply of money cannot stimulate investment over long periods. The traditional argu-

---

[71] See pp. 147–48.

[72] The essentials of Keynes' argument are well brought out by Modigliani, "Liquidity Preference and the Theory of Interest and Money," *loc. cit.* Other leading articles bearing on the problem may be found in the three volumes published for the American Economic Association, *Readings in Business Cycle Theory, Readings in the Theory of Income Distribution,* and *Readings in Monetary Theory.*

ment is that such a process involves "forced" saving which can only be maintained by an ever-increasing supply of money which it is not practicable to provide. Such secular increases of money supply have, however, occurred in the past, and it would be sheer speculation to insist that savers and workers come to anticipate the upward trend of prices and to make contracts only at prices which take price-level movements into account.[73] The fact is that neither on the level of theoretical analysis nor of history has the influence of money supply on investment been established for a cyclically disturbed environment.

D. The Progress of Capital Formation

The history of economic thought exhibits a marked cyclical swing between periods when hopes of cumulative progress were dominant and periods living under the shadow of the fear of stagnation.

Adam Smith's *Wealth of Nations* asserted a theory of steady progress. The increasing division of labor, he argued, makes for larger output and larger capital stock. From this flow higher incomes and so a larger population. This in turn means a wider market, still greater division of labor, a spur to invention, and so still more rapid capital formation.

Ricardo and John Stuart Mill turned their eyes away from the possibilities of increasing returns. Their stress was on diminishing returns attributable to the pressure of population and capital on a limited supply of land. For a time the increased income of the saving classes tends to speed the process of capital formation by raising the current supply of saving. Moreover, invention and improvement are forces working to raise the productivity of capital. But in the end, the tendency to diminishing returns to capital applied to scarce land would be controlling. Profit rates would fall to that practical minimum at which they no longer afforded either a source of saving or a sufficient risk premium and reward for investment. Saving and investment would both cease and a stationary state supervene. Stagnation at full employment was the destination of economic development.[74]

---

[73] An expanding money supply, of course, need not involve rising prices. If productivity is increasing, it may simply mean that prices tend to stand at a high level relative to costs. But both costs and prices may be stable or falling.

[74] Marx's views were equally stagnationist. But since he was an early scoffer at Say's Law, he saw a secular decline of investment demand as a cause of aggravated crisis and depression. His views, therefore, are markedly similar to the theories of stagnation dominant today. Cf. Joan Robinson, *An Essay on Marxian Economics* (London, 1942), Ch. 5; Maurice Dobb, *Political Economy and Capitalism* (London, 1937); P. M. Sweezy, *Theory of Capitalist Development* (New York, 1942), Ch. 6, 12.

The neoclassical writers, deriving their outlook from Marshall, beheld a fairer future. For them, the Malthusian ghost was already laid. Now it was capital pressing on a limited supply of land and of labor as well. But to even the score, there was a stronger faith in the possibilities of invention and improvement in widening the field for capital. This faith was partly founded on the demonstrated progress of science and on a conception of science as a process of cumulative advance without limit. And, partly, it was founded on an intuition of the possibilities of increasing returns, a process whereby capital accumulation, by increasing income, broadened the market, and so created ever larger opportunities for the application of capital. In essence, their theory marked a return to Adam Smith.[75] F. H. Knight has pronounced the verdict of this school on the specter of stagnation:

It rests on the questionable assumption that accumulation could proceed without opening up new demand by occasioning invention and discovery, and in any case is reasonably supposable only as a vague limit at the end of an indefinitely long course of development. During this process any prediction of given conditions tends to become fanciful. The reasonable prediction is that over long periods changes tending to raise the rate of return will more or less predominate during some intervals and changes of the opposite kind in other intervals.[76]

The relative optimism of this outlook was nourished by a century and a half of rapid growth and capital accumulation. But for many, perhaps most, economists it was not proof against the shock of the depressed thirties. The virtual cessation of advance which marked that decade, its very low levels of investment, its persistent unemployment, its disappointing recovery, made a contemporary impression which caused theorists to search for an explanation, not merely in *ad hoc* circumstances, but in some deeper-rooted change in the basic conditions of economic life. The result is the modern theory of stagnation. We may fairly call it Hansen's Theory.[77]

---

[75] Young, *op. cit.*

[76] "Capital and Interest," *Encyclopedia Brittanica*, 1946, IV, 779–801; also in *Readings in the Theory of Income Distribution*, pp. 384–417. Cf. A. C. Pigou, "Economic Progress in a Stable Environment," *loc. cit.*

[77] Although some of the ideas were foreshadowed by Keynes, the theory was given its leading expression by A. H. Hansen in "Economic Progress and Declining Population Growth," *Am. Econ. Rev.*, Mar. 1939, XXIX, 1–15; also in *Readings in Business Cycle Theory*, pp. 366–84; *idem, Fiscal Policy and Business Cycles; idem,* "Some Notes on Terborgh's 'The Bogey of Economic Maturity,'" *Rev. Econ. Stat.*, Feb. 1946, XXVIII, 13–17. Literature based on similar ideas is voluminous. See the bibliography in *Readings in Business Cycle Theory*, pp. 483–84. Reliable systematic exposition is provided in Benjamin Higgins, "Concepts and Criteria of Secular Stagnation," in *Income, Employ-*

The primary objective of this theory is to assert the existence of a tendency toward chronic and growing unemployment and to offer an explanation for it. The full implications of the theory are, therefore, beyond the scope of the present paper.[78] One of its main props, however, is the idea that net investment tends to decline, after a point, in developed capitalist economies. It is this proposition which is of particular interest here.

The outlook of Hansen's theory is dominated once more by the assumption of diminishing returns. At a given level of technical knowledge, the yield of increments to capital stock tends to sink as its quantity increases relative to labor supply and resources. Increasing returns may be characteristic of the early stages of a country's development, but the economies of Western Europe and the United States of America are mature. At a given level of technical knowledge, therefore, the current inducement to net investment will fall unless population growth and the discovery and development of resources keep pace with capital formation. Moreover, if we may assume that investment outlets generated by past developments have been fully exploited, the marginal productivity of capital will rise or fall together with the level of population growth, resource discovery, and technical progress.

Of these three stimuli, it is argued that population growth and resource discovery are clearly declining in strength. The third factor, technical progress, may indeed be proceeding with undiminished vigor, but it cannot be expected to offset the enfeeblement of the first two. One reason is that with the accumulation of wealth, innovation turns in a capital-saving direction. When capital equipment was scant, few opportunities existed for reducing costs by saving capital. But as the mass of equipment increases, more and more improvements have the effect of economizing capital. A second reason is that the composition of demand changes, as per capita income rises, in the direction of greater emphasis

---

ment and Public Policy: Essays in Honor of Alvin H. Hansen (New York, 1948), pp. 82–107, and *idem,* "The Theory of Increasing Under-Employment," *Econ. Jour.,* June 1950, LX, 255–74.

[78] For the same reason, we neglect the theories of R. F. Harrod, "An Essay in Dynamic Theory," *ibid.,* Apr. 1939, XLIX, 14–33, and *idem, Towards a Dynamic Economics* (London, 1948); and E. D. Domar, "Capital Expansion, Rate of Growth and Employment," *Econometrica,* Apr. 1946, XIV, 137–47; *idem,* "Expansion and Employment," *Am. Econ. Rev.,* Mar. 1947, XXXVII, 34–55. These theories, though often referred to as theories of growth, are, properly speaking, theories of the requirements of steady growth at full employment. They make no assertions with respect to the likely development of capital formation over time.

on services compared with commodities. And services, supposedly, are less heavily capitalized. Thus the stream of innovations must be increasing if the level of investment is to remain even level. It must increase still more rapidly to offset the effects on investment of retarded growth of population and resources.[79]

If we accept these views about the time trends in the three dynamic factors, it is argued that we must infer an actual decline in capital formation. For even though the supply of saving rises with per capita income, this will not stimulate investment. The elasticity of the schedule of the marginal efficiency of capital with respect to interest rates is very low, and the response of interest rates to an increase in the supply of saving is extremely limited. This, of course, assumes that the inducement to invest is already deficient compared with saving. At this point, indeed, increases in saving are worse than useless, for they generate declines in income which cause a further deterioration in the expected yield of investments.

So far as it is concerned with the demand for additional capital, Hansen's theory represents a departure from the neoclassical view in that it expresses a more limited faith in the possibilities of opening new outlets for capital through the advance of knowledge. Briefly stated, the basis for this change in view is found in calculations—admittedly only suggestive—which "point unmistakably to the conclusion that the opening of new territory and the growth of population were together responsible for a very large fraction—possibly somewhere near one-half—of the total volume of new capital formation in the nineteenth century."[80] With these important outlets for investment rapidly narrowing down, it seems too sanguine to think that technical progress can speed up sufficiently to close the gap, particularly in view of the growing tendency for invention and consumption to take a capital-saving direction.

The argument is attractive, but it is not difficult to enter a plausible rebuttal. The experience of the 1940's has made the outlook for population growth far less gloomy than it appeared to Hansen in the late thirties and early forties.[81] The same decade has belied predictions, at least so far as the United States is concerned, that the population appears to be

---

[79] A third reason is stressed by Michael Kalecki, *Studies in Economic Dynamics* (London, 1943), pp. 89–92. Innovation stimulates new investment, but it causes the liquidation of old capital in competing uses.

[80] Hansen, "Economic Progress and Declining Population Growth," *loc. cit.*, p. 9.

[81] J. S. Davis, *The Population Upsurge in the United States*, Food Research Inst., War-Peace Pamphlets, No. 12 (Stanford, 1949).

approaching stabilization in geographical distribution.[82] Again, very large portions of the world, even outside the sphere of communist control, remain unsettled or only partly settled. And, while climate and location interpose obstacles to development, science is steadily reducing these barriers. Even within the settled areas, the discovery and creation of resources proceeds at a rapid pace—witness, among other things, the rapid advances in agricultural productivity. Meanwhile, there are signs that the pace of advance of pure science is accelerating and that deliberate devotion of resources to technological exploration is becoming more and more extensive. That much technical progress will be capital saving may be taken for granted. But such innovations need not be alternative to capital-using innovations; they may also be additional. And services are becoming increasingly capitalized. Is it clear, for example, that a dollar spent on education or medical care requires less capital in buildings, equipment, and personnel training than a dollar spent on a representative commodity?

A second differentiating mark of Hansen's theory is its implicit assumption that capital yields diminishing returns, at least in advanced economies. Perhaps it does; but are we at all sure that, on balance, an increase in the scale of the market in the United States does not still permit economies more sizeable than the diseconomies it causes through pressure on resources and otherwise? If it does, the inducement to invest can feed on itself, at least so far as secular trends go, with capital formation limited by the supply of saving and the size of the capital goods industries.[83] It seems right to conclude that, so far as the barebones of Hansen's theory are concerned, it is plausible but far from completely persuasive. Its detailed contentions and implications need more careful examination than they have yet received. In particular, those drawn to

---

[82] *Ibid.*, p. 21.

[83] Along the same lines, we must take note of the opinion of at least a portion of neoclassical thought about the character of the returns to capital. Witness H. C. Simons, who asserts that: "in the sense of potential 'social yield' or of marginal efficiency under free-market conditions, investment opportunities are and have been nearly limitless. Holding fast to Cassel notions, I believe that the productivity curve for new capital is extremely flat; that investment, proceeding at the maximum rate consistent with high thrift, would have little effect for the significant future, even failing large accretions of innovations, on yields in this sense." "Hansen on Fiscal Policy," *Jour. Pol. Econ.*, Apr. 1942, L, 170. Cf. F. H. Knight, "Diminishing Returns from Investment," *ibid.*, Mar. 1944, LII, 26–47. For contrary views, see Keynes, *op. cit.*, pp. 374–77, and D. McC. Wright, "Prof. Knight on Limits to the Use of Capital," *Quart. Jour. Econ.*, May 1944, LVIII, 331–58.

the subject might do well to regard the phase of assertion and counter-assertion as closed and a phase of empirical study as the need of the times.

In the terminology used in earlier portions of this essay, the basic elements in Hansen's theory are time trends in the determinants of *potential* productivity. They bear particular comparison, therefore, with the neoclassical theory which depends on the very same elements. Hansen's theory has, however, been both supported and attacked in the light of considerations relevant to the difference between potential and effective productivity. Briefly stated, the argument is that the development of capitalism has also raised a series of barriers to the exploitation of potential productivity. These barriers are identified as business monopoly,[84] labor unions, government intervention in economic life by taxation, regulation and direct participation, and hindrances to foreign investment.

These barriers between the potential and effective productivity of capital are regarded by Hansen and his adherents as developments strengthening their main case.[85] By others, however, they are considered as a full-fledged alternative explanation for such evidence of declining investment opportunity as has appeared.[86] The nub of the issue is the question whether the substantial elimination of the special barriers, to the extent that they are judged to be removable, would also eliminate the tendency to declining investment opportunity. Hansen and his adherents, while welcoming policies designed to reduce obstacles to investment, believe such policies would not be sufficient. His critics believe they would.

The gap between potential and effective productivity was also used by Schumpeter to accommodate a systematic theory of the progress of capital formation which is basically antagonistic to Hansen's theory and, in the main, also at variance with the views of Hansen's opponents outlined above.[87] His view is a logical extension of his general theory about capital formation. For it turns neither on some autonomous change in the taste for saving, nor on an independent decline in opportunities for investment, but on the metamorphosis through which the entrepreneur-

---

[84] Hildebrand, *op. cit.;* E. D. Domar, "Investment, Losses, and Monopolies," in *Income, Employment, and Public Policy,* Ch. 2.

[85] Cf. Domar, "Investment, Losses, and Monopolies, *loc. cit.;* Higgins, *op. cit.*

[86] E.g., H. C. Simons, *op. cit.;* H. S. Ellis, "Monetary Policy and Investment," *Am. Econ. Rev., Proc.,* Mar. 1940, XXX, 27–38; S. H. Slichter, "The Conditions of Expansion," *Am. Econ. Rev.,* Mar. 1942, XXXII, 1–21.

[87] *Capitalism, Socialism and Democracy,* Ch. 10–14.

ial function passes as capitalism develops. This is, of course, utterly consistent, for Schumpeter saw both saving and investment opportunity as the creations of enterprise.

As capitalism develops, the vigor of enterprise begins to decline. In part this is due to the emergence of a political and social environment which is hostile to business, which reduces its rewards, and limits the scope of its activities. The appearance of this hostile milieu stems from the fact that the position of the business class, both its status in society and its power in politics, is progressively undermined. As firms grow in size and experience, the entrepreneurial function tends to become routinized, an affair for salaried employees; so the businessman gradually loses his chief moral title to social leadership. Next, with the spread of pecuniary values and commercial habits of thought, the bourgeois class loses its main political supporter, the old aristocracy, whose romantic sway is inconsistent with the spirit of calculation. The growth of big business also destroys another important political ally, the small tradesman and artisan. And finally, the rational and critical attitude fostered by capitalism nurtures an intelligentsia whose questions do not stop at the "credentials of kings and popes." It goes on to dissect private property and the system of bourgeois virtues themselves. It rationalizes dissatisfaction with existing institutions and ruling classes and so provides the necessary intellectual leadership for anticapitalist forces. The result, as stated, is the gradual appearance of political and social conditions unfavorable to business activity, taxing its gains, regulating its movements, and limiting its scope.

Quite as important as these environmental changes, however, is the transformation which occurs in the nature of capitalist motivation. The same rational spirit which is responsible for the material triumphs of business also leads businessmen to a critical analysis of their own goal. This was the creation of a great personal fortune in order to found and support a family and home. But the income statement of the proceeds and costs of home and family, as modern businessmen compute it, shows a psychic deficit. And as these institutions cease to be the centers and goals of bourgeois life, the driving force of enterprise begins to disappear.

For Schumpeter, all this meant a gradual reduction in the pace of capital formation—at least under capitalism. This may not become visible, the effects of random causes and special circumstances being what they are, for many years. But it constitutes a persistent force that will be controlling in the end. It does not mean breakdown or chronic unemployment necessarily, for the saving motive will weaken with the investment drive. But, with the passing of the function of the individual entrepreneur, it does mean the socialization of economic activity.

All these theories admittedly are of limited application at best. They are hypotheses intended to illuminate the latter stages of the economic and sociological processes of industrialization, but not its beginnings or its life course. They are, moreover, restricted to capitalistic economies and so do not apply to countries in which capital formation is determined or heavily influenced by the decisions of central authority. If we restrict the application of Hansen's theory, for example, to countries in which population growth is markedly retarded and which already enjoy relatively high per capita incomes, it may be said to be relevant to perhaps 20 per cent of the world's population.[88] Even within this limited sphere, however, there are doubts about the applicability of the theories as interpretations of observable events, as distinct from predicted future events. For it is not clear which, if any, advanced capitalist countries have as yet given evidence of a persistent decline in the level of capital formation.

Insofar as such evidence may be found, moreover, there is doubt about the relative validity of the rival theories now in vogue and, it must be added, about their fitness compared with other theories that may be or have been propounded. Modern theoretical literature, for example, puts little stress on certain older ideas that have often been advanced to explain the laggard pace of British and French advance in recent decades. It has been plausibly contended, for example, that these countries are now suffering a penalty for their early lead in the industrial race. Their older equipment, the specialized experience of their population and their geographical layout make it more difficult for them than for their newer rivals to take full advantage of modern techniques. And their older industries now feel the competition of more recently equipped competitors.[89] If this line of argument has validity, it implies that any observed retardation in the pace of capital formation may be but temporary and that the turn of the old countries will come again as time presents oppor-

---

[88] J. J. Spengler, "The Population Obstacle to Economic Betterment," *loc. cit.,* pp. 343–54.

[89] Thorstein Veblen, *Imperial Germany and the Industrial Revolution* (New York, 1915), pp. 128–33. See also Rutledge Vining (Testimony before the Interstate Commerce Commission, Dockets No. 29885–6, pp. 47–53), who applies the same ideas to the experience of New England compared with other regions in the United States. Chang employs similar arguments in comparing the pace of advance of a number of leading industrial countries. *Op. cit.,* pp. 111–12.

tunities for renewing old equipment and gradually loosens the industrial and geographical ties of their people.

Finally, all this bears only on the question of maturity and its concomitants. With so much of the world undeveloped, and with so many of the relatively advanced countries in the full tide of capital accumulation, the theory of the progress of capital formation needs filling out. What is the path by which a country passes from its precapitalistic doldrums into a state of industrial animation? Is there not a cumulation of investment opportunities and of the means of exploiting them in these earlier stages? If so, what are the specific developments by which the process of capital formation gathers strength? What obstacles must be surmounted and what adjustments must an economy make in the training and allocation of its labor force, in the composition of its output, in its domestic and foreign trade? Is the nature of these adjustments very similar from case to case, or does it differ widely depending, say, on a country's physical endowment and location? We now have an uncertain and incomplete gerontology of capital formation. A paedology and a theory of maturation are utterly lacking.

III. PROBLEMS OF RESEARCH

The foregoing survey of the scope and content of the economics of growth serves to illustrate its far-reaching character. It is, in fact, to be regarded as one of the major branches of economics, coordinate with the economics of resource allocation and income distribution and the economics of short-term, or cyclical, fluctuations. As such, there are few, if any, facets of economic life and, therefore, few, if any, subjects in economics that are foreign to it. This, then, may be said to be the first of the difficulties which the study of growth poses. It is extremely many-sided and will call for the cooperation of specialists in all the major branches of economics.

These various branches are relevant from a special point of view, namely, in their bearing on long-term change. And that means that the causes, or factors, which become relevant are not merely the relatively objective, relatively easily definable, variables with which economics has usually dealt, but others far less familiar. We shall be involved not only with numbers of workers, machines, acres, tons, or square yards of commodities, and the like; we shall also need to consider less easily grasped attributes like mobility, industry, enterprise, thriftiness, knowledge, and skill and their diffusion. The first problems that this raises are those of sheer definition, observation, and measurement. These problems have seldom been faced in the past, because so long as our interests lay in short-run questions, these less tangible factors could be taken to be constant and so neglected. From the viewpoint of long-term problems, however, they are variables of first-rate importance.

To understand the causes and processes of economic growth, moreover, it will not be enough to relate these and similar growth factors to output change. We shall also want to understand and explain the movements of these immediate determinants. And such explanations will involve investigations which, in almost every instance, lie outside the normal boundaries of economics. The location of those boundaries hitherto has been fixed by the reach of money income as an explanation of behavior. Economics, in fact, if not in intention, has been the science which studied the implications of changes in pecuniary advantage. But population growth, changes in industrial and financial organization, technological progress and its diffusion, the changing vigor of enterprise, differences in industrial and geographical mobility—none of these can be adequately, or probably to any considerable extent, understood in terms of pecuniary advantage. The economics of growth is, therefore, the field of work in which the dependence of economics upon its sister social sciences appears in a supreme degree.

The study of economic growth also presents in aggravated form that universal problem of economics and of social science, the distillation of dependable uniformities from a process of cumulative change. A dependable law implies some stable system of structural characteristics (tastes, propensities, motives, physical obstacles, organization, law, etc.) which cause a set of recognizable tendencies to emerge in the relations among variables. Social structure, however, is notoriously in flux, so that in practice it is some sort of relative stability on which we must depend —relative usually to the period of time that is relevant. But the longer the period, the less likely are we to find the degree of stability we need. No one can say ahead of time how grave an obstacle this will be, but it will certainly be far more serious than in studies of short-term fluctuations in which it has already proved disturbing. Long-term growth presumably constitutes a process of cumulative rather than repetitive change to a greater degree than other economic phenomena.

The study of economic growth, therefore, stands closer to history than do other economic subjects. Not only will study of the past, even the distant past, furnish us the bulk of the necessary data, but it seems unlikely that, for the foreseeable future, the economics of growth can be much more than economic history rationalized here and there to a limited degree as uniformities in the process of development are established. The sweeping visions of Marx, Sombart, Weber, and others will, no doubt, color and direct our thoughts and work, but the generalizations we trust will be less profound and of narrower application.

These doubts and fears are no more than natural. The work of finding uniformities in the variety of historical change and national difference has hardly begun. Economists so far have preferred the easier job of discovering the necessary implications of arbitrarily chosen premises. The study of the political, psychological, and sociological foundations of economic life has been even more neglected. Economists have preferred to cultivate a science of pecuniary advantage. The study of economic growth will not permit them to indulge these proclivities. The insights which traditional theory can furnish will, of course, have to be worked to the limit. But we may expect that limit to be reached sooner in studies of secular change than elsewhere. If the economics of growth attains the rank it ought to have in our subject, we should expect to see history, geography, psychology, and sociology take a prominent place in the training of economists in the future. Experience suggests that we cannot be sanguine about the strength of these allies. But more than ever, our problems seem to lie within their domains, and a closer federation is in order.

COMMENT
Simon Kuznets

General agreement with Abramovitz' discussion permits, and the lack of space compels, limiting this comment to a few supplementary observations on statistical studies of the economic growth of nations.

They suggest the following conclusions: (a) During the last century, the rate of growth in national product, and particularly in product per capita, differed strikingly among the various countries. (b) On the whole, such growth was greater in countries that, at the beginning of the period, had relatively high levels of economic performance; and the consequence has been greatly to widen international differences in per capita incomes. (c) Wherever substantial growth in per capita product occurred, it was accompanied by a shift away from agriculture—although the process may have been, in part, increasing differentiation and transfer of activities from the countryside, rather than a genuine shift from agricultural cultivation. (*d*) Accompanying industrialization were the increasing urbanization of the population, the extensive spread and intensive penetration of business and financial institutions, and all the associated corollaries.

Most important is the impression of diversity, even among the few countries for which long statistical records of economic growth are available. Thus, with respect to the relation between rates of growth of (*i*) population and (*ii*) per capita product—an important tenet in the "stagnation" doctrine—we find all combinations: of high (*i*) with high (*ii*) —e.g., United States and Japan; of low (*i*) with high (*ii*)—e.g., Sweden; of high (*i*) with low (*ii*)—e.g., Italy, and as far as tenuous records go, India; and of low (*i*) with low (*ii*)—e.g., France. We find combinations of relatively high proportions of savings and capital formation with high rates of growth (e.g., Japan); moderate proportions of capital formation with high rates of growth (e.g., Sweden and partly the United States); relatively high proportions of capital formation with moderate rates of growth (e.g., Great Britain from 1870 to 1914). There is variety among countries in the nature of the industries that lead in the process of growth; in the relative supply of natural resources and the rate of growth attained; in the extent of reliance upon foreign trade and capital imports.

If one adds to this picture the diversity in historical heritage and in the character of the dominant social institutions, aspects that do not lend themselves to statistical treatment, the difficulties that study of economic growth faces can be readily understood—even if the period of empirical reference is limited to the last century. To be sure, the picture might become less puzzling were a longer period to be brought into view: the increasing inequality, during the last century, in the spread of the industrial system across the face of the globe may seem more comprehensible if it is viewed as another case, if more strikingly worldwide, of a similar phase in the spread of many earlier systems of economic and social organization. Yet, the variety of growth experience remains impressive, however we may try to reduce it by looking at it in longer perspective.

Certain important, if obvious, conclusions follow. First, in evolving, as well as evaluating, theoretical hypotheses as to economic growth, any attempt to go beyond mere "lists" of factors would have to be made in clear recognition of the types of countries and the periods for which the processes of growth are to be explained. Second, since the impression of diversity suggested above exists in terms of concepts evolved in static analysis, a question may be raised whether part of the difficulty is in the concepts. For example, if certain elements in consumption are strategic in increasing labor's productivity, and it is thus possible to secure higher rates of growth by increasing consumption (and reducing capital formation) as a proportion of national product, is it desirable to maintain a distinction between such consumption and capital formation as means of increasing labor productivity? Third, with the greatly widened differences among nations in structure and levels of economic performance, the basis for across-the-board comparisons, of regression analysis in which the capital-product ratios for the United States and Honduras appear on the same diagram, and an inference is drawn as to capital needs of China, is all the more tenuous—if it ever was adequate. These comparisons require close statistical and historical analysis of the economic growth of each country—where the interrelations of the various components and factors in the longer-term changes may be adequately probed. Fourth, in such analysis, it would be possible and necessary to build a bridge between the more narrowly economic and the demographic and social phenomena, and emphasize the processes of adaptation (by migration and redistribution) of population and other resources to changing opportunities.

The recent surge of interest in problems of economic growth is largely an aftermath of current events. It is clearly *not* an organic outgrowth of continuously and increasingly effective work on the problem leading to a scientific discovery, the latter stirring interest and stimulating research on a new foundation—perhaps an idyllic picture of what happens in the experimental natural sciences. In fact, this recent interest comes after decades during which the problem has been neglected in the traditional corpus of economic theory, and ruled out by some economists as not the proper concern of economics. It may well prove that the contribution of economic analysis, in the accepted meaning of the term, to the study of problems of economic growth, can be only very limited, and that the flurry will subside leaving no lasting results. But the response to the spur of current events has been and is likely to be heroic efforts to struggle with a complex problem with inadequate means—with excesses of zeal that are only natural in view of the relevance of immediate results to grave problems of policy. In such conditions, the broad review presented by Abramovitz is valuable in providing both a perspective, and an indication of directions of further work—of a type whose results could be subjected to the critical test of reference to accumulating empirical observations.

COMMENT

Harold F. Williamson

A satisfactory theory of the economics of growth would identify the principal factors in the process and indicate the extent to which they are relatively dependent or independent variables; it would furnish the analytical tools necessary to show causal relations; it would be susceptible to empirical verification; and its relevance would not be restricted temporally, spatially, or to any particular cultural or institutional pattern. Merely to state these specifications is to question whether a thoroughly satisfactory theory can ever be developed. The subject matter involved in the process is so complex and presents so many imponderables that precise generalizations will certainly be difficult to formulate. These obstacles have not and should not discourage further explorations. Between an ideal theory and the present state of knowledge there exists a large area which challenges us to expand the scope of our understanding; an area which, in part at least, is more susceptible to analysis and useful generalizations than have thus far been developed.

Abramovitz lays proper emphasis on the historical importance in economic growth of the discovery and application of new production functions and the process of capital formation. His survey indicates, however, the unsatisfactory state of our understanding of the process of how new production functions are discovered and how this process may be brought into the analytical framework of the economics of growth. Schumpeter and others, by treating new production functions as exogenous factors, have made more fruitful attempts, although within limited institutional or cultural settings, to analyze their effect on economic growth.

Even in the field of capital formation, which forms the most valuable substantive portion of the essay, the results are disappointing. Despite the great attention given to the subject by economists, much of present-day capital theory is subject to serious limitations, which are brought out explicitly by Abramovitz. For example, the problem of full employment to which Keynes and his followers have addressed themselves has relatively little meaning for most underdeveloped areas.

Hansen's stagnation model represents a specialized case, not very useful for historical analysis; nor does it represent a situation that is likely to face the larger part of mankind for a long time to come.

Economists generally have been too much concerned with static models and too culturally bound by a Western European framework of institutions to make the contributions to the subject of the economics of growth that might reasonably be expected from the profession. This reluctance to depart both from static models and from a given institutional pattern is understandable. Many of the most pressing economic problems lend themselves to this approach. Moreover, the precision of theoretical analysis tends to be inverse to the number of variables which have to be considered whose dependence or functional relationships are not known. Unfortunately, the usefulness of theoretical analysis is also likely to be inverse to its precision. This is especially true when we attempt to apply our theories of economic growth to different cultural or institutional patterns.

Nor have the economic historians, with few exceptions, made notable contributions to our understanding of the subject. This has come from a preoccupation with segments of the process and from a reluctance to generalize about their subject matter.

An expanding body of literature has already contributed much to a better understanding of the problems involved in analyzing the economics of growth and has indicated how important it is to enlist the support of natural and social scientists generally. With the growing recognition of its importance, it is not too much to expect that economists and economic historians alike will devote more attention to the subject. Some of the difficulties that lie ahead have been outlined by Abramovitz in the concluding portion of his essay. His plea for greater cooperation among the practitioners of all relevant disciplines is well taken. But cooperative ventures are likely to fail in the absence of well-defined objectives and leadership. To give these is primarily the responsibility of the economists and economic historians. Theirs is the major task of indicating what phases of the economics of growth need further exploration. More specifically, they should identify those elements which have important effects on economic growth, but which lie, or seem to lie, outside the analysis; they should incorporate as many of these elements as is logically possible into the theoretical framework; and finally, they should call for specifications from those in other disciplines on the behavior of elements which are clearly autonomous, with the purpose of discovering how these elements influence or enter into the economic system.

5

SOME BASIC PROBLEMS IN
THE THEORY OF THE FIRM

Andreas G. Papandreou

The concept of the firm which is employed by econo-
mists in their teaching and research clearly reflects the frame of reference
they have selected in dealing with the problems of their discipline. This
frame of reference has been aptly called the *action* frame of reference.[1]
It consists of five basic concepts: The *act,* the *agent,* the *end,* the *situation,* which includes both means (elements of the situation over which
the agent exerts control) and conditions (elements of the situation over
which the agent cannot exert control), and finally, the *norm,* that is, the
principle which relates means to ends. The norm postulated by the economist is that of rationality. The agent is conceived as engaging in action
which maximizes a utility index (an ordinally structured preference system), given the constraints inherent in the situation.

The concept of the firm has been built to fit the specifications of
this frame of reference. This has been accomplished through the postulation of the concept of the entrepreneur, which to all intents and purposes displaces that of the firm in analysis. This result is attained in a
fairly simple manner. The firm emerges as soon as the owners of productive services sell them to an entrepreneur for a definite price. When this
set of transactions is consummated the owners of the productive services
cease to be of analytic concern to us. We then turn to the entrepreneur,
who thus becomes our sole object of analysis as far as the behavior of the
firm is concerned. This tour de force enables the economist to retain his
schema of an acting individual agent, even in the case of the firm, which
may legitimately be regarded as a "collective" of some sort. This probably is the key to the interesting fact that the economist has not evolved
a theory of conscious cooperation. On the contrary his main and lasting

---

[1] Cf. Talcott Parsons, *The Structure of Social Action* (New York, 1937; 2nd ed.,
Glencoe, 1949), Ch. 2 for a discussion of the action frame of reference.

contribution lies in the formulation of the properties of unconscious co-operation via the system of markets.

The adequacy of the economist's frame of reference in dealing with the wide variety of behavior problems which do not involve conscious interdependence among the acting agents cannot be seriously subjected to question. As soon as we leave the realm of unconscious interdependence, however, and attempt to deal with problems of deliberate cooperation we find ourselves increasingly falling back on concepts and generalizations whose relationship with the main body of thought is more or less tenuous. The duopoly or oligopoly problem is a case in point. Although interesting work dating back to Cournot had been done on the "small numbers" case within the basic conceptual frame of reference employed by the economist, effective incorporation of these issues into the main body of thought did not seem feasible until the advent of the theory of games.[2] The same comment is in order in connection with the conscious cooperation which takes place within the firm. Whenever the economist becomes concerned with such problems as "union participation in management," or the "separation between ownership and control" he has to fall back on concepts and generalizations which are not part and parcel of his main frame of reference. Concern with such matters has been the province of the institutional economist, an economist, that is, who in one way or another employs much of the sociologist's or the social psychologist's method and vocabulary.

It will be argued in this essay that the literature of the last two decades has provided the means whereby the conceptual frame of reference of the economist can be widened to incorporate without strain the concepts which are necessary for the consistent treatment of problems of conscious cooperation. The contributions which are considered crucial in this respect are three. There is, first, the contribution of Chester Barnard, who in his *The Functions of the Executive*[3] has laid the foundations for a theory of conscious cooperation which is consistent with the frame of reference employed by the economist. There is next the monumental work of Neumann and Morgenstern on the theory of games. Finally, Herbert Simon's work has brought together under one conceptual roof Barnard's concept of organization and Neumann and Morgenstern's concept of a game of strategy.[4]

In the part immediately following, an attempt will be made to pre-

---

[2] John von Neumann and Oskar Morgenstern, *Theory of Games and Economic Behavior* (Princeton, 1944; 2nd ed., 1947).

[3] Cambridge, Mass., 1938.

[4] H. A. Simon, *Administrative Behavior* (New York, 1945).

sent a frame of reference which will enable the economist to deal with problems of intrafirm structure without doing violence to his main conceptual schema.[5] This model will in turn lay the foundation for a systematic consideration of two related problems: first, the relationship between social structure and the structure of "power" and "control" over the firm, and secondly, the relationship between the character of the preference system of the firm and the cultural milieu in which it has grown.[6]

I. THE CONCEPT OF THE FIRM IN THE LIGHT OF THE THEORY OF ORGANIZATION

A. The Concept of Organization

The fundamental building block of a conceptual frame of reference which assigns a central position to conscious cooperation is provided by Chester Barnard's concept of *organization*. Organization is defined as a "system of consciously coordinated activities or forces of two or more persons."[7] It should be stressed that it is only the system of personal interactions that makes up the fabric of organization. Organization is not conceived, then, as a *group* of persons; rather it is conceived as an *action field,* as a system of consciously interdependent actions of two or more persons. When we consider persons in their roles as members of an organization, we regard them in their purely functional aspects, as mere phases of cooperation. The persons as such, whether they be conceived as physical, biological, or psychological and social entities, do not belong to organization.

Closely related to the concept of organization is the concept of a cooperative system. Organization is an element of the cooperative system; so are the persons whose activities constitute organization, and the physical plant which goes hand in hand with persons and organization. Persons and physical plant constitute a cooperative *system* (rather than an aggregate) by reason of the fact that the activities of the members are consciously coordinated toward the achievement of at least one definite end.[8]

---

[5] The decision has been made not to consider in this essay the contributions of the social psychologists or the industrial sociologists. Although their work is rich in empirical findings, the task of relating their conceptual frame of reference to that of the economist cannot be carried out within the confines of this essay.

[6] It must be stressed at this juncture that these basic problems are the only aspects of the theory of the firm which will be considered in this essay.

[7] *Op. cit.,* p. 73.

[8] *Ibid.,* p. 65.

The following conditions must be met for organization to emerge: first, persons must be willing to contribute activity to the system; secondly, they must share a common goal; thirdly, deliberate communication must be possible and present. The first two conditions must be met if the pattern is to be considered consciously cooperative. The third condition, deliberate communication, must also be met if conscious coordination and, therefore, organization is to emerge. Herbert Simon, who on the whole accepts the Barnard schema, prefers to state the problem in the language of the theory of games.[9] The cooperative pattern emerges when the participants prefer the same set of consequences. If anticipations concerning one another's behavior are correct, all will act to secure these consequences. In the absence of deliberate communication, however, the pattern may be expected to be highly unstable. Conscious coordination is the device or process whereby each participant is informed as to the strategies selected by the others.

Organization in Barnard's sense obtains whenever the activities of two or more persons are consciously coordinated with a view of achieving a common goal.[10] Organization is, therefore, ubiquitous. It extends from the simplest and most unstructured cooperative activities to the most complex and imposing structures. The act of exchange may be chosen as an example of the simplest sort of organization. Willingness to participate, joint goal (in some sense), and deliberate communication are all present. To the act of exchange which constitutes simple organization can be contrasted the complex organization which typically obtains in the case of the firm. The firm is in fact a cooperative system possessed of an organization which is both stable and complex. Stability in this connection refers to the nonephemeral character of at least a part of the interactions which are included in the enterprise. Complexity refers to the fact that (typically) the firm's organization is made up of a system of simple or unit organizations. The process of communication in a complex organization cannot be left to chance. It becomes specialized in centers of communication. These fairly stable centers of communication make up the executive (sub-) organization of the firm. The executive-administrator is regarded within this frame of reference as a communica-

---

[9] *Op. cit.*, pp. 72–73.

[10] The reader must be warned that the discussion of the concept of organization in this essay is confined to what Barnard calls *formal* organization. To formal organization Barnard contrasts *informal* organization. The latter refers to the set of interactions among persons which are not governed by a common goal and which, therefore, are not consciously coordinated. The concept of informal organization is akin to the social psychologist's concept of the group.

tion center, as the functionary who informs the participants of one another's strategies so that the cooperative goal may be achieved. Communication of the strategies involved in the process of cooperation is a
necessary condition for the performance of the executive role. It is not a
sufficient condition, however. The executive is not a mere center of communication. He also wields *authority* over the participants. The executive function, therefore, implies the issuing of coordinating *and* authoritative communications to those who contribute activities to the firm's
organization. Authoritative coordination lies at the heart of the concept
of the firm. Since authority plays such an important role in the concept
of the firm selected in this essay, it is necessary to provide a definition of
the term. Following Barnard and Simon we may define a communication
as authoritative if the recipient accepts it as determining the premises of
his choice of action "without deliberation on his own part on the expediency of those premises."[11]

B. The Process of Coordination

The conception of the firm as a cooperative system permits the organization theorist to set up a "rational" model of the firm closely resembling that of the economist; but, at the same time, it enables him to
employ much of the available sociological and psychological material.

The rational model of the firm as constructed by the organization
theorist resembles that of the economist in that rationality is attributed
only to the executive organization or some segment thereof (corresponding closely to the economist's concept of the entrepreneur), while the
economist completely removes from his model all agents other than the
entrepreneur. The organization theorist, while including in his model
the activities of the operative (nonexecutive) staff, views them as being
partly rational and partly nonrational. In so doing, however, he does not
destroy the purely rational character of the total construction. This is accomplished by regarding the activities of the operatives as manipulable
components of the system. The sociological and psychological considerations enter the rational administrative action model as *data* in a means-
ends problem, in the same fashion that end systems, technologies, and
institutions enter the rational action model of the economist. Organization theory and the economist's theory of the firm are seen to converge,

---

[11] Simon, *op. cit.*, p. 125. Simon has introduced, in this connection, the concept of
the "area of acceptance." The area of acceptance may be defined as that subset of all actions which may be performed by an employee with respect to which he is willing to accept the executive communication as guiding his behavior.

in fact, as soon as we introduce organizational techniques as data into the latter, side by side with the technological data.

Adoption of the rational model implies that we regard the executive organization of the firm or some segment thereof (which might be identified as the apex of the executive pyramid) as seeking to achieve ends with scarce means in a rational manner. This implies that administrative action is regarded (within the confines of the model) as efficient. Efficiency in turn implies that the means employed in the attainment of an end system are minimized or conversely that the ends attained from a given set of means are maximized.

The organization goals constitute the fundamental value premises of the system.[12] We are not concerned at this juncture with the manner in which these goals are formulated and the reasons for their acceptance by the executive as guiding his actions. This will concern us in detail at a later stage of the argument. All that needs to be emphasized here is that these goals are best regarded as being related to one another through a utility index of some sort. Nor is it necessary that we consider them to be ultimate ends; it would be preferable to consider them as intermediate stages in a means-ends chain in which they function as value indices of some sort. The goals of the firm—in the sense just described—must be contrasted sharply to what may be called the *function* of the firm. Function, in this sense, refers to the intended output of the firm, whether it is a service or a commodity. The function of a shoe manufacturing firm, for instance, is the production of shoes. It should be clear that when we talk about the utility index, the value premises accepted by the executive as guiding his actions, we make no commitment on the number or type of ends that enter the system nor do we make a commitment relating to the manner in which they are ranked. The statement is perfectly general, permitting any interpretation which is suitable in any concrete cases we care to study. It is conceivable, for instance, that the function of the firm may enter explicitly the value premises accepted by the executives as guiding their actions. Concern with "service" in this sense may, in fact, be prevalent in the case of government corporations, public utilities, etc. It is also possible that the conservation of the firm may become one of the ends sought by the executives. Students of administration seem to be convinced that this is typical rather than unusual, at least in the case of the large concern.

Given the goals of the system, the (rational) executive engages in

---

[12] Cf. *ibid.,* Ch. 3.

action which will enable the firm to attain them in an efficient way. This process involves (1) substantive planning, (2) procedural planning, and (3) execution of both plans.[13] Substantive planning essentially refers to the construction of the firm's budget,[14] whereas procedural planning refers to the construction of the psychological environment of decision necessary for the emergence of the organization. Substantive planning, procedural planning, and execution of the plans should not be conceived as a series of separate steps but rather as an integrated whole.

The structure of the system of communications and authority is the key to the procedural plan. This involves much more than the preparation of an organization chart specifying the channels of communication and authority. If the persons contributing activities to the firm's organization were regarded as rational agents, not much more than the organization chart would be needed. Under such conditions the operative could be considered as substituting organizational value premises for his private value premises and proceeding to act efficiently in a more or less automatic fashion. This construction implies that the operative (or, in fact, any contributor of action to the organization of the firm) substitutes a preference system communicated to him by the executive for his own personal preference system.[15]

The model of organization just presented is pegged upon the assumption of rational action on the part of all the participants in the organization of the firm. If it is recognized, however, that action is partly rational and partly subject to habit and the stimulus-response pattern, the procedural plans must elaborate the structure of internal influences as well as of authority which will provide the appropriate stimuli and lead to the establishment of the repetitive patterns which are necessary for the efficient attainment of the organizational ends. Learning theory and social psychology will provide the information necessary for the formulation of the appropriate procedural plan. The inculcation of loyalty to the organization and to the organizational goals, the development of efficient patterns of action and high morale become most important under these circumstances.

The distinction between influence and authority must be elaborated somewhat if we are to avoid making some of the conventional er-

---

[13] *Ibid.,* p. 96.

[14] Cf. G. F. Thirlby, "Notes on the Maximization Process in Company Administration," *Economica,* Aug. 1950, XVII, 266–82.

[15] For a discussion of these issues, see Simon, *op. cit.,* Ch. 6, 10.

rors of students of administration. In a complex organization, centers of communication are established which issue information to the participants concerning one another's strategies. When these communications are accepted by the recipient as determining the premises of his choices "without deliberation on his own part on the expediency of those premises,"[16] a relationship of authority exists between the issuer and the recipient of the communication. Authority, we have already seen, is of the essence in the structure of the firm. Authority in this sense, however, need not be exercised exclusively in a downward direction, though it is undoubtedly predominantly exercised in this manner. It may be exercised sideways and even in the upward direction. The structure of authority as it is depicted in organization charts refers not to the actual pattern of authority, but rather to that expected to prevail in the "normal" course of events. Influence implies suggestion and persuasion rather than command. The recipient of influence may accept a communication as governing his action; he does so, however, following "deliberation on his own part on the expediency" of the premises contained in the communication. The structure of influence is obviously of crucial significance in the functioning of an organization, especially in view of the fact that it is difficult to identify and control its sources.

Executive organizations in large or complex firms are themselves complex. This complexity expresses itself in a twofold manner. First, the lines of authority become elongated. Secondly, at any one level of this vertical scale of authority, executive work is divided into specialized function segments, giving rise to what may conveniently be called horizontal decentralization of authority. A large and complex firm, then, is almost invariably associated with an executive process which is decentralized both vertically and horizontally. With respect to the vertical decentralization of authority it is important to contrast *peak coordination* to inferior or subordinate coordinating activities. Peak coordination includes all the executive tasks performed at the apex of the executive pyramid. Authoritative and conscious coordination at its peak levels is carried on with a sense of the whole and in view of the total complex relationships of the firm to its social and physical environment. The internal and external equilibria of the system are sought simultaneously against the constellation of data confronting the firm. At levels inferior to that of peak coordination, this complex totality is lost. The outstanding characteristic of the peak coordination level of the executive organization is that it is not subject to horizontal decentralization. It should be clear, of

---

[16] *Ibid.,* p. 125.

course, that the fact that peak coordination is not subject to horizontal decentralization does not imply that the function must be performed by a single person. It is possible to allocate this function to a group rather than to an individual (an "organization" in Barnard's language). Although, then, peak coordination must be carried out by a single agency, the "singleness" of this agency must allow for subtle qualitative and quantitative variation in its composition.

G. F. Thirlby prefers the term *maximization center* for describing what has been called peak coordinator in this essay.[17] The substantive plan of the firm, according to Thirlby, is incorporated into the operating budget which is formulated by the maximizing center. The executive function at lower levels than that of peak coordination does not consist merely in the execution of the rigid orders of the peak coordinator. The task of selecting strategies, the task of selecting among alternative courses of action, is distributed, in general, throughout the organization. "Initiative may be exercised: (*a*) within the tolerance limits allowed by standing orders; (*b*) in the planning process leading to the board's decision which lays down standing orders."[18] The extent to which strategy selection is delegated down the lines of authority varies from case to case. What is crucial to keep in mind, however, is this: *the extent and character of the delegation is an integral part of the procedural plan selected by the peak coordinator.*[19]

C. The Process of External Influence

In the preceding section we considered the flow of authority and influence *within* the firm as they relate to the attainment of the firm's

---

[17] *Op. cit.*, p. 267.

[18] *Ibid.*, p. 271.

[19] A number of empirical studies have been published during the last decade dealing essentially with the problem of location of the "decision-making" function in the contemporary enterprise. Clearly the outstanding study is R. A. Gordon's *Business Leadership in the Large Corporation* (Washington, D.C., 1945). It is mandatory reading for all concerned with problems of enterprise structure. P. E. Holden, L. S. Fish, and H. L. Smith's *Top-Management Organization and Control* (Stanford, 1941) is one exception to the run-of-the-mill management studies in that it combines a conceptual framework and case-study material. It seems on the whole, however, to be more normative than observational-analytical in character. The Harvard Graduate School of Business Administration studies of the board of directors, despite their informative character, completely lack a conceptual framework. Such generalizations as are presented in these studies merge with normative considerations to produce a list of more or less loosely stated recipes for running a business. I am specifically referring to J. C. Baker, *Directors and Their Functions* (Boston, 1945), M. T. Copeland and A. R. Towl, *The Board of Directors and Business Management* (Boston, 1947), and M. L. Mace, *The Board of Directors in Small Corporations* (Boston, 1948).

goals. Both the goals toward which the firm strives, however, and the manner in which they are attained are subject to powerful and all-pervasive influences *from outside* the firm.[20] This is just another way of saying that the firm is a component of a much broader cooperative system which, in its informal aspects, becomes coextensive with what we call society. In a typical firm-and-market economy we are confronted with a process of cooperation which is partly conscious and partly unconscious. Within the firm, cooperation is of a deliberate character, with the conscious coordination of activities supplied by the firm's executive organization. In contrast to this, cooperation as it concerns the relations among firms (for that matter, as it concerns the relations among "units" in general), is unconscious; the interfirm or interunit cordination is supplied by the system of markets.[21]

No less important is the unconscious influence provided by the mores, folklore, customs, institutions, social ideals, and myths of a society which lay the foundation for formal organization. More immediately relevant to any one firm's behavior are the standards and values of the groups and communities with which it comes into contact as an organization, as well as the groups, communities, and organizations to which its members belong. It should be clear that the preference system of the firm, as well as the attitudes of the participants in the firm's organization toward such things as cooperation, authority, efficiency, innovation, etc., must be profoundly affected by the broader community within which the firm operates.[22]

Side by side with these unconscious societal influences we find influences exercised consciously by a variety of organizations, groups, and persons which in one way or another are affected by the firm's behavior (i.e. constitute "interest groups"). This set of influences is highly heterogeneous; in order to make some headway, therefore, in the analysis of their consequences upon firm behavior some attempt at classification must be made.[23] To begin with we are concerned here with conscious

---

[20] The reader should be warned that the term "influence" is used in this connection in the loose lexical sense rather than in the technical sense imparted to it by Simon's definition. Hereafter, whenever we employ the term in its technical sense, we shall italicize it.

[21] In this connection see R. H. Coase, "The Nature of the Firm," *Economica,* Nov. 1937, IV, 386–405.

[22] For an excellent presentation of these issues the reader is urged to see H. A. Simon, D. W. Smithburg, and V. A. Thompson, *Public Administration* (New York, 1950), Ch. 3.

[23] See Gordon, *op. cit.,* Ch. 7, and G. C. Means in National Resources Committee, *The Structure of the American Economy* (Washington, D.C., 1939) Pt. 1, Ch. 9, for two attempts at presenting a consistent system of concepts.

external influences rather than those of an *internal* nature. The latter have already been discussed in some detail in the preceding section. An influence is regarded as being internal if it is exercised by a participant in the organization (in the Barnard sense) during the process of conscious cooperation. It follows that the highest level of authority (in the sense of channels of authority expected to hold under "normal" conditions) from which internal influences can be exercised over the organization is that of the peak coordinator. The peak coordinator may himself be influenced by communications (or anticipations of communications) issued by stockholders, creditors, a union, and so on; such influence, however, will not be regarded as internal since it is not a component of the system of activities which are coordinated by the organization's executive.

Conscious external influences may be broken down into two categories: (1) the exercise of *influence* and (2) the exercise of authority. External *influence* and authority may be exercised over a firm by: (*a*) the government (in its sovereign aspects); (*b*) groups earning income by contributing factor services to the cooperative system (i.e., owner-stockholders, lenders of money, suppliers of goods on lease, operative labor, executive and professional labor); (*c*) buyers of the firm's product; (*d*) sellers of products and services to the firm; (*e*) competitors in the factor and product markets; (*f*) other persons, groups, or organizations which take interest in its operations. The degree of influence that such groups are in a position to exercise probably varies with their "power," whatever this ambiguous term may be taken to mean.

One final distinction seems necessary at this juncture. When the exercise of influence has as its immediate object the peak coordinator, it may either affect his conception of the broad value premises, the preference system of the organization, or it may affect the objective environment, the factual premises of his decision.[24] In the former case the results sought by the organization are modified or even radically changed as a result of the influence exercised. This implies that a new strategy will be selected. In the latter case the results sought are not affected, but, since the factual premises are changed, the strategy will have to be modified.[25]

---

[24] The distinction between factual and value premises is discussed at length in Simon, *op. cit.*, Ch. 3.

[25] It should be stressed that the value premises of enterprise strategy selection may be significantly affected as a result of the exercise of internal influence and authority in the upward direction. Executives at levels below that of peak coordination may at times be very influential in the formulation of the preference system of the firm. Such influence is regarded as internal since it is exercised by participants in the firm's organization in their capacity as participants rather than as a "bargaining" group. In this connection see E. S. Mason, "Price and Production Policies of Large-Scale Enterprise," *Am. Econ. Rev., Proc.*, Mar. 1939, XXIX, 61–74.

D. Some Implicit Issues

Although no attempt has been made to define the firm, it must be clear from the context that the firm is considered as a cooperative system possessed of a unique executive organization—an organization, that is, which converges to a peak coordinator.[26] The awkward term "peak coordinator" has been chosen advisedly in order to avoid associating the functionary with any one agent or group of agents designated by some conventional title, such as president, or chairman of the board, or executive council or the finance committee, etc. Just as we avoid all commitments as to the title borne by the peak coordinator in any one concrete case, we make no commitment as to the legal status of the firm. The firm may be a corporation or a group of corporations or a part of a corporation, or it may be a partnership or a proprietorship or some combination of some or all of the above.

This discussion raises the question of the *frontier* of the firm. We must be able to recognize whenever we are confronted with a concrete institution or legal entity, whether we are dealing with a plant (a segment of a firm), a firm, or a multifirm. The economist's basic criterion in establishing the frontier of the firm is provided by the notion of profit maximization. In the words of Robert Triffin "the frontier of the firm will be the frontier of the maximizing unit."[27] It is preferable, however, not to employ the concept of profit maximization inasmuch as this begs a number of questions which will be considered subsequently. The concept of the profit-maximizing plan of the firm may be replaced by the concept of *a* plan, in general, with a corresponding operating budget. A plant's plan must of necessity be a subset of the firm's plan. The firm's plan or budget, however, is *not* a subset of some other plan. The objection might be raised, however, that in the case of a multifirm this is exactly what takes place. The issue is important enough for the frame of reference under discussion to merit consideration.

When a group of firms subjects some segment of its behavior to the coordinating influence or authority of the group (or some organization which in some sense or other represents the group) a multifirm may be said to exist. The legal form selected and the source of the "power"

---

[26] A question may be raised concerning the status of a one-man "firm." Since in this case organization is absent, and since organization is an element of our definition of the firm, it follows that a one-man "firm" is not a firm at all. For some purposes this implication of the definition is undesirable. For our purposes it is of no consequence.

[27] *Monopolistic Competition and General Equilibrium Theory* (Cambridge, Mass., 1940), p. 94.

to coordinate may vary from case to case. Typically both cartels and combines constitute multifirms. It is argued here that the member firms' plans are *not* subsets of the multifirm's plan; rather the multifirm's plan should be regarded as a composite of mutually consistent subsets of the participating firms' plans. The interfirm coordinating communications are aimed at modifying some of the factual premises of firm strategy selection, and thus lead to the exclusion of some of the strategies which otherwise would have been available to the member firms. In any case it must be clear that the plan of the multifirm cannot contain the plan of the firm. If it did, the multifirm would become a "firm" and its member units would become "plants."

II. THE STRUCTURE OF EXTERNAL INFLUENCE

The preceding part was devoted to the formulation of a conceptual frame of reference which assigns a central position to conscious cooperation. In this part we propose to consider some of the empirical evidence available on the matter of external influence over the firm. There can be no doubt that the structure of external influence is of central concern to the student of firm behavior. The preference system of the firm is intimately related to the origin and character of *influence* and authority exercised over the firm. Therefore, the selection of an appropriate model for the analysis of firm behavior will be greatly facilitated by knowledge concerning the structure of influence over the firm.

In attempting, however, to arrive at some empirical generalizations concerning the character of the influence exerted by various interest groups over the firm, we are forced to sacrifice the generality of the model of organization presented, and to make definite commitments concerning the empirical counterparts of some of the concepts developed in the model. These commitments will, in general, become evident as the argument progresses. It is probably sufficient at this juncture to state that the firm is identified with the large modern corporation. The tentative empirical generalizations put forth in this part are subject to this restriction.

A. Stockholders and Creditors

The thesis, so dramatically enunciated by Berle and Means, that ownership has been separated from "control" as a result of the diffusion of stock ownership—a consequence of the growth of the large corporation—has not gone completely unchallenged.[28] The Securities and Exchange Commission arrived at the conclusion that approximately three-fourths of the corporations studied were "more or less definitely under ownership control."[29] Robert Gordon has successfully argued, however, that the conclusions of the Securities and Exchange Commission are based on a more or less mechanical manipulation of statistical data on the distribution of stockownership.[30] Both Gordon's study and an independent investigation by the author of this essay tend to support the Berle and Means thesis that the "property atom" has been split as a consequence of the growth of the large corporation.[31] To be sure, the data on the distribution of stockownership support both the thesis that there is diffusion of ownership and the thesis that there is concentration of ownership. There is nothing contradictory in this. To establish, however, that stockholdings are distributed in a strikingly unequal fashion and that there is susbtantial concentration of stockownership in the hands of minority groups of stockholders does not automatically imply that "control," "leadership," "authority," and "influence" are exercised by these minority groups. Gordon's careful study of the role of the stockholder in the large corporation furnishes some of the answers to these vexing questions. We shall attempt to summarize his findings, though presenting them whenever possible within the frame of reference developed in this essay.

At the start, a distinction must be made between small stockholders and large stockholders or stockholder groups, the terms "large" and "small" referring to the proportion of stock outstanding owned rather than the absolute dollar figures. The prevalence of the small stockholder in the large or giant corporation is not open to dispute. Stockholdings of less than 1 per cent aggregated well over half the value of the common stock of 176 giant corporations.[32] With respect to the small stockholder we are forced to the conclusion that his capacity to exert influence over

---

[28] A. A. Berle, Jr. and G. C. Means, *The Modern Corporation and Private Property* (New York, 1932). See also James Burnham, *The Managerial Revolution* (New York, 1941), for a somewhat different interpretation of the same phenomena.

[29] Temp. Nat. Econ. Com., *The Distribution of Ownership in the 200 Largest Nonfinancial Corporations,* Monog. 29 (Washington, 1940). Paul Sweezy, "The Illusion of the 'Managerial Revolution,'" *Sci. and Soc.,* Winter 1942, VI, 1–23, also has challenged the thesis that ownership has been separated from control. Consideration will be given to the broader implications of the controversy in Pt. IV.

[30] Gordon, *op. cit.,* Ch. 2, 8.

[31] A. G. Papandreou, *The Location and Scope of the Entrepreneurial Function* (Cambridge, Mass., 1943), unpublished thesis in Harvard University Library.

[32] Gordon, *op. cit.,* p. 159.

the large corporation is insignificant. This is the result of the lack of interest in and/or ability to organize for the exertion of influence in stockholders' meetings. The proxy machinery, though largely a management instrument, "becomes a partial—and by no means completely satisfactory—substitute for complete disfranchisement."[33] The growth of nonvoting stock and the narrowing of the range of matters on which stockholder vote is legally necessary have both contributed to the passivity of the small stockholder.

One sort of influence of the small stockholder over the corporation must be recognized, however. There are undoubtedly limits beyond which no management would care to go in disregarding the interests of the small stockholder. If these limits were transgressed, management could well expect "activation" of the passive small-stockholder group (possibly under the leadership of some small but powerful minority) and censure of its actions. The peak coordinator, to state the matter more formally, must take account of this potentiality as a factual premise in the development of enterprise strategy.

It is not easy to arrive at generalizations concerning the degree to which large minority interest groups exert influence over the large corporation in the formulation of its strategy. It must be admitted, however, that practically all degrees of influence can be found—ranging from the most passive to active participation in the executive process. In some cases members of large minority interest groups participate actively in the performance of the executive, and possibly even the peak coordination, function. In such cases the minority group may be regarded as affecting substantially the value premises (the preference system) of executive decision making. Where this is not true, it is likely that minority groups exert *influence* (ranging from "substantial" to "little") affecting the factual premises of executive decision making. Seldom do minority groups exert authority, and when they do it is unlikely that they exercise it with respect to the value premises of decision making (except, of course, in the cases where they actively participate in the peak coordination function).

Intimately associated with the problem of ownership "control" is the question of the role of the board of directors in the large corporation. The degree of influence exercised by the stockholder group must needs be related to the manner in which boards of directors are instituted, to

---

[33] *Ibid.*, p. 161. The SEC has attempted to improve practices relating to the use of the proxy machinery under power granted to it by section 14(a) of the Securities Exchange Act of 1934.

their composition and to the role which they play vis-à-vis the executive organization of the firm. Gordon's findings on the functions of directors support the view that seldom do boards of directors perform the peak-coordination function. The board of directors does not, in general, constitute a group independent from and superior to, the executive group. Its membership is partly drawn from the executive ranks—and, even when this is not true, its constitution is largely determined by the executives. In many cases, therefore, the board of directors may be conceived as a management instrument, i.e. as an organization subject to the coordination supplied by the executives for the attainment of the goals of the enterprise. This interpretation of the role of directors in the large corporation does not imply that they exert no influence over the peak coordinator. It does imply, however, that, in general, boards of directors exercise *influence* rather than authority, and that insofar as they do exercise *influence* they tend to affect the factual rather than value premises of enterprise strategy selection.

The general picture of the relationship between ownership and influence in the large corporation clearly supports the view that the importance of the owner group has declined substantially with the advent of the giant corporation. This conclusion, however, is open to misinterpretation and misuse. Although it is certain that ownership in the large corporation generally lacks the position necessary to influence significantly the structure of the preference system of the enterprise, it does not follow that the peak coordinator will fail to attach a significant weight to the interest of the stockholders in the formulation of the preference system of the firm. The peak coordinator and, more generally, the executives of the enterprise are subject to the subtle but all-pervasive influences exercised on them by the standards, values, and myths of the broader community in which they function. In a private enterprise society these standards, values, and myths can be relied upon to influence the executive to take "due account" of the interests of the owner. Unfortunately, it is impossible to assess the significance of this factor: this should not lead us, however, to a casual underestimation of its importance. Another element in the picture which should not be neglected is the extent of stockownership on the part of the executive group. Absolute, not relative, measures are relevant in this context. Any executive who has a substantial "dollar stake" in an enterprise is apt to be influenced to some extent by his role as an owner. The ownership stake of executives in the large industrials is substantial. It is somewhat less substantial in the utilities, and tends to be rather negligible in the case of the railroads.[34] The importance of this consideration should not be exaggerated, of course, since executive compensation is quantitatively much more important than earnings from stockownership. Still, it serves to modify rash generalizations concerning the insignificance of the stockholder interest in enterprise strategy selection.

The importance of the creditor or financial group also seems to have declined in recent years. Included in the financial group are the commercial, private, and investment bankers. The power of the financial group to influence the behavior of business firms derives primarily from two sources. To begin with, bankers can employ their bargaining power to establish some degree of continuing influence over firms which either borrow from them or make use of financial services supplied by them. Secondly, bankers in any city (especially large commercial banks) are apt "to be the rallying point and to provide the leadership for the city's financial interests."[35] In this leadership role bankers may be in a position to exert substantial influence over management of both small and large corporations. This leadership role shades imperceptibly into the relatively high status which bankers must have in any community, at least from the point of view of the business executive.

Gordon recognizes the importance of these considerations; he feels, nevertheless, that the degree of influence exercised by the banker over the large enterprise has been exaggerated. Generally speaking, bankers are apt to exert much influence over firms during periods of financial stress, reorganization, merger, and rapid expansion, i.e., in situations that enhance the bargaining power of the banker. Under such conditions and, in most cases, for the duration of the period of great need of funds, they may exercise some authority as well as *influence*. Almost invariably, however, their authority and *influence* are restricted to the range of problems which are generally referred to as "financial." It is, therefore, probably correct to surmise that bankers, insofar as they exercise any influence over the firm by reason of their bargaining power, tend to affect the factual premises rather than the value premises of strategy selection. At times, however, they may be successful in affecting the value premises, the preference system of the firm, particularly in re-

---

[34] *Ibid.*, pp. 297–304. See also R. A. Gordon, "Ownership and Compensation as Incentives to Corporation Executives," *Quart. Jour. Econ.*, May 1940, LIV, 455–73; J. C. Baker, *Executive Salaries and Bonus Plans* (Boston, 1938).

[35] Gordon, *Business Leadership*, p. 189, n. 1.

spect to the liquidity attitudes of the executive.[36] In their role as a high status group they may be able to exert moderate influence over the enterprise by affecting not only the factual premises but also the value premises of enterprise strategy selection.

It is generally agreed that the influence of the banking interests over the firm has declined significantly during our times.[37] Increased reliance of the large successful corporation on internal financing may partly account for this. The growing participation of insurance companies and other financial institutions in the investable funds market has undoubtedly contributed to this decline in the importance of the banker. Increasingly important is the role of government as a supplier of funds. The advent of World War II accelerated this tendency, and preparation for meeting the eventuality of a third world war may be expected to carry the process even further.

B. Labor

The appraisal of the role of labor as an interest group vis-à-vis the business firm, especially in relation to its influence on the executive of the corporation, is somewhat obstructed by the heated verbal debate between the spokesmen of management and labor which has accompanied the power struggle between organized labor on the one hand and management on the other. The broader social implications of this conflict will be considered at a later stage of this essay. We are presently concerned with the evaluation of the degree to which labor is in a position to exercise influence over the executive organization of the firm.

The outstanding document on the subject has been written by Neil W. Chamberlain.[38] The ability of labor, as an interest group, to exert influence over the firm is dependent upon the degree to which it is organized for such action. The mechanism of collective bargaining, supported by the power to strike, renders the exercise of its power legitimate within the framework of our legal institutions. It is well known, of course, that labor has achieved dramatic success (not without signifi-

---

[36] *Ibid.,* p. 201, n. 24.

[37] *Ibid.,* pp. 214–21; Paul Sweezy, *The Theory of Capitalist Development* (New York, 1942), Ch. 14.

[38] *The Union Challenge to Management Control* (New York, 1948). This book constitutes mandatory reading for those who wish to gain valuable insights into the nature of the problem. Other relevant contributions are: Gordon, *Business Leadership,* pp. 255–58; C. E. Lindblom, *Unions and Capitalism* (New Haven, 1949); S. H. Slichter, *Union Policies and Industrial Management* (New Haven, 1949); C. S. Golden and H. J. Ruttenberg, *The Dynamics of Industrial Democracy* (New York, 1940).

cant setbacks, however) on both the political-legal level and on the level of utilization of its legal power in its dealings with employers. Although there are reasons for expecting that the growth of its power over the firm will continue, the feeling is quite general that it will proceed somewhat more slowly and less dramatically.

The main direct source of influence of labor over the executive organization of the firm is the employment contract. This has been defined by Simon as a contract in which the employee agrees to accept the authority (in the Barnard-Simon sense) of the employer and the employer agrees to pay the employee a stated wage.[39] The union, representing labor at the bargaining table, can affect not only the wage rate, but also the area of acceptance of authority, i.e. the range of behavior with respect to which the employee will accept executive communications as guiding his actions. The union can go even beyond this, however, by specifying the "physical" and "social" conditions under which executive communication will be accepted as guiding the action of its members. As soon as these possibilities are appreciated, it becomes evident that labor, if effectively organized, can establish substantial authority over the peak coordinator of the firm, extending over as wide a range of matters as it deems relevant to its interests and as its power permits it to invade. The experience of the last twenty years can leave no doubt about the determination and ability of labor to widen this range. The extent to which it has been successful is evidenced by the great concern of management over the "encroachment on its prerogatives" by the unions.

It is highly likely that the growing ability of labor to exercise authority over the firm's peak coordinator is restricted to the factual premises of enterprise strategy. Despite the high degree of union penetration of "management areas," the socio-cultural climate mitigates the likelihood that unions can exert significant influence in the process of formulation of the value premises of enterprise strategy. This seems to be the case today, though it must be admitted that future developments may bring significant changes in this respect.

The influence we have just examined is exercised directly by labor over the peak cordinator of the firm, and is analogous in many respects to the influence exercised over him by the other interest groups. Labor unions, however, are in a position to exercise influence at the lower levels of the executive hierarchy as well as directly on the operatives.

---

[39] H. A. Simon, "A Formal Theory of the Employment Relationship," *Econometrica*, July 1951, XIX, 293–305.

This raises serious problems of coordination which have been debated vigorously by representatives of unions and management. Insofar as the influence exercised by the unions at these lower organizational levels contradicts the authority of the executive the efficiency and even the life of the concern may be seriously endangered. Chamberlain is convinced that this feature of the conflict between labor and management can be eliminated by the acceptance by both contestants of the need for "functional integration."[40] This essentially amounts to recognition by the union that its representatives can act at the lower levels only within the limits established by the peak coordinator in conformance with his agreement with the unions. The clear implication of this notion is that union representatives, insofar as they participate in the process of co-ordination of the activities which make up the firm's organization, must assume the responsibilities of the role of the executive along with its privileges.

C. Government

The influence of government has increased in a striking fashion during the last quarter century. Government means so many things, however, and its influences take such a variety of forms that the discussion here must of necessity be restricted to the broadest and most general considerations.

Government, in this context, includes federal, state, and local governments in their legislative, executive, and judicial aspects. The government in its sovereign aspect exercises authority over all its citizens and subordinate organizations. With respect to the private firm not "affected with a public interest" government's authority is aimed at affecting the factual premises of strategy selection whether its communications ("laws," "orders," "decisions") take a prohibitory or a prescriptive form. With respect to government corporations, however, and firms "affected with a public interest" its authority clearly extends to the formulation of the value premises, the preference system of the organizations.

Government exercises indirect influence on all firms by participating actively in the economic process, i.e., by directly affecting the flow of funds and the counterflow of goods and services. Developments of the last quarter century have given special importance to this type of influence. Fiscal policy has come to be considered as the most essential

---

[40] Chamberlain, *op. cit.*, Ch. 10–12.

instrument of national planning.[41] Government has also increasingly engaged in influencing its constituency by means of modern methods of mass communication. Public opinion climate formation and direct appeals to businessmen and other interest groups may elicit behavior patterns somewhat more consistent with the interests of government.

Government is itself subject to the pulls and pressures exerted on it by the various national interest groups. It may be hypothesized, in fact, that its behavior is a vector of this multitude of influences or forces exercised upon it.[42] One of the most important functions of government is the maintenance of the centripetal cooperative aspects of society despite the centrifugal or conflict forces in operation. The resolution of important conflicts or the development of a *modus vivendi,* if resolution is not likely, undoubtedly constitutes one of the central tasks of government. It is clear, therefore, that the problem of "control" over the business firm must be of immediate interest to government. Some of the authority it exerts over the firm is aimed at resolving the conflict of the interest groups which are vying for the "control" of the firm. A great deal of labor legislation, of the regulation of the securities market, and even some of the antitrust laws are aimed at this resolution of conflict over the "control" of the firm.[43] However, the more actively government participates in the resolution of conflict over the firm the more likely it is that the contestants will shift their battleground from the firm level to the political level. "Control" of the government may then become the means for establishing "control" of the firm. There are signs that we are steadily moving in this direction. Needless to say such a development will undermine most of the institutions associated with a "decentralized society."

D. Conclusions

The brief survey of the structure of external influence over the large, modern enterprise strongly supports the following conclusions: (*a*) the influence of stockholders has declined with the advent and growth of the modern corporation; (*b*) the influence of financial

---

[41] See Arthur Smithies, "Federal Budgeting and Fiscal Policy," *A Survey of Contemporary Economics,* Vol. I, H. S. Ellis, ed. (Philadelphia and Toronto, 1948), Ch. 5; also, the present volume, Ch. 9.

[42] A stimulating analysis of the problem of influence exercised on government by business groups can be found in R. A. Brady, *Business as a System of Power* (New York, 1943).

[43] It should not be forgotten, of course, that the law of property still is the main instrument for resolving issues of this order.

groups also has declined; (*c*) labor's influence has grown by leaps and bounds and may be expected to continue growing with the passing of time; (*d*) government's influence has also increased spectacularly; (*e*) management has become the focus of forces pulling the enterprise in different directions.

These empirical findings have been presented within a conceptual framework with the following general features: (*a*) The peak coordinator is conceived as the highest level of intrafirm authority. He formulates the operating budget of the firm. This amounts to the selection of a strategy. The selection of a strategy, in turn, requires the specification of some value premises (preference system) and factual premises. (*b*) The peak coordinator is subject to a variety of influences some of which affect the value premises while others affect the factual premises of his decisions. (*c*) The preference system accepted by the peak coordinator as guiding enterprise behavior is regarded as being a resultant of all the influences which affect the value premises of enterprise strategy selection. If the peak coordinator were free of immediate, direct, conscious influences, his own value system and, therefore, the ethos of his own culture and subculture would be dominant in the formulation of the value premises of enterprise strategy selection. If the peak coordinator must accept the authority of one or more groups (with respect to value premises), their value system and, therefore, the ethos of their culture and subculture will be dominant. The developments of the last half-century support the hypothesis that the peak coordinator has been subjected to a changing structure of conscious influence.

The changes in the structure of enterprise which attend the growth of the modern corporation in size and national importance have been discussed quite intensively in the literature of the last two or three decades. Much has been written on the "separation of ownership and control," on "management control," and the "encroachment upon management prerogatives" by unions. These developments raise serious problems both of analysis and public policy.

There is general awareness of the developing contradiction within the structure of public policy. Our law of property and laws of incorporation (supported by judicial decision and interpretation) still support the construction that the board of directors plays a role of agent, trustee, or fiduciary to the stockholders of the corporation. The fundamental legal limitation on the action of the board is merely one of intent. Insofar as they take the interest of the stockholders into account they are free practically to do anything they wish with company property. We are familiar with the fact, however, that, at least in the majority of the corporations, the board of directors is rather passive. We are also aware of the fact that the connection between the mass of stockholders and the board of directors is a very loose one, to say the least. Some of the legislation enacted (namely laws pertaining to securities markets, reorganizations, public utility structure, etc.) aims at preserving the power of the stockholder and the traditional relationship between director and stockholder. Other types of important legislation, especially labor legislation, have tended to give legal status "to an interest in the affairs of the corporation by a party other than the stockholders."[44]

It is interesting to note that even business executives and business students are increasingly giving lip service to the notion that the boards of directors (or management) are trustees for the owners, *and* labor, *and* customers, *and* the public. It must be recognized, of course, that statements by managers or directors to that effect need not imply adherence to such principles in decision making—at least as far as the value premises of decision making are concerned. They do imply, however, that the forces of change have been so successful that new verbalizations, slogans, and myths are necessary for the daily conduct of business.

Government policy is undoubtedly largely the resultant of the pressures and counterpressures of the various interest groups vying for "control" of the firm. Insofar as this is true we may expect government to sanction developments which are supported by the new "balance of power" in the economy. Although this approach may lead to interpretation of current government policy it cannot provide us with criteria as to what government policy *should* be from the point of view of the economy or the nation as a whole. Before we are in a position, however, to establish optimum policy measures we must be acquainted with the *behavior consequences* of the structural changes which we are presently considering.

III. DO FIRMS MAXIMIZE PROFITS?

A. Rationality and Profit Maximization

The assumption that firms maximize profits has dominated economic analysis for a long time. Nevertheless, the concept of profit maximization is seldom stated unambiguously; and, even when it is stated

---

[44] Chamberlain, *op. cit.,* p. 19, n. 18.

with precision, its relation to the broader body of theory is rarely made explicit. In recent years, however, the assumption has come under fire as being unrealistic, especially in the case of "management controlled" corporations. Increasingly, economists tend to qualify the assumption by listing conditions under which it might not be true. In what follows we propose to consider the issue in some detail.

It is worth pointing out at the outset of the discussion that we are not concerned primarily with the question of whether firms do *in fact* maximize profits. Excessive concern with the realism of the assumption —in the sense of direct correspondence with the "facts"—suggests an inadequate conception of the role of theory construction. The validity of the assumption must be judged primarily by reference to its capacity to lead to tentatively valid derived propositions about empirical data.

It is often supposed that the assumption of profit maximization rests on the same universal grounds as the assumption of utility-index maximization or rationality. This is not correct however. Profit maximization does imply rationality of course; but rationality is consistent with maximization of other things as well as profits. Profit maximization can be derived from utility-index maximization only through the imposition of a restriction on the character of the index. As soon as the distinction between profit maximization and utility-index maximization is carefully drawn it becomes possible to distinguish between *efficiency* and profit maximization in an unambiguous fashion. Efficiency relates to rationality, that is to maximizing a utility index. It implies maximization of ends with a given set of means or the minimization of means in the attainment of a given set of related ends. Efficiency is implicit in profit maximization, but efficient behavior need not be profit-maximizing behavior. A business firm may be efficient without seeking to maximize profits.

Ideally rationality implies that the actor has a well-ordered preference system, that he has perfect knowledge concerning the means-ends relationships, and that he acts to maximize his end system. Actually he is confronted with a means-ends chain. Each link in the chain must be considered as an intermediate end (with respect to the preceding link) and as an intermediate means (with respect to the succeeding link). In general, we prefer not to state the preference system in terms of the ultimate ends. The higher the level of the ends in the means-ends chain, the more difficult it becomes to establish the relationship between means and ends and hence the more difficult it becomes to ascertain whether action is rational or not.[45] Profit may be regarded as a value index in terms of which we rank the ends which enter our preference systems. As soon as we select profit as the *ranking criterion* of an end system, rational behavior must involve profit maximization.[46] Thus profit-maximizing behavior can be derived from rational behavior when we specify that the ranking criterion of our preference system is profit.[47]

Profits may be introduced into the theory of choice in a somewhat different way. Profit may be regarded by the theorists as one among many related goals sought by the entrepreneur. In such constructions profit maximization is replaced by the more general notion of preference-function maximization. Hicks' classic statement that "the best of all monopoly profits is a quiet life" was made in this vein.[48] This suggestion has led to a fuller treatment by Benjamin Higgins, Tibor Scitovsky, and Melvin Reder.[49] Higgins points out that profit maximization is a survival condition in perfect competition. Its force is much weaker, however, in the case of nonperfect competition since under such conditions the entrepreneur may be expected to have margins with which to work and with which to satisfy desires other than the desire for profit. Higgins proceeds to classify the desires or forces which lead to nonprofit-maximizing solutions into three categories: those which lead the entrepreneur to produce at a point below the profit-maximizing output; those which lead him to produce at a point above that output; and, finally, those that make him stay where he is, whether he is producing an output above or below the profit-maximizing output. Leisure (Hicks' "quiet life") leads to the first case. Desire to own a large firm, power, prestige, etc., may account for the second case. The third case arises either as a result of "just price" ideas or as a result of reluctance to experiment. Higgins' formal presentation involves the introduction of indifference curves

---

[45] See Simon, *Administrative Behavior*, Ch. 4.

[46] Where profit is the ranking criterion not ranking but measurement takes place. It seems best, however, to use the expression "ranking criterion" even in this case in order to maintain the generality of the concept.

[47] In this connection, see Talcott Parsons, "The Motivation of Economic Activity," *Can. Jour. Econ. Pol. Sci.,* May 1940, VI, 187–202; reprinted in *idem, Essays in Sociological Theory Pure and Applied* (Glencoe, 1949), Ch. 9.

[48] J. R. Hicks, "The Theory of Monopoly," *Econometrica,* Jan. 1935, III, 1–20.

[49] Benjamin Higgins, "Elements of Indeterminacy in the Theory of Non-perfect Competition," *Am. Econ. Rev.,* Sept. 1939, XXIX, 468–79; Tibor Scitovsky, "A Note on Profit Maximization," *Rev. Econ. Stud.,* Winter 1943, XI, 57–60; Melvin Reder, "A Reconsideration of the Marginal Productivity Theory," *Jour. Pol. Econ.,* Oct. 1947, LV, 450–58.

(relating profit to output) into the standard textbook dollars-output diagram. Tangency of the net-profits curve to an indifference curve maximizes the entrepreneur's utility index.

Scitovsky's paper deals more specifically with the leisure *versus* income problem as it relates to the entrepreneur. The leading conclusion of Scitovsky's argument is that profits will be maximized only if the entrepreneur's choice between more or less activity—or between more income and more leisure—is independent of his income. In all other cases utility-index maximization leads to outputs which do not maximize profits. Reder's paper contains a wealth of suggestions. He, too, claims that profit maximization must be regarded as a very special case.[50]

B. Profit Maximization and Uncertainty

As soon as we introduce dynamic and uncertainty considerations, new issues arise in connection with the profit-maximization construction. It should be noted at the outset that the introduction of time (even in a trivial or perfunctory way) reduces the potency of the profit-maximization assumption in producing operationally meaningful theorems. Since the entrepreneur must now be assumed to be maximizing the present value of his assets (or some related magnitude) his horizon and expectations must be known before statements concerning his behavior in any one period can be derived from the profit-maximization assumption. In other words, any number of current outputs may be consistent with profit maximization even in the case of single-valued expectations —expectations, that is, which are held with certainty. In the absence of knowledge concerning entrepreneurial horizon and expectations the profit-maximization construction becomes an empirically irrelevant tautology.[51]

Recognition of the fact that expectations are not single-valued will generally force us to substitute preference-function maximization for profit-maximization analysis. Gerhard Tintner's work has illuminated this aspect of the problem considerably.[52] His approach is struc-

---

[50] An interesting discussion of the problem can also be found in William Fellner, *Competition among the Few* (New York, 1949), pp. 169–74.

[51] The Lester-Machlup controversy is relevant at this juncture. See B. F. Haley, "Value and Distribution," *A Survey of Contemporary Economics*, Vol. I, pp. 11–13, for a discussion of the issues involved and for bibliographical references.

[52] Gerhard Tintner, "The Theory of Choice under Subjective Risk and Uncertainty," *Econometrica*, July–Oct. 1941, IX, 298–304; *idem*, "A Contribution to the Non-Static Theory of Choice," *Quart. Jour. Econ.*, Feb. 1942, LVI, 274–306; *idem*, "The Theory of Production under Non-Static Conditions," *Jour. Pol. Econ.*, Oct. 1942, L, 646–

tured on the generally accepted frequency-ratio analysis. Tintner distinguishes four cases: (1) subjective risk with respect to prices and interest, with the assumption of perfect knowledge concerning technical-technological conditions; (2) subjective uncertainty with respect to prices and interest, also on the assumption of perfect knowledge concerning technical-technological conditions; (3) subjective risk with respect to technical-technological conditions; (4) subjective uncertainty with respect to technical-technological conditions.[53] Risk refers to a situation in which the entrepreneur is confronted with a joint probability distribution of the anticipated prices, interest rates, and (in the third case) technical-technological conditions, where the parameters of the distribution are known with certainty (probability of 1). Subjective uncertainty is present if the parameters of the joint probability distribution are not anticipated with certainty. In this case there exists an *a priori* probability distribution of the joint probability distribution. Tintner's solution of the choice problems consists in the postulation of a *risk preference functional,* in the case of subjective risk, and an *uncertainty preference functional* in the case of subjective uncertainty, which must be maximized by the entrepreneur. The implication of the solution clearly is that the mathematical expectation of anticipated discounted profits (the weighted arithmetic mean of discounted net profits with the probabilities as weights) will not be maximized except in a special case. This means, in somewhat different words, that the entrepreneur may be just as concerned with other features of the probability distribution of anticipated net profits (such as its dispersion, kurtosis, skewness, etc.) as he is with the mathematical expectation.

G. L. S. Shackle's recent contribution to the theory of expectations deserves comment.[54] Shackle takes strong exception to the traditional approach of dealing with the problem of expectations. His basic objection to the traditional approach is that numerical probability calls for both uniformity of some sort in the conditions of experiment and a "large" number of such experiments. Even if this difficulty were to be overcome somehow, the entrepreneur would still be faced in many cases with decisions which for *him* are virtually *unique.*[55] Shackle's novel

---

67; *idem,* "A Contribution to the Non-Static Theory of Production," in *Studies in Mathematical Economics and Econometrics,* Oscar Lange, Francis McIntyre, T. O. Yntema, ed. (Chicago, 1942), pp. 92–109.

[53] Tintner, "The Theory of Production under Non-Static Conditions," *loc. cit.*

[54] *Expectation in Economics* (Cambridge, Eng. 1949).

[55] *Ibid.,* Ch. 7.

way of attempting to deal with the problem takes the following general form: He formulates first a *potential surprise function, y* $= f(x)$, which gives, for each value of x (where x stands for the "values" of hypothetical outcomes), the surprise y, which the entrepreneur expects himself to feel if x turns out to have that value.[56] It must be emphasized that zero potential surprise need not mean certainty; it merely means that the entrepreneur would not be surprised at all if that particular value of x were realized. With an interesting tour de force, Shackle proceeds to epitomize the potential surprise function. For any given degree of surprise, the greater the absolute (either gain or loss) value of x, the more our attention will be aroused; while, for any given value of x, the greater the degree of potential surprise, the less our attention will be aroused. Thus indifference curves can be drawn such that all points on any one of them have equal capacity to arouse interest or attention. In general, we should expect two points of tangency (one in the gain, the other in the loss region) between the potential surprise curve and the indifference curves. These two points are named *focus-gain* and *focus-loss*. According to Shackle the entrepreneur's attention will be *focused* exclusively upon these two hypothetical outcomes. Finally, we can construct an "indifference map of uncertainties," from which, given the focus-gains and the focus-losses of any two courses of action, we can identify the course of action which will be preferred by the actor. The indifference curves relating focus-gains to focus-losses are assumed to be positively inclined, since presumably increases in focus-losses must be compensated for by increases in focus-gains.

Shackle's treatment of the subject of expectations is both promising and stimulating. It is clear, however, that its value remains to be demonstrated in empirical work. In this respect, of course, it is neither superior nor inferior to the traditional approach. What is important from our point of view, however, is this: even if we adopt the Shackle approach the profit-maximization construction must yield to a broader statement.[57]

[56] See Ralph Turvey, J. de V. Graaf, and W. J. Baumol, "Three Notes on 'Expectation in Economics,'" and Shackle's reply in *Economica*, Nov. 1949, XVI, 336–46.

[57] It is not possible to consider here other developments in the theory of expectations and uncertainty. It seems advisable, however, to call the attention of the reader to some outstanding performances in this field. Among the earlier statements of the problem the following might be mentioned: Helen Makower and Jacob Marschak, "Assets, Price and Monetary Theory," *Economica*, Aug. 1938, V, 261–88; Jacob Marschak, "Money and the Theory of Assets," *Econometrica*, Oct. 1938, V, 311–25; A. G. Hart, "Anticipations, Uncertainty, and Dynamic Planning," *Jour. Bus. Univ. Chicago* (Special Supplement), Oct.

C. Conclusions

Concisely stated, the few preceding paragraphs mean that we should proceed to substitute general preference-function maximization for profit maximization. No doubt this procedure will reduce our chances of being wrong. This protection from error, however, is gained at a cost. It is much harder to derive operationally meaningful theorems concerning firm behavior from a construction which is directly based on preference-function maximization than to do so from the profit-maximization construction. The relative development of the theory of the firm (based on profit maximization) as contrasted to that of the consumer (based on utility-index maximization) testifies to the validity of this argument. If economists wish to replace profit maximization with preference-function maximization, they must take steps to make certain that their procedure will not be rendered meaningless from an empirical point of view. It is necessary to experiment with ideal types in which specific commitments are made about the shape of the preference function maximized by the entrepreneur. This calls, of course, for substantial work both in the general area of expectations (and the manner in which they are related to the flow of events) and in the area of "structure of control" over the firm.

It is a major thesis of this essay that the preference function maximized by the peak coordinator is itself a resultant of the influences which are exerted upon the firm. The peak coordinator is conceived as performing the integrating function; he is conceived as formulating the preference system of the enterprise. He does so, however, under the "weight" of the unconscious and conscious influences exerted upon him. This formulation contains one disturbing possibility. It must be evident that if influence takes the form of authority, and if authority is simultaneously exercised by two or more interest groups in a contradictory manner, the peak coordinator will not be able to formulate a consistent preference system.[58] It may be necessary, under such conditions, to drop

---

1940, XIII, 1–98. Among the more recent performances the following deserve special mention: Milton Friedman and L. J. Savage, "The Utility Analysis of Choices Involving Risk," *Jour. Pol. Econ.*, Aug. 1948, LVI, 279–304; Jacob Marschak, "Role of Liquidity under Complete and Incomplete Information," *Am. Econ. Rev., Proc.*, May 1949, XXXIX, 182–95, and Milton Friedman's, R. M. Goodwin's, Franco Modigliani's and James Tobin's discussion of the paper, *ibid.*, pp. 196–210; Jacob Marschak, "Rational Behavior, Uncertain Prospects, and Measurable Utility," *Econometrica*, Apr. 1950, XVIII, 111–41.

[58] In this connection see K. J. Arrow, "A Difficulty in the Concept of Social Welfare," *Jour. Pol. Econ.*, Aug. 1950, LVIII, 328–46.

the action frame of reference in favor of a behavioristic interpretation.

In this connection we should mention Kenneth Boulding's recent book which contains many interesting suggestions concerning the concepts of utility and profit maximization.[59] *Homeostasis*—or maintenance of the "state" of the organism—is, according to Boulding, a construction more general than that of maximization. The concept of equilibrium, in other words, is more general than the concept of maximum. A maximization approach, as a special case of the equilibrium approach, yields useful results only in cases where the agent (organism, in Boulding's terminology) *consciously* recognizes a divergence from the maximand as a stimulus to action. Boulding thinks that preference-function maximization as an analytical device can be employed successfully in the case of the firm. The labor unions, however, are an outstanding example (among others) of organizations whose behavior could be approached more effectively through the more general nonmaximum analysis. A nonmaximum approach is tantamount to a behavioristic approach. A relationship among variables can be postulated as soon as the nature of the "state" which is to be maintained is specified. Empirical generalizations concerning behavior may be conceived as variants of the homeostatic approach.

Armen A. Alchian's "Uncertainty, Evolution, and Economic Theory,"[60] is worthy of special mention in connection with the formulation of behavior models. The economic system is conceived as containing a process of selection of the fittest; it is conceived as adopting those firms which, in a world of uncertainty, have happened to have made the appropriate decisions regardless of the process. Positive profits are the mark of success and viability. The process of reasoning or motivation through which this success was achieved is not significant. Alchian offers two models in his paper. The first is an "adoptive model dominated by chance." It is skillfully asserted that random behavior, involving no conscious adaptation, may lead to predictable resource allocation, given the adopting mechanism of the economic system. The second model includes conscious adaptation which takes the form of imitation of the successful and /or trial and error. Alchian arrives at the interesting conclusion that the economist can employ the tools he has developed for dealing with conditions involving certainty to "predict the more adoptable or viable types of economic interrelationships that will be in-

---

[59] *A Reconstruction of Economics* (New York, 1950), Ch. 2.
[60] *Jour. Pol. Econ.*, June 1950, LVIII, 211–21.

duced by environmental changes even if individuals themselves are unable to ascertain them."[61]

Whether we choose a behavioristic or an action frame of reference we must always take pains to impart empirical meaningfulness to our model. The way to achieve such meaningfulness, if we restrict ourselves to the action frame of reference, consists in formulating a variety of ideal types, making commitments in each case about the shape of the preference function to be maximized, and testing (whenever possible) the operationally meaningful hypotheses which can be derived from them. Whether we like it or not, it seems that we are on the road to developing and testing a variety of formulations rather than a single set of postulates.

IV. ENTERPRISE IN A CHANGING WORLD

A. The Concept of Entrepreneurship

The term *entrepreneur* has heretofore been used as interchangeable with the term *peak coordinator*. Emphasis was placed throughout on the *function* which was identified as peak coordination rather than on the person or persons performing it. The peak coordinating function has been defined as the supply of conscious and authoritative coordination at the apex of the organizational structure. Coordination, in turn, is conceived as the deliberate provision of communications which "integrate" the strategies of the cooperating participants in order to produce the system of actions which we have named *organization*.

This particular definition of entrepreneurship is, of course, arbitrary. It is consistent, however, with the general properties of the organization frame of reference presented in this essay. It is unfortunate that the term entrepreneur has come to mean so many different things and to be associated with so many different conceptual frames of reference.[62] This is especially disturbing in view of the fact that the role assigned to the entrepreneur is a crucial one in almost all the dominant conceptual schemata. The entrepreneur as the "organizer-manager," the entrepreneur as the "risk-bearer," the entrepreneur as the "innovator," are concepts which have played and are still playing an important role

---

[61] *Ibid.*, p. 220. In this connection we should also mention Boulding's ecological approach, *op. cit.*, Ch. 1.

[62] For a concise review of the meanings attributed to the term see J. H. Strauss, "The Entrepreneur: The Firm," *Jour. Pol. Econ.*, June 1944, LII, 112–27.

in economic analysis.[63] Beyond their variety of analytical uses the terms entrepreneur and enterprise have come to be most important in the structure of American "ideology." Enterprise almost invariably suggests "freedom," "progress," "change," and "dynamic leadership." Under these circumstances it becomes extremely difficult to use the concept of entrepreneurship in a value-neutral and analytically meaningful manner. There can be no doubt that the goals of scientific investigation would be served well if we were to drop the term entrepreneur from the professional vocabulary. In view of the fact, however, that the chances of this occurrence are almost nil, we should strive to become as precise and exacting in the use of the term as conditions permit.[64]

Though the subject cannot be discussed at length here, a few comments may point the direction in which conceptual clarification of the term entrepreneur might proceed. A distinction is needed between the concept of the entrepreneur as a *function* and as an *ideal type*. When we talk about risk-bearing or innovating or combining the factors of production, we are thinking of functions performed within a structural-functional system.[65] Again, when we talk about the "owner-manager-risk-bearer" or the "owner-manager-innovator" or the "nonowner-manager," and so on, we are constructing ideal types which are handy for expository and heuristic purposes. It should be clear, for instance, that the separation of ownership and "control" need not be construed as eliminating the function of the entrepreneur in the Knightian sense. The peak coordinator in a "management-controlled" corporation may be likened to Knight's "independent" entrepreneur (who in this case also performs the management function). The entrepreneur, in this case, does not have to persuade the contributors of capital that he is capable of performing the entrepreneurial function. His power position vis-à-vis the contributors of capital is such that he does not need their approval or consent. Knight's formulation does contain, however, an ideal type

---

[63] The two classics in this area are F. H. Knight, *Risk, Uncertainty and Profits* (Boston and New York, 1921), and J. A. Schumpeter, *The Theory of Economic Development,* trans. Redvers Opie (Cambridge, Mass., 1934).

[64] The Research Center in Entrepreneurial History, Harvard University, has been doing much stimulating work in this area. The reader is referred to their serial publication, *Explorations in Entrepreneurial History,* R. R. Wohl and H. G. J. Aitken, ed. (mimeographed). See also, A. H. Cole, F. H. Knight, J M. Clark, and G. H. Evans, Jr., "Symposium on Profits and the Entrepreneur," *The Tasks of Econ. Hist.,* Dec. 1942 (Suppl. to the *Jour. Econ. Hist.,* Vol. II), pp. 118–46.

[65] See Parsons, *Essays in Sociological Theory Pure and Applied,* Ch. 1–2.

corresponding to the function of bearing the risk in a world of uncertainty, namely, that of the *capitalist-entrepreneur*. It cannot be doubted that the separation of ownership and "control" is fatal to this ideal type. Similarly, Schumpeter's innovation is a function which may be performed in institutional settings completely different from the private-property and decentralized-economy setting which is crucial, however, for Schumpeter's entrepreneur as an ideal type.[66]

If the distinction between function concepts and ideal-type concepts is made with clarity and precision, any number of constructions of the term entrepreneur may be made, each one of them useful in its own context and in relation to its own domain of concepts. The definition of entrepreneur proposed in this paper is clearly a function definition. It can be used in a variety of ideal-type constructions. In fact, for each set of external influences a different ideal type can be constructed which can be employed meaningfully in the analysis of the behavior of the firm under the specified set of influences.

B. Social Change and Business Enterprise

It has been clear, particularly in Part II, that there is an historical dimension to the issues presented in this essay. The advent of the large or giant enterprise with the attending increase in the area of conscious co-ordination of economic activity, the rapid growth of the executive or managerial and white-collar classes, the separation of ownership and "control," the growth of labor and government into significant sources of influence over enterprise—all these and other developments are rightly claimed to have altered both the character of enterprise and the social structure within which enterprise operates. Journalists, sociologists, political scientists, and economists have produced a voluminous literature dealing with various aspects of these developments. We can do no more here than concern ourselves with two issues which seem to be immediately relevant to the topic of this essay: first, in what way have these changes in the institutional setting affected enterprise behavior? Secondly, does the cumulation of all these changes amount to a new and significantly different societal structure? If it does, we must adjust our thinking with respect to both analysis and policy to the new social realities.

With respect to enterprise behavior a number of suggestions have been made. It is often claimed, for instance, that the time horizon of the

---

[66] J. A. Schumpeter, *Capitalism, Socialism, and Democracy* (New York and London, 1942), p. 134.

large modern enterprise is much wider than that of the small-scale enterprise which (typically) preceded it. Easterbrook goes so far, in fact, as to suggest that for the "bureaucratic" organization maximization of the period of existence may be the appropriate "principle of selection."[67] The notion that time horizon is positively correlated with size of enterprise is plausible. It will not help us much, however, either from an analysis or a policy point of view, if we leave matters at this stage. The implications of a widening time horizon must be worked out with precision and must lead to commitments concerning the shape of the preference functions maximized (typically) by the "bureaucratic" enterprise, before we can appraise the significance of the change and put it to good analytical or policy use.

The large or giant modern enterprise is also claimed to be more rational than its small-scale predecessor. The methods of scientific management and accounting techniques employed by the former constitute evidence, it is argued, of its greater efficiency. Insofar as this is true it should make the economist's action frame of reference (with the implicit commitment that action is rational) more meaningful today than it has been in the past. At the same time, however, it is claimed that a giant enterprise is subject to inefficiencies which are associated with the "dead weight" and inflexibility of its "bureaucratic" structure.[68] In the same vein it is argued that the "professionalization of management" which attends the growth into dominance of the modern enterprise must affect the character of the end system formulated for the enterprise by the entrepreneur. Also, the growing independence of the "managers" from the contributors of capital, the increasing power of labor unions, and the spectacular growth of government participation in economic life must have affected the preference system of the firm significantly. It must be repeated, however, that it is insufficient to point the direction in which these developments are apt to affect the behavior of the firm. It is necessary to proceed to the formulation of models which lead to operationally meaningful propositions. Until then our thinking will, of necessity, be restricted to the speculative and expository levels.

One last suggestion may be discussed in this connection because of the wide support it has been receiving of late. Many authors have proposed that organizational preservation or conservation or maintenance

---

[67] W. T. Easterbrook, "The Climate of Enterprise," *Am. Econ. Rev., Proc.*, May 1949, XXXIX, 323–35.

[68] In this connection see Gordon, *op. cit.*, Ch. 14, and TNEC Monog. 11, *Bureaucracy and Trusteeship in Large Corporations* (Washington, D.C., 1940).

of market position are more relevant "principles of selection" than profit maximization.[69] In an economy of oligopolistic markets and giant firms, maintenance of organization and position must be of crucial importance to the peak coordinator. Though this cannot be doubted, effective analytical use of these insights must await the elaboration of their implications for firm behavior. Some suggestions are in order in this connection. The maintenance of organization or maintenance of market position insights may be developed systematically within either an action (maximization) or a homeostatic (nonmaximum) frame of reference. Boulding's asset-ratio preference theory seems to fit best the maximization formulation, provided we include among the assets of the firm such things as market position, etc. The behavioristic approach would be restricted to working out the implications of maintaining a given "state."

To the second question or issue we raised, namely, whether or not the changes that have taken place in the structure of our economy amount to a new society, the answer given by most seems to be, "Yes." Clearly the outstanding contribution in this field is Schumpeter's *Capitalism, Socialism, and Democracy*. Schumpeter's argument is so elaborately spun and touches on such a variety of issues, economic, cultural, and social, that it is impossible to do it justice in this essay. One aspect of his analysis, however, is so immediately relevant to our argument that we cannot afford to pass over it. The new society, for Schumpeter, is the product of successful capitalism. Employing an analysis which resembles in many respects the Marxian schema, he argues that the very success of capitalist enterprise has laid the foundations of its own withering away. The rise of the new bureaucratic and scientifically oriented large enterprise, itself the result of the creative genius of the capitalist-entrepreneur, has led to the routinization of innovation, to the "expropriation" of the owners, and to the emergence of a large and powerful bureaucracy which does not regard itself as the servant of the *rentier*-owner. In his words, "Dematerialized, defunctionalized, and absentee ownership does not impress and call forth moral allegiance as the vital form of property did. Eventually there will be *nobody* left who really cares to stand for it—nobody within and nobody without the precincts of the big concerns."[70] Social revolution is taking or has taken place. The "battleground" is the enterprise itself. The "revolutionary" is the

---

[69] See Oswald Knauth's *Managerial Enterprise* (New York, 1948). R. B. Heflebower has developed an intriguing analysis of firm behavior in terms of market position in a manuscript which has not been published as yet.

[70] *Op. cit.*, p. 142.

capitalist-entrepreneur, himself the victim of his own "revolution." The heir apparent is the "manager," the "planner," the "bureaucrat."

James Burnham's *The Managerial Revolution* does not compare well with Schumpeter's brilliant work. Burnham's main theme is provoking, but his argument on the whole is thin and insensitive to the complexities of the problem he has set himself to resolve. Burnham has missed completely what Schumpeter has so aptly called the "Cultural Indeterminateness of Socialism."[71] Much too much is deduced from a rather simple set of assumptions. Burnham's argument is cast in the language of dialectic materialism. He travels the same road as the Marxists as far as the future of capitalism is concerned, but he parts company with them concerning the interpretation of the process of the "struggle for power" which is involved in the demise of capitalism and, therefore, concerning the character of the society which is to succeed (or has succeeded) capitalist society. Not the working class but the managers will displace the capitalist ruling class. The new society is, therefore, not a classless but a class society. Despite the shortcomings of the Burnham thesis it undoubtedly contains a kernel of truth. Despite the pronounced cultural differences between the Nazi society and the U.S.S.R., and between both of them and the British and American social structures, their development in the last two or three decades suggests the presence of a common leitmotiv. The emergence of a large bureaucracy in both the private and the public spheres, and the tendency toward centralization in the over-all direction of the economic process are common to all of them. But we don't need the argument of the "managerial revolution" to understand these developments. Schumpeter's analysis is both more exacting and more plausible than Burnham's thesis. It is important to note, however, that both Burnham and Schumpeter base a major part of their argument on the separation of ownership and "control." Almost all studies of current social change give a very prominent place to the Berle and Means thesis.[72] Few are those who are prepared to discount its importance.

If it is true that we are undergoing a social revolution of such magnitude the question of policy toward such problems as the separation of ownership and control, or labor participation in "management," or the ineffectiveness of the board of directors in the large corporation, must be regarded in a new light. To begin with we cannot seriously entertain

---

[71] Schumpeter, *op. cit.,* p. 170.

[72] Peter Drucker's *The New Society* (New York, 1949) is an outstanding example among them.

the notion that we can reverse the process. A good many of these developments must be accepted as more or less permanent features of the new *status quo*. Then again, even if we are willing to accept some of these developments as inevitable elements of our new social environment, and even if we are quite clear in our minds about the appropriate objectives of public policy, we cannot formulate policy until we have taken stock of the behavior implications of the new social structure. Herein lies the task of the economist.

COMMENT
Richard B. Heflebower

The essay on "The Theory of the Firm" presents a frame of reference for the study of the firm rather than a review of the conclusions about its conduct. The author rejects the usual framework because in it the firm is an "ideal type" formulated to fit its prescribed role in partial-equilibrium theory. What is proposed is conceptual autonomy for the firm, gained by treating it as a case of the general phenomenon of social organization. Where such organization involves conscious cooperation as it does in the firm, the key role is that of the "peak coordinator" who determines the ends of the organization and the means of coordination for achieving the ends. The stockholders come in as one, but not an unique one, of the various "external influences" on the firm's ends. These ends are not defined, but would be encompassed in the logically impeccable, but meaningless concept of "preference-function maximization." This substitute for profit maximization does not prescribe either the content or functional character of ends, and avoids logical defects which the author finds in the theory of profit maximization under conditions of uncertainty.

Viewing the firm as a case of the general problem of organization facilitates the study of its structural attributes and motivation when it is a going concern. While most economists would deny that they still hold to the classical view of the firm as a perfect reflector of impersonal market forces, they do indeed choose those attributes of the firm which fit into their explanation of how economic organization is achieved through unconscious cooperation in the market. Thus, implicitly, the firm as an organization is denied the role of an independent influence.[73] Once this

---

[73] The idea expressed here should not be confused with the zone of discretion enjoyed by an oligopolist, which stems from the structure of the market in which he sells.

restrictive view is dropped, attention is focused on the firm as a system of communication and coordination under authority. In this system, the "peak coordinator" establishes the machinery and policy guides by which others make particular operating decisions. Such a concept of organization invites a new look at the alleged diseconomies of large-scale management and at the enlarged scope of coordination under authority in vertical integration or even socialism. It also suggests that the response of the firm to particular market developments may be conditioned significantly by its broader interests, which include concern about the virility and life of the organization as such. If so, the process by which coordination among firms and households is achieved in the market may differ substantially from that in the models now used.

Indeed, Papandreou's framework reinforces some recent suggestions about motivation. To the extent that the organization is of significance apart from any one of its activities or members, the ends system of the peak coordinator, who is faced by uncertainty, calls first for building an organization whose attributes maximize the firm's ability to avert the ill consequences of unfavorable surprises and only secondarily to take advantage of favorable surprises.

Difficulties arise when one takes the necessary second step of considering the firm as part of the operating market system. The problems are really those of the relation of peak coordination to ownership, for in Papandreou's model, the peak coordinator need not be pecuniarily motivated or affected. Such a model by-passes the large share of business still done by owner-controlled enterprises. Even in going concerns whose stock is loosely held, the peak coordinator must either be pecuniarily affected by market developments, or be guided by ends which correlate with the financial results of the firm's operations, for otherwise the system of unconscious cooperation could not be as orderly as it is.

More basically, it is not possible to include in the peak coordinator's role important functions related to capital investment. This is true whether one is concerned with investment decision making or with risk assumption. At the initiation of the enterprise, when expansion requires external financing, or when major changes of direction of the firm's activities are contemplated, owners' formal and often active consent must be obtained. Because of that and because of the peculiar relation of entrepreneurial capital to the necessarily anticipatory character of production, the owners' role is different in kind from that of other "external groups."

Such considerations emphasize that the theory of the firm must explain initiation as well as the operation of the enterprise, and it must show how firms react to, and modify, their pecuniary environment. Only by these means, can we see how well, and why, the enterprise system works and compare it with alternative means of organizing economic affairs.

COMMENT
Edward S. Mason

Papandreou, in considering the limits of the firm, rejects Triffin's notion that these limits will be "the frontier of the maximizing unit," on the ground that this "begs a number of questions" concerned with what is maximized. He favors the concept of limitation set by a plan or budget. In the absence of any clear-cut definition of what is included in a "plan" or "budget," this concept seems to raise at least as many questions as the rejected notion of maximization. A third conception could have been adapted from Barnard's phrase, quoted with approval, "authoritative communication lies at the heart of the concept of the firm." (P. 187.) Following this suggestion, the limits of the firm might be said to be the limits of authoritative communication. The absence of any very clear-cut definition of the frontier of the firm seems to lead the author into difficulties in his treatment of combines and cartels, which he lumps together as "multifirms."

The discussion of the organization of the firm leans very heavily on Barnard and Simon, whose contributions, together with those of von Neumann and Morgenstern, are considered to be "crucial." Papandreou argues that this framework of thought "has provided the means whereby the conceptual frame of reference of the economist can be widened to incorporate without strain the concepts which are necessary for the consistent treatment of problems of conscious cooperation." (P. 184.) By this he appears to mean that the firm has been shown to be capable of that rational action long attributed by economists to the entrepreneur, a figure that, in earlier analysis, served to represent the firm.

If this is so has the contribution of this literature to economic analysis really been a large one? Papandreou's answer is that the "organizational theory" of the firm enables the employment of "much of the available sociological and psychological material." The author does not show, however, nor, probably, would the space allotted him permit, how the incorporation of this material helps to explain the action of the firm. The writer of this critique must confess a lack of confidence in the marked superiority, *for purposes of economic analysis,* of this newer concept of the firm, over the older conception of the entrepreneur.

A consideration of the goals or purposes of the firm leads the author to an acceptance of rational action as characteristic of firms, but he denies that the concept of rationality implies any particular goal, including profit maximization. A concern for "service," a maintenance of the life of the firm, power, prestige, or a number of other possible goals are as consistent with the postulate of rationality as profit maximization. Unfortunately, however, they are not equally consistent with the utility of economic analysis in any problem-solving sense. It would be awkward, to say the least, if in attempting to assess the probable effect on quantity supplied of a given price increase, we were confronted by a group of firms, all acting rationally, but toward quite different goals.

Part III of the paper, concerning the question of profit maximization, correctly emphasizes that the important matter is not whether profits are "in fact" maximized, but whether the assumption of profit maximization can and does lead to useful empirical results. After considering many subtle arguments for and against profit maximization under static assumptions and after emphasizing the indefiniteness of meaning attaching to the concept under conditions of uncertainty, Papandreou leaves this reader with no very clear-cut notion of whether or not he regards profit maximization, in any sense, to be a useful tool of economic analysis. But this critic suspects that, confronted with a specific economic problem, not only Papandreou but other authorities, cited in this section, would find some simple concept of profit maximization a very useful tool indeed, at least in achieving a first approximation.

The literature on the question whether control of the large firm lies in the hands of ownership, management, or other individuals or groups is surveyed in Part II. What is missing, however, are useful comments concerning what difference if any, it makes. This reader, and he suspects many others, has read for years about the separation of ownership and control, about the new concept of corporate property, etc., without developing any clear-cut notion as to how economic analysis should be reshaped to fit these obviously epoch-making innovations. Nor have we been given much guidance here.

Many other matters are discussed in this exceptionally comprehensive survey of recent literature on the "Theory of the Firm." What this critic would like to convey, however, is a moderate skepticism concerning the claims here made for the accomplishments of the last two decades in this area of economics.

6

ECONOMICS

OF AGRICULTURE

D. Gale Johnson

Writings and researches in the economics of agriculture generally have little more in common than the fact that they deal with some phenomenon related to agriculture. This diversity is due mainly to two considerations. First, the economics of agriculture is almost as broad in scope as the economics of an entire economy. International trade, business cycles, money, banking and credit, taxation, monopoly, labor—in short, the whole gamut of subject matter specialties—are legitimate game for the agricultural economist. Second, the individuals whose stock in trade is agricultural economics have brought a wide variety of approaches to the subject. Some of these approaches have little relevance to what is normally considered to be economic analysis, and yet there has been a ready market for them. Unless we think that Gresham's law applies to the survival of economic methods and ideas, we must accept the various approaches as fulfilling some kind of a demand.

Agricultural economics as a field of specialization developed, in large part, on the basis of farm management work.[1] Farm management, which might be defined as the analysis of the entrepreneurial problems of the farmer, got its start in the first decade of this century. Of more than passing significance to later developments in the field was the fact that the early practitioners were not economists. These pioneers were, among other things, horticulturists, biologists, and various other kinds of applied natural scientists. As a consequence, despite the efforts of a few men who were trained as economists, much farm management work has been somewhat barren of economic analysis and concepts. In

---

[1] For an exhaustive survey of the early history and later developments of agricultural economics, see H. C. Taylor, *The Story of Agricultural Economics* (Ames, 1952).

223

fact, until the last decade or decade and a half, much the same was true of most of the work done by agricultural economists.[2]

This survey, however, does not concern itself with farm management. In 1939, one of my critics, T. W. Schultz, published a critique of farm management work as it existed at that time.[3] He argued that farm management work had not been fruitful either in aiding individual farmers in making their decisions or in relating the actions of individual firms to the economy as a whole.[4] He believed that this was true because farm management analysis had not been based upon an adequate analytical footing.

In 1947 my other critic, J. D. Black, and three of his former students published an exhaustive treatise on farm management.[5] Not only does this book provide the best available statement of the basic propositions of farm management, but it also provides, at several points, systematic criticisms of research methods and results, thus relieving the present writer of responsibility in this direction.[6]

Recently there has occurred among some of the younger farm management workers a concerted effort to integrate more closely the theory

---

[2] On this point, see T. W. Schultz, "Scope and Method in Agricultural Economics Research," *Jour. Pol. Econ.*, Oct. 1939, XLVII, 705–17. This article was a review of a series of bulletins on the scope and methods of research in agricultural economics edited by J. D. Black. In response to a criticism by Schultz that the series contained too little economic analysis, Black wrote: "An important reason that there is not more theoretical analysis in the reports is that the editor of the series, and sometimes one or two others working closely with him, could find no more time for working into the field. The qualitative analyses for several of the subfields had to be left to the 'specialists' in them, and in a few instances nothing much came forth. Nevertheless, Professor Schultz probably underestimates the amount of such analyses in the series. . . . There is much (qualitative analysis) . . . distributed among the projects under the head of 'Basic Concepts,' etc. It was believed that it would be more acceptable associated with definite problems than offered as a solid chunk in one place. The resistance to theory among the rank and file of agricultural economists was pretty strong in 1930–33 and has not largely abated yet." (J. D. Black, "A Reply," *ibid.*, pp. 719–20.)

[3] "Theory of the Firm and Farm Management Research," *Jour. Farm Econ.*, Aug. 1939, XXI, 570–86. This critique was discussed, in general somewhat unsympathetically, by H. C. M. Case, S. W. Warren, G. W. Forster, D. C. Mumford, and R. S. Kifer, "Farm Management Research," *ibid.*, Feb. 1940, XXII, 111–37.

[4] These criticisms had been advanced earlier by two specialists in farm management, W. W. Wilcox, "Types of Farming Research and Farm Management," *ibid.*, May 1938, XX, 417–29, and Sherman Johnson, "Adapting Farm Management Research to New Opportunities," *ibid.*, Feb. 1939, XXI, 98–106.

[5] J. D. Black, Marion Clawson, C. P. Sayre, and W. W. Wilcox, *Farm Management* (New York, 1947).

[6] I refer especially to Ch. 21, "Farming Costs," and Ch. 22, "Measures of Success and Factors in Success in Farming."

of the firm and farm management research.[7] However, as yet the empirical work done by this group has not emerged. The difficulties of successfully integrating the received theory of the firm and the analysis of the problems of the individual firm are numerous, and it is not to be expected that an immediate revolution will occur.

The present survey is restricted to a somewhat limited aspect of the total arena within which agricultural economists have operated. I have restricted it to an analysis of the interrelations between agriculture and the rest of the economy. I have included not only the analyses of how these interrelationships function but also a review of various policies and programs that have been adopted to modify the functioning of the market system as it affects agriculture.

I. THE RELATIVE ECONOMIC POSITION OF FARM PEOPLE

Analyses of the interrelations between agriculture and the rest of the economy have started generally from certain presumptions about the relative economic position of farm people. During the past three decades, most policy proposals have been based on the belief that the incomes of farm people, in some average sense, were below the incomes of nonfarm people. Though this belief is frequently expressed and little or no support adduced for it, a number of economists have attempted to marshall evidence to support the view that real farm incomes were, in fact, less than nonfarm incomes. On the whole, the evidence has been of two sorts —data on incomes, and migration rates of farm people.[8]

---

[7] For a general review of the growing interest in economic theory, see the articles by Irving Fellows, H. B. James, E. O. Heady, G. L. Johnson, and E. J. Nesius in the *Jour. Farm Econ.*, Nov. 1950, XXXII, 1100–81.

[8] An attempt to answer the same question is sometimes made by direct comparisons for farm and nonfarm people of a long list of consumption items and general services available. Items compared frequently include food consumed, quality and amount of housing, years of education, number of doctors per 100,000 population, and local governmental expenditures. (See Walter C. McKain, Jr. and Grace L. Flogg, "Differences between Rural and Urban Levels of Living: Part I. Nationwide Comparisons," Bur. Agric. Econ., U.S. Dept. Agric., 1948, mimeo.) The results of such comparisons will almost always be inconclusive. If any one consumption item is greater for farmers than nonfarmers, it is impossible to say anything about the relative levels of living. And it is usually found that farm food consumption is greater (and of higher nutritional quality) than is that of city dwellers. It should also be noted that comparisons of expenditures for education or roads in rural and urban communities are meaningless until we know something about relative costs. For a similar analysis, but somewhat more restrained, see O. V. Wells, "Agriculture Today: An Appraisal of the Agricultural Problem," *Farmers in a Changing World*, 1940 Yearbook of Agriculture (Washington, 1940), pp. 387–90.

A. The Income Data

The Bureau of Agricultural Economics—an indispensable source of data about agriculture—publishes two series of farm-nonfarm income comparisons. One shows the per capita income of farm and nonfarm people, and the other shows the income from agriculture per farm worker and the average annual wage per employed worker. Data from these two comparisons are given in Table 1 for selected periods and years.

TABLE 1

INCOME COMPARISONS BETWEEN FARM AND NONFARM PERSONS

A. Per capita Incomes of Farm and Nonfarm Population

Year	Farm[a] (dollars)	Nonfarm (dollars)	Farm/Nonfarm (per cent)
1935–39	244	595	41
1940	262	686	38
1942	520	1,019	51
1946	693	1,294	54
1948	949	1,517	63
1950	829	1,563	53

B. Annual Farm Income Per Worker and Annual Wage per Employed Industrial Worker

Year	Farm Worker[b] (dollars)	Industrial Worker[c] (dollars)	Farm/Industrial (per cent)
1935–39	475	1,217	39
1940	457	1,341	34
1942	916	1,908	48
1944	1,283	2,400	53
1946	1,505	2,333	65
1948	1,699	2,872	59
1950	1,504	3,114	48

SOURCE: B.A.E., *The Farm Income Situation*, July–Sept., 1951, pp. 18–19.
[a] Includes all income accruing to farm people, including the income from nonfarm sources.
[b] Includes only income from agriculture and is the sum of realized net operator income and total farm wages.
[c] Includes nonsalaried employees in manufacturing, mining, and Class I railroads.

These data are frequently used to support the view that farm incomes are low. Even at its peak in 1948, per capita income of the farm population was only 63 per cent of the nonfarm, while in 1946 the income of all farm workers (including the operator) averaged 65 per cent of the annual wage income of the employed industrial worker. During the last half of the thirties, these ratios were roughly 40 per cent.

In 1942 Black used the data on per capita incomes of the farm and nonfarm populations as a basis for comparison. However, he suggested that certain modifications must be made to any income series comparing farm and nonfarm incomes. First, income from nonagricultural sources must be included, data not then generally published. Second, farm-produced food and fuel, which are valued in income estimates at farm prices, should be valued at the prices city consumers would have to pay. Third, an adjustment should be made to allow for the fact that housing rents, which are included as income on farms at about $25 per person per year for 1937–40, probably represent a lower level of costs for housing than is usual in the cities; but Black did not estimate the adjustment that should be made. Fourth, Black argued that an adjustment should be made to allow for the fact that a smaller proportion of the farm population is in the labor force than is the case with the urban population. As a consequence, per capita earnings may normally be expected to be lower in agriculture, and likewise the costs of maintenance—since it costs less to maintain a child than an adult of working age.[9] Black concludes: "Perhaps if liberal allowance is made for all of these shortcomings and differences, the $217 and $652 we started with as farm and nonfarm per capita income as of the year 1940 might be changed to something like $450 to $500 as against $635. This still leaves a pretty wide gap."[10]

Black assumes that the correct procedure for estimating the gain to farm families of the availability of food at farm prices is to value it at retail prices. This adjustment, however, must surely overestimate the importance of low-priced food to the farm family. The retail price to the city family includes costs for processing services that farmers do not get when they consume food produced on their own farms. More important, however, farm families consume more food than they would if they in fact paid retail prices for all of it. This is a general problem of index numbers to which we will return later.

Koffsky has provided the only systematic published comparison of the purchasing power of farm and urban incomes.[11] He compared the costs of two budgets—one for farm families and one for urban families —both at farm and at urban prices. For the lowest income groups for which sufficient data were available, he found that the farm budget cost 30 per cent more in the city than on the farm; for more nearly average

[9] J. D. Black, *Parity, Parity, Parity* (Cambridge, Mass., 1942), pp. 112–13.

[10] *Ibid.*, p. 113.

[11] Nathan Koffsky, "Farm and Urban Purchasing Power," Conference on Research in Income and Wealth, *Studies in Income and Wealth* (New York, 1949), Vol. XI, pp. 153–178. See also the excellent comment by Margaret G. Reid, *ibid.*, pp. 179–206.

income groups, the corresponding figure was 27 per cent.[12] As one would expect, most of the difference in the cost of the farm budget at urban prices rather than at farm prices was in food.

Koffsky utilized his data to make a comparison of the real incomes, for 1941, of farm operators (including unpaid family workers in units equivalent to a farm operator) and of factory workers. Farm earnings per worker averaged $928, while the annual wage earnings of factory workers were $1,479. Thus the factory worker received 59 per cent more than the farm operator and unpaid family workers (counted as equal to one-half an operator) and presumably paid only 27 per cent more for his budget.

The comparison that Koffsky makes is open to several criticisms. First, the total income from agriculture, including the income from land and capital, is attributed to the farm labor, while only labor income is used in the case of the factory worker. Either the nonlabor income of factory workers should be added or the nonlabor income (about 20–25 per cent) of the farm worker should be deducted. Second, the estimated difference in the cost of living is an upper limit of the differences mentioned earlier.[13] Third, the estimate of the number of operators and unpaid family workers may be too high.

The comparison that Koffsky made raises certain questions that have not always been given adequate consideration. What is the purpose of the comparison? Are we interested in comparing family incomes? If so, we should compare total family income from all sources. Or are we interested in comparing returns to comparable resources? If so, we should include in our comparisons only the earnings of the resources to be compared. Koffsky straddles the issue. He compares total farm returns per worker to wage income of factory workers. The first comparison is legitimate for some welfare problems, while the second is the only meaningful one if we wish to judge the economic efficiency of our economy.[14]

---

[12] *Ibid.*, pp. 170, 172.

[13] For development of this point, see Ragnar Frisch, "Annual Survey of General Economic Theory: The Problem of Index Numbers," *Econometrica,* Jan. 1936, IV, 1–38.

[14] Family incomes are a function of the quantities of resources owned and the rates of return obtained on these resources. Consequently, knowledge that real family incomes in two occupations differ is not sufficient to determine that output can be increased by a transfer of resources from one occupation to another. If the rates of return to all comparable resources are equalized and family incomes differ markedly, it may well be that society will want to take steps to modify the distribution of resources or control over resources by various procedures such as direct grants or by more nearly equalizing the access to educational opportunities, whether or not this results in a net increase in national output.

Second, if we are comparing returns to farm and nonfarm resources, we must have a concept of comparable resources. Market data cannot tell us which groups of nonfarm workers possess the same skills and abilities that farm workers can and do supply. Can the average farm worker perform the average factory job?

Third, the cost-of-living difference which Koffsky calculated is the upper limit of the probable true difference. If it cost 27 per cent more to buy the farm budget at urban prices, an actual increase of money income of 27 per cent given to a family moving from the farm to the city would permit them to achieve a higher level of satisfaction than they had enjoyed on the farm if their preferences did not change. With the new set of relative prices, the family could achieve the same level of satisfaction with less than a 27 per cent increase in income by reducing their consumption of products with higher relative prices in the city and increasing their consumption where relative prices are lower. However, the use of the upper limit will aid in answering the question whether real farm incomes are substantially below nonfarm incomes.

Fourth, the cost-of-living difference is undoubtedly not uniform for all income groups. Koffsky attempted to correct for this by recognizing that as incomes rise, the proportion of total expenditure spent on food declined. But there is another change in consumption and expenditure patterns associated with income changes which was not recognized, namely, that the proportion of food expenditure consisting of home-produced foods declines as income increases. At the lowest income level which Koffsky used, about 68 per cent of the money value of all food was home produced. At the income level of twice this (roughly the average farm operator's income), the percentage that was home produced was 55.[15] Rough calculations indicate that recognizing this factor would have given a price level difference of the city over the farm of 24 per cent instead of 27 per cent for the average farm operator income level.

Income comparisons between agriculture and the rest of the economy are complicated by the definition of a farm implicit in all of our agricultural statistics. The Census definition of a farm results in the inclusion in the farm population of many families who rely upon agriculture little, if at all, for a means of livelihood. In addition, large segments of agriculture are essentially noncommercial in that much of the production is used for home consumption. Such families depend upon farming for their living, but seem to be so isolated from the main stream of mar-

---

[15] U.S. Dept. Agric., *Rural Family Spending and Saving in Wartime,* Misc. Pub. 520, Tab. 7.

ket activity that it would be worth while to exclude them from the data when income comparisons are made.[16]

Three attempts have been made to compare the incomes of the approximately half of the farm families that produce about 90 per cent of the agricultural output. The present writer estimated that in 1939 the labor return to family labor on commercial farms was about $600 while the annual wage income of employed industrial workers was $1,278. In 1944 the two figures were $1,540 and $2,400. If the farm incomes are increased by 25 per cent roughly to express the difference in purchasing power of incomes, there was a wide disparity in 1939, reduced to about 20 per cent in 1944. Farm labor incomes of family workers in real terms may have been higher in 1948 than the labor incomes of employed industrial workers.[17]

A somewhat similar approach is to estimate labor incomes from agriculture by regions, since most of the subsistence farms are found in the South and many of the part-time farms in the East. When this is done, it was found that in 1945 labor incomes on farms in three regions were very closely equal to, if not greater than, the income of employed industrial workers after adjustment for cost-of-living differences.[18] If the data were adjusted to include nonfarm income, a fourth region would probably have reflected equal real returns. What was true in 1945 would have continued through 1948.

A third technique has been used, based on the classification of farms in the 1945 Sample Census of Agriculture. Brandom and Allison estimated that in 1944 the average per capita incomes on commercial family farms (in number 3,244,000) and on large-scale farms (102,-000) had per capita incomes (including nonfarm income) of $875. All persons not on farms had incomes of $1,311 in the same year.[19] If farm

---

[16] For an excellent discussion of the characteristics and problems of the other 3 million farm families, see Joint Committee Print, 82nd Congress, 1st Session; prepared by W. W. Wilcox and W. E. Hendrix. In 1944 there were roughly 1.6 million part-time farmers; 0.4 million low-income farms operated by families with operators under 25, over 65, or by widows or disabled persons; and 1.0 million by able-bodied male operators with an average gross value of products of $875 and with the upper limit being $1,800 gross (perhaps $1,000 net).

[17] Data on farm labor returns for 1939 and 1944 are from D. G. Johnson, "Allocation of Agricultural Income," *Jour. Farm Econ.,* Nov. 1948, XXX, 739. Later years were estimated by same method. Income of employed industrial workers is from B.A.E., *Agricultural Outlook Charts,* 1951, p. 22. The labor income of hired workers on the commercial farms is about two-thirds that of family workers.

[18] D. G. Johnson, "Functioning of the Labor Market," *Jour. Farm Econ.,* Feb. 1951, XXXIII, 70–78.

[19] G. E. Brandom and H. E. Allison, "Per Capita Incomes on Commercial and Non-Commercial Farms," *ibid.,* May 1951, XXXIII, 122–23.

incomes are adjusted upward by about 25 per cent, they were still about 20 per cent below nonfarm incomes. A part of the remaining difference may be attributed to the smaller proportion of the farm than of the nonfarm population that is in the normal working ages.[20]

B. The Migration Data

Because of the many problems of determining the appropriate measures of real income, the "comparability" of income receivers, and the number of income receiving units in agriculture, additional evidence on the differences in real returns to the labor resource in agriculture and nonagriculture has been brought to bear by analysis of migration statistics.

During the last forty years there has been a fairly continuous migration out of agriculture. By decades since 1910, the following net migration has taken place: 6 millions, 6 millions, 3 millions, and 10 millions (for 1940–48). These data indicate that roughly 25 million persons, on balance, left farms.[21] Some of the migration undoubtedly represented retirement—the Iowa farmer living in Long Beach—but our knowledge of the age distributions of migrants indicates quite clearly that most of the migrants are quite young (under 35 years). Despite this amount of migration, farm population has declined by only seven millions in the past four decades.[22]

Migration out of agriculture is required to achieve a redistribution of the labor force necessitated by the relatively high birth rates of farm people. In addition, the changing character of our economy has required (during at least the last four decades) a decline in the absolute number of farm workers if the real returns to farm labor relative to nonfarm were not to fall. Consequently, one would expect that real returns to farm labor would generally be below the real returns in nonfarm occupations requiring comparable skills and capacities. It is through a differential in real earnings that "in a free society, reallocations of human resources are achieved and a changing equilibrium is achieved."[23] Davis argues, if I interpret him correctly, that except for the depression following World War I and 1932–36, the income differential was not larger than is implied by the need to transfer labor out of agriculture in the

---

[20] In 1940, 29.3 per cent of the farm population was under 14 years of age; of the urban population, 19.8 per cent was under 14. The same proportions were over 65.

[21] Actually there is a strong crosscurrent of migration—for every three moves away from farms, there have been about two moves back.

[22] See Series Census-B.A.E., 16A, *Estimates of Farm Population: 1910 to 1950.*

[23] J. S. Davis, "American Agriculture: Schultz' Analysis and Policy Proposals," *Rev. Econ. Stat.,* May 1947, XXIX, 82, 86.

numbers implied by factors mentioned at the beginning of the paragraph.

Schultz and Black state that during most of the last several decades farm incomes have been below nonfarm incomes by so substantial an amount that it can be said that a significant disequilibrium existed in the allocation of labor.[24] In other words, agriculture was faced with a serious excess supply of labor.

In support of his view, Schultz argued that the relationship between the rate of migration and changes in farm prices and incomes relative to nonfarm were inconsistent with the proposition that agricultural incomes were roughly in balance with nonagricultural incomes.

From 1929 through 1944 the rate of migration tended to rise at the same time relative farm prices and incomes rose, and the rate fell in the converse situations. Thus from 1930 through 1934, agricultural income per farm worker was 33 per cent of the average industrial wage income and net off-farm migration averaged 200,000 per year; from 1935 through 1939, the income ratio was 45 per cent and migration averaged 560,000 per year; from 1940 through 1943 the income ratio was 62 per cent and civilian migration averaged 1,160,000 per year and other net withdrawals from the farm population averaged 900,000 annually.[25]

The major difference between the views lies in the presuppositions about the barriers to mobility. One position seems to imply that the barriers have not been very significant and that the income differential required to achieve the readjustment in the labor resource has not been an unacceptable one. The other view rests on the presumption that recurrent periods of high unemployment and the slow rate of expansion of the economy represent significant barriers to movement and created, at least for 1920 through 1940, an income difference so substantial that it would have been wise public policy to have tried to speed up the movement of labor out of agriculture.

C. Summary

The available data supports the view that during most of the interwar period real farm labor returns were substantially below nonfarm labor returns. This is revealed by both the income comparisons and the

---

[24] T. W. Schultz, *Agriculture in an Unstable Economy* (New York, 1945), Ch. 4; J. D. Black, "The Problem of Surplus Agricultural Population," *Internat. Jour. Agrarian Affairs*, Oct. 1939, I, 7–24, esp. 12–15.

[25] Schultz, *Agriculture in an Unstable Economy*, pp. 94–100.

relationship between migration rates and changes in relative incomes.

There has been only one year since 1910, except for the demobilization period following World War II, that there has been a net migration into agriculture—and this was 1932. If farm labor returns never are high enough to induce net movement back into agriculture and only occasionally reach equality with nonagricultural returns, as Black has argued,[26] the recurrent periods of unemployment that tend to pile up population on farms mean that, over the average of a lifetime, farm labor returns will be below nonfarm. I believe that this proposition is valid. If it is, it implies the need for study of the ways in which we can improve the functioning of the labor market in a manner that will expedite the transfer of labor from farm to nonfarm employment.

II. THE NECESSITY FOR LABOR TRANSFER OUT OF AGRICULTURE

There has been a continuous exodus of labor from farm to nonfarm occupations for most of the present century. This is not a phenomenon restricted to American agriculture since a similar development has occurred—and must occur—in every nation as it has become industrialized. While the classical economist was concerned that levels of living could not be increased because of the difficulty of expanding food output due to the operation of the law of diminishing returns and the apparent fixity of the land supply, most students of agriculture in recent decades have been concerned by the need for, and difficulty of, transferring resources, especially labor, out of agriculture. Though the general outline of the processes at work that induced a decline in the significance of agriculture in an expanding economy has been well known for some time,[27] the last decade has witnessed two developments of importance. One has been a more detailed and complete specification of the models of the functioning of the economy; the second has been the various attempts made to estimate the parameters involved.

There have been several expositions of those aspects of an economy

---

[26] *The Problem of Surplus Agricultural Population,* pp. 12–15.

[27] See, for example, O. E. Baker, "Changes in Production and Consumption of Our Farm Products and the Trend in Population," *Annals Am. Acad. Pol. Soc. Sci.,* Mar. 1929, CXLI, 97–146. If there has been during the last decade an important advance in the general understanding of the process of adjustment, it has resulted from placing greater emphasis upon the functioning of the factor markets. Earlier writings of agricultural economists tended to emphasize the operation of product markets and movements in relative product prices. Consequently, most policy proposals advanced by the economists were concerned with raising the level of farm prices and did not reflect the possible need for speeding the adjustment in resources.

with a rising level of real per capita income that affect the proportion of the total resources that can be employed in agriculture if these resources are to receive approximately the same level of real returns as similar resources employed elsewhere.[28] The technique used has been generally that of comparative statics.

Studies in this area have attempted to explain the past shifts in the importance of agriculture; but several have also attempted to use the same approach to forecast the future level of agricultural employment or the prospects for the level of agricultural returns if employment should not change. The general model of the economy can be used in either role. The difference, of course, is that the estimate of the future requires extrapolating the course of the significant economic variables, such as real national income and population, and the magnitude of certain parameters, such as the income and price coefficients in the demand-for-food equation. Because of the many pitfalls involved in forecasting such variables as population or real national income, I shall review certain aspects of the efforts to describe the functioning of the economy as it has operated in the past, as related to labor transfer.

The authors cited agree that the quantity of resources that can be employed in agriculture at as high real returns for the same resource as are earned elsewhere is related to the following variables—population growth, real per capita income,[29] tastes and preferences of consumers,

---

[28] Schultz, *Agriculture in an Unstable Economy,* esp. Ch. 3–5; J. M. Brewster, "Farm Technological Advance and Total Population Growth," *Jour. Farm Econ.,* Aug. 1945, XXVII, 509–26; H. A. Simon, "Effects of Increased Productivity upon the Ratio of Urban to Rural Population," *Econometrica,* Jan. 1947, XV, 31–42; J. D. Black and Maxine E. Keifer, *Future Food and Agriculture Policy* (New York, 1948), esp. Ch. 7, 8, 13, 14. B.A.E., *Long-Range Agricultural Policy, a Study of Selected Trends and Factors Relating to the Long-Range Prospect for American Agriculture,* Committee Print, Committee on Agriculture of the House of Representatives, 80th Congress, 2nd Session, March 10, 1948; Sherman Johnson, *Changes in American Farming,* U.S.D.A. Misc. Pub. 707 (Washington, 1949). See also M. R. Cooper, G. T. Barton and A. P. Brodell, *Progress of Farm Mechanization,* U.S.D.A. Misc. Pub. 630 (Washington, 1947).

[29] In his analysis, Brewster tends to ignore the effect of per capita income upon the demand for food on the ground that the physical quantity of food consumed per capita (as measured in pounds) has hardly changed since 1909. This assumes that the weight of food consumed is an adequate measure of the quantity of farm resources required in its production, a presumption which he does not attempt to prove. Brewster accepts an estimate that during 1935–39 per capita food consumption was about 15 per cent less than it would have been under full employment conditions. But he then argues: "Having once reached this maximum . . . per capita consumption would offer no additional outlet for increased farm production." (Brewster, *op. cit.,* p. 511.) Thus Brewster seems to assume a zero income elasticity of demand under full employment conditions.

and technological developments in agriculture. A fifth factor—changes in net foreign demand—is also accepted.

A. Estimation of the Influence of the Variables

The use of the general models implicit in the writings in this area requires estimating the changes in the variables and determining how each variable is actually related to the phenomena under consideration (the supply of or demand for farm products).

1. *Population Growth.* Over past periods ranging up to 80 years, we have fairly accurate estimates of the U.S. population from the Census.[30] From the decade 1870–79 through 1930–39, there was an almost continuous decline in the rate of growth of population. Between 1870 and 1880, population increased by 30 per cent, while between 1930 and 1940 the increase was 7 per cent and roughly one-half the average increase of the two preceding decades. Until 1930, the absolute increase per decade was surprisingly constant. In all of the writings cited, the implicit or explicit presumption is that the growth in demand for food (at a given real price) is related proportionately to the growth in population. No attempt is made to show this, apparently because it seems obvious.

2. *Real per Capita Income and the Income Elasticity of Demand for Farm Products.* As we all know, the measurement of national income is extremely difficult and subject to considerable inaccuracy. Yet we accept the available data for what they purport to be.[31] National in-

---

[30] Estimating future population seems to be a somewhat more difficult task and subject to fairly wide error. In estimates published in 1937 and 1938, Thompson and Whelpton indicated a 1950 population ranging from 137.1 to 144.2 millions, but their upper estimate was low by 8 millions. Estimates made in 1943 proved to be as much in error. Estimates made two years later were still low by 6 to 7 millions. Even estimates made by the Census Bureau in early 1949 were low by almost 3 millions for 1950.

Schultz, Black, and workers in the B.A.E. relied upon population forecasts made in the mid-forties for their predictions of postwar food demand. The estimate which guided Schultz' work indicated a 1960 population slightly smaller than the actual 1950 population. In all cases the slowing down of population growth was greatly overestimated. For an excellent discussion of the accuracy of population forecasts, see J. S. Davis, "Our Amazing Population Upsurge," *Jour. Farm Econ.,* Nov. 1949, XXXI, 765–78.

[31] We could, perhaps, do a little better than this. Kuznets estimates that the national income increased by $59 billions (in 1929 prices) between 1875 and 1925. Of the total increase, $21 billions can be attributed to the increase in the number of gainfully occupied, $23 billions to increases in income per gainfully occupied within each major industry group, and $15 billions to changes in the distribution of workers among industries. See Simon Kuznets, *National Income, a Summary of Findings* (New York, 1946), pp. 45–49. Almost all of the increased income due to interindustry shifts in employment represented

come (measured in constant dollars) per capita has apparently increased at a compound rate of roughly 2 per cent per annum since 1870.

Growth in per capita real income is related to the growth of demand for farm products through the income elasticity of demand. Numerous estimates of the income elasticity of demand for food at retail, based on budget studies, indicate that the income elasticity of demand may be about 0.5 to 0.6.[32] Other estimates of the income elasticity of demand have been made from time-series data. Stone and Mack obtained estimates of 0.53 and 0.54, respectively.[33] Tobin and Girshick and Haavelmo obtained estimates of 0.27 and 0.25.[34] The difference between the higher and lower groups of estimates seems to be due to the estimates of food consumption used. Stone and Mack utilized the Department of Commerce series of estimates of consumers' expenditures on food deflated by the Bureau of Labor Statistics price index for food. Tobin and Girshick and Haavelmo relied upon the Bureau of Agricultural Economics estimates of per capita consumption of food—a price-weighted quantity index.

Assuming that both series measure what they are presumed to measure, the deflated Commerce series would reflect the quantity of food consumed, including services attached thereto, more accurately than the BAE price-weighted quantity index. The first index permits changes in the composition of consumption that represent different demands for resources to be reflected; the BAE index largely excludes these within any one food group. For example, if consumers increase their demand of high-quality beef relatively to low-quality beef, this will be reflected by

---

the relative decline in the proportion of the labor force engaged in agriculture. Much of the increase in the national income of $15 billions attributed to this change may not reflect a change in real income, but only that money incomes—for a given level of national income—are higher in urban than in farm employment. If the real incomes per worker in agriculture and in the rest of the economy had been the same at both dates, none of the increase in national income attributed to the interindustry shifts would have represented an increase in real national income. However, real incomes per worker in agriculture were probably below real incomes elsewhere throughout the period and a part of the $15 billions of increase did represent a rise in real income. But it is certainly incorrect to treat all of it as such.

[32] See Schultz, *Agriculture in an Unstable Economy*, pp. 65–68, for a review of studies based on budget data collected prior to 1940. Two recent studies should be noted: James Tobin, "A Statistical Demand Function for Food in the U.S.A.," *Jour. Royal Stat. Soc.*, Pt. 2, 1950, CXIII, 113–40; and Ruth P. Mack, "The Direction of Change in Income and the Consumption Function," *Rev. Econ. Stat.*, Nov. 1948, XXX, 239–58.

[33] Richard Stone, "The Analysis of Market Demand," *Jour. Royal Stat. Soc.*, Pt. 3–4, 1945, CVIII, 286–382; Mack, *op. cit.*

[34] Tobin, *op. cit.*; M. A. Girshick and Trygve Haavelmo, "Statistical Analysis of Demand for Food: Examples of Simultaneous Estimation of Structural Equations," *Econometrica*, Apr. 1947, XV, 79–110.

the deflated Commerce series but not by the BAE. Likewise, if consumers increase their demand for services attached to food, the Commerce series will reflect this and the BAE series will not.

In terms of the analysis of the growth in demand for farm products, the above estimates of income elasticity are not what we need, for two reasons. First, they relate only to food. Second, they represent estimates of income elasticities at the consumer level and do not indicate the income elasticity of demand for farm resources. In recent years, the farmer has received about one-half of the consumer expenditures for food in retail stores.

The income elasticities estimated by Tobin and Girshick and Haavelmo for the retail level are probably fairly satisfactory estimates of the income elasticity of demand for food products at the farm level, though perhaps a trifle low. This is true because the BAE index of food consumption, even though weighted by retail prices, largely measures the input of farm food products. If consumers do not shift their consumption consistently from products which in the base period had a low proportion of the retail price, represented by marketing services, to those products with a high proportion (or vice versa), changes in the index will reflect the farm good product input. However, the index will fail to reflect two types of changes in the demand for farm resources. One type is the increase in demand for the better grades and qualities. If their production requires more farm resources, the index will not show it. Second, the index will underestimate the true changes in consumption for years after the base period if there takes place an increase in the relative costs of producing the commodities for which demand relatively increases, as compared to the costs of these commodities for which demand relatively falls. Where there are substantial changes in income, the underestimate may be important.

Two studies of the income elasticity of demand for farm products at the farm level are worthy of mention. For the period 1920 to 1943, Tintner found an income elasticity of 0.3.[35] The estimate of production used was the BAE series of the volume of production for sale and home use—a price-weighted quantity index. Louis Fourt, in an unpublished study, estimated the income elasticity of demand for farm products to be about 0.4.[36] His analysis was based upon an estimate of production ob-

---

[35] See Gerhard Tintner, *Scope and Method of Econometrics, Illustrated by Applications to American Agriculture* (Statistical and Social Inquiry Society of Ireland, 1949), p. 12.

[36] L. A. Fourt, "Economic Progress, Income and the Marketing of Farm Products" (1950, unpublished).

tained by dividing cash receipts from farming by the index of prices received by farmers.

3. *Tastes and Preferences of Consumers.* Except in a very broad way, we know relatively little about changes in the tastes and preferences of consumers. Generally speaking, we tend to reserve tastes and preferences for a catch-all to which we relegate a persistent and unexplainable residual in our empirical demand equations. Such studies generally indicated a downward drift in the demand equation for food,[37] a result consistent with the reduction in physical work in our economy which has reduced the need for caloric intake.

4. *Technological Change.* The sources of growth in the supply of farm products are (1) changes in the quantities of inputs used and (2) changes in the production function.[38] Most, though not all, of the changes in quantities of inputs used are within the control of farm firms and resource suppliers. In recent decades, public decisions with respect to land development, reclamation, and soil conservation have added to the quantity of land available without much reference to the market returns on the resources involved. However, changes in the amounts of resources used in farm production are not as autonomous as are changes in demand.

Changes in the production function, or technological advance, are probably both induced and autonomous. Thus far we do not have any reliable evidence to indicate the relative importance of the two sets of forces. If all changes in techniques were costless to the farmer and cost reducing, technological change would be autonomous. However, many forms of technological change require new investment and since the amount of farm investment is closely related to the level of farm income, technological change may be related to the level of farm income. In other words, a new method of production which is relatively profitable at any known level of prices may be adopted more rapidly at higher than lower levels of prices. However, the contrary hypothesis that low relative prices force farmers to search for cost-reducing techniques cannot be disproven from available data.

---

[37] See, for example, Girshick and Haavelmo, *op. cit.,* p. 109, and note the signs of the residuals found by Tobin, *op. cit.,* p. 133.

[38] The impression is given in some of the references noted in footnote 28 that changes in farm labor productivity (the ratio of farm production to the number of workers in agriculture) is an adequate measure of technological change. This impression is an erroneous one. The ratio of output to a single input may change for one of two reasons— a change in the proportions of the factors and a change in the production function representing technological advance. With a given technology and a decline in the quantity of one factor used, the ratio of output to the quantity of factor will increase.

Table 2 gives a rough indication of changes in the level of farm output, the quantity of inputs used, and the ratio of inputs to output for selected years since 1910.

Insofar as the ratio of inputs to outputs is a suitable measure of technological change, these data, as well as others,[39] indicate that there was little change between 1910 and 1920. There was a small change during the twenties, though it is obscured by the low crop yields in 1930. There was a substantial change during the thirties (from perhaps an index of 110 for the late twenties to an index of 95 in the late thirties). This was a greater change than occurred between 1940 to 1948. However, the choice of the base period for the price weights of the index of

TABLE 2

INDEX NUMBERS OF TOTAL PRODUCTION INPUTS, TOTAL FARM OUTPUT, AND INPUT PER UNIT OF OUTPUT, UNITED STATES, SELECTED YEARS, 1910–48
(1935–39 = 100)

Year	Total Production Inputs	Farm Output	Inputs per unit of Farm Output
1910	91	79	115
1915	99	88	112
1920	107	92	116
1925	103	93	111
1930	108	95	114
1935	97	96	101
1940	103	110	94
1945	115	129	89
1948	122	140	87

SOURCE: B.A.E., *Farm Production Practices, Costs and Returns*, Stat. Bull. 83, pp. 6–7, 74, Indexes of inputs and outputs are price-weighted quantity index with 1935–39 prices used as weights. 1935–39 = 100.

inputs significantly affects the relationship between inputs and outputs. Between 1935–39 and 1946–48, there have been substantial changes in the relative prices of inputs, with the price of labor rising most. Labor is the one major input which has declined substantially in quantity used during the last ten years. However, the reweighting of the input index does not change the picture prior to 1930.[40]

The uneven course of technological change in agriculture over the past forty years makes it difficult to predict its future course.[41] However,

[39] D. G. Johnson, "The Nature of the Supply Function for Agricultural Products," *Am. Econ. Rev.,* Sept. 1950, XL, 539–64.

[40] One further reservation is in order. The technique used in estimating the change in the ratio of inputs to outputs assumes that the inputs are perfect substitutes, one for the other. If the combination of inputs changes through time and if the elasticity of substitution is less than unity, the technique used to arrive at the results indicated in Table 2 may underestimate the change in output due to changes in techniques.

[41] For a more complete discussion, see J. D. Black, *The Rural Economy of New England* (Cambridge, Mass., 1950), Ch. 30.

a satisfactory explanation of the relatively slow technological advance from 1910 to 1930 seems possible. During the first part of the period, the existing technology was based upon horses and mules and the tools and equipment which could be used with animal power. Given the limitations of the source of power and the relatively immature state of crop and livestock breeding programs, little technological advance was possible. During the twenties, agriculture was shifting to mechanical power. The tractor was still a fairly cumbersome machine and was not well adapted for handling the cultivation of row crops. Farmers did not eliminate an equivalent number of horses when a tractor was employed—in part because of inertia, in part because some seasonal tasks still required about as many horses as before.

It is perhaps not unreasonable to assume that improved technology would increase farm output by three-fourths of one per cent per annum over the next decade without any increase in the quantity of resources employed. The actual change in output would also depend upon the quantity of resources employed.

5. *Net Foreign Demand.* The four variables or relations that have been discussed above are largely exogenous influences upon the demand or supply of farm products. It is questionable whether the same can be said of changes in net foreign demand (exports minus imports). It is true that many changes in net foreign demand are not related to changes in the comparative advantage of agriculture in our economy. For example, changes in tariff rates can and have affected the net foreign demand for agricultural products. Likewise, differences in the rate of growth of incomes or of population in the United States and elsewhere could be important. But over the long pull, it is probable that our transition from a large net exporter of food to a net importer of food is a consequence of a steady change in the comparative advantage of our agriculture due to essentially domestic influences. In other words, agriculture cannot now compete with other sectors of the economy for domestic resources and sell in foreign markets as effectively as it did fifty years ago. The loss in "competitive position" could be due to (1) a greater rate of technological advance in nonagriculture than in agriculture in the U.S.; (2) a change in the proportions of factors in agriculture due to the relative fixity of the quantity of land; or (3) an unwillingness of agricultural workers to accept the same relative money incomes today that they accepted earlier. Of course, appropriate changes in the relations specified in the rest of the world could have the effect of reducing the comparative advantage of American agriculture. It should be noted that the decline

in the comparative advantage of American agriculture has not been the subject of a rigorous investigation. Because we do not know what has caused the decline of net exports, we have no alternative but the unsatisfactory one of considering the cause to be exogenous; and this is the procedure generally used.[42]

B. Implications

Population, per capita real income, and tastes and preferences each act to influence the level of demand for farm products. The level of technology influences the quantity of farm resources required to produce a given amount of farm products. Net foreign demand tends to have a generally equilibrating role, indicating general changes in the comparative advantage of agriculture. Because of the close relation between the family, the firm, and the farm labor supply, population growth also affects the supply of farm labor, a point discussed somewhat later.

Agricultural economists have placed considerable emphasis upon changes in population growth as a significant influence determining the level of demand for farm products and thus the quantity of labor that could be employed in agriculture. Holding the appropriate things constant, it is not hard to discover the reason for the emphasis upon population as a major influence in determining well-being in agriculture in an advanced nation such as our own. If the income elasticity of demand for farm products is 0.25 and the "population" elasticity is 1.0, a given percentage increase in population will increase the demand for farm products four times as much as the same percentage increase in real per capita income. This may well explain why agricultural economists have given little thought to the interrelations between population and real per capita income. All of the analyses assume that the two are independent. Yet, with a given level of technology and a given supply of natural resources, a larger population in a nation might well result in lower per capita income, though greater total income. The fact that in the United States

---

[42] In his early comments on this article, Black has suggested that some of the decline in our net food exports has been due to the effect of rising consumer income on the variety of foods and fibers that are demanded. Since our climate is somewhat limited in diversity, this explanation is a reasonable one. Black also suggests that U.S. agriculture has been slow in intensifying production to the point implied by maximum profit to the firm and that more output could be produced at lower cost. He further argues, however, that import barriers abroad would check the exports resulting from further intensification. However, our own import barriers, particularly on sugar, wool, and fats and oils, maintain imports at a lower level than would prevail in a free-trade situation.

rising real per capita income and increasing population have occurred together is not adequate support for the belief that the two are causally related, except for the possibility that within a given social-cultural climate, higher real incomes may induce a higher birth rate.

But there is a second implication of population growth, namely, with reference to the problem of labor transfer because the fertility rate of rural farm women is considerably greater than that of rural nonfarm or urban women. For 1935–40 the net reproduction rate for farm women was 130 per cent higher than for urban women, and 44 per cent higher than for rural nonfarm women. The urban net reproduction rate has exceeded unity since 1900 only during the last half-dozen years. If one averages the net reproduction rates of the latter part of the thirties and of the forties, using the population distribution by rural-urban residence for 1947 as weights, total U.S. population would increase about 20 per cent in one generation (about 28 years), but the rural farm population (assuming no migration) would increase about 70 per cent and the urban population would decline slightly. Thus population growth adds to the labor transfer problem by materially contributing to the potential farm labor supply and contributing only moderately to the nonfarm population and labor supply.

It should be added, however, that even if the U.S. population were stable, labor transfer away from the farms would be required. Given the structure of birth rates, farm population might increase as much as 40 per cent in a generation without migration. But the transfer problem would be smaller with no population increase than it would be with a large one. Consequently, population growth is not an unmixed blessing to agriculture.

In agriculture much of the research and education that has been responsible for the technological change of the last several decades has been financed by the public in general. While the technological change that has occurred in agriculture has contributed to the rise in real income in our economy, it has increased the magnitude of the labor transfer problem by reducing the demand for farm labor. The question of the long-run effects of publicly supported research and education upon the real incomes of farm people has not been adequately investigated. It seems reasonable to argue that the effects have been beneficial. This point cannot be developed here, but if the long-run demand elasticity is near unity (because of the availability of substitutes or foreign demand and supply conditions) an unchanging farm technology in an otherwise progressive society is not likely to promote increasing real incomes in agriculture.

III. AGRICULTURAL POLICY AND THE FARM INCOME DIS-ADVANTAGE

Agricultural policy has many facets, but almost every proposal has been related to the desire to mitigate an actual or presumed income disadvantage of farm people. Fashions have changed, however, during the past four decades. Major programs that were well established by the end of the twenties included systematic and extensive support of agricultural research and education at several levels (high school, college, and adult education through the extension service), provision of credit to farmers through government-sponsored agencies, the provision of numerous inspection, regulatory and information services related to the marketing and processing of agricultural products, and the special treatment of farm cooperatives.

During the twenties a search was made for new tools to attack the problem of low farm incomes. This time the emphasis turned more directly to the market itself. Numerous schemes involving export dumping were discussed, and two such measures were passed by Congress, only to be vetoed by President Coolidge both times. The Federal Farm Board was established in 1929 with a $500,000,000 revolving fund to be used to stabilize farm prices, but the fund failed to revolve and the Farm Board passed out of the picture in 1933. The main residue that the Board left for posterity was one of its reports, in which it argued that price stabilization was impossible unless production was kept in line with the amount actually moving into consumption.

Following 1933 the rallying point of most efforts to increase farm incomes has been parity price. Parity price, as originally defined in the Agricultural Adjustment Act of 1933, is a price calculated for each commodity that gives that commodity "a purchasing power with respect to articles that farmers buy, equivalent to the purchasing power of agricultural commodities in the base period." Except for tobacco, the base period was established as August, 1909 through July, 1914. Some of the subsequent modifications of parity are discussed below.

The nature of farm price programs can perhaps be best illustrated by showing how price support operations might function under existing legislation, the Agricultural Act of 1949, for a perishable commodity and a durable commodity. Let us assume that the perishable commodity is butter. The Secretary of Agriculture announces a support price at 90 per cent of parity (he may establish it at 75 to 90 per cent in general). This gives a support price of $0.60 for butter of a certain grade at Chicago. The market price would go below this; consequently, the Secretary offers to buy butter at $0.60 and accumulates stocks. At the same time, he may impose a quantitative import restriction on butter. If market price does not rise above $0.60 within a few months to permit him to dispose of the stocks, several alternatives are available. Butter may be dumped abroad; it may be transferred free or at a low price to relief agencies or to the school lunch program; it may be diverted to a "lower" use such as for soap production; or it may actually be destroyed (as has happened to several million bushels of potatoes). In addition, the Secretary could make the support price conditional upon producers entering into a marketing agreement under which they would agree to limit their sales of butter.

The durable product might be cotton. A support price of 90 per cent of parity would be announced (it could be as low as 75 per cent under certain supply conditions). Farmers might be required to reduce cotton acreage if they wish to avail themselves of the loan privilege; in any case, the Secretary could require that they vote marketing quotas to maintain the loan rate. The farmers that agree to restrict acreage have the loans, which are nonrecourse in nature, as well as certain conservation payments as incentives. Those who do not restrict acreage must abide by the marketing quotas, or any excess sales are taxed at rates ranging up to 50 per cent. If output is restricted sufficiently by the program, the Secretary has no additional problems. If not, farmers will offer cotton for loan and the government may accumulate stocks. If stocks are accumulated in too large volume, the Secretary may dump cotton abroad (import quotas would have been imposed previously) or offer it for sale for some domestic uses at low prices.

From 1933 through 1950 the government paid out to agriculture in direct payments in accordance with the provisions of the various agricultural price support programs about $8.8 billions; it suffered monetary losses in its price support operations for perishable commodities of $1.5 billions and about $0.6 billions for storable commodities—a total of $10.9 billions. (Something over $1.5 billions of the direct payments should be attributed to efforts to alleviate some of the undesirable effects upon farm production of price control during World War II.)

There has been a running debate over the past fifteen years among agricultural economists concerning the farm price programs. This debate can be summarized partially around the following points: (1) criticism and appraisal of the existing price programs; and (2) proposed alternatives to these programs.

A. Criticism and Appraisal of Farm Price Programs

Many agricultural economists have argued that parity price is not an appropriate objective to guide any price policy.[43] The basis for the conclusion was essentially economic; changing demand and supply conditions through time require changing relative prices among agricultural products and between farm products and all other products. Parity prices, if made effective, will in some cases lead to increases in output of commodities in cases where the usual price adjustments would dictate declines. Attempts to prevent such responses to relatively high prices lead to all sorts of restrictive devices—production control, import quotas, output destruction, and so on. Not only does adherence to parity prices disrupt effective use of resources within the United States, but the objective of parity prices and attempts to achieve it have constituted a major breach in our program for promoting more liberal foreign trade policies in this and other countries.[44]

There is fairly general agreement that the farm price programs have not resulted in as serious a misuse of agricultural resources as had been feared. This result is largely due to the inability of production control to limit output effectively.[45] Farmers found it possible to increase output per acre on the acreage-restricted products and to find alternative uses for acreage that they would otherwise have devoted to the restricted products. The result was heavy accumulations of stocks of durable commodities by 1941, for example; but World War II solved this embarrassing problem, just as the Korean conflict eliminated the more recent possible debacle.

Another major element of criticism arose as a consequence of the distribution of the gains from the program. First, the program tends to concentrate its income transfers in the higher income brackets within ag-

---

[43] J. S. Davis, *On Agricultural Policy, 1926–1938* (Stanford, 1939), esp. pp. 367–72, 389, 475–78; T. W. Schultz, *Redirecting Farm Policy* (New York, 1943), pp. 6–19; G. S. Shepherd, *Agricultural Price Policy* (Ames, 1947).

[44] D. G. Johnson, *Trade and Agriculture, a Study of Inconsistent Policies* (New York, 1950).

[45] T. W. Schultz and O. H. Brownlee, "Effects of Crop Acreage Control Features of AAA on Feed Production in 11 Midwest States," Agr. Exp. Sta. Res. Bull. 298 (Ames, 1942); Shepherd, *op. cit.*, pp. 58–65.

riculture, and there is only a very loose relation between the aggregate amount of transfer and the over-all economic position of farmers. Witt and Hopkins found that in Iowa in 1939–40 the direct payments to farmers coincidental with the price programs were more than twice as great for the farmers in the highest third of the income range as for those in the bottom two-thirds.[46] Any gains to farmers that came from higher prices due to the programs have gone mainly to the highest income groups in agriculture.[47]

There have been two beliefs that have lent support to the view that the price support program has had generally favorable effects on balance. One view, expressed by Tolley, Bean, and Ezekiel, is that a farm price program with its attendant controls was required to offset the monopolistic character of labor and business.[48] This view has had, and still has, wide support in popular and political circles.

A second view is that general income transfers to farmers through higher prices and direct grants have not had serious effects upon the allocation of resources between agriculture and the rest of the economy and may have had desirable consequences.[49] Wilcox has argued that higher farm incomes due to governmental action have led to an increase in investment in agriculture, particularly in laborsaving machinery. The increased investment has been desirable because of the high returns to investment in agriculture and because the introduction of laborsaving capital has induced migration from middle-sized family farms. In addition, higher incomes may aid migration by providing the financial resources necessary.

The main assumptions of Wilcox' analysis may well be valid, namely, that marginal returns to capital in agriculture are higher than elsewhere, that higher farm incomes lead to significant additional investment, that the introduction of laborsaving machinery may induce

---

[46] Given in T. W. Schultz, *Production and Welfare of Agriculture* (New York, 1949), p. 156.

[47] D. G. Johnson, "High Level Support Prices and Corn Belt Agriculture," *Jour. Farm Econ.*, Aug. 1949, XXXI, 509–19.

[48] H. R. Tolley, "An Appraisal of the National Interest in the Agricultural Situation," *Am. Econ. Rev., Proc.*, Feb. 1941, XXX, 119–20; Mordecai Ezekiel and L. H. Bean, *Economic Basis for the Agricultural Adjustment Act*, U.S.D.A. (Washington, 1933), pp. 40–48.

[49] W. W. Wilcox, "High Farm Income and Efficient Resource Use," *Jour. Farm Econ.*, Aug. 1949, XXXI, 555–57; *idem*, "Effects of Farm Price Changes on Efficiency in Farming," *ibid.*, Feb. 1951, XXXIII, 55–65. See also J. M. Brewster and H. L. Parsons, "Can Prices Allocate Resources in American Agriculture?" *ibid.*, Nov. 1946, XXVIII, 938–60.

migration, and low incomes may limit migration because the required financial resources are lacking. But this does not prove that government-supported farm prices at relatively high levels are the most adequate policy solution. If one wishes to increase incomes in agriculture while at the same time increasing the real value of the national output, direct approaches to achieve the required resource transfers seem to offer more significant results. Efforts to improve labor mobility and to adapt credit forms and institutions more specifically to the peculiar circumstances of farmers would be more likely to meet the above objectives than would higher farm prices. This is particularly true in the case of the lower-income farmers since higher prices will not increase their incomes sufficiently to permit the required adjustments, a point recognized by Wilcox.

B. Proposed Alternatives and Modifications

There have been numerous proposals for modifying the farm price programs.[50]

Perhaps the most far-reaching of such proposals was the scheme of forward prices advanced by Schultz in 1940.[51] This proposal rejected the idea of parity prices. It was proposed that all price supports be set at the estimated level that would clear the market (actually slightly below this level) and that these prices be announced prior to the time that production planning occurs. No production control was visualized and, in general, any difference between the forward price and the actual market price would be paid directly to the farmer, thus allowing the market to allocate the available supply of a product among consumers. A storage program was suggested, however, to stabilize the quantities of storable products coming to market as a means of reducing the impact of yield variability upon production and consumption.

---

[50] For various proposals not specifically commented upon, see the following: Association of Land-Grant Colleges and Universities, Committee on Post-War Agricultural Policy, *Post-War Agricultural Policy* (n.p., 1944); W. H. Nicholls, "A Price Policy for Agriculture," *Jour. Farm Econ.*, Nov. 1945, XXVII, 743–60; see also 17 other articles on price policy in the same issue; B.A.E., *What Peace Can Mean to American Farmers: Agricultural Policy*, U.S.D.A. Misc. Pub. 589 (Washington, 1945); Committee on Parity Concepts, "Outline of a Price Policy for American Agriculture for the Post-War Period," *Jour. Farm Econ.*, Feb. 1946, XXVIII, 380–97; L. J. Norton and E. J. Working, "A Proposal for Supporting Farm Income," *Illinois Farm Economics*, Dec. 1945–Jan. 1946, No. 127–128, pp. 309–13; *idem*, "Supporting Farm Income," *ibid.*, April–May 1946, No. 131–132, pp. 345–51.

[51] T. W. Schultz, "Economic Effects of Agricultural Programs," *Am. Econ. Rev., Proc.*, Feb. 1941, XXX, 127–54; *idem, Agriculture in an Unstable Economy*. See also D. G. Johnson, *Forward Prices for Agriculture* (Chicago, 1947).

The most important argument for forward prices was that they would reduce the effect of price uncertainty upon the allocation of agricultural resources. It was argued that price uncertainty promoted inefficient use of farm resources by discouraging the employment of enough capital in agriculture to bring down the marginal product of capital to approximately the level of the interest rate. In addition, price uncertainty made it difficult to allocate a given supply of resources among alternative products in a way that would maximize farm income. It was believed that a central "expert" body could do a better job of price forecasting than several million farmers and that forward prices would reduce price uncertainty as well as transfer it from the farmers to the government.

In the event of a depression, advocates of the forward price proposals usually would make an exception to the rule that the prices be established at the short-run equilibrium level. It is argued that during a depression, when labor transfers out of agriculture are essentially stopped, a transfer of income to agriculture through the price system will not have many undesirable effects. Such a transfer may be a political necessity; in any case, the payments involved, if not covered by taxes, would aid in recovery from a depression and would, at the same time, prevent hardship among farm people.

The major underlying supposition behind the proposal is that during periods of full employment no planned income transfers should be made to agriculture. If the returns to farm resources are "too low," the underlying cause—excess quantity of resources—should be attacked directly by measures designed to increase migration.

In general, Black supports the basic desirability of forward prices, but his specific proposals imply some modifications.[52] He believes that attempts to forecast short-run price variations should not be made, and that instead, support prices approximating the long-run equilibrium level would be more desirable. In addition, he believes that the total gross income rather than the price should be stabilized, thus reflecting the effect of yield variations. Black emphasizes the desirability of adopting measures to improve the nutritive content of the national diet, particularly for low-income consumers, through a plan resembling the food stamp plan of a decade ago.

The general proposition that efforts should be made to expand

---

[52] Black and Kiefer, *Future Food and Agricultural Policy,* esp. Ch. 21.

consumption as an alternative to production restriction has been analyzed by several other economists. Waugh, Hoffman, Gold, Southworth, Schickele, Coppock, and Stigler made contributions to theoretical discussions.[53] Cochrane and Shepherd attempted empirical estimates of the possible expansion of consumption or of farm income as a result of increasing food availability to low-income consumers.[54]

The plans to increase the food consumption of low-income consumers all involved some form of price discrimination or restricted income transfer. Southworth showed that of the three main techniques for increasing food consumption—price discrimination, an unrestricted income transfer, and an income transfer restricted to food—the third would increase food consumption the most and the second the least. Proposals such as the food stamp plan or food allotment programs have been criticized on several grounds, but the one of most interest to economists relates to the welfare aspects. Is it acceptable social policy to make an income transfer that is restricted to expenditure upon food? If the transfer is made by price discrimination, the condition of resource efficiency that requires the equality of marginal cost and price is violated. If the transfer occurs through a money grant that must be spent upon food, the individual receiving the grant cannot equalize the ratio of prices of food and other commodities with the rate of substitution between food and other commodities. In either case, it can be shown that the losers could afford to bribe those gaining to give up the food subsidy scheme, and return to a single price plus an unrestricted income subsidy. The proponents of the measure must argue that these criteria are not as important as others and that the objections rest upon acceptance of consumer sovereignty which in democratic societies has been disregarded frequently, as illustrated by free public education and public health measures.

Several interesting, if somewhat impractical, proposals have been made for farm price and income maintenance schemes not requiring a

---

[53] N. L. Gold, A. C. Hoffman, and F. V. Waugh, *Economic Analysis of the Food Stamp Plan*, U.S.D.A. (Washington, 1940); Herman Southworth, "The Economics of Public Measures to Subsidize Food Consumption," *Jour. Farm Econ.*, Feb. 1945, XXVII, 38–66; Rainer Schickele, "The National Food Allotment Program," *ibid.*, May 1946, XXVIII, 515–33; F. V. Waugh, "Market Prorates and Social Welfare," *ibid.*, May 1938, XX, 403–16; George Stigler, "Social Welfare and Differential Prices," *ibid.*, Aug. 1938, XX, 573–86, and rejoinder by F. V. Waugh, *ibid.*, pp. 587–89.

[54] W. W. Cochrane, *High-Level Food Consumption in the United States*, U.S.D.A. Misc. Pub. 581 (Washington, 1945); G. S. Shepherd, "Changing Emphases in Agricultural Price Control Programs," *Jour. Farm Econ.*, Aug. 1944, XXVI, 487–500.

general drain upon the Treasury but financed by special taxes upon farm products or farm incomes.[55] These schemes, though varying in detail, are based on the proposition that farm prices and incomes are very unstable in a cyclical sense. Consequently, a system of taxes and subsidy payments could be devised to reduce the amplitude of fluctuation of farm incomes. The taxes would be levied during periods of full employment and/or inflation, and the subsidies would be paid in the contrary circumstances. Such a system would contribute to lessening deflationary and inflationary pressures that arise in agriculture.

Some of the proponents of the schemes have argued that they would be self-financing since the subsidy payments to farmers could be equated to the tax receipts. Burch has argued that the tax incidence would not fall entirely upon farmers if the supply of farm products was responsive to income or price changes.[56] However, this analysis ignores the positive production effects of the receipt of subsidies at other times. Even though farm output were reduced when the taxes were levied, the output would rise when subsidies were paid. And some types of production adjustments, such as those due to labor transfer between agriculture and the rest of the economy, might not be seriously affected since the long-run income prospects in agriculture would not be affected by the proposals. The latter statement assumes that over a reasonably short period of time, say a decade or two, taxes and subsidies would be equal. Given our ability (or inability) to predict changes in national income and employment, it must be admitted that the probability of such equality is not large. It should also be noted that the proposals would lead to higher retail prices of farm products at the peak of the cycle and lower prices at the trough than would otherwise occur. Whether or not this would be desirable is largely a political proposition.

The most serious objection to such proposals is that they represent a particularistic solution to a problem that arises due to the general in-

---

[55] Geoffrey Shepherd, "A Farm Income Stabilization Program Could Be Self-financing," *ibid.*, Feb. 1948, XXX, 142–50; F. V. Waugh, "Excise Taxes and Economic Stability," *ibid.*, Aug. 1948, XXX, 399–410; H. G. Halcrow, "Analyzing the Tax Load of Agriculture—Discussion," *ibid.*, Feb. 1949, XXXI, 280–81; D. G. Johnson, "The High Cost of Food—A Suggested Solution," *Jour. Pol. Econ.*, Feb. 1948, XLVI, 54–57; H. G. Halcrow and R. E. Huffman, "Great Plains Agriculture and Brannan's Farm Program," *Jour. Farm Econ.*, Aug. 1949, XXXI, 497–508; H. G. Halcrow, "Farm Price Production and Income Policy," *Proc. West. Farm Econ. Assoc.*, 21st An. Meeting, p. 41; and E. L. Barber, "Modifying the Federal Income Tax to Promote Greater Stability of Farm Income," *Jour. Farm Econ.*, May 1948, XXX, 331–39.

[56] D. W. Burch, "Fluctuating Farm Income and the Tax System," *ibid.*, Feb. 1951, XXXIII, 108–14.

stability of the economy. It is undoubtedly preferable to seek more general solutions based on satisfactory fiscal and monetary management of the economy.

A number of economists, perhaps those who were somewhat more realistic politically, have worked for improvement within the general structure of the present price programs, particularly by suggesting modifications (modernization) of the parity price formula. In this group should be included O. V. Wells, Walter Wilcox, and H. C. M. Case, in addition to J. D. Black. The modernization consisted of giving up the 1910–14 relative prices within agriculture and substituting a moving average of relative prices, usually the most recent decade, tied to the average of the 1910–14 parity relationship. These economists, and others, undoubtedly believed that price parity was to be with us for some time and one should make the best of it, even if the best is none too good.

At the end of the decade, it cannot be said that the economists' proposals had received wide support in political circles, though the Agricultural Act of 1948 included several provisions which many economists had advocated. The Act provided for a more up-to-date parity formula such as Black and Wells had supported; it provided for relatively low levels of price supports such as had been approved by most economists including the Committee on Parity Concepts of the American Farm Economics Association; it permitted forward pricing; it made possible direct payments to farmers rather than the maintenance of prices in the market place; and the Act provided for a schedule of support prices that would vary inversely with the level of yields or output. However, these features never went into effect.

But the Brannan Plan emerged upon the scene and created such political tension and dissension that the end result was the Agricultural Act of 1949, which involved the highest average level of price supports of any of the recent proposals, with the possible exception of the Brannan Plan.[57] The Act specifically prohibits the use of direct price support payments to farmers and requires production limitations, even when farm prices are relatively favorable in comparison with actual experience during the past thirty years.

And even those that supported modernization of the parity formula

---

[57] See George Mehren, "Comparative Costs of Agricultural Price Supports in 1949," *Am. Econ. Rev., Proc.,* May 1951, XLI, 717–46, and comment by J. D. Black, *ibid.,* pp. 747–54. For a well-balanced discussion of the major features of the Brannan Plan, see Schultz, *Production and Welfare of Agriculture,* pp. 176–87.

can take little solace in how their ideas were distorted. Though the Agricultural Act of 1949 provides for using the relative prices for a recent ten-year period for most commodities, it prohibits the use of the new parity prices for the important farm commodities whose parity prices would have been reduced thereby. Consequently, the modernization resulted in raising average effective parity prices and did little to improve the relative prices within agriculture.

In closing this section, it should be remarked that the basic weakness of all attempts to improve economic well-being in agriculture through price policy is that most of the gains go to those farmers who have the highest income. In recent years, this has certainly included large numbers of farm families whose level of income is substantially above the national average. Furthermore, it may be suggested that since the farm families on the half or less of the farms that produce at least 90 per cent of the agricultural output have real incomes roughly equal to (if not above) the national average, some of the possible advantages for certain price proposals, such as forward prices, may be much less important than they were a decade ago.

IV. DESIRABLE DIRECTIONS FOR RESEARCH

Research in the economics of agriculture does not seem to have kept pace with the changing circumstances of agriculture. There are grounds for asking whether the areas of research being emphasized are the significant ones. The agricultural economist is a tool user rather than a tool creator, and therefore the importance and relevance of his work depend mainly on the nature of the problems that he studies. If his task were largely to expand and strengthen the analytical structure of economics, the particular empirical problems chosen for study would require justification only in terms of their contribution to the development of theory. But the agricultural economist is primarily a specialist in applied research, and both the demand for his wares and the social significance of his work depend upon his ability to analyze emerging, important problems of the farm and of the nation.

The economist is all too frequently guided in his selection of research topics by fads or by what were major issues a decade or two earlier. One sees this clearly in much of the research and prescription with regard to monetary and fiscal problems during the past decade, based largely on the events of the thirties, with its fear of deflation and unemployment. In agriculture, at the moment, research on marketing problems is in ascendancy, but it is doubtful that this ascendancy is a consequence of the importance of the field, given the fact that Congress has appropriated a liberal amount of money. No one has raised seriously the question whether this investment in research in the marketing of agricultural products is likely to reveal greater degrees of "inefficiency," however defined, than would similar amounts spent on study of other products, such as consumer durables. In addition, most agricultural economists have failed to adjust their perspective to take account of the improved income position of commercial farmers, the better allocation of resources that comes with full employment, the marked changes in relative prices of factors, and the scale effects of economic development.

Any attempt to indicate desirable directions for research in agricultural economics must recognize at least three fairly distinct objectives. First, there is the research that contributes to adult education, especially to that of farm people because the Land Grant colleges have a major responsibility in their extension programs to emphasize significant social, political, and economic issues. Economists at these institutions have the responsibility of conducting research that will be useful in developing such educational programs. Second, it is necessary to provide data and analytical techniques that will be of use to farm operators in making their farm decisions. The third objective entails research that will contribute to a better understanding of economic processes as they concern interrelations between agriculture and the rest of the economy, and the allocation of resources within agriculture. Each of these objectives is important; each merits research resources.

1. The first objective points to research that will aid farm people and persons in government and elsewhere, who have specific responsibilities to agriculture, to act more rationally as citizens in making the necessary public decisions. The research required is mainly of an expository and descriptive nature, but descriptive in terms of meaningful analytical propositions. It is surprising how little research material there is that is useful to extension workers in economic education. One major area in which economic education is much needed pertains to the effect of government activity, as reflected through monetary and fiscal actions, upon the functioning of the economy. Another is the effects of various governmental regulative activities, such as production controls, marketing quotas, price controls, rationing, and various types of subsidies, upon the size of the national product. A third is the character of the important influences in an industrial economy that determine the level of farm income and the quantity of resources employed in agriculture. A fourth

area might well be the analysis of the determinants of the varying levels of farm income in the different regions of the United States and of various nations throughout the world. Such research and education could contribute appreciably to the development of a more meaningful program of action by the United States in aiding economic change in low-income areas of the world, including some agricultural areas of the United States.

2. A large fraction of the total research and educational efforts in the field of agricultural economics is designed to aid individual farmers in making rational decisions. Much research in farm management has not been particularly productive, but this is not because there do not exist numerous problems to challenge the economist. Three may be mentioned. The advisor to a farm operator must be in a position to describe the results of changing resource combinations. Undoubtedly, many experienced individuals are able to indicate, with a fair degree of accuracy, the effects of changing resource use; but the knowledge is of the nature of an art and cannot be systematized sufficiently to be taught effectively. Research that will aid in specifying the production function should be directed along two lines. One approach is to utilize observations derived from records of actual farm operations. As yet statistical techniques are not entirely adequate to the task of permitting a highly reliable estimate of the significant phases of the production function. One highly complex difficulty is the measurement of the management input. Another is that the inputs and outputs on a farm are consequences of decisions made by the farm operator and are not experimental data. Unless great care is taken in the analysis of the data, one ends up with a statistical distortion of the production function as extreme as Moore's positively sloping demand function. The other approach is through the design of experiments and the analysis of experimental data. Most experimental work in agriculture, e.g., in feeding or in the use of fertilizer, is not now designed in a way that will help the economist to estimate the marginal returns to various inputs. (All too often, these experiments are not even designed so that they will effectively answer the questions asked by the experimenters themselves!) Such experiments have a pragmatic purpose, namely, to indicate the most efficient way of doing a certain task. The usual procedure is to compare only two or usually no more than three ways of conducting an operation (such as rate of feeding cattle); this is insufficient to determine whether the particular techniques or rates chosen for the experiment are the most efficient out of the total available alternatives. Since efficiency, from the farmer's view-

point, is defined in terms of profitability, what is required is an estimate
of the functional relation between the input(s) and the output. The
economist should contribute to the development of experiments that
will provide such data.

A second area of needed research is the effects of risk and uncertainty upon the structure of the farm firm and the appraisal of various
methods of adapting the firm to variable and uncertain outputs and
prices. In agriculture, production planning is subject to greater elements
of uncertainty than it is in most other fields of production activity. The
success or failure of farm firms all too frequently depends upon Dame
Luck. A period of high yields or low yields, both due to factors beyond
the control of a farmer, may well determine the economic fate of a
farm family for one or two decades.

A third area of research is the analysis of the process of farm en-
largement and consolidation. The low-income areas of agriculture are
largely synonymous with the areas of small farms. Even if migration
were to reduce markedly the population dependent upon agriculture
in such areas, past experience does not indicate that the land abandoned
or released would be recombined into farming units of sufficient size.
Quite frequently the land remains idle. While this nonuse of such land
may represent its best use in some cases, it is probably true that there is
a system of farming, given the appropriate technology and adequate
capital, that would make possible a rent on most of such land. The
validity of the last statement requires investigation, of course, but the
important point is that the growth process of farm firms where size adjustments are required deserves careful study.

3. Within the framework of the third objective, there are several
fairly specific research problems which appear to be important. One is
the mobility and migration of labor, both between agriculture and the
rest of the economy and between agricultural areas. In this case the
agricultural economist may well be able to contribute to a general theory
of resource mobility. It must be admitted that economics does not have
an acceptable, empirically verifiable theory of resource mobility. A general framework is available, but the framework is hardly suitable for
predictive purposes. Another is the measurement and analysis of technological change in agriculture and the rest of the economy. Changes
in the relative and absolute employment of resources in agriculture depend, among other things, upon changes in production efficiency. Perhaps more important, the rate of growth of the national product depends
upon technological change and may well be more dependent upon such

change in the future than in the past because of recent and prospective population expansion. Many statistical and analytical problems are involved in measuring technical change, but the analysis of factors affecting the rate of change may be even more complex and difficult—and, also, more important.

Another is the analysis of the interrelations between economic fluctuations in agriculture and in the rest of the economy. Much support for agricultural policy rests on the presumption that economic fluctuations in agriculture may result in inflation or deflation in the economy as a whole. While I believe this view to be unfounded, it would be desirable to have a more complete understanding of the character of the interrelations involved.

The above views do not constitute a magic formula for changing the basic nature of research in the economics of agriculture. The emphasis upon the various objectives that must be considered, and by inference the various individuals and groups of people for whom the research is intended, rests upon important distinctions. So much of the research in this field falls between various stools because no clear idea exists as to the major purpose of the research.

It is necessary to reiterate that the agricultural economist should try to anticipate the emerging important problems rather than wait for them to develop. There are risks, of course, in doing so, but there can be only failure in working on the obsolete problems of a decade or two ago.

COMMENT
John D. Black

The major point that needs to be made about this essay is that the author deliberately chose to limit his analysis of developments in the economics of agriculture to a narrow sector of the field, and to omit altogether the phases of the economics of agriculture that would have supplemented where most needed the thirteen essays in *A Survey of Contemporary Economics,* Volume I. Of that volume, I once wrote as follows: "The planners of this volume were apparently thinking of economics as 'political economy' in the main. This is highly significant in view of the fact that this collection was planned by a committee of the American Economic Association. How much longer it is going to take what is called economics today to broaden out to include private affairs instead of just public affairs is difficult to anticipate. After all, it is only a few decades since the departments of economics in our universities were called departments of political economy. Such broadening is greatly needed. We spend our lives mostly as firms, or families, or single individuals, producing and consuming goods and services. If economic science is to serve humanity, as, for example, we expect chemistry and medical science to serve it, it must become much more, relatively, an economics of private production (including marketing) and consumption, and less exclusively a science of national aggregates and the affairs of the state."

We do have, of course, a sort of private business economics in our schools of business or commerce. But our professors in departments of ecnomics are not generally satisfied with it. It is not likely to suit them better until they themselves take a hand in its development and evolve within it a body of principles and relationships much more ample than the present highly sterile theory of the firm.

Both logically and pedagogically the private economics of the individual business unit, farm, and household should come first. Then should follow analysis of the complex of interunit relationships that give modern society its dominant character. These interunit relationships are among business firms of the same type and of different types, and between them and farms and households. They need to be considered as they exist within such social units as cities and their surrounding trade areas, and within other sorts of economic areas, and finally, within the total economy and the nation and among nations.

Not to have used the economics of agriculture on this occasion to show the nature and possibilities of intraunit analysis, and then of interunit analysis within larger aggregates, is particularly unfortunate because in the better of the departments of agricultural economics in this country, there is evolving the kind of integration of private and aggregative economics that the science of economics so much needs, and which does not occur when private economics is in a school of business and aggregative economics in a department of economics. To have traced this evolution would have been singularly helpful.

To be more specific, the particular division of economics in which this essay could have supplemented the first volume to best advantage is production economics. All told, in one place or another in that volume, there are perhaps a dozen pages of what may be called production economics theory. A good deal of headway has been made in developing a body of production economics of agriculture. To label all of this as "farm management" is highly inaccurate. For example, the volume, *Farm Management* by Black, Clawson, Sayre, and Wilcox, which Johnson cited in his essay, pretty well covers the whole field of the production economics of agriculture, albeit on an undergraduate level. And there is much already developed production economics of agriculture that could not be included in a volume with that title.

In keeping with the foregoing, Johnson's treatment of the government agricultural programs omits almost entirely their production economic aspects. The middle A in the AAA of the Agricultural Adjustment Act of 1933 stood for adjustment, and that adjustment was primarily production adjustment. This represented an evolution out of the "Outlook" program of the U.S. Department of Agriculture, initiated in 1923.[58] It is true that most of the Congressmen who voted for the measure expected it would raise prices of farm products. Still, it was very far from being just a price support measure. The Act of 1948 restored some of its production adjustment character.

Johnson's Parts I and II are very well handled indeed, and he has performed a very useful service in bringing together the analyses bearing on the balance between agriculture and the rest of the economy.

COMMENT
Theodore W. Schultz

The adage, "Grow more corn to produce more hogs, to buy more land, to grow more corn," has come to characterize the feverish efforts at economic development of countries and peoples the world over. But ultimate purposes aside, little is yet known on how to induce such development and what its effects are upon the different sectors of the economy. Some valuable lessons may be had from what has happened in the United States, especially from studies which endeavor to explain the uneven development within agriculture.

Johnson's essay, which is restricted to the more important relations between agriculture and the rest of the economy under circumstances of rapid economic development, brings some of these lessons to the fore. It is clear from his essay that some progress has been made in un-

---

[58] See J. D. Black "The Role of Public Agencies in the Internal Readjustments of the Farm." *Jour. Farm Econ.*, Apr. 1925, VII, 153–75.

derstanding the functioning of the economy when fundamental factor supplies and product demands undergo marked changes over time. The essay is much more than a survey of the published materials, for it necessarily reflects the results that have been emerging from Johnson's researches in this field.

I wish that space might have permitted Johnson at least to outline the possible explanations for the very uneven economic development within U.S. agriculture. Why have some parts of agriculture been bypassed and others advanced so little in output per worker? There is also the question of occupational and locational effects of economic development. France appears to have been spared this particular "farm problem." Thomson[59] found that real returns earned by human agents in agriculture and in industry, in France, from 1901 to 1948, despite wars and serious inflations, stayed about equal. The explanation appears to be (1) a slow rate of economic development; (2) relatively low birth rates in farming communities; (3) the adoption of few new and better production techniques in agriculture; and also (4) national efforts to shelter agriculture of France by restrictions on trade.

The factors shifting the demand schedule for farm products are on firmer ground, both conceptually and empirically, than those underlying supply. This, I believe, is apparent in Johnson's essay. But it should be possible now to make some real headway in explaining shifts in the supply schedule of farm products. The input indices developed by Barton, Cooper, and Brodell[60] and others in the Bureau of Agricultural Economics, despite imperfections in the data on which space limitations prevent me from commenting, represent a valuable new tool with which to gauge the elasticities of substitution among the several classes of inputs and with which to approximate the value of the increase in the output per unit of input from advances in production techniques. The supply schedule of farm products in the United States has shifted far to the right; in 1950, 75 per cent more products were forthcoming at about the same relative price than in 1910. There have been two fundamental developments: one has altered the supply of inputs available for agricultural production and, as a result, the quantity of nonfarm inputs was

---

[59] Procter Thomson, *The Productivity of the Human Agent in Agriculture: An International Comparison,* Ph.D. thesis, University of Chicago, 1951.

[60] See, M. R. Cooper, G. T. Barton, and A. P. Brodell, *Progress of Farm Mechanization,* U.S.D.A. Misc. Pub. 630 (Washington, 1947) and G. T. Barton and M. R. Cooper, "Relation of Agricultural Production to Inputs," *Rev. Econ. Stat.,* May 1948, XXX, 117–26.

four times as large in 1950 as in 1910; the other has been the very successful "production" of new and better production techniques by the agricultural experiment stations, U.S. Department of Agriculture, and others. The outcome is that total inputs rose much less than outputs from 1910 to 1950; with 1910–14 input prices as weights, total inputs rose 33 per cent, which represents an upper limit in measurement; and using 1946–48 input prices, inputs rose only 14 per cent, a lower limit in gauging this development.

There is another major problem on which work is far enough along to indicate promising results. This is the problem of the instability of farm prices. It is being approached in two parts, i.e., the farm price effects of the instability of the general level of prices, and the large short-term movements of farm prices which are a consequence of (1) very inelastic demand and supply schedules; (2) large and abrupt shifts in the demand schedule which occur frequently; and (3) substantial variations in production caused by weather and other exogenous factors which occur from time to time.

7

PUBLIC

FINANCE

C. Lowell Harriss

Essays in the first volume touched upon many developments in public finance, especially problems dealing with the levels of employment and of prices and with federal budgeting, commonly termed "fiscal policy."[1] Consequently, the discussion here focuses deliberately on other topics.

I. GOVERNMENT EXPENDITURES

The tremendous growth of government expenditures, here and abroad, has been one of the striking economic developments of recent years. Economic analysis of these changes has dealt primarily with the probable effects on the levels of employment and prices.[2] The economic effects of some specific types of spending have been studied.[3] On the

---

[1] See in particular, Arthur Smithies, "Federal Budgeting and Fiscal Policy," *A Survey of Contemporary Economics,* Vol. I, H. S. Ellis, ed. (Philadelphia, 1948), Ch. 5.

[2] J. F. Due, "Government Expenditures," *Fiscal Policies and the American Economy,* K. E. Poole, ed. (New York, 1951), Ch. 5, and P. J. Strayer, "Public Expenditure Policy," *Am. Econ. Rev.,* Mar. 1949, XXXIX, 383–404, discuss some of the more detailed problems. I exclude the literature of "welfare economics" because it is covered elsewhere in this volume; one good discussion from the point of view of public finance is H. M. Somers, "Dépense publique et bien-être économique," *Rev. de Sci. et de Légis. Finan.,* Jan.–Feb.–Mar. 1951, XLIII, 1–24; he expresses skepticism about the usefulness of the "compensation principle." The literature dealing with the broad problem of increasing governmental influence—writings of Hayek, Von Mises, Wooton, Clark, for example—touches on another phase of the general topic.

[3] A. H. Hansen and H. S. Perloff, *State and Local Finance in the National Economy* (New York, 1944) presents some analyses, especially on such topics as the national interest in state and local health, education, and many other spending programs; yet there is a tendency to underestimate the seriousness of costs, and the data are now out of date. Major American economic journals contain few references to articles which might be classed here.

261

whole, however, the analytical results are generally unsatisfactory. Economists specializing in public finance have generally concentrated on taxation. Perhaps there is not much more the economist can say about spending. The nature of the problems, especially the unavailability of bases for appraising results, makes study difficult. Description, plus the statement of rather obvious generalities, may about exhaust the possibilities.[4]

A contrasting tendency is implicitly to identify "economy" with "nonspending." The need for broader and more objective analysis is huge. And it should be possible for the economist, cooperating with other specialists—engineers, educators, medical doctors, social workers, diplomats, and military leaders—to help in answering important questions. Unequivocal answers cannot be expected, if only because the problems are so huge, the objectives are not precise, and the conflicts cannot all be resolved.

II. TAX SHIFTING AND INCIDENCE

Some developments in shifting theory are to be noted, but the area of agreement has probably been reduced rather than increased. Primary interest has shifted to the "economic effects" of a tax, a broader concept not defined uniformly but including the effects on output, investment, disposable income, and other items. The inappropriateness of partial equilibrium analysis for study of the effects of major taxes is now widely recognized. Moreover, some economists question the value of analysis of major taxes without explicit consideration of the effects of the expenditure of the tax funds. Little has yet been accomplished in such extensive coverage.

The subject of property tax shifting has developed slightly. Rent controls have made shifting more difficult in some cases, and the deductibility of property taxes in computing income subject to income taxes (which are imposed at many different rates), makes the net cost of the property tax on a particular property vary somewhat from owner

---

[4] The treatment of government expenditures in national income computations may be misleading. The assumptions that (*a*) (most) government employees yield services equal in value to the wage or salary payment; (*b*) materials used by government agencies provide services equal in value to their cost; and (*c*) transfer payments are neutral may all be satisfactory for computing national income, but they give absolutely no help in determining whether society is getting the best result reasonably possible or whether more or less could advantageously be devoted to such activities.

to owner.[5] The theory of property tax capitalization has received little attention; Shoup's study notes that the simple theory needs modification if the tax affects interest rates and thereby the rate used in capitalization; the spending may create benefits which offset burdens or differentials in taxes.[6]

Most economists, apparently, still hold that the personal income tax rests primarily on the recipient of the income, or, more precisely and not insignificantly so, on him, his family, and possibly others he does or might help. This traditional conclusion has received popular and professional challenge, however, especially as applied to wages and salaries. When there is a strong union, when demand is high and inelastic (as for armaments), when the margin for bargaining is not narrow, employees may push harder, and the employer resist less, than if the income tax were lower (especially if the employer himself is subject to a high marginal tax rate, in some way working on a "cost plus" basis, or subject to profit renegotiation). The traditional reply that less employment in the firm would follow, tending to increase the availability of labor and to reduce wage rates in other parts of the economy, would not necessarily apply in a generally inflationary situation.[7]

Another way in which the income tax may be shifted is by changing the supply (or demand) of labor or other productive resource. By reducing the income left for the individual's disposition, the tax reduces the attractiveness of work for compensation relative to other uses of time. The higher the rate at the margin, the less will a person be able to retain from effort yielding taxable income. He may exert himself less or direct his efforts to uses yielding nontaxable "income." The amount

---

[5] The number of persons subject to highest bracket income tax rates is small. Their part of the total demand for real estate is too slight to raise prices by the full value of the tax deduction they enjoy; they are less burdened by the tax than an owner subject to lower income tax brackets.

[6] Carl Shoup, "Capitalization and Shifting of the Property Tax," *Property Taxes* (New York, 1940), pp. 187–201; a more general theoretical analysis which shows how the results may vary according to numerous different sets of conditions is H. A. Simon, "The Incidence of a Tax on Urban Real Property," *Quart. Jour. Econ.,* May 1943, LVII, 398–420; Simon, however, fails to take account of all reasonable possibilities, so that his conclusions cannot necessarily be extended to other sets of conditions.

[7] Such shifting of the personal income tax is certainly uneven, partly because the amount of tax varies from employee to employee (though most persons having roughly similar jobs will probably be subject to the same marginal rates) and partly because of the wide differences in bargaining positions. The persons in weak bargaining positions will pay in higher prices (or lower property incomes) some of the income tax of those who got wage increases.

of labor offered in the market may be reduced, permitting those working to obtain higher rates; thus the income tax is to some extent shifted to people in their capacity as purchasers or property owners.

This argument assumes that demand for labor does not fall to offset fully the reduction of supply. Since persons reducing their money income by working less, or not working more, will probably spend less, the assumption may well be questioned. In an inflationary situation, however, demand may be great enough to press wages higher. The argument also assumes that people have real choice in the amount of work they will do. Certainly, there is much choice when labor demand is high —housewives have opportunities to get jobs paying money; employees may choose about working overtime or as to the amount of vacation they take or whether they may be absent from work without serious worry about criticism. Others with considerable freedom of choice are persons on commission; those deciding whether to retire; young people beyond the compulsory school age; and employees with good opportunities for earning tax-exempt income (growing food, fixing a house, doing things for the family).[8]

Another consideration—"labor" is not homogeneous! Differences in quality are large. High rates of payment go generally for relatively desirable activities (at the margin). The progressive income tax impinges especially on such activities. Therefore, the supply of such labor may be affected relatively more than the supply of more ordinary labor. The one systematic study, however, concludes that as to business executives the evidence shows little effect on executive effort.[9]

For the great masses of income recipients, marginal tax rates have not been high enough to exert a major effect on effort; tax consciousness has lagged behind increases in tax rates; and other pressures or inducements to work have been high. Moreover, some persons who have a choice will work more when taxes are high in order to be able to maintain their money purchases.

The personal income tax also falls on interest, dividends, rent, and other earnings. By reducing the net return, and especially by reducing the source of supply (business earnings for reinvestment), the personal income tax will undoubtedly reduce the supply of capital, tend to raise the price, and shift a portion of the tax to users—unless demand is re-

---

[8] The effects of any such reactions are broader than shifting of the income tax. They include the reduction in specialization and the breaking down of the market, with probabilities of loss of real social income.

[9] T. H. Sanders, *Effects of Taxation on Executives* (Boston, 1951), Ch. 1, 3, 5.

duced equally. Yet, the overwhelming consensus remains that the personal income tax rests predominantly on the economic units (families) on which it is imposed.[10]

The main development in the theory of shifting of business taxes has been the increasing acceptance of a conclusion reached, but not widely accepted, many years ago. The base on which business income taxes are imposed is not the net profit of economic theory; consequently, the older conclusion that a tax on net profit cannot be shifted (from the owners of the business) does not necessarily apply to present taxes on business income. These taxes reduce the net return to investors or risk-takers. The funds offered for such investment will be reduced, because of the lowered net attraction and also because business earnings are an exceptionally important source of such capital. The reduction in supply will tend to force up the gross return, until the prospective *net* rate is enough to equal the return available elsewhere. Reduction in the amount of capital will reduce output below what it would otherwise be; the product price will be higher than it would otherwise. In this way, some of the tax is shifted to consumers, and by a method which the businessman may not fully appreciate. Therefore, the tax is increasingly recognized as a mass consumption tax, like sales and pay-roll taxes. However, as some investment is thus shifted to nontax lines—bonds and durable consumer goods—their net yields will tend to fall, reducing also the net rate expected on taxed investment; some of the tax on business income is shifted to investors generally.

Another consideration has had influence. Increases in demand have helped to increase business earnings. Prices, however, have not always been "free"; some businesses have not taken full advantage of opportunities to increase prices; or various kinds of government control have been effective. Where control over price has been exercised by sellers, by utility commissions, by renegotiators of prices of military goods, and conceivably by price control agencies, one consideration has been the profit after taxes; some business income taxes, therefore, are shifted to consumers in higher prices.

Another possibility has received more attention. Persons buying

---

[10] See Richard Goode, "The Income Tax and the Supply of Labor," *Jour. Pol. Econ.*, Oct. 1949, LVII, 428–37; M. H. Gillim, *The Incidence of Excess Profits Taxation* (New York, 1945), pp. 11–34; H. M. Somers, *Public Finance and National Income* (Philadelphia, 1949), pp. 170–96; Duncan Black, *The Incidence of Income Taxes* (London, 1939), *passim*. It should be noted that sales taxes may have somewhat similar effects; if some items—leisure, home-produced food, laundry done at home—are exempt from a sales tax, a person may choose to produce them for himself rather than earn money to buy them.

common stock or other assets (resulting from past investment) whose income is taxed will pay a price which will provide an expected yield after tax equal to the best yield obtainable elsewhere (including, of course, assets whose income is not subject to tax). Consequently, an increase in expected future taxes will lower the current selling price of the asset and fall on the current owner; new buyers will bear none (or less) of the tax. Some such capitalization is generally conceded, but economists have learned little about the amount, the permanence of the adjustment, and the effect on yields of other assets.

Except in the case of certain public utilities, the earnings needed to pay preferred dividends are taxed, but since the preferred dividend is fixed, all of the tax will fall on the earnings for the common stock before any touches the earnings for the preferred. Increases in tax rates, unless shifted to consumers, tend to be especially burdensome to owners of common stock in corporations making more than nominal use of preferred stock.

The theory of the shifting of sales taxes was refined by the application of developments in price theory. The most complete analysis was made by Due.[11] The results vary widely, depending upon which of the many possible combinations of assumptions seems most relevant. Under the conditions that have prevailed in recent years most of the taxes have doubtless been shifted to consumers, with pyramiding in some cases. The more general the tax, of course, the less useful the method of partial equilibrium analysis. A sales tax falling on most items of consumption, or a set of excises yielding very large revenues, may have enough effect on the total economy, especially with the spending of the tax funds, to change relative prices and the price level more than infinitesimally.[12]

The general view is that payroll (social security) taxes on the employee rest on him, while those on the employer fall partly on the employer (stockholders) but mostly on the consumer, as they become costs covered by price.[13] Yet most of the complications noted in the discussion of personal income and business taxes appear; additional con-

---

[11] J. F. Due, *The Theory of Incidence of Sales Taxation* (New York, 1942). Several articles have appeared, making numerous refinements. The analysis is too complicated and the applicability too small to permit review here.

[12] See J. F. Due, "The Incidence of a General Sales Tax," *Pub. Finance,* Sept. 1950, V, 222–30. In the U.S., sales taxes or excises, by changing "parity" prices for agricultural products, may start a more complicated set of forces.

[13] Sam Arnold, "Forward Shifting of a Payroll Tax under Monopolistic Competition," *Quart. Jour. Econ.,* Feb. 1947, LXI, 267–84, shows how the tax will reduce somewhat the net income of the employer under conditions that may prevail fairly widely.

siderations are that more or less direct, but highly uneven, benefits are associated with the taxes, and coverage is not universal. To date, rates have been low (except on railroads and their employees), but they are scheduled to rise, and proposals are seriously advanced to make much heavier use of pay-roll taxes (for health insurance). The shifting and incidence of pay-roll taxes may warrant more intensive analysis if the rate should rise to, say, 15 per cent from the present level of around 4 per cent.

Theories of shifting and incidence of death and gift taxation remain necessarily indefinite.[14] Fundamentally, of course, heirs or potential heirs get less because of the tax. Sometimes, however, the tax may in some meaningful sense fall on the person who owns the property to be transferred (or his family) and who consumes less in order to leave his heirs more; the tax may, for example, induce purchase of life insurance and payment of the tax with funds that would otherwise not become part of the estate. I doubt that we shall ever know the relative importance of these considerations. The former, I think, is the more important. Large fortunes are most unlikely to be maintained by insuring with funds that can come out of reduction of consumption—tax rates are simply so high that preservation of large fortunes is impossible. Yet "estate planning" is now common among families with large fortunes, so that the property owner controls the shifting of death and gift taxes to a large extent.

III. THEORIES OF PROGRESSION

The development of reliable guides for treating people differently has not received the attention it deserves. Economists have long been concerned with this problem as it relates to taxation. There is probably a widespread belief that since minimum, or some other subjective, sacrifice doctrine or an apparently more objective "ability-to-pay" principle —or some confused mixture—leads logically to progressive taxation, we have the major esssential for solving practical problems. Yet our intellectual position is weak. The older criticisms of this crude view have been elaborated by Fagan.[15] He formulates seven assumptions which must be proved to substantiate the major sacrifice theories: (1) the use

---

[14] The arguments are summarized by J. K. Hall, "Incidence of Death Duties," *Am. Econ. Rev.*, Mar. 1940, XXX, 46–59. His conclusion, that the tax falls on the transferor, seems to me wrong, but discussion appears to me singularly unpromising.

[15] E. D. Fagan, "Recent and Contemporary Theories of Progressive Taxation," *Jour. Pol. Econ.*, Aug. 1938, XLVI, 458–85.

of sacrifice as a criterion can apply only to income above a subsistence minimum; (2) the principle of diminishing marginal utility is valid for increasing rates of money income; (3) there is no change in personal sensibilities as income increases; (4) utility curves are reversible, or more simply, to make a man poorer takes away only the utility that was added when he was earlier made richer by the same amount; (5) all persons have the same utility systems; (6) the marginal utility of income is unchanged by expenditure; (7) the real costs necessary to earn a given rate of income, and domestic needs, are the same for all taxpayers. Two other assumptions have less general application. All of the assumptions are shown to be false or of restricted applicability. The result is a devastating attack on positions which most economists probably hold as a major item of faith. Fagan's own constructive position somewhat resembles that of Wagner and Simons. He endorses a "socio-political" theory; he believes that someone can develop an ethical foundation as a guide to treating people differently; it will require an objective analysis of the conditions of welfare, drawing upon knowledge of physiology and psychology. If this job can be done, it is ahead. Simons emphasized another type of justification for progressive taxation: the desirability of checking the tendency of economic inequality to cumulate.

A more limited, but useful, guide has recently been emphasized: persons in essentially similar circumstances should be treated similarly.[16] It is surprising how many questions this very limited guide will help solve. Yet it leaves open the issue of deciding *what* differences properly justify differences in tax burden—and *how much*. Though it may be easy to get agreement that a family with a $10,000 income should be taxed more heavily than a family of the same size with an income of $8,000 or $9,999, we must also find some basis for deciding how much. Little progress in this direction has been recorded.[17] One can easily con-

---

[16] Groves terms it "neutrality." H. M. Groves, "Neutrality in Taxation," *Nat. Tax Jour.,* Mar. 1948, I, 18–24.

[17] The provision of fairness and of justice has been a main function of government. Yet we have little to guide us in deciding what is more or less fair. The shifting of economic decisions from the impersonality and even ruthlessness of the market to government may bring abuse of high ethical concepts. The frequency with which we use the term "fair" must imply that we have enough idea of its meaning to apply it in specific situations. Yet the literature of public finance, where the concepts have a long history of attempted application, reveals a shallow understanding. An exception, written by a student of taxation, though not with a tax orientation, is E. N. Cahn, *The Sense of Injustice* (New York, 1950).

coct realistic possibilities that will disturb our sense of fairness; and when tax rates are high, the discrepancies are not small.

Tax progression received new support in the late 1930's from the now familiar argument that reduction in voluntary saving in much of the Western world then seemed desirable. Some of the apparent professional disregard of problems of fairness and equity in taxation undoubtedly resulted from this new justification for palatable policies.[18]

IV. DISTRIBUTION OF THE TAX BURDEN

For public policy formation, it would be useful to have reliable knowledge on how our tax burden is distributed. Distribution by income groups is obviously of interest, and since public policy is concerned with many other groupings—urban-rural, young-old, sick-well, saver-nonsaver, stockholder-nonstockholder, owner-occupant-renter, veteran-nonveteran, by occupations, by geographic area, etc.—it would help to know how they are affected differently by taxes and by government spending. We now have at best critically incomplete information. Roughly one-third of our total tax bill, the personal income tax, can be distributed moderately well among "taxpayers" on the basis of their "income."[19] Since some other data are available linking income and other characteristics, we can make cross-classifications which throw some light on the distribution of the personal income tax by these other characteristics. For the other two-thirds of the tax bill, however, our position is deplorable.

The major reason is obivious—we make heavy use of taxes which are not related directly to income or, as a group, to other factors in which we are interested. Moreover, we are far from certain about their final incidence.

Two major studies have been published in the postwar period. Adler estimated the distribution of both taxes and the benefits of government spending by the income of consumer units.[20] He compares 1938–39 with 1946–47. He finds that under his assumptions, both

---

[18] I know of no discussion of the implications of tax progression on a world basis. The responsibilities this country has undertaken to finance others makes this topic of more than passing interest to our children.

[19] But they are neither families nor individuals but a mixture, and one that contains other elements, notably unincorporated businesses.

[20] J. H. Adler, "The Fiscal System, the Distribution of Income, and Public Welfare," *Fiscal Policies and the American Economy,* Ch. 8.

taxes and expenditures have an equalizing effect, with the dividing point in 1946–47 the $4,000–$4,999 income group. The estimates are admittedly subject to a large margin of error and are not of much help for other than the broadest analysis. Musgrave and his associates did a more thorough job in estimating the distribution of taxes for 1948.[21] Their discussion of conceptual and methodological problems is advanced. The findings are less satisfactory than the analysis of principles, for the obvious reason that the best statistics are not good enough. Fortunately, different assumptions are made and examined, with breakdowns for the major taxes. All show a total tax burden (federal, state, and local combined) which is regressive below $1,500 (consumer-unit income), then generally proportional to $5,000, moderately progressive to somewhat over $6,000 and sharply progressive thereafter. Unfortunately, the open-end class is $7,500 and over, so that the range where progression is obviously steep is not shown. In general, taxes as a percentage of income are found to be about as high at the under $1,000 level as at the $6,000 level in two cases and at the $5,000 level in the other.[22]

Some other work has been done but not all has been published. Due estimated the total burden of federal excise taxes on a family with a given pattern of consumption,[23] and Crum estimated the distribution of the corporation income tax for 1941.[24]

V. DEVELOPMENTS OF MAJOR AMERICAN TAXES

A. The Personal Income Tax[25]

As the personal income tax during this period has become the major source of American tax revenue, students of public finance have become increasingly concerned about its imperfections because of heavy

---

[21] R. A. Musgrave, J. J. Carroll, L. D. Cook, and L. Frane, "Distribution of Tax Payments by Income Groups: A Case Study for 1948," *Nat. Tax Jour.*, Mar. 1941, IV, 1–53.

[22] A criticism of Musgrave's findings by R. S. Tucker, "Distribution of Tax Burdens in 1948," *Nat. Tax Jour.*, Sept. 1951, IV, 269–85, appeared too late for review here.

[23] J. F. Due, "Federal Excise Taxation," *Bull. Nat. Tax Assoc.*, Dec. 1947, XXXIII, 66–79.

[24] W. L. Crum, "The Taxation of Stockholders," *Quart. Jour. Econ.*, Feb. 1950, LXIV, 15–56. He assumes that the corporation income tax falls on stockholders. The striking, but not surprising, result is the gross inequality, especially the heavy burdens on stockholders with modest incomes. The data are for 1941, when corporation tax rates were lower than today.

[25] State income taxes are so varied, and their *net* burden is so small relative to the federal burden, that use of space to discuss changes in their role does not seem justified.

increases in rates.[26] War emergency and the pressure of changing post-war forces have worked to impede refinement even on points attention to which has seemed desirable to most students. Yet some notable changes were made.

Current payment with a large amount of collection at source (withholding) began during the war and appears to be working with fair success. A related change has been the *simplification of the personal income* tax as applied to the vast majority of taxpayers. Most taxpayers have an easy way to obey a law which is otherwise very complicated and to escape inequalities growing out of differences in personal situations.

The biggest structural change has been the *splitting of income* between husbands and wives, provided in 1948. The inequality of treatment between residents of community property states and other states became a matter of general concern as tax rates rose greatly. One solution was for states not having the community property system to change their property laws to establish this system, and several did so. Not all state constitutions would have permitted such changes, however. The Treasury tried unsuccessfully to induce Congress to "solve" the problem by compelling all husbands and wives to file joint returns, and thus to pool their incomes for computing tax rates. Congress adopted the opposite policy, permitting all married couples to treat their combined income as two incomes of half the total amount. The great mass of taxpayers received no benefit, others received little, but some received very large tax reductions.[27] The net tax on married couples with large incomes was reduced substantially, the distribution of total tax burden changed, and the revenue potential of the income tax was made more dependent upon tax rates, which, to yield a given revenue, must be higher because the base in the upper brackets is smaller.

1. *Definition of Income.* The importance of the definition of "income" for tax purposes has increased as income taxes have risen. This definition, for example, determines part of the basis for differentiating taxes imposed on different persons or families, i.e., the equity problem; moreover, business, social, and personal life will be influenced, deliberately or indirectly, by special tax treatment of different elements of "income." Though there has been extensive discussion of

---

[26] A valuable treatment by an economist is W. S. Vickrey, *Agenda for Progressive Taxation* (New York, 1947). Joyce Stanley and Richard Kilcullen, *The Federal Income Tax* (New York, 1948; 1950 suppl.), present a competent legal exposition which an economist interested in a technical legal problem could understand.

[27] In 1951, a single individual earning $15 a week and a married person with two children earning $140 a week paid the same marginal tax rate.

the definition of taxable income, most attention has been given to specific problems rather than general concepts.

What analysis there has been of broad concepts is well illustrated in the contrasting positions of Simons and Fisher.[28] The former argued that the concept of income appropriate for tax purposes is the accrual concept which Haig had formulated many years earlier, plus gratuitous receipts; Fisher, on the other hand, held that income is what is consumed (regardless of source of funds) and that receipts which are saved are not income. Simons criticized Fisher's proposals chiefly because they ignored the accumulation of economic power through saving. Fisher countered that society needs savings. Simons' definition[29] is widely accepted by the few economists who have written on the problem, but with some modifications, notably the inclusion of gifts and bequests in the income of the recipient (on this point he himself came to have doubts). This agreement on principle should be valuable in approaching the solution of specific problems, but, unfortunately, the analysis of specific problems must often consider conflicting principles.

One important specific problem is the failure to include in "income" the net *value of services of durable consumer goods,* especially owner-occupied dwellings, and home-produced food and services provided within the family. Very different is *interest from municipal* (state and local government) *bonds,* which by statute is excluded from taxable income but which is certainly considered income by economists. The exclusion results from policy considerations. The Treasury has occasionally asked Congress to remove the specific exclusion, partly to increase tax yields but also to remove a major method of defeating the progressive features of the income tax. There are too few persons subject to highest bracket personal income tax rates to bid municipal bonds to a price which fully offsets the tax advantage. There is a true buyer's surplus. The Treasury has neither proposed publicly, nor endorsed, compromises which would retain for state and local governments the

---

[28] H. C. Simons, *Personal Income Taxation* (Chicago, 1938) and *Federal Tax Reform* (Chicago, 1950); Irving Fisher and H. W. Fisher, *Constructive Income Taxation* (New York, 1942). In 1942 the Treasury proposed a graduated tax on spendings, to be superimposed on the regular income tax. The objective was to discourage spending, not to provide a better tax definition of income as Fisher urged. R. E. Paul, *Taxation for Prosperity* (Indianapolis, 1942), gives brief attention to this episode.

[29] ". . . the algebraic sum of (1) the market value of rights exercised in consumption and (2) the change in the value of the store of property rights between the beginning and the end of the period in question." *Personal Income Taxation,* p. 50.

interest savings they enjoy and in most cases "need" greatly, and which would take from bondholders only the tax savings which exceed the benefits to state and local governments. Such a compromise would yield about $300 million a year additional revenue to the Treasury at no cost to state and local governments. In view of the huge increase in such debt in the last few years, and the increase in federal tax rates, the prevailing view of students is that the problem is more serious than ever before.[30]

Another major problem of defining taxable income, the treatment of *capital gains and losses*,[31] continues to receive professional and popular attention. Starting with the practical and judicial requirement that, to be taxable, income must (generally) be realized, we must recognize that in our economy taxpayers have considerable freedom in the timing of realization of gains and losses; they can, therefore, time realization with tax considerations in view. Capital gains are generally an important part of large incomes. The problem is complicated further by the fact that in our economy some types of "income" can be converted to "capital," and vice versa, so that differences in tax treatment can sometimes be exploited by more or less artificial manipulation of property. Moreover, Congress has never provided that gains unrealized at death be taxed as income; *permanent* avoidance thus remains possible.[32] Other considerations add to the difficulty of solving the problems. Professional economists seem to be in general agreement that capital gains and losses should be included somehow in the base of an income tax,[33] but they are far from agreement on the best methods.

High tax rates increase the importance of the question, What *deductions from gross income* should be allowed in figuring the net income which is appropriate for tax purposes? The main consideration is the relative treatment of taxpayers, but revenue and economic allocation problems are also involved. Presumably, the specific exemption

---

[30] A well-balanced and original study is now available: L. C. Fitch, *Taxing Municipal Bond Income* (Berkeley, 1950).

[31] L. H. Seltzer, *The Nature and Tax Treatment of Capital Gains and Losses* (New York, 1951), analyzes the issues and the statistics thoroughly.

[32] H. C. Simons, *Federal Tax Reform* (Chicago, 1950), pp. 44–52, emphasized this point. This failure to assure an ultimate accounting of gains increases the difficulties of allowing generous deduction of losses. Any treatment which, like the present, permits permanent escape will encourage recognition of losses and holding on to gains.

[33] For a qualified exception see H. L. Lutz, *Public Finance* (New York, 1924; 4th ed., 1947), pp. 338–45.

covers enough to support life (though it is far below what federal minimum wage legislation would imply is "necessary" as a minimum).[34] Why grant anything more? The most compelling answer is that when most businesses (i.e., their owners) and professional persons are taxed under the personal income tax, at least some of the costs of getting the income must be deductible if the owner is to be treated fairly. A second answer is that some deductions may seem desirable as a matter of social policy.

There has yet been little writing on what has within a few years become a matter of more than trivial importance—whether in computing taxable income one can count as a deductible expense the costs of going to and from work, of general or specialized training, of moving from one job to another, of hiring someone to care for children, of clothing and its maintenance, of tools and equipment, of insurance and retirement payments, of entertainment, etc.[35] Differences between the attractiveness of jobs will be increased by tax differentials arising out of such considerations. There is a parallel problem of whether certain benefits ("fringes") should be included in gross income. Should medical services, or lunches, or transportation, or uniforms, or provision of recreation facilities, or "expense accounts," or pension contributions provided by an employer be included in the employee's gross income? What was once a problem of a few executives, professional men, and movie stars now affects millions of families significantly.

The *deductibility of taxes and interest* also becomes a more serious problem as tax rates rise. For some purposes it would seem that taxes and interest should be deducted only if the benefits they yield are included in gross income (or represented by lower deductions elsewhere, e.g., labor costs); in the case of business activity this condition presumably prevails. In personal life, however, most of the benefits for which interest and taxes are paid are not represented by values in gross income as computed for tax purposes. No carefully reasoned and statistically complete analysis of the deduction allowed *charitable contributions* has appeared.[36]

---

[34] There has been some move to make the exemption more generous in apparently meritorious cases; blind persons and everyone over 65 years old get a double exemption. Yet this type of aid provides no help to the persons with greatest need (i.e., those with very low incomes), and great help to persons with large incomes.

[35] The literature intended for tax practitioners contains much more on this subject than more narrowly economic literature. Of the latter Vickrey, *op. cit., passim,* is the most systematic. Sanders, *op. cit.,* Ch. 8, finds a confused situation in expense allowance policies of corporations.

[36] The Treasury has tried to require more reporting and to restrict somewhat the control of founders and successors of exempt foundations and trusts, but to date little has

Nor have economists written much about the new deduction, added in 1942, for *unusual medical and dental expenditures*. The reason cited by the Treasury in proposing the deduction was that "normal" health costs could reasonably be budgeted and in a sense covered by the specific exemption; extraordinary medical costs are not reasonably foreseeable; they are compelling and should not be discouraged or made more difficult by taxes; and, while huge in relation to specific family budgets, their total is not great enough to bring large loss of revenue.[37]

Different problems of income definition pertain more specifically to businesses, incorporated or not, and are receiving more and more attention. One such problem is the treatment as a deductible cost of the *cost of equity capital,* and to a smaller extent the value of services of the owner in excess of (or below) payments made to him. Interest is growing in the difference between the economist's concept, which recognizes such items as costs, and the contrasting concept of the framers of tax laws (and of the accounting profession). The tax advantage obviously rests with debt financing or leasing and renting as contrasted with equity financing.[38] It also rests with the distribution of corporate earnings, to the extent that distribution is desired by stockholder officers and members of their families as salaries rather than as dividends.[39]

The tax treatment of *depreciation and obsolescence* has received considerable attention. In the past the major problem of principle was timing. In the 1930's when each tax year was a separate unit with no allowance for losses of other years, timing might determine, in fact, whether or not any tax advantage would be gained from deductible depreciation. What was deducted in loss years was forever lost taxwise. For

---

been done. More and more resources are coming under the control of such bodies, which are themselves generally exempt from taxes. The tax aspects are described systematically in J. K. Lasser, *How Tax Laws Make Giving to Charity Easy* (New York, 1948).

[37] There are certainly abuses, such as some "recuperating" trips to Florida in January; hair-splitting lines have been drawn. There may be instances in which some of the tax "relief" is absorbed by doctors in the form of higher charges than they would otherwise make; in this respect, the deductibility differs from others in which the price—interest, taxes, business costs—is set by the market rather than by individuals taking account of personal "ability to pay."

[38] H. M. Groves, *Postwar Taxation and Economic Progress* (New York, 1946), pp. 31–35.

[39] G. E. Lent, "Bond Interest Deduction and the Federal Corporation Income Tax," *Nat. Tax Jour.,* June 1949, II, 131–41, found that up to 1942 there was no evidence of a trend for corporations to rely more heavily on debt financing but to cut the use of preferred stock. The Federal government, in dictating railroad reorganizations, put the Treasury ahead of former bondholders as claimants on future earnings by transforming debt to equity.

a decade, however, there has been enough recognition of losses of other years to reduce greatly the possibility that a firm will lose entirely the tax advantage from depreciation. Yet the question of when deduction is to be taken retains significance. In general, the Treasury imposes an inflexibility so rigorous as to demonstrate its inherent inappropriateness in a world of change. It is argued that businesses tend to use for their own investment planning the depreciation schedules set by the Treasury, that these schedules overstate the economic life of much equipment, and that consequently businesses have been slow in scrapping equipment to replace it with newer.[40] In addition to the psychological factor is the fact that the necessity of paying higher taxes in early years (because of the low depreciation allowance) reduces the funds left available for new purchases even by businesses which can correctly estimate the relative superiority of new equipment and which are unable or unwilling to borrow and buy or to lease. As a spur to modernization, more generous depreciation rates have been urged. They were provided during World War II and are now available for writing off investment in facilities certified as necessary for defense purposes.[41] Most discussion has rested on the implicit assumption that tax rates would not rise and might fall. If an increase in tax rates, and especially a rising level, is likely, however, there is some tax advantage in postponing deductions.

Perhaps even more attention has been given to another depreciation problem, that resulting from increases in the cost of replacing equipment.[42] Our economy, and our tax system, have not been built for inflation. On the basis of current prices, depreciation of much property has been inadequate to permit retention of enough funds to replace the productive capacity that has been disappearing; taxes on businesses may consequently have been higher than the production "facts of life" would justify. The problem has been widely recognized, but apparently considered of temporary significance—and in any case difficult to solve. Noth-

---

[40] E. G. Keith, "Repercussions of the Tax System on Business," *Fiscal Policies and the American Economy,* pp. 341–42; G. I. Terborgh, *Depreciation Policy and the Postwar Price Level* (Chicago, 1947); L. H. Kimmel, *Depreciation Policy and Postwar Expansion* (Washington, 1946). Depreciation allowances for tax purposes are fixed by administrative rather than legislative action, and the range of discretion is wide.

[41] Amortization in not more than five years has been provided in both cases. When the useful economic life is longer than the period of accelerated amortization, and when tax rates are high *temporarily,* firms may benefit greatly from such treatment.

[42] E. C. Brown, "Tax Allowances for Depreciation Based on Changes in the Price Level," *Nat. Tax Jour.,* Dec. 1948, I, 311–21. Accounting literature has contained many discussions of this problem.

ing has been done taxwise. If prices rise more or less chronically while tax rates are very high, however, the need for action will increase; businesses will become more generally aware of the problem and take it into account in making investment decisions; though the net effects may be obscure, they would seem certainly to include discouragement of investment by raising the prospective return necessary.

Depletion presents a problem which has been badly confused. Special treatment is granted owners of oil and many other natural resources. They are allowed, for tax purposes, to deduct as current costs, while the resource is being used up, amounts which are not limited to the owner's investment. In the case of oil and gas the deductions often come to many times the investment. Moreover, the costs of exploration and development can be charged to *current expense* when made, without reducing the base for future depletion of any resources discovered. Owners of oil and some other natural resources receive vastly favored tax treatment. The Treasury has tried to persuade Congress to remove or reduce the favoritism, but the benefits were extended rather than reduced.[43]

Many other problems of defining income for tax purposes remain. Some are too small to have stimulated much interest on the part of economists.[44] Yet they give rise to inequalities and distortions which are not clearly desirable. They are generally too complex or too firmly embedded to make popular discussion of any practical promise; the exemption of social security benefits and of the interest earned by assets invested in life (and other) insurance, corporate reorganizations, involuntary conversion, and nonbusiness losses are a few examples. Some will determine business decisions. The economist should know, at least, that the income tax is now unbelievably complex, especially as applied to businesses; that it employs no clearly nor consistently defined income concept; that the concept applied offers many bases for differences in the treatment of persons, families, and businesses, differences which can

---

[43] The present generous depletion provisions aid the *successful* firm, not the poor wildcatter who has consistently bad luck. An excellent analysis is D. H. Eldridge, "Tax Incentives for General Enterprise," *Jour. Pol. Econ.,* June 1950, LVIII, 222–40. The Treasury's views and the statements of representatives of oil and other industries will be found in *Revenue Revision of 1950: Hearings . . . ,* Ways and Means Committee, 81st Congress 2d Session, pp. 178–492. The spokesman for the oil industry did not really meet the Treasury's basic arguments. For discussion of contrasting treatment of a problem which is similar in respect to risk, see J. K. Butters, "Taxation of New Product Development," *Harv. Bus. Rev.,* Summer 1945, XXIII, 451–59.

[44] Simons, *Federal Tax Reform,* Ch. 4–6, provides a notable exception.

sometimes be deliberately manipulated by a well-informed and favorably situated taxpayer and which can in no sense be said to represent considered public opinion or the best judgment of professional economists. And, as tax rates rise, these differences become of increasing concern.

2. *Timing of Income.* Economists, tax accountants, and tax attorneys have devoted much of their writing over the last decade to one or another of the problems of "timing," when a receipt or deduction item is to be taken into account. Two have already been noted—capital gains and losses and depreciation. Timing is important chiefly (*a*) because when tax rates are progressive, a fluctuating income will be taxed more heavily than one with the same total amount received in equal yearly amounts[45] and (*b*) because postponement of tax gives the income recipient more funds (temporarily) for business, other investment, or consumption. There is general consensus that timing problems can be solved only by the introduction of averaging, but there is no agreement on the best form.

The most refined plan is cumulative averaging. The tax each year would be computed as follows: the income for all years since the initiation of the system, including that of the current year, would be added and divided by the number of years; the tax on this average would be computed and multiplied by the number of years; from the total would be deducted the tax paid in earlier years; the difference would be the tax due in the current year.[46] It meets the major requirements except for administrative simplicity; yet, even on this score, the burdens of the *serious* complexities could be placed on the Treasury, which could handle them with a few experts. And, like any good averaging plan, it would permit great simplification of many other parts of the law; most timing problems, notably depreciation, would be eliminated. It is doubtful whether the taxpayers affected would understand and accept the plan. The Treasury has been unsympathetic. Moreover, valid criticism may be levied against a system which uses the distant past in computing current tax liabilities. When the value of money may change as much as it has, some allowance for general price level changes would be necessary. Less ele-

---

[45] There are two exceptions. The most important arises when the fluctuations are *within* the first bracket; the other, when the fluctuations are over the highest bracket. The biggest single change now arises when income fluctuates around the top of the exemption level, where the rate jumps from zero to about 25 per cent. The splitting of income in effect doubles the first bracket for married couples and thus reduces the number of families needing averaging. A good brief discussion is Roy Blough, "Averaging Income for Tax Purposes," *Accounting Review*, Jan. 1945, XX, 85–96.

[46] Vickrey, *op. cit.*, 164–97.

gant proposals may even be superior.[47] One of apparent promise has been proposed by Holt; he suggests using a weighted moving average (for five years) to determine the tax rates to be applied to the current-year income with the complicated features handled largely by tables prepared by the Treasury and which for the taxpayer would be simple.

Congress has not seriously considered—nor has it had presented to it—much in the way of averaging. Yet for business losses it has taken positive action. Under the New Deal the ability to offset business losses of one year against profits of another was completely abolished (because, to avoid budget deficits, it was felt that revenue must be obtained, even at a high price in equity and business health). A new tack was taken during World War II, and the statute came to provide that losses of businesses (incorporated and unincorporated) could be carried back two years and forward two years. The Treasury and some students of taxation came to feel that carry-forwards were better than carry-backs, and in 1950 the law was changed to provide a much longer carry-forward, five years, but a carry-back of one year only.[48]

Another timing problem which Congress recognized specifically was the valuation of inventory in computing costs. When prices are rising or falling, the net earnings for any given period will depend in part upon the prices attributed to the inventory consumed during the period. When prices are rising, the inventory on hand at the beginning of the period will have cost less than its replacements at the end of the period. If the early value is used in estimating costs, the total computed costs would not enable the firm to duplicate its accomplishment. Yet, under generally accepted accounting practice, this principle of estimating costs was used by business for its own purposes and by the government for tax purposes. The sharp rise and fall of prices from 1936 to 1938 dramatized the distortion possibilities, and Congress took the first of several steps to permit some businesses to use a more stabilizing principle. Firms that met certain strict requirements could choose a "last-in-first-out" (LIFO) instead of "first-in-first-out" (FIFO) basis. Rather few firms

---

[47] C. C. Holt, "Averaging of Income for Tax Purposes." *Nat. Tax Jour.*, Dec. 1949, II, 344–61. See also Simons, *Federal Tax Reform*, pp. 40–44; Groves, *Postwar Taxation and Economic Progress*, pp. 223–36.

[48] U.S. Treasury and Joint Committee on Internal Revenue Taxation, *Business Loss Offsets* (Washington, 1947; mimeo.). Professional opinion is divided on the relative merits of carry-forwards and carry-backs. Shoup has recently pointed out that a carry-back should tend to make businesses less willing to spend money carelessly because of high marginal rates of tax; the larger their pretax profit, the greater their cushion if they have losses in later years which they can carry back. C. S. Shoup, "Some Considerations on the Incidence of the Corporation Income Tax," *Jour. Finance*, June 1951, VI, 187–96.

adopted LIFO during the 1940's, even though for some years the tax advantages were tremendous. Butters analyzes the issues and summarizes business reaction to date.[49]

Big tax benefits, of which the timing of tax liability is one of the largest, stimulated the business use of pension plans under high wartime tax rates.[50] The employee does not pay the income tax at the time the employer contributes the payment (and gets his tax deduction) but later when the pension is paid and when there is little or no salary to force the pension into a high tax bracket. Moreover, the income earned by the assets in the pension fund is not taxed except when the beneficiaries receive it. The cumulative advantage can be large. During World War II, corporations, especially those subject to excess profits tax and price renegotiation, could contribute to pension funds at little cost; moreover, executives found that drastic increases in personal income taxes made it difficult to save "adequately" for their own retirement out of salary after tax. In 1942 Congress changed the statute, specifying more clearly, and tightening somewhat, the conditions under which (a) the firm's contributions would be deductible in computing its tax; (b) the pension fund earnings would not be taxable; and (c) the employees would be taxed only when pensions were received. Because taxes are a determining consideration, Congress in setting general rules and the Treasury in administering them have vast power in determining how provisions for retirement will be financed. Recently, as a result of strong union demands, huge amounts have gone into pension plans. The tax loss to the Treasury has been large; the tax benefits have accrued to a limited section of the public.[51]

3. *The Tax Unit.* Another problem of progressive taxation is the determination of the taxpaying unit. If different tax rates are imposed on different types of units (incorporated and unincorporated businesses) or on units with different amounts of income (the typical situation of the personal income tax), accidents, irrelevant factors, and deliberate adjustment can become important.

One major development has been noted: the splitting of income permitted in the case of husbands and wives.[52] Other problems affecting

---

[49] J. K. Butters, *Effects of Taxation, Inventory Accounting and Policies* (Boston, 1949).

[50] We now have a good economic analysis of the subject as it pertains, primarily, to corporation executives. C. A. Hall, Jr., *Effects of Taxation, Executive Compensation and Retirement Plans* (Boston, 1951).

[51] One current issue is the treatment of owners and employees of unincorporated businesses and the self-employed; they cannot now use tax-benefited pension plans.

[52] This action has so dated the large pre-1948 literature that review does not seem appropriate here.

the family as the tax unit have received attention, e.g., the broadening of the scope of dependency. Yet the fact remains that a family of more than husband and wife that has income from property can reduce its total tax by distributing the property so that the income goes to owners subject to lowest marginal rates. The general trend of legislation, judicial decisions, and administrative practice has been to make such distribution less attractive;[53] donors must give up even more of the attributes of ownership than before to obtain income tax savings. Tax-unit problems arising out of family partnerships have been prominent. Owners of unincorporated businesses have a potential device for splitting income by making members of the family partners and thus moving income to lower brackets. Sometimes such formal changes are merely recognition of what has actually been a fact—the wife as a true economic partner; most of these situations, however, are now covered by the split-income provision. Children, brothers, and other relatives, however, may be made partners and taxes reduced. A legally valid partnership, however, does not have to be recognized for tax purposes, and revenue agents reputedly scrutinize new family partnerships carefully.

Corporation tax rates have been lower generally than those on income of prosperous individuals. The transfer of income not needed for consumption to a corporation one can control may bring large tax advantages. Long before our period economists tried to devise ways by which the earnings of the more or less artificial units which are recognized under property law could be taxed under a personal income tax. The rules have been tightened, but the penalty rates are "bargains" compared with highest personal income tax rates.[54] Moreover, penalties can be avoided by bringing in as owners members of more than five families, or by investing modest fractions in real estate or "operating" companies. Persons of substantial wealth are thus not in fact prevented from keeping that part of their investment income destined for reinvestment out of the personal income tax stream, while retaining control and the benefits of corporate management.

B. The Corporation Income Tax

The taxpaying-unit problem of most interest is that growing out of the corporation income tax. This tax began in 1913 as a device for col-

---

[53] Tax literature, especially that written for attorneys, has given this development much attention. Though the legal problems are highly complex, the text summary of the economic issues is not seriously oversimplified.

[54] I know of no better statement than Simons' brilliant comments, *Federal Tax Reform*, pp. 84–86.

lecting at source the personal income tax on dividends, following roughly British precedents.[55] Yet the tax now has a separate existence, and, except among some (but not all) professional economists, corporations are widely held to have taxpaying capacity of their own. The change has come about without extensive public discussion of the basic issues prior to the decisions, and the economy is saddled with a system which, though deplored, is apparently destined to become more, rather than less, widely used.

The views of professional economists have not changed fundamentally during recent years. They generally agree that taxes must eventually be paid by persons, not things. Though the federal civil service contains professional economists of high competence, they have been doing little to guide public thinking on this topic, and policy-making has been dominated by other considerations.[56] Yet, even among economists who agree that the corporate entity is not a good agency to use to tax people, there is no agreement about how it should be treated—except that it cannot be ignored.

At the beginning of our period, the 1936 tax on undistributed profits was, in fact, being repealed with such general relief to business that the persuasions of economists still fall on deaf ears.[57] When World

---

[55] The British, taking a step "backward" after World War II by adding a tax on corporations presumably distinct from their owners or customers, cited U.S. policy in "justification."

[56] Treasury and Presidential leadership has rested with men whose interests have not run to taxes. Treasury statements on taxes hardly pretend to be objective and comprehensive. On undistributed profits the Treasury focuses attention on the *owners* of corporations, but when proposing changes in corporation tax rates it has been unwilling to consider explicitly the effects on stockholders or consumers. The determining premise is that much stock is owned by persons of wealth; the judgment is that they should be taxed more heavily than they will be under the personal income tax. Other possibilities are disposed of by ridicule. The "widow-and-orphan" problem seems to need no serious thought since not all widows own stock! The problem of pensioners has not yet come to be so derisively ignored. A more formidable obstacle to clear analysis has been the fact that corporation earnings have generally been satisfactory even after high taxes. Another reason lies with business leadership, where intelligent and vigorous criticism of the corporation income tax has been the exception. The inroads have been gradual. The personification of business entities has been common. Business taxes have seemed better to some executives than high personal income taxes. Shifting has not been difficult in an inflationary period in which the federal government, as an important buyer, has been willing to absorb business taxes in the prices it pays. The disrepute of "business" under the New Deal, the dominance of stagnation views with their implications of the "dangers" of business savings, and the absence of appreciation of the historical role of reinvested earnings provide some explanation.

[57] An objective analysis is now available. G. E. Lent, *The Impact of the Undistributed Profits Tax, 1936–37* (New York, 1948).

War II revenue needs had to be met, corporations were held to be appropriate units for taxation on "normal," as well as on undistributed and "excess," earnings. The same philosophy prevails today in official circles, though it is widely questioned by professional economists.[58] Yet many economists apparently endorse some tax on corporation earnings. Disregarding minor reasons which, at best, would justify a small fraction of current taxes, the overwhelming argument is that abolition would be disrupting, its effects uncertain, and the revenue loss not easily recouped.[59] But to approve corporation taxation is no more to approve a 52 per cent rate than approval of alcohol is approval of drunkenness.

Corporations are now generally taxed on their earnings and the stockholders on the dividends they receive.[60] In recent years this "double taxation of dividend income" has been widely condemned. While revenue needs remain high, however, the prospects of relaxation are slight. The major difficulty in principle is that corporations *do* have a legal and economic existence which often (but not always) separates them from their owners. If the corporation is not taxed as such, the income which is not distributed in dividends is not taxed, though someone benefits. Only if we could be certain of adequate, eventual tax accounting for such income, could we feel justified in overlooking temporary avoidance.

The criticisms of "double taxation" of dividends are mainly (*a*) that it penalizes a peculiarly valuable type of investment; (*b*) that it puts a premium on debt financing, with resulting inflexibilities and economic strains in times of stress and exaggeration of earnings in times of

---

[58] One of the few serious professional defenses of business taxation is Paul Studenski, "Toward a Theory of Business Taxation," *Jour. Pol. Econ.,* Oct. 1940, XLVIII, 621–54; I doubt that this defense was intended to apply to taxes at present rates. Of the extensive literature I suggest Richard Goode, *The Corporation Income Tax* (New York, 1951), Groves, *Postwar Taxation and Economic Progress;* Simons, *Federal Tax Reform;* and Keith, *op. cit.,* as generally expressive of responsible professional views.

[59] We need a careful analysis of the relative merits of corporation taxes and sales taxes as mass levies on consumption. For some reason, possibly the fear of labor unions, government economists have not been permitted to release their analyses of how, under present spiraling conditions, corporation income taxes are inflationary. In fact, despite its anxiety to discourage inflation, the administration has urged higher taxes not only on producers generally but even on *regulated public utilities!* I predict that within five years even government economists will get sufficiently restless over escalator clauses, vast government buying regardless of price, and parity prices to press for forthright analysis of corporation taxes.

[60] There are many tax-exempt corporations. There has recently been some attempt to restrict these exemptions, especially as applied to some cooperatives and businesses owned by universities. In endorsing such changes, the Treasury and Congress have implied a theory of shifting of corporation taxes to consumers which is inconsistent with the theory implied in the (unformulated) justifications of taxation of other corporation earnings.

prosperity; (*c*) that it imposes taxes on persons with incomes below the personal exemption as well as taxes that are poorly adjusted to reasonable standards of tax distribution; and (*d*) that it conceals the cost of government.

The major possible solutions are (*a*) to extend to the great mass of relatively small and closely owned corporations the privilege of being taxed as partnerships; (*b*) to give (common) stockholders credit against their personal income tax for the tax paid by the corporation, granting refunds where appropriate (the traditional British treatment); (*c*) to permit the corporation, in computing its own taxable income, to deduct dividends paid (as it now deducts interest)—in essence the undistributed profits tax; (*d*) to exclude some dividends from income subject to personal income tax or to grant some other consideration at the personal level.[61]

It is not possible to examine these proposals. None is ideal. And what is best under one set of conditions might not be best under another. In the late 1930's, many economists favored the undistributed profits tax method, partly on the grounds that it would encourage the payment of dividends, thus stimulating stockholder consumption. Today, economic conditions would dictate the opposite policy since saving seems highly desirable. Yet other considerations, notably equity, might still be overriding. Much depends upon other parts of the tax system, such as provisions for taxing capital gains and losses.

One complication is the tremendous variation among corporations. The small business often has some choice in that its owners can escape double taxation by avoiding the corporate form. Yet retention of some earnings in the business may be desired, and if the corporation tax rate is less than the personal rate, the corporate form of organization may be preferable. Earnings can be plowed back, free of personal income tax. For many firms, however, such action is impossible, and the tax burdens of the corporate form seem too great. Disincorporation follows, as during World War II. If corporations with small incomes are taxed at lower rates, as at present, there will be some tendency to splinter corporations and use two or more firms to increase the number of tax units. As a practical matter, disincorporation is often impossible; important advantages of the corporate form must be sacrificed.[62]

Attention has been given to how the tax encourages shift of owner-

[61] U.S. Treasury Department, *The Postwar Corporate Tax Structure* (Washington, 1946), remains one of the best analyses of the problem.

[62] The capriciousness, crudeness, and inequality of our tax system are illustrated by the difference in tax liability resulting from the form of legal organization. For scores

ship to governments (notably in the case of electric utilities) and to tax-exempt institutions. One recent study has shown how taxes affect decisions to sell businesses. In some cases they stimulate mergers and in many more they "distort" decisions.[63] Another of the more interesting studies of this period showed how taxes impede growth of small firms.[64]

C. Excess Profits Taxation[65]

"Excess profits" taxation is again topical. Unfortunately, we as yet have no comprehensive description and analysis of World War II experience. We face a major issue with much experience and little generally accepted analysis. Like so many bad taxes, from the gabelle to the tax on freight transportation, this is endorsed because it yields revenue.

On one point economists would doubtless be in unanimous agreement—designation by executives of government or by Congress that certain business receipts are "excess" does not necessarily make them so economically. The objectives are mixed.[66] Is the tax to take gains arising from national tragedy? Is it to get "excess" profits no matter how obtained? Is it to raise revenue? Is it to create a symbol that will aid in solving other problems (notably controlling wage rates and nonfarm prices)?

The prospect of the owners of incorporated businesses benefiting from the tragedy of war is widely held to be repulsive. Yet it is also widely assumed that many employees and farmers will, and should, get more income (for more output?) after military spending begins.[67] In a short-run war situation, of course, the risk-inducing function of profits

of thousands of businesses there can be large tax benefits from one form of organization rather than the other. Yet the best form will vary from year to year, the costs of shifting may be large, and the accuracy of choice depends upon the acumen of the tax advisor. Economists have written little about the taxation of "business" as such, even though such a tax impedes our major mechanism for creating income.

[63] The technical tax considerations can be extremely complex. J. K. Butters, John Lintner, and L. W. Cary, *Effects of Taxation, Corporate Mergers* (Boston, 1951).

[64] J. K. Butters and John Lintner, *The Effects of Federal Taxes on Growing Enterprises* (Boston, 1945).

[65] Suggestions for taxing increases in personal income have received support. I agree with Hewitt that such a tax would be undesirable. W. H. Hewitt, "The Taxation of Increases in Personal Income," *Bull. Nat. Tax Assoc.*, Oct. 1947, XXXIII, 11–16.

[66] J. R. Hicks, Ursula K. Hicks, and Laszlo Rostas, *The Taxation of War Wealth* (Oxford, 1941). See Gillim, *op. cit.* Still one of the best analyses is C. S. Shoup, "The Taxation of Excess Profits," *Pol. Sci. Quart.*, Dec. 1940, LV, 535–55; Mar. and June 1941, LVI, 84–106, 226–49; K. J. Curran, *Excess Profits Taxation* (Washington, 1943); Simons, *Federal Tax Reform*, pp. 38–40.

[67] One reason corporation earnings are singled out may be a statistical accident; unlike wages, they appear as one huge unit rather than as a series of much smaller receipts by individual stockholders or levies on innumerable consumers.

may be slight; existing capital is "sunk," and new investment will be guided and controlled by other forces. Other functions, however, may be important, especially the function of inducing businesses to economize and that of providing capital for growth of successful firms. The longer the period, the greater the constructive role of corporate earnings.

In 1940 there appeared general support for a tax on "excess profits," but no consensus on how to define "excess." One possibility was to tax earnings above some "normal" rate, regardless of whether they were attributable to war spending; the other was to tax earnings above those in the prewar period; the latter would be more nearly a tax on profits resulting from the war. Congress provided both bases and gave each corporation its choice. (The same kind of choice is offered in the 1950 "excess" profits tax.) Businessmen convinced Congress that the general rules did not fit many firms. Some averaging was provided, and special treatment was given some firms in atypical situations, such as growing firms. Then in 1942 a very complex "relief" provision was inserted; its administration proved very difficult.

Economists do not agree about the desirability of excess profits taxation, chiefly because of inability to attach relative weights to arguments whose logic is not questioned. The tax can certainly remove some possibilities of private benefit from national misfortune.[68] Yet no tax will recoup all such personal benefits; nor will the personal income tax, applying to owners of unincorporated businesses, be an adequate substitute where the tax on corporations does not apply. On the other hand, some of the increase in income during a war will be due to new invention or other innovation.

If professional thinking had advanced by 1950, there was little evidence of an effect on government officials. The Administration proposed a tax on "excess" corporation earnings. There was no explicit comparison of alternative ways of raising revenues; there was no serious discussion of the merits of this tax as a revenue-raising device. Since the Treasury proposed fairly generous credits for determining normal income, many problems which in principle were difficult could be passed over as unimportant in practice.[69] The government has another method of recoup-

---

[68] I know of no professional economist who advocates the tax on the ground that businessmen in search of profits incite war so that a tax to take the profit out of war will help preserve peace.

[69] A semantic problem puts opponents at a disadvantage. How can one oppose "excess"? Little public interest could be aroused in the hard problems. Elementary economics textbooks now distinguish between long- and short-run necessary costs. This distinction is vital in making tax policy; the years move along, and decisions for the short-run

ing profits arising out of war spending—contract renegotiation. This point is valid except that renegotiation does not extend to all firms selling to the government's prime contractors, some of which may make large war profits which can be reached by an excess profits tax (if the firm is incorporated). Moreover, other businesses exempt from renegotiation may benefit from armament spending as a result of a general increase in money incomes.

There has been increasing agreement that tax rates high at the margin are wasteful and somewhat inflationary. A relatively small present or future benefit justifies spending tax dollars. Such spending wastes resources and tends to raise prices. Firms become less determined to hold the wage line. Why not bid up prices if in doing so the firm can get needed supplies? The criticism has merit, but we have no consensus on how much.[70] There has been increasing recognition that excess profits taxation reduces the effectiveness of profits in guiding resource allocation and in financing the growth of successful firms.[71] Skepticism of the effectiveness of profit as a tool for resource allocation may be justified, but alternatives should be examined no less skeptically. Advocates of the tax have not, to my knowledge, met these arguments comprehensively. This area needs study and, since the tax seems here to stay, we should search for ways to offset its adverse effects.[72]

D. Death and Gift Taxes

Estate, inheritance, and gift taxes have received little legislative or academic attention. On the whole lawyers have been more active than economists in serious study of the problems.[73] Economists have long held

---

have a way of surviving. What is "excess" for a few years may be absolutely essential for ten years.

[70] Some economists unduly belittle the argument that an excess profits tax may be inflationary. Major effort has been spent trying to teach the public that the source of inflation is the government deficit and that since taxes reduce the deficit they are deflationary. Perhaps we should give more attention to the question, Why is spending so large? Excess profits taxes tend to increase spending.

[71] D. T. Smith, "Thinking Ahead, 'Excess Profits Tax,' " Harv. Bus. Rev., Nov. 1940, XXVIII, 129–32.

[72] The new tax is sufficiently more generous at critical points than the final World War II law to reduce grounds for concern at this (1952) time. The danger is that growing pressure for revenue will lead to removal of the present comparatively lax features. At any specific point the economist is likely to find it impossible to make a convincing intellectual defense of one position as against another close by.

[73] A summary which the serious economist can understand is S. S. Surrey, "An Introduction to Revision of the Federal Estate and Gift Taxes," Cal. Law Rev., Mar. 1950, XXXVIII, 1–27. A brilliant analysis of Supreme Court decisions, showing how

that death taxes can raise revenue with apparently less personal sacrifice than other taxes; that they do little to discourage personal initiative and, in fact, force potential heirs to work more industriously; that they have less adverse influence on businesses and on resource allocation than income or other taxes raising equal revenues; that they check the tendency of economic inequality to accumulate; and that they can be administered relatively easily because the courts must participate if property is to be transmitted at death. A more recent merit claimed by some economists is that these taxes provide an effective offset to new savings. The attention of professional economists has generally been passing and uninformed; at best, the merits just listed are realized imperfectly, but the imperfections are inadequately understood.[74]

The capriciousness of our transfer tax system is inadequately noted. The taxes are sometimes heavy, especially on large estates. They cut great fortunes and, with the income tax, drastically change the economic position of the rich. They also induce the wealthy to put property into tax-exempt trusts and foundations. They induce splitting of fortunes within families. The marital deduction is giving (older) women greater economic power than they would otherwise have.[75] Death taxes tend to induce the wealthy to invest in highly liquid assets and to tie up property in trust for long periods.[76] They sometimes induce family businesses to merge with larger firms.[77] They reach, imperfectly it is true, some property which escapes income tax, notably state and local government bonds, capital gains unrealized at death (including oil fortunes made under the generous provisions of the income tax), residences, jewelry, and art objects.

---

legal reasoning has shifted, is Louis Eisenstein, "Estate Taxes and the Higher Learning of the Supreme Court," *Tax Law Rev.,* Apr.–May 1948, III, 393–565; Simons, *Federal Tax Reform,* pp. 37–38, goes to the heart of the problem and recognizes the difficulties of devising a satisfactory system.

[74] In 1948, when income tax splitting was provided, Congress enacted an apparently parallel "marital deduction," in effect, estate splitting. The highly complex provision in essence exempts from death tax property passing to a surviving spouse up to half of the total estate. The gift tax contains a comparable exemption. By thus changing the definition of taxable estate, Congress made drastic cuts in tax liability in many cases. A married person can easily transmit more than a third of a million dollars with little tax; yet without proper planning, the tax might be over $65,000.

[75] This is developed by Charles Looker, "The Impact of Estate and Gift Taxes on Property Disposition," *Cal. Law Rev.,* Mar. 1950, XXXVIII, 44–70.

[76] C. L. Harriss, "Liquidity of Estates and Death Tax Liability," *Pol. Sci. Quart.,* Dec. 1949, LXIV, 533–59; J. A. Pechman, "Analysis of Matched Estate and Gift Tax Returns," *Nat. Tax Jour.,* June 1950, III, 153–64.

[77] C. L. Harriss, "Estate Taxes and the Famiiy-Owned Business," *Cal. Law Rev.,* Mar. 1950, XXXVIII, 117–49.

For a person of wealth no form of activity can be as remunerative as planning to minimize the taxes on his estate.[78] The law sometimes seems fickle and uncertain. The complexity of the federal estate and gift taxes defies description. To the intricacies of property law are added many others which the nonexpert observer would not foresee. The result is an incredibly difficult, uncertain, and sometimes inconsistent tax.

We need a thorough analysis of possible objectives of death taxes and of the means needed to realize them.[79] For obtaining a desirable adjustment of tax to the individual who pays, an accessions (inheritance) tax form may be more appropriate than the estate tax form; the tax could be graduated according to the total amount a person received throughout his lifetime in gratuitous receipts from all sources.[80] The treatment of gifts and bequests as income of the recipient has also been suggested.[81] I know of no analysis of these proposals that is adequate as a basis for a professionally responsible recommendation. How desirable is the further reduction of large fortunes,[82] and what are the relative merits of death and income taxation for achieving this objective?

The gift and estate taxes could be integrated into a single cumulative transfer tax to eliminate the present possibilities of double use of lower bracket rates.[83] The use of long-term trusts to pass the benefits of property from one generation to another without tax should be made impossible.[84] The estate, gift, and income taxes should be coordinated to eliminate inconsistencies.[85]

---

[78] R. H. Montgomery and J. O. Wynn, *Montgomery's Federal Taxes—Estates, Trusts and Gifts* (New York, various years) present the possibilities in terms which the non-specialist can understand.

[79] Louis Shere made this point in comments in *Am. Econ. Rev.,* May 1950, XL, 406–09.

[80] The most complete defense of such a proposal is H. J. Rudick, "What Alternative to Estate and Gift Taxes?" *Cal. Law Rev.,* Mar. 1950, XXXVIII, 150–82.

[81] Simons, *Personal Income Taxation,* Ch. 6; Shere, *op. cit.*

[82] The economic and social aspects of large and modest fortunes seem to have received little study, and the material is inadequate for supporting policy decisions.

[83] C. L. Harriss, *Gift Taxation in the United States* (Washington, 1940). The problems have been faced in detail and legislation drafted. Advisory Committee to the Treasury Department, *et. al., Federal Estate and Gift Taxes, A Proposal for Integration and for Correlation* (Washington, 1947); this report is an example of cooperative work of practicing attorneys and government officials; unfortunately, the compromises needed to get agreement obscure some of the more troublesome issues.

[84] Vickrey, *op. cit.,* suggests a "bequeathing power" tax. I fear that nothing short of this ingenious, but highly complicated, device would do the job completely. In 1950 the Treasury urged much less ambitious action but was apparently not given a chance to present the details of its plan.

[85] A. W. DeWind, "The Approaching Crisis in Federal Estate and Gift Taxation," *Cal. Law Rev.,* Mar. 1950, XXXVIII, 79–116, presents a plan based largely on income

One ghost reappeared—the proposal that death taxation should be "returned to the states."[86] The case for federal participation in the light of current conditions has been well stated.[87] The major argument is that federal action is necessary to assure states a minimum of power to tax transfers at death. If left to themselves, some states would compete for wealthy residents by removing death taxes and imposing no gift tax; other states desiring to tax transfers at death would be seriously frustrated. But, though federal participation is essential, the states might well be given a larger fraction of the revenue. Groves makes this distinction and points out more specific problems.

E. Sales Taxes

The 1930's saw the widespread state adoption of more or less general retail sales taxes, more use of gasoline taxes, new liquor taxes, and the federal taxation of numerous commodities and services. The dominant view of economists at the time was that most such taxes were undesirable relative to other methods of financing government spending. The traditional condemnation—that such taxes tend to bear heavily on the poor, who, for humane reasons, should not have their living standards depressed—was reinforced by the new objection that such taxes retarded recovery. Exceptions were often made for (a) the gasoline tax on the grounds that offsetting direct benefits were received in the form of highway outlays and (b) liquor taxes on the grounds, essentially, that poor people should be taxed to sobriety.

Increased uses and new justifications for commodity and service taxes were found in World War II. A commodity tax that raised the price of an item would discourage its consumption, lead to unused capacity in the industry, and thus stimulate the industry to accept orders for military goods. Some of these taxes (e.g., those on luggage, cosmetics, etc.) were justified on the grounds that the thing taxed was not a

---

tax rules and providing complete transfer tax exemption of interspousal transfers. For a general survey of state death taxes see H. M. Groves, Luther Gulick, Mabel Newcomer, *Federal, State and Local Government Fiscal Relations* (Washington, 1943), pp. 469–96. The peculiar dominance of the federal government in this field reduces the practical significance of state problems—for large estates; the tax on small estates is seldom large enough to present significant problems for the economist.

[86] Committee on Postwar Tax Policy, *A Tax Program for a Solvent America* (New York, 1945), Ch. 10; Republican Party platform of 1948, *N.Y. Times,* June 23, 1948, p. 6.

[87] H. M. Groves, "Retention of Estate and Gift Taxes by the Federal Government," *Cal. Law Rev.,* Mar. 1950, XXXVIII, 28–43.

vital necessity;[88] consequently, the revenue could be obtained without serious personal hardship.

These taxes as a "system" have received little economic analysis,[89] but the Treasury has made good quality studies of most of the individual taxes.[90] Postwar conditions in the industries affected varied widely. An omniscient and omnipotent power playing with these taxes as an organist on his keyboard might have manipulated them to great social advantage. In such a dream world, while postwar shortages were serious, the federal excise tax might have been varied to balance the quantities offered and quantities demanded, taking the "gray-market margin" for the Treasury. At the same time, the taxes on products of industries with unused capacity could have been reduced or eliminated. Such delicate control, however, seems impossible because Congress cannot act quickly enough or with enough objectivity.

Many wartime levies were to terminate six months after the end of hostilities. At the end of hostilities, however, Congress and the President agreed that the taxes should be retained, even taxes which seemed deplorable (notably those on transportation and communication). This episode was instructive. It illustrates the difficulties of planning for a future which is uncertain; it also illustrates a difficulty similar to some in our tariff history. Revenue became a dominant consideration, justifying actions that would otherwise have seemed highly undesirable; also, the necessity of considering many specific items created just as many specific vested interests which could combine in the familiar logrolling manner and effectively prevent action limited to a few cases. The more general

---

[88] The term "luxury" was sometimes used but not defined by Treasury or other supporters. The implied justification of these taxes on equity grounds is flimsy. Tastes and needs vary tremendously. "Luxuries" seem to me the relatively unimportant things to the individual, best discovered as the things on which the marginal units of income are spent. The only way to tax luxuries fairly is to tax income and thus let each person cut out of his consumption the items he chooses. This line of reasoning is a variant of the point associated with welfare economics that specific taxes on commodities and services, as contrasted with income taxes (ignoring effects on leisure), change patterns of consumption to the detriment of the consumer. J. R. Hicks, *Value and Capital* (London, 1939), pp. 38–41; Margaret F. W. Joseph, "The Excess Burden of Indirect Taxation," *Rev. Econ. Stud.,* June 1939, VI, 226.

[89] For estimates of the burden of these taxes on typical families, see J. F. Due, "Federal Excise Taxation," *loc. cit.,* pp. 66–79; a more detailed treatment is R. E. Manning, *Federal Excise Taxes* (Washington, 1947).

[90] These studies are generally available in mimeograph. See also G. E. Lent, "The Admissions Tax," *Nat. Tax Jour.,* Mar. 1948, I, 31–50. We now have a good analysis of liquor taxation, T. Y. Hu, *The Liquor Tax in the United States, 1791–1947* (New York, 1950).

and uniform the tax, the less the problem of specific pressures, which can mass heavy weight.

In 1950 the Treasury presented a carefully prepared plan for reducing excises; hearings ran to nearly 3,000 pages, chiefly on excise taxes. The testimony was unusually interesting and instructive about particular industries, their problems, and their relation to the national economy. The testimony is valuable in showing how complex an apparently simple tax may be.[91] At the margins, a host of troublesome problems can arise, and, though the results they produce are not earth-shaking, they can mean a lot to the persons affected. Perhaps the economist is justified in making policy recommendations before thoroughly exploring such situations when tax rates are low, but if the tax is high enough to exert a major influence, I doubt that professional responsibilities are met until such problems have been examined. And this is a job that requires much detailed knowledge of industry.[92]

The conflict in Korea ended the immediate prospect of excise tax reductions and stimulated interest in raising excises. Many students of public finance have endorsed such a policy; it is unfortunate that we have so little serious and unbiased analysis of past experience. The more items we subject to special excise taxes, however, the closer we come to a general sales tax, with the important exception that variation in rates under special taxes may (and may not) improve the system of relative prices in adjusting quantities consumed and produced. Increasing recognition is being given to the fact that special commodity taxes enter into prices, and to the extent that stabilization of a price index becomes important, special taxes may defeat that objective; it may be useful, therefore, to impose taxes that will have little or no effect on price indices used in fixing other prices (the Bureau of Labor Statistics index used in wage contracts and the index used in determining farm parity prices). Ad valorem may be preferable to specific taxes because in a period of rising prices the former will adjust automatically and tend to keep relative burdens in line.

---

[91] Especially sophisticated for such an occasion was the testimony of Leon Henderson, based on detailed staff studies. House of Representatives, Committee on Ways and Means, *Hearings on . . . Revenue Act of 1950* (Washington, 1950), pp. 948–1002.

[92] Though it is easy to recommend a tax on manufacture of automobiles and parts, most of us would doubtless have great difficulty deciding wisely what phases of repair and rebuilding should be taxed. Does the tax on sporting goods hurt private educational institutions (government schools are tax exempt) significantly (cutting salaries, reducing scholarships, or increasing the "need" for government aid)? Does the tax on admissions hurt symphony orchestras? Is the 20 per cent cabaret tax responsible for the widespread abolition of opportunities for dancing at dinner, and, if so, how useful, fair, equitable, beautiful, or otherwise meritorious is the purpose served thereby?

Any program should include a study of objectives, and each specific proposal should be examined in the light of these objectives; this examination should include careful consideration of the structure of the tax, and should have the active participation of the industry. It is highly desirable to rationalize the present taxes, most of which have not been changed (except for rate increases) for almost a decade, were imposed without industry consultation, and when pressure for speed was so great that detailed study was not even attempted. Many of these taxes were shown by 1950 testimony to be subject to criticism on technical grounds.[93] Finally, the benefit considerations should not be ignored, though, except for increases in automotive taxes, I think of no clear cases for the application of this principle.

A general federal sales tax is again a subject of general discussion. Much of the literature is polemical and superficial; the discussion is seldom related to alternatives. Still among the best studies are those made by the Treasury in 1943.[94] The weight of the argument favors a retail sales tax rather than a tax at the manufacturing or wholesale level. A retail tax was held less likely to interfere with price control and less likely to be pyramided. It would produce more revenue for any given rate because the base would be larger, due to higher prices and greater potential coverage (such as services and secondhand goods). It would be more adaptable to special needs (e.g., exemption of articles entering business costs and of sales to state and local governments); it would reach inventories in the stocks of retailers and wholesalers; it would apply more uniformly to consumers; valuation would be easier (especially of products of integrated firms); determination of taxable transfers would be easier. The chief advantage of taxes at the manufacturing or wholesaling level would be a smaller number of firms to watch and a generally better quality of records.

Some analysis of state sales taxes has been published but little of general interest. Perhaps the main point is that such taxes give a prompt increase in yield during inflation. Though few general sales taxes have been added, many special excises have been adopted and rates of older ones raised.[95]

---

[93] State experience might have prevented some mistakes, but state rates have been too low to dramatize the problems. A good analysis is J. F. Due, "Retail Sales Taxation in Theory and Practice," *Nat. Tax Jour.*, Dec. 1950, III, 314–25.

[94] Division of Tax Research, U.S. Treasury, *Considerations Respecting a Federal Retail Sales Tax,* in mimeograph and also in Committee on Ways and Means, *Hearings on . . . Revenue Revision of 1943* (Washington, 1943), pp. 1095–1272.

[95] R. G. and Gladys C. Blakey, *Sales Taxes and Other Excises* (Chicago, 1945).

Traditional academic antagonism to sales taxation seems to be weakening.[96] The possible adverse effects of increased income tax rates worry us more than a few years ago. Before the economics profession gives the tax its blessing, however, a thorough study of all alternatives is needed; the study should certainly include analysis of the structure of the tax. The possibilities of a tax on "value added" also warrant serious analysis.

F. Poll Taxes

There has been one development in the *economic* theory of the poll tax. A flat tax imposed without regard to effort or consumption would have the great merit of not affecting incentives adversely or "distorting" patterns of consumption. The necessity of paying such a tax in cash would doubtless induce some additional effort in the market economy.

G. Property Taxation

Our period witnessed a further decline of academic interest in the property tax. The *relative* fiscal importance of the tax itself dropped. As late as 1940 it was still the country's most important source of tax revenue. Today it is overshadowed, though it is still the main tax source of local governments. Yields have risen, though less than might be expected in view of the rise of real estate prices and the amount of new construction. The net "burden" of property taxes has fallen not only because of the depreciation of the dollar but also because the rates of income tax, from which the property tax is in effect partially deducted, have risen. The relative urgency of property tax problems has declined, yet much of the accomplishment of local government depends upon their solution.

Generalization about the property tax is hazardous because it is administered by tens of thousands of jurisdictions. A feature that is important in one case is insignificant in another. A few of the major unsolved problems of interest to an economist should be noted. What valid basis do we have for judging whether the tax conforms to reasonable criteria of fairness? Since the tax is not on "net worth" but (some fraction of)

---

[96] See A. M. Henderson, "The Case for Indirect Taxation," *Econ. Jour.*, Dec. 1948, LVIII, 538–53; the title is misleading because Henderson tends to endorse traditional views and to attach little importance to the leisure problem. For a criticism of the criticism that sales taxes induce poorer allocation of resources, see E. R. Rolph and G. F. Break, "The Welfare Aspects of Excise Taxes," *Jour. Pol. Econ.*, Feb. 1949, LVII, 46–54.

gross assets, since much falls on businesses and is presumably passed on to consumers, since some falls on pure land rent, since some has been capitalized—how can the tax really be evaluated? How much allowance should be made for difficulties of administration?[97] How much allowance should be made for benefit?

No major change in the views of students of public finance appears to have developed.[98] The major argument for the tax on improvements is that it provides a revenue source for local governments. As applied to tangible personal property (machinery, furniture, jewelry, etc.), the tax is still such a hopeless mess that little serious defense is attempted, and for intangible personal property (bank accounts, stocks, mortgages) the traditional tax finds no informed defenders except on the ground that since laws do exist, they should be enforced. Some use is being made of income tax data to locate ownership of intangible property. The possibility of a general tax on net worth, or a capital levy, has received some attention, but no one draws on our wealth of sad experience with the administration of property (and death) taxes.[99]

VI. SOCIAL SECURITY[100]

One major development has been the growth of the social security system and of the "insurance" and the various grant-in-aid programs. There is a considerable monographic literature discussing the problems and the accomplishments of benefit programs, and the unsolved problems of need. The attention of professional economists has focused more on financing, especially intergovernmental relations. The most important fact about the development of analysis during the period is the absence of progress in balancing the harm done by taxes against the benefits of the spending.

The pay-roll taxes themselves are substantial burdens on covered

---

[97] This tax shares with estate and gift taxes the difficulties arising out of the use of a base which does not result from market transactions.

[98] I believe that less emphasis should be placed on capital value and more on physical characteristics. There are two arguments: many of the services of local government are not related directly to value but rather to size or other feature; the tax on capital value will tend to retard new construction relative to a tax based on number of square or cubic feet. C. L. Harriss, "Alternative Bases for Real Estate Taxation," in Tax Policy League, *Property Taxes* (New York, 1940). Another possibility would be greater use of service charges.

[99] Hicks, Hicks, and Rostas, *op. cit.,* is probably the best discussion.

[100] The field of social security has a more or less independent existence. I have not been able to review the literature as thoroughly as the importance of the subject would justify.

employees and, through employers, on the general community (including persons who do not qualify for benefits). By prewar standards these burdens are heavy enough to be a source of major concern. Yet they have been so overshadowed by other increases, and so intermixed with benefits, that they have received little professional attention. The Old Age and Survivors' Insurance program, however, remains underfinanced in the sense that accruing benefit rights exceed tax collections.

VII. STATE AND LOCAL FINANCE

Major professional attention has focused on national problems. They have been the most dramatic and have involved considerations which have dominated professional interest in the last two decades—the levels of employment and prices. State and local governments, however, have had help from professional economists, and official reports and specialized journals contain numerous studies which in less troubled times would have had greater general interest than has been the case.

By 1940 most states had abandoned important use of the property tax, had adopted other taxes, and had assumed very different expenditure programs from those at, say, the end of World War I, or even in 1930. State financing of welfare (spurred by federal grants) was the most dramatic change, but state payment for education and highway construction had also grown. Income and sales (and pay-roll) taxes had become major revenue producers. Local governments had increased spending, primarily for welfare; though still overwhelmingly dependent upon the property tax, they were getting more than earlier from state governments and a few new taxes.

The war years witnessed a dramatic change. General prosperity brought increased revenues while restrictions on construction, the decline in welfare needs, inertia in adjusting wage rates to price increases, and declining interest rates reduced outlays or accounted for their failure to increase. On balance these governments reduced their debts and accumulated large reserves. Yet, in ways that are less easily measured, there was "capital consumption"—deterioration of physical assets and loss of position in the employment market.

In the postwar period outlays increased for both current and capital purposes, debt rose, and reserves fell. Forces which for generations have led to growth in government spending—increased population, rising prices, settlement in new areas (e.g., suburbs), higher standards of service—have operated to the financial embarrassment of many state and local governments. The present prospect is mixed; unit costs of service will rise, but the quality and quantity may fall because of inability to obtain real resources or unwillingness to vote funds; needs are large and obvious, and are now increased by pressures for civil defense. Prosperity reduces demands for welfare payments and eases tax collection. Most probable on balance is serious financial strain.

States in the postwar period have made few major changes in their revenue systems except in rates and in the introduction of new excises (notably on tobacco products).[101] More interesting, probably, are the changes in local systems. The trend has been to find supplements to the property tax. Using old powers or ones newly granted by state legislatures, local governments (school districts as well as giant cities) have imposed many new taxes.[102] Most striking, perhaps, are a dozen or so municipal taxes on earnings—not on all sources of income—generally on a gross basis, and at flat rates without exemptions. The experience is encouraging, but the taxes have many defects in principle. Their administration has weaknesses but is supported powerfully by the use of withholding.[103] Low rates and the disadvantages of alternatives remove some of the stigma from the defects. Some local governments have adopted sales taxes. Most are in California, where the local tax is combined with the state tax. Excises on specific items have been adopted in many communities. Admissions taxes are also found, and some Pennsylvania governments have added severance taxes on coal. The host of other levies that can be found in one place or another make a list that resembles the list of taxes (also licenses and fees) in "backward" countries.

Many local governments face extremely difficult revenue problems. Few economists have given this subject the serious attention it deserves. Local and state government finances are not adjusted to inflation, and in a period of chronically rising prices, these governments will have a most difficult time.

VIII. FEDERAL-STATE-LOCAL FISCAL RELATIONS

Federal-state-local fiscal relationships have received much study and still seem no less perplexing than a decade or two ago.[104] We have

---

[101] A summary of Census data is R. W. Lindholm, "State Fiscal Activity, 1945–49," *Nat. Tax Jour.*, Sept. 1950, III, 242–47.

[102] For a criticism of this general policy see M. Grodzins, "State Municipal Fiscal Relations: A Critical Commentary." *ibid.*, Mar. 1950, III, 1–17.

[103] Tax Institute, *Income Tax Administration* (New York, 1949), pp. 305–58.

[104] Groves, Gulick and Newcomer, *op. cit., passim;* R. M. Haig, "Federal-State Financial Relations: A Conscientious Governor Studies a Senate Document," *Pol. Sci. Quart.*, June 1944, XLIX, 161–75.

no machinery by which governments at similar and at different levels can negotiate and reach effective and binding agreements (except by the cumbersome "compact" mechanism). The Supreme Court refuses to settle the major issues. The balance of power in Congress and in many state legislatures gives some groups, notably rural areas, far greater power than either their numbers or their contribution to economic life justify.

Constructive steps have been taken. Most states have enacted reciprocity legislation to prevent the taxation by more than one state of the same shares of corporation stock in an estate. The federal government has amended postal legislation to aid states to check avoidance of cigaret taxes by out-of-state purchase. Many states help each other by exchanging information, and the federal government makes its records available at a modest charge to aid in enforcing state income and other taxes.[105] The Supreme Court has generally sanctioned extensions of state power to tax items or acts entering, or closely associated with, interstate commerce; broad powers have been granted states in enforcing sales and use taxes.

In expenditures the major item of general interest has been the development of welfare and unemployment insurance programs under the inducement or practical coercion of the federal government. Matching grants have provided the main inducement in recent years. Conditions of widely varying practical importance are attached to such grants.[106] Tully examined the crediting device.[107] It in effect forced states to adopt unemployment insurance. It can be made to permit either a large or a small amount of local variation within a generally uniform national pattern. In one sense it weakens local autonomy; in another, it protects some states (presumably a majority) from a kind of competition which gives a few states power to defeat others.

Separation of sources, giving certain governments exclusive control over some taxes, has some merit, especially for the few taxes which local governments can administer effectively. Tax sharing, collection by one government and giving part of the revenue to another, has supporters. Simons urged federal sharing of the basic (normal) personal income tax on a collection basis;[108] the balance of power in Congress would probably

---

[105] T. C. Atkeson, "Organizing Cooperative Tax Enforcement," *Proc. Nat. Tax Assoc., 1949* (Sacramento, 1950), pp. 372–78.

[106] See B. L. Johnson, *The Principle of Equalization Applied to the Allocation of Grants in Aid* (Washington, 1947). A compact summary by an economist who has participated in these studies is Paul Studenski, "Federal Grants in Aid," *Nat. Tax Jour.,* Sept. 1949, II, 193–214.

[107] A. M. Tully, *The Tax Credit* (Albany, 1948).

[108] Simons, *Federal Tax Reform,* p. 33.

result in a sharing formula benefiting sparsely settled areas at the expense of others.

The deductibility of one tax in computing another has received considerable attention.[109] The federal government has, of course, become the major claimant on income for taxes. Yet in one respect it has left other governments taxing power by permitting individuals and businesses to deduct many state and local taxes in computing income subject to federal tax. For the system as a whole there is hardly net gain. But individual governments may appear to gain in taxing power, especially the power to use progressive personal income taxes.[110]

Problems which seem to call for action tempt us to try to use the mighty coercive power of the federal government. Sometimes functions traditionally left to state and local governments or to the market are involved—e.g., education, medical services, and housing.[111] Whether net gains from federal financing of such activities would be registered could be decided only by someone who knows the prospective benefits and the damage done by the taxes involved. No single program of federal extension is likely to be critical in weakening local government, the area in which individual participation in affairs of government is possible; but, as Simons emphasized, many actions may combine into a total which can fatally threaten local governments and one foundation of the "good society."

IX. TAX ADMINISTRATION

There has been considerable writing on various problems of tax administration, and much of it and of other work has resulted in substan-

---

[109] See H. E. Klarman, "Income Tax Deductibility," *Nat. Tax Jour.*, Sept. 1948, I, 241–49.

[110] If a community wished to get entertainment or transportation or food or housing or utility services (from municipal plants!) at less net cost, it could do so by paying for them with taxes deductible in computing federal income tax.

[111] A recent article proposes, as a goal of federalism, "fiscal equity," defined as the achievement of equality "in those objective economic circumstances traditionally employed in the calculation of national government tax burdens." The essence is the use of geographical discriminations in the federal income tax to achieve geographical uniformity in the net burdens and benefits of all government taxes and spending. J. M. Buchanan, "Federalism and Fiscal Equity," *Am. Econ. Rev.*, Sept. 1950, XL, 583–99. I find this argument disturbing, though the ethical goal which is the central thesis has appeal. The basis for application is so oversimplified as to be seriously misleading. How can benefits be evaluated? How good are the objective criteria used in distributing national tax burdens? How far should government try to neutralize the differences between prosperous and unprosperous areas?

tial achievements. The most familiar development is probably the most important—income tax withholding. Without such improvements it is hard to imagine what would have happened as the income tax became a mass levy at high rates. Other less striking but important developments include experiments with joint auditing and exchange of information, improvements in methods of assessing property, and the intensive analysis of a carefully selected sample of income tax returns to aid in devising more effective methods of general audit. The last demonstrated that the quality of income tax administration was far below reasonable goals.[112] Despite the good results that have been achieved here and there in tax administration, the opportunities and the need for improvement are probably far greater than generally recognized. The strains are now heavy indeed.[113]

X. DEBT MANAGEMENT[114]

I merely mention debt management—my space is limited, the issues which have absorbed professional attention are largely monetary, and things are in flux.

Murphy has now given us an "inside" description of Treasury debt management during World War II.[115] Perhaps the most interesting point is the emphasis on "tailoring" issues to get the maximum benefits of a discriminating monopolist. The Treasury's essentially short-run criteria of benefit became evident in the postwar inflation. In contrast, most of the technical (nonmonetary) literature on federal debt issuance and management is of limited interest and passing significance. Serious discussions of technique have been combined with discussions of the broader monetary issues.[116]

---

[112] Bureau of Internal Revenue, U.S. Treasury, *The Audit Control Program* (Washington, 1951). The Bureau has tried for years to convince Congress that it has not had enough staff.

[113] A summary of important legal problems of tax administration, and some other tax problems, is: C. A. Peairs, Jr., "General Principles of Taxation: An Initial Survey," *Tax Law Rev.*, Mar. and May 1951, VI, 267–311, 471–506.

[114] Space limits preclude reference to management of state and local governnment debt. On the whole, there seems to have been an increase in the quality of planning of issues and managing the debt outstanding. A recent study is International City Managers' Association, *Municipal Financial Administration* (Chicago, 4th ed., 1949), Ch. 11.

[115] H. C. Murphy, *The National Debt in War and Transition* (New York, 1950).

[116] Simons seems to me to have cut to the heart of the problem better than anyone else, but his major analysis, as well as that of other writers, lies largely in areas deliberately excluded from my essay. H. C. Simons, "On Debt Policy," *Jour. Pol. Econ.*, Dec. 1944, LIII, 356–61; *idem*, "Debt Policy and Banking Policy," *Rev. Econ. Stat.*, May 1946, XXVIII, 85–89.

XI. INTERNATIONAL TAX PROBLEMS

Only brief listing can be made of developments in the international sphere. The United States has negotiated special treaties to reduce taxes on various kinds of international economic actions (relating primarily to income and to transfers at death) and to improve administration.[117] The relations of taxation to foreign trade and investment have received serious study. The most comprehensive was prepared for the United Nations.[118] The possibility of using tax stimulants to encourage foreign investment has received occasional mention (e.g., to help in the growth of underdeveloped areas, or to ease the "dollar shortage"); the potential aid seems small in relation to the costs.[119] The International Institute of Public Finance was revived; the Fiscal Division of the United Nations has sponsored and published several descriptive and analytical studies.

XII. CONCLUSION

Public finance presents the economist with difficulties which are probably more troublesome than in most other subdivisions of the discipline. Since public finance makes up almost one-third of the nation's entire economic activity, the potentialities for good and evil are by no means trivial. Wise judgments require competence in specialized areas each of which may require full-time concentration. The specific problems of public finance always touch intimately one or more other technical subjects, and the problems arise because they are practical. The student of public finance must therefore face questions the answers to which in much other analysis are assumed.

The significant problems involve evaluation of alternative governmental policies. This evaluation requires a determination of relative merits which much other economic analysis can assume to result from the operation of the market and the price system. The recent growth in public finance has added other difficulties for analysis. The growth has been both large and sudden. The adjustment to date may be very different from that of the next ten years. Studies become dated quickly; few

---

[117] See M. J. Wasserman and J. F. Tucker, "The United States Tax Treaty Program," *Nat. Tax Jour.*, Mar. 1949, II, 3–50; Tax Institute, *op. cit.*, pp. 377–433.

[118] Fiscal Division, Department of Economic Affairs, *The Effects of Taxation on Foreign Trade and Investment* (New York, 1950); this study contains a good bibliography.

[119] L. L. Ecker-Racz, "Tax Stimulants to Foreign Investment," and H. S. Bloch, "A Realistic Approach to International Tax Problems," *Proc. Nat. Tax Assoc., 1949* (Sacramento, 1950), pp. 136–51.

things written even five years ago can still be accepted without question, simply because conditions have changed so much.

Moreover, major government spending programs have become so large that they impinge upon each other, and taxes have become so high that they not only touch each other but also affect expenditure programs more or less directly. Choices, to varying extent, are mutually exclusive, and policies are somewhat self-defeating. Spending to boost prices of agricultural staples increases costs of foreign aid, and of aid to Americans on relief; income taxes make it harder for parents to pay college tuition, and demands for federal aid to higher education are voiced. In somewhat different words, the partial analysis which so generally serves in the study of economic problems becomes less and less satisfactory for the analysis of *major* issues of public finance.

The absence of close connection between benefit and liability for payment makes comparison of the two difficult. Beneficiaries of spending programs are likely to be biased in evaluating the results, and the economist may have little chance of turning elsewhere to get an appraisal. The study of some phases of tax problems requires evidence from the taxpayer, who may very well not be impartial.[120]

Considering these difficulties, many of the accomplishments have been impressive. In addition to what I have mentioned, there has been much good work on concrete problems, work too specific to have been mentioned here.[121] Serious thought has also been given to the over-all view. With few exceptions the studies with broad scope suffer because of superficiality enforced (*a*) by a desire to condense into a few hundred (or even a few dozen) pages analysis of scores of problems, each of which is relevant and important and needs extensive discussion and integration; (*b*) by the objective of informing and persuading intelligent laymen, requiring simplification beyond the possibilities of the subject matter; (*c*) by a general inadequacy of developed theory combined with an unwillingness to face tough problems; and (*d*) by efforts to be "politically realistic." Though economists (and the community) look to

---

[120] Questionnaires seem to me to hold less promise than intensive interviews and detailed case studies. The latter, of course, are more expensive. Two recent studies illustrate the point. L. H. Kimmel, *Taxation and Incentives* (Washington, 1950) based on 200 replies to 1,000 questionnaires leaves me uneasy and unsatisfied, if only because so many of the questions could not be framed to yield meaningful and unequivocal answers. Butters, *op. cit.*, covering a more limited field but drawing upon questionnaires supplemented by exhaustive and penetrating interviews, gives a clearer picture.

[121] For an excellent bibliography see Tax Institute, *The Tax Institute Bookshelf* (Princeton, pub. quarterly).

government financial action to do more and more things, improvements in the logical, philosophical, analytical, and inductive foundations for guiding policy decisions have not kept pace.

COMMENT

Roy Blough

This chapter should prove very useful to all readers interested in public finance, and highly challenging both to the economist who specializes in this field and to the graduate student who is considering his choice of a field of specialization. Not only does the chapter record the important institutional and intellectual developments in public finance over the past generation; it also points up the major problems that, at least relatively speaking, have been neglected. But since the function of the critic is to criticize, I turn to another, albeit less important viewpoint.

The nonspecialist, or general reader, may derive from the chapter an unflattering picture of developments in public finance over the past generation. In this picture, it appears that while there have been some important institutional developments, and while a great deal of work has been done in analyzing specific issues of federal taxation, the theory of tax justice has lost ground, no adequate theoretical analysis has been made with respect to public expenditures, and there is little evidence of major attack on the central economic problems of public finance. Unfortunately, there is much that is true in this picture, but, in my opinion, the developments have been more constructive than the general reader may conclude.

Several factors contribute to making the picture less than life-size. In the first place, for various appropriate reasons certain topics, namely, fiscal policy, fiscal measures relating to welfare economics, and the public debt have been excluded from the scope of the chapter. This exclusion has the effect of stripping the field of public finance of some of its most important aspects. While the reader is warned of the situation, he is likely to find it difficult to bear continually in mind the fact that the excluded topics are integral and important parts of public finance. They are integral parts of public finance because, on the one hand, the making of policy decisions in public finance without reference to these topics would lead to untenable conclusions and, on the other hand, the economic analysis of these topics without regard to the general theoretical system of public finance and to the detailed characteristics of fiscal institutions would run the risk of serious error.

In the second place, the very considerable emphasis placed on institutional developments in the chapter may tend to obscure the intellectual advances. It was appropriate, perhaps necessary, to describe institutional developments. Institutions in public finance are "ideas in action." Keeping up with institutional developments is a heavy load for the student of public finance, but one that he must carry since much of the constructive work in the field could not be done without an intimate knowledge of fiscal institutions. But emphasis on institutions does not give a sense of intellectual advance, perhaps because they are in a continual state of flux.

In the third place, the approach to the distribution of the tax burden is made largely through the discussion of many specific federal tax issues. This approach tends to fragmentize the treatment of developments regarding the various major considerations on which tax policy decisions are based. Analyses that are made issue by issue are important for deciding specific questions of policy, but the central ideas that are applicable to all issues tend thereby to be obscured. For example, I doubt if the reader would get from the chapter an adequate notion of the organized studies that have been made regarding economic effects of taxation, particularly effects on incentives, or of certain recent systematic developments of ideas of tax fairness, which although less precise than earlier treatments are more realistic. It may also be noted that in the discussion of specific issues, the recognition of valid conflicts of interest and the process of weighing competing public values may not come through very clearly to the reader.

Finally, the frequent references that are made in the chapter to unsolved problems tend to divert attention from what has been accomplished.

It is certainly not my intention to suggest that all is well in the field of public finance. I agree entirely with Harriss that very much remains to be done. The need for substantial work in the field of public expenditures seems to be particularly important. It may be that the failure to move forward more rapidly in this area reflects an unwillingness by economists specializing in public finance to do with public expenditures what they have done with taxes, namely, to spend a long time in the study of institutions and processes. Out of such study might be expected to grow generalizations of importance both for the science of economics and for expenditure policy.

The most constructive approach to public finance would seem to require a combination of attitudes. One of these is the recognition that close coordination is necessary between the economic aspects and the political science and public administration aspects of the subject. The other is the recognition that theories of public finance in all of their ramifications should be geared into the central framework of economic doctrine and, insofar as there are applicable bodies of doctrine in political science and public administration, into these as well.

COMMENT
Simeon E. Leland

Harriss has written a good essay. His is a topical approach, not a review of literature or a history of ideas.

Scholars in the field now seem to emphasize two things: (1) fiscal policy; and (2) personal income taxation. In the first volume of the *Survey* the bundle of problems embraced under the title of fiscal policy was discussed. Methods and problems of taxation were largely neglected. The present essay attempts to remedy this defect. Its coverage is good. It presents a brief sketch of the trend and development of taxation policies, mainly at the federal level where most scholars now focus their attention. Harriss seems convinced that during the last two or three decades few significant contributions, either to the improvement of income tax practices or to the advancement of theoretical discussion, have been made. Most of the problems are old ones—the new literature seems barren of fundamental additions. Refinements, new qualifications, or restatements have, of course, been added.

Even the literature added in the last twelve years does not impress Harriss. The books cited in his essay are few. Henry Simons is the author most frequently and approvingly cited. The bulk of the literature is in periodicals, many of which are noted in the review. Is the result as disappointing as the lack of citations by Harriss would indicate?

It seems safe to say that the greatest economists of the generation have not been primarily interested in taxation. The closest approach to public finance they have made has been in connection with fiscal policy. Here they made indelible the importance of taxation, public spending, and borrowing in our economic life. The subject of public debts, however, has been raised in importance far more than this essay would indicate. The classical scholars dealt mainly with the problem of payment; the modern student must deal primarily with debt management and the impacts of debt policy on monetary matters. This literature is good, and more extensive than the essay indicates, but with space limits as rigid as were imposed, the author should not be too harshly criticized. His conclusion emphasizes how vast is the field he had to compress. He is certainly correct that "the logical, philosophical, analytical, and inductive foundations for guiding policy have not kept pace" with the growth of the public fisc.

One area generally neglected by public finance scholars is that of social security. They either do not realize or are unwilling to concede its importance. For most of them pay-roll taxes represent regressive taxation rather than contributory insurance payments. They give the subject little attention in their writing or teaching. Harriss has given it too scant attention. Relevant articles of high quality are not cited.

State and local taxation is played down in the essay—as it should be. The decline of the property tax is pointed out, but three other facts seem to need increased emphasis. First is the growth of expedients to finance local governments. Second, and related, is the increasing role of transfers (monetary payments in some form or other) from central to subordinate governments. Third is the rise of state sales taxes. The discussion of that subject is mainly as an adjunct of federal finance. But the states have proved that retail sales taxes can be successfully enforced. Also, it was the states—a few like Wisconsin—which taught the federal government how to make personal and corporate income taxes effective. On the other hand, the federal government did not demonstrate—as it could have—that its excises might have been utilized more fully to help channel or retard wartime consumption. Both sets of governments, however, have failed to make best use of death and gift taxes—as Harriss himself, here and elsewhere, has clearly pointed out.

Really significant advances in the analysis of the incidence of taxation are not reported. Harriss indicates that "primary interest has shifted to the 'economic effects' of a tax" but, aside from the Harvard Business School studies, he mentions no significant additions to the literature. The area is one for future exploration, especially since high tax rates require intensive study lest they produce deleterious economic effects. Undoubtedly, in the period under review, public finance scholars have had to be more concerned with the ways of financing a war and its aftermath than with theoretical analysis or the economic effects of taxation. Yet, with the prospect of high-level taxation for years to come, the economic consequences of these measures can no longer be neglected.

8

INTERNATIONAL

INVESTMENT

Norman S. Buchanan

"International Investment" is a loose phrase at best. Although in general economics the word investment now usually means expenditure on factors of production to create capital goods, this usage has not carried over to give a logically parallel concept of international investment. The term includes more than the creation of capital goods beyond the national boundaries or profit-seeking commitments abroad. The recent stress on national income analysis has emphasized international investment as being the net positive or negative change in a country's claims on the rest of the world. But even this usage is quite unilluminating for many problems; and certainly the meaning of international investment is not restricted to the special sense appropriate in national income analysis. Perhaps the essential idea is investment—however defined—outside the legal, monetary, fiscal, and economic system of the country from which the investment is made. At any rate, independent jurisdiction in these matters gives rise to many of the problems which make international investment a special branch of economic study.

This looseness of the term international investment inevitably allows considerable latitude of choice as to what one should include and what omit in an essay for a volume of this kind. While the writer readily concedes that, with equal or greater justification, a different selection of topics and emphasis might have been made, the ensuing pages are organized under the following headings: (I) International Investment and the Disintegration of the World Economy; (II) Foreign Investment, Domestic Employment, and International Stability; (III) Nonprivate Capital Transfers in the Postwar Period; (IV) Capital Movements on Private Account since the End of World War II; and (V) Unresolved Problems in International Investment.

307

I. INTERNATIONAL INVESTMENT AND THE DISINTEGRATION OF THE WORLD ECONOMY

Much of the contemporary thinking on international investment problems goes back to the 1930's, when traditional views on international investment underwent profound changes. In part these changes are directly traceable to what actually happened to international investment during the world depression; but no less are they traceable to the profound changes wrought by the depression in the objectives and means of economic policy in which international investment had to be included. In other words, present-day views on international investment are partly a consequence of the perverse behavior of international capital movements during the depression and partly a result of the fact that economic policy in many countries has extended its scope and recast its objectives. Much that is nowadays common coin in discussions of international investment would have had an alien ring two decades ago. Consequently, it may be worth while to trace briefly how these views arose and have carried forward to the present day.

A. International Investment and the Structure of World Trade before 1930

The world depression brought an end to international investment of the traditional sort. Viewed in retrospect, this investment is seen to have been an important, if unnoticed, segment of the world trading system. It was partly responsible for the particular pattern which trade flows had assumed and for the ease with which international settlements were financed. To regard the international capital flows as merely items which balanced the trade flows is, in a measure, misleading since the investments were often for the very purpose of adding new flows of raw materials and foodstuffs to international commerce. Only in a statistical sense did international investments and their derivatives balance the trade accounts. International investment and multilateral international commodity trade had almost an organic connection with one another. Yet even the essential outlines of this complementarity were not clearly described until the world economic depression of the 1930's had seriously damaged the foundations on which it rested and the effectiveness with which it functioned.[1]

---

[1] More than any other single writer Folke Hilgerdt has emphasized the importance of the interconnections between investment flows and trade flows in the kind of multilateral

B. Impact of the Depression on Old and New Countries

As the world economic depression spread and deepened it generated an air of gloom and apprehension which stifled international investment.[2] Falling prices, declining world trade and new trade barriers not
only checked fresh investments abroad but also raised doubts as to the
soundness of previous commitments. But this cessation of new foreign
investments and the effort to repatriate earlier investments brought great
difficulties to many countries which their policy-makers still vividly
recall.

For the more mature industrial and semi-industrial countries the
problem was to accommodate the national economy to the attempted
sudden withdrawal of short-term funds on foreign account.[3] Insofar as
these withdrawals were achieved they necessarily were at the expense of
the country's foreign exchange reserves: domestic deposits were canceled
against a release of assets held abroad. But the shrinking foreign exchange reserves increased the fears of other foreign creditors that transfer might soon be impossible; consequently, they too sought to withdraw
their commitments before it was too late. In these circumstances a modest run on a currency could easily develop into a panic, especially if spec-
ulators' transactions reinforced, rather than allayed, existing apprehensions.

The traditional response of the banks to a fall in their foreign exchange reserves was, of course, higher money rates and a contraction of
the currency with the object of improving the trade balance and foreign
exchange reserves via a fall in the country's price and income level relative to the rest of the world. But this familiar route to recovery was
blocked by several obstacles during the depression. First, it rather implic-

---

trading system which came to an end after 1930. See, League of Nations, *The Network of
World Trade* (Geneva, 1942); *idem, Industrialization and Foreign Trade* (Geneva, 1945);
and Folke Hilgerdt, "The Case for Multilateral Trade," *Am. Econ. Rev., Proc.,* Mar. 1943,
XXXIII, 393–407.

[2] As is well known, new American investments abroad fell off sharply in 1929 as
against 1928, i.e., before the depression really got under way. But this is usually explained by the very high interest rates available in New York in 1929 rather than by a
reassessment of the prospective yields available on foreign investments. See also, Ilse
Mintz, *The Deterioration of the Quality of Foreign Bonds* (New York, 1951).

[3] It has not seemed necessary to document the few pages that follow with numerous
references. The purpose is not to try to sketch the international financial history of the
1930's but merely to show how this helped to mold current attitudes on international investment problems. For an excellent account of this whole period, see Ragnar Nurkse,
International Currency Experience (Geneva, 1944).

310 · *A SURVEY OF CONTEMPORARY ECONOMICS*

itly assumed that the particular country's rate of expansion or contraction was out of line with that of the rest of the world. But if a number of countries were in a similar position, i.e., with dwindling foreign exchange reserves, and their exports were highly competitive, then even severe deflation might not much improve foreign exchange reserves and so make possible the capital withdrawals. Moreover, the traditional theory had envisaged modest, rather than gigantic, shifts in the trade balance and had been formulated for "normal" capital transfers having direct effects upon the circular flow of income rather than for speculative movements and flight transfers on a large scale. Finally, there was the obvious impropriety of imposing still further deflation on economies already experiencing serious unemployment. National governments found prices and wages less than completely flexible; unemployed workers were restive and at times menacing. How much distress the country would endure out of respect for the convenience and safety of creditors was a delicate question which governments had to decide. It is not surprising that most of them chose exchange control rather than continued deflation.

Thus for the more developed countries it was chiefly the mechanism for international short-term transfers which broke down during the depression with such disastrous results and drove them into controlling capital movements as a means of self-preservation.

The less developed debtor countries suffered difficulties of a different kind from foreign investments.[4] For them the problem was how to maintain debt service on previous borrowings in the face of falling food and raw material prices and a virtual cessation of new capital inflows from abroad. During the 1920's many of them had adjusted their economies to a substantial stream of capital from the creditor countries so that the maintenance of service charges was really no problem as long as new investments continued. But once new loans stopped, they had actually to adjust sufficiently to reverse the capital flow. This was more of a change in their balance of payments than they could conveniently manage. Moreover, the world depression produced sharp price declines for their principal export products so that foreign exchange receipts from exports fell off. Confronted, as they often were, with a foreign demand for their exports which was often highly inelastic with respect to price and yet highly elastic with respect to income (e.g., industrial raw materials), they had little chance of maintaining, let alone improving, their foreign exchange position. In these circumstances they were forced, on the one hand, to cut imports severely and on the other, to halt debt

---

[4] See, Nurkse, *op. cit.,* Ch. 8, and *passim.*

service transfers and/or default on their obligations as debtors. Neither was pleasant. The cut in imports meant both halting development projects which had to have capital goods from the industrialized countries and making scarce those consumers' goods manufactures which had become part of their standard of consumption. In some cases, too, the growth of industrial crops under foreign direction had forced a dependence on imported food; without means of payment, food imports had to be reduced as well.

To default on debt service or to block its transfer meant impairing the country's credit rating. Since many of these countries were anxious to develop their economies, they wished to preserve their credit rating and future borrowing capacity. Moreover, they began to be skeptical of the virtues of developing their economies via export industries whose markets were so sensitive to the level of business activity in the industrialized countries. Apparently, these markets could quickly become unprofitable and leave the country with its citizens in acute distress and a balance-of-payments problem that seemed to have its origin in the prior acceptance of investment from abroad. If foreign capital were to be genuinely helpful to these countries, it had probably better be hedged about with certain restrictions as to its use and also available in a stream which would not suddenly dry up.

Thus for the less developed countries the depression underscored the risks to the receiving country of long-term capital investment from abroad. It was too uncertain in its flow to be relied upon. It tended to concentrate on primary industries with volatile markets abroad. But though the markets for tea or tin might collapse, the native laborers still had to eat. Capital imports appeared less attractive than they had during the enthusiasm of the 1920's. Perhaps the policy of allowing foreign capital to come in without let or hindrance and to develop industries for the world market needed careful re-examination. At least some countries believed they were justified in reasoning along these lines.[5]

C. The Reorientation of the International Investment Problem

The unfortunate depression experience of many countries with foreign investments and international capital flows helped to bring to an

---

[5] "Immediately before the war, however, a distinct change appeared in the attitude of undeveloped countries toward new investment. Instead of passive acceptance, they were prepared to substitute active acceptance or active rejection." C. P. Kindleberger, "Planning for Foreign Investment," *Am. Econ. Rev., Proc.,* Mar. 1943, XXXIII, 348. See also the thoughtful article by L. H. Jenks, "British Experience with Foreign Investments," *The Tasks of Economic History,* Dec. 1944 (Suppl. to the *Jour. Econ. Hist.,* Vol. IV), pp. 68–79.

end the *laissez-faire* attitude of most governments towards movements of capital across their borders. But this change of attitude towards international capital movements was merely another manifestation of the much broader shift on the part of national governments with respect to the ends and means of national economic policy. The "Keynesian Revolution" engulfed many an official who had never read Keynes. It was unlikely, in the general sweep towards positive economic policies designed to achieve full employment, that earlier attitudes towards international investment would hold firm.

Amongst economists, international investment (like so much else) got caught up in the emphasis upon the relation between broad economic aggregates—employment, investment, saving, etc.—and what these theoretical formulations implied for economic policy.[6] Instead of discussions of international investment in terms of motivation, purpose,[7] etc., the tendency was rather to adopt Joan Robinson's treatment of making international investment simply the net change in the foreign balance equivalent to the difference between exports and imports in any period—essentially a derived residual, not causative in itself but fraught with consequences for the interest rate, domestic investment, and home employment.[8] In other words, international investment questions tended more and more to enter and leave the forum via the side door, while the main entrance was reserved for full employment, fiscal policy, exchange policy, or trade controls. Moreover, economists became increasingly distrustful of markets and the market mechanism in general (including the

---

[6] At least this is presumably true. The later 1930's are singularly barren of publications dealing with international investment problems other than those dealing with problems of capital flight, exchange control and direct trade controls.

[7] Insofar as Carl Iversen's *Aspects of the Theory of International Capital Movements* (Copenhagen and London, 1935) and C. P. Kindleberger's *International Short-Term Capital Movements* (New York, 1937) may be taken as standard works in English on international investment down to 1939, or even much later, there was much emphasis on the different types of capital movements—real and monetary, long-term and short-term, normal and abnormal, equilibrating and disequilibrating, speculative and income, autonomous and induced, etc.—and how these tended to react upon foreign exchange rates, trade flows, price levels, relative prices and incomes, etc., in the lending and receiving countries. These classifications were not mutually exclusive nor was any single pair of terms sufficient in itself to carry the whole analysis.

Iversen, Kindleberger, and others also emphasized the close interdependence between capital movements and other items in the balance of payments. They stressed that capital transfers and goods transfers had to be linked at all times and that the cause and effect relationship might run either from foreign lending to changes in exports or imports or from trade deficits and surpluses to foreign borrowing and lending.

[8] Joan Robinson, *Essays in the Theory of Employment* (London, 1937), pp. 183–209.

international capital market) and more attracted to the alternative of economic direction through national policy.[9] Thus it came about that events in the real world combined with developments in other branches of economics to shunt discussions of international investment questions on to rather different lines after, say, 1936. The traditional view that national governments should allow foreign capital to enter and leave the country at the discretion of private capitalists rather gave way to the view that national economic interests of a broader nature—full employment, exchange stability, etc.—must come first if a conflict arose.

This overriding concern with full employment questions and the widespread emphasis on macro-economic analysis also affected the treatment of international investment problems in other ways. There were attempts to distinguish between different types of capital movements in terms of their effects on the national economy, and to seek ways and means by which "desirable" types could be encouraged and the rest controlled or prohibited.[10] More important, however, was the fact that macro-economic analysis pointed up the inference that there was no need, from the point of view of employment, of limiting the international investment concept merely to private transfers in search of profits abroad. Indeed, the national income equations made easy the transition from the view that public investment at home would aid domestic employment to the view that public investment abroad would have the same result. But this way of looking at matters only came fully into its own during and after World War II.

These trends in economic thinking, which rather subordinated international investment questions to issues deemed more important, persisted down to the outbreak of World War II. Down to 1939 new international investment not only never regained its predepression volume but was probably actually smaller than international disinvestment. Pri-

---

[9] "Historically, the interwar period will probably be remembered as a period of retreat from the price system, when all sorts of temporary or provisional measures were adopted to regulate economic activity. . . . This was perhaps even more true of the international mechanism than of domestic markets. . . ." L. A. Metzler, "The Theory of International Trade," *A Survey of Contemporary Economics,* Vol. I, H. S. Ellis, ed. (Philadelphia, 1948), p. 253.

[10] The conception of "desirable," of course, varied considerably from country to country. For the more developed countries, perhaps the emphasis was predominantly on the risks and dangers of "refugee transfers" and speculative movements, and rather less on long-term investments. For the underdeveloped countries, the emphasis was rather more on the kinds of industries into which foreign capital might safely be allowed to go and the relative merits of portfolio and direct investments. But the important point is that the virtues of international investment per se were no longer taken for granted.

vate investors showed little enthusiasm for shouldering the risks of blocked balances and political instability; the wise, if unvalorous, course seemed to be to husband their capital in a safe refuge. Apparently, investors felt that the uncertainties of administrative discretion by exchange control authorities overshadowed the profit possibilities of foreign ventures. If they invested abroad at all it was chiefly in areas in which their government had political domination and control or in countries where political risks were nominal or nonexistent, e.g., the British Dominions or the United States.

D. Earlier Approaches to the Postwar International Investment Problem.

Broadly speaking, the 1939 attitudes towards international investment problems were resurgent in the earlier planning for the postwar international economy. Early in the war the Economics Section of the League of Nations began a series of studies on postwar international economic problems which stressed that international investment would have to have an important role in the postwar world, both in the "transition" period and afterwards, if a viable international economy were to be reconstructed.[11] In a measure, these studies somewhat redressed the balance between the traditional pre-1930 views on the virtues of international investment and the depression-born view that tended to subordinate it to full employment policy. The League studies showed how intimate was the connection between the "network of world trade" and the pattern of international investments. But they also showed that planning for the postwar world must take account of the depression experiences with international capital flows and devise instrumentalities to prevent their recurrence.

Other studies which appeared during the war also emphasized both the important role that international investment could play in the postwar world and some of its weaknesses and dangers as exemplified during the 1930's.[12] The now classic volume, *The United States and the World Economy*, by H. B. Lary *et al.*, appeared in 1943 and contained a long analysis of capital movements from and to the United States (by R. L. Sammons) which was both factually more complete and analytically

---

[11] The particular studies referred to above would include, *Europe's Trade* (Geneva, 1941); *The Network of World Trade; Europe's Overseas Needs, 1919–1923 and How They Were Met* (Geneva, 1943); *The Transition from War to Peace Economy* (Geneva, 1943); *Economic Stability in the Post-War World* (Geneva, 1945); and Nurkse, *op. cit.*

[12] At its annual meeting in January 1943 the American Economic Association devoted a session to the topic of foreign investment.

more enlightening than anything that had previously appeared. This study particularly stressed the importance of stabilizing and increasing the flow of American dollars to other countries via import transactions and foreign lending. The sources of this instability, it emphasized, were mainly two: ". . . (1) The extraordinary amplitude of fluctuations in domestic economic life . . . ; and (2) the erratic behavior of capital movements, reflecting the sudden shifts of American interest in foreign investments and the fluctuating preferences of foreigners for American securities and dollar balances."[13] These authors further argued that the United States would be well advised to formulate an investment program ". . . on a comprehensive and long-range basis and executed at a reasonably regular rate. . . . The responsibility for developing such programs will doubtless be borne chiefly by the governments concerned, and much of the capital may have to be provided through official agencies."[14] More and more one encountered the phrase "foreign investment policy" with respect to the world after the war, a phrase which, in this writer's opinion, hardly would have been used even as late as 1939. The international investment problem was being given a new setting.

One really new problem in international investment, however, began to attract attention even in the early days of World War II. This was the problem of the "underdeveloped areas" and the means to their improvement.[15] In some respects this was an old problem in a new form. But its political aspects and its new drive made it almost a new problem. It became increasingly obvious during the war years that it would have to come in for serious attention when the war was over. But surprisingly enough it attracted relatively little attention among economists until well after the war.

Thus the depression experience had left its mark: postwar foreign investment would have to differ in important respects from prewar foreign investment. It was generally agreed that short-term capital move-

---

[13] *Op. cit.*, p. 12.

[14] *Ibid.*, p. 19. See also the early and similar proposals by R. B. Bryce, "International Aspects of an Investment Program" in *Postwar Economic Problems,* S. E. Harris, ed. (New York, 1943).

[15] Among earlier publications on this problem the following may be mentioned: P. M. Rosenstein-Rodan, "Problems of Industrialization of Eastern and Southeastern Europe," *Econ. Jour.,* June–Sept. 1943, LIII, 202–11; *idem,* "The International Development of Economically Backward Areas," *Internat. Affairs,* Apr. 1944, XX, 157–65; H. Frankel, "The Industrialization of Agricultural Countries," *Econ. Jour.,* June–Sept. 1943, LIII, 188–201; *International Development Loans,* Nat. Planning Assoc., Planning Pamphlets, No. 15 (Washington, 1942); and H. D. Fong, *The Post-War Industrialization of China,* Nat. Planning Assoc., Planning Pamphlets, No. 12, 13 (Washington, 1942).

ments would bear watching in the interests of domestic employment. It was conceded, too, that uneven flows of capital were acutely troublesome to capital-importing countries; but since the prospective lenders (chiefly the United States) were thought likely to have trouble holding employment at sufficiently high levels, some writers saw the opportunity to link the interests of borrowers and lenders in a mutually happy solution. And beyond all this the prospective capital-importing countries with their depression and wartime experiences so freshly in mind had strong views concerning the role of foreign capital in their own national economic development. Thus international investment—of the proper kind and for the proper purposes, of course—was to play a new role which would assist the lending countries with their problems and aid the borrowing countries to achieve economic betterment.

In a very real sense the Bretton Woods Agreements of 1944 sought to formalize these views on international investment (and much else) in documents which countries with widely varying economic problems and interests could yet accept.[16] After Bretton Woods there were some grounds for hoping that future international investment might be made to flow in the proper directions and in adequate volume.

II. FOREIGN INVESTMENT, DOMESTIC EMPLOYMENT, AND INTERNATIONAL STABILITY

The flow of events just sketched had erosive effects upon the traditional theory of international investment. Moreover, the depression saw the theory of aggregate income and employment develop and ramify in a remarkable fashion. In the main these latter theoretical developments were not immediately related to the theory of international investment. But in due course their relevance to international investment was made explicit.

A. International Investment and the Transfer Problem

The contemporary emphasis in the theory of the balance of payments and adjustments therein is more upon changes in income and employment as between countries and rather less upon the effects of mon-

---

[16] The Fund Agreement (Article VI, sec. 3) allowed members to "exercise such controls as are necessary to regulate international capital movements . . ." and the special circumstances of the transition period were recognized in Article XIV, sec. 2 to give countries further protection. But it was the International Bank for Reconstruction and Development that was expected to usher in a renaissance in international investment.

etary expansion and contraction upon relative prices as the mechanism of adjustment. While earlier economists were not unaware of income changes as adjustment mechanisms leading to equilibrium in the balance of payments, they lacked, in Metzler's words, ". . . a theory of employment or income, and were therefore unable to explain just how far the adjusting process could go."[17] Moreover, by implicity taking full employment for granted secondary, tertiary, and subsequent changes in income and employment were, in effect, ruled out. But once these assumptions are cast aside, the effects of foreign lending and borrowing upon the economies of the participants can become exceedingly complex theoretically.

Perhaps the first, and still the most systematic, attempt to unravel these complexities was by Metzler in 1942.[18] He undertook to examine the effects in the lending and borrowing countries of a capital transfer where the marginal propensities to consume, to import, and to invest are not identical in the two countries and where the two economies are, by assumption, below the level of full employment. Metzler then inquires whether the induced income changes and resultant changes in exports and imports will suffice to effect the capital transfer. To solve his problem Metzler uses three tables—each with a different set of propensities for the two countries—and with each table he examines the effects (I) of reducing income in the paying country and increasing it in the receiving country by the amount of the transfer; (II) of reducing income in the paying country by the amount of the transfer but with no primary expansion in the receiving country; and (III) where the primary expansion of income occurs in the receiving country but there is no primary contraction in the paying country. Metzler ascribes the primary changes in income in parts I, II, and III of his three tables to the fiscal policy adopted by the respective governments. As might be surmised, this analysis is too complicated to be fully presented here.

What emerges from Metzler's analysis, however, are the conclusions: (1) that if both countries are stable in isolation—i.e., the marginal propensity to consume, plus the marginal propensity to import, plus the marginal propensity to invest are together less than unity—then the induced changes in incomes and trade balances will not suffice

---

[17] *Op. cit.,* p. 218.

[18] L. A. Metzler, "The Transfer Problem Reconsidered," *Jour. Pol. Econ.,* June 1942, L, 397–414, reprinted in *Readings in the Theory of International Trade,* H. S. Ellis and L. A. Metzler, ed. (Philadelphia, 1949). It seems unnecessary to revert to the earlier (1929) discussion of the transfer problem between Keynes and Ohlin relating to German reparations which is reprinted in *ibid.*

to effect the capital transfer; (2) that if one of the countries is unstable in isolation—i.e., the sum of the marginal propensities exceeds unity— then the capital transfer can be effected via induced changes only if the unstable country allows the transfer to affect its income directly. But Metzler makes it clear that he regards "stability in isolation" as by far the most probable state of affairs in the real world. Consequently, for his model, he concludes that induced income changes will not suffice to effect the capital transfer.

Metzler's analysis, however, also implies that the expansionary effects of foreign lending upon income may come from either or both of two sources: first, from the fact that the lending comes out of new money or idle balances (fiscal policy of type III above); or second, from the fact that the marginal propensities to spend in the borrowing country are greater than those of the lending country. In other words, foreign lending may activate funds that would otherwise remain idle or not be created or, on the other hand, it may transfer them to foreigners having a higher propensity to spend than income receivers at home. In either event the result will be expansionary.

Metzler's discussion is highly illuminating. But in applying his results to the real world it must be remembered that the analysis throughout assumes unchanging propensities throughout the sequences, and that prices, exchange rates, and interest rates in both countries are also assumed not to vary. Without these rigid assumptions the model would probably be unmanageable. One should perhaps also bear in mind in relating Metzler's model to actual countries that there is no mention of how large the capital transfer is assumed to be, relative to other components in the respective economies: the assumed transfer might produce a mere ripple in one economy but a near tidal wave in the other. Finally, for the trade figures to get as badly out of balance as they do in some of the tables it must be assumed that importers have access to virtually unlimited lines of credit. But these comments relate only to the applicability of the analysis to countries in the real world and not to the analysis itself.

Much of the substance of Metzler's contribution seems to have been independently developed by Salant and Machlup (and extended by others) in their studies of the repercussions of income changes in one country upon the rest of the world.[19] But to examine their studies prop-

---

[19] W. A. Salant, "Foreign Trade Policy in the Business Cycle," *Public Policy*, Vol. II (Cambridge, Mass., 1941), reprinted in *Readings in the Theory of International Trade;* Fritz Machlup, *International Trade and the National Income Multiplier* (Philadelphia, 1943), esp. Ch. 8 and pp. 178 ff.

erly would draw this essay over into an exposition of comtemporary international trade theory in general. For a review of these contributions the reader is referred to Metzler's essay, "The Theory of International Trade" in *A Survey of Contemporary Economics,* Vol. I.

B. Foreign Investment and Domestic Employment

After all the discussion during the late 1930's of the "stagnation thesis" as applied to the American economy it is not surprising that American economists began to speculate about the possibilities of maintaining high-level postwar employment via the vent of foreign investment. As World War II wore on, and it became clear that postwar American foreign economic assistance would be mandatory, the relations between home employment and foreign investment took on immediate relevance.[20]

Even viewed narrowly, and so without reference to foreign policy objectives and humanitarian impulses, the question of the relation between domestic employment and investment abroad had several sides.

First was the question of the efficacy of foreign investment as a means of raising home employment. This question was explicitly analyzed, *inter alia,* by Randall Hinshaw in 1945.[21] He first questioned the customary linking of the employment levels of the 1920's and the then flow of investment abroad: the net outflow from the United States as an annual average for the years 1924–30 only exceeded by $10 million the return flow from amortization, sales of holdings, and receipts of interest and dividends. While it is dangerous causally to tie together items drawn from opposite sides of the balance of payments, Hinshaw's main contention was not historical, but rather to show by some interesting tables that in order to maintain a constant export surplus of any given amount, i.e., to provide a constant stimulus to home employment, new lending would have to proceed at variously sharply rising rates, depending upon the yield and amortization flows assumed. This led Hinshaw to conclude that while large foreign investments ". . . may be an effective method of achieving full employment, it is hardly a feasible method. . . ."[22] And he added that for maintaining employment, long-term loans at low interest rates were most suitable.

The relation between the return flow of amortization and interest

---

[20] Eugene Staley, *World Economic Development* (Montreal, 1944), was probably the first explicitly to link postwar oversaving in the American economy with foreign investment; see pp. 41–46, and *passim.*

[21] "International Investment and American Employment," *Am. Econ. Rev., Proc.,* May 1946, XXXVI, 661–71.

[22] *Ibid.,* p. 670.

(or dividends) and new lending was subsequently worked out more precisely in 1950 by E. D. Domar by using equations designed to allow for different types of amortization formulas.[23] Domar's more precise formulations underscored the point that if the rate of growth of new lending were greater than the rate of interest, then the return flow need never exceed the gross outflow—whatever the amortization rate. If the percentage annual rate of growth is equal to, or smaller than, the rate of interest, however, the inflow will sooner or later come to equal or exceed the gross outflow of new lending. But this broad statement inadequately describes the range of possibilities formally analyzed by Domar.[24]

The main thesis of Domar's contribution, however, is doubtless not the mathematical equations developed but the suggestion that there is no *a priori* reason why foreign lending should not be so conducted as to avoid any eventual net inflow.[25] But if the rate of growth of new investment is to exceed the yield, it is reasonably clear that private investment alone will not suffice. For either the yield rate must be very low, with a modest rate of growth, or moderate yield rates must evoke a high growth rate. For Domar the answer lies in very low (2 per cent or less) rates on government lending abroad so that the yield rate on private and public lending combined is made equal to the rate of growth of new loans. Loan operations so conducted "could become a major instrument of a wise foreign economic policy."[26]

---

[23] "The Effect of Foreign Investment on the Balance of Payments," *Am. Econ. Rev.,* Dec. 1950, XL, 805–26.

[24] It should be pointed out that Domar reasons throughout on the assumption that the amortization rate and the interest yield rate are the same for all loans made. He recognizes (p. 811, n.) that this is unrealistic since amortization and yield rates will differ from loan to loan. But his remark that this possibility would require "some averaging method" seems hardly to cover the difficulty. For example, for equity investments or direct investments there is no yield rate which could be put into a formula; there is no yield rate except in retrospect or in anticipation. And there is no amortization rate for equities, although there may be repatriation of initial investment.

[25] "If we can invest abroad for three years without injuring our economy or the borrowers', and for five years without running into trouble, why not for any number of years? If absolute figures make us feel uncomfortable, why not think in terms of some fraction of our growing (it is expected) national product?" *Ibid.,* p. 808.

[26] This conclusion, it seems to this writer, is not well considered. It is probably politically unrealistic, but leave that aside. The real difficulty is the commitment—as a policy—to make government loans available at a nominal interest charge at some high preannounced rate. Having so committed itself, the government would be hard-pressed either to find enough sound loans to match the commitment or to differentiate between one country and another as loan recipients. And to evolve criteria for rejecting loan appli-

The compound-interest phenomenon which gives such hair-raising results in foreign investment applies equally to domestic investment or to a host of other economic magnitudes. But it is well known that interest and dividends, far from being an ever growing proportion of national income, have actually shrunk as a fraction of the whole. The reasons seem to be that some investments are outright losses which yield nothing and that even good investments come to an end through exhaustion, technical change, or shifting wants. Wars, inflation, and possibly a secular decline in yield as capital accumulates have also been factors of major importance. Consequently, even sizeable foreign investment commitments in the years ahead are unlikely to mean that debt service will grow to astronomical figures.[27]

Even were the lending country prepared to act as Domar's equations suggest it might be wise for it to act, however, borrowing countries would probably soon eschew the role which he assigns to them. As they develop economically, they will be better able to supply their own capital needs without borrowing abroad. Most potentially borrowing countries in such a scheme already resent their present dependency upon the wealthier countries, and many of them are fearful of becoming politically or culturally dominated by their creditors. Consequently, they often wish to borrow as little as possible—grants are something else again—from abroad and to form their own capital as soon as they can. If their economic development at all conforms to previous historical experience, they would be able to do so.

Surely it is not necessary, however, to choose between, on the one hand, a crescendo of foreign lending which gives a perpetual export surplus and, on the other, an avoidance of foreign lending altogether. It seems wiser to assume that in the years ahead considerable foreign lending on private and public account will occur and to face up to the domestic problems that this may present.

---

cants—where some large sum is already publicly earmarked for the purpose—which will be accepted as fair and reasonable in the face of rejection and so not generate ill will is to impose a nearly impossible assignment on those charged with policy administration.

[27] Being prepared to expect losses in foreign investment in the sense that not all ventures or loans turn out as well as, or better than, expected is not the same thing as making loans which, *at the time they are made,* hold only a dim prospect of the terms of the agreement between borrower and lender being fulfilled. All manner of unforseen developments may make any particular foreign investment turn into an outright loss, but the commitment did not assume that they would do so. But to make commitments as loans which are known to the negotiators to be little more than disguised gifts is a breach of honesty and good faith. And this does not mean that outright grants of assistance for political reasons have no place in foreign policy.

322 · *A SURVEY OF CONTEMPORARY ECONOMICS*

Nevertheless, both the actual shift from an active to a passive balance of payments and the possible adverse consequences of a passive balance of payments per se have given economists concern in recent years.[28] Let us consider the latter point first.

The concern over the deleterious effects of a passive American balance of payments has taken several forms. In its simplest version it no more than draws attention to the fact that imports are "leakages" and a depressant on income. If, in a simplified model, net exports are expansionary for income and employment one must conclude, logically, that net imports leave the opposite effect. Imports, by definition, augment the aggregate supply of goods in the home market but, at least immediately, add nothing to domestic money incomes. With the insistent demand abroad for American exports such as has recently prevailed, and which seems likely to continue for some time to come, foreigners probably will not accumulate idle dollar balances unless American export controls, as in World War II, force them to do so. If the net import surplus goes entirely for debt service and liquidation, then one is forced to guess as to what the public or private recipients thereof are likely to do with the funds and how this would affect employment. Possibly, in private hands the proportion of income saved from interest and dividends would be rather high and might therefore be a depressant on income. But can the same be said for debt service income on government loans? In view of the diverse possibilities, generalization is probably impossible.

Other writers have based their apprehensions of an import balance for the United States on more concrete considerations. It is often urged, for example, that the dilemma of a net creditor status for the United States lies in the danger that, without tariff reductions, most importable goods have too low a price and income elasticity of demand in the American market to yield large enough dollar proceeds to foreigners, while, on the other hand, major cuts in the American tariff would force drastic adjustments in the structure of American industry and employment. The elasticity argument has been favored by non-American, especially European, writers, but certain Americans are not sanguine as to the latter-day flexibility of the American economy, even granted Congressional acceptance of lower tariff duties.

---

[28] See, for example, the papers by Randall Hinshaw and H. B. Lary and the comments by R. F. Mikesell, J. J. Polak and J. P. Young in *Am. Econ. Rev., Proc.*, May 1946, XXXVI, 672–86, 710–16; also W. S. Salant, "The Domestic Effects of Capital Export under the Point Four Program," *ibid.*, May 1950, XL, 495–510.

It is not easy to assess these arguments since they are essentially expressed judgments on matters of fact for which reliable data are not to be had. Perhaps economists have been too prone to accept the purported statistical findings that price elasticities of demand for exports are typically below unity, notwithstanding Haberler's repeated insistence to the contrary and Orcutt's recent severely critical review of the statistical findings.[29] As for the adaptability of the American economy to the competition of increased imports without falling into a slump, this is again a matter on which factual data are sparse indeed. But the remarkable ease with which the American economy shifted from war to peace production after 1945 or with which it accommodated to a drop in net exports from $11.5 billion in 1947 to $2.2 billion in 1950 should at least call in question some of the more fearful views often expressed on this score.

C. *International Investment and International Economic Stability*

Well before the end of World War II, there were frequent assertions that means must be devised to stabilize the flow of international investment.[30] Article I(v) of the Agreement establishing the International Bank makes one of its purposes "to conduct its operations with due regard to the effect of international investment on business conditions in the territories of members. . . ." And from time to time various economists have re-emphasized the potentialities of international investment as a stabilizing device.[31] Yet, at present writing, the problem is about as far from solution as it was a decade ago.

Perhaps the primary reason is that the actual postwar world has been substantially different from the anticipated postwar world and has

---

[29] See G. H. Orcutt, "Measurement of Price Elasticities in International Trade," *Rev. Econ. Stat.*, May 1950, XXXII, 117–32.

[30] See, for example, U.S. Dept. of Commerce, *The United States in the World Economy* (Washington, 1943), Ch. 3 and *passim;* League of Nations, *Economic Stability in the Post-War World,* Ch. 13.

[31] Most recently, for example, the report of the U.N. Group of Experts, *National and International Measures for Full Employment* (Lake Success, 1949), pp. 54 ff., which proposes that lending countries through their governments should commit themselves to a foreign investment "target." This target would then be met by putting at the disposal of the International Bank any difference between this target figure and loans made through other channels.

Jacob Viner, in an otherwise critical review of this document, seems to accord some support to this proposal. See his "Full Employment at Whatever Cost," *Quart. Jour. Econ.,* Aug. 1950, LXIV, 401–03.

necessitated both larger capital transfers and transfers different in character from those contemplated. Most international capital transfers since 1945 have been for relief and economic reconstruction in which political considerations in the broadest and best sense were never wholly absent. Such transfers lend themselves scarcely at all to contracyclical considerations. Moreover, in the last half dozen years, cyclical problems have been of distinctly secondary importance in the international economic scene—far more pressing issues have crowded the agenda.

Somewhat similar prospects are in view for the years immediately ahead. Any large-scale revival of private international investment is probably unlikely. Loans and grants for economic development and for political purposes may run to large figures. But neither policy lends itself well to contracyclical considerations.[32] To be sure, if the more industrialized countries should fall into a slump, they might wish to push economic development more vigorously abroad.

In a world, however, where more and more the aim is to insulate national price levels from one another by direct controls, where exchange controls are preferred to adjustments in exchange rates, and where almost any deflationary tendencies are viewed as a threat to full employment at home—in such a world, foreign borrowing is likely to appear as the only "feasible" means of dealing with balance-of-payments problems. International stability in this special sense may be attainable by a policy of generous international lending. It is perhaps only one aspect of the broader proposition, now popular in some quarters, that the burden of adjustment in balance-of-payment problems should rest with the creditor country.

Perhaps the future may show that the earlier postwar conceptions of the international stability problem in relation to international investment require reformulation. Perhaps the problem is not essentially a "business-cycle" problem but rather one of working out some kind of *modus vivendi* whereby internal national economic stability for the industrialized countries and economic development for the low-income countries will not be constantly running afoul of efforts to reap the advantages of international specialization and trade. The older view that a country should adapt its internal economy to whatever extent called

---

[32] While international investment for economic development is better suited to this purpose than politically motivated transfers from the point of view of the investing country the same cannot be said from the point of view of the developing country. These countries are likely to resent deeply any adaptation in their plans forced upon them by economic considerations in the more industrially advanced countries. Nevertheless, it must be admitted that the possibilities of linking economic development plans with measures for promoting international economic stability are not wholly bleak.

for by its balance-of-payments position finds few supporters today. But the alternative view that a worsening of a country's balance-of-payments position calls for adjustment abroad but not at home—or that foreign credits should sustain the internal *status quo* economically until the country finds it convenient to make some internal adjustment—would appear to be an equally unworkable basis for an international system. International investment can probably never be a satisfactory substitute for internal adaptation even if the supply of loans were completely elastic. What seems to be called for is some kind of cooperative approach between countries which recognizes this fact, but also recognizes that the "real costs" can be more equitably shared than they have customarily been and that international investment can contribute to this end. No one (least of all this writer) yet sees, probably, how these objectives may be achieved and what kinds of international machinery and controls they would require. Yet it may be true that this, rather than smoothing international business cycles, is more nearly the crux of the international stability problem.

III. NONPRIVATE CAPITAL TRANSFERS IN THE POSTWAR PERIOD

Probably, few persons supposed that the end of World War II would see an immediate upsurge of private international investment or that even if it occurred it would suffice to re-establish a viable international economy. The problems to be faced and the sums needed immediately following the war were not appropriate to private finance. The European belligerents were economically weak: capital destruction and undermaintenance joined with demoralization to hold production at a low level; intra-European trade was almost at a standstill; Germany presented special problems; and from the longer-term point of view, the liquidation of prewar investments combined with the accumulation of wartime debts appeared to be a millstone which could not soon be cast aside. There was much speculation as to how high a level of real income the European nations could sustain, even after the immediate postwar difficulties were cleared away.

The direct capital contributions of the American economy via its government to the solution of these postwar problems amounted to a large figure—something more than $5.2 billion as an annual average from 1946 through 1950. In 1939 the total portfolio and direct long-term investments of the United States were estimated at $10.8 billion;[33] in other words, in any two postwar years the United States government

---

[33] *The United States in the World Economy*, p. 23.

has provided dollar grants and loans to the rest of the world nearly equal to total American long-term investments abroad in 1939. In the five years 1946 through 1950, the total of $26 billion is about equal to the estimated total value of *all* international investments of all countries in 1944. Even with allowance for differences in the purchasing power of the dollar now and in earlier years, the sums transferred to foreign countries by the American government since the end of the war are still large. They are much smaller, of course, measured against American national income.

A. International Capital Transfers as Public Grants

This essay cannot describe the many postwar programs under which the American government has transferred capital to foreign countries nor appraise their effectiveness in attaining their purposes. It may not be out of place, however, briefly to examine the apparent rationale of these transfers. The logic of private international investment is pecuniary gain. What, ostensibly, is the comparable logic for transfers on public account?

For the first phase—the interval of direct relief—the answer is obvious: the objective was simply a humane desire to lessen the distress following upon the cessation of hostilities coupled with an apprehension that unrelieved hunger and suffering might threaten political stability. Even before the war ended the view was widely proclaimed that relief was a government responsibility, not a task for private charity. As will be seen from Table 1 the American contribution to UNRRA and post-UNRRA relief was $2.38 billion. These were outright grants.[34] As Table 1 shows, the United States government also made direct contributions to relief through other channels.[35]

---

[34] So far as can be determined, the United States government made almost no outright grants for relief after World War I. Relief was then considered a job for private charity. The United States government did, however, accept foreign government obligations for surplus supplies sold on credit ($599 million) and for relief supplies furnished on credit ($141 million). About $10.9 million was spent for feeding children and for similar programs for which no obligations of foreign governments were taken. See, 80th Congress, 1st Session, Senate Committee on Finance, *Foreign Assets and Liabilities of the United States* (Washington, 1948), pp. 6–8. Even before World War II ended, the American government was providing relief in reoccupied areas in Europe.

[35] The figures on grants in Table 1 from *Report to the President on Foreign Economic Policies* (Washington, 1950)—the "Gray Report"—were compiled from Dept. of Commerce data (as revised) but do not correspond at all closely with those published in *Foreign Assets and Liabilities of the United States,* pp. 35 ff. The latter are considerably larger. But presumably the Gray Report figures, being more recent, have a greater claim to accuracy.

TABLE 1

United States Government Grants, other Unilateral Transfers, and Loans to Foreign Countries, 1946–50

[Millions of dollars]

Type of Aid	1946	1947	1948	1949	1950
A. Unilateral payments:					
Lend-lease	178	......	......	......	......
UNRRA and post-UNRRA	1,529	761	83	2	......
Civilian supplies distributed by the armed forces	539	1,009	1,468	1,082	500
Transfers to Philippines	61	91	130	203	166
Chinese aid	15	......	167	97	23
Korean aid	......	......	......	39	57
Greek-Turkish aid	......	74	349	171	62
International Refugee Organization	......	15	89	71	33
Interim aid	......	12	544	......	......
European Recovery Program	......	......	1,397	3,730	2,757[1]
Mutual Defense Assistance Program	......	......	......	......	516
Other	132	288	135	190	181
Total unilateral payments	2,454	2,250	4,362	5,585	4,295
Less: Unilateral receipts	166	303	205	264	175
Equals: Net unilateral payments	2,288	1,947	4,157	5,321	4,120
B. Long-term loans and investments:					
Lend-lease credits	547	......	1	4	1
Surplus property including ship sales	787	273	168	30	2
Export-Import Bank loans	945	797	454	163	193
United Kingdom loan	600	2,850	300	......	......
Subscriptions to:					
International Bank	318	317	......	......	......
International Monetary Fund	5	2,745	......	......	......
European Recovery Program	......	......	476	428	163
Other	146	161	17	54	55
Total long-term loans and investments	3,348	7,143	1,416	679	414
Less: Repayments	86	294	443	205	287
Equals: Net long-term loans and investments, including to International Bank and International Monetary Fund	3,262	6,849	973	474	127
Less: Subscriptions to International Bank and International Monetary Fund	323	3,062	......	......	......
Equals: Net long-term loans and investments, excluding to International Bank and International Monetary Fund	2,939	3,787	973	474	127
C. Outflow of short-term capital (net)	−250	108	−87	173	−10
Total net unilateral payments and total capital movement, excluding to International Bank and International Monetary Fund (A + B + C)	4,977	5,842	5,043	5,968	4,237

[1] Includes aid to Indonesia $38 million.

Source: U.S. Department of Commerce with revised data to end of 1950 as supplied to the author through the courtesy of Robert L. Sammons.

The second phase of United States Government postwar capital transfers to foreign countries dates from the international financial crisis in the summer of 1947. By then it was clear that to restore order and viability to economies abroad and some semblance of a rational international economic system was a far more formidable task than had been earlier believed. In the first half of 1947 alone, the United Kingdom drew $1.5 billion on the American credit of $3.75 billion. By August 20, 1947, when the convertibility clause in the agreement was suspended, total drafts had amounted to $3.35 billion. Since this loan had been expected to care for the British current account deficit until 1951, something had clearly gone wrong.[36] A different attack on the postwar international economic problem seemed necessary.

The response of the American government to the convertibility crisis was the Marshall Plan proposal, which resulted in the Foreign Economic Assistance Act in April, 1948[37]—a scheme to achieve certain basic political ends by explicitly economic means.

What was the rationale of the Marshall Plan Program as a venture in international capital transfers on public account? Broadly speaking, the reasoning seems to have taken the following lines. The vital interests of the United States required that communism in Europe be checked, both as an immediate internal danger and a latent external threat. The immediate danger was that economic distress would strengthen communist and other dissident groups throughout Europe. Consequently, national governments would be weakened and harassed in their domestic affairs unless and until there was an improvement in economic well-being. The latent threat was that weak governments responsible for disorganized national economies were an open invitation to the USSR to extend its domination over the whole of Europe. The broad strategy emerging from this analysis, therefore, was to strengthen national economies by a broad attack on fundamental economic difficulties and, simultaneously, to enhance their collective economic strength by achieving greater intra-European economic cooperation. Both efforts, if successful, would check the encroachment of communism upon American

---

[36] For a succinct recent account of the crisis and its causes see H. S. Ellis, *The Economics of Freedom* (New York, 1950), pp. 97–100; also J. H. Williams, "The British Crisis: A Problem in Economic Statesmanship," *Foreign Affairs,* Oct. 1949, XXVIII, 1–19; Hubert Henderson, "The Moral of the British Crisis," *Rev. Econ. Stat.,* Nov. 1949, XXXI, 256–60.

[37] Few economic measures have been as fully documented—by careful studies, special reports, expert testimony, and elaborate exhibits—before their passage through Congress as was the Foreign Economic Assistance Act of 1948. Since, in all probability, something sizeable had to be done after Secretary Marshall's speech, it is not so clear for whom all this research and expert testimony was felt to be necessary.

national interests.[38] But a program of this kind would require the United States to commit real capital resources on a substantial scale.

The economic logic had two main threads: one was that economic welfare could not improve until output increased, increased output required increased real investment, and the necessary increased investment could not be provided quickly enough out of domestic resources. The other thread ran in terms of the interrelations between internal economic strength, balance-of-payments difficulties, and the barriers blocking a vigorous intra-European and international trade. In brief, economic aid under the Marshall Plan should concentrate upon substantially increasing economic efficiency in the individual participating countries while simultaneously emphasizing the substantial gains to be had from economic integration through international specialization and exchange.[39]

Between 1948 and the end of 1950, the United States government committed $8.4 billion in grants and $1 billion in loans under the European Recovery Program (ERP).[40]

These dollar transfers were, on the whole, highly effective insofar as the purpose was to restore production, increase investment, quiet unrest, and stop the drift to communism in the participating countries. By

---

[38] These aims of course harmonized with long-term American policy objectives with respect to multilateral trade at stable exchange rates without exchange controls or direct trade controls. (See *infra*, p. 331.) A revival of something approximating a rational international economic order was held to be unattainable without the active participation of European countries, especially the United Kingdom. But these longer-term objectives, despite the public emphasis they received, were probably of minor importance in getting the Marshall Plan adopted.

[39] See Title I of the Foreign Economic Assistance Act of 1948 where the goals were stated in the following terms: "(1) Promoting industrial and agricultural production in the participating countries; (2) Furthering the restoration or maintenance of the soundness of European currencies, budgets, and finances; and (3) Facilitating and stimulating the growth of international trade of participating countries with one another and with other countries by appropriate measures, including reduction of barriers which hamper trade."

As the program developed the American authorities increased their emphasis on point (3); in the early stages it was comparatively neglected in favor of the production goals. A British writer has summarized the assumptions of the American authorities as follows: "The countries of Europe were considered by Mr. Marshall's experts to be underproducing . . . they were considered to have learnt nothing from the past and to be determined . . . to get back to the state of things prevailing before the war. If they would get together . . . and generally so organize their affairs as to secure the advantages of mass production and mass sales in an internal market of 200 million people, they would begin to be in a fair way to resolving their difficulties; . . . and the money invested by the American people in a recovery introduced by these means would be money well spent." A. D. Marris, *Prospects for Closer European Economic Integration* (London, 1948), p. 7.

[40] See Table 1 *supra*. The $8.4 billion in the text above includes the "interim aid" grants of $556 million recorded for the years 1947 and 1948. Perhaps one ought also to include "Greek-Turkish" aid and some part of the "civilian supplies distributed by the armed forces" but these have been omitted.

330 · A SURVEY OF CONTEMPORARY ECONOMICS

the close of 1950, industrial production in Western Europe was about 40 per cent above the 1938 level as against only 10 per cent above in 1948.[41] For the whole of Europe, total net investment in 1949 was over $7 billion (in 1938 prices), which was roughly 25 per cent higher than prewar. With Germany excluded, net investment in Europe in constant prices in 1949 was about 60 per cent above 1938. The amounts committed to investment in the Marshall Plan countries have been one of its striking achievements, although there were important differences between countries as to its kind and allocation.[42]

The struggle against inflation was fairly successful up to the outbreak of the Korean war in June, 1950, but at present writing, inflation has again become a major problem in most ERP countries. As of June, 1950, the cost of living indexes in only three countries—Austria, France, and Iceland—had risen more than 20 per cent over the 1948 level.[43] But since then the cost of living has again moved upwards as a consequence of higher prices for primary products. The fact that not all these price increases in primary product imports had yet been reflected in cost-of-living prices by early 1951 was a source of grave concern.[44] Doubtless,

[41] *Fed. Res. Bull.,* Apr. 1951, XXXVII, 368. Of course, the Marshall Plan was by no means wholly responsible for this result.

[42] The above figures are drawn from Economic Commission for Europe, *Economic Survey of Europe in 1949* (Geneva, 1950), p. 39, which report contains a wealth of information on the direction of the investment flows, investment per head, and sources of finance. Perhaps the most striking fact is the growing importance of public investment.

[43] U.N., *Econ. Bull. for Eur.,* Third Quarter 1950, II, 89.

[44] See, Economic Commission for Europe, *Economic Survey of Europe in 1950* (Geneva, 1951), Ch. 5 for an extended discussion of the reappearance of the inflation problem and its implications for European economic affairs. The following figures drawn from the U.N. *Monthly Bulletin of Statistics* show the rise in the cost of living indexes and raw material price indexes for a few selected European countries between June, 1950 and April, 1951:

COUNTRY	COST OF LIVING		RAW MATERIALS	
	June '50	April '51	June '50	April '51
Belgium	365	411	365*	478
Denmark	179	198	252	350
France	107	126	119	206
Finland	971	1,093	1,036	1,526
Norway	171	197	232	315
Sweden	161	181	205	277
U.S.A.	166	180	198	233

* General wholesale price index

The Economic Commission for Europe reported in January, 1951 that, "Specific controls which had been relaxed or abandoned have in some cases been re-introduced. The control of imports and exports has also been adjusted in certain countries with a view to influencing internal prices." *Econ. Bull. for Eur.,* 3d Quarter 1950, II, 17.

no amount of advance planning could have foreseen the Korean War and the resulting world scramble for raw materials.

The success of the Marshall Plan in achieving its broader economic objectives is more questionable. Insofar as the purpose was to eliminate balance-of-payment problems (especially the "dollar shortage"), direct exchange and trade controls, and substantially to increase multilateral intra-European and international trade, the Marshall Plan had only a qualified success. European trade improved but much of it was still bilateral, even in 1951; exchange controls and direct trade controls were still common practice. If the ERP outlays were (in part) an investment to finance the change-over from economic nationalism and bilateralism to an international economic order built around price and market mechanisms, then the returns were disappointing: either the "business risk" inherent in the effort was greater than anticipated or "political factors" supervened. Explanations from both sides are readily available in the recent literature.

On the one hand are those who insist that the ERP analysis of Europe's postwar economic difficulties was essentially faulty because it assumed that Europe's economic weakness was temporary and hence temporary assistance in the form of grants and loans would effect a cure. These writers have insisted that the "dollar shortage" is chronic and the problem intractable, through any orthodox measures, for the foreseeable future. Consequently, unless the United States were prepared to effect large dollar transfers more or less indefinitely—a kind of perpetual ERP—most of the world (not only European countries) must resort to bilateralism, bloc arrangements, and discrimination against dollar imports to achieve viability.[45]

---

[45] Thomas Balogh probably has been the most insistent proponent of this view and has expounded it in various publications. So far as this writer is aware, his first exposition of it was in his essay "International Aspects of Full Employment" in Oxford Institute of Statistics, *The Economics of Full Employment* (Oxford, 1944). But in this essay the treatment was more oblique—and apparently less pessimistic as to the long-term economic prospects of Europe—than in his more recent writings. See *The Dollar Crisis* (Oxford, 1949) or his essays, "Exchange Depreciation and Economic Readjustment," *Rev. Econ. Stat.*, Nov. 1948, XXX, 276–85, and "The United States and International Economic Equilibrium," *Foreign Economic Policy for the United States,* S. E. Harris, ed. (Cambridge, Mass. 1948).

But Balogh is not the only writer partial to the view that the dollar shortage may be chronic. See, for example, C. P. Kindleberger, *The Dollar Shortage* (New York and London, 1950), *passim,* but especially Ch. 8; also R. G. Hawtrey, *The Balance of Payments and the Standard of Living* (London and New York, 1950). It should be added, however, that these writers and others are not of one mind as to the causes of the chronic dollar shortage nor as to the policies necessary in the circumstances. See, for example, Horst Mendershausen, "Foreign Aid with and without Dollar Shortage," *Rev. Econ. Stat.*, Feb. 1951, XXXIII, 38–48.

Other observers would hold that the failure of ERP to solve European balance-of-payment problems and establish multilateralism was not primarily because of any chronic economic weakness in Western Europe but because the postwar economic policy of European governments has assigned balance-of-payment problems a low priority in comparison with full-employment objectives, social welfare measures, and the virtues of a planned economy. Consequently, both the will and the ability to adjust the internal economy to the trade balance have been weakened. Perhaps, too, a planned economy in a democratic setting has a bias towards inflation on the one hand and autarchy on the other.[46] None of these factors was favorable to the trade policy objectives of the European Recovery Program.

To assess these (and other) competing analyses of the reasons for the limited success of the Marshall Plan with regard to its broader objectives would necessitate going far beyond the legitimate scope of the present essay. But perhaps this initial, large-scale venture into international public investment does suggest some tentative conclusions as to the scope and limits of such capital transfers for achieving political ends.[47]

Viewed *ex post*—from the Marshall Plan (and similar) experience —the efficacy of international capital transfers to achieve political objectives abroad would probably now be acknowledged to be somewhat less than was earlier believed in many quarters. Two considerations seem to support this view.

First, it has come to be increasingly recognized that the international side of a country's economy is inseparable from the domestic: any policy with respect to the one has inescapable policy implications for

---

[46] "In current economic planning there are few indications of the development of such international specialization . . . current tendencies are in the opposite direction . . . most European countries tend to increase the range of commodities produced at home and thus to reduce their economic dependence on their neighbours." Economic Commission for Europe, *Economic Survey of Europe in 1948* (Geneva, 1949), p. 228.

[47] The basic political fact is that the United States has been forced into a position of major responsibility in international affairs. In this role it has had to look beyond its own borders for its security and internal well-being and so weigh the consequences of political and economic developments in other countries. On this basis a "dollar shortage" can be created by the simple agreement between the United States and any other country that dollar assistance would contribute to their vital common interests. Consequently, international capital transfers on public account find their political justification *ex ante* in what they promise to yield in changes abroad favorable to the interests of the transferring country. Broadly speaking, capital transfers are only useful, of course, where there is already some community of vital interests among the parties to the transfer. See Horst Mendershausen, *op. cit.*, where this mode of reasoning is developed at some length.

the other. National policy-makers may give primacy to either, provided they accept the other as secondary and substantially predetermined. But this poses a problem. A capital transfer from one sovereign state to another by gift or loan may be made with certain stipulations as to the use of the foreign balances so acquired. But it carries no right to interfere in internal policy. Consequently, except in the most dire circumstances, the capital transfer has little leverage in shaping domestic policy. The best that can be hoped for is that a clear statement of objectives will elicit policies in other countries which, with foreign assistance, will make the stated objectives attainable.

The objectives of the United States in making postwar capital transfers to other countries have been stated many times. A recent official version runs as follows:

> We are working toward the ultimate goal of a peace which rests upon the firm foundations of an expanding world economy. It is, therefore, important that we continue our efforts to encourage world trade and capital investment throughout the world. Only in this way can the nations of the world achieve rising standards of living through sound and self-supporting economies . . . it is still possible and necessary to make progress in the direction of a system of multilateral and nondiscriminatory trade.
>
> We must, therefore, continue to work for such a system. We must try to establish an adequate system of international payments. We should encourage other countries to adopt the necessary monetary and fiscal measures which can assure sound currencies and obviate the need for direct trade restrictions. We must make sure that our own house is in order—that we have eliminated unnecessary barriers to imports, and that our policies in such fields as agriculture and shipping are so adjusted that they do not impose undue burdens on world trade.[48]

Such statements invariably get a firm nod of approval at international conferences and even at home most governments profess their loyalty to these aims. But all the same since 1945 most governments and their electorates (including the American) have either desired or felt compelled to bend foreign economic policy to domestic economic policy rather than the other way about. To make much progress towards "unobstructed international trade and investment" meant either forcing internal adjustments, or modifying domestic policies, or both. Yet, few governments have thought these changes either desirable in themselves in relation to their real costs, or really feasible in the context of the internal and external political realities with which they were confronted. Consequently, while never denying the virtues of multilateral trade and

---

[48] "Gray Report," p. 15.

investment and their appurtenances, few governments saw their way clear to move in that direction—despite the Marshall Plan. Large public investments abroad seem to depend for their effectiveness upon foreign governments adopting policies consistent with the aims which the investing country desires to accomplish. Yet, the investing country can only hope this will occur; it may not interfere in internal affairs abroad to attain it.

The second reason for somewhat doubting the efficacy of international capital transfers on public account to achieve basic policy changes in other countries is the growing conviction that perhaps the obstacles thereto are not basically economic but rather social and cultural. The belief that only economic difficulties have restrained other nations from reverting to private initiative as the mainspring of the economic system has been wavering: the United Kingdom was particularly disillusioning to Americans in this regard since such a large stake had been placed on its early return to convertibility and multilateralism. But there was no discernible eagerness abroad to embrace the allegedly self-evident virtues of private enterprise and international trade and exchange without direct controls. American policy had either misjudged the political temper in other countries, or the magnitude of the problem was many times greater than the American authorities had believed. And there has been a growing suspicion that the former was nearer the truth. In any case, the causal connection between foreign economic assistance and a revamping of internal political objectives is far from straightforward. Perhaps a large question mark should follow many of the standard pronouncements and slogans on the political returns from international public capital transfers until political complexities abroad are better analyzed and comprehended.

These comments on the efficacy of international investment in the political arena are not meant to suggest that the Marshall Plan was a mistake. Rather the intention is somewhat to question the glowing confidence with which public capital transfers are still proposed as the obvious solution to a host of international problems. Judged by experience to date, such transfers can be quite effective in achieving concrete, immediate, economic objectives within particular countries. Measured against the broader objectives for which these specific projects were essentially means, the results have been less gratifying.

B. The International Bank for Reconstruction and Development

Up to December 31, 1950, the International Bank for Reconstruction and Development had made loans totaling slightly more than $1 billion of which $363 million were still undisbursed. All but $19 million were repayable in United States dollars. Of this total the Bank borrowed $260.6 millions (all but $10.6 million in the United States) and provided the remainder out of its own assets. In addition it had guaranteed loans amounting to $25.6 million.[49]

As matters have worked out the Bank has increasingly emphasized its "Development" rather than its "Reconstruction" functions until this is now almost its exclusive interest.[50] The importance of the Bank in the whole problem area of the underdeveloped countries and the means to their improvement goes much beyond what might be inferred from the loans it has actually made. Aggregate loans have not been large, relative to the alleged capital needs of the underdeveloped countries. But the Bank has probably given more careful study to the problems confronting these countries in their quest for development than any other organization. Moreover, it has had a valuable background of practical experience in meeting these problems in the obstinate, concrete form in which they exist in the real world. Consequently, the Bank's judgment as to the ways and means by which the Bank can assist in their solution deserves careful attention. But before considering the Bank's positive views on these problems and its own proper role, let us briefly consider the criticisms which have been leveled at it.

The criticisms of the Bank have been along two lines: first, the

---

[49] *International Financial Statistics,* Feb. 1951, IV, xiv. The Bank may assist borrowers through three channels: through loans directly from its own resources, through funds borrowed in the capital markets under its own obligation and through guaranteeing loans made by private investors. See *Agreement,* Article IV, Sect. 1(a). Of their subscriptions to the capital of the Bank, member countries were required to pay in 20 per cent of which 2 per cent was to be in gold or in U.S. dollars and the remaining 18 per cent in their own currencies. Before the 18 per cent can be loaned, the country in question has to grant permission (see Article IV, Sect. 1[b]). As of June 30, 1950, there was a long list of currencies amounting to $114.5 million which, though held by the Bank, were still restricted as to use. "Unrestricted currency" holdings of the Bank—those of the United States, United Kingdom, Belgium, and Canada—were, by contrast, only $3.7 million. See, *Fifth Annual Report,* p. 52.

[50] The financing of economic reconstruction and the "transition period" are clearly stated among the "purposes" of the Bank in its Articles of Agreement in Article I (i) and (v). But fairly soon after the war it became apparent that these tasks were much larger and more difficult than the Bretton Woods agreements had provided for. The British loan in 1946 and later the Marshall Plan in 1948, as well as the special aid programs to China, Korea, Greece, and Turkey (see *supra* Table 1, p. 327) dwarfed to insignificance anything the Bank might have done towards financing economic reconstruction or the special problems of the transition period. See *Third Annual Report* (Washington, 1948), p. 8.

In May, 1947, the Bank loaned $250 million to France and in August, 1947, $190 million to the Netherlands, $40 million to Denmark and $10.8 million to Luxembourg, chiefly for the purchase of capital equipment for economic reconstruction.

broad contention that its resources are too small and its outlook too narrow to deal with the underdeveloped areas problem; second, that even granted its limited financial resources the Bank has followed, and continues to follow, misguided policies.

Those who contend that the Bank has followed mistaken policies chiefly stress three points. First, that the "specific project approach" towards loans for economic development as employed by the Bank represents too literal an interpretation of sections 4 and 5 of Article III and should be abandoned in favor of granting loans for general development purposes. Closely related to this criticism is the second, which would have the Bank jettison the policy of limiting its loans to the direct foreign exchange costs of the particular project being financed. These critics would have the Bank take account of the indirect, no less than the direct, foreign exchange drain of development programs. Third, and finally, the Bank has been criticized for being "too commercial" in its attitude towards prospective borrowers by being too paternally prudent and charging too high interest rates.

Other critics are convinced that these and other weaknesses of the Bank make it hopelessly inadequate to handle the problems of economic development. This school of thought presumably would scrap or circumvent the Bank and substitute a new, larger institution with powers to make large long-term, general-purpose loans at very low or even nominal rates of interest. They would contend that only an "imaginative," large-scale, many-sided attack on the underdeveloped areas problem without delay holds any real promise of success. Because of space limitations the present essay can only note that these views exist and not attempt either to describe them in detail or evaluate them.[51]

The Bank has not been unmindful of these criticisms.[52] Broadly

---

[51] A good account of these various views on how economic development should be financed will be found in United Nations, *Methods of Financing Economic Development in Under-Developed Countries* (Lake Success, 1949). In particular see the extracts from the report of the U.N. Sub-Commission on Economic Development with its Annex A, prepared by Mr. V. K. R. V. Rao, proposing a new organization called the United Nations Economic Development Administration (UNEDA).

The memoranda included in this report are more critical of the Bank's policies by implication than by direct statement. But perhaps this is merely obeisance to the traditional amenities of international conferences.

[52] See the *Annual Reports* of the Bank, and United Nations, *Methods of Financing Economic Development,* pp. 89–102; but especially the statements by W. A. B. Iliff, L. B. Rist, D. C. deIongh, officers of the Bank, and the address by Eugene R. Black, the President of the Bank, in *Fifth Annual Meeting of the Board of Governors, Summary Proceedings* (Washington, 1950). The remarks that follow are mainly based on the last document.

speaking, the Bank believes that its critics, on the one hand, misconceive the process of economic development and how the Bank can assist it and, on the other, disregard the obligations and responsibilities put upon it by the Articles of Agreement. The Bank insists that economic development is a slow process and that, despite assistance from without, the major effort must come from within the developing country. The Bank also believes that hasty development without careful programming based upon a realistic appraisal of economic potentialities will only result in wasted resources, whether saved at home or borrowed from abroad. Consequently, the Bank is of the view that it should not lend its assistance to proposed undertakings and programs which are without demonstrable economic merit. In the words of W. A. B. Iliff, Director of the Loan Department:

> There are only two criteria from which the Board and the Management of the Bank are not prepared to depart . . . first, the Bank is not prepared to invest in any member state more than the Bank feels that the member state has a reasonable prospect of servicing; secondly, the Bank is not prepared to invest in any program or project unless it is satisfied with the economic merits of that project. The phrase "economic merits" is used in its widest possible sense.[53]

The Bank insists that these two criteria must be the basis of its loan policy.[54]

These lending criteria have had a direct relation to the Bank's continued insistence that it must establish the investment merits of its obligations among private investors if its total loans are to be larger than its own capital. The market had to be carefully cultivated, in the Bank's view.[55] This meant circumspection in its lending operations.

Finally, the Bank on numerous occasions has expressed its firm conviction on two points: first, that the major portion of the capital necessary for economic development must come from within the country itself; second, that foreign financial assistance should come chiefly from

---

[53] *Ibid.,* p. 37. Mr. Iliff offers a number of examples to show that the Bank has not applied these criteria in a narrow way.

[54] Article III, Sect. 4 (v) states ". . . the Bank shall act prudently in the interests both of the particular member in whose territories the project is located and of the members as a whole."

[55] "In the United States, institutional investors, such as insurance companies, banks, and trusts, constitute the largest group of potential purchasers of securities issued or guaranteed by the Bank . . . there were only a few states where institutional investors could legally invest in the Bank's securities. Unless this situation could be remedied, there was little prospect that the Bank would be able to sell any substantial amount of its securities in the United States." International Bank for Reconstruction and Development, *Third Annual Report,* pp. 28–29.

private sources.[56] The Bank's view is that the success of its efforts along these lines must be weighed at least equally with its actual lending operations.[57]

There is thus a great gap between the Bank's conception of economic development and that of its critics, within and without the underdeveloped areas. This gap is not visibly narrowing.

It may well be, however, that these differences of opinion between the Bank and its prospective borrowers are really only a surface manifestation of a rather fundamental cleavage between the developed and underdeveloped countries on the ends and patterns to be sought in economic development and the means to their achievement.[58] In other words, while both groups of countries "believe in" economic development they, in fact, hold different convictions as to what economic development should be moving towards and what vehicles are suitable for its advance: what the poorer countries want to achieve may be at odds with what the industrialized countries want to usher into existence.

The already developed countries, broadly speaking, conceive of economic development as moving forward within an international economy. Their view of economic development tends to emphasize comparative cost principles, regional specialization, and substantial, if not exclusive, reliance upon prices and markets to organize and guide production. This tends to mean that—at least initially—further development in the low-income areas would build upon already established primary product industries. As these develop further and increase their efficiency, ancillary industries would grow up around them. The traditionally mutually profitable interchange of raw and semiprocessed primary products for manufactures from the older countries would continue and expand. Private capital from abroad would assist this expansion. Industry and commerce would thus develop "naturally" as local capital accumulated and the requisite technical, managerial, and professional skills diffused amongst the people.[59]

---

[56] See *ibid.,* p. 20.

[57] See, for example, *Fifth Annual Report,* pp. 7–19.

[58] Cf. the excellent pamphlet, "The Strategy of World Development," *Planning,* No. 327 (London, 1951).

[59] The above omits the political motives the Western industrialized countries have for developing the poorer countries, which center around limiting communist expansion and the fact that the underdeveloped areas are at present indispensable sources of many strategic raw materials. See, for example, "Gray Report," p. 49 and *passim,* and International Development Advisory Board, *Partners in Progress* (Washington, 1951). The latter report particularly puts emphasis on strategic considerations.

If economic development is essentially so conceived, then the emphasis is upon gradualism, private enterprise, resort to the price system, international specialization, domestic capital accumulation and fairly direct linkages between foreign borrowing, expansion of exports, and debt service maintenance.

The underdeveloped countries, however, tend to conceive their own economic development in different terms. They believe—contrary to the prevailing view in the developed countries—that their development should stress industry and manufactures for home consumption, diversification of their economic structure, and lessened dependence upon the already developed countries. They seem to be convinced that to continue being primary producers for the world market means a continuance of low levels of income, economic "dependency," political weakness, and a generally humble role in world affairs. They tend to be distrustful of the price system and wary of private entrepreneurs.[60] Planned development, a "balanced" economic structure, and a substantially *lessened* dependence on other countries via the world economy seem to be the themes which they stress and reiterate.

Economic development on this pattern implies a different pace and different amounts and kinds of assistance from the already developed countries. If development stresses creating industries to serve the home market, then outside assistance must be in the form of very long-term loans at nominal interest rates or outright grants. For while a heavy import balance may be necessary to achieve the desired development, the plans do not contemplate an early export surplus to service loans from abroad. If the development plans also contemplate heavy outlays for education, health, housing, etc.—as they usually do—then these will further reinforce the case for very long-term loans at low interest rates and for straight grants. Finally, many underdeveloped countries feel that population pressures, political unrest, etc., force them into a broad-scale assault on the development problem: in their view the traditional sequences of development offer little hope of success.[61]

The foregoing suggestion that between the developed and underdeveloped countries there may be a really basic cleavage on both the objectives and means of economic development cannot, unfortunately, be adequately explored here. If there is anything in it, however, perhaps the present controversy centering about the World Bank and financial

---

[60] Cf. *supra,* Part I.

[61] Cf., U.N., *Methods of Financing Economic Development,* and the various discussions in the U.N. Sub-Commission on Economic Development.

techniques in development does not bring the real crux of the difficulties into the open.

But regardless of whether more than methods of finance and the World Bank are at issue in current discussions of the economic development problem, this much can be said: there is an enormous difference between the sums from abroad which the underdeveloped countries feel they must have for development purposes and the sums which the industrialized countries are (apparently) prepared to provide. How these differences will be resolved into an accord from which economic development can move forward is far from clear. The United States—as implicitly or explicitly the only major source from which such international transfers are likely to proceed over the foreseeable future—can neither ignore the problem nor fail to weigh carefully the ramified implications of the available alternative solutions.

C. The Export-Import Bank and International Lending

The present Export-Import Bank dates from July 31, 1945, when the United States Congress approved a new act raising the limit on *outstanding* loans and guaranties by the Bank to $3.5 billion (from the previous $700 million) and removed the prohibition on loans to foreign governments in default on their debts to the United States.[62] Only the Bank's activities since June 30, 1945, are considered here—total loan authorizations prior to June 30, 1945, amounted only to $1,268 million of which $336 million were still undisbursed.[63]

As of June 30, 1950, the Bank had total credit authorizations outstanding of $2,786 million and uncommitted lending authority of $714 million. Between July 1, 1945, and June 30, 1950, the Bank authorized new credits of $3,521 million and actually disbursed $2,652 million. Measured by authorizations granted, the period of greatest activity was from July 1, 1945, to July 1, 1946; measured by actual disbursements the most active period was January 1, 1946, to June 30, 1947. Indeed, in this eighteen months period, the Bank was making disbursements at

---

[62] The original Export-Import Bank was established by Executive Order (No. 6581) on February 2, 1934, with the immediate purpose of assisting the finance of foreign trade between the United States and the USSR. A second Export-Import Bank to finance trade with Cuba was created by Executive Order (No. 6638) on March 9, 1934. The two banks were merged in 1935. The Export-Import Bank Act of 1945, in addition to raising the Bank's lending authority, also gave it an independent status and vested its management in a full-time board of directors of which the Secretary of State was a member *ex officio*. For a good brief account of the Bank see D. B. Marsh, *World Trade and Investment* (New York, 1951), Ch. 31.

[63] *First Semi-Annual Report to Congress* for the period July–December, 1945, p. 52.

a rate of over $1 billion per year; and more than half of its total disbursements up to June 30, 1950, occurred in these same eighteen months. The Bank's disbursements are shown in Table 1, *supra,* p. 327.

Notwithstanding the Bank's statutory purpose, its credit facilities since mid-1945 have been mostly used for economic reconstruction and economic development.[64] The credits for economic reconstruction went chiefly to European countries.[65] The credits for economic development have gone mainly to Latin America, China, Indonesia, Israel, and Turkey for the purchase of materials, equipment, supplies, and services from the United States for undertakings ranging from shrimp vessels for Mexico to hotel construction in Venezuela.[66]

Finally, and ancillary to its main activities, the Bank (as of June 30, 1950), at the direction of the Administrator for ECA, had granted loans and credits amounting to $1,045 million and issued guaranties totaling $22.8 million. But these funds were advanced to the Bank by the Administrator for the purpose.[67]

Thus the recent history of the Export-Import Bank well mirrors the changing character of the international economic problem as viewed from the United States since the end of World War II. In the months immediately following the cessation of hostilities, the Bank used its enlarged resources primarily for financing economic reconstruction. When

---

[64] From July 1, 1945, to March 31, 1950, the Bank's authorized credits of $2,846 million went 35 per cent for reconstruction, 34 per cent for economic development, 23 per cent for lend-lease requisitions, 6 per cent for cotton purchases, and 2 per cent for "other" purposes. Percentages calculated by the writer from figures in National Advisory Council on International Monetary and Financial Problems, *Semi-Annual Report to the President and to the Congress,* for the period Oct. 1, 1949—March 31, 1950 (Washington, 1950), p. 21.

[65] *First Semi-Annual Report to Congress,* pp. 16–17. As the Bank has pointed out, ". . . the crucial fact was that only the United States, and Canada to a lesser extent, were in a position to supply quickly the large quantities of goods needed by liberated and war-devastated countries." *Ibid.,* pp. 9–10. Thus the Bank felt forced into the position of having to pay primary attention to the urgent needs of European countries—with the end of lend-lease and before the International Bank or the Marshall Plan—and (probably) only minor attention to the credit status of the borrower. In fact, the "capacity of the borrower to repay" is listed fifth in a list of six factors considered in making the reconstruction loans. *Ibid.,* p. 10.

[66] The *Tenth Semi-Annual Report to Congress,* App. C, gives brief statements of the purposes for which credits were advanced under particular loans.

[67] Credits and guaranties so provided for under the Foreign Economic Assistance Act of 1948, as amended (Sections 111[c] [2] and 111[b] [3]) are not to be included in calculating the loan limits imposed on the Bank by the Export-Import Bank Act of 1945. In other words, the Bank essentially acted for ECA and on its directive. It had no independent authority in these matters.

the responsibility for economic reconstruction in the broad sense was shifted to ECA, the Export-Import Bank after an interval of relative inactivity in 1948 and early 1949 expanded in the direction of economic development. As stated in its *Ninth Semi-Annual Report* (p. 4):

Loans by the Bank, however, are likely to be especially needed in underdeveloped areas where basic transportation and similar facilities, which may not represent attractive investments to private capital, are needed and where general conditions may not for some time be sufficiently stable to attract private investment.

But the special role of the Bank as against that of the International Bank for Reconstruction and Development seems to be decidedly unclear. Other than vague references to the desirability of "coordinating" the activities of the two Banks one finds little. Presumably the authorities are convinced that there is need for a strictly American lending agency to assist economic development which can take account of political realities at home and abroad.

IV. CAPITAL MOVEMENTS ON PRIVATE ACCOUNT SINCE THE END OF WORLD WAR II

Since the end of World War II, as Arthur Salter has remarked, "Private foreign investment (in which the general investor risks his money) either in portfolio or in direct investment has been practically non-existent."[68] The movements of United States private long-term capital are shown in Table 2. Moreover, as another study has pointed out, reinvested earnings accounted for $1,015 million as against actual new capital commitments of $1,386 million during the period 1946–48. Finally, of this $1,386 million, $1,004 was in petroleum.[69]

This failure of private international investment to regain its vigor since 1945, or even since 1929, has caused genuine concern. Some ERP countries have looked hopefully to private investment as a source of funds after the Marshall Plan. The government of the United States has repeatedly emphasized its wish to shift the burden of foreign financial assistance to private hands—both to reduce its fiscal load and to put capi-

---

[68] Arthur Salter, *Foreign Investment,* International Finance Section, Princeton University, Essays in International Finance, No. 12, Feb. 1951, p. 38.

[69] *Surv. Curr. Bus.,* Nov. 1949, XXIX, 18–23. According to a recent official report total U.S. private investments abroad had the following dollar values in billions of dollars: 1945, 14.7; 1946, 15.6; 1947, 17.0; 1948, 18.3; 1949, 19.3. The estimated value of U.S. government investments abroad rose correspondingly from $2.1 billion in 1945 to $13.5 billion in 1949. Nat. Advis. Coun. Internat. Mon. Finan. Prob., *op. cit.,* p. 10.

tal transfers abroad upon an investment basis in the narrower sense. Yet the flow of private foreign investment remains small.

The main reason—apart from still vivid recollections of the 1930's —why private capital has not flowed abroad since World War II seems to be that investors have viewed the risks "peculiar to foreign investment" as too high in relation to the prospective returns. At least in the

TABLE 2

NET OUTFLOW OF UNITED STATES PRIVATE DIRECT-INVESTMENT CAPITAL, BY AREA, 1946–49
(Millions of dollars)

Year and Industry	Total	Canada	Latin American Republics	ERP Countries	ERP Dependencies	Other Europe	All Other Countries
1946: Total...............	182.4	37.9	58.5	18.0	6.1	0.8	61.1
Petroleum industry.......	170.0	12.0	103.0	7.0	4.0	(1)	44.0
Other industries..........	12.4	25.9	−44.5	11.0	2.1	.8	17.1
1947: Total...............	723.5	13.0	441.7	47.4	53.0	1.1	167.3
Petroleum industry.......	487.0	37.0	257.0	20.0	50.0	1.0	122.0
Other industries..........	236.5	−24.0	184.7	27.4	3.0	.1	45.3
1948: Total...............	645.1	37.8	321.0	48.2	68.5	5.2	164.4
Petroleum industry.......	486.0	44.0	205.0	38.0	61.0	2.0	136.0
Other industries..........	159.1	−6.2	116.0	10.2	7.5	3.2	28.4
1949: Total...............	834.4	103.2	480.4	33.8	38.3	13.3	165.4
Petroleum industry.......	677.0	54.0	397.0	10.0	34.0	13.0	169.0
Other industries..........	157.4	49.2	83.4	23.8	4.3	.3	−3.6

(1) Less than 50 thousand dollars
NOTE: Breakdown between petroleum and other industries is subject to revision. Detail will not necessarily add to totals because of rounding.
SOURCE: U.S. Department of Commerce. Data as given in "Gray Report" p. 121.

United States—by far the largest potential source of private foreign investment—investors have felt that the risks of war, of confiscation, of political instability abroad, of exchange control blocking of earnings and principal, etc., have made foreign commitments quite unattractive compared with available domestic opportunities. And since 1945 these risks have been growing rather than shrinking. When corrected for risk, the prospective yields on foreign investment have not compared at all favorably with those from domestic investment.[70]

[70] Informed opinion has usually contended that inconvertibility and confiscation were the most serious risks "peculiar" to foreign investment. See, for example, *Hearings on Foreign Investment Guaranties,* U.S. Senate, Banking and Currency Committee Hearings on S. 2197, 81st Cong., 1st Sess. (Washington, 1949).

Efforts to overcome these "risks peculiar to foreign investment" have elicited three different types of proposals in the United States—none of them wholly satisfactory:[71] first, those proposals which would attack the problem by the negotiation of bilateral "investment treaties" between the recipient and investing country (the United States); second, the negotiation of multilateral "codes of fair treatment" of foreign investment; third, proposals that the United States government should offer guaranties to American private investors against loss from those risks "peculiar to foreign investments." Each group of proposals has several variants and they are not necessarily mutually exclusive—certainly the third could be combined with either the first or second, for example.

While space does not permit any adequate treatment of these three types of proposals in the present essay, it should be pointed out that they raise more complex issues than might at first appear. Furthermore, their actual efficacy in promoting a healthy and substantial flow of private international investment is problematical.

Multilateral investment codes and bilateral investment treaties may be considered together since their objectives are broadly similar, i.e., to bind the contracting parties by agreement to a specified behavior pattern in the treatment of foreign investments.[72] From one point of view these agreements are an attempt to put foreign investors on equal terms with domestic investors with respect to property rights, taxation, access to the courts, incorporation, joint participation rights, employment requirements, etc., with allowable exceptions, of course, for industries dealing with national defense or to conform with other expressions of national public policy, e.g., ownership of mineral rights only by nationals. Other clauses would deal with the transfer problem, the means and procedures for "fair and just" compensation in the event of expropriation or dispossession, etc. Alternatively, however, such agreements may be regarded as efforts to harmonize widely differing national viewpoints on economic and social policy sufficiently to induce a flow of capital investment. But if the basic preconceptions from which the contracting

---

[71] For a thoughtful discussion of this range of problems see W. A. Brown, "Treaty, Guaranty, and Tax Inducements for Foreign Investments," *Am. Econ. Rev., Proc.,* May 1950, XL, 486–94.

[72] The League of Nations in its last days received and published a report of a committee of technical experts on this topic. See, League of Nations, *Conditions of Private Foreign Investment* (Princeton, 1946). See also, International Chamber of Commerce, *Draft International Code of Fair Treatment for Foreign Investments* (Paris; no date, but believed to have been published in 1949).

governments approach the problem of foreign investment are poles apart, no consensus is likely to emerge on what constitutes "fair treatment," "confiscation," "discrimination," etc.[73]

Unfortunately, countries nowadays have markedly different conceptions of the "proper" approach to economic and social questions. Consequently, multilateral agreements on codes of fair treatment cannot now be negotiated. This impasse has led the United States government to enter upon bilateral investment treaties with Uruguay and Italy, and a new treaty of "Friendship, Commerce, and Navigation" with Colombia which is more specific on investment matters than such treaties customarily have been. Informed opinion holds that in present circumstances bilateral agreements of this type are all that can be achieved for the time being.

Proposals to guarantee private international investment against loss from those risks "peculiar to foreign investment" were first officially suggested in President Truman's "Point IV" of his inaugural address in 1949. Subsequently, a bill (S. 2197) was proposed and hearings held thereon which would have given the Export-Import Bank certain guarantee powers, but no Congressional action resulted.[74]

If the risks peculiar to foreign investment—apart from ordinary business risks—are those of transfer, confiscation, seizure, and expropriation, and, lastly, war destruction, a scheme to guarantee private investors against these risks raises a number of difficulties. For instance, what would be the limit of the guaranty and to what investments would it apply? S. 2197 used the term "productive" investments, but in the context this phrase is not self-evident in meaning. In the case of countries using multiple exchange rates, or where exchange rates altered be-

[73] This is well illustrated in the controversy over the investment provisions of the Havana Charter or the wrangling in the subcommissions of the Economic and Social Council of the United Nations. See, for example, Clair Wilcox, *A Charter for World Trade* (New York, 1949); and U.N., *Methods of Financing Economic Development*, pp. 113–28.

What the prospective borrowing countries regard as a basic, minimum protection of their fundamental sovereign rights in the treatment of foreign investments within their domain is viewed by prospective investors, resident in a country basically devoted to the principles of private property and enterprise, as virtually a denial of any protection to the foreign investor whatsoever.

[74] S. 2197, 81st Cong., 1st Sess. was to amend the Export-Import Bank Act of 1945. The proposed guaranties were restricted to "productive" investment and to those risks peculiar to investment abroad. See *Hearings on Foreign Investment Guaranties*, Senate Committee on Banking and Currency, 81st Cong., 1st Sess. (Washington, 1949). The proposal seems to have generated little enthusiasm, either in those who might have benefited from its provisions or in official government circles.

tween the time of the investment and the invoking of the guaranties, what exchange rate would be applicable? What would be the status of foreign currencies or other assets acquired by the government under the guaranty against inconvertibility? If the guaranties are to apply only to investments made subsequent to the legislation is this not unfair to those investors who earlier shouldered the risks themselves, and would not the guaranties thus subsidize those who would compete with them abroad? These and other questions are all inherent in any guaranty of private investments abroad. The proposal is not as simple and straightforward as it appears at first.[75]

Thus, little success has so far attended those efforts and proposals designed to lessen the risks of private foreign investment in the disordered world of the present day. It is generally agreed that a restoration of the free flow of private capital could be highly beneficial to lending and borrowing countries alike. But up to the present there has been little consensus on the terms and conditions on which it would move or would be allowed to enter.[76]

V. UNRESOLVED PROBLEMS IN INTERNATIONAL INVESTMENT

Notwithstanding the many international capital transfers of recent years and the considerable thought and discussion the topic has received, much of it remains in an unsettled and unsatisfactory state. Perhaps part of the difficulty lies farther afield in the still tenacious belief that there is some kind of a "normal" world from which the last two decades have been a protracted aberration, but an aberration nonetheless. But may

---

[75] See also Yuan-Li Wu, "Government Guarantees and Private Investment," *Am. Econ. Rev.*, Mar. 1950, XL, 61–73 for a discussion of other difficulties and a proposal for a new international agency for the investment of private funds abroad. Wu appears to be hopeful about the potentialities of international investment codes.

[76] Had space permitted, some attention might properly have been devoted to "clandestine capital movements" on private account in the post-World War II period. For those interested in this topic, the following may be mentioned: Lionel Robbins, "Inquest on the Crisis," *Lloyds' Bank Review*, Oct. 1947; Williams, *op. cit.*, pp. 3–19; M. L. Hoffman, "Capital Movements and International Payments in Postwar Europe," *Rev. Econ. Stat.*, Nov. 1949, XXXI, 261–65; J. H. Adler, "Clandestine Capital Movements in Balance of Payments Estimates," *Quart. Jour. Econ.*, Aug. 1950, LXIV, 477–82, and "Comment" by Florence Jaffy and "Reply" by Adler, *ibid.*, Feb. 1951, LXV, 142–47; A. O. Hirschman, "Types of Convertibility," *Rev. Econ. Stat.*, Feb. 1951, XXXIII, 60–62; R. G. D. Allen, "Note on Statistics of the Balance of Payments," *Econ. Jour.*, Mar. 1951, LXI, 179–96. Unfortunately, the very nature of these capital movements is such that all evidence concerning them will be as well hidden as possible, and therefore no reliable estimates of their amount, direction, or volatility are easily compiled.

not the kind of normality in international affairs which the world once knew—and to which it would indeed be comforting to return—have become instead the abnormal, the unusual, the occasional, the not-to-be-expected state of affairs? Perhaps the only foreseeable "normality" in international affairs is a long succession of "abnormal" situations for which imperfect solutions will have to be improvised as the occasion demands. This might be a better frame of reference than the one which seems to have so largely shaped international economic policy in recent years, namely, that if only this or that program—Bretton Woods, UNRRA, British Loan, Marshall Plan, ECA, GATT, Point IV, NATO, etc.—be carried through successfully, all will be back in normal order and should give no further trouble. This is speculation, of course, and it would be improper in an essay on international investment to push the point further: its relevance, if any, is collateral or oblique.

(1) Regardless of the foregoing, however, the political economy of international capital transfers on public account would bear more careful analysis than it has received. The causal sequence between foreign financial assistance and political change favorable to the transferring country has several weak links. Financial assistance is not an all-purpose weapon for any difficulties that block the achievement of the objectives of foreign policy. Not all political attitudes abroad have an economic base. Furthermore, foreign financial assistance can easily boomerang, with results quite the reverse of those intended. The postwar experience is not without examples. And other instances may arise in the near future when the repayment clauses in certain postwar loan agreements become operative. If the "project approach" is inadmissible in capital transfers for political ends—as it probably is—then the logic and strategy of these transfers will need to be developed considerably beyond their present crude state. Possibly, too, international good will may be a nonpurchasable commodity in foreign affairs.

Where the transfers are formalized in a loan agreement, other difficulties arise. In private loans the creditor acquires certain contingent rights which become operative in the event of nonperformance by the debtor. There is an established procedure for settling differences through the courts. And if worse comes to worst the settlement proceeds through bankruptcy to liquidation. In all events, the obligation can be ultimately liquidated according to legal procedures understood and accepted by both parties from the outset. There is no such recognized procedure for intergovernmental loans. In the event of nonperformance or nonpayment, the lending government can only open "negotiations" with the borrowing government which may drag on for many years with little result beyond growing animosity and resentment. These are important difficulties in intergovernmental loans for political ends and they remain unresolved.

None of the foregoing is to suggest that international capital transfers on public account have no proper place in the contemporary world. The prospects are for more rather than fewer transfers of this type. But if so, the relation between ends and means in such transfers needs further study, and perhaps the machinery for handling negotiations between the parties needs overhauling.

(2) One of the most vexing problems still on the agenda is to resolve the disputes concerning the role of foreign capital in economic development. Countries intent on economic development generally hold views which diverge widely from those current either in the International Bank or in countries in a position to make capital available for the purpose. Apart from the simple fact that the International Bank and the prospective creditor countries are currently making available much smaller sums than the countries seeking development believe to be their due, there are several genuine problems which warrant careful study.

First among these is that of developing some basic principles concerning the role of foreign capital in economic development. In reality this is a congeries of problems with numerous interrelations. For instance, what proportion of the total investment for economic development can safely come from abroad? The balance-of-payments problem has been analyzed with useful results.[77] But beyond this are such problems as whether some industries or some types of undertakings are more suitable for foreign financing than others and, if so, what are the applicable criteria. Again, if foreign capital is to provide some portion of the investment, what are the relative merits of the "project approach" and the general assistance approach? Finally, if the investing country holds to certain economic beliefs, e.g., concerning the proper sphere of public and private enterprise in economic development, should it then insist that these be recognized as a condition of granting loans or credits?

Secondly, starting from the assumption that capital imports for economic development are both desired and desirable, what are the

---

[77] J. J. Polak, "Balance of Payments Problems of Countries Reconstructing with the Help of Foreign Loans," *Quart. Jour. Econ.*, Feb. 1943, LVII, 208–40. But see the critical article by A. E. Kahn (dealing with Polak's article and some efforts of the present writer) entitled, "Investment Criteria in Development Programs," *ibid.*, Feb. 1951, LXV, 38–61.

means and devices by which foreign assistance can best be rendered? For example, in what circumstances and for what purposes are outright grants preferable to loans? The meaning of the word loan has become thoroughly blurred in recent years, while in official circles the line between a credit and a grant or gift must be wobbly indeed. Yet it is hard to believe that in the long run desirable results will flow from such loose distinctions. Is it not possible to distinguish the circumstances and purposes for which loans are appropriate from those calling for outright grants? Lastly, where does assistance in kind, technical or other, stand in relation to loans or grants?

Third among the unresolved problems of international investment for purposes of economic development is the question of how far should the donor or lending country emphasize the international aspects of the development schemes of the countries to which it makes capital transfers. Each individual national development plan may be well conceived if considered in isolation. But a number of countries working separately may evolve development plans which, in the aggregate, are incompatible or mutually contradictory. Unless the countries transferring capital for purposes of aiding economic development are indifferent as between autarchical tendencies and promoting a viable world economic system, they must presumably go beyond the individual country approach to economic development problems. From the long-term point of view, there is little merit in making capital transfers to developing countries if they are likely to develop in directions that make continued outside assistance indispensable. Yet, any firm insistence on these points is almost certain to evoke the familiar charge that capital assistance from the more industrialized countries is inevitably accompanied by political interference.

Part III, B of this essay drew attention to the divergent views, between developed countries and those intent on development, on the general pattern such development should follow and the means to its achievement. These differences have been brought into sharper focus recently over the world-wide shortage of raw materials and primary products.

Evidence accumulates that various factors—the spread of industry geographically, the revival of European industrial production, defense and war-preparedness programs, and the general tendency of durable goods consumption to show striking increases—are pushing up the demand for raw materials and primary products at a rate that is alarming in comparison with existing sources of supply. If so, the aspirations of the underdeveloped countries and the needs of the rest of the world come directly in conflict: the industrialized countries need more minerals, fibers, oils, and foods and need them quickly; the underdeveloped countries are no less convinced that this is *not* the kind of development they want and that the exploitation of their natural resources by foreign capital will bring them more harm than good. Does this mean, unless matters are to reach an impasse, that some new means must be devised which will allow both the industrialized and underdeveloped countries to satisfy their requirements, at least in part, and what kind of international investment arrangements does this call for? Finally, if international investment, even if wisely and generously applied, can only slowly solve the raw material shortage as new sources of supply are discovered and brought into production, so that a shortage still persists, what new problems are then posed, and can capital transfers help solve them? Perhaps by the time this essay appears in print, the economists associated with the President's Raw Material Policy Commission will have come up with some answers.

COMMENT

Ragnar Nurkse

A recent criticism of the "traditional" type of international investment, put forward by H. W. Singer,[78] suggests a question which the preceding essay, while presenting very fairly the broad issues involved, does not explicitly discuss. Why is it that private business investment abroad has tended in the past—in the last few years as well as in the nineteenth century—to concentrate on primary production for export and to keep away from industries working for the domestic market in economically backward areas? The obvious explanation is the poverty of the local consumers. The inducement to invest is limited by the size of the market, as Allyn Young[79] suggested in his reinterpretation of Adam Smith's famous thesis. The size of the market, in its turn, is determined by productivity; and productivity is largely a result of the application

---

[78] "The Distribution of Gains between Investing and Borrowing Countries," *Am. Econ. Rev., Proc.,* May 1950, XL, 473–85.

[79] "Increasing Returns and Economic Progress," *Econ. Jour.,* Dec. 1928, XXXVIII, 527–42; also in *Readings in Economic Analysis,* R. V. Clemence, ed. (Cambridge, Mass., 1950), Vol. I.

of capital. But the incentive to apply capital is limited by the size of the market, and so the circle—some call it vicious—is complete.

What can be done to enlarge the market? Although in backward areas Say's Law may be generally valid, it never is valid in the sense that the output of any single industry, set up by foreign capital, can create its own demand. The expansion of the market can be realized only through a process of balanced growth, whereby people in different industries, working with more and better tools, become each others' customers.[80] An individual foreign investor may not have the inducement, or even the power, to break the deadlock formed by low productivity, lack of real buying power, and inadequate investment incentives. The doctrine of balanced growth leaves plenty of room for international investment, but there is no guarantee that, even if we abstract from political and other risk factors, the motives that guide individual investors and entrepreneurs will induce an automatic flow of funds from the rich to the poor countries. The marginal productivity of capital in the latter, compared with the former, may be high indeed, but not necessarily in private business terms.

Private investment is attracted by markets, and for the poorer countries the big markets in the past were the markets for export to the great industrial centers. Foreign investment in extractive industries working for export is not to be despised, since it brings with it various direct or indirect benefits. Why is even this type of investment now flowing out in only a small trickle? Aside, again, from political impediments, perhaps a part of the answer is that the export markets for primary commodities are not enjoying the same rate of secular expansion as that which came about in the nineteenth century from the extraordinary growth of population as well as productivity in the Western industrial countries, and also from Britain's willingness to sacrifice her own agriculture to the requirements of international specialization. Synthetic substitutes in recent decades have affected unfavorably the demand for a number of staple products. The present (1951) raw material boom is widely regarded as being due to special circumstances which may not last.

Thus the theory of international investment on private business account boils down, in the main, to an attempt to explain, not why capital moves, but why it does not move.

It may be worth noting, however, that the direct business investments on which so much reliance is now being placed, for the financing

---

[80] See P. N. Rosenstein-Rodan, "Problems of Industrialization," *loc. cit.*, p. 205.

of economic development abroad, were not predominant even in the heyday of private foreign investment. Of Britain's total overseas investments outstanding in 1914, 30 per cent was in loans to governmental authorities, 40 per cent in railway securities, and 5 per cent in public utilities.[81] This does not leave any major proportion for the strictly "colonial" type of investments in mines and plantations producing for export, which are often, but with questionable accuracy, taken to be typical of foreign investment before 1914. Hence the use of inverted commas in the first line of this comment.

This is not in contradiction with Buchanan's essay, which does not enter into the more distant past of international investment. It seemed best to use this space for one or two supplementary notes on matters ably set forth in the essay.

COMMENT
John H. Williams

A survey of international investment presents a task of unusual difficulty when, in a single paper, one undertakes to review the facts, the literature, the lessons for theory and policy, and the large unsettled questions. Buchanan has handled very judiciously the problems of selection and emphasis involved. Though the essays in this volume are primarily "to serve the needs of economists who are not themselves specialists in the field," this essay should provoke further thinking by the specialists. Particularly good is the last section on "unresolved problems," but throughout the essay one has the feeling that the writer is animated by a spirit of pioneering in new areas of economic policy, which do not admit of the oversimplifications to which systematic theory all too readily lends itself. By its premises, classical international trade theory was ill equipped to deal with international investment. It was static equilibrium analysis, which rarely got beyond "trade adjustment" and the "transfer problem," and failed to deal with the processes of growth and change. This emphasis was carried further by Keynesian economics, with its "closed economy" assumptions and its goal of full employment through

---

[81] Herbert Feis, *Europe, the World's Banker, 1870–1914* (New Haven, 1930), p. 27. The total is incomplete, but even with allowance for this, the percentages given would not be significantly lowered.

internal policy, protected by direct external controls, exchange-rate variations, and the like.

Part I is an excellent survey of the impact of Keynesian economics on international investment theory and policy, as worked out, not by Keynes himself, but by his disciples. Buchanan's treatment is well balanced. I like his reservations on (as well as his praise of) Metzler's essay; his commonsense treatment of some of the more extravagant of the leverage studies—how foreign investment can support home employment; and his remarks on the great riddle of internal-external adjustments—how to combine full employment with an internationally viable economy. Perhaps most people would now agree that the classical economists insisted too much upon adjustability of supply, and particularly internal adjustability to external change; but surely Keynesian economics has unduly simplified the problem by its emphasis on "effective demand," as a sort of mechanical cure-all, implying, as Buchanan says, "adjustment abroad but not at home," or foreign credits (or grants?) "to maintain the internal *status quo*."

One of the most difficult parts of the task was to present in short compass an adequate survey of postwar developments. This is admirably done, particularly in the section on "nonprivate capital transfers in the postwar period." It is of course difficult to make appraisals without more historical perspective. I agree with Buchanan that the Marshall Plan experience, though probably exceeding expectations as to industrial expansion, still leaves a large question as to whether (pre-Korea) it was achieving its fundamental purpose of creating a viable Western Europe. Certainly no "integration" or "coordination of investment" has been achieved, and even the progress toward "liberalization of trade and payment" within Western Europe has been limited and precarious. Now Korea and the rearmament program raise new questions, create new inflationary pressures, worsen terms of trade, and increase balance-of-payments deficits.

I can select only one further topic. In his last section, and also in the earlier discussion of underdeveloped countries, Buchanan shows awareness of what I increasingly feel to be the dominant problem of international investment in our time—a problem closely related to the viability of Western Europe, the future of underdeveloped countries, and our own role as creditor country. Even before Korea, there was developing a change in the world relation between industrial output and primary production. Industrial output has increased (pre-Korea) 50 per cent above prewar, while raw materials (except petroleum and aluminum) are scarcely above prewar, and according to some estimates, food supply (outside the United States) has declined. One contributing factor has been the increased level of industrial output in Europe, but a main cause has been the expansion here; before the war we consumed a third of the world's metals, and now (pre-Korea) a half. One important question may be whether the expansibility of industrial output in more advanced countries is so much greater than that of primary production by techniques applicable in less developed countries that this gap will continue to widen.

This world imbalance, reversing the relations of the preceding three-quarters of a century, comes while sharply divergent views are developing, as between borrowing and lending countries, on the purposes of international investment (or grants). In addition to resolving this divergence, we must, as Buchanan says, plan international investment as a whole with a view to seeing that the parts fit together to create a better balanced world. As part of such planning we may need to think not only of our role as foreign investor but also of the implications for our own internal production pattern. We may well be faced with the need for a kind of international sharing that goes beyond the mere making of loans and grants into questions of how the composition of our production and trade can promote a more stable world.

NATIONAL ECONOMIC PLANNING

9

Paul A. Baran

The two decades that constitute the proximate frame of reference of the present—necessarily sketchy—survey have witnessed a truly spectacular growth of practical and theoretic endeavors in the field of economic planning.

In the socialist sector of the world—the USSR, the countries of eastern and southeastern Europe and China—economic planning has developed (or is developing) into the effectively controlling principle of economic organization. In the advanced capitalist West, doctrines of economic planning have largely displaced earlier concepts of economic liberalism and exercise a powerful influence upon economic policies and economic thought. In backward capitalist areas, planning is increasingly accepted as the indispensable tool of economic progress.

Tempting as it would be to examine the causes and ramifications of this far-reaching social and intellectual development, the present account must confine itself to a brief report on a few of its salient features —leaving aside many important aspects of the planning problem as well as foregoing the discussion of the profound crisis of the capitalist order to which the ascendance of economic planning appears to be the historical response.

In what follows, Part I will consider planning for full employment under advanced capitalism; Part II, planning for economic growth under backward capitalism; and Part III, planning under socialism.

I. PLANNING UNDER ADVANCED CAPITALISM

A. The Background

1. *The Neoclassical Dilemma.* Although "from the time of the physiocrats and Adam Smith there has never been absent from the main

body of economic literature the feeling that in some sense perfect competition represented the optimum solution,"[1] serious doubts about the reliability of the "invisible hand" have disturbed not only John Stuart Mill, but even the more complacent Marshall, Wicksell, and Pigou (to name only the most outstanding).

One deep discomfort arose from the realization that the distribution of wealth was such that even if earnings were in accordance with the marginal productivity theory, perfect competition would yield anything but an optimum distribution of income (and optimum allocation of resources). The other was caused by the divergence of social and private utilities, or—using the apt formulation of Max Weber—by the discrepancy between private and social rationalities that characterizes even the construct of perfect competition.

Troublesome as these faults were, matters were even worse in the real world with which "perfect competition" had never had much in common. There the growth of monopoly, immobilities and indivisibilities of factors, inequalities of bargaining positions and opportunities, political and economic privileges of all sorts, accounted for economic (and social) results that were greatly at variance with what one might have expected on the basis of a study of the mirage of perfect competition.

The way out of this perplexity was seen by the neoclassical writers in a moderate amount of government intervention. To quote Samuelson again ". . . [they] recognize[d] that in these circumstances any interference (à la Robin Hood) with perfect competition which transfers income from rich to poor would be beneficial."[2] Also, interference that would aim at the elimination or reduction of monopoly or at some rectification of the neglect of social rationality by the private enterprise system, such as building of public schools, hospitals, and the like, would have been regarded by the neoclassical economists as, on the whole, desirable.

Yet their professed sympathy for social reform and public regulation was essentially alien to the main body of their thought. Resting upon the assumption of full employment of resources, the reasoning of the neoclassical school left little room for changes in prevailing institu-

---

[1] P. A. Samuelson, *Foundations of Economic Analysis* (Cambridge, Mass., 1947), p. 203.

[2] *Ibid.,* p. 206. However: "It is the part of responsible men to proceed cautiously and tentatively in abrogating or modifying even such rights as may seem to be inappropriate to the ideal conditions of social life." Alfred Marshall, *Principles of Economics* (London, 1890; 8th ed., 1921), p. 48.

tions. The only way in which the poor could become better off was through increased productivity that under competitive conditions would raise real wages. Otherwise there was little or nothing that could be done to improve their wretched position. Unless benefits for the poor were to be obtained by a redistribution of income *among the poor themselves* (which would be patently beside the point and possibly even detrimental by disturbing wage differentials that were assigned an important function in the allocation of resources), such benefits could only be secured by reducing the share of total real income accruing to the rich in form of profits, rent, and interest. Since the propensity of the rich to plow back their earnings into productive enterprise was regarded as sufficiently bolstered by the forces of competition and the puritan injunction to thrift, any reduction of the income going to them was expected to cause a diminution of the "surplus" available for investment, as well as of the incentives to invest on the part of the capitalist class. As a result, economic progress would necessarily slow down, and the picayune improvements of the lot of the poor that possibly could be secured by redistributive measures would be more than offset by the subsequent retardation of the growth of output and real income.

Placed against the background of this "iron law" of basic economic interrelationships,[3] the advocacy of governmental intervention had inevitably a hollow sound. It reflected the anxieties of the small businessman helplessly watching the rise of his large-scale rival, it expressed the bewilderment of the common man whose daily experiences hardly tallied with the optimism of a Bastiat or a J. B. Clark, it served as an indication of the noble sentiments and high ethical standards of its protagonists—but also as a testimonial of their starry-eyed disregard for the elementary principles of sound economics.[4] This is where the matter

---

[3] Cf. A. C. Pigou, "Some Aspects of Welfare Economics," *Am. Econ. Rev.*, June 1951, XLI, in particular 301–02.

[4] Even so, it represented a threat to dominant interests by supplying ammunition to social reform movements and by encouraging the development of trade unions. It was left to Pareto, who was contemplating social reality not through the looking glass of English moral philosophy but from the more austere position of a "disinterested" aristocratic observer, to formalize an attitude that expressed adequately the monopolistic answer to the Mill-Marshall-Pigou "revolt of the middle classes." By repudiating the validity of interpersonal comparisons of utility, Pareto purged political economy of all the reform implications disturbing the British (and German) economists. As it was impossible (in his opinion) to make any scientific statements concerning cardinal utility, any judgment on distribution of wealth and income became to him an ethical value proposition beyond the realm of economic science. Taking from the rich and giving to the poor became nothing that could be recommended by economics, since even the notion "rich" and "poor" lost meaning in the Pareto frame of reference. What appeared as common sense to Smith,

rested for a number of relatively harmonious decades that witnessed an unprecedented economic growth of the Western world. The advances attained overshadowed the stupendous price that had to be paid for progress[5]—the criticisms of the competitive process could be countered by pointing to its readily observable triumphs.

Yet towards the end of this exceptional epoch an old malignant disease began assuming major proportions. To be sure, large unemployment had existed in earlier phases of the capitalist age; it was not until the twenties of our century, however, that in conjunction with other social and political developments it became a powerful threat to the continuity of the existing social order.

2. *"The New Economics."* It was in an attempt to face the urgent issue of unemployment that The New Economics[6] of J. M. Keynes laid the foundations for planning for full employment under capitalism. Its central insight is actually very simple. It repudiates Say's Law, and recognizes as the outstanding characteristic of the capitalist process—as Karl Marx did some eighty years earlier—the absence in the market automatism of a "built-in" mechanism keeping aggregate effective demand on a level requisite for the maintenance of full employment.

In the absence of any such mechanism, the state has to assume responsibility, when unemployment develops, for measures calculated to raise aggregate effective demand to a level compatible with full utilization of human resources. Should private investment under full-employment conditions (once they are reached) decline below the level of intended savings, the state should stand ready to take such steps as may be called for to offset the deficiency in private spending.

That is, however, where the role of the state (and economic planning under capitalism) end. Once the necessary steps are taken to assure the attainment and the maintenance of full employment, traditional economics comes back into its own. Only to the extent to which great inequalities of income and misallocation of resources stand in the way of promoting high levels of income and employment, should govern-

---

Ricardo, Mill, Marshall, Pigou—not to speak of the uninstructed man in the street—turned out to be a nonscientific ethical preference, with the economist's preference counting no more than anyone else's. Schumpeter completed the structure by rationalizing and glorifying monopoly.

[5] Cf. Paul Mantoux, *The Industrial Revolution in the Eighteenth Century* (London, 1928), as well as Friedrich Engels, *The Condition of the Working Classes in England* (London, 1920).

[6] This is the title of a useful collection of papers related to Keynesian economics edited by S. E. Harris (New York, 1947).

mental economic planning be concerned with income distribution and resource allocation. Keynes sees "no reason to suppose that the existing system seriously misemploys the factors of production which are in use. . . . It is in determining the volume, not the direction of actual employment that the existing system has broken down."[7]

B. The Tool Box

The state can attempt to fulfill its functions in a number of alternative ways. Yet, whichever way is chosen, the indispensable prerequisite of an active participation of the government in the process of determination of the level of income and employment is the ability to prognosticate more or less accurately the behavior of various economic aggregates exercising an important influence on the level of business activity in a capitalist economy. The analytical tools provided by Keynes and the economists following his lead appeared to render such prognostication feasible.

The most important among them is the concept of the consumption function relating aggregate spending on consumers' goods and services to national income. This relationship was treated as fairly stable, thus permitting the isolation of the volume of currently intended savings.[8] Such confidence as there was in the stability of the consumption function was, however, severely shaken during the last decade. The postwar experience has drawn attention to the level of accumulation or decumulation of assets as a powerful determinant of the volume of consumers' expenditure.[9]

An even more trenchant argument questions the usefulness of the

---

[7] J. M. Keynes, *The General Theory of Employment Interest and Money* (New York, 1936), p. 379. Cf., however, on p. 157: "There is no clear evidence from experience that the investment policy which is socially advantageous coincides with that which is most profitable."

[8] From the original $C = C(Y)$ the expression changed to $C = C(Y - B - W)$ where B stands for withholdings of income payments to individuals on the part of business, while W represents the net withdrawings of income on the part of the government (tax collection less transfer payments). Should both B and W be regarded themselves as functions of the size of GNP and the above relationship accordingly rewritten $C = C[Y - B(Y) - W(Y)]$ the original concept of the consumption function would be restored— although deprived of its original simplicity. It is questionable, however, whether B and W can be properly regarded as functions of GNP or whether their behavior is more or less independent of changes in GNP. Cf. P. A. Samuelson, "Simple Mathematics of Income Determination," *Income, Employment and Public Policy, Essays in Honor of Alvin H. Hansen* (New York, 1948), pp. 133–55.

[9] Cf. E. E. Hagen, "The Reconversion Period: Reflections of a Forecaster," *Rev. Econ. Stat.*, May 1947, XXIX, 95 ff., as well as the literature referred to therein.

entire concept. It was pointed out that the "community's propensity to consume"[10] has little to do with the choice as between consumption and saving. The overwhelming majority of the population, even in countries as rich as the United States, save a negligible part of their income, and —what is even more important—of total savings accumulated by the nation.[11] Thus under conditions of full employment *all* personal savings constitute only a small part of total savings, and savings from what some tax laws define as "earned income" an almost negligible part.[12] The bulk of the savings that have to be offset by intended investment if full employment is to be maintained consists of *business savings* and of such savings as are directly influenced by corporate profits and corporate decisions concerning dividends.[13] In other words—even if it were established that the "propensity to consume" schedule is stable enough to yield a predictable relationship of consumption to disposable income—this relationship would account only for a fraction of total savings.[14] The remainder depends on the depreciation-reserves-dividends-spending decisions of boards of directors, decisions that cannot be very well attributed to the working of some general psychological laws—in any case very "unreliable customers in economics," to use Schumpeter's expression.[15]

---

[10] This is, in itself, a rather misleading notion inasmuch as it places the "responsibility" for any given allocation of income as between consumption and saving (and therefore indirectly for any given level of employment) on society at large rather than on that class in society that is in the position to make decisions in regard to saving or consumption.

[11] Cf. Moses Abramovitz, "Savings and Investment: Profits *vs.* Prosperity," *Am. Econ. Rev.,* June 1942 (Suppl.), XXXII, 56; for the postwar period: Council of Economic Advisers, "The Annual Economic Review," *The Economic Report of the President* (Washington, 1951), App. B, p. 223; and, J. N. Morgan, "The Structure of Aggregate Personal Saving," *Jour. Pol. Econ.,* Dec. 1951, LIX, 528 ff.

[12] This is even more pertinent if the analysis refers not to the United States or Great Britain but to the rest of the world where the savings of the "public" are altogether negligible, where virtually all the savings are accumulated by business, and possibly landowning, interests.

[13] This point is stressed in an unpublished paper, "An Analysis of Retained Business Receipts," by Lorie Tarshis. Cf. *Surv. Curr. Bus.,* July 1950, XXX, 10, Table 5— making due allowance, of course, for the years of the war when special conditions boosted individual savings.

[14] It is interesting that the most outstanding recent work on the consumption function—*Income, Saving and the Theory of Consumer Behavior,* by J. S. Duesenberry (Cambridge, Mass., 1949)—nowhere even mentions that what it is dealing with is nothing but this small share of what has to be offset by investment if full employment is to be maintained.

[15] Schumpeter goes too far when he maintains that " . . . of course, practically all business savings which in turn, constitute the greater part of total savings—is done with a specific investment purpose in view," since some of it may be done for speculative pur-

Yet there is very little light that The New Economics sheds on what determines business expenditures. Accounting for investment goods (including construction) as well as for inventories and gross exports, this sector of aggregate demand is treated as an independent rather than dependent force in the process of income generation.[16] A certain, presumably small, part of it is regarded as "induced" by changes in income, but the bulk of it is looked upon in Keynesian writings as "autonomous," i.e., as motivated not by *actual* variations in income and demand but by *anticipations* of future changes in aggregate demand, in the demand for particular products, or expected changes in the relation between prices and costs.

Although some progress has been achieved by government agencies (Securities and Exchange Commission and U.S. Department of Commerce) as well as by some private organizations in polling business about its investment plans, not much reliance can yet be placed upon such surveys. "To great extent we still rely today largely on hunches and anticipation of other people's behavior, just as the forecasters did before Keynes' writing."[17]

With the predictions concerning personal and business expenditures based thus on highly tenuous estimates, the decisions concerning governmental revenues and outlays are derived from little more than "enlightened guesses." The fiscal authorities are not even able to gauge reliably the impact of their own actions (more or less spending or taxing) on aggregate income since the magnitude of the multiplier obviously depends on the relationships just referred to.

The foregoing may be fully accepted by an advocate of governmental planning for full employment. Granting that the government's ability to prognosticate adequately the behavior of the relevant economic aggregates is deficient, and that therefore planning for government intervention cannot go beyond groping for the right set of measures at any given time, he may abandon the ambition to "plan" for periods longer

---

poses or in order to assure a steady flow of dividend payments. J. A. Schumpeter, *Capitalism, Socialism and Democracy* (New York and London, 1942; 3rd ed., 1947), p. 395.

[16] "The 'blade' of investment carves out economic fortune; the 'blade' of the propensity to consume remains stationary while the carving is done." A. F. Burns, "Keynesian Economics Once Again," *Rev. Econ. Stat.*, Nov. 1947, XXIX, in particular p. 262.

[17] Gerhard Colm, "Fiscal Policy," *The New Economics*, p. 461. Needless to say, the part of business demand that is linked to foreign trade is, if anything, even less predictable, dependent as it is not on domestic conditions but on the still less tractable developments in foreign countries.

than a few months and take the position that a "flexible" fiscal policy accompanied by other "flexible" arrangements is all that is needed to achieve the substance of the desired result. As suggested by the authors of *National and International Measures for Full Employment,*[18] whenever unemployment should reach certain predetermined magnitudes, inflationary measures would be called for; whenever the price index rises to some agreed-upon level, deflationary measures would be in order. It is held that with sufficiently rapid reactions on the part of the authorities, in particular if such rapid reactions could be presumed by the public on the basis of experience, employment could be maintained on a stable and satisfactory level.

C. The Application

Yet the acceptance of this principle or, for that matter, even the availability of a sufficiently powerful forecasting apparatus in the hands of the government does not per se indicate the specific policies that may be adopted to promote and sustain full employment. Recognizing that aggregate demand tends to be insufficient to provide a market for full employment output (at given prices), the government can embark upon a variety of programs for the expansion of investment, consumption, or both.

(1) While certain nonfiscal measures may be taken in order to improve business conditions, governmental planning for full employment is associated primarily with fiscal policy. The government may seek to expand aggregate effective demand by a reduction of taxes. The effectiveness of this procedure, occasionally dubbed "deficit without spending," is predicated upon the condition that the governmental deficit thus incurred be large enough to make up, in conjunction with the multiplier effect, the deficiency in aggregate effective demand.

If the marginal propensity to spend should prove to be low, the requisite deficit may assume major proportions—may in fact exceed the entire normal expenditure budget of the government.[19]

(2) The disposable income in the hands of individuals and businesses may be expanded by an *increase of government expenditures.*

---

[18] United Nations Group of Experts (Lake Success, 1949).

[19] For a brief and simple presentation of this and other variants of fiscal policy see A. H. Hansen, "Three Methods of Expansion through Fiscal Policy," *Am. Econ. Rev.,* June 1945, XXXV, 382–87. For a masterful analysis of the implications of the alternative methods see Michal Kalecki, "Three Ways to Full Employment," *Economics of Full Employment* (Oxford, 1944), pp. 39 ff., as well as Nicholas Kaldor's App. B to William Beveridge, *Full Employment in a Free Society* (New York, 1945).

Such an increase may be financed through higher taxes,[20] through governmental borrowing, or through printing of new money.

(*a*) *"Leaf-Raking."* This kind of expenditure is by definition not associated with any purchase of useful objects on the part of the government. Digging ditches or building pyramids are the examples of this kind of governmental outlays used by Keynes, and they illustrate adequately the nature of the spending involved.

(*b*) *"Social Service Investment."* In this case the government acquires for the amounts spent *useful objects* such as schools, hospitals, parks, and roads. Their distinguishing feature is that the services that they render either do not enter the market at all, or if they so enter do not normally compete in the market with goods and services produced by private business. An important limitation of spending programs (*a*) and (*b*) is that their scope is limited by the potential of the construction (and related) industries. To be sure, this potential may be expanded, but such expansion may be difficult in the short run in view of the immobility of various factors, and moreover, may be irrational in terms of social priorities.

(*c*) *Foreign Aid.* In their effect on *domestic* real income, direct governmental purchases of goods and services for shipment abroad or giving money to foreigners for purchases of domestic products are identical with the type of spending under (*a*).

(*d*) *Military Spending.* While obvious political arguments may justify it, it combines the negative features of both "routes" (*a*) and (*b*).

(*e*) *Investment in Productive Enterprise.* Of all forms of governmental spending, this one would involve governmental economic planning that goes far beyond attempts at anticipation and compensation of short-run aggregate demand deficiencies. It would call for active participation of government in the determination not only of the volume of new investment but of its direction as well. Accordingly, it would require governmental operation of productive plant and facilities. For successful implementation of such economic policy, the government would have to possess advance information on the specific investment plans of private business so as to be able to arrive at appropriate deci-

---

[20] The "balanced budget" or the "unit multiplier" methods are of almost exclusively theoretical interest. If the deficiency in aggregate demand that is to be offset is at all large, the adoption of this strategy would require an exorbitant level of taxation. See the excellent summary of the argument in Samuelson, "Simple Mathematics," *op. cit.,* as well as the literature cited therein.

sions in regard to its own investment projects. It would have to be guided in its investment policies by its own knowledge of existing or potential technological improvements, as well as by its own estimates of future demand.[21] It frequently would have to "invade" fields in which investment is curbed by prevailing monopolistic controls, and would have to operate in other fields in which investment is lacking in view of insufficient attractiveness of profit prospects to private interests (low-cost housing, for example).

The "complementarity" of this approach undoubtedly entails considerable difficulties. The government's decision to invest in a certain industry could not properly be made without certainty about private undertakings in that area. Private investors in their turn would have to weigh possible governmental operations as one of the major factors determining the profitability of a departure. If expectations of monopolistic profits—at least for a certain period—constitute a propelling force of new private investment, the ever-present danger of governmental engagement in the same line of output may well become an important deterrent to private venture. If plowing back of profits by existing firms is predicated upon their ability to maintain certain market and price structures, the threat of governmental "undercutting" may well paralyze the expansion or maintenance of privately owned facilities.

The resulting decay of the "capitalist climate" and of the capitalists' willingness to invest may progressively increase the aggregate investment deficiency and force a corresponding expansion of government investment, if full employment is to be preserved. Not that the only way of offsetting a lack of private investment is governmental *investment*. As pointed out by Kalecki,[22] "both public and private investment should be carried out only to the extent to which they are considered useful. If the effective demand thus generated fails to provide full employment, the gap should be filled by increasing consumption and not by piling up unwanted public or private capital equipment." Yet it is not unlikely that in the foreseeable future in most capitalist countries, the alternative to insufficient private investment would have to be expanded governmental investment rather than increased consumption. In that case an "investment strike" on the part of business, accompanied possibly by a shrinkage even of existing productive enterprises, may force the govern-

---

[21] This is not to suggest that such demand would have to be exclusively "guessed"; the government's plans of its own future activities may influence the nature of further demand.

[22] *Op. cit.*, p. 53.

ment to nationalize the declining industries in order to maintain or to expand them according to requirements.

(*f*) *Spending on Consumption.* "Investment dollars are high-powered dollars. Consumption dollars are, too."[23] An expansion of income and employment can also be secured by governmental sponsorship of private or collective consumption. The only requirement for this kind of spending to result in a relatively large increase in total income and employment is that the initial beneficiaries should be people with a high marginal propensity to spend. Schemes such as food stamp plans and free school lunches for children aim at the fulfillment of this requirement. If satisfaction of collective rather than individual wants is to be preferred, this approach may partly merge with the one outlined under (*b*).

This type of spending is clearly preferable to public works of the (*a*) variety. It may even be more advantageous than financing of productive investment, if—as mentioned above—such investment should be considered redundant. Wherever urgent investment remains unattended to because of its insufficient appeal to private business, this type of spending on current consumption may be a luxury that a nation attempting to utilize its resources rationally could ill afford.

D. The Obstacles

The methods thus briefly listed differ among one another in their short-run efficiency and in their impact on long-run economic development. The goal of full employment may be attainable at some cost by each and all of them. It should be borne in mind, however, that the approach outlined in the preceding sections applies only to advanced capitalist countries where unemployment of manpower caused by insufficiency of aggregate demand is accompanied by underutilization of plant and equipment. Where this is not the case, as in less developed countries, where the human unemployment is not "Keynesian" but "structural" or "disguised," the planning authorities face altogether different problems. We shall come to this aspect of the matter in Part II.

But even with respect to highly industrialized countries, fiscal policy does not represent a simple cure of underemployment. The difficulty, if not impossibility, of prognostication of the measure of the aggregate demand deficiency is an obvious cause of possible excessive governmental spending—and of inflationary effects of a full-employment policy.

---

[23] Samuelson, "Simple Mathematics," *op. cit.,* p. 137.

Also, shortages of certain products, as well as increases in monopoly power appearing under full-employment conditions (or even before full employment is reached) are likely to generate inflationary pressures. The resulting rises in the cost of living and trade union demands for higher money wages are bound to give new turns to the inflationary spiral.

Needless to say, full employment accompanied by inflation is neither a stable nor a tolerable state of affairs. Undermining the possibility of rational calculation, generating a state of permanent uncertainty, progressively depleting the working capital stocks of enterprises, continuous inflation endangers the entire elaborate credit structure of the capitalist economy and creates a dangerous cleavage between debtors and creditors.

The inflationary concomitants of a fiscal policy directed toward the attainment and *maintenance* of full employment thus present the planner for full employment with a rather unpleasant dilemma: either giving up the full-employment goal and being content with considerably less than full employment or else adopting appropriate fiscal policy measures and supplementing them with a battery of physical controls and governmental administrative interventions.

This indeed is a Hobson's choice. The former course implies the abandonment by the protagonists of planning for full employment of their basic claim that *full* employment can be attained and maintained within the capitalist system. The latter alternative involves political and social problems that are crucial to the entire concept of planning for full employment—that are, however, largely neglected in the literature of The New Economics.

What is at issue is the theory of the state. As mentioned above, the Keynesian concept of economic planning is based on the identification of the state with "society as a whole," of governmental action with *volonté générale.* In this thinking—developed perhaps most explicitly by A. P. Lerner—the government is seen as an essentially neutral *instrumentality* that can be employed for the furthering of the interests of the "public," the "community," or whatever other term may be used to designate the rather undifferentiated sum total of inhabitants of a given country that constitutes "society" in the liberal frame of reference.[24]

The only hurdles that are to be overcome are stupidity and ignorance. "The effects that the government should consider are primarily

---

[24] To be sure, this view of the state is fully compatible with the recognition of the existence of so-called "pressure groups" that play such a prominent role in political science literature. Yet the very notion of the "pressure group" presupposes the existence of some neutral entity upon which the pressure is being exerted.

the effects on the *public* in whose interests the government is supposed to be acting. . . ."[25]

This abstract notion of the role of the state in the socio-economic process is, however, hardly a fruitful hypothesis for adequate comprehension and prediction of actual behavior of government. This attitude, treating all social and political matters as a "frightful muddle" (J. M. Keynes), ignores the paramount importance of the *interests* of the class exercising a controlling influence in society, excluding thus from consideration of social and economic development all its essence and all its propelling forces.

To be sure, class interests in general and the interests of the ruling class in particular do not prescribe unique courses of action in every given situation. Nor are the contents and precise definition of these interests always certain.[26] Still, to use Robbins' apt distinction, the "objective" interests are on the whole ascertainable, even if the "subjective" interests are frequently moot.[27] The dissolution of this dichotomy, the raising of the subjective appraisals of interests to the level of comprehension of their objective contents, may be all the "amplitude of freedom" that is left to rational argument in social and economic matters. That this "amplitude of freedom" is very narrow and that it is *without* rather than *within* its confines where the causes of all important economic and political departures are to be sought, is perhaps *the* most important insight gained thus far by social science.[28]

One need not go far in the acceptance of any particular theory of

---

[25] A. P. Lerner, "An Integrated Full Employment Policy," *Planning and Paying for Full Employment,* A. P. Lerner and F. D. Graham, ed. (Princeton, 1946), p. 164. Or ". . . private enterprise and public enterprise are both useful instruments for serving the public welfare, and . . . the issue between them is best resolved in each particular instance by the pragmatic economic test of which is able to operate more efficiently" (A. P. Lerner, "Foreign Economic Relations of the United States," *Saving American Capitalism,* S. E. Harris, ed. (New York, 1948), p. 279)—as if both private and public enterprise were engaged in a contest of performance with an impartial and disinterested arbiter handing down the verdict. While the naïve rationalism of this writer was neither fully shared by J. M. Keynes nor is entirely acceptable to the more responsible representatives of the Keynesian school, it expresses adequately the basic attitude underlying the entire approach.

[26] The usually striking divergence of long-run and short-run interests may by itself give rise to considerable doubts as to what *actually* promotes the best interests of a social class in a concrete historical constellation.

[27] Lionel Robbins, *The Economic Basis of Class Conflict* (London, 1939), p. 4.

[28] A somewhat similar conclusion arrived at from altogether different premises is expressed by F. H. Knight: ". . . it is a . . . pernicious idea that by education a society can lift itself by its bootstraps." "Principles in Economics and Politics," *Am. Econ. Rev.,* Mar. 1951, XLI, 23.

the state to recognize that various schemes of government planning and
action for full employment under capitalism must be considered with
regard to their compatibility with the controlling interests in a capitalist
society.[29] From the point of view of the short run, the important question
may be the relationship of the necessary measures to the "subjective" interests involved. As far as the long run is concerned, it is the extent to
which the government's economic plans and activities serve or hamper
the "objective" interests of the capitalist class that will decide their fate
within the capitalist order. The former problem, urgent as it is in day-
to-day political decisions, need not detain us any longer. Not only is it
possible to assume, it is even possible empirically to observe that where
subjective *misapprehensions* about the nature and implications of full-
employment measures blocked their acceptance by the dominating interests, such misapprehensions were eventually disspelled by rational argument and actual experience. Yet where resistance to governmental
intervention in economic affairs stems from *correctly* assessed objective
interests of the capitalist class, the vigor and tenacity of the opposition
become overwhelming, and policies that are in conflict with those interests are doomed.[30]

Examined in this light, however, only a few of the "routes" to full
employment briefly referred to above appear to be realistic within the
capitalist system, while others are either (in the long run) inconsistent

---

[29] "In all societies—from societies that are very meagerly developed and have barely
attained the dawnings of civilization, down to the most advanced and powerful societies—
two classes of people appear: a class that rules and a class that is ruled. The first class, always the less numerous, performs all political functions, monopolizes power and enjoys
the advantages that power brings, whereas the second, the more numerous class, is directed
in a manner that is now more or less legal, now more or less arbitrary and violent. . . ."
Gaetano Mosca, *The Ruling Class* (New York: McGraw-Hill Book Co., Inc., 1939), p. 50.

[30] What would seem to be in contradiction with the above thesis is only apparently
so. Such infringements upon the objective interests of British capitalism as have occurred
from 1940 to 1950 and that were laid at the door of the Labor government are much more
attributable to special circumstances or to the emergencies of the war and postwar period
than to specific policies of the Labor administration. They were therefore accepted without
much ado by the representatives of the British business classes. ". . . with the partial exceptions of transport and steel, all of the nationalization, or seminationalization programs
were based squarely on findings, and in large part on recommendations, which had been
made by Conservative-dominated fact-finding and special investigating committees. . . .
Even the nationalization of the iron and steel industry seems to have been mainly the
realization of a plan for reorganizing the industry which had been advanced by the Iron
and Steel Federation itself. . . . To cap it all, the top planning machinery evolved by the
Labor government represents a relatively minor adaptation of wartime controls to somewhat altered peacetime circumstances." R. A. Brady, *Crisis in Britain* (Berkeley and Los
Angeles, 1950), p. 41.

with the maintenance of a private enterprise economy or else presuppose political changes that would be tantamount to a fascization of the political order of capitalism.

The approach closest to the heart of business interests is what was classified above as "nonfiscal measures" as well as "deficit without spending." The former, if properly undertaken, may be conducive to an improvement of the "business atmosphere," while the latter, not interfering with the freedom of action of business, and not resulting in any expansion of governmental participation in economic affairs, is acceptable as "countercyclical planning" even to those who are decidedly opposed to all economic planning on the part of the government.[31]

Matters are much more complex with respect to fiscal measures involving increases in governmental spending.[32] Clearly, the "balanced budget" or "unit multiplier" method are altogether out of question as far as the business class is concerned. Requiring, as it does, a level of taxation that would "nationalize" and redistribute the bulk of national income (and accordingly destroy the value of a large part of privately owned assets) it ". . . implies nothing less than a social revolution."[33] Equally distasteful would be a full-employment strategy referred to above as "investment in productive enterprise." Such a policy would progressively push the government into extensive participation in business activities and would, in all likelihood, create conditions necessitating a further expansion of the governmental sector of the economy. Only little foresight is needed to envisage a more or less complete nationalization of private enterprise as the end of this process, and even less insight to see the unacceptability of this course to the business class and to a government operating within the framework of a capitalist society.

Nor are large-scale subsidies to consumption consistent with the functioning of a healthy capitalist order. Not only could such subsidies raise the floor under the wage level, providing the wage earner with a subsistence minimum regardless of employment and thus changing his relative valuation of income and leisure,[34] but what is perhaps more im-

---

[31] Cf. Milton Friedman, "A Monetary and Fiscal Framework for Economic Stability," *Am. Econ. Rev.,* June 1948, XXXVIII, 245 ff.

[32] For an interesting discussion of business attitudes toward deficit spending see S. S. Alexander, "Opposition to Deficit Spending for the Prevention of Unemployment," *Income, Employment and Public Policy,* pp. 177–98.

[33] P. M. Sweezy, "Duesenberry on Economic Development," *Explorations in Entrepreneurial History,* Feb. 1951, pp. 182 ff.

[34] Schemes could conceivably be devised, however, under which consumption subsidies would be paid not to unemployed but to employed persons and made proportional to their wages.

portant, such unearned payments, if they assumed major proportions, would be alien to the fundamental system of ethics and values associated with the capitalist system. The compulsion of "earning one's bread in the sweat of one's brow" is cement and mortar of a social order the cohesion and functioning of which are predicated upon monetary incentives. Reducing the necessity to work for a living, the distribution of a *large volume* of free goods and services would shatter the social discipline of the capitalist society and weaken the positions of social prestige and social controls crowning its hierarchical pyramid.

Not much choice is thus left to the planner for full employment in a capitalist society—with all available alternatives hardly conducive to a rational utilization of resources and to long-term growth of welfare and productivity. "Leaf-raking," the most wasteful of them, may actually meet with the least opposition on the part of the controlling interests. Building schools, hospitals, and roads may readily at an early stage violate overriding social priorities, and constitute thus a manifest misallocation of resources. Foreign investment and armaments are obviously readily expandable outlets of spending—yet the exploration of their implications would lead us far beyond the scope of the present essay and into the realm of the theory of imperialism.

E. Alternatives

Confronted with a battery of formidable obstacles, planning for full employment under capitalism can thus hardly live up to the expectations of its protagonists.

1. *Abandonment of Full Employment.* They may—as mentioned above—abandon their goal of *full* employment and resign themselves to a countercyclical governmental policy designed to smooth cyclical fluctuations and maintain employment and income at some "adequate" level —markedly below what could be termed complete utilization of available human resources.

In this way, inflationary pressures and their undesirable concomitants could be avoided. The continuous existence of an "industrial reserve army" (Marx) would keep labor "in its place," would assure the maintenance of work discipline in the capitalist enterprise, would preserve the social "command position" of the entrepreneur by safeguarding his fundamental source of social power: the ability to hire and fire.

It is highly questionable, however, whether this arrangement offers a workable solution of the "liberal dilemma." In the first place, only rich countries may be in a position to forego a large share of potential output, to waste another portion of it on unproductive purposes, and to reduce the income of the working members of society by what would be needed to prevent destitution of the unemployed. In countries where the per capita national product is less lavish such a policy may constitute an obvious and unbearable irrationality.

Even more serious may be the consideration that the workability of the "industrial reserve army" device is much less certain now than it would seem to have been in the heyday of capitalist efflorescence. Now that the trade unions have attained a powerful position, *large-scale* unemployment may periodically be necessary if the bargaining power of labor is to be sufficiently reduced for the social conditions briefly outlined above to be achieved.[35] Large-scale unemployment, involving seven to eight million "statistically" unemployed may well be beyond what could be called the "margin of political tolerance." The economically "necessary" reserve army may be very much larger than the politically possible one.

If the political impossibility of tolerating unemployment large enough to assure prevention of inflation and the maintenance of the capitalist "climate" should *force* the government to transcend the goal of only "adequate" employment and push it into larger expenditures needed for the maintenance of full or nearly full employment, all the perplexities that were to be avoided would be with us once more.

2. *Fascism.* To be sure, there is a way of disposing of them. Instead of relying on an "industrial reserve army" to make the trade unions "reasonable," labor can be *forced* to be reasonable. Instead of counting on the normal contractual relations of the capitalist market to generate the necessary labor discipline, such discipline can be *imposed* by administrative means.[36]

The requisite set of compulsory measures could not be adequately administered, however, by a constitutional, democratic government under normal "nonemergency" conditions—"perhaps only a totalitarian

---

[35] "On an average of good and bad years (statistical) unemployment should be higher than five to six million—seven to eight perhaps. This is nothing to be horrified about because . . . adequate provisions can be made for the unemployed." Schumpeter, *op. cit.,* p. 383; cf. also John Jewkes, *Ordeal by Planning* (New York, 1948), pp. 78 ff., for similar views and estimates.

[36] "The Nazis succeeded in overcoming the problems created by full employment because they had first broken the labour movement. Discipline in industry was ensured by substituting terror, along with a mystical propaganda appeal, for the fear of unemployment. The vicious spiral was cut at the root by fixing wages." Joan Robinson, *The Problem of Full Employment* (London, 1943), p. 36.

state could muster sufficient economic (and political) power to enforce a solution upon the contending parties possibly by eliminating one of them as an organized force."[37] Should there be any doubt which of the "contending parties" would be eliminated as an organized force, A. P. Lerner helps to dispel it: "If we are to enjoy very high levels of full employment without inflation, it may be necessary to give up the determination of wages by collective bargaining,"[38] and rely upon ". . . compulsory arbitration for wage determination in which both the worker and the employer get a fair deal."[39]

We return thus once more to elementary notions of the theory of the state. With all the basic institutions of the capitalist society left intact, with all its essential property relations unaffected, with the economic and political status of the business class, if anything, enhanced, it would be nothing short of fatuous to assume that a government resting upon such a socio-economic foundation could be a "neutral" entity acting *not* in the interests of the economically dominant class in society but on behalf of the general "public." Such "neutrality" was always claimed by fascist governments and their spokesmen;[40] it would seem to be redundant at this time to provide an elaborate proof of the mendacious nature of that pretense.

In fact, on few matters is there so much consensus, among all competent students of fascism, as well as documentary evidence (accumulated in war crimes trials in Nuremberg and elsewhere) as on the finding that big business dominated the policies of Germany's fascist state. Nor was this a purely German phenomenon. Matters were no different in Italy,[41] or in Japan where a dozen so-called Zaibatsu families controlled

---

[37] M. W. Reder, "Problems of a National Wage-Price Policy," *Can. Jour. Econ. Pol. Sci.,* Feb. 1948, XIV, 58.

[38] A. P. Lerner, "Rising Prices," *Rev. Econ. Stat.,* Feb. 1948, XXX, 26.

[39] A. P. Lerner, "Money as a Creature of the State," *Am. Econ. Rev.,* May 1947, XXXVII, 316.

[40] "The freedom from doctrines and dogmas . . . results in the fact that economic policy in the national socialist state is determined by considerations of expediency and, without prejudice applies such measures as are necessary in any given case for the economic welfare of the people." Eberhard Barth, *Wesen und Aufgaben der Organisation der gewerblichen Wirtschaft* (Hamburg, 1939), p. 9, as quoted by Franz Neumann, *Behemoth, the Structure and Practice of National Socialism 1933–1944* (Toronto-New York-London, 1944), p. 233.

[41] ". . . the middle class composition of the fascist party determined the *form* of the fascist action; the forces that gave the action of the fascist leadership direction and contents was all the time the big bourgeoisie." Ignazio Silone, *Der Faschismus, seine Entstehung und seine Entwicklung* (Zurich, 1934), p. 166 (translated from the German by the writer).

exclusively the economic (and not only economic) policies of the fascist-militarist government.[42]

There is no reason to assume that all these and similar cases were purely fortuitous, and that "strong" governments in other capitalist countries that would seek to solve the problems attendant upon full-employment policies by a destruction of trade unions and by an authoritarian fixing of the share of national income going to labor would not also be fascist regimes dominated by the most influential and powerful class in society. Yet the nature of the regime is bound to influence decisively the choice of "routes" that it adopts in order to provide for full employment. Controlled by capitalist interests, it cannot engage in "spending on productive enterprise" since such spending is essentially inimical to capitalist institutions. All the more is it inclined to use the "military expenditures" route towards full employment. Not only is this device highly acceptable to big business, it is also fully in keeping with the fascist ideology prone to consider domestic economic problems in terms of "living space," "co-prosperity zones," and "national power."[43]

The machinery of regulation that has been developed by fascist governments, and that embraced more or less closely coordinated controls over wages, prices, investment, credit, foreign trade, etc., has been amply described in the literature.[44] After a lengthy period of groping it evolved into a set of measures directed towards three interrelated objec-

---

[42] "The predominance of the business group in Japan's ruling coalition has not been established during the course of the war. It was, in fact, already fully expressed in the Cabinets which both preceded and followed the Manchurian invasion of September 18, 1931 . . . all the way down to Pearl Harbor. . . . Thereafter the forced growth of heavy industry and the still greater concentration of vested monopoly interests in the furtherance of which the authority of government was liberally drawn upon, merely confirmed and extended the dominant position occupied by the Zaibatsu in the Japanese regime." T. A. Bisson, *Japan's War Economy* (New York: Macmillan Co., 1945), pp. 203 f.

[43] The pursuit of military might as the most important "route" to full employment does not preclude—in fact calls for—a marked improvement in the living conditions of the population. Stemming from the mere existence of full employment, such an improvement represents the indispensable condition for the political stability of the fascist-militarist regime. Under certain circumstances it may even result in a far-reaching identification of popular ideologies with those of the fascist rulers. Cf. Oscar Lange, Review of Paul M. Sweezy, *The Theory of Capitalist Development, Jour. of Philosophy*, July 1943, XL, 378–84, as well as Sweezy's reply in his Preface to the second printing, *The Theory of Capitalist Development* (New York, 1946).

[44] In addition to the already cited work by Franz Neumann, cf. K. E. Poole, *German Financial Policies, 1932–1939* (Cambridge, Mass., 1939); Maxine Y. Sweezy, *The Structure of the Nazi Economy* (Cambridge, Mass., 1941); Otto Nathan, *The Nazi Economy* (Durham, 1944); Thomas Balogh, "The National Economy of Germany," *Econ. Jour.*, Sept. 1938, XLVIII, 461 ff.

tives: (1) maximization of total output by means of full employment and highest exertion on the part of the working members of society; (2) maximization of the volume of resources extractable for armaments and related (political) purposes by rigorous controls of mass consumption; (3) avoidance of inflation by an authoritarian division of real income among the social classes.

At hardly any time—not even during the war—did these objectives lead to an adoption of what may be termed a coordinated, consistent plan. In the main they were approached by *ad hoc* measures that added up, as time went on, to a maze of rules and regulations covering all aspects of economic and social life. Inefficient as it was, this system of controls was developed to its bureaucratic perfection in Germany, and represents still the greatest experiment of peacetime economic planning under capitalism.[45]

3. *Laborism.* There has been suggested, however, another formula that could represent a possible solution of our dilemma. The "contending party" to be sacrificed on the altar of full-employment equilibrium would not be labor but the capitalist class. Under this arrangement, which one could call with Schumpeter the rule of "laborism," the government would no longer be dominated by business interests but by the other party to the contest—the trade unions.

A trade union administration determined to abolish bargaining over the distribution of the social product by eliminating one of the two decisive claimants would have to be a much stronger government than a regime sponsored and supported by the business class, since its task would be considerably more complex. Indeed, the claimant whom it would wish to "abolish" would be the economically and socially ruling class in society, entrenched in traditional positions of property and power, resting upon an elaborate structure of custom, habit, and prevailing social values. Compared with the magnitude of this undertaking, the task of fascism was easy. Outlawing the unions, or still better "taking them over," and suppressing their political mouthpieces was actually all that was needed to destroy them as an "organized force." To be sure, such an action militated against the political institutions of democracy, vio-

---

[45] The mode of operation and the efficiency of the German economic organization are discussed in detail in: United States Strategic Bombing Survey, *The Effects of Strategic Bombing on the German War Economy* (Washington, D.C., 1946). Cf. also Emile Despres' review of this report in *Rev. Econ. Stat.,* Nov. 1946, XXVIII, 253 ff., and the reply by P. A. Baran and J. K. Galbraith, *ibid.,* May 1947, XXIX, 132 ff. Cf. also B. H. Klein, "Germany's Preparation for War: A Re-examination," *Am. Econ. Rev.,* Mar. 1948, XXXVIII, 56 ff.

lated such notions as freedom of assembly, organization, and speech. It did not disturb, however, the basic socio-economic structure of the capitalist order. It was in other words a *political* revolution neither accompanied nor followed by what could be termed a social transformation.[46]

What is envisaged in "laborism's" advent to power is, however, precisely the opposite: with the continuity of political institutions maintained, with the structure of social values and ideologies unaffected, the prevailing *economic* and *social* system is expected to be radically altered. To make matters still less realistic, this drastic overturn in the basic economic order of a capitalist society is expected to be carried out by an organization that by its very nature constitutes an integral part of that society. Set up not to abolish collective bargaining but to secure it, brought up not to flout the market mechanism but to gain a place in it, educated not to combat the institutions of a capitalist society but to grow into one of them—the trade union movements in advanced capitalist countries such as the United States or Great Britain are constitutionally and ideologically unable to assume dictatorial political powers needed to undertake revolutionary changes in the economic and social structures of their societies.

Where in extraordinary political constellations they achieve political power they become frustrated by the very circumstances to which they owe their political success, and assimilate themselves to the conventional functions of a government in a capitalist society, wholly unable to adapt that government to their original plans and purposes. Nor could it be different. The nature of any particular government depends in the last analysis not on the individuals that happen to hold official positions; it is crucially determined by the socio-economic structure of the society over which it presides.[47]

Yet, assuming that a "laborist" administration were to succeed in squaring the circle, in "suppressing" the capitalist class in a capitalist society, the contradictory nature of the resulting situation is easily visualized. In attempting to serve the interests of its supporters, it would seek

---

[46] The speed and ease with which the societies of Western Germany, Italy, and Japan reverted after the war to a prefascist *political* order, this reverse calling for no changes in their social and economic structure, offers an excellent historical illustration of the distinction made above.

[47] To adapt Schumpeter's brilliant analysis of a social class to the very similar problem of government "for the duration of its collective life, or the time during which its identity may be assumed each [regime] resembles a hotel or an omnibus, always full, but always of different people." J. A. Schumpeter, *Imperialism and Social Classes* (New York, 1951), p. 165.

to counter possible aggregate demand deficiencies by efforts to increase consumption, be it through outright spending on consumption benefits (food subsidies, etc.) or through appropriate tax policies accompanied by transfer expenditures.

The "laborist" government would have to deal with inflationary pressures that would appear once full employment is reached (or approached), by freezing wages on some level agreed upon with the trade unions and by the enactment of suitable measures to enforce stable prices.

On the basis of available experience there can be little doubt that such a policy would have a highly discouraging effect upon private investment. Compelled to pay high wages, exposed to trade union demands concerning working conditions, unable to increase prices to allow for increased costs, subject to rigorous controls of a hostile administration, the businessman would find it rational not only to refrain from new investment but possibly to abstain from maintaining his enterprise in working order.

As far as the employment aspect of the matter is concerned, the "laborist" government may have no strong reasons for worry. The deficiency in aggregate demand caused by the growing inadequacy of private investment could be made up by further expansion of governmental spending on consumption, social services, and the like. Yet such a policy would imply neglecting the maintenance and necessary expansion of the nation's productive plant and would obviously be unacceptable to any responsible government. In other words: confronted with an "investment strike" on the part of the capitalist class, the laborist administration would find itself compelled either to retreat and to grant such concessions to the business community as may be needed to restore the confidence of the investor or else to undertake on an ever-expanding scale investment and operation in the field of productive enterprise.[48]

In the former case the rule of "laborism" would rapidly draw to a close; a policy of yielding to "economic necessities" would deprive it of its original mass support without endearing it to its capitalist opponents.

---

[48] The British experience is succinctly summed up by Aneurin Bevan: "There is no way in which it is possible for anybody to carry out a plan in the modern state involving stability of employment, involving the proper dispersal of industry, involving all the things that we mean by effective control over economic life, unless the power has passed from the hands of the oligarchs into the hands of democrats. . . . Parliament is made responsible for the government of the nation and for overriding social policies, but private property has all the levers." *Democratic Values,* Fabian Tract No. 282 (London, 1950), pp. 7, 9.

Should the latter course be adopted, "laborism" would begin transcending the framework of a capitalist society and enter the road to all-out socialization.

II. PLANNING UNDER BACKWARD CAPITALISM

A. The Issues

The burning issue confronting underdeveloped countries[49] is not that there is at times insufficient employment of available men *and* available capital equipment but that the existing quantity of capital goods (and land) is inadequate to assure a level of productivity that would provide the backward countries with tolerable standards of livelihood.[50] The only way to prevent a continuous deterioration of living standards (apart from mass emigration unacceptable to other countries, or a slowing down of population growth that cannot be expected under prevailing conditions)[51] is to assure a steady increase of total output at least large enough to offset the rapid expansion of the population.

An obvious source of such an increase is the vast multitude of entirely unemployed or ineffectively employed manpower.[52] There is no way of employing it usefully in agriculture, where the marginal produc-

---

[49] For a somewhat more extensive discussion of what follows in this section, cf. P. A. Baran, "On the Political Economy of Backwardness," *Man. School Econ. Soc. Stud.,* Jan. 1952, XX, 66–84.

[50] There is no simple definition of what is to be considered a backward area. P. N. Rosenstein-Rodan suggested to this writer that all countries where the per capita annual income is lower than some $150 to $200 should be regarded as "underdeveloped." *Partners in Progress,* A Report to the President by the International Development Advisory Board (Washington, 1951), presents (pp. 102 ff.) a listing of underdeveloped areas the population of which is estimated at 1,075,273 thousand (for midyear 1949). This list does *not* include continental China nor the countries of eastern and southeastern Europe. If those countries are taken into account, the estimate of the population living under conditions of economic backwardness would reach approximately 1.8 billion people, i.e. nearly three-quarters of the world's total.

[51] A decline in the growth of population". . . will require a tremendous increase in production, an increase that . . . can bring rising standards of living and new vistas of health and individual welfare to the world's most poverty stricken peoples," F. W. Notestein, "Population, the Long View," *Food for the World,* T. W. Schultz, ed. (Chicago, 1945), p. 52 and *passim.*

[52] The majority of this manpower are "disguised unemployed," i.e., "persons who work on their own account and who are so numerous, relatively to the resources with which they work, that if a number of them were withdrawn for work in other sectors of the economy, the total output of the sector from which they were withdrawn would not be diminished even though no significant reorganization occurred in this sector, and no significant substitution of capital," United Nations Group of Experts, *Measures for the Economic Development of Under-Developed Countries* (New York, 1951), par. 17.

tivity of labor tends to zero. It could be provided with opportunities for productive work only by transfer to industrial pursuits.[53] For this to be feasible, large investments in industrial plant and facilities have to be undertaken. Under the conditions obtaining in underdeveloped countries such investments are not forthcoming for a number of important and interrelated reasons.

Disregarding capital imports, the only source from which investment can be provided is the "economic surplus" currently generated by the economic system. There are no hard and fast rules by which its magnitude can be established. It represents the difference between gross national product and aggregate *essential* consumption, and is therefore usually larger than voluntary saving. The definition of what constitutes "essential consumption" is clearly elastic and would greatly depend on the country and period under consideration.

The crucial hurdle obstructing the development of underdeveloped countries is that even such meager "economic surplus" as could be mobilized from their small aggregate incomes is usually frittered away on unproductive purposes. With a very uneven distribution of income, large individual incomes exceeding significantly what could be regarded as "reasonable" requirements for current consumption accrue, as a rule, to a relatively small group. Many of them are large landowners maintaining a "feudal" style of life with large outlays on housing, servants, travel, and other luxuries. Their "requirements" for consumption are so high that there is little room for saving.

Other members of the "upper crust" receiving incomes markedly surpassing "reasonable" levels of consumption are wealthy businessmen. Yet their drive to accumulate capital and to expand their enterprises is continuously counteracted by the urgent desire (or social compulsion) to imitate in their living habits the socially dominant "old families," to prove by their conspicuous outlays that they are socially (and therefore also politically) not inferior to their aristocratic partners in the socially ruling coalition.

But if the social structure existing in the underdeveloped countries and the values held by their upper income groups depress saving markedly below some hypothetical magnitude of available "economic surplus," the will to reinvest funds in productive enterprise is effectively curbed by other factors. One of these is a strong reluctance on the part of

---

[53] "The economic case for the industrialization of densely populated backward countries rests upon [the] mass phenomenon of disguised rural unemployment." Kurt Mandelbaum, *The Industrialization of Backward Areas* (Oxford, 1945), p. 2.

the businessmen to damage their carefully erected monopolistic positions by creation of additional productive capacity.[54] More important, however, is the absence of suitable investment opportunities, paradoxical as this may sound with reference to backward areas.

The shortage of investible funds and the lack of investment opportunities represent two aspects of the same problem. A great number of investment projects, unprofitable under prevailing conditions, could be most promising in a general environment of economic expansion. Large-scale investment is predicated upon large-scale investment. Roads, electric power stations, railroads, and houses have to be built *before* businessmen find it profitable to erect factories and to invest their funds in new enterprises.[55]

Nor is there usually land going to waste in backward areas that is fit for agricultural purposes and at the same time readily accessible.[56] The expansion and improvement of agricultural production would normally require considerable investment. In underdeveloped countries such investment is just as unattractive to private interests for agricultural as for industrial purposes.

Approached thus via agriculture, an expansion of total output would also seem to be attainable only through the development of industry. Only through increase of industrial productivity could agricultural machinery, fertilizers, electric power, etc., be brought within the reach of the agricultural producer. Only through an increased demand for labor could agricultural wages be raised and a stimulus provided for a modernization of the agricultural economy. Only through the growth of industrial production could agricultural labor displaced by the machine be absorbed in productive employment.

If and when investment projects are undertaken in spite of all adversities, the "economic surplus" required to support them is frequently provided not by an intended contraction of resource utilization elsewhere in the economy, but by inflation. It is clear that the quantity of resources withdrawn from the lower income groups through the mechanism of inflation is considerably larger than what would correspond to the amount of spending that initially ignited the inflationary development. In advanced countries the resulting redistribution of real income in favor of

---

[54] *Measures for the Economic Development,* par. 35.

[55] "An underdeveloped country is poor because it has no industry, and an underdeveloped country has no industry because it is poor." H. W. Singer, "Economic Progress in Underdeveloped Countries," *Soc. Research,* Mar. 1949, XVI, 1–11.

[56] ". . . in most countries where under-employment is acute, nearly all the cultivable land is already cultivated." *Measures for the Economic Development,* par. 21.

the business class—socially undesirable as it may be—has the possibly redeeming effect of leading to an accelerated formation of physical capital.[57] In underdeveloped countries, however, waste accompanies iniquity. The customs and spirit of their high-income receivers being what they are, increasing profits and windfall gains resulting from inflationary price movements produce a higher propensity to embark on unproductive expenditures on the part of the monied groups of the population.[58]

All the domestic obstacles standing in the way of economic development in backward capitalist countries, as well as the hurdles resulting from the international setting of the underdeveloped economies, find their expression in the balance-of-payments difficulties continuously experienced by backward areas. Their discussion would take us, however, beyond the scope of the present account.[59]

B. The Remedies

Left to itself, the situation appears as a "system not only of vicious circles, but of vicious circles within vicious circles, and of interlocking vicious circles."[60] Not that in the course of time some progress might not be attained by the normal functioning of the price and profit mechanism, by international capital movements, and the like. Whether such progress would be rapid enough to prevent major human catastrophes in many underdeveloped countries is highly conjectural. It is undeniable, however, that not much time is left for the transformation of the economies of the backward areas.

True, this is not the first time the population of the underdeveloped countries has experienced misery. But it is the first time that hundreds of millions of human beings have become convinced that because of new scientific knowledge and new technical skills their misery is not necessary. In Asia, in Africa, in Latin

---

[57] The German inflation following the end of the first World War is a case in point.

[58] The usefulness of the "ideal-type" model presented above, which is not meant to depict accurately the situation in any one particular underdeveloped country but attempts to bring into relief the problem faced by all of them, is confirmed by various empirical studies referring to specific countries. See for instance the *Report to the President of the United States by the Economic Survey Mission to the Philippines* (Washington, D.C., 1950), p. 2.

[59] The reader will find an interesting treatment of the problems related to the balance of payments of underdeveloped countries in: J. H. Adler, *The Underdeveloped Countries, Their Industrialization* (New Haven, 1949); J. J. Polak, "Balance of Payments Problems of Countries Reconstructing with the Help of Foreign Loans," *Quart. Jour. Econ.*, Feb. 1943, LVII, 208–40; reprinted in *Readings in the Theory of International Trade,* H. S. Ellis and L. A. Metzler, ed. (Philadelphia, 1949).

[60] Singer, *op. cit.,* p. 5.

America, that conviction is growing. And the people of these lands are determined to solve their economic problem.[61]

In an effort to overcome backwardness, the government could undertake a variety of planning measures. A fiscal policy of capital levies and highly progressive taxation could syphon off surplus purchasing power, and eliminate nonessential consumption. The savings thus enforced could enable the government to step in and make the requisite investment wherever private capital refrains from undertaking required industrial projects or wherever monopolistic controls block the necessary expansion of plant and facilities.

In addition, an entire arsenal of "preventive" devices is at the disposal of the authorities. Inflationary pressures resulting from developmental activities (private and public) could be reduced or even eliminated if outlays on investment projects could be offset by a taxation system providing for a corresponding and simultaneous contraction of spending elsewhere in the economic system.

In the interim, speculation in scarce goods and excessive profiteering in essential commodities could be suppressed by rigorous price controls. An equitable distribution of mass consumption goods in short supply could be assured by rationing. Diversion of resources in high demand to nonessential purposes could be prevented by allocation and priorities schemes. Strict supervision of transactions involving foreign exchanges could render impossible capital flight, expenditure of limited foreign funds on luxury imports, pleasure trips abroad, and the like.

The combination of these measures could accomplish a radical change in the structure of effective demand in the underdeveloped country and a reallocation of productive resources to satisfy society's need for economic development.

C. The Obstacles

The mere listing of the steps that would have to be taken in order to assure an expansion of output and income in an underdeveloped country reveals the implausibility of the view that they could be carried out by the governments existing in most backward capitalist countries. The reason for this impossibility is only to a negligible extent the absence of a competent and honest civil service needed for the administration of the program. A symptom itself of the political and social marasmus prevailing in underdeveloped countries, this lack cannot be remedied without

---

[61] Stringfellow Barr, *Let's Join the Human Race* (Chicago, 1950), p. 5.

an attack on the underlying causes. Nor does it go near the roots of the matter to lament the lack of satisfactory tax policies in backward countries or to deplore the absence of tax "morale" and "discipline" among the civic virtues of their population.

The crucial fact rendering the realization of a developmental program illusory is the political and social structure of the governments in power.

> In our judgment, there are a number of under-developed countries where the concentration of economic and political power in the hands of a small class, whose main interest is the preservation of its own wealth and privileges, rules out the prospect of much economic progress until a social revolution has effected a shift in the distribution of income and power.[62]

If to appease the restive public, blueprints of progressive measures such as agrarian reform, equitable tax legislation, etc., are officially announced, their enforcement is willfully sabotaged. The government, representing a political compromise between landed and business interests, cannot suppress the wasteful management of landed estates and the conspicuous consumption on the part of the aristocracy, cannot suppress monopolistic abuses, profiteering, capital flights, and extravagant living on the part of the businessmen.

III. PLANNING UNDER SOCIALISM

A. "Socialist Economics"

Although the social and political structure of the country where planning is to become the guiding principle of economic organization appears basic to all discussion of its contents and direction, most of the literature on socialist economics pays hardly any attention to this aspect of its subject matter. Wholly in the tradition of all utopian thought on the subject of "good society," this literature escapes into a painstaking discussion of the economic organization of an "established" socialist order characterized primarily by "consumers' sovereignty." It would be redundant to attempt here a summary of its "notably abstract" contents.

---

[62] *Measures for the Economic Development*, par. 37. "The landowners in the higher middle class hold the balance of power in Parliament and in the main political parties, there being few Egyptians of prominence who are not owners of land. This common interest in land results in great solidarity among the well-to-do who influence the Government and make the passage of progressive legislation very difficult whenever it threatens their interest." A. M. Galatoli, *Egypt in Midpassage* (Cairo, 1950), p. 86.

Not only was such a survey recently presented,[63] but the material involved bears only a tenuous relation to realistically conceived problems of economic planning.

The writings in question could perhaps be interpreted as a normative endeavor to elaborate rules for an "ideal" economic organization and conduct, compliance with which would yield an economic "optimum." They "might be considered as providing a theoretic basis for the work of a Central Planning Board seeking to rationalize the planning system of a socialist state."[64] Yet this claim can hardly be sustained. As Bergson has pointed out in his celebrated contribution to welfare economics,[65] the contents of any "optimum" are determined by the values adopted in its formulation; the stipulation of the means by which such an "optimum" could be attained is therefore evidently meaningless without reference to those basic ends—in particular, since " 'means' are also 'ends.' "[66] This observation, true as it is in its incontrovertible generality, constitutes undoubtedly an advance from the transparently ideological doctrine identifying "welfare" under the specific existential conditions of a capitalist society with human "welfare" at large.[67] It represents, however, only the first "critical" (in both senses of this word) step towards a concrete, historically relevant doctrine of welfare and of economic planning for welfare.

Indeed, "ends" and "values" taken as "given" in economic analysis (in keeping with the practice advocated notably by Lionel Robbins)[68] do not fall from heaven but constitute themselves moving forces and important outcomes of the concrete socio-economic process. The range of values, objectives, and means within which the relevant choices are to be made is thus fairly closely delineated by the essential characteristics of

---

[63] Abram Bergson, "Socialist Economics," *A Survey of Contemporary Economics,* Vol. I, H. S. Ellis, ed. (Philadelphia, 1948), Ch. 12.

[64] Ibid., p. 412.

[65] "A Reformulation of Certain Aspects of Welfare Economics," *Quart. Jour. Econ.,* Feb. 1938, LII, 310–34; reprinted in *Readings in Economic Analysis,* R. V. Clemence, ed. (Cambridge, Mass., 1950), Vol. I, pp. 61–85; and briefly restated by the author in "Socialist Economics," *op. cit.*

[66] "Socialist Economics," *op. cit.,* p. 413.

[67] An identification implicitly assumed by Marshall and Pigou. It is worth noting that Bergson himself who was the first to insist on the relationship between value judgments and "optima" concepts has also "fallen into the trap" of implicitly accepting individualistic behavior as supplying the value judgment underlying his "welfare function." This was shown in the brilliant essay by K. J. Arrow, *Social Choice and Individual Values* (New York, 1951), *passim* but in particular p. 72.

[68] *An Essay on the Nature and Significance of Economic Science* (London, 1932).

the stage of social and economic development, as well as by the interests of the class ruling at any particular time. Not much useful purpose is therefore served by considering planning in a socialist society as directed towards the attainment of "optima," the contents of which are borrowed from the individualistic value system of the capitalist world or from some personal predilections of the writers.

After all, one of the crucial *raisons d'être* of a socialist society would seem to be the pivotal function accorded in it to *social organs of control* carrying out measures the social merits and implications of which could not be properly assessed by individuals. What is more, it is presumably the purpose of whatever political action is taken to establish a socialist system to create such social organs of control that would limit consumers' sovereignty (*and mould consumers' preferences*) in the interest of the community as a whole in preference to an arrangement in which it is the capitalist enterprise which performs this function for the benefit of private interests.[69]

This does not by any means imply that the Central Planning Board would "sovereignly" or "arbitrarily" brush aside the preferences of the public and be guided by the whims of its members. On the contrary, the Board's policies may be fully compatible with ". . . a principle likely to be accepted by socialists . . . of giving people what they want where there is no good reason for a contrary policy."[70]

However, it is precisely the *meaning* of this maxim that is at issue. The actual process of determination of the nature and direction of economic activity, of the share of output devoted to consumption or investment, of the assortment and quality of various products placed on the market may well represent a historical *novum* defying categories inherent in our conventional frame of reference. The Planning Board would be obviously subject to strains and stresses of its rapidly changing social environment and would have to respond to the wishes and needs of a society involved in a revolutionary transition. It would thus neither substitute its own preferences for those of the people nor efface itself by merely executing the desires of the consumers—desires expressing a value scheme representing a holdover from a social structure of an ear-

---

[69] Thus the notion of "consumers' sovereignty" is misleading under capitalism, where not "the consumer is king" but the producer holds firmly the reins of power in his hands. Cf. Maurice Dobb, "Economic Theory and Socialist Economy—A Reply," *Rev. Econ. Stud.*, 1934–1935, II, 144 ff., and Alfred Sherrard, "Advertising, Product Variation, and the Limits of Economics," *Jour. Pol. Econ.*, Apr. 1951, LIX, 126–42.

[70] A. P. Lerner, "Economic Theory and Socialist Economy," *Rev. Econ. Stud.*, Oct. 1934, II, 53.

lier historical phase. It would strive to promote an attitude on the part of the population that would be conducive to the attainment of some new "optimum."[71]

It is the inability to perceive this interaction that bars a realistic approach to the problems of socialist planning on the part of liberal economists interested in the problem of socialism. *"Liberalism takes the individual as given* and views the social problem as one of right relations between given individuals."[72] Is it astonishing that from such a position one cannot visualize a social system the entire concept of which is built upon the recognition of the decisive influence of the social structure upon the nature, values, volitions, and actions of the individual?

It must be stressed that a radical reorientation of all aspects of social existence could not unfold under the rein of unfettered individual freedom. Nor would it be reasonable to assume that perfect social consensus would support the revolutionary measures involved. Directed as they would have to be against vital interests of previously privileged classes, violating many short-run preferences of others, such a revamping of the socio-economic structure would necessarily involve compulsion. The extent of such compulsion would vary from country to country depending on prevailing conditions—it is hardly conceivable that it could be altogether absent anywhere. "It is highly doubtful whether the achievements of the Industrial Revolution would have been permitted if the franchise had been universal. It is very doubtful because a great deal of the capital aggregations that we are at present enjoying are the result of the wages that our fathers went without."[73]

In advanced and backward countries alike, the problem facing the Board would be not slow adjustments to small changes—the main prerequisite for the applicability of the rules derived from static analysis—but choice among few technological alternatives involving large indivisibilities and "fixed coefficients." Attempting to cope with such perplexities, the Board would look in vain for guidance to the literature on socialist economics.[74]

---

[71] Whether this would be done indirectly by influencing social values or more directly by staging advertising campaigns for some commodities, by suspending the production of others or by manipulating prices of still others is a matter of technical detail that would have to be settled on grounds of expediency. Cf. Maurice Dobb, *op. cit.,* pp. 144 ff.

[72] F. H. Knight, *Freedom and Reform* (New York and London, 1947), p. 69.

[73] Bevan, *op. cit.,* p. 12.

[74] "Thus the proposition that the marginal value productivity of a factor must be the same in every use—it being understood that values are proportional to the marginal

386 · *A SURVEY OF CONTEMPORARY ECONOMICS*

To be sure, those rules can be and have been reformulated in a way sufficiently general for them to refer to all situations in which a rational allocation of resources is accepted as a desirable objective. "If we so order the economic activity of the society that no commodity is produced unless its *importance* is greater than that of the alternative that is sacrificed, we shall have completely achieved the ideal that the economic calculus of a socialist state sets before itself."[75] It is clear, however, that such a general principle, common sense though it is, offers no help whatever to the Planning Board confronted with actual choices. The decision concerning the relative *importance* of various alternatives would have to be made without the assistance of the welfare economist.

Not that the Planning Board could not make such decisions rationally. In making them, however, it could not rely on any ready-to-use prescription of economics but would have to perform a duty essentially germane to its function in a dynamic society. It would have to engage in the task of "social engineering," i.e., formulate social *priorities* in the light of economic, political, and possibly defense requirements of any given situation. In this endeavor it would constitute, actually, only a part of the "brain trust" of a socialist society—executing social decisions and participating at the same time in formulating them by providing indispensable information on "what is possible."[76]

At the peril of some oversimplification it may be said that the Board would permit consumers' preferences to determine the composi-

---

rates of substitution of the individual households—clearly obtains only if the principle of consumers' sovereignty prevails as an end." Bergson, "Socialist Economics," *op. cit.,* p. 430. Cf. also Eduard Heimann, "Developmental Schemes, Planning, and Full Employment," *Planning and Paying for Full Employment,* A. P. Lerner and F. D. Graham, ed. (Princeton, 1946).

[75] A. P. Lerner, "Statics and Dynamics in Socialist Economics," *Econ. Jour.,* June 1937, XLVII, 253 ff. (italics supplied).

[76] It may be worth pointing out that the foregoing in no way supports the contention of Max Weber, Mises, Hayek, Brutzkus, and others, that a rational calculation would be impossible in a socialist society. Under static assumptions with "consumers' sovereignty" determining the allocation of resources it is just as possible under socialism as under competition. So much is fully established by Barone, Lange, and others. Under dynamic assumptions, in particular under conditions of rapid change in all "data," no mechanical devices can assure such rationality, either under capitalism or under socialism. In the former system, it is the entrepreneur who decides what is "rational"; in the latter, the Planning Board. The advantages of the discretional powers of the entrepreneurs, frequently seen in the fact that owing to large numbers their errors may cancel out, are greatly reduced under conditions of large-scale business and considerable uniformity of business opinion, and are anyway decisively outweighed by the superior knowledge, disinterestedness, and ability to encompass the needs of society as a whole on the part of the Planning Board.

tion of output *within* the Board's relevant "priority classes." On the other hand, the desire of some consumers to have resources transferred from a higher "priority class" to a lower (e.g., from the production of work clothes to the production of fancy neckwear) may be resisted by the Planning Board.

It goes without saying that most of these problems disappear or lose much of their urgency as soon as the Board's "autonomous program" has accomplished its purpose and significantly raised the country's total output, or attained whatever other objectives appeared urgent during the transition from capitalism to socialism. Loosening the Board's priorities schedules, this development would, at the same time, widen its "priority classes"—in other words, increase the area of the Board's indifference with respect to the allocation of resources. In the meantime, the redistribution of income will have fully affected the structure of consumers' demand, and the "taste-moulding" activities of the Planning Board will have resulted in a new pattern of consumers' preferences.

Where the Board's "autonomous program" was small from the very beginning, where in other words developmental requirements loomed less large in the early stages of economic planning, the transitional period would be accordingly shorter and simpler. In such conditions the interference of the Board with the preferences of the consumers would be necessitated merely by shortages resulting from the change in the social structure, and by the "taste-moulding" endeavors of the Board. It is clear that the sacrifices and discomforts resulting from such disregard of consumers' preferences would be less stringent than those springing from severe scarcities.

B. The Soviet Experience

It is perhaps the very limited extent to which economic theory can offer help to a Central Planning Board engaged in the administration of a system in the throes of economic development and in transition from capitalism to socialism that accounts for the conspicuous paucity of theoretic publications on economic planning on the part of Soviet economists. Indeed, as was suggested above, an economic science that has drawn its inspiration from the study of the "coordinating operation of the market and at times the failure of the market to achieve a coordination of decisions"[77] is not geared to deal with problems confronting an economy in which the "coordination of decisions" is a function of a cen-

---

[77] Oscar Lange, "The Scope and Method of Economics," *Rev. Econ. Stud.*, 1945–46, XIII, 26.

388 · *A SURVEY OF CONTEMPORARY ECONOMICS*

tral political body. Nor are possibly other branches of social sciences which are designed to study the processes taking place in capitalist (and precapitalist) societies as yet in the position to provide insight as to the regularities characterizing the behavior of such an authority.[78]

It could hardly be otherwise. Although the basic philosophy of the Central Authority may determine the goal of its activities, its concrete policies are shaped by the specific circumstances prevailing at any given time.

Even if it were possible to establish some regular pattern of the authority's reaction to any set of specifiable economic and political conditions, an attempt at a general theory of its policies would be necessarily jeopardized by the impossibility of anticipating adequately domestic and international developments determining, and *themselves determined by,* its actions.

Thus the experience of Soviet planning has lent itself very little to theoretical summaries; and most useful writing on the subject has been by necessity of a historical character.[79] Whether in monographs dealing with relatively short periods and with special aspects of the Russian planning effort or in larger treatises seeking to encompass the entire period since the Revolution,—students of Soviet planning have had to analyze the policies of the Russian government as caused by, or themselves causing, specific economic and political constellations. It is by no means fortuitous therefore that efforts at a comprehension of Soviet economic reality in terms of conventional economic theory reached their apex in the years of the New Economic Policy, i.e., at a time when the "coordination of economic decisions" was still largely entrusted to the market mechanism, and have become increasingly rare and unrewarding in the ensuing two decades, in the years in which economic planning has become the effectively governing principle of Soviet economic life.

A brief consideration of the problems that the Soviet planners are called upon to solve may serve to render the foregoing more explicit.

---

[78] See, however, Nathan Leites, *The Operational Code of the Politburo* (New York, 1951), for an attempt to establish a pattern of *political* conduct of the Soviet leadership, an attempt that illustrates, if anything, the sterility of the generalizing formalism characteristic of much of modern social sciences.

[79] "La methodologie sovietique de planification a grandi avec la pratique de l'administration de l'economie socialisée. Cette discipline scientifique n'était enseignée dans aucune chaire universitaire au monde. On ne pouvait l'etudier dans aucun manuel. Les oraticiens sovietiques ont été obligé d'apprendre la science de planification par l'experience de leurs propres erreurs et lacunes qu'ils ont dû decouvrir et rectifier." Stanislas Stroumiline, *La Planification en U.R.S.S.* (Paris, 1947), p. 29.

1. *The Determination of the Long-run Goal of Economic and Social Development.* It goes without saying that decisions under this heading represent the bases of all plans and policies pursued by the Soviet government. Although strongly affected by the ideology (and social basis) of the ruling party—and to that extent explicable in its terms—they are powerfully influenced by the specific conditions under which they have to be made. The tasks confronting the Soviet government have turned out to be quite different from what was anticipated in earlier Marxist thought. Indeed, although political developments in Russia permitted the seizure of political power by a socialist party, the economic and social prerequisites for a socialist order were entirely absent. Fully aware of this contradiction, the Bolsheviks had no intention of immediately establishing socialism (and comprehensive economic planning) in their hungry and devastated country.[80]

Their plan was rather to resist all internal and external attempts to overthrow the socialist regime and to preserve political power until the victory of socialism in Europe's leading industrial nations. All economic measures in the years immediately following the Revolution were subordinated to this basic purpose.[81] Once socialism had prevailed in the advanced countries of the world, the fortress of Russia's economic and social backwardness was expected not to be stormed by a frontal assault but to succumb to a carefully planned flanking operation. Aided by highly developed socialist countries such as Germany and Great Britain, socialist Russia was to approach slowly, although much faster than before, the levels of productivity and welfare attained in the Western world. "The

---

[80] "Not 'introduction' of socialism is our *immediate* task, but *immediate* transition merely to control by the Soviets of Workers' Deputies over the social production and distribution of products." Lenin, "On the Tasks of the Proletariat in the Present Revolution," (April 7, 1917) as translated in E. H. Carr, *The Bolshevik Revolution 1917–1923* (London, 1950), p. 80.

[81] "The Party proclaimed the country an armed camp and placed its economic, cultural and political life on a war footing. . . . It took under its control the middle-sized and small industries in addition to large-scale industry, so as to accumulate goods for the supply of the army and the agricultural population. It introduced a state monopoly of the grain trade, prohibited private trading in grain and established the surplus-appropriation system under which all surplus produce in the hands of the peasants was to be registered and acquired by the state at fixed prices, so as to accumulate stores of grain for the provisioning of the army and workers. Lastly it introduced universal labor service for all classes. . . . All these measures which were necessitated by the exceptionally difficult conditions of national defense and bore a temporary character were in their entirety known as War Communism." *History of the Communist Party of the Soviet Union (Bolsheviks); Short Course* (Moscow, 1949), pp. 282 ff.

achievement of socialism was . . . thought of by Lenin at this time primarily in terms of world revolution."[82]

The New Economic Policy that followed the phase of War Communism was still merely a set of temporary measures, designed to promote a recovery of the national economy from the catastrophic depths into which it had been plunged by war, foreign intervention, and revolution. The purpose of those policies was not, any more than that of the earlier ones, the introduction of a socialist economic system, but the creation of transitional conditions that would permit the socialist government to retain political power until the triumph of socialism in the West.

The picture changed drastically in 1924. The failure of the last revolutionary attempt in Germany (the Hamburg uprising in the fall of 1923) placed the Soviet government face to face with an essentially new situation. It had become clear that the expectation of an early victory of Western socialism was erroneous, that socialism in Russia was isolated. This implied, however, that the Soviet regime in Russia, considered earlier as an essentially provisional arrangement for the duration of the "holding out" phase, had to stabilize itself for an indefinite period separating it from the world revolution, and to build "socialism in one country."[83]

Such stabilization was predicated upon a number of crucial conditions. First, the regime had to be able to meet Russia's urgent need for economic development—without any significant foreign assistance;[84] secondly, the economic growth of the country had to be so directed as to render it as immune as possible to economic blockade or outright military aggression deemed probable under conditions of "capitalist encirclement"; and third, the living standards of the population had to be improved and the internal political and economic basis of the socialist regime strengthened and broadened.

---

[82] Carr, *op. cit.*, p. 107.

[83] Cf. Stalin's *Report to the XVIII-th Congress of the CPSU* on March 10, 1939, where he developed also his modification of the theory of the "withering away" of the state under socialism. The meaning of that new orientation is frequently misunderstood. As Rudolf Schlesinger points out, "What was really discussed was not whether it was possible to build an ideal type of Socialism in one country but whether what could be built in one country should be supported or opposed." *The Spirit of Post-war Russia, Soviet Ideology 1916–1946* (London, 1947), p. 103.

[84] For a short review of the foreign economic relations of the USSR, cf. P. A. Baran, "The U.S.S.R. in the World Economy," *Foreign Economic Policy for the United States,* S. E. Harris, ed. (Cambridge, Mass., 1948).

These objectives became the guiding principles of the Five Year Plans of which the first was enacted in the spring of 1929.[85]

2. *The Determination of the Speed of Attainment.* The policies followed at any given time are only partly determined by long-term goals. The other coordinate is provided by the decision concerning the *tempo* at which the realization of these ends is sought. To be sure, the speed with which the long-term goals are to be attained is far from independent of the nature of the goals themselves. Indeed, the development of an integrated economy independent of foreign markets and able to support technically no less than economically its own further growth calls primarily for expansion of basic industries. This in itself necessitates certain minimum rates of advance. In the absence of an already existing elaborate framework of an industrial economy, every major industrial project requires outlays far in excess of its own cost. These outlays have to be synchronized if waste is to be avoided; plants consuming electric power have to be built at the same time as power stations are erected, coal mining has to be expanded simultaneously with the construction of blast furnaces, and dwellings for workers have to be built where new factories are established.[86]

What is more, prevailing technological standards impose indivisibilities that have to be taken into account in the determination of the investment program of any given year. Neither automobile factories nor hydroelectric plants can be acquired piecemeal or in such sizes as might be convenient. Even if adoption of units smaller than technologically optimal, or of a technology less capital intensive than the most advanced should appear rational at any particular moment, such policy might prove to have been myopic in the longer run.

At the same time, the nature and the rate of investment decided upon for the initial period of the program exercises a powerful influence upon the speed of expansion in ensuing periods. The basic industries constructed during the first period produce the investment goods to be used in the next; the volume of saving needed in the next period is thus greatly influenced by investment decisions made earlier.[87]

---

[85] For the history of the planning effort at that time see Friedrich Pollock, *Die Planwirtschaftlichen Versuche in der Sowjetunion, 1917–1927* (Leipzig, 1929), *passim,* and Maurice Dobb, *Soviet Economic Development since 1917* (London, 1948), pp. 230 ff.

[86] Cf. Dobb, *loc. cit.*

[87] Correspondingly, a program directed towards economic development via consumers' goods industries implies automatically not only smaller initial investment but also much lower rates of subsequent growth.

If the goal of expansion of basic industries necessarily implied rather high rates of speed in the execution of the development program, the Soviet government's appraisal of the international situation and of the dangers threatening Russia's external security suggested even higher *tempi* of growth.[88]

To some extent the accelerated preparation for defense coincided with the general industrialization program. Calling for emphasis on basic industries and mining as the essential prerequisites for current and potential expansion of military output, it reinforced the reasoning underlying the Soviet broad plan of economic development. On the other hand, suggesting dispersal of industry, erection of parallel plants, and the industrialization of the more distant areas of the Soviet Union, it prevented full utilization of available "external economies" and thus increased the magnitude of the required investment. It stimulated, however, the development of the backward regions of the USSR—highly desirable on its own account.

No such harmony, tentative as it may have been, existed with regard to the third fundamental objective: strengthening of the internal basis of the regime and improvement of the standard of life. That goal would have pointed to an altogether different strategy and to altogether different rates of development.

What is necessary in such a situation is a decision on the magnitude of the "economic surplus" that can be used for investment (and defense) purposes in any given period. If great urgency is attached to the attainment of the developmental (and/or defense) goals, consumption standards may be fixed at "rock bottom." This "rock bottom" is indicated by the need to preserve health and productive efficiency of the population and to maintain political stability.

It goes without saying that the reduction of current consumption to such "rock-bottom" levels is highly undesirable. Under conditions of strain that would inevitably result from such "belt tightening," even small hitches in production, let alone crop failures, may easily give rise to major difficulties.[89] Moreover, the political and economic costs of mo-

---

[88] "We are 50–100 years behind the advanced countries. We have to traverse this distance in ten years. We will either accomplish it or else we will be crushed." Joseph Stalin, *Problems of Leninism* (11th ed., Moscow, 1939), p. 329. (Translated from the Russian by the writer.) It is interesting to note that this statement was made on February 4, 1931, i.e., exactly ten years prior to Germany's invasion of Russia.

[89] This is the reason for the stress placed by the Soviet authorities on the accumulation of sizeable reserves of all important consumers' goods. Cf. G. Sorokin, *Sotsialisticheskoie Planirovanie Narodnogo Khosiaistva SSSR* (Socialist Planning of the National Economy of the USSR) (Moscow, 1946), p. 24.

bilizing the marginal amount of the "surplus" may be entirely out of proportion to the advantages that can be derived from it for the developmental program. Thus the First Five Year Plan, although programming extremely high rates of expansion, was very far from scheduling a reduction of consumption to "rock-bottom" levels. In actual fact it anticipated an increase of consumption by as much as 40 per cent over the quinquennium.[90]

The decision on the magnitude of the "economic surplus" extractable from the economy for investment purposes is thus of an eminently political and socio-psychological nature. It has to take into account not only the "margin of social and political tolerance" but also the effect of any level of consumption on incentives and efficiency. It has to depend, moreover, on the possibility and the cost of securing control over the "economic surplus" by the governmental authorities.[91]

3. *The Mobilization of the "Economic Surplus."* The authorities can secure the resources needed for investment, defense, social services, administration, and the like in a number of alternative ways. Some of the criteria by which the choice has to be made are purely technical—the reliability, convenience, and cost of various procedures. Where the resources involved represent a large share of an absolutely low aggregate income, as is the case in the Soviet Union, political considerations assume prime importance. The mobilization of the "surplus" has to be so organized as to minimize the political resistance to what is bound to be an unpopular policy. At the same time the distribution of the burden of the program among various social groups and classes has to be calculated so as to strengthen the social and political basis of the regime. Much of the controversy in Russia in the late twenties and early thirties centered around this issue.

The best procedure for withdrawing from the population the share of its money income which is required to meet the government's outlay is an income tax. Under the conditions prevailing in the Soviet Union prior to the industrialization period this method of raising revenue was beset with considerable difficulties. As far as the urban population was concerned, the tax could be readily assessed and collected. Matters were much less simple with regard to the rural sector of the economy. Neither

---

[90] Dobb, *Soviet Economic Development*, p. 235. This increase did not materialize in view of unexpected difficulties associated mainly with the peasants' resistance to collectivization.

[91] On the share of national product devoted to investment, cf. Abram Bergson, "Soviet National Income and Product in 1937," *Quart. Jour. Econ.*, May and Aug. 1950, LXIV, 208–41, 408–41; also P. A. Baran, "National Income and Product of the U.S.S.R. in 1940," *Rev. Econ. Stat.*, Nov. 1947, XXIX, 226–34.

the assessment of income accruing in agriculture nor the collection of the tax from subsistence farmers appeared to be a manageable task. The fiscal authorities were confronted with strong resistance on the part of the peasants—only recently freed of the tax and rent burdens of the Czarist days—and measures of enforcement of the tax assessments, such as removal of produce in kind or confiscation of livestock, were bound to provoke profound hostility against the government and were politically intolerable.

Another method of securing the resources needed for the realization of the governmental program is the expansion of the earnings of the government-owned and operated sector of the economy (industry, transportation, trade, etc.). This could be accomplished by keeping industrial prices low in relation to prices of agricultural products—combining, however, such a price policy with a wage policy leaving large profits in the hands of the nationalized enterprises. Such a course, favoring the agricultural population, would place the burden of the program upon the shoulders of industrial workers. Even if it could have been made to yield sufficient revenue—a doubtful assumption in view of the relative smallness of the government sector of the economy prior to its expansion under the Five Year Plans—it would have been politically wholly unacceptable.

The accumulation of profits in the governmental sector of the economy could be brought about not merely by an appropriate wage policy but also by raising the prices charged for its output. The obvious advantage of this procedure as compared with relying on industrial wage policy alone is that it distributes the burden of the accumulation process between the urban and the rural sectors of the population.[92]

Yet this strategy, involving the "opening of the scissors," i.e., a shift in relative prices in favor of industry, could be and was effectively counteracted by the "kulaks," i.e., peasants in possession of marketable surpluses, who refused to exchange on terms proposed by the government. While rural demand for some products of the nationalized sector was sufficiently inelastic to enable the government to obtain for them certain quantities of agricultural produce, the general tendency of those agricultural producers that mattered was either to reduce their output or to increase their own consumption of agricultural produce, rather than to trade on terms below what they considered to be a "parity" ratio.

---

[92] This policy could be and was—actually not according to plan—reinforced by inflationary developments accompanying almost the entire period of the first two five-year plans.

At the peril of overemphasizing one aspect of the problem at the expense of others, it may be said that the collectivization of Soviet agriculture was motivated to a large extent by the necessity of overcoming this crucial hurdle. To be sure, expansion of agricultural output and release of agricultural manpower for industrial employment—possible only through transition to large-scale farming and through mechanization of agricultural production—were by themselves objectives of tremendous importance. However, without a reorganization of the agricultural economy assuring the possibility of "syphoning off" agricultural surpluses, progress in agricultural production would have only slowly affected the volume of agricultural output available for nonrural consumption.

By transferring the disposal of agricultural output from individual peasants to government-supervised collective farm managements, collectivization destroyed the basis for the peasants' resistance to the accumulation policy. From now on the share of agricultural output consumed on the farm could be fixed by direct apportionment to collective farm members, while farm consumption of nonagricultural commodities could be regulated by fixing the prices paid by the government for the marketed share of agricultural output and charged by the urban sector of the economy for goods supplied to the farm population.

The way was thus open for wage and price policies to become the main instruments for mobilization of the "economic surplus" of the entire economy. The total of wages paid (including the apportionment in kind to collective farm members) is calculated to absorb the share of total product allotted to consumption, while the government secures control over the part of national income to be devoted to investment, defense, social services, administration, etc., through the profits of the government-controlled enterprises.

These profits could be transferred in their entirety to the government, which could use them to defray its planned outlays. In actual fact a more complicated procedure is employed. A large share of the profits is paid over to the government in the form of an "advance." This "advance," called "turnover tax," is contributed to the State budget immediately following the marketing of the factory's products, *independent of cost accounting.*[93] The balance of the profits—the difference between the wholesale price net of turnover tax and cost—appears as profits *sensu strictu.* A share of these profits is paid to the government at the end

---

[93] M. I. Bogolepov, *The Soviet Financial System* (London, 1945), p. 9 (italics supplied).

of the accounting period as "deductions from profits," while the remainder is left with the enterprises for various stipulated purposes.[94]

There are a number of reasons for the employment of this cumbersome device. One is that "the State cannot wait for periodical balance sheets to be issued in order to determine how much a given establishment has accumulated."[95] Payment (or nonpayment) of the turnover tax serves thus as a rapidly reacting indicator of the extent to which productive plans are fulfilled by the individual enterprise. Equally important perhaps is the consideration that "flooding" of individual enterprises with vast profits not to be surrendered until the end of an accounting period would generate an atmosphere of "quasi-prosperity" in their managerial offices and exercise an adverse effect upon the effort to assure economical conduct of plant operations. Moreover, this arrangement prevents accumulation of "artificial" profits generated *within* the industrial system and not representing a withdrawal of "economic surplus." ". . . Since a very large part of what is produced by heavy industry is consumed by State-owned industry . . . prices of industrial equipment either do not include the turnover tax or only at a very low rate. . . ."[96]

This is not the place for a detailed description of the Soviet financial system.[97] Suffice it to add that the "turnover tax" and the "deductions from profits" account for the bulk of the "economic surplus" generated in the country. The balance appears in the form of small amounts of profits reinvested locally, the even less significant income taxes, various minor business taxes, loans from the public and the like.

4. *The Allocation of the "Economic Surplus."* Most of the "economic surplus" is channeled through the government budget into a variety of purposes. While a share of it serves to support the military establishment, governmental administration, and social and cultural undertakings, the balance is used to carry out the investment program.

Two types of problems have to be solved in determining the use of these investment funds. The *total* must be divided among different in-

---

[94] Approved local investment, payment of bonuses to employees, erection of welfare establishments (work canteens, rest homes, etc.).

[95] Bogolepov, *loc. cit.*

[96] *Ibid.*, p. 10.

[97] Good treatments of the subject will be found in Bogolepov, *op. cit.*, Dobb, *Soviet Economic Development*, Alexander Baykov, *Soviet Economic System* (Cambridge-New York, 1947), and in the Russian language in K. N. Plotnikov, *Budzet Sotsialisticheskogo Gosudarstva* (The Budget of the Socialist State) (Moscow, 1948), and N. N. Rovinski, *Gosudarstvenny Budzet SSSR* (The State Budget of the USSR) (Moscow, 1949).

dustries, and a choice has to be made concerning the technical form that investment should take in any particular case.[98] The former issue is to a large extent prejudged by the decisions concerning the goal and tempo of the developmental program. Once these decisions are made, "the problems of economic planning seem to acquire a resemblance to the problems of military strategy, where in practice the choice lies between a relatively small number of plans, which have in the main to be treated and chosen between as organic wholes, and which for a variety of reasons do not easily permit of intermediate combinations."[99]

This choice between "a relatively small number of plans" seems to be made by an appraisal of the feasibilities and implications of the available alternatives. Certain specific bottlenecks—shortages of steel or machine tools or transportation facilities—may dictate the selection of a plan calling for the least quantity of the critical item. The need to concentrate scarce managerial or technical talent on one construction project rather than dissipating it on a number of undertakings may dictate the preference for a certain technological process.

Such a preference, in turn, may temporarily preclude investment even of relatively small quantities of resources to other branches of the economy, although the advantages that such investment may promise could be large. "The economic plan singles out each time the leading branches of the national economy, the crucial links that have to be grasped for the entire chain of economic development to be pulled up."[100]

The consecutive plans are thus characterized by the nature of the "link" singled out. "The crucial link of the first Five Year Plan was the heavy industry with its heart piece—machine building. The decisive links in the second and third Five Year Plans were the leading branches of the heavy industry—metallurgy, machine building, fuel, energetics, chemistry. Under the conditions of the Patriotic War the crucial link in the plan was military production."[101] It is this concentration upon the highest priority tasks that gives the Soviet economy the character of a "target economy." At any particular time certain highest priority objectives command exceptional attention. This frequently results in transi-

---

[98] Maurice Dobb, "A Note on the Discussion of the Problem of Choice between Alternative Investment Projects," *Soviet Studies*, Jan. 1951, II, 291.

[99] Dobb, *Soviet Economic Development*, p. 6. "Much substitution in production arises through shifts in the extent to which alternative processes are used, rather than through variation in factor combinations in the individual process." T. C. Koopmans, "Efficient Allocation of Resources," *Econometrica*, Oct. 1951, XIX, 455 ff.

[100] Sorokin, *op. cit.*, p. 22 (translated from the Russian by the writer).

[101] *Ibid.*, p. 23.

tory "disproportionalities." The fulfillment of one target is accompanied by lags in the attainment of others. The next period witnesses, then, a shift of emphasis to the backward "links" that have to be pulled up for the "chain" to be straightened out.

This strategy of local advances followed by a subsequent consolidation of the conquered terrain is dictated, however, by the specific conditions of the Russian economy, and may well represent a particularly effective method for a rapid development of underdeveloped countries. Where slow growth rather than urgent structural change should constitute the guiding principle of the economic effort, the pattern of "campaigns" and "targets" may be inappropriate, and investment could be allocated in relatively small portions among different branches of the economy with a view to equating their productivities on the margin.

However, the decision about the production targets and the distribution of the investment funds among different *branches* of the economy leaves unanswered the question how to choose between different *modes* of producing the desired output. The solution of this problem suggested by conventional theory (the ratios of costs of factors to their respective marginal value products should be the same for all factors) would provide no succor to the planning authority. Even if sufficient continuity of substitution could be assumed, the Planning Board would have to consider not only the *social* costs involved in the employment of an additional quantity of a factor, but also—and this is most important—take into account the impact of its own activities on the future relative scarcities of factors.

Thus the existence of a large rural surplus population may have suggested (and still suggests) that in Russia strong preference should be given to techniques employing much labor and little capital. Yet such advice would overlook the large social cost of transferring a man from the village into industrial occupation. The additional industrial worker must be provided with urban dwelling space. Paid the going industrial wage, he must be assured of the quantity of food, clothing, etc., that is usually consumed by industrial workers.[102] Even if his product in the new occupation should exceed the cost of his sustenance in the city, it may be impossible for technical and/or political reasons to extract the requisite additional food from agriculture. True, the "disguised unemployed" had contributed previously nothing or little to total agricultural output while consuming a certain quantity of food. That food came, however, from

---

[102] This quantity itself is largely influenced by political considerations!

his family's table and constituted no drain on the sparse "marketed share" of agricultural output.

Since the expansion of agricultural output and the increase of agricultural supplies available to the cities require not only large-scale investment but also a considerable amount of time, the physical limitations on the amount of food that could be placed at the disposal of the urban population may by themselves call for the selection of capital-intensive rather than labor-intensive techniques of production.

The same conclusion may be arrived at if it is considered that the abundance and "cheapness" of currently available labor is only a temporary condition *preceding* the realization of any given stretch of the developmental program. The Planning Board, aware of the aggregate demand for labor entailed by its own plans, has to bear in mind therefore that relatively soon, during the life-span of the equipment that is to be installed, labor may turn from a relatively ample to a relatively scarce factor.

These very general considerations may suffice in the present context. A lively and extensive discussion of possible formal criteria to be followed in making specific investment decisions has been taking place in the recent Soviet literature; it would exceed by far the available space to present here a detailed account of its contents.[103] The Planning Board itself has not yet stated, to my knowledge, what principles it follows in making the relevant decisions. It is most likely, however, that the Soviet economist Chernomordik expresses the official view.

Our advocates of the employment of a coefficient of effectiveness to solve the problem of comparing alternatives try to equip themselves with some kind of a slide rule to mechanize the labor of project-making. This mathematical method only serves, in the last analysis, to divert attention from the real problem: the comprehensive study of the basic processes of the economy; ascertainment of the effect on the national economy of any particular capital construction.[104]

5. *The Balance Sheet.* The investment decisions of the Central Authority as well as of managements on lower (plant and regional) levels are combined with the estimates of the magnitude and composition of consumers' goods supply and checked for mutual consistency in the so-

---

[103] Condensed translations of the relevant articles are published in *Soviet Studies* as well as in the *Current Digest of the Soviet Press.* Norman Kaplan has presented an excellent summary and analysis of the debate in: "Investment Alternatives in Soviet Economic Theory," *Jour. Pol. Econ.,* Apr. 1952, LX, 133–44.

[104] D. I. Chernomordik, "Effectiveness of Capital Investment and the Theory of Reproduction: Towards a Statement of the Problem," *Voprosy Ekonomiki* (June, 1949), pp. 78–95, translated in *Soviet Studies,* Apr. 1950, I, 359–63.

called "national-economic balance sheets." To describe the procedure involved, it may be best to present an extensive quotation from the work of a Soviet economist:

The balance sheets and distribution plans as drawn up at the present time include: firstly, material balance sheets (in kind) showing the proportions of the material elements of reproduction; secondly, value (price) balance sheets showing the proportions in the distribution of financial resources and ensuring proper proportion in the distribution of the social product in respect of its material form and its value; thirdly, balance sheets for labour power.

Material balance sheets (in kind) consist of the following: 1) balance sheets of industrial products which, considering the main purpose for which they are to be used, represent the elements of the fixed funds of the national economy that ensure fulfillment of the construction program of the national-economic plan (equipment and building materials), 2) balance sheets of industrial and agricultural products, which considering the main purpose for which they are to be used, represent the elements of the circulating funds of the national economy that ensure fulfillment of the production program of the national-economic plan (metals, fuel, electric power, chemicals, agricultural raw materials), 3) balance sheets of industrial and agricultural products, which, considering the main purpose for which they are to be used, represent articles of individual consumption.

The material balance sheets and distribution plans, which are approved by the Government, cover products of national-economic importance as well as products which require centralized distribution because of their shortage. During the war the number of items of funded products, i.e. products distributed by the centre, had to be considerably enlarged.

Value balance sheets consist of the following: 1) balance sheet of the population's money income and expenditure, 2) the State Bank's cash plan, and 3) the state budget.

The income side of the balance sheet of the population's money income and expenditures covers the wage fund of the workers and office employees and other incomes of the urban population; the expenditure side covers expenditure by the population in buying goods at state and cooperative stores, paying for services and other money expenditures. The chief purpose of this balance sheet of the population's money income and expenditure is to ensure proper proportion in planning the volume of trade, the wage fund and the money income of collective farmers. This balance sheet serves as a basis for drafting the trade plan and also for planning the wage fund in the national economy.

The State Bank's cash plan serves as an important means for planning money circulation. The income side accounts for money received by the State Bank from trade turnover and payments by state organization; the expenditure side accounts for payments made against the wage fund and other money expenditures. The State Bank's cash plan makes it possible to determine the volume of currency emissions required for the ensuing period.

The state budget is a most important financial balance sheet which determines the distribution of the bulk of the national income. The main items of revenue in the state budget are accumulations of the socialist economy in the form of profits and turnover tax, and money received from the population in payment of taxes, subscriptions to state loans, etc. The expenditure side of the state budget consists of disbursements made in financing the national economy (production and capital construction), social and cultural development, administrative expenses and expenditures on defence. The function of the state budget is to ensure the financing without deficit of the national economy with the aid of the country's internal financial resources.

The labour power balance sheets include: 1) the balance sheet for labour power in the state economy, which determines the demand for labour power and skilled personnel in the various branches of the national economy, and the principal sources for recruiting labour for it (training the state labour reserve schools, organized hiring of labour), 2) the balance sheet of labour power in the collective farms, which determines the utilization of collective-farm labour resources for carrying out the plan of agricultural production and for work in industry.

The balance sheets system in the national-economic plan makes it possible correctly to solve the problem of planning resources, consumption and distribution in the national economy.[105]

The method thus briefly sketched represents a merely formal solution of the task of maintaining a general dynamic equilibrium of the Soviet economy. Whether it assures a smooth functioning of the economic system depends obviously on the magnitudes that are entered in that generalized "input-output" matrix.[106] The degree of accuracy that is attained in the estimation of the shape of the technological transformation functions, of the volume of actual production in individual plants, and of consumption of various goods by the consumers, determine the extent to which the plan is able to avoid disproportionalities and waste.

There can be no doubt that both have characterized the working of Soviet planning—particularly in its earlier phases. Yet the causes of these deficiencies may have been primarily associated with the historical setting of the Russian planning effort rather than with the principles underlying it. The breakneck speed of the "target-economy" calling for the "leading links" strategy accounted for continuous occurrence and re-

---

[105] A. D. Kursky, *The Planning of the National Economy of the U.S.S.R.* (Moscow, 1949), pp. 129 ff. The remainder of the chapter from which the above is cited contains additional valuable information on the methodology of Soviet planning. Cf. also Sorokin, *op. cit., passim.*

[106] The problems involved in elaborating such a matrix are akin to those discussed in W. W. Leontief, *The Structure of the American Economy, 1919–1929* (Cambridge, Mass., 1941), in particular p. 34, although the difficulties that have to be overcome in the planning practice may not be quite as stupendous as suggested by Leontief's analysis. It may be sufficient for the "central" matrix to include only the "leading links" of the economy, leaving a great deal to the functioning of the decentralized economic units.

currence of major successes in some parts of the economy and equally serious "gaps" in others; the poverty of the country made it impossible until the late thirties to accumulate sufficient reserves to permit a rapid plugging of those "gaps"; and the lack of personnel scientifically trained for planning work on all levels caused avoidable mistakes in the preparation of the estimates determining the relationships embodied in the plan.

The "hitches" that occur in the functioning of the system become less frequent and less costly as their causes gradually disappear. Slowing down the speed of industrialization, filling the "pipelines" of the economy with the indispensable stocks of food, raw materials, fuel, etc., the availability of adequately prepared planning officials, combined with growing levels of literacy and civic responsibility on the part of the population, lead to a progressive improvement of the actual performance of the economic system.[107]

As Maurice Dobb points out, ". . . the notion that successful development from one economic situation, with its given combination of resources and configuration of demand, to another might be a more crucial test of the contribution made by an economic system to human welfare than the attainment of perfect equilibrium in any given situation seldom commanded attention."[108] Such attention, on the part of social scientists, is however urgently called for by the problems faced by many relatively advanced nations, but faced especially by the multitudes living in the world's underdeveloped countries.

Very little of what constitutes the main body of our customary economic theorizing would seem to be of much help in solving these perplexities. What the Soviet experience strongly suggests is the need for concrete historical research into the social and political prerequisites for economic growth and development. The "standards of perfection" evolved in the writings on "economics of socialism" offer no guidance in the effort to conquer backwardness, squalor, and oppression. "The advocacy of impossible changes is advocacy of no changes at all." The contribution that economic science can make to the solution of the prob-

---

[107] An impressive testimonial of efficiency was the rapid conversion and reallocation of the Russian industry during the war, as well as its reconversion and growth during the postwar years. On the latter, cf. Abram Bergson, J. H. Blackman, and Alexander Erlich, "Postwar Economic Reconstruction and Development in the U.S.S.R.," *Annals Am. Acad. Pol. Soc. Sci.,* May 1949, CCLXIV, 52 ff., as well as the more recent statements on the "Results of the Fourth (Postwar) Five Year Plan," *New Times,* Apr. 25, 1951, XVII (Suppl.).

[108] *Soviet Economic Development,* p. 3.

lems of a planned economy is more likely to be found on the lines suggested by Wassily Leontief and "linear programming" than in the refinements of "optimum conditions" pertaining to an imaginary world. This contribution would be amply rewarded—by the continuous "feedback" linking realistic economics with the demands and issues of reality. What this implies, however, is that in a rationally organized society the economist of our days would be one of the "disguised unemployed" to be transferred to the position of "social engineer" helping to understand and to create the conditions for economic and social progress.

COMMENT
J. K. Galbraith

It is not easy for the critic to come to grips with Baran's brilliant and persuasive essay. The author leaves few obvious handholds for disagreement; his argument is closely reasoned and impressively buttressed by authority. Yet, in my own case at least, I found myself eventually exposed to conclusions which I would not have reached without the author's compelling guidance and which, when eventually tested against the facts of everyday existence, seem to me substantially in error.

I have no complaint, along the foregoing lines, with the author's treatment of planning in the backward countries. His analysis of the barrier to progress that is imposed by corrupt and reactionary ruling groups seems to me sound and useful. Perhaps there are more exceptions than he implies. One might at least hope that India, for example, is finding some sort of path of evolutionary development, as Puerto Rico has shown a similar possibility on a small scale nearer at hand. But there are great elements of truth in his argument, and for these I am willing to settle.

I am not able to challenge generally his treatment of planning in socialist countries. I am troubled as to why his state which, as the mirror of conflicting and dominating pressures, acts as a barrier to rational economic action in the advanced capitalist country (or confines it to leaf-raking and arms building), ceases to be a barrier in the socialist state: Are there in such countries no group interests organized, if not around profit, at least around power, prestige, and bureaucratic status? May not these limit or frustrate development? But I profess to no real competence in the theory of socialist planning and, since the editor is aware of this, I assume that the division of labor between critics was designed to give this part of the task to my colleague.

My considerable difference with Baran concerns the advanced capitalist countries and the possibility that they can assume a reasonably intelligent and rational control over their economic destiny. The net of his conclusion is they cannot; a pervasive conflict with capitalist attitudes will confine action to meaningless expedients such as make-work or worse. It would seem to me, nonetheless, a reasonable conclusion from the recent history of the United States, the Scandinavian countries, the United Kingdom, and the more advanced of the other British Commonwealth countries that this is not so.

In Germany between the wars we had a demonstration of almost classic clarity of the contradictions in a parliamentary democracy between dominant capitalist attitudes and effective action to improve welfare and to increase and stabilize employment. The outcome in fascism was the one which the author's analysis makes inevitable. But in outlining this new road to serfdom it seems to me that the author tends, as did Hayek, his precursor though not necessarily his mentor in dismal prophecy, to identify the German case with the world. Germans are not thought to be people of high political capacity. Is it not possible that they have failed where the improvisation and compromise of others have succeeded and might continue to succeed?

If we stick with employment and stabilization of output as the central goals, it seems to me there is substantial evidence to this effect. In most of the advanced countries—Germany is still a noteworthy exception —tax systems have been developed and even redesigned to free income when output declines and to collect more when it rises; there are now automatic subventions to worker and agricultural incomes to cushion any drop; it would seem certain that in the advanced Western countries there is a state of mind which not only admits of, but demands, positive management of taxation and public expenditure to stabilize income and employment. Things which cannot be done in principle are being done, albeit imperfectly, in practice.

There are two reasons why they are possible. For one thing, I cannot believe that the state is nearly so devastatingly a possession of business as the author believes. Neither is it a possession of labor or a disembodied and detached arbiter—the alternatives in the author's somewhat overly exclusive categories. In fact, it is something of all three and more. It is, as everyday observation surely suggests, a focus of many and changing pressures among which that of business, though surely important, is not exclusive. The result is not favorable to a precise full-employment policy, but it is not inimical to an imprecise one.

This brings me to the author's second mistake which grows out of a kind of perfectionism which leads him to dismiss as a failure what is not ideal. The kind of employment policy toward which, in my view, the advanced capitalist countries have been making their way will never work perfectly. It may involve inflation at some times; unemployment at others; some misuse of resources at still others. But none of these things need be fatal and certainly not the latter. Especially in the United States, wealth provides what may be a generous margin for error. It is idle to suppose that an employment policy can be executed with precision; it is quite possible to suppose that it can be so executed as to keep the economy within its margins of tolerance and these may be quite generous.

COMMENT
Adolph Lowe

Baran's essay is an original contribution to, rather than a survey of, the contemporary economics of planning. It so happens that I find myself in wide agreement with the tenor, though not always with the temper, of his arguments. Yet in the interest of readers who look for factual information, I wish it were possible to close both the factual and the literary gaps in Baran's presentation. Due to limitations of space all I can do is to enumerate some of the issues a consideration of which should not be absent from a well-rounded picture.

1. The first comment refers to the *aims* of economic planning. Baran discusses two: full employment in advanced capitalism, and economic growth in underdeveloped regions, including the Soviet Union. But the theory and practice of planning in advanced capitalist countries has recently been concerned with, at least, two additional aims.

First, economic growth, understood as adjustment to the shift in the world's economic balance, has become a primary concern also in the Western world, particularly in Western Europe. This concern centers upon two main issues: planned improvement of domestic productivity and supra-national integration. Most of the planning measures taken by the British Labor government were to serve the former purpose, as does the Monet Plan in France or the "National Budget" in Norway. Pointers of the latter tendency are Benelux, the European Payments Union, the Schuman Plan, and the various schemes of European economic unification which followed in the wake of the Marshall Plan.[109]

But in recent years a second aim of economic planning has come to the fore which may, in the long run, have an even stronger impact upon the structure of the advanced capitalist countries including the United States: preparation for defense. As a consequence, the experience with "war economics" and its theoretical interpretation may supply a better equipment for the solution of this generation's economic problems than do the most advanced treatises of peacetime economics.

2. This leads to a comment upon the *techniques* of economic planning. In concentrating upon the full-employment issue, Baran naturally focuses his attention upon monetary and fiscal policies. But it is unfortunate that he regards direct controls as an alternative, rather than a supplement, to "indirect" planning techniques, and even exclusively as a fascist alternative. In the state of permanent "overemployment," which the preparedness economy of the years ahead is likely to create, an elastic combination of both techniques may well form the major challenge to theory and practice.

A word must be added about planning in underdeveloped countries. Baran reaches his pessimistic conclusion by making large-scale industrial development the central point. But all the time actual development has been progressing in many regions, notably in parts of Latin America, India, and certain countries of the Near East. This was possible because small-scale techniques have proved very effective in overcoming the bottlenecks of capital scarcity and low labor skills in certain agricultural and industrial projects.[110]

3. Perhaps the most important aspect in Baran's exposition is his continuous emphasis on the *socio-political environment* within which planning takes place. Certainly economic planning is a matter of social rather than of technical engineering, and the planner has, at least in the early stages, to take the social framework as his strongest datum. However, in accepting this postulate, one need not agree with the sweeping strokes with which Baran paints the images of his three social types.

He doubts that the democratic structure in the countries of advanced capitalism is strong enough to sustain the shift in political and social power which successful planning requires. And yet, stability of em-

---

[109] For details see S. E. Harris, *Economic Planning* (New York, 1949).

[110] See H. G. Aubrey, "Small Industry in Economic Development," *Social Research*, Sept. 1951, XVIII, 269–312.

ployment and security against aggression are aims so fundamental for survival that the pressure groups of democratic societies may subordinate to them their sectional aspirations. It is true that the problem of labor incentives becomes crucial, once the "stick" of unemployment is removed. But the evidence we have of the United States or Britain does not prove a serious abuse of trade union power, nor the ineffectiveness of the remaining "carrot." One cannot deny that Baran points to a possible alternative. But in the present state of international affairs the inner solidarity, at least of the Anglo-American societies, is likely to prove strong enough to carry essential measures of economic planning.

One would hardly venture a similar prediction for the present social order in the underdeveloped regions generally. There, in certain cases, political and social change, and possibly revolution, will have to precede planning for economic growth. But again this is not true of countries like Mexico, Chile, Uruguay, India, Turkey, or Israel. Their social regimes, though only in few instances compatible with standards of Western democracy, seem capable of progress by reformist means. Their growth would then appear to be a genuine economic task based on a combination of domestic planning and foreign aid.

Finally, while overpessimistic with regard to the noncommunist part of the world, Baran may well be too optimistic in evaluating the long-term strength of the Soviet social fabric. One cannot take an unlimited power of resistance to strains of forced development simply for granted. The danger grows with the incorporation into the Soviet orbit of societies with different social traditions.

4. In conclusion, a comment is due to Baran's treatment of the *full-employment* issue. In spite of his reservations against the Keynesian conclusions, he has identified himself with the Keynesian assumption that the ultimate cause of capitalist unemployment is "voluntary" underconsumption. Logically this hypothesis is tenable. But the statistical data covering the last fifty years suggest other primary causes: undersaving and "forced" underconsumption owing to technological displacement. At any rate, planning for full employment will have to take into account all types of large and sudden changes. It has, in other words, to utilize the results of business-cycle research.[111]

---

[111] See *Conference on Business Cycles Held under the Auspices of the Universities-National Bureau Committee for Economic Research* (New York, 1951), pp. 375–403.

10

METHODOLOGICAL

DEVELOPMENTS

Richard Ruggles

The preceding essays in both volumes of *A Survey of Contemporary Economics* have been concerned with the presentation and appraisal of recent work in specific fields. In these essays, attention has already been devoted to developments in the methodology of each of the fields.[1] To present these specialized methodological techniques in detail would be unnecessarily repetitious (and presumptuous), besides being impossible in the allotted space. On the other hand, the restriction of this essay to explicit methodological controversies would be excessively dull, and would present a distorted picture of methodological developments. Instead, a framework will be developed as a basis for discussing broad methodological approaches, certain recently developed research techniques, and some of the methodology implicit in current economic research. The discussion will be developed as follows. Part I will contain an arbitrary breakdown of the research process, using the latter term in its broadest sense. There is nothing basic or original in this classification scheme; it has been drawn up entirely with reference to the task at hand. Part II will concern itself with the examination of specific broad methodological approaches, in terms of the framework erected in Part I. This section will also contain a brief review of recent explicit discussions in the economic literature on these approaches. Part III will consider the methodological implications of certain specific techniques which are recent developments in the field of economic research. Finally, Part IV will examine some of the changes in the methodologies which are

---

[1] For bibliographical material on the special topics discussed, e.g., econometrics, dynamic analysis, etc., the reader is referred to the essays on these topics. Bibliographical notes in this essay will be confined to those sources to which direct reference is made in the text.

implicit in current economic research, and the factors affecting the choice and use of these various specific methodologies.

I. THE PROCESS OF ECONOMIC RESEARCH

For the purpose of this survey, economic research will be viewed as a process involving four consecutive stages of analysis. These stages are: (1) the exploration of the problem; (2) the theoretical development of hypotheses; (3) the empirical testing of hypotheses; and (4) the evaluation of conclusions. For a given research project these steps are cumulative in the sense that the carrying out of any particular stage of analysis automatically requires that the previous stages have already been carried out in some manner or other. On the other hand, earlier stages of analysis can proceed independently of the stages that are supposed to follow. It is possible, of course, that the attention of any one research worker or group may be directed only to one stage of the analysis, or that several stages may be merged together. All stages are necessary, however, in order to cover the full range of economic research. Furthermore, a research project which is primarily concerned with the exploration of the problem (Stage 1), for example, may be highly dependent on the empirical testing (Stage 3) carried out in other research projects.

1. *The Exploration of the Problem.* This stage of analysis relates to the scope and purpose of research. Although it may be vague and confused in many instances, it still remains a matter of basic importance. Before any question can be investigated, the problem must be defined, either implicitly or explicitly. No data can be collected without first deciding what is to be collected. No hypothesis can be made without first considering the general subject and range of the problem. Economists sometimes inherit their problems, perhaps without really realizing it, and in other cases they enter the analysis after the problem has been set up by previous work in the area. But often considerable stress is laid upon this first stage of analysis, and specific techniques are used to delineate the range of the problem and to obtain a more definite formulation of the issues involved. Some research workers do not go beyond this point, but rather are content to spend all of their energies in setting up the problem to be studied. Once a formal hypothesis is formulated, even in a fairly crude way, this first stage can be considered finished.

2. *The Theoretical Development of Hypotheses.* After the purpose and scope of the problem have been decided upon, further research

usually takes the form of developing the hypothesis. This is the domain of theory in the process of research. At this juncture the original scope and purpose of the project may be altered considerably to fit the convenience of the research worker. Simplifying assumptions may be introduced, or consideration may be restricted to special aspects of the problem, so that a specific hypothesis may be developed more fully. Attention is focused on the nature and the interrelation of various alternative hypotheses, and various conditions and assumptions are set up within which the analysis is to be carried on. Since every hypothesis entails certain assumptions and has certain implications, theorists also have the task of analyzing hypotheses to reveal their implicit assumptions and their logical consequences. It is often possible to prove by theoretical means alone that an hypothesis is inconsistent with itself or that it is in contradiction to a related hypothesis. This stage of analysis, then, considers the logical basis and the logical implications of the hypothesis. All research which goes beyond problem-raising must enter this stage.

3. *The Empirical Testing of Hypotheses.* Considerable discussion has revolved around the question of whether economics should test its theorems directly, or indirectly by testing its postulates.[2] One cannot help but feel, however, that the differences of opinion have been more terminological than substantive. For the purpose of the present survey, therefore, any theorem or postulate for which empirical testing is proposed will be included within the coverage of the term "hypothesis." Estimation of parameters and conditional or actual predictions which are based on empirical information are essentially of the same nature as the direct empirical testing of hypotheses. They involve obtaining the "best" fit of empirical data to a previously formulated theory. As additional empirical data become available, these estimations of parameters and predictions may be considered to be hypotheses, and tested accordingly. Not all hypotheses are operationally meaningful, in the sense that they could conceivably be refuted by empirical data.[3] Of those hypotheses which can be tested empirically, the majority can only be tested in the negative sense, i.e., refuted; only hypotheses which refer purely to unique

---

[2] See Lionel Robbins, *An Essay on the Nature and Significance of Economic Science* (London, 1932; 2nd ed., 1935); F. S. C. Northrop, *The Logic of the Sciences and the Humanities* (New York, 1948), pp. 247 *et seq.;* and J. R. N. Stone, *The Role of Measurement in Economics* (Cambridge, 1950), pp. 12–14.

[3] This is not to say that all hypotheses which are not operationally meaningful and so cannot be proven either correct or incorrect by any empirical means are useless and nonsense; such a statement is itself an hypothesis which is not operationally meaningful, and to assume it to be correct is simultaneously to declare it to be nonsense.

events can ever be considered proven correct. The most that can be said for all other hypotheses is that their conclusions are not contradicted by the empirical evidence at hand. Some empirical testing is of an extremely simple nature; the maker of the hypothesis simply relies on his own experience and casual observation to check it. On the other hand, empirical testing can become an extremely elaborate stage of analysis requiring masses of information and highly developed techniques. In any case the stage of empirical testing of hypotheses requires as a prerequisite the existence of hypotheses to test, and it serves the function of eliminating those hypotheses which can be proven wrong. By this' process those hypotheses which are not in contradiction with empirical data tend to remain in the body of economic doctrine.

4. *The Evaluation of Conclusions.* For many economists, it is not enough to test whether or not a given hypothesis is contradicted by empirical information; the problem of the importance of the resulting conclusion in terms of value judgments still remains. Where the analysis is at all complex, the evaluation of the significance of the conclusions will be an aggregation of value judgments derived from some social or individual system of ethics and tastes. This final stage of the analysis arises because economists tend to be socially oriented, and do not like spending their energies on trivial and irrelevant issues. Although most economists prefer, if possible, to avoid some of the more controversial value judgments, it is usual to allow some of the more general ethical considerations to enter into the evaluation of conclusions.

Methodology can now be defined as the manner in which these various stages of analysis are approached, and the importance given to each stage in a specific research project. Every research project thus may have a unique methodology, since the substance of the work will in large part determine the relative accent laid upon the different stages of analysis and upon the different approaches utilized. By considering methodology in this manner, it becomes possible to discuss the differences among various specific methodologies, and to make observations relating to the trend of methodological developments. The following section will discuss the relation of a number of methodological approaches to the four stages of analysis set up above.

II. METHODOLOGICAL APPROACHES

It would be possible to make an almost endless list of methodological approaches, and any reasonably limited classification must necessarily do injustice to those working on the periphery of fields and force a false simplicity upon the others. For this summary survey, however, limitation is unavoidable. The principal approaches will therefore be discussed in the following classification: (1) mathematical economics; (2) statistical methods; (3) econometrics; (4) institutional economics; and (5) speculative economics.

A. Mathematical Economics

One of the most striking aspects of methodological developments in the past twenty years has been the increase in the application of mathematics to economic theory.[4] Mathematical economics applies only to the second stage in the research process, the theoretical development of hypotheses; there is no fundamental difference between the function served by mathematical economics and the function served by nonmathematical economic theory.[5] No matter how highly developed mathematical economics may become, it can never do more than study the logical bases of hypotheses and their interrelationships. Some consideration of the general problem to be studied and of possible hypotheses (i.e., Stage 1) is necessary before any mathematical techniques can be used, and some type of empirical testing (i.e., Stage 3) is necessary if the abstract formulations of mathematical economics are to proceed beyond purely formal analysis. Mathematical economics is limited in exactly the same way that any concentration on economic theory is limited; it is only a portion of the total research process. One of the greatest dangers attaching to the increasing use of mathematical techniques, therefore, lies in the possibility that too much will be claimed for it; a high degree of refinement at this stage combined with neglect of other stages can only produce a relatively low order of research. Abstract theory in and of itself may be rather sterile, unless and until it can provide the basis for the succeeding stages in the research process.[6]

The great advantage of mathematical economics undoubtedly lies in its usefulness in handling certain complicated relationships among economic magnitudes. Even Stigler concedes this point:

---

[4] This is not to say that mathematical economics is a recent innovation—witness the tradition embodied in Walras, Pareto, and Slutsky, not to mention Marshall, Edgeworth, and Pigou.

[5] For discussion of this role see Gerhard Tintner, "Scope and Method of Econometrics," University of Cambridge, Department of Applied Economics, Reprint Series No. 22 (1949), p. 2.

[6] To the extent that mathematical economics is mathematics instead of economics, concentration on it may lead eventually not only to better economics, but also to better understanding of all fields related to mathematics. But this is mathematics, not economics.

Without mathematics one can give only an intuitive proof of complicated relationships such as those expressed by Euler's theorem, Slutsky's equation, the theory of general equilibrium, and certain theorems in the theory of games. . . . There are types of economic analysis some of which even the non-mathematical economists have deemed important that can be executed more swiftly, more surely, and more completely with the mathematical method.[7]

This is a substantial claim. The fact that some analysts develop unwarranted theoretical formulations solely for the sake of using specific mathematical techniques is not to be held against mathematical economics, but rather is poor execution of the mathematical method.

The proponents of the mathematical method have held, further, that the use of symbolic methods is an aid to clear thinking and the advancement of analysis, because those using this abstract language are forced to formulate their concepts unambiguously,[8] and succeed in making clear to each other the exact reasons for their divergent results.[9] These arguments stress the point that good mathematical practices can improve loose thinking. Much confusion would be avoided, it is felt, if each economist were to write down the system of equations he has in mind, insert the specific values of their parameters, show lagged relations explicitly, specified as to length (sometimes zero), and finally test the consistency and completeness of the theory by counting the variables and equations.[10]

It certainly cannot be denied that much confused thinking could be clarified by applying some of the logical steps which are used in rigorous mathematical procedure, but the converse of the proposition may also be true. Many of the absurdities arising from the poor use of mathematics could be overcome if mathematical economists would spend more time on the problems of making the analytically useful and valid classifications and definitions that characterize good literary economics. There are many examples of the inexact use of mathematics; the use of symbols does not force economists to formulate their concepts unambiguously. Both the Greek and Roman alphabets are full of symbols for confused ideas. In Stigler's terms,[11] "The history of science gives us good reason to believe that every concept of modern science will be found to

---

[7] G. J. Stigler, *Five Lectures on Economic Problems* (London, 1949), p. 40.

[8] P. A. Samuelson, *The Foundations of Economic Analysis* (Cambridge, Mass., 1948), p. 92.

[9] Jacob Marschak, "On Mathematics for Economists," *Rev. Econ. Stat.,* Nov. 1947, XXIX, 269–70.

[10] *Loc. cit.,* p. 270.

[11] *Op. cit.,* p. 40.

be ambiguous at some future time. Therefore a snobbish mathematics would be unusable at present. It is as if one were to assert that language is only for the expression of pure thoughts: we also have mathematical pornography." In most mathematical presentations of economics, the problem of defining the concepts for which the symbols stand is given little attention. In one fairly recent book employing the mathematical method,[12] thirty-one definitions are given in less than two pages; commonly, mathematical economists devote one paragraph to this task. The broadness of the definitions is usually sufficient to permit the symbols to fit a wide variety of different concepts, and this, of course, has the effect of giving spurious exactness to the mathematical presentation. Klein has explicitly recognized this situation in his preface, when he points out that the estimates in his volume are based on data already outmoded because of the conceptual changes, as well as the purely statistical revisions, made by the Department of Commerce in their national accounts data.[13] The conceptual changes in the Department of Commerce's definitions of the gross national product and consumers' expenditures, for example, were sufficient to affect the results obtained by the particular analysis employed, even though these changes in concept are not discernible in the mathematical presentation of the theoretical framework. Such possible variations in definitions are frequently of significance for the analysis, but are far below the level of specification normally used in mathematical economics. The inexactness of the definitions of the variables used thus can lead to the use of the same symbol for what are significantly different concepts. It is not a fault of mathematical economics that it is vague—there is nothing per se in the use of symbols that increases vagueness—but, on the other hand, it is not arguable that the use of symbols per se will reduce vagueness.

A further problem in the application of mathematics to economics arises in connection with the meaning and appropriateness of certain operations. For example, transitivity of relationships may unconsciously be assumed by the analyst where it is not warranted, or the implications of purely additive relationships may not be fully appreciated.[14] The misuse of mathematical assumptions should not, of course, be considered a

---

[12] L. R. Klein, *Economic Fluctuations in the United States, 1921–1941* (New York, 1950), pp. 102–04.

[13] *Loc. cit.*, p. viii.

[14] J. M. Clark, "Mathematical Economists and Others," *Econometrica*, Apr. 1947, XV, 77.

fault of mathematics. On the other hand, this same point has another facet: the utilization of mathematical techniques does not necessarily increase the validity of the analysis. Blind application of specific mathematical procedures is not a substitute for good logical reasoning.[15]

The question of whether or not the mathematical economist should provide a translation of his methods and results into words remains the occasion for much of the controversy regarding the mathematical method. Samuelson[16] has maintained that the translation of mathematical economics back into literary economics is not only unrewarding from the point of view of advancing science, but involves, as well, mental gymnastics of a peculiarly depraved type. Clark,[17] on the other hand, takes the view that mathematical economists are an able and growing sect, using an esoteric method and special language which makes their results increasingly inaccessible to the general economist. He makes a plea for communicability, suggesting that the work of the mathematical economists should be put in such a form that the general economists can satisfy themselves that the results have been verified and their significance properly evaluated. Stigler[18] would go further than Clark, maintaining that translation is not only desirable, but absolutely necessary from the point of view of the economics profession. He feels that translation would reduce the danger that the mathematical economist has fallen in love with mathematical form, and would also reduce the possibility that small problems will be solved elegantly while larger problems are missed. In addition, and more importantly, Stigler feels that it is the fundamental obligation of the scholar to submit his results and methods to the critical scrutiny of his competent colleagues in a comprehensible manner, and that the profession contains many very able economists whose mathematical attainments are meager or less; every mathematical economist, he feels, could, if he would, state clearly in the language of words the assumptions and conclusions of his analysis, even where the details of proof must be shrouded in a fog impenetrable to the nonmathematical economist. Failure to provide adequate translation Stigler considers to be attributable either to laziness, snobbishness, or a sense of

---

[15] Samuelson points out that it is the acceptance of the mathematician's customary canons of exposition and proof, whether in words or symbols, that is important. ("Economic Theory and Mathematics—An Appraisal," *Am. Econ. Rev., Proc.,* May 1952, XLII, 56–66.)

[16] *The Foundations of Economic Analysis,* p. 6.

[17] *Op. cit.,* p. 75.

[18] *Op. cit.,* p. 45.

shame at the abstractness of the analysis. E. B. Wilson[19] takes much the same position, when he states that there is a small group of economists who are well trained in mathematics and who apparently choose to write for one another rather than for economists in general. Like Stigler, Wilson believes that the mathematical economists have something important to say, but that not much will be accomplished by them until and unless economists in general can understand why their contributions are important.

Marschak[20] gives another possible way out of the problem of translation; he suggests that all economists should learn sufficient mathematics so that translation will not be necessary. But as Baumol has pointed out,[21] the hope that there exists some way in which a reasonably thorough grounding in mathematics can be obtained in x easy lessons is doomed to frustration in view of the variety in the types of mathematical techniques employed. With relatively little expenditure of effort and a reasonable training in elementary mathematics, Baumol feels, the average economist can undoubtedly learn to work his way through certain specific writings which have had some recourse to mathematical method, but if a relatively untrained individual attempts to follow the continuing developments in even a limited field the quest is likely to turn into an endless pursuit, as he attempts to integrate in his own mind new developments which bring with them an increase in the variety of mathematical techniques. Furthermore, to carry out original work and make substantial contributions to an area of mathematical economics, efficiency demands a wider horizon than just that of the mathematical techniques already in use in economic analysis. In other words, mathematical economics does require a specialization in mathematical techniques, rather than casual interest in the area. As Samuelson points out, mathematics can even be a hindrance, since it is only too easy to convert a good literary economist into a mediocre mathematical economist.[22]

In practical terms, fortunately, the problem of translation is not as insoluble as the wealth of controversy seems to indicate. In the first place, the word "translation" has considerably different connotations to different people. Mathematical economists in general would probably not, as a matter of principle, be averse to a discussion in words of their

[19] "Review of Haavelmo's *The Probability Approach to Econometrics*," *Rev. Econ. Stat.*, Aug. 1946, XXVIII, 143.

[20] *Op. cit.*, p. 269.

[21] W. J. Baumol, "Notes on Some Dynamic Models," *Econ. Jour.*, Dec. 1948, LVIII, 16.

[22] "Economic Theory and Mathematics—An Appraisal," *loc. cit.*

assumptions, general methods, and conclusions. What they would object to is a literal step-by-step transformation of their mathematics into words solely for the purpose of popularizing their work with the general economists; this they feel is impossible to do and is unjustified.[23] General economists, on the other hand, do not really want a labored and complicated translation; they only want to be told what the investigator is trying to do, what he is assuming, what general method is being employed, and what results his analysis has achieved. The fact that some mathematical economists write for each other is not particularly undesirable; it would only become unhealthy if there were no one who bridged the gap by working in both general literary economics and in mathematical economics, and if there were no communication between the two groups. There is a strong possibility that as mathematical economics develops, the increasing variety in the types of mathematics required will necessitate specialists in specific areas, and a problem of "translation" among these areas will also arise. To state that translation is always desirable is to say that all economics should be written so that any well-educated, intelligent, but untrained member of society could understand—and while much of the economics which is written today falls into this category, to specify it as an ideal would seem to be unduly restrictive.

It is unfortunate that the rapid development of mathematical economics has tended to split economists into literary and mathematical factions. The proponents of the mathematical method tend only to speak of mathematics in relation to confused literary thinking, and those opposed to speak only of poor mathematics in relation to clear and logical thinking. Mathematical training will never turn a great economist into a mediocre economist, but on the other hand, as Stigler points out,[24] it will not "turn a mediocre economist into a great economist—a proposition with which most mathematical economists will immodestly agree."

B. Statistical Research

Statistical research can be defined broadly as the collection and manipulation of numerical observations. This definition of statistical

---

[23] As R. G. D. Allen indicates ("The Mathematical Foundations of Economic Theory," *Quart. Jour. Econ.*, Feb. 1949, LXIII, 111–12), the mathematics in a considerable amount of economics is coming to be the steel framework of the structure rather than the scaffolding; in such cases it may no longer be proper to follow Hicks' procedure —in *Value and Capital* (Oxford, 1939) and *A Contribution to the Theory of the Trade Cycle* (Oxford, 1950)—of giving a complete nonmathematical treatment with the mathematics in separate appendixes.

[24] *Op. cit.,* pp. 38–39.

research can refer either to the exploration of the problem (Stage 1) or to the empirical testing of hypotheses (Stage 3). It is not directly applicable to the theoretical development of hypotheses (Stage 2). Not all information, of course, can be cast into useful statistical form. This was well pointed out by Wallis in his review of the Kinsey Report,[25] and by Tintner,[26] who admits that in many areas (such as historical research) data are too scarce to permit reliance on statistical methods, and that in other areas (such as the study of economic institutions and the legal framework) methods other than purely statistical ones will be found more appropriate.

The general problem of transforming empirical information into statistical data is related to this point. It is unfortunately true that the statistical investigator can consciously or unconsciously force empirical information into classifications which are inapplicable and misleading. Like the use of symbols in mathematical analysis, numerical data can give a false impression of concreteness and accuracy to statistical analysis. The people who collect basic data are usually aware of the variety of definitions which are masked by one single classification grouping; no matter how much time is spent on wording questions, the same question will be interpreted differently by different respondents. Purely statistical techniques can rarely handle this problem. Those who are involved in the analysis of statistics obtained by others unfortunately often lose sight of these transformation problems—this is one of the reasons that accounting has become a lucrative art. Numerical data by themselves are inadequate; besides figures, a considerable amount of information is required on the nature of the definitions, insofar as they are known, and on the manner in which the methods of collection condition these definitions. One of the more disturbing features of the tremendous growth in statistics and statistical analysis in recent years is the paucity of meaningful information on the definitions, sources, and methods used in acquiring the data, and the almost complete failure on the part of the analysts using the data to take account of what little information is available.[27]

---

[25] W. A. Wallis, "Statistics of the Kinsey Report," *Jour. Am. Stat. Assoc.,* Dec. 1949, XLIV, 464.

[26] *Op. cit.*

[27] For example, definitions, sources, and methods used in deriving national accounts data for various countries are not generally available. This has not, however, prevented these data from being widely used for international comparisons, even though gross incomparabilities are known to exist, by both academic economists and official groups.

A considerable amount of "economic design"[28] is necessary if the data which are collected are to be useful for analytic purposes. This is not to say that every compiler of basic materials brings to his task a brilliant mind and a host of extraordinary skills. There are vast volumes of statistical data which are mute testimony to the fact that their authors did not adequately concern themselves with the problems of economic and statistical design; the fact that a problem requires skillful treatment does not mean that it will of necessity receive it. One of the major difficulties encountered in obtaining basic statistical data arises because most economic information is a by-product of the operation of the society and its administration. In diverting such material to economic analysis, it is often necessary to make special adjustments to the original tabulations to make them internally consistent and comparable with other related series of economic data. Since it is often impossible to accomplish this task successfully, and since it is usually laborious and thankless, the end result is that statistical series very frequently are neither fully consistent with themselves nor comparable with each other.

The term "statistical analysis" is so broad as to be almost meaningless—any analyst using empirical data may be using statistics, but this does not say much about his method. A better specification of the exact nature of a given approach can be obtained if statistical analysis is split into the following subgroups: (1) probability analysis; (2) time series analysis; and (3) informational techniques. These categories are obviously not mutually exclusive; a given statistical analysis may incorporate elements of each.

1. *Probability Analysis.* The major use of probability analysis by economists has been with reference to the empirical testing of hypotheses (Stage 3). According to Snedecor,[29] the outstanding characteristic of the present-day professional statistician is his interest and skill in the measurement of the fallibility of conclusions. Economics has borrowed considerably from the applications of probability theory to other fields in the sciences and social sciences, but in recent years considerable attention has been focused on the development of special techniques for applying statistical inference to economic problems. The development of sam-

---

[28] The term "economic design" is used by Stone, *op. cit.,* p. 10, to refer to the problem of defining economic facts in terms of the theoretical principles that are to be used in interpreting and relating them.

[29] G. W. Snedecor, "On a Unique Feature of Statistics," *Jour. Am. Stat. Assoc.,* Mar. 1949, XLIV, 1.

pling theory permitted economists to deal with "errors" of observation in sample data and to study the effect of increasing sample size. In testing economic hypotheses, observational "errors" were taken into account, but the hypotheses themselves were generally considered to be exact formulations. Recent work on statistical inference in economics has taken a different approach; instead of considering the theory to be tested as exact, many of the current formulations specify a random variable as a part of the theory itself.[30] In other words, a stochastic scheme is set up, and the total system is related to the statistical data. Despite the progress which has been made, however, the task of building a fully satisfactory technique on this basis is still left for the future. As Tintner points out,[31] the foundations of probability theory are still disputed and will remain so for some time to come, and there is not very much agreement about the methods to be used in statistical inference. Nevertheless, it cannot be denied that the methodological experiments in this area are stimulating and suggestive.

2. *Time Series Analysis.* Using the broadest possible definitions, it could be said that all empirical analysis involves time series analysis. As Kuznets points out,[32] any item of statistical evidence concerning society is part of an historical series; even a frequency distribution, a cross section measured at one point of time, must be viewed as a unit in a time series. Other economists, however, have interpreted the term "time series analysis" much more narrowly. Frickey, for example, states that time series analysis is the decomposition of time series into their component parts of secular, cyclical, seasonal, and irregular movements.[33] For the purposes of this discussion, analysis of the interrelations of the time patterns of series of economic data or the decomposition of a single time series will be defined as time series analysis. It can refer either to the exploration of the problem (Stage 1) or to the empirical testing of hypotheses (Stage 3). With reference to Stage 1, time series analysis has been used to organize and refine raw data in a manner which might make them more suggestive in helping to define the problem. With reference to Stage 3, time series analysis is involved whenever the test-

---

[30] For discussion of the basic approach see the chapter on "Econometrics" by Wassily Leontief in the first volume of this *Survey;* also Trygve Haavelmo, "The Probability Approach in Econometrics," *Econometrica,* July 1944, XII (Suppl.).

[31] *Op. cit.,* p. 7.

[32] Simon Kuznets, "Conditions of Statistical Research," *Jour Am. Stat. Assoc.,* Mar. 1950, XLV, 1.

[33] Edwin Frickey, *Economic Fluctuations in the United States* (Cambridge, 1942), p. 3.

ing of hypotheses necessitates the interrelation or the processing of time series data. It is obvious that probability analysis may be used as an integral part of time series analysis in either Stage 1 or Stage 3; the two techniques are not mutually exclusive, but may be employed together on any specific problem.

In practice, much of the work on time series suffers from the fact that probability analysis has not been used as much as it should have been, or that it has been misapplied. Some of the people working in this area have recognized the dangers inherent in attaching significance to the results of specific techniques of time series analysis—certain of these techniques would yield definite results even if applied to series of random numbers. Yet all time series work is not free from this taint; processing and decomposition of time series data can be very dangerous because it is easy for the investigator to obtain results which proceed not from the data but from the process of adjustment and manipulation.[34]

3. *Informational Techniques.* Only a small portion of the statistical research work which is carried out in economics can properly be classified as either probability or time series analysis. For want of a better name, those techniques which are used in the remainder of statistical research will be termed "informational." Like the statistical methods discussed above, these techniques can be used with reference to either the exploration of the problem (Stage 1) or the empirical testing of hypotheses (Stage 3). Informational statistical research is devoted primarily to the task of obtaining and presenting statistical data, rather than processing the data. Data of this sort form the foundation of what is known about the nature and structure of the economic system. In many cases such information is sufficient to disprove a simple hypothesis without the use of further specialized techniques. Much of the most effective statistical analysis is of this extremely unelaborate type, bringing pertinent information to bear on specific problems by presenting the statistical data which are available.

The question of the classification of data is one of the more important problems arising from the use of information techniques, and it has not received as much attention as it should from economists in general. Problems of classification arise not only in the design of statistical collection, but also whenever any substantial aggregation of data is necessary. The price of order and simplicity in the presentation of statistical information is lack of flexibility and the consequent burial of information.

---

[34] A. F. Burns, "Frickey on the Decomposition of Time Series," *Rev. Econ. Stat.*, Aug. 1944, XXVI, 136.

Every simple classification system constitutes more or less of a strait jacket, preventing the use of the data in other forms. On the other hand, the abandonment of a simple classification system can rapidly lead to masses of unrelated and incoherent figures. One of the major weaknesses of informational techniques, commonly, is the lack of an adequate statistical framework which can produce order without rigidity. The plethora of data flooding the shelves and filing cabinets of economists is not necessarily a good omen of progress; it could mean that economics is heading for a statistical chaos wherein all data are internally inconsistent over time and incomparable with each other. Each economist, through proper selection, could then prove his own hypotheses and disprove those of his colleagues.

C. Econometrics

According to the definition chosen by Leontief,[35] econometrics can be considered to be that "type of economic analysis in which the general theoretical approach—often formulated in explicitly mathematical terms—is combined—frequently through the medium of intricate statistical procedures—with empirical measurement of economic phenomena." In terms of the preceding discussion, econometrics is thus a unification of mathematical economics and statistical analysis;[36] it is this unification of theoretical and factual studies which was accented by Frisch in his opening editorial in the initial issue of *Econometrica*.[37] To a considerable extent the remarks made in connection with mathematical economics and statistical analysis are equally applicable to econometrics,[38] but the unification of the two techniques raises a number of other points which deserve separate mention.

---

[35] *Op. cit.,* p. 388.

[36] A considerable portion of the work which is currently designated econometric is concerned with the application of a specific probability approach to the statistical verification of dynamic economic models. However, not all probability analysis is econometric, nor does the use of dynamic models alone necessarily mean that the investigator is embarked on an econometric analysis. Furthermore, since econometrics is defined as the unification of mathematical economics with statistical analysis, it is proper to include as econometric many things which are not concerned with an explicit probability approach and which do not use either dynamic analysis or explicit models. The use of probability has already been mentioned in connection with statistical analysis (see pp. 419–20); dynamic models will be considered in relation to recently developed techniques of economic analysis in Part III.

[37] Ragnar Frisch, "Editorial," *Econometrica,* Jan. 1933, I, 1.

[38] The major point which is relevant here is that since econometrics is dependent on statistical analysis it may be unable to cope with those factors which have not been—or cannot readily be—cast into a quantifiable form. R. A. Gordon ("Business Cycles in the Interwar Period: The 'Quantitative-Historical' Approach," *Am. Econ. Rev., Proc.,* May 1949, XXXIX, 52) criticizes the econometric approach to business-cycle research on these

First, by combining mathematical economics and statistical analysis the first three stages of the research process have been brought together; the charge that a specific technique is applicable only to a portion of the research process, which was made in connection with both mathematical economics and statistical analysis, is no longer as valid. By carrying out the different stages of research in closer conjunction with each other, a considerably greater degree of economic design can be employed in the research, and the resulting analysis will benefit by greater consistency and integration than would have been possible otherwise. The empirical testing of economic theories is often hampered by the fact that the theory is not in a form that lends itself to testing by currently available statistical material. The concepts and definitions specified by theory are seldom identical with those which are available in existing empirical data. Similarly, statistical analyses made without benefit of definite economic theories are never quite explicit about just what problem is being considered, what the exact implications of the statistical analysis are, and how this statistical analysis is related to other statistical findings and to economic theory in general. By designing the economic theory in such a manner that it can be tested by available data, and by simultaneously providing a theoretical framework for the statistical analysis, econometrics is able to overcome many of the difficulties which are normally inherent in the separation of the various stages of research.[39]

It should be noted, however, that the econometric approach is not completely self-contained, and that some of the apparent self-containment may be spurious. Generally speaking, the econometric approach does not place very much emphasis on the exploration of the problem (Stage 1) but rather prefers to concentrate its attention on the theoretical development and testing of hypotheses (Stages 2 and 3).[40] In criticizing the work of Burns and Mitchell,[41] Koopmans[42] states the position held by many econometricians. He holds that there should be a fuller

---

grounds, and this same point is fully admitted by most econometricians themselves; see T. C. Koopmans, "The Econometric Approach to Business Fluctuations," *ibid.,* p. 70; Tintner, *op. cit.,* p. 4; and Jan Tinbergen, *Business Cycles in the United States of America, 1919–1932* (New York, 1939), p. 11.

[39] These remarks would, of course, also apply to a unification of nonmathematical theory with statistical analysis. Although no one has applied a specific name to this combination of techniques, it is probably considerably more common, in practice, than the application of econometrics.

[40] It is, of course, obvious that econometrics per se is unrelated to the evaluation of the significance of conclusions in value terms (Stage 4).

[41] A. F. Burns and W. C. Mitchell, *Measuring Business Cycles* (New York, 1946).

[42] T. C. Koopmans, "Measurement without Theory," *Rev. Econ. Stat.,* Aug. 1947, XXIX, 163.

utilization of the concepts and hypotheses of accepted economic theory as a part of the process of observation and measurement, since such a method promises to be shorter and perhaps even the only possible road for successful economic analysis. Koopmans arrives at this conclusion by pointing out that for the purpose of systematic and large-scale observation of any many-sided phenomenon, theoretical preconceptions about its nature cannot be dispensed with, and the attempt to do so is a detriment to the analysis.[43] He thus infers that Stage 1 is not a profitable part of econometrics, at least at the present time. However, an effective argument can also be made on the other side of the question. Just because theoretical preconceptions, whether implicit or explicit, are a necessary part of any empirical work, it does not necessarily follow that every empirical investigator should concern himself with the development of a complete and articulated theory which is intimately related to existing economic theory before he makes any investigation of empirical material. Every theoretical preconception has behind it preconceptions of an empirical nature which, in turn, are based on a selection, from casual experience or from previous research, of information believed to be important according to some other theoretical preconception. Koopmans' phrase "measurement without theory" emphasizes the absurdity of a purely empirical approach, but so, equally well, might the phrase "theory without significance" point out the meaninglessness of theory developed entirely without relation to empirical concepts. As was pointed out in the first part of this paper, the interaction of theory and empirical information is part of the infinite series which is the research process, and it is impossible to operate with either one alone. What Koopmans is really arguing is that there should be a formal consideration of specific theoretical economic models, combined with informal empirical observation, prior to any formal recourse to statistical data. Proponents of the so-called empirical approach, on the other hand, would reverse this prescription, saying that those who would make economic theories should have more knowledge about the real world than is possible through casual observation, and on this ground they would urge the examination and study of statistical information, combined with some loose theoretical structure, prior to the creation of any formal hypothesis or complex theoretical structure.

This discussion of whether every analyst should take existing economic theory into account before embarking on statistical research is

---

[43] *Loc. cit.*

somewhat reminiscent of the advice Schumpeter used to give aspiring students. Schumpeter claimed that the curse of economics was that there were too many scholars and not enough fools. Scholars, he pointed out, were always very cautious, and educated themselves on a subject before they formed any definite opinions about it. As a result they carefully read each other's works, thought about the problems in the same contexts, and took over from each other the mass of preconceptions and basic assumptions which are necessary to scholarly work. Thus scholars tend to be sheep following the lead of the past and differing from each other not in broad scope but only on minor details. Fools, on the other hand, are much less apt to read the works of scholars, because they couldn't understand them if they did. For this reason it is the fools who do the more original thinking: they are not hampered by the preconceptions of scholars. It is the fools, then, who provide the original creative inventions which the entrepreneur-scholars then come along and exploit by refinement and integration into the body of accepted doctrines. The moral of this story is that the approach of the fool is not entirely foolish; learning may impede the progress of knowledge as well as aid it.[44]

In terms of the Koopmans vs. Burns and Mitchell controversy, the universal use of the existing concepts and the hypotheses of accepted theory as a basis for the process of observation and measurement might well be a serious impediment to hypothesis seeking and discovery. Econometricians often tend to start by taking over problems from the explicit formulations of existing theory, using statistical data only at the testing stage. Scant attention is given to the exploration of the problem, and the statistical material is not brought to bear at this level. The empiricists who were being criticized by Koopmans were trying to spend their time on the prospecting and probing phase (Stage 1), and, as Vining points out,[45] they cannot therefore be criticized in terms of an efficiency concept which is applicable only to the testing stage. There is

---

[44] Schumpeter's awareness of the necessary role of preconceptions is well revealed in his discussion in "Science and Ideology" (*Am. Econ. Rev.*, Mar. 1949, XXXIX, 359), where he stated in part: "That prescientific cognitive act which is the source of our ideologies is also the prerequisite of our scientific work. No new departure in any science is possible without it. Through it we acquire new material for our scientific endeavors and something to formulate, to defend, to attack. Our stock of facts and tools grows and rejuvenates itself in the process. And so—though we proceed slowly because of our ideologies, we might not proceed at all without them."

[45] Rutledge Vining, "Koopmans on the Choice of Variables to be Studied and of Methods of Measurement," *Rev. Econ. Stat.*, May 1949, XXXI, 78.

nothing inherent in econometrics as such that prevents it from encompassing the exploration of the problem (Stage 1) and bringing statistical information to bear at this level, but it is true that much of the logical neatness of the method would be lost in the process. Furthermore, even where statistical material is brought to bear on the exploration of the problem, it is not always completely satisfactory; sometimes the analysis is limited by the use of a single body of data, first to develop explanatory schemes and second to test these same schemes.[46] It has already been noted that the dependence on statistical data has limited the applicability of econometrics to those aspects of the problem which can be handled quantitatively. However, even within this orbit, as Leontief points out,[47] further progress of quantitative economic analysis will depend upon the success of the essentially nonstatistical search for promising analytical insights as much as upon the final statistical sifting of the empirical "pay dust."

D. Institutional Approaches

Twenty years ago there was considerable discussion in the *American Economic Review* on the meaning and nature of the institutional approach and its role in economic analysis.[48] Some of the participants[49]

---

[46] Again, this is not necessarily an inherent characteristic of econometrics. As Leontief points out (*op. cit.*, p. 407), research workers other than those who are econometricians face this same problem.

[47] *Op. cit.*, p. 403.

[48] Round Table Discussion, "Economic Theory—Institutionalism: What It Is and What It Hopes to Become," *Am. Econ. Rev., Proc.*, Mar. 1931, XXI, 134–41; Morris Copeland, "Economic Theory and the Natural Science Point of View," *Am. Econ. Rev.*, Mar. 1931, XXI, 67–79; E. M. Burns, "Does Institutionalism Complement or Compete with 'Orthodox Economics'?" *ibid.*, pp. 80–87; J. R. Commons, "Institutional Economics," *ibid.*, Dec. 1931, XXI, 648–57; Round Table Discussion, "Institutional Economics," *Am. Econ. Rev., Proc.*, Mar. 1932, XXII, 105–16; P. T. Homan, "An Appraisal of Institutional Economics," *Am. Econ. Rev.*, Mar. 1932, XXII, 10–17; J. E. Shafer, "Institutional Economics of Professor Commons," *ibid.*, June 1932, XXII, 261–64; J. R. Commons, Comment on J. E. Shafer, *ibid.*, pp. 264–69; N. L. Silverstein, Comment on P. T. Homan, *ibid.*, pp. 268–69; W. C. Mitchell, "Commons on Institutional Economics," *ibid.*, Dec. 1935, XXV, 635–52.

[49] Homan, *op. cit.*, pp. 15–16: "It is my opinion that an institutional economics, differentiated from other economics by discoverable criteria, is largely an intellectual fiction, substantially devoid of content. . . . If institutional economics be broadly defined, it is practically co-extensive with economics. If narrowly defined in connection with a Veblenian origin, it consists mainly in a few thin essays, critical, hortatory, and hopeful. If not defined at all, it is a miscellaneous body of works associated with a group of economists reputed to be institutionalists. In ultimate conclusion, one may record a conviction that the current controversy between a posited institutional economics and a posited neoclassical economics is obsolete, unreal, silly, and beside the point. . . . Its roots nearly

complained of the futility of the discussion of institutional economics, claiming that it could not be defined and that its usefulness was past; but institutionalism was not without its defenders. One of them, William Jaffe,[50] defined institutionalism as an approach in which the analyst uses institutions not so much as the constant background of his analysis but rather as determining forces in that analysis, and in which the explanation of economic relationships is looked for in changes in institutions. It is this, Jaffe says, that makes the whole thing "positively irritating" to the classical economist. The source of the irritation is the institutionalists' attempt to explain economic phenomena in ways other than those consecrated by the customs, habits, and usages of the guild of economists. But, Jaffe continues, "the so-called institutionalists by no means confine themselves to the role of innocent passive victims of the irascible orthodox tempers. They are actively irritating; there is something infuriating about the way they relegate the *a priori* and abstract method to the scrap heap."

In the last twenty years the spirit of the institutionalists has permeated the whole of economic analysis and has become more or less integrated with the other approaches. The revolutionary fervor is gone, yet in many fields of economics the imprint of institutionalism remains. The term institutional today is usually reserved for those analysts who are working in applied fields and who use in their research the large available body of empirical material on the institutions in these areas. Theory is not usually discarded, but the focus of interest is often shifted to the analysis of the specific institutional factors which are found in a given situation.

The advantage of institutionalism lies in its ability to deal with those factors which are not readily amenable to the present state of quantitative measurement, as well as those which can be handled statistically. As was pointed out in the section on statistical analysis, statistical data on specific subjects frequently are unavailable, or the problems of achieving adequate and comprehensive transformations of empirical information into statistical form may prove to be insurmountable. In such situations, recourse to the institutional approach may yield a much more satisfactory explanation than the use of incomplete and invalid statistical procedures.

---

a generation ago grew in an absurd anti-rationalism and an equally absurd and satisfied traditionalism. It has had its day and done its work and may be consigned to the lower regions without sorrow."

[50] Round Table Discussion, "Economic Theory—Institutionalism: What It Is and What It Hopes to Become," *loc. cit.*, pp. 139–41.

The vagueness of the institutional approach and the looseness or absence of established techniques thus produces a certain freedom and flexibility, but at the same time it is likely to produce a chaotic lack of system. As a result, although institutionalism is useful for *ad hoc* analysis, it is not conducive to a rapid cumulative growth of generalized knowledge.

In its modern sense, institutionalism can refer to any of the four stages in the research process, although of course it may be combined with other techniques at any of the stages. Because of its tendency to focus attention on the descriptive aspect of a given field, the institutional approach often lays considerable stress on the exploration of the problem (Stage 1), and in many cases the analysis proceeds no further than this. In fact, it is quite possible that no problems are ever specified; the work is concerned entirely with the informational presentation of material. It should be remembered, however, that even if this is conceived to be the sole task of the institutionalist, Koopmans' contention about empiricism is still applicable[51]—no study can start out with just the bare facts of economic life; some purpose and some preconceptions are necessary before anything can be done.

E. Speculative Analysis

This last category of methodological approaches is largely residual, in the sense that any analysis which does not follow mathematical procedures, use statistical analysis, or rely on other collected empirical (institutional) information may be considered to be speculative. This is the time-honored approach in economics; introspection and casual observation are relied upon to provide the substance of the analysis, and logic to provide the framework. All stages of the research process can be handled by speculation, and this has been one of the more unfortunate aspects of this approach. For some people speculation may be work, but for others it is sheer joy; and economics has tended to attract those who revel in speculating about speculative speculations. The beauty and symmetry of these creations have given them endurance, and they have provided us with much of our present-day economics.

It is easy to disparage speculation, but its role can also easily be underestimated. The integration of the stages of the research process and the interrelation of the various methodological approaches is usually accomplished through the liberal use of speculative analysis. Speculation is

---

[51] "Measurement without Theory," *loc. cit.,* p. 163. H. M. Fletcher, in Round Table Discussion, "Institutional Economics," *loc. cit.,* p. 107, made the same point with respect to institutionalism.

still really one of the main components of all economic analysis. Few techniques are fully automatic and independent of judgment, and wherever judgment enters, speculation is rampant. There is a substantial cumulative aspect to speculative analysis, for knowledge is cumulative, and to the extent that general knowledge forms the basis of much casual observation, speculation in one period starts with the substantive achievements of the previous period.

III. RECENT DEVELOPMENTS IN SPECIALIZED TECHNIQUES FOR ECONOMIC RESEARCH

Any survey of methodological developments in economics would be incomplete if it did not give some explicit attention to certain specific techniques of economic analysis which have evolved in recent years. These specific techniques do not themselves constitute "method" in the broader sense in which the latter term has been used in this survey; rather they can better be considered uses or applications of various methodologies in specialized procedures designed with reference to particular problems or particular bodies of material. Any such specific technique of economic analysis obviously has methodological implications, in much the same manner that any piece of economic research has methodological implications. To the extent that these techniques are used in current economic research, the methodologies inherent in them are important, and examination of them will throw additional light on the general picture of methodological developments.

To warrant consideration in a survey of methodological developments, it seems reasonable to require that a given technique display a recent and continuous history of developmental work and attempted use, even if only in rudimentary form. Many of the techniques now in the developmental stage may never be integrated into anything like general use. Others are now at such an early stage that they cannot really be classed as techniques; rather they are suggestive ideas which may at some later time serve as a basis for the development of definite techniques— the extremely suggestive ideas contained in von Neumann and Morgenstern's *Theory of Games and Economic Behavior,* for example, are as yet relatively unexploited in terms of workable techniques. As purely suggestive ideas they have had little impact on the actual methodology of economics. If in the future they are developed further, they may at that time influence methodology, but to regard them as current influences upon methodological change is to enter the area of speculation.

There are two general areas of specialized techniques which can meet this criterion. The first is the area of classificatory frameworks, embodying the specific techniques of national income accounting, input-output tables, and money-flows accounts. The second is the area of "model building," which, although by no means a new idea in economics, has been considerably elaborated and extended over the past two decades. Descriptions of the techniques in these areas and their methodological implications will cast considerable light on the role of these specific techniques in methodological developments.

A. Classificatory Frameworks

In discussing the various specific classificatory techniques which have been developed recently, it will be useful first to describe briefly the nature of each, pointing out the manner in which they developed and the forces which were important in determining their characteristics, and outlining roughly their present form and content. It will then be possible to consider the methodological implications of the group of techniques as a whole, and of each of them individually in comparison with the others.

National income accounting in its present form is the result of gradual development over a number of decades. The history of this development in terms of the relevant economic literature is given in the essay on "Development and Use of National Income Data" by Carl Shoup.[52] For present purposes, it is sufficient to consider the nature of the evolutionary change in national income accounting as a classificatory framework.

In its early stages, national income was conceived of as the total of all the incomes in the nation. It was thought of primarily as an aggregate, an economic construct, which it was interesting to measure for a variety of reasons; one of these reasons was, of course, the belief that a time series of aggregate national income would reflect changes in the welfare of the nation. The various processes of computing this aggregate had a profound effect on the development of national income as a classificatory device. Briefly, it became obvious that national income aggregates might be estimated in three different ways. First, it would be possible to add up all the income payments—wages, salaries, interest, dividends, entrepreneurial income, and profits—received by individuals. Second, it would be possible to estimate the total income payments made

---

[52] *A Survey of Contemporary Economics,* Vol. I, H. S. Ellis, ed. (Philadelphia, 1948), pp. 288–313.

by the various industries in the economy, by computing and adjusting the value added of each. Finally, national income would again be reflected by adding up the total expenditures of individuals and the government and the total saving (or investment) in the economy. In the process of making such estimates, problems arose regarding the treatment of various items and the adjustments that should be made to preserve the conceptual equality of the three ways of computing national income. Items such as transfer payments, depreciation, direct and indirect taxes, inventory change, and various types of government outlays raised numerous problems. Because of such problems it became necessary to formulate in both conceptual and empirical terms explicit breakdowns of the national income aggregate for each of these three different points of view.

As the different breakdowns of the national income aggregate were statistically implemented, it became obvious that various aspects of the changing composition of national income were in themselves of interest, and that even the changes in specific components were useful as separate statistical series of economic information. Quite probably the functional and structural relationships indicated by these breakdowns had considerable influence as suggestive stimuli for economic theory at this time. And conversely, the development of aggregative economic theory during the thirties had considerable impact on the direction which the work on national income took. The Keynesian $Y = C + I$ was none too clear in its definitions, and in the attempt to fit statistical data into simple aggregative models, attention was of necessity directed to such additional economic constructs as disposable income, personal income, and gross national product.

World War II brought with it the need for over-all statistics which would be useful in setting up production goals and in calculating the inflationary pressures which would be generated because of the diversion of production for military uses. Both in the United Kingdom and in the United States, this need resulted in the development of a set of accounts for the various economic sectors, in which inter-sector income flows could be recorded. Accounts for five sectors (producers, consumers, government, the rest of the world, and capital) are characteristically included in the set. The first four of these show, for each sector, the sources of income on the one side, and the allocations of this income to expenditure and saving on the other side. The fifth is a balancing account, showing, on the one side, total saving in the economy, and on the other side, gross investment. These sector accounts served as a framework into which statistical data were fitted. Postwar problems of readjustment and economic recovery have led to refinement and extension of this framework for domestic uses, and also to meet the needs of comparative analysis of different national economic systems.[53] The classificatory procedures which were designed within the various countries with reference to their own domestic economies are, as might be expected, not fully satisfactory in terms of comparing the economies of different countries, and a great deal of further work in this area is needed.

Input-output tables as a framework for the classification of statistical data are a much more recent development than national income concepts; the first major work on this subject, *The Structure of the American Economy, 1919–1939,* by Wassily Leontief, was published in 1941. An input-output table is designed primarily to show the interindustry relationships in the economy. These relationships are extremely important in any study of the physical production functions of the various industries, and thus to any evaluation of the capabilities of the economy for producing a given bill of final goods, or any analysis of the repercussions of a given impact (such as the necessity for defense production) on the industrial structure of physical production. The present needs of defense mobilization may well bring about a rapid development in the use of input-output tables as a classificatory device, in much the same way that World War II fostered the development of national income accounting.

The conceptual basis of an input-output table is rather simple. Economic activity is visualized as recorded in a huge accounting system, which shows the receipts and the expenditures of each of the different industries, together with the income and expenditure of the government, of individuals, and of the rest of the world. The classification of industries can be shown in any desired degree of fineness, from, for example, the eight major industrial groups employed by the Census to the more than 400 industry groups used in the latest BLS studies. The expenditures of an industry or sector appear as the purchase of input items. These expenditures on inputs are classified, for each industry and sector, according to the industry or sector from which the purchase is made. When, for instance, the steel industry pays wages, it is paying for labor inputs received from the household sector. When it purchases coal, it is getting material inputs from the coal-mining industry in return. The receipts of an industry or sector, on the other hand, arise from the sale of outputs.

---

[53] See for example *A Simplified System of National Accounts,* published by the National Accounts Research Unit of the Organization for European Economic Cooperation, Paris, 1950. This work has now been superseded by a more recent version entitled *A Standardized System of National Accounts,* which is available in mimeographed form.

The output of each industry and sector, like the input, is classified by industry, this time according to the industry receiving the output. For the steel industry, output would be classified according to the industries which buy the steel. The same industry and sector breakdown is used for classifying both the expenditures (inputs) and the receipts (outputs), so that it is, of course, possible to arrange all the data in one symmetrical matrix. Any one cell in this table represents an input item from the point of view of the industry which purchases it, and an output item from the point of view of the industry which sells it. If the conventional input-output table is read down the columns, it shows the set of inputs which are absorbed by each industry and sector; if it is read across the rows, the same table shows the disposition of the output of each industry and sector.

Statistical implementation of an input-output table requires an enormous quantity of information, and in consequence, very few countries have been able to draw up such tables. Sets of data for the United States are available at the present time only for the years 1919, 1929, and 1939. A much more detailed set of data is now in preparation for 1947. The early input-output tables for the United States relied primarily upon data derived from the various censuses and available only for census years. More recently, the inputs of various individual industries have been studied directly, in an attempt to obtain greater detail and specification than is contained in the census data. As yet, systematic sampling has not been employed extensively; instead, the studies which are made are intensive studies of the processes and inputs employed in an individual industry.

As a system of classification, input-output tables differ from national income accounts in that they highlight the interindustry relationships, which the national accounts treat as intermediate and eliminate from the system completely. National income accounting usually does show the industrial structure of the economy in supplementary tables, in terms of gross national product or national income originating by industry, but such tables cannot show the to-whom, from-whom interindustry sales and purchases. Input-output tables, however, are customarily restricted solely to this one to-whom, from-whom basis of classification: transactions are shown in terms of the industry purchasing and the industry selling, and not by any other criterion. Thus, for example, the national accounts can show the expenditures of consumers, the government, and the capital sector classified by type of final good, but input-output tables would show these expenditures classified only by the industries in which such goods originate. The two classification systems differ because they consider the economy from what are essentially two different points of view. An input-output table is concerned with production as a physical transformation process, and looks upon the economy as a set of completely interdependent producing industries. The interesting economic problem, from the input-output point of view, is the nature of this industrial interdependence, and the manner in which any impact on the system as a whole, such as defense mobilization, technological change, or population growth, will alter the structure of production. National income accounting, on the other hand, is to a greater extent concerned with income, and the manner in which it arises as a result of decision-making in the economy. In emphasizing this decision-making process, the functional as well as the to-whom, from-whom aspects of the transactions shown are important. Accent is placed upon the effect of the government's taxation and expenditure policy, the investment decisions of producers, and the saving and spending decisions of consumers. The system of interrelated income and expenditure accounts makes possible the examination of the income-generating effects of any given change, and its cumulative effect upon prices, output, and employment.

Both of these frameworks are extremely useful as bases for classifying information about the operation of the economy; unfortunately, however, the development of the two systems has not been integrated or even correlated in most countries. Those who advocate national income accounts are not really interested in the input-output presentation, and those working on input-output relationships feel that their approach is the only reasonable one to follow. But there obviously is no inherent contradiction in the two systems of classification; they are supplementary rather than alternative. Integration of the two into one single classification system having all the features of both is not only possible, but has been successfully carried out in both the Netherlands[54] and Denmark.[55] For each of these countries a single comprehensive table is available which yields the to-whom, from-whom interindustry relationships of an input-output table and the functional classifications for the various sectors in the manner of national income accounts. Such an integrated presentation has obvious advantages, since it permits both types of analysis

---

[54] See *De Nationale Jaarrekeningen: doeleinden, problemen, resultaten.* No. 8 der Monografieen van de Nederlandse Conjunctuur, Centrael Bureau voor de Statistiek (The Hague, 1950).

[55] See *Nationalproduktet og Nationalindkomsten, 1946–1949,* Det Statistiske Departementet (Copenhagen, 1951).

to be carried on within the same framework. One of the greatest disadvantages of the coexistence of a number of unintegrated general classification systems is that the many minor and usually irrelevant and chance differences prevent the analyst from moving from one system to another. With respect to input-output tables and national income accounting, for example, the treatment of financial intermediaries is likely to differ, not for any particular analytic reason, but solely because the systems are developed without reference to each other.

Money-flows accounts are the newest of these three general systems of classification; it is only now in what are really the initial stages of development.[56] But it represents a logical extension of the same sort of technique as national income accounting and input-output tables. The money-flows system of classification is addressed specifically to the study of the use of money and credit in producing, distributing, and exchanging wealth. It is designed to provide an integrated system of measurements which will aid in answering questions about both the magnitude and the significance of monetary and credit flows. In the present stage of development of the money-flows work, accounts showing the sources and uses of funds are set up for each of nine sectors in the economy.[57] These accounts cover such categories as borrowing, debt repayment, and changes in holdings of cash, deposits, government bonds, accounts receivable, and other financial assets, as well as the more traditional income and expenditure categories.

The money-flows accounts bear a closer relationship to national income accounting than to input-output tables. However, the money-flows accounts include many nonincome and nonexpenditure items which are explicitly excluded from the national income accounts, so that they are applicable to a whole range of problems which are beyond the scope of national income accounting. Like national income accounting, the money-flows accounts focus on decision making, but with the insistence that economic activity and the decision-making process are broader than simply current production and current income. Thus the impact of a given credit restriction on decisions could be traced through the framework of the money-flows accounts, whereas it could not be analyzed adequately in terms of the national income accounts alone.

---

[56] A book by Morris Copeland on the subject of money-flows is now in the process of publication by the National Bureau of Economic Research.

[57] These sectors are: (1) consumers; (2) corporate business; (3) noncorporate business; (4) the federal government; (5) state and local government; (6) banking; (7) life insurance companies; (8) other investors; and (9) the rest of the world.

In relation to the national income accounts and to input-output tables, the money-flows accounts are complementary, again, rather than alternative. There seems to be considerable evidence that those working on money-flows are cognizant of this fact—at least with respect to national income accounting—and are utilizing existing national income accounting concepts insofar as they are applicable.

Wealth accounts, finally, should be noted in passing. Systematic work is beginning to be done in this field.[58] Conceptually, every economic unit has a balance sheet, in which its assets and liabilities can be entered. In setting up national wealth accounts, a classification system must be devised for combining and consolidating these individual balance sheets such that useful interrelations among industries and sectors are preserved, both in terms of evaluating the physical capacity of various industries and in terms of analyzing the decision-making process of different groups. Such a classificatory framework would accent the analytic importance of statistical data on the types and the quantity of the assets held by the various industries and sectors. Information of this type would be useful in connection with all three of the classificatory systems described above; national income accounts, input-output tables, and money-flows accounts are all concerned only with the current transactions which take place in the economy, and analyses employing any of the three would benefit from the use of a capital, as well as a current, account.

In terms of their own methodology, these classificatory systems are examples of informational statistical presentations. They can, of course, be used for more complex statistical analyses, but in general complex statistical techniques are not used in developing them. Mathematical economics has been used to some extent in the development of the theoretical structure of the various systems. Institutional economics has played a very important part in determining appropriate functional and sectoral classifications.

National income accounting as a specific technique has already had a significant impact on the general body of economic research activity. Input-output, while less generally used, is, as will be pointed out in the next section, coming into more active use; one reason it is not more widely used is the present lack of statistical implementation on a scale comparable to that of the national income accounts. The money-flows

---

[58] For a recent survey of work being done in this area see Conference on Research in Income and Wealth, *Studies in Income and Wealth,* Vol. XIV (New York, 1951).

accounts and the wealth accounts, while they probably do forecast the path of future methodological developments, are at present severely limited by lack of data.

The urge to develop such classificatory frameworks is characteristic of economic research activity in this period, and as such it has distinct methodological implications. The most striking methodological influence of which it is a symptom is the closer interrelation which is evolving among the stages of research. Theorists, in the interest of making their theories more realistic and more nearly capable of being tested empirically, have given serious attention to the erection of statistical frameworks suitable to both the data and their theories. The development of such frameworks was of necessity a matter of successive approximation; the initial theoretical framework would have to be revised drastically upon preliminary exploration of empirical material. Gradually, by working back and forth between the theoretical framework and the empirical material, a more adequate framework would be obtained. But the evolution of these classificatory systems cannot be explained solely in terms of the changing orientation of the theoretical economist. With the increasing volume of economic statistics, statisticians and others involved in the day-to-day use of these statistics were forced to develop systems of aggregation which would preserve as many as possible of the meaningful relationships among the data, and at the same time reduce the sheer volume of the material with which they were confronted. Again, a process of successive approximation was involved, wherein the analytic and policy uses of the data dictated which elements of it should be amplified or disaggregated, and which elements could be consolidated or truncated.

These two developments tended to bring theorists and statisticians closer together. Analysts working on the exploration of problems (Stage 1) used the evolving classificatory frameworks as tools in their work. Analysts working on the development of hypotheses (Stage 2) tended to formulate those hypotheses in terms of the concepts of the classificatory frameworks, partly because of the power of suggestion, and partly because doing so made the concepts operationally more meaningful, in the sense that they became amenable to immediate empirical testing. And analysts working on the testing of hypotheses, finally, began to find that theory and data were now more nearly comparable in form, so that testing became both easier and somewhat more valid. The function which has been served and will increasingly be served by these classificatory frameworks thus is that of introducing more integration into the research process.

B. Model Building

In its broadest sense, the term "economic model" can be used to refer to any theoretical structure involving economic magnitudes. The connotations of this phrase in present-day economic parlance, however, are very different from this. The phrase has come to refer specifically to the description of the working of the economic system in terms of a set of simultaneous equations expressing all the interrelationships among the measurable economic magnitudes which determine the operation of the system.[59] The variables in these simultaneous equations can be either exogenous or endogenous. The exogenous variables are those which the analyst considers to be outside the economic system, such as wars, weather, population growth, and governmental activity. The endogenous variables are those which are considered to be determined by the operation of the economic system, such as prices, wages, employment, the rate of interest, profits, and output. The equations in the system can express a number of different types of relationships. First, an equation may be simply a definitional identity, such as is given by the statement that consumers' expenditures plus personal saving equal disposable income. Second, an equation may express a technical relation, such as the production function which gives the technological relation of inputs to outputs. Third, an equation may specify certain institutional relations, such as that between a corporation's profits and the corporate profits tax which the firm pays. Finally, an equation may give the behavior relations among variables, as does the consumption function showing the behavior of individuals with respect to the consuming of their income.[60] These different equations are sometimes referred to as structural equations, since they show the basic structure of the economic system. When the number of independent structural equations is equal to the number of endogenous variables, and the exogenous variables are given, the system of equations is complete. (Obviously, any model can be made complete by reclassification of the unknown endogenous variables in the system as given exogenous variables.)

The form in which such models were first used was fairly simple. A relatively small number of variables was included in the system, and

---

[59] For a fuller discussion of models and their development see the chapter on "Econometrics" by Leontief, *A Survey of Contemporary Economics*, Vol. I.

[60] *Statistical Inference in Dynamic Economic Models,* T. C. Koopmans, ed. (New York, 1950), Ch. 2, "Measuring the Equation Systems of Dynamic Economics," by T. C. Koopmans, Herman Rubin, and R. B. Leipnik.

these were, for the most part, of an extremely aggregative nature. Such over-all magnitudes as national income, the level of prices, total consumption, total investment, total saving, the level of employment, the interest rate, and the stock of money were included. This sort of analysis was termed macro-economic, in distinction from the micro-economic analysis of traditional value theory which examined the behavior of the individual firm or the single consumer. The models employed in this macro-economic analysis almost universally involved the assumption that macro and micro relationships were identical and that no serious problem of aggregation was involved. Thus it was assumed that the (macro) behavior pattern of output per man-hour for the economy as a whole directly corresponded to the (micro) behavior pattern of output per man-hour in a representative plant, whereas in fact, of course, any relative expansion or contraction of highly productive sectors, industries, or plants would lead to a situation where the over-all and the individual changes in output per man-hour would not be similar. Most models in this early period were static, in that they did not attempt to take into account the functional relationships among economic variables at different points of time. What the models did engage in was comparative statics, i.e., the investigation of the characteristics of the model in one position of equilibrium in comparison with another position of equilibrium, without regard to the transitional process involved in the adjustments among variables. The static functional relationships which were employed in these models were almost always of a simple, usually linear, nature, thus entailing the assumption that the rates of change of the variables with respect to each other were constant. This means, of course, that such things as marginal cost and the marginal propensity to consume would be constant in such models.

At first, the major use of models was in theoretical analysis. The relative importance of certain assumed relationships could be illustrated more clearly, and comparison among different theoretical structures was somewhat simpler, if theories were all cast into the same general form.[61] By changing given assumptions, it was also possible to analyze the repercussions of these changes upon the operation of the model.[62] As models came into more general use, it was natural that they should be directly

[61] An example can be found in L. R. Klein, *The Keynesian Revolution* (New York, 1947).

[62] For a simple dynamic model of this type, see P. A. Samuelson, "Interactions between the Multiplier Analysis and the Principle of Acceleration," *Rev. Econ. Stat.,* May 1939, XXI, 75–78; also in *Readings in Business Cycle Theory,* Gottfried Haberler, ed. (Philadelphia, 1944), pp. 261–69.

related to the national income data which were being developed at approximately the same time. The statistical data were "fitted" to the models by the method of least squares, and parameters were obtained for the structural equations. The models at this stage in their development were still relatively simple, and the statistical techniques employed could also be relatively simple. Considerable interest came to be attached to the use of such models and their parameters for the purposes of projection. This interest was stimulated by the problem of the "inflationary gap" during the war, and the fear of a postwar collapse in demand which would lead to unemployment.

At about this point in the development of the use of models, considerable dissatisfaction with their static nature began to be expressed.[63] Dynamic analysis had generally been avoided because of the increased complications which it introduced into the models. By its inherent flexibility, dynamics emphasizes the impossibility of exploring all conceivable models. But, as Samuelson points out,[64] the economist has no choice but to enter the study of dynamics; for otherwise there is little possibility of presenting a reasonably realistic description of such phenomena as speculation, cyclical fluctuation, and secular growth. The introduction of dynamic models accented the set of economic problems related to the stability of the system. It was no longer sufficient to show how a model might determine a given equilibrium in a static sense; rather it now became necessary to explore the question of whether the dynamic model envisaged was explosive in its operation through time. The use of dynamic analysis has undoubtedly made possible, and will increasingly make possible, a closer approach of theory to reality, but it has had the effects which were feared, as well as those which were hoped for: the complexity of models has been increased to such an extent that modern model building is becoming an exercise in mathematics as well as economics, and as such has developed into a special area requiring extensive specialized training.[65]

Simultaneously with the introduction of dynamics into the theoretical development of models, econometricians became increasingly concerned with two problems which arise in the statistical estimation of the parameters of the endogenous variables in an equation system. These

---

[63] See A. G. Hart, " 'Model-Building' and Fiscal Policy," *Am. Econ. Rev.*, Sept. 1945, XXXV, 531–58.

[64] "Dynamic Process Analysis," *A Survey of Contemporary Economics,* Vol. I, p. 374.

[65] See the discussion in Part II above with regard to mathematical economics.

problems have appeared in the literature as (a) the problem of identification, and (b) the problem of random disturbances.

The identification problem has been discussed a great deal in econometric literature, with varying terminology. As Koopmans points out,[66] an attempt to systematize the terminology and to formalize the treatment of the problem has been made over the past few years by various authors connected in one way or another with the Cowles Commission. The nature of this problem can perhaps most simply be seen with reference to the traditional example of the estimation of parameters in the case of demand and supply equations. When the observed data are the results of shifts in both the demand and the supply curves, as well as movements along both schedules, the observed price-quantity combinations are not sufficient on the basis of the usual theoretical model to derive the parameters which indicate the influence of price changes on supply and demand, and the parameters remain unidentified. (The problem of identification thus occurs, even when the problem of statistical error is not present.) Of course, if one schedule did not shift, and the other did, the parameters of the unchanging schedule could be identified. It is only through the use of additional information such as this (or such as the exact shift in both schedules) or by further specification of the model itself, that the identification problem can be solved. Different models will differ considerably in the kinds and degrees of their identification powers.[67] Considerations of this nature, of course, introduce further complications into the already complex systems of dynamic models.

The problem of random disturbances arises because it is unreasonable to presume that any relations in equation systems other than definitions should be satisfied exactly. No matter how careful the analyst is to obtain an exhaustive list of all determining variables, he cannot logically hope to include all the relevant factors. Instead, therefore, he tries to introduce only the principal systematic influences, omitting the vast number of minor variables, the effects of which show up as random disturbances of the main relationships. Prior to the introduction of the probability approach to model building, exact equation systems without a random variable were used, and statisticians could legitimately claim that economists did not present their models in such a form that they rep-

---

[66] T. C. Koopmans, "Identification Problems in Economic Model Construction," *Econometrica*, Apr. 1949, XVII, 126. This article contains an excellent bibliography on this problem.

[67] For a discussion of this point see Leonid Hurwicz, "Generalization of the Concept of Identification," in *Statistical Inference in Dynamic Economic Models*, pp. 245–57.

resented well-specified statistical hypotheses. Models which have been made more realistic, in a statistical sense, by the introduction of a random disturbance into each of the structural equations (except the definitional equations) are termed "stochastic models." By specifying the distribution of the random (stochastic) variables in each equation, it is possible to estimate parameters of the system. This use of statistical inference in relating models to empirical data has added one more dimension to model building: the mathematician-economist must now become a theoretical statistician.

One final point should be raised in connection with the current development of aggregative dynamic stochastic models. Econometricians have generally come to recognize that the aggregative nature of the models is a serious problem, since the behavior equations valid for relations among micro-variables may not, in fact, be valid for macro-variables. Various theoretical solutions to this problem have been offered on the aggregative level. One partial solution based on a different method of attack is to disaggregate, and introduce many more equations into the model. This procedure has been followed in linear programming, in which the data of the input-output tables are used to develop an economic model. A set of simultaneous equations is developed in which the input-output relations of each industry are described by treating the technical input coefficients as independent structural parameters. This approach assumes these coefficients to be invariant with respect to output (thus the equations themselves are linear), indicating that constant returns to scale are assumed. Since the coefficients are also independent of the prices of cost factors, relative inputs of various factors are not responsive to price changes, and thus input factors are not substitutable for each other. This lack of substitutability is probably the major weakness of this approach. For a great many problems, however, linear programming and related models based on input-output data promise to be most realistic and useful.

From a methodological point of view, the development of model building represents an additional step in the evolving integration of the economic research process which has repeatedly been emphasized throughout this survey. Model building has fostered a greater unification of the formulation of theoretical structures (Stage 2) with the statistical testing of these formulations (Stage 3). As a principal tool of econometrics, model building has placed considerable emphasis on mathematical economics, and on the probability approach to statistical analysis. Much of the work done in the area so far has been primarily concerned with the development of methods of analysis; in this connection, the stimulus which is given to the development of sets of statistical data which can be used in its statistical testing is also important.

IV. METHODOLOGY IN CURRENT ECONOMIC RESEARCH

The discussions in Parts I and II were designed to provide a frame-work for the examination of methodology, and Part III presented some of the recent developments in specialized techniques for economic re-search. The discussion in this section will attempt to utilize this frame-work and classification of specialized techniques with reference to se lected portions of current economic research activity. The work of three types of research groups will be considered: (1) private economic re-search organizations; (2) governmental research work; and (3) aca-demic research work.

A. Private Economic Research Organizations

The work of these groups can be divided into two categories: (*a*) basic research, and (*b*) policy-oriented and applied research. The Na-tional Bureau of Economic Research, the Cowles Commission, and the Michigan Survey Research Center will be considered briefly as examples of the first type of organization. The Twentieth Century Fund, the Com-mittee for Economic Development, the Brookings Institution, and vari-ous business research groups will be considered as examples of the sec-ond type.

The National Bureau of Economic Research has devoted a consid-erable part of its energies to business-cycle research.[68] Much of its work in this area is concerned with the exploration of the problem (Stage 1). The statistical techniques used are usually not very complex: time series are presented and decomposed into trend, seasonal, and cyclical elements. Little attention is devoted to the hypotheses and assumptions inherent in the treatment of this empirical data, and in general no elaborate theoret-ical framework is erected. Thus Stage 2 of the research process is usually truncated. The empirical testing of hypotheses (Stage 3) is not sharply differentiated from the exploration of the problem (Stage 1).

In this area of business-cycle research, the work of the National Bu-reau has been the subject of considerable methodological controversy.

---

[68] The publication list of the National Bureau lists nineteen separate books and an additional twenty papers published on business cycles. The methodological discussion here refers mainly to the central work, Burns and Mitchell, *Measuring Business Cycles*.

On the one hand, it is held that the attempt to dispense with theoretical preconceptions has had a detrimental effect upon the analysis.[69] On the other hand, it is questioned whether the National Bureau methods have stayed within the bounds of objectivity or whether they too have engaged in "illicit theorizing."[70] These two criticisms are not necessarily incompatible with each other. As was stressed earlier in this paper, it is not possible to dispense entirely with theoretical preconceptions. When an attempt is made to do so, the theoretical preconceptions simply become implicit and remain unexplored. In the business-cycle research of the National Bureau, this methodological difficulty becomes quite clear in connection with the notion of the reference cycle.[71] It is implicitly assumed that the decomposition of time series is a legitimate tool for cycle research, that cycle averages are meaningful, and that various phases of a cycle can be identified. These assumptions in turn imply an essentially one-dimensional basic pattern of cyclical fluctuation in the economy.[72] For reasons such as these, some reviewers have questioned the whole National Bureau program of business-cycle research.[73]

With reference to the use of specialized techniques, the National Bureau has not only utilized the classificatory frameworks of national income accounting and money-flows, but it has in fact been one of the foremost groups in developing these techniques. This work of the National Bureau can be looked upon as a highly developed exploration of the problem (Stage 1), where procurement and arrangement of statistical data are designed in such a way as to provide raw material for further exploration of problems (Stage 1) and for the testing of hypotheses (Stage 3).

The methodology implicit in much of the empirical work of the Cowles Commission is in direct contrast to that employed by the National Bureau. Little effort is spent on the exploration of the problem (Stage 1); instead, attention is immediately focused on the theoretical development of hypotheses (Stage 2). Mathematical economics is the principal approach used at this point in the research process. A great deal of the effort of the staff of the Cowles Commission is devoted to the development of special empirical testing techniques (Stage 3). Fairly elaborate techniques of statistical inference are employed. Just as the Na-

---

[69] Koopmans, "Measurement without Theory," *loc. cit.*, p. 163.

[70] E. S. Shaw, "Burns and Mitchell on Business Cycles," *Jour. Pol. Econ.*, Aug. 1947, LV, 292.

[71] For a discussion of the reference cycle, see Burns and Mitchell, *op. cit.*

[72] Koopmans, "Measurement without Theory," *loc. cit.*, p. 165.

[73] *Ibid.*, p. 172; Shaw, *op. cit.*, p. 298.

tional Bureau in much of its work concentrates on Stage 1 in order to provide empirical material for further research, so the Cowles Commission in much of its work concentrates on Stage 2 in order to provide a theoretical examination of statistical inference which will be applicable to the empirical testing of hypotheses.[74]

In those cases where the work of the Cowles Commission has not accented statistical inference, it has often been concerned with the theoretical development of hypotheses (Stage 2). The general methodological approach of one such work, Lange's *Price Flexibility and Employment*,[75] has been subjected to a searching criticism by Milton Friedman.[76] First, Friedman pointed out, in order to obtain generality in the theory, Lange was willing to keep his analysis exceedingly abstract, and to consider an indefinitely large number of unspecific variables and unspecified functions; but this merely means the addition of terms and the insertion of commas without any essential increase in complication. The appearance of generality is thus obtained without its substance, and the theory itself is essentially nonoperational. Second, classifications were used that have no direct empirical counterparts. The concepts of positive, negative, and neutral monetary effects, for example, constitute a catalog of theoretical possibilities, not empirical realities. These criticisms by Friedman strike at the heart of a great deal of this sort of theorizing, which attempts to obtain generality through simple symbolic presentations. Although various writers for the Cowles Commission have used such an approach, it is perhaps somewhat unfair to lay sole responsibility for such methodology on them, when there is so liberal a use of it by so many economists.

The Survey Research Center at the University of Michigan employs a methodology which is in contrast to both the National Bureau and the Cowles Commission. The outstanding distinguishing characteristic of the Survey Research Center is the use of primary sample data. The exploration of the problem (Stage 1), the theoretical development of the hypothesis (Stage 2), and the empirical testing of the hypothesis (Stage 3) are all integrated around the analysis of sample data. The major technique employed is statistical analysis of a probability type, and inasmuch as the principal reliance is on primary sample data, many of the problems of aggregation are not encountered.

---

[74] For example see *Statistical Inference in Dynamic Economic Models*.

[75] Oscar Lange, *Price Flexibility and Employment* (New York, 1944).

[76] Milton Friedman, "Lange on Price Flexibility and Employment," *Am. Econ. Rev.*, Sept. 1946, XXXVI, 613-31.

These examples of basic research organizations serve to point up the wide diversity in methodologies which exist from group to group; despite these differences, however, these organizations have one important feature in common. From the point of view of methodology, such groups are generally more willing than others to experiment with complex and involved techniques of research—they are interested in the development of prototypes of methods which are applicable to more general use.

In contrast with such basic research groups, policy-oriented research organizations are not concerned with the development of method, but are rather interested in the realization of immediate meaningful results. In general, this results in considerable accent on the exploration of the problem (Stage 1) and the evaluation of conclusions (Stage 4), with consequent truncation of Stages 2 and 3. The surveys of the Twentieth Century Fund are somewhat representative of the best work of this type. There is considerable dependence on statistics of the informational type, but no elaborate techniques of processing the data are ordinarily developed. Institutional information is woven into the analysis to make it more realistic. The Brookings Institution is somewhat less institutional in its approach, and places more reliance on economic constructs and aggregations. The research reports of the Committee for Economic Development are less uniform in their methodological approaches, since they tend to be written by consultants having wide differences in background. Since many of the authors are drawn from universities, however, the work of the Committee for Economic Development often places greater accent on the development of hypotheses (Stage 2), but elaborate methodological techniques are not usually employed. Little if any formal attention is given to the empirical testing of hypotheses.

Applied economic research organizations are in general less well known but much more numerous than other research groups. For the most part, such groups concentrate heavily on the exploration of the problem, giving summary treatment to the remainder of the research process. The final output of these groups tends to be of an empirical nature, containing a great deal of institutional information and some informational statistical material. Such applied economic research is often of a case study nature. The case study has a considerable methodological advantage in that problems of aggregation are not serious, and in that nonquantifiable information can be integrated into the analysis more easily. On the other hand, it is limited by the partiality of the analysis, and by the lack of articulation of the hypotheses. Furthermore, what empirical information is available is usually used to develop the hypothesis, so that no adequate empirical testing is possible. And research projects in these applied areas are commonly of such a specialized nature that hypotheses developed in the context of one situation are not relevant to the special- ized conditions of other situations, so that the work in applied research is not as cumulative as that concerned with more general problems.

The impact of policy-oriented and applied economic research on basic economic analysis should not be underestimated. Such work has served to give theoretical economists better grounding for Stage 1 of their analyses and to provide materials for Stage 3. Conversely, economic theory has become more and more integrated into the work of policy- oriented and applied research groups.

B. Government Research

Certain government agencies have as one of their principal func- tions the collection of primary economic data. In addition to this direct effort on collection of primary economic data, a large body of informa- tion is provided as a by-product of the regulatory and administrative ac- tivities of the government. The provision of statistical series for eco- nomic research should be viewed as a part of the total research process, providing material for both the exploration of the problem (Stage 1) and the empirical testing of hypotheses (Stage 3). The impact of the growth of statistics on economic methodology has been great; one of the major differences between economic research today and that of fifty years ago is the increasing use of empirical information. To the extent that economics can be considered a science, it is because of this growth of empirical information.[77]

Almost all government agencies do some economic research, in ad- dition to providing basic data. In some cases, to be sure, the research process consists in keeping track of the pieces of paper that flow into the agency, reading *The New York Times,* attending meetings, and on the basis of these activities, adding additional memos to the general flood. In

---

[77] According to Stigler ("A Survey of Contemporary Economics," *Jour. Pol. Econ.,* Apr. 1949, LVII, 93–105), recent economics documented by Vol. I of the *Survey* does show the triumph of statistics over history as a source of empirical knowledge. In part, Stigler feels that this is due to the fact that the contributors to the *Survey* were relatively young. He feels that the neglect of history has had an obvious incidence not only on the essays in the *Survey* but also on contemporary economics in general. Whether the youth- ful bent towards statistics is because of the absence of memories or whether it is a natural development of economics more readily recognized and accepted by younger members of the profession can only be determined by the passage of time.

other cases, however, a concerted effort is made to carry out systematic research on a particular subject. The methodology employed in many cases is quite similar to that already described in the section on policy-oriented foundations. Considerable accent is placed on Stage 1 (the exploration of the problem), and little attention is generally given to Stage 2 (theoretical development). The empirical testing which is done (Stage 3) is usually of a fairly simple nature. Stage 4, the evaluation of conclusions, obviously is given great importance, since policy formation is the object of such research.

Certain government agencies have also played a considerable role in the development of classificatory frameworks. The development of such subjects as national income accounting, input-output, and money-flows owes much to the active participation of various government agencies. In this work, considerably more attention has of necessity been given to Stage 2 of the analysis (the theoretical development of hypotheses), so that the frameworks will be more meaningful for economic analysis.

C. Academic Economic Research

In the space allotted to this essay, it is not feasible to make a comparative analysis of the methodology of specific academic authors or of specific pieces of research done in academic institutions; the discussion in this section will therefore be confined to examining the general nature of academic research in terms of the methodological framework erected in Parts I, II, and III.

Relative to the work carried out in most research foundations and in the government, academic research tends to place less emphasis on the exploration of the problem (Stage 1). Academic economists commonly inherit their problems; the scholarly approach starts with reading everything other scholars have written on a subject, and this serves as a direct substitute for a more empirical approach. The theoreticians, furthermore, consider their work on Stage 2 to be the core of all economic research, from which all other work should spring.[78] There is a widespread lack of

---

[78] This point is well illustrated by the following excerpt from J. R. Hicks, *A Contribution to the Theory of the Trade Cycle* (Oxford: Clarendon Press, 1950), p. v: "The title of this book is at once a claim and a disclaimer. I do believe that the argument which I am going to set out is quite likely to be the main part of the answer to the great question with which I am concerned—why it is that these rather regular fluctuations in trade and industry have gone on occurring, from the beginnings of industrialism up to the present. That is claim enough; but I want to make it clear at the outset that I am not claiming any more. I am not by any means positive that the answer which I have found is the right

coordination between the theoretical development of hypotheses (Stage 2) and their empirical testing (Stage 3), in that the theoretical developments which are set up cannot easily be tested empirically.[79] The empirical testing of hypotheses (Stage 3), like the exploration of the problem (Stage 1), tends to be somewhat neglected. "Facts" are often cited as giving support to one side of a controversy or contradicting the other side, but it is not unusual for both sides to cite the same facts and differ on their interpretation and meaning.[80] This situation can exist because of the vagueness both in the conceptual content of the theory and in the definitions of the empirical constructs. Stage 4, the evaluation of results, is not neglected by most academic economists. Economic theoreticians are apt to move directly from the development of an hypothesis to the policy implications of that hypothesis, and to the evaluation of the results for society as a whole. Just as some of the research foundations and government agencies tend to combine Stages 1 and 4, with a minimum of explicit attention to Stages 2 and 3, academic economics has concentrated on Stages 2 and 4, giving less attention to Stages 1 and 3. Theory is translated into policy without too much concern for the empirical verification of the theory.

With respect to the specialized techniques of analysis, academic economists are essentially pioneers and experimentalists, and this gives a somewhat spurious appearance of changing methodology, even when there has been little change in the actual approaches and techniques used for *substantive* analysis. The recent developments in mathematical techniques, for example, would appear from the literature on the subject to

---

answer; one cannot begin to be sure of that until one has tested one's theory against the facts, and I am well aware that any testing which I have been able to do has been extremely superficial. If the theory which is here offered stands up to theoretical criticism, the next stage will be the concern of statisticians, econometrists, and (most of all) economic historians, who will have to see whether it does prove possible to make sense of the facts in the light of these hypotheses. All I hope to have shown is that the theory is reasonable in itself, and that it would serve to explain the kind of phenomenon which has been experienced.

"Even on the purely theoretical side, I am very conscious that much remains to be done. If a provisional answer is given to the main question, that answer raises further questions, and many of these are left unexplored. The main argument itself has got some weak links, which need strengthening. But there are plenty of people whose hands will itch to get on with these jobs. At the point where I leave it, the inquiry looks like branching out in many directions. That is a good point at which to write a progress report, which is all that this 'contribution' claims to be."

[79] See the discussion of Friedman on Lange above, p. 445.

[80] Stigler ("A Survey of Contemporary Economics," *loc. cit.*) claims that the dominant characteristic of the recent period in academic economic research is its reliance on casual empirical information. He cites the theoretical nature of the *Survey* as proof.

be a major revolutionary change, but as yet the number of economic works which use highly developed mathematical techniques for substantive analysis is relatively small. It is surprising how much economic research employing mathematics is meant to be experimental and illustrative of method rather than productive of substantive results. There can be no doubt, however, that the introduction of mathematical techniques has influenced the direction which economic analysis has taken and which the future developments can be expected to take.

In conclusion, there is one fairly common characteristic of academic economics which has not yet been mentioned. Problems which might be solved but are relatively unimportant are put aside, while the major efforts of academic economists go into the larger and (at present) insoluble problems. Ultimate aims are thus sought directly. Economics might well progress faster if the dictum of von Neumann and Morgenstern,[81] that "the great progress in every science came when, in the study of problems which were modest as compared with ultimate aims, methods were developed which could be extended further and further," were more widely appreciated.

D. Factors Influencing Methodological Development

Preliminary consideration of methodological development might give the general impression that it was purely an evolutionary process, in which the more successful methods naturally and inevitably supplanted less successful methods. Such a situation may be true to some extent, but it is highly conditioned by two other major factors which also shape methodology. These are: (1) the changing scope of economics; and (2) the industrial organization of the profession.

In the not too distant past, much of economics was concerned with exploring the implications of a relatively small number of self-evident postulates. It was on this basis that much of classical economic theory was constructed. An outstanding feature of such economics was its lack of accent upon the use of empirical data; both the institutionalist movement of the early twenties and the current emphasis on empirical investigations have been in reaction to the irrelevance and unreality of "orthodox" economics. The result has been a considerable shift in the scope of economics. For example, the field of industrial organization has traditionally centered around such questions as oligopoly, duopoly, monopolistic competition, and the problem of uncertainty, but more recently

---

[81] John von Neumann and Oskar Morgenstern, *Theory of Games and Economic Behavior* (Princeton, 1944), pp. 6–7.

there has been considerably more interest in such questions as the process of decision making in the firm, factors affecting price policy, and the basis of investment decisions. Whether, as Stigler claims,[82] the institutionalist movement marked a high point of dissent against traditional economics, and whether institutionalism failed, is both a matter of definition and a question of personal judgment. But the depression of the thirties did nothing to strengthen the traditional concept of the scope of economics; rather it proved to be a stimulus to the gathering and using of empirical information, with a minimum of classical economic theory. World War II continued this process. The result has been a considerable change in methodology, considering the research process as a whole. The charge made by Stigler[83] that the period immediately past, in academic economics, has been one "of the clever gadget and the plausible surmise —the age of the easy answer" is probably very true. But it may also be true that the period was—and is—one of transition, resulting from the changing scope of economics. The change which is required to make good use of the information which is now or will in the near future be available is a very considerable one, and it cannot be accomplished overnight.

Much in the manner that method is highly related to the scope of economics, it is also highly related to the industrial organization of the economics profession. Each of the various types of economic research group discussed above operates within a specific institutional setting which profoundly affects the methodology it employs. The methodology of the profession is thus a function of both the institutional settings and the relative importance of the different types of research group.

Organized research permits methods to be employed which are entirely different from what is possible in individual research. Division of labor and mass processing of data are possible, thus permitting the use of complex methodology. For the basic research organizations, however, this advantage is somewhat offset by uncertainty with respect to future income, which makes long-range planning of any magnitude difficult. As a result, small projects involving only one or two people tend to be supported, and true group research is much less prevalent than might be expected. Policy-oriented and applied economic research groups, on the other hand, are under considerable pressure to produce immediate results which will be comprehensible to those supporting them. This usually means that complex methods are avoided, and simple, direct, although

[82] "A Survey of Contemporary Economics," *loc. cit.,* p. 104.
[83] *Loc. cit.*

perhaps less productive, approaches are utilized. Government research activity is in many ways institutionally similar to that of the policy-oriented and applied economic research groups. It is usually necessary that the research be designed so that immediate and relevant results which can be used for policy purposes are forthcoming. The work is therefore generally geared to the digestion of masses of data in a fairly simple informational manner.

In academic economic research, finally, the institutional setting is especially important in shaping methodology. Economists seem to thrive on publication rather than research, and it is easier to publish by writing about the writings of others. Controversy is thus encouraged: the more that is written about what has been written, the more there is to write about. In view of this, plus the genuine intellectual appeal of the literature, it is not surprising that many academic economists become unduly addicted to this approach. Furthermore, university staffs are organized for teaching rather than research, so that it is common for an economist to find himself alone in his research interests. Coverage of a wide range of special fields by a teaching staff is not conducive to the establishment of a well-integrated research group, so that most academic research is of necessity an individual rather than a group undertaking. Unlike members of research groups, the academic economist does not have service organizations at his command. Special compilations of data cannot be obtained easily, and elaborate machine handling of data is usually out of the question. The academic economist is therefore forced to fall back on published aggregated data—which are usually not well suited to his particular purpose. It is no accident that the concept of the scope of economics which gives primary emphasis to Stage 2 originated in this sort of institutional setting.

These observations on the industrial organization of the economics profession emphasize the difficulties in the way of the development of economics as an empirical science. Economic foundations interested in basic research are too few and too poorly supported to accomplish this task. Other economic research foundations and government agencies have the resources and materials at their command, but they are of necessity interested in short-run results rather than long-run objectives. Within academic economics, institutional factors seriously restrict the choice of methodology. As a result, it may be impossible, at least in the present period, to develop methods which are suitable for an empirical economics—the academic economics which was characterized by Stigler as casually empirical may remain so into the future.

E. Conclusion

Some readers may have been bothered by the emphasis which has been given in this section to the diversity of individual methodologies. But the possible differences among methodologies are many. The accent placed on the various stages of analysis may differ, and different approaches and techniques may be employed. The component parts of the various different methodological approaches are basically the same, but the possible variation in combinations is very great. Many of the controversies on method would have been unnecessary if the participants had clarified the differences in their concepts of the scope of economics, and if they had made the purposes of their analyses more evident; it is too often true that a writer is accused of using an inadequate method when, in fact, he is simply concerned with a different problem from that envisaged by his critic. The wide diversity of economic methodologies which are found in current use is an extremely healthy sign—there can be, obviously, no one "best" method, applicable to all problems in economics, no matter what one's concept of scope is. Differences in problems require differences in the accent which is laid upon the various stages of the research process; some may be amenable to particular techniques of analysis, and some to others. The important problem for advancing economics is not that of determining which particular methodology should be employed, for methodology is merely a means to an end. The end is the accumulation of a body of knowledge which will be of assistance in understanding important economic problems, and to the extent that any methodology fosters this end, it can be considered good methodology.

COMMENT

Evsey D. Domar

This paper is concerned not with methodology as a part of the philosophy of knowledge, but rather with a description of present-day economic research. By choosing, or being told to choose, this orientation, the author missed his opportunity to say something worth while on an interesting, if difficult, subject, and produced instead an odd mixture of classifications, observations, and exhortations in which even the essential purpose of economic (or perhaps of any other) research somehow gets lost. This purpose is not to "obtain an exhaustive list of all determining variables" (p. 441), but on the contrary to try to get along with as few variables as possible. Its essence consists not in copying economic reality, as he seems to imply—this would be both impossible and useless—but in extracting from it a few easily manageable key factors and constructing from them a model, which may be expressed in words or symbols, or even implied, but which for a given purpose can be used as a substitute for reality itself. The nature and purpose of this process of abstraction is a source of much confusion which the paper makes no attempt to dispel. Contrary to the widely held notion, such a model is not intended to be a factual statement about real processes, and different and even contradictory models can be legitimately set up regarding the same process. The familiar assumption that firms maximize profits does not imply that they actually so behave, but that useful results can be obtained if this assumption, which can be so easily manipulated, is substituted for the actual and undoubtedly very complex behavior.

However much I disagree with the author's approach to economic methodology, there is space here for but a few brief remarks directed at specific parts of the paper. The description of the several research techniques in Part II shows neither the relation between the content of research and techniques, nor between general economic changes and the content of research. With the increasing emphasis on the control of our economic environment and the consequent expansion of governmental activities, problems which could be dealt with by common sense or with simple two-dimensional diagrams have tended to recede in importance and to be replaced by larger questions regarding the working of the whole economy which involve complex chains of causation, frequently of a reciprocal nature and operating over different intervals of time. To handle them by intuitive common sense requires a most unusual ability, while even a modest mind can get some results by means of an explicit mathematical model. As Leontief once put it, "A doubtful reader . . . can ascertain the limitation of his own common-sense intuition by trying to hazard at least an approximate solution of a system of three simple linear equations with three variables; or, after having found the right answers mathematically, by trying to guess out intuitively what effect a change in one of the constants would have on the values of all three unknowns."[84] The present flowering of mathematical economics is not due to the whims of a few theoreticians, but to the nature of problems confronting us. But it should be made clear that the solution of a model is a

---

[84] W. W. Leontief, *The Structure of the American Economy, 1919–1939* (2nd ed., New York, 1951), p. 34.

solution of a logical system and nothing else; to endow it with economic significance is a very fine art.

The recent revival of interest in "institutional economics" is another example of how new problems affect economic research. The stimulus comes from studies of economic development which reveal the striking absence in many countries of such economic amenities as a disciplined labor force, a tolerably well-trained and reliable industrial and governmental bureaucracy, a banking system, and what not, and thus lead to the construction of institutional models which will, I hope, make this branch of economics less sterile and more purposeful.

Finally, a word about the input-output technique discussed in Part III and sandwiched between national income and money-flow accounts as if it were just another method of classifying economic information. It is, of course, much more than that: a system for dealing with simultaneous and reciprocal relationships among economic variables, in contrast to the one-directional causation on which most of our analysis is still based. Its enormous possibilities (for instance in the construction of dynamic systems) are not revealed in the paper.

COMMENT

Milton Friedman

Ruggles' thorough essay presents a thoughtful analysis of the trees at the almost inevitable cost of paying little attention to the forest. A few words about the forest may accordingly be in order.

In his admirable book on *The Scope and Method of Political Economy*, John Neville Keynes distinguishes among "a *positive* science . . . [,] a body of systematized knowledge concerning what is; a *normative* or *regulative science* . . . [,] a body of systematized knowledge discussing criteria of what ought to be . . . ; an *art* . . . [,] a system of rules for the attainment of a given end"; comments that "confusion between them is common and has been the source of many mischievous errors"; and urges the importance of "recognizing a distinct positive science of political economy."[85]

Unfortunately, the confusion is still common—as is indeed indicated by Ruggles' inclusion of the "evaluation of conclusions" in his schematization of the current research process on a par with the develop-

---

[85] (London, 1891), pp. 34, 35, 46.

ment and testing of hypotheses, and his description of this step as "an aggregation of value judgments derived from some social or individual system of ethics and tastes." The emergence of a distinct field of "welfare economics" is, I believe, the only methodological development of recent decades that can be regarded as a significant movement toward distinguishing positive from normative economics. And even this development has had rather more effect in lending the appearance of scientific respectability to discussions of what "ought to be," and in asserting the dependence of policy conclusions on basic value judgments, than in promoting recognition of "a distinct positive science of political economy."

A major reason for distinguishing positive from normative economics is precisely the contribution that can thereby be made to agreement about policy. Any policy conclusion necessarily rests on a prediction about the consequences of doing one thing rather than another, a prediction that must be based—implicitly or explicitly—on positive economics. I venture the judgment that currently in the Western world, and especially in the United States, differences about economic policy among disinterested citizens derive predominantly from different predictions about the consequences of taking action, differences that in principle can be eliminated by the progress of positive economics—rather than from fundamental differences in basic values, differences about which men can ultimately only fight.[86]

Perhaps the chief obstacle to a fully accepted and articulated positive economics is the difficulty of testing the validity of tentative hypotheses in the social sciences. The ultimate goal of a positive science is the development of a "theory" or "hypothesis" that yields valid and meaningful (i.e., not truistic) predictions about phenomena not yet observed. And the only relevant test of an hypothesis is comparison of its predictions with what occurs: the hypothesis is rejected if its predictions are contradicted ("frequently" or more often than predictions from an alternative hypothesis); it is accepted if its predictions are not contradicted; great confidence is attached to it if it has survived many opportunities for contradiction. Unfortunately, in the social sciences we can seldom contrive experiments to test particular predictions, free from disturbing influences. We must use evidence cast up by the "experiments" that happen to occur. Such evidence is abundant and often as conclusive as that from contrived experiments. But it is far more difficult to interpret, and this

---

[86] An obvious example is minimum wage legislation, which proponents predict will reduce poverty, opponents predict will increase poverty. Both evaluate it by the same objective.

hinders greatly the permanent weeding out of unsuccessful hypotheses. They are always cropping up again.

One manifestation of this difficulty has been the attempt to find an easier test of hypotheses, to suppose that hypotheses have "assumptions" whose conformity to reality is a test of their validity different from and additional to the test by implications or predictions. The associated desire for descriptive realism indirectly fostered mathematical economics, with its emphasis on Walrasian general equilibrium analysis as an escape from the *ceteris paribus* of partial equilibrium analysis; it explicitly motivated monopolistic competition analysis and explains its popularity, which derived from a belief that the "assumptions" of the previous analysis were "unrealistic," rather than from any recognized contradiction of its predictions; it was the battle cry of institutionalism and the closely related emphasis on extensive statistical studies of economic phenomena; it has been manifested most recently in the belief that a theory can be tested by asking questions of consumers, producers, and the like.

These tendencies have produced real and valuable improvements in the formal "language" available for describing economic interrelationships and in our detailed knowledge of the phenomena to be explained by economic theory. But they have left something of a vacuum in the equally vital intermediate area of theories or hypotheses that have implications about important phenomena susceptible of contradiction through observation. Alfred Marshall's emphasis on the construction of an "engine for the discovery of concrete truth" has tended to be submerged under the urge for descriptive realism.

INDEX OF NAMES

SUBJECT INDEX

A

Acceleration principle, 74

Advertising, effect of, on consumption, 59

Aggregation, problems of, 47, 80–81, 421, 439, 442

Agricultural Acts of 1948 and 1949, 243–44, 251–52

Agriculture, economics of; *see also* Farm management
in general, chapter 6
economic position of farm population
in general, 225–33
income, 226–31, 259
migration from farms, 231–32
farm price programs
alternatives and modifications, 247–52
countercyclical taxes and subsidies, 249–50
criticisms and appraisal, 245–47
forward price proposal, 247–48
typical programs, 243–44
in the U.S.S.R., 394
labor transfer out of agriculture, factors responsible for
in general, 233–43
consumer tastes, 238
foreign demand, 240–41
population growth, 235
real per capita income, 235–38
technological change, 238–40
production theory, 257–58; *see also* Farm management
research suggestions, 252–60

Allocation of resources; *see* Resource allocation

Area surveys—consumption, 39, 48–49, 61, 67, 72

B

Backward areas; *see* Economic development of underdeveloped areas

Balance of payments, theory of, 317–19; *see also* International investment

Bond yields, effect of tax exemption, 272

Brannan Plan, 251

Budget studies—family, 43, 227–29; *see also* Area surveys—consumption

Business cycles
agricultural prices and incomes, 250–51
consumer goods, 75–76

Business cycles—*Cont.*
economic growth, 144, 148, 167
international aspects, 309–11, 315, 323–25
intersector propagation, 256
labor mobility, 232
population factors, 104–5, 115–16, 123
research methodology, 443–44

C

Capital flights, international, 309–10, 314–15, 381

Capital formation; *see also* International investment
in general, 146–76
government expenditures for, 363–65, 369
population factors, 113–14, 116
private, response of, to labor government, 376
underdeveloped areas, 378–81; *see also* Economic development of underdeveloped areas
U.S.S.R., 391–93
war conditions, 285–86

Capital gains and losses, 273

Capital theory deficiencies, 156, 181

Capitalism; *see also* Planning, national
environment for capital accumulation, 173–75
evolution of, 217–19
resource allocation, 35

Capitalist motivation, 158–60, 174, 217, 220

Cohort analysis, 87

Collective bargaining
alternatives in inflation, 372
variables encompassed, 201
welfare economics analysis of, 17–18

Collectivization of agriculture, 395

Comparative advantage of U.S. agriculture, decline in, 240–41

Compensation principle
payments, 13–14, 25
policy implications, 35

Competition, perfect
economic progress, 24
inapplicable to real world, 356
profit maximization, 207
size of decision unit, 25

467

This book has been set on the Linotype in 12 point Garamond No. 3, leaded 1 point. Chapter numbers are in 24 point Spartan Medium. The chapter titles and author's names are in 18 point Spartan Medium italics. The size of the type page is 27 by 45½ picas.